Dictionary of Literary Biography • Volume Forty

Poets of Great Britain and Ireland Since 1960
Part 2: M-Z

Dictionary of Literary Biography

Documentary Series

Yearbooks

Dictionary of Literary Biography • Volume Forty

Poets of Great Britain and Ireland Since 1960
Part 2: M-Z

Edited by
Vincent B. Sherry, Jr.
Villanova University

A Bruccoli Clark Book
Gale Research Company • Book Tower • Detroit Michigan 48226

Manufactured by Edwards Brothers, Inc.
Ann Arbor, Michigan
Printed in the United States of America

Library of Congress Cataloging in Publication Data
Main entry under title:

Poets of Great Britain and Ireland since 1960.

(Dictionary of literary biography; v. 40)
"A Bruccoli Clark book."
Contents: Pt. 1. A-L — Pt. 2. M-Z.
Includes index.
1. English poetry—20th century—History and crit-
icism. 2. English poetry—20th century—Bio-bibliog-
raphy. 3. English poetry—Irish authors—History
and criticism. 4. English poetry—Irish authors—
Bio-bibliography. 5. Poets, English—20th century—
Biography—Dictionaries. 6. Poets, Irish—20th cen-
tury—Biography—Dictionaries. I. Sherry, Vincent B.
II. Series.
PR611.P58   1985   821'.914'09   85-12979
ISBN 0-8103-1718-4 (set)

Contents

Contents

Dictionary of Literary Biography • Volume Forty

Poets of Great Britain and Ireland Since 1960
Part 2: M-Z

Dictionary of Literary Biography

George MacBeth

(19 January 1932-   )

Lawrence R. Ries
Skidmore College

SELECTED BOOKS: *A Form of Words* (Swinford, Oxfordshire: Fantasy Press, 1954);

Lecture to the Trainees (Oxford: Fantasy Press, 1962);

The Broken Places (Lowestoft, Suffolk: Scorpion Press, 1963; New York: Walker, 1968);

Penguin Modern Poets 6, by MacBeth, Edward Lucie-Smith, and Jack Clemo (Harmondsworth: Penguin, 1964);

A Doomsday Book (Lowestoft, Suffolk: Scorpion Press, 1965);

Noah's Journey (London: Macmillan, 1966; New York: Viking, 1966);

The Colour of Blood (London, Melbourne & Toronto: Macmillan, 1967; New York: Atheneum, 1967);

The Night of Stones (London: Macmillan, 1968; New York: Atheneum, 1969);

Jonah and the Lord (London: Macmillan, 1969; New York: Holt, 1970);

A War Quartet (London: Macmillan, 1969);

The Burning Cone (London: Macmillan, 1970);

The Orlando Poems (London: Macmillan, 1971);

Collected Poems, 1958-1970 (London & Basingstoke: Macmillan, 1971; New York: Atheneum, 1972);

The Scene-Machine (Mainz: B. Schott's Soehne, 1971);

Shrapnel (London: Macmillan, 1973);

Prayers (Shirley, Solthull: Aquila, 1973);

A Poet's Year (London: Gollancz, 1973);

My Scotland: Fragments of a State of Mind (London: Macmillan, 1973);

Shrapnel and A Poet's Year (New York: Atheneum, 1974);

© *Jerry Bauer*

The Transformation (London: Gollancz, 1975);

In the Hours Waiting for the Blood to Come (London: Gollancz, 1975);

The Samurai (New York: Harcourt Brace Jovanovich, 1975; London: Quartet, 1976);

The Survivor (London: Quartet, 1977; New York: Harcourt Brace Jovanovich, 1978);

Buying A Heart (London: Omphalos, 1978; New York: Atheneum, 1978);

The Seven Witches (London: W. H. Allen, 1978; New York: Harcourt Brace Jovanovich, 1978);

Poems of Love and Death (London: Secker & Warburg, 1980; New York: Atheneum, 1980);

A Kind of Treason (London: Hodder & Stoughton, 1981);

The Katana (New York: Simon & Schuster, 1981);

Poems from Oby (London: Secker & Warburg, 1982; New York: Atheneum, 1983).

PLAY PRODUCTIONS: *The Doomsday Show*, London, 1964;

The Scene-Machine, Kassell, Germany, 1971; London, 1972.

OTHER: *The Penguin Book of Sick Verse*, edited, with an introduction, by MacBeth (Harmondsworth: Penguin, 1963; Baltimore: Penguin, 1965);

The Penguin Book of Animal Verse, edited, with an introduction, by MacBeth (Harmondsworth: Penguin, 1965);

Poetry: 1900-1965, edited by MacBeth (London: Longmans/Faber & Faber, 1967);

The Penguin Book of Victorian Verse, edited, with an introduction, by MacBeth (Harmondsworth: Penguin, 1969);

The Falling Splendour: Poems of Alfred Lord Tennyson, edited by MacBeth (London & New York: Macmillan, 1970);

The Doomsday Show, in *New English Dramatists 14* (Harmondsworth: Penguin, 1970);

The Book of Cats, edited by MacBeth and Martin Booth (London: Secker & Warburg, 1976; New York: Morrow, 1977).

George MacBeth was one of the original members of that coterie of poets that gathered under the wings of, first, Philip Hobsbaum and, then, Edward Lucie-Smith in the mid-1950s. These poets, partly in reaction to the orthodoxy of Movement poetry and partly in pursuit of their own stated poetic, "that the principle by which words work in poetry is something open to rational examination," became known as the Group. MacBeth's association with the Group was never based on stylistic cohesion, but rather benefited him through regular contact with critical and creative concepts of other writers. From this base he has become one of the most prolific and diverse poets of the past several decades.

George MacBeth was born on 19 January 1932, in the mining village of Shotts in Scotland to George MacBeth and Amelia Morton Mary Mann MacBeth. When he was four, his family moved to Sheffield. His memories of his childhood there during the war, especially the death of his father, would inform much of his later work. He attended New College, Oxford, where he graduated in 1955 with first-class honors in Classical Greats. His public career has been as a producer for the BBC, preparing programs on literature and the arts. Since 1976 MacBeth has divided his time between England and the United States. Although a native of Scotland, his poetry resonates more with the neuroticism of the modern city than with the rural tranquillity of his own country.

Few poets have generated the kind of lightning-rod criticism that has crackled around MacBeth's poetry. Such criticism is partly in response to his subject matter, partly in response to his style. While dealing with such traditional themes as personal suffering, psychological horror, and the grotesque effects of war, MacBeth imbues the material with his own brand of macabre humor and satiric wit. The effect is a poetics of black humor, a garish seriousness melded to hysterical fantasy. MacBeth's obsession with dark themes is matched by his versatility of style. He is a trickster, willing to pull out all stylistic stops in order to achieve his poetic ends. Sixteenth- and seventeenth-century verse forms are found intermingled with syllabic verse. He has a facile hand when playing with poetic form, and often the reader is distracted from the substance of the poem by the poetic sleight of hand. The tension aroused by this gamesmanship has led critics to be wary of his art. His formal dexterity is often seen as camouflage or misdirection for his inability to deal substantially with his thematic material. One critic has even suggested, "Maybe George MacBeth is a hoax."

MacBeth himself delights in the notoriety that surrounds him. His book jackets frequently carry the most barbed of his critics' comments. Neither the Movement nor the Group prepared the public for MacBeth's poetry. His ability to twist language and verse to any end is viewed with horror by many who praised the same quality in W. H. Auden. In addition, MacBeth is willing to fail reaching for poetic effect rather than wait for the exact line or meter. He is often a poet of quantity rather than quality; as he explains, "the important thing is to thrash out huge quantities of fairly well-written poetry. If it doesn't last, who cares?"

Ironically, MacBeth's very first volume of poetry, *A Form of Words* (1954), is destined to last, and has indeed become a collector's item. This slight volume appeared contemporaneously with the birth of the Movement, but MacBeth was able to keep his distance from those poets. He does acknowledge early influence from Ted Hughes, especially in his interest in animal violence, but he is less respectful of the Movement poets' care and deliberation: "The Movement weren't prepared to churn out a bad poem about the most important experience of their lives. A willingness to do that seems to me the first essential of an important poet." *A Form of Words,* both in title and substance, shows the influence of William Empson, an influence that seemed almost omnipresent in the early and mid-1950s. As a result, the poems are heavy in verbal and stylistic playfulness, and hint at a retreat from life into style.

This first volume was important not only for launching MacBeth's poetic career but also for providing him with direction and focus. Perhaps most important it brought him into contact with the Group, with whom he met regularly for the next nine years to discuss the writing of poetry.

A pamphlet, *Lecture to the Trainees* (1962), preceded his second book of poetry, *The Broken Places* (1963), by a year. The long wait between *A Form of Words* and *The Broken Places* might have raised expectations of a change in direction, a change in voice. The second book, however, reconfirms and accentuates what was good and bad in the first. The technical expertise is still there, and technique has become an object in itself. Several of the poems are pure intellectual experiments that few will enjoy. There is a considerable body of syllabic verse in this volume, a verse form that had become popular in England during the 1950s, for it provided a low-key, unobtrusive structure while demanding a high level of technical rigidity. The thematic direction of the poetry is suffused with MacBeth's preoccupation with cruelty and violence. But he brings a macabre vision to this subject and refuses to displace the unpleasant sadism of contemporary life with dreamy visions of a pastoral world. His dark sympathies have bought him little grace among critics, but he clings firmly to his vision. The notes appended to certain poems often contain greater shock effects than the poems themselves. The note to "The Son," for example, explains, "A mortuary attendant rapes the body of a dead woman. He associates her with his mother, who died of a liver disease." The poem itself has little that is shocking

George MacBeth, 1964 (Evening Standard *Collection, BBC Hulton Picture Library*)

and is quite simply a well-wrought poem. But the same critics who had a difficult time with Thom Gunn's pseudofascist poems found themselves even more upset with MacBeth's surrealistic grotesqueries. His poetry was labeled "sick," "unpleasant," and "sadistic" (*London Magazine,* October 1965). But the general critical impulse was, and remained for some time, not to discuss MacBeth thematically, but to accuse him of avoiding substance through his slick and contrived technique. Norman MacCaig raised the question whether MacBeth was "a writer with a compulsive interest in technique because he has no compulsive themes" (*New Statesman,* 7 June 1963).

At this time, also, MacBeth edited for Penguin the first of several books he would prepare for them, *The Penguin Book of Sick Verse* (1963). If he was spoiling for a literary fight, this book was certain to help his cause. Ian Hamilton had said in the *London Magazine* (December 1963) that *The Broken Places* was marked by a "gratuitous nastiness of tone and subject." MacBeth did little to deflect this kind of criticism when he remarked in his introduction to *The Penguin Book of Sick Verse,* "The primary aim of this anthology has been to amuse." Then he presented eight sections of sick verse: illness, mental breakdown, visions of doom, world weariness, corpse love, lovesickness, cruelty, and sick jokes. The *Times Literary Supplement* (9 January 1964) treated the entire book as a sick joke and dismissed it and its editor in harsh, denunciatory terms.

MacBeth himself seemed to thrive on the criticism he was receiving. Although nine years separated *A Form of Words* and *The Broken Places,* the following years would see almost a yearly volume of poetry from him. In addition, he published many of his poems individually in pamphlets through the small presses (Scorpion, Sceptre, Fantasy, Turret) and even had several published privately.

A Doomsday Book (1965) develops the two directions that his earlier volumes had indicated: a high playfulness in technique and theme, and a lonely, detached personal voice. Here he throws out the syllabics for which he had previously shown fondness and seems determined to demonstrate that his technical wizardry is as effective within the confines of straightforward Victorian stanzaic and rhyme schemes. The childlike element in his poetry is much in evidence, both when he sees the poem as an elaborate game and when he writes poems about real or imagined animals. "The Ski Murders" for example is slick and inventive: the incidents of a detective story are arranged in alphabetical order like encyclopedia entries. The poem as game remains a constant in MacBeth's literary credo, and he has not been deterred by the unsympathetic response this kind of poetry has received. Perhaps the best work in this volume are those poems in which he is able to establish a small, personal voice. He reaches back into memories of childhood for poems such as "The Return" and "A Dirge," creating moments of loneliness and fear, but without the self-indulgence of certain confessional poets.

The Colour of Blood (1967) is a deliberate attempt to join technique and integrity, to wed the high technical accomplishment to significant thematic patterns. There is both gain and loss in this attempt: the personal voice is once more absent, but the language has become more resourceful and vital. Instead of the familiar Scottish landscape, MacBeth gives us Arabian, Indian, and Jewish backgrounds. He presents a series of dream monologues in elaborate stanzaic form. These poems are dense and intricate, and the author has provided notes which present the context for several, although as before the poems can stand without them. The note for "The Blood-Woman" informs the reader that the poet is "waiting for a Muse whose embraces will

drain his blood." The poems work best when the dream quality is self-contained within the poem, as in the opening lines of "The Suicides": "I dream of whales. I feel upon my skin / Far seas beat." There are still some games, as in those poems called "Chinese Synopses," in which he arranges letters up and down on the page to imitate Chinese typography. C. B. Cox in a review in the *Spectator* (28 July 1967) called these experiments "complete hocus-pocus." For the most part, the joining of a language rich in metaphor and crisp in detail to his vital vision was well received by critics who earlier had balked.

MacBeth, beneath his laissez-faire exterior, seems to have paid attention to his critics, because each new volume, for better or worse, appears almost to be a direct response to the criticism of the preceding one. In his more perverse moments, he takes what was healthy in his earlier work and man-

Dust jacket for MacBeth's 1967 book, which was well received by some of the same critics who had earlier criticized his themes and techniques

Dust jacket for the 1971 book in which the adventures of MacBeth's mythical protagonist parody Ted Hughes's Crow

ages to make it, if not sick, weak. *The Night of Stones* (1968) was greeted as "a flamboyant disaster" (*Poetry,* November 1970). The poetry has become even less clear than the difficult dream poems of *The Colour of Blood;* there are surreal excursions through rituals of blood and transfiguration. He haunts the page with appalling scenes of bloodshed and nuclear holocaust, but these fail generally to take on tragic dimension because the poet seems unable to respond with a full emotional range to the human condition. This failure is best illustrated by the long opening poem, "Driving West," to which is attached a long explanatory note. The note itself is almost too complex to digest, but the poem's fourteen pages of dense surrealism are mainly interesting for their frequent display of cinematic technique: flashbacks, close-ups, mixed-time sequences. This poem, like others in the volume, disappoints in not holding the attention and by not engaging the emotions. There is an effective poem about dogs, "At Cruft's," which is an amalgam of eighteen short poems that effectively capture the physical characteristics of various species of dogs through clever poetic devices. And there are, of course, the almost

by now obligatory word and sound games that are based on vowel or numerical analyses of other poets' works. One poem is in a language that MacBeth invented for the occasion. The sense of play in poetry is similar to a chess game; it relies on both parties understanding the strategy. In this volume the delight remains almost exclusively with the creator. *Choice* stated succinctly, "This new collection is a disappointment."

A War Quartet (1969) returns to his personal experience of World War II and represents an innovative, energetic attempt to make sense of that experience. In an earlier interview, MacBeth had remarked that his father had been killed by a dud antiaircraft shell in Sheffield. Later the young MacBeth was bombed out of his home, an experience that, he felt, gave him as direct connection with the war as a serving man. The personal experience is transformed into four extended poems in blank verse that survey four major arenas of the war: the tank battles of North Africa, the aerial dogfights of the Battle of Britain, German submarine warfare, and the Russian campaign. In his introduction, MacBeth states that he is aiming at documentary surrealism, and that he uses astrological references to take the place of Homer's gods. Although this effort to deal with serious issues in a serious way was generally received as an improvement over his previous skillful posturing, the book was not considered a success. When he concentrates on immediate physical experience, his poetry is effective and moving. But much of this work is overwritten, and the artificial devices keep the poet from addressing issues directly. The obscurity of the private dream monologues was carried over to this treatment of historical events.

The Burning Cone (1970) and *The Orlando Poems* (1971) move MacBeth's poetry only slightly beyond the areas he has already explored. Impersonality once again dominates the tone and perhaps even more than in earlier poetry form provides a cover for the poet's own persona. In "Snow Leopard," the death of a cat is manipulated into a

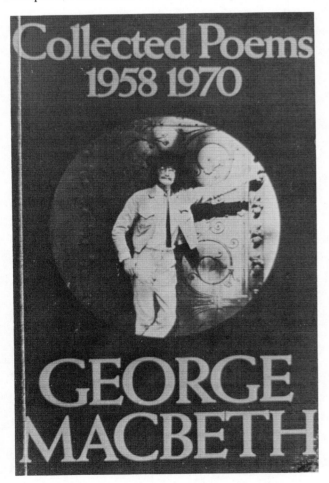

Front cover for the 1971 volume for which MacBeth chose his most-representative and most-valued poems from eight full-length collections, a large number of pamphlets, and two volumes of children's verse

complex dream sequence. "A Christmas Ring" consists of fifteen sonnets that trip over their own ornate diction. He renders Keats's "Ode on a Grecian Urn" in an inventive, sexy bit of modern slang. "A Light in Winter" works because MacBeth's disembodied tone of emptiness metes out this tale of adulterous love so exactly. *The Orlando Poems* tell of the varied adventures of a mythical protagonist and, in parody of *Crow*, honor MacBeth's debt to Ted Hughes. Unfortunately the stylistic and intellectual mockery fall far short of the original, and more than any previous volume this one loses itself in trivializing word play.

In 1971, Macmillan published *Collected Poems, 1958-1970.* Whether it is worthwhile for a poet to have a collected edition in mid-career is debatable; for MacBeth it provided an opportunity to garner both the most valued and the most representative from eight full volumes of poetry, a large number of separately published pamphlets, and two volumes of children's verse. The critical response to the individual publications had been mixed: angry, admiring, frustrated, laudatory.

He divided this collected edition into five sections: 1) public crisis—family deaths; 2) white goddess poems; 3) poems for children; 4) poems for performance; and 5) new poems. The selections show his versatility and technical dexterity, his facile arrangements of sound on the page as well as his intense journeys to the psychological, dark interiors. His tonal range is especially remarkable; he can achieve almost any effect he desires through his verbal acrobatics. What take on lesser stature are the earlier charges of outrageousness, gratuitous violence, and self-obsessed exhibitionism. With many of the minor performances omitted, an impressive collection remains. Not all sections are equally attractive or pleasing. The fourth section, which contains many of his experiments such as nonsense syllables and exploded typography, is sometimes entertaining and clever, sometimes wearisome. His poetic jokes, he said in the foreword, were "written for those who (like myself) regard themselves as children." The most satisfying poetry of this edition is found in the semiconfessional poems that deal with the pain and beauty of the quiet dark corners of life. Although his characters may never achieve tragic stature, the details of their human isolation bring them sympathetically to life. If they appear cold, they reflect the iciness of contemporary relationships. Even his poetic pranks and sick jokes ("The Auschwitz Rag") cannot totally conceal the pain. As a mid-career volume, *Collected Poems* is impressive for what has

PRAYERS

George MacBeth

Front cover for MacBeth's 1973 pamphlet of poems addressed to various fauna and flora

been accomplished, for what was and is still to come.

Shrapnel (1973) and *A Poet's Year* (1973) were originally published as slight separate volumes, and in 1974 they were republished together as a single volume. The title of the first refers to the bomb fragments MacBeth as a child used to pick up in the Sheffield streets. He sees these fragments of shrapnel as "the remains of a gigantic jig-saw of violence and pain." As in the past, he is most successful when he returns to the war of his childhood in poems such as "The Sirens," "The War," and "The Passing Ones," in which he captures those painful, unguarded moments of a small boy whose father had been needlessly killed by shrapnel. The opening poems, a litany of St. Francis-like prayers to a strange assortment of deities, are still a bit too whimsical and the pain is at times buried under literary form; but here MacBeth almost always keeps his tone under control. If, however, *Shrapnel* works because he has successfully fused, as the *Hudson Review* (Spring 1975) said, "the personal, social, and aesthetic," *A Poet's Year* seems rather disjointed

and devoid of a unifying voice. The title simply indicates that this book is an accumulation of what MacBeth wrote between September 1971 and September 1972. His earlier volumes, including *Shrapnel,* had a strong organizing voice in the background, even when that voice was strident or discordant. Here one senses that it has not been a very good year for the poet (there is no entry for October) and that he has given us, almost in ironic contrast to the volume it is paired with, the fragments, the shrapnel, of his adult life, complete with a haunting sense of loss. "On the Death of May Street," a slow elegy to the destruction of a street named after his grandmother, is symbolic of time that tramples everything of value in this volume. In the very first poem, "The Stones," the poet stands before the only building to survive the Allied raid in 1944 on Darmstadt; the final poem, "Time Passing," concerns the loss of a watch in the sea.

In 1973, MacBeth published a book of autobiographical reminiscences, *My Scotland: Fragments of a State of Mind.* These prose poems were written in short bursts between August 1969 and September 1970, and confront in a different literary and psychic way many of the issues he had dealt with earlier. The book is divided into five sections; each section is composed of a series of short prose pieces describing Scottish people and places. The speaker is a modest persona who, in exile, is attempting to recreate the Scotland of the 1930s that his parents knew. This book was an important piece of self-evaluation for MacBeth, for his examination of lost worlds assisted him in finding a firmer foothold in his own poetic landscape. He also began to explore fiction at this time as a new mode of expression. *The Transformation,* the first of four novels written in the 1970s, was published in 1975.

When *Buying a Heart* appeared in 1978, he had developed a more relaxed voice, even when he put on stage the old props: blood, corpses, Gothic tales. The title poem, which refers to an ox's heart that he bought to feed his cat, speaks calmly and directly of the peace the poet has made with the world: "I have to/accept the disquieting thought of/inevitable change, whether I/like it or not." There are several excellent poems on food ("How to Eat an Orange," "An Ode to English Food"), as well as a ghost tale ("Last Night"), and a chilling, hilarious story of Gothic revenge ("Amelia's Will"). He also returns to experimental verse for the first time in several volumes with the inventive "Crazy Jane's A.B.C.," illustrated by Robin Lawrie, a pop comic-strip story, "The Silver Needle," and another parody of *Crow,* "The Greedy Book." This is a fine

ON THE ROAD FROM WISBECH

Coming, they come
At me in white,
Going, they go
In awesome red,
Coming, they move
In pairs, in light.
In darkness now
Like zombies, dead

And glowing with
An after-life,
They pass along
In easy twos,
Arrowing for
A distant strife
And governed by
Their nervous shoes.

They glint like rubies
Far ahead
On rings. They seem
To glide like blood.
Coming, they bear
White flames to wed,
Spattering me

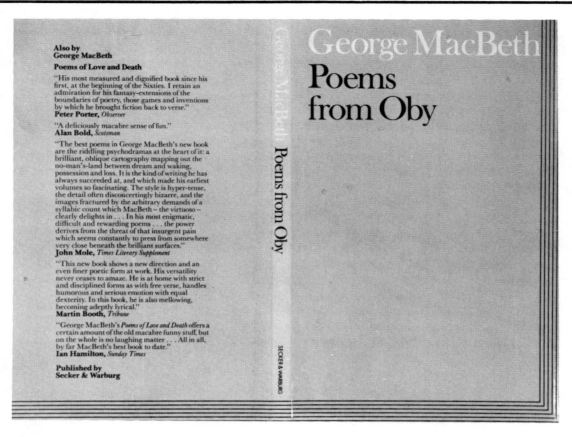

Dust jacket for MacBeth's 1982 book. The poet, who bought an old rectory in the parish of Oby in 1979, calls this book "the fruit of a new involvement with the countryside."

group of poems that received little critical acclaim. *Choice* (June 1979) called it "a little unattractive volume" that exhibited "bad taste in diction." *London Magazine* (June 1979) noted that "a good number of the poems seem to have been flung together in a hurry."

His 1980 volume, *Poems of Love and Death*, dispelled such criticism, for he returns to the controlled looseness of syllabics to confront the issues with which he has always been most successful: personal loss, wounded and wounding love, silent pain. MacBeth has developed for himself a dignified, mature tone, nurtured on a sense of suffering that has gradually grown more real, more intimate. In "The Creed," the poet speaks in his own voice of "the insurgency of pain / That will go, and will come again." Such knowledge, and acknowledgment, breathes an acute tenderness and lyricism into poems such as "The Gift," "In the Same Room," and "An Hour Ago." Up until this point, MacBeth's career had been that of a poet in search of a voice;

these poems assured us that he had found an appropriate one.

Poems from Oby (1982) confirmed and strengthened the direction of the previous volume. In the foreword MacBeth acknowledges the evolution in theme and style that has been occurring— "less diversified by comic and performance and experimental elements"—and attributes this growth to his own coming to terms with the world: "the luck of settlement, finding a piece of land to feel secure on, and someone to live there with." The poems themselves exhibit further moderation, an anecdotal tone, and themes of sensitive caring. "Thoughts on a Box of Razors" could have easily reached for the rawness and shock of his earlier work, but here MacBeth writes fourteen thoughtful sonnets that conclude in a thematic statement that summarizes the entire volume: "Wholeness is frail."

George MacBeth has always been a controversial poet, with both the critics and the popular audience. His reception in America has been warmer than in England, partly because the Americans are comfortable with his style of kinkiness. Sometimes he offends by trying; often he offends when he does not try. His poetry has always moved in two directions: inventive, quirky experiments, and personal poetry carved out in highly crafted verse. As a result, his poetry has frequently been damned and praised in the same review, for seldom have the two sides of MacBeth pleased the same sensibility. There is also some obvious critical discomfort in not being able to place him neatly in some literary niche. M. L. Rosenthal once called him "the Unidentified Flying Object of British verse," and Harry Morris, in the *Sewanee Review* (Spring 1971), said that his poetry is the product of "so much talent so frequently misdirected." Roger Garfitt notes that early on he acquired the reputation "as the *enfant terrible* of English poetry." But if one puts aside what has become at least in part a cultivated infamy, George MacBeth remains an interesting experimenter who is gradually refining his strengths, winnowing his weaknesses. His evolution over the past three decades shows clearly a developing sensibility for the isolated psyche as well as a talent for the craft of poetry that has few equals. In those efforts where these two qualities blend into a balanced achievement, his poetry stands among the best there is today.

References:

D. M. Black, "The Poetry of George MacBeth," *Scottish International* (Edinburgh), August 1968;

Roger Garfitt, "The Group," *British Poetry Since 1960*, edited by Michael Schmidt and Grevel Lindop (Oxford: Carcanet, 1972), pp. 29-49;

The Poet Speaks, edited by Peter Orr (London: Routledge, 1966), pp. 131-136;

M. L. Rosenthal, *The New Poets: American and British Poetry Since World War II* (New York & London: Oxford University Press, 1967), pp. 194-195, 260-262.

Papers:

The University of California, Los Angeles, and the State University of New York, Buffalo, have collections of MacBeth's papers.

Derek Mahon
(23 November 1941-   )

Brian Donnelly
Carysfort College

BOOKS: *Twelve Poems* (Belfast: Festival Publications, Queen's University, 1967);

Design for a Grecian Urn (Cambridge, Mass.: Erato Press, 1967);

Night Crossing (London & New York: Oxford University Press, 1968);

Ecclesiastes (Manchester: Phoenix Pamphlet Poets, 1969);

Beyond Howth Head (Dublin: Dolmen Press, 1970);

Lives (London: Oxford University Press, 1972);

The Snow Party (London & New York: Oxford University Press, 1975);

In Their Element: A Selection of Poems, by Mahon and Seamus Heaney (Belfast: Arts Council of Northern Ireland, 1977);

Light Music (Belfast: Ulsterman Publications, 1977);

The Sea in Winter (Dublin: Gallery Books, 1978; Old Deerfield, Mass.: Deerfield Books, 1979);

Poems 1962-1978 (London: Oxford University Press, 1979);

Courtyards in Delft (Dublin: Gallery Books, 1981);

The Chimeras (Dublin: Gallery Books, 1982);

The Hunt by Night (London: Oxford University Press, 1982);

A Kensington Notebook (London: Anvil Press, 1984).

TELEVISION: *Shadows on our Skin,* adapted from a novel by Jennifer Johnston, BBC 1, 1980;

How Many Miles to Babylon?, adapted from a novel by Johnston, BBC 2, 1981;

The Temptation of Eileen Hughes, adapted from a novel by Brian Moore, ITV (London), to be broadcast at a future date;

First Love, adapted from a novel by Ivan Turgenev, ITV (London), to be broadcast at a future date.

OTHER: *Modern Irish Poetry,* edited by Mahon (London: Sphere, 1972).

Derek Mahon is one of a significant number of poets from Northern Ireland who came to prominence in the late 1960s and early 1970s. He has published five full collections of verse to date, as well as a number of shorter volumes of poems, and is widely regarded as one of the most talented and original voices in contemporary poetry.

He was born and grew up in the city of Belfast, Northern Ireland, and was educated at the Royal Belfast Academical Institution (1953-1960), and at Trinity College, Dublin (1960-1965), where he majored in French. He began writing verse early, and his first publication, *Twelve Poems,* appeared in 1967. After leaving Trinity Mahon spent the next five years (1965-1970) teaching and doing odd jobs in England, France, Ireland, Canada, and the United States. In 1970 he settled in London on a more or less permanent basis and began a career as a freelance journalist, writing book reviews for the *Observer,* the *Listener, New Statesman,* and the *Times Literary Supplement.* He served as drama critic for the *Listener* (1971-1972) and as features editor for *Vogue* magazine (1974-1975) before returning to his native Northern Ireland in 1977 as writer in residence at the New University of Ulster, Coleraine, County Derry.

At the end of 1979 Mahon left the New University to work in the features department of the BBC. He wrote screen adaptations for television of novels by the Irish writers Jennifer Johnston and Brian Moore, as well as a dramatization of Ivan Turgenev's *First Love.* In 1981 Mahon was appointed poetry and fiction editor of the *New Statesman* in London, a position from which he has since resigned.

Mahon's career has been typical of the careers of many contemporary poets who divide their time between creative work in verse and the business of earning a living in the more lucrative areas of teaching, literary journalism, and public readings of their poetry. In Mahon's case there has been a creative interplay between his work as a poet and his other professional activities. His wide and eclectic reading as a reviewer has surely influenced his preoccupations as a poet and has often colored the texture and tone of his verses. On the other hand, the finely attuned ear of the poet and his creative intelligence have made him one of the most consistently interesting book reviewers, especially when the work under consideration is singular, quirky, or outside the mainstream of current fashion and taste. Likewise, his fine adaptations of novels for television reflect one of the most striking qualities found in his poetry: an acute ear for the nuances and inflections of the speaking voice as seen in his many fine monologues and verse letters.

Derek Mahon has published four major books of poems: *Night Crossing* (1968), *Lives* (1972), *The Snow Party* (1975), and *The Hunt by Night* (1982). His shorter publications such as *Beyond Howth Head* (1970) and *Courtyards in Delft* (1981) have formed the substance of these volumes, and his *Poems 1962-1978* (1979) collects most of the poems published up to 1978 as well as a substantial number of previously unpublished works. It should be noted that Mahon tends to revise many poems when including them in later books. Most of the revisions are fairly minor, such as the alteration of a few words; occasionally a poem is given a new title and an epigraph or dedication is added or dropped; but in some instances the form and/or content are significantly altered. Mahon has also published a "version" of Gerard de Nerval's *Les Chimères, The Chimeras* (1982), which further reflects his skill as a translator who can render the feel and substance of the original work and, at the same time, make the utterance entirely his own.

All of Mahon's books are remarkably homogeneous, and, though there is an ever increasing technical and rhetorical sureness from book to book, his main subject matter remains singularly consistent. Indeed it is possible to view his whole work as variations upon certain recurrent themes. The opening poem in *The Chimeras,* "El Desdichado," is unmistakably Mahon and shows some of the most individual characteristics and preoccupations of his work as a whole. The speaker in this short lyric expresses his sense of loss and isolation with a precision and control that mask passion and evoke a detached pathos: "I am the widower—dim, disconsolate—/The Aquitainian prince in the ruined tower./My star is dead, my constelled lute/Emblazoned with the black sun of despair." As in many of his earlier poems the quiet formality of the diction and the tightly controlled stanzas create a feeling of detachment between the speaker and the plight which his words express. This detachment can be seen most obviously in "A Disused Shed in Co.

Courtesy of Bernard Stone,
The Turret Book Shop

Wexford" (in *The Snow Party*), a long poem which many of Mahon's admirers regard as his most impressive achievement so far. Here he characteristically brings the inanimate world to life—in this instance "a thousand mushrooms" locked away in a shed of a derelict country hotel. His unsentimental rendering of their existence builds a convincing and moving metaphor of all the persecuted and forgotten peoples in human history. The poem succeeds largely through the fine evocation of the atmosphere and the details that work upon the narrator's sensibilities. The condition of the mushrooms is vividly described in a series of lucid images which poignantly create the essence of suffering and of loss: "What should they do but desire?/So many days beyond the rhododendrons/With the world waltzing in its bowl of cloud,/They have learnt patience and silence/Listening to the rooks querulous in the high wood." Or, "Spiders have spun, flies dusted to mildew/And once a day, perhaps, they have heard something—/A trickle of masonry, a shout from the blue/Or a lorry changing gear at the end of the lane."

The theme of loss, exile, and isolation is a recurring preoccupation in Mahon's work as is his related fascination with figures who live on the fringes of society. An awareness of being cut off from the lives of ordinary folk occupies a central place in the verse, and many of his most characteristic poems have a lonely, isolated figure or an odd-man-out at their center. We encounter such figures in all of Mahon's books; in, for example, poems such as "Grandfather," "My Wicked Uncle," and "The Death of Marilyn Monroe" in *Night Crossing;* "The Last Dane," "A Dying Art," and "As God is my Judge" in *Lives;* "A Refusal to Mourn" and "Going Home" in *The Snow Party;* and "An Old Lady," "Knut Hamsun in Old Age," and "Ovid in Tomis" in *The Hunt by Night.* In his creation of characters who are totally removed from any contact with normal social life Mahon reveals his affinity with Samuel Beckett, a writer whose spare and often bleak lyricism has probably influenced Mahon as much as W. H. Auden, Louis MacNeice, and the French poets of the late-nineteenth century and earlier-twentieth century. For example, in "Exit Molloy," the fourth section of "Four Walks in the country near Saint Brieuc" (in *Night Crossing*), he has succeeded in capturing the tone of the Beckett character, a tone of bewildered and resigned detachment from the sufferings of the body, heightened by characteristic pedantry.

Mahon, whose career since leaving high school has removed him from his native Ulster and into the uncertain world of free-lance writing in England and elsewhere, has an obvious personal understanding of the conditions of exile, uncertainty, and cultural alienation. In the final stanzas of "Afterlives" (in *The Snow Party*) he memorably describes his feelings on stepping ashore in war-torn Belfast, off the boat from England in 1974:

> And I step ashore in a fine rain
> To a city so changed
> By five years of war
> I scarcely recognize
> The places I grew up in,
> The faces that try to explain.
>
> But the hills are still the same
> Grey-blue above Belfast.
> Perhaps if I'd stayed behind
> And lived it bomb by bomb
> I might have grown up at last
> And learnt what is meant by home.

Unlike some other contemporary Ulster poets, such as Seamus Heaney and John Montague, Mahon has rarely attempted to confront the troubles in his native province from a direct historical and social perspective. Nevertheless, his unease with the role of poet and cultured commentator, whose roots are deep in a society governed by guns

and sectarian clichés, has found complex expression in his work. In "Rage for Order" (in *Lives*) he asserts the case for poetry which seems, in a city like Belfast at least, to be "a dying art,/an eddy of semantic scruples/in an unstructurable sea." The poem ends on the positive assertion that, nevertheless, "it cannot be/long now till I have need of his/desperate ironies." But this seems more a statement of faith than of reason, as was his contention that "a good poem is a paradigm of good politics— of people taking to each other with honest subtlety, at a profound level." Mahon's later unease with the so-called civilizing powers of literature in a culture like Northern Ireland's is more persuasive and deeply felt. In his long, discursive, and splendidly controlled verse letter "The Sea in Winter" (in *Poems 1962-1978*), he confesses that "all the time I have my doubts/About this verse making. The shouts/Of souls in torment round the town/At closing time make as much sense/And carry as much significance/As these lines carefully set down." The only hope is that "One day,/Perhaps, the words will find their mark/And leave a brief glow on the dark. . . ."

When Mahon's poetry does "glow" it is when memory and imagination illuminate aspects of everyday life that are unremarkable in their ordinariness. In this respect he is no latter-day William Wordsworth of the *Lyrical Ballads* celebrating the wild flowers of the fields. His fascination is with such things as the banal day-to-day existence of life in the modern city. For example, in an early poem, "Glengormley" (in *Night Crossing*), he celebrates the humdrum life of a Belfast suburb with characteristic irony and playfulness. In the later "The Sea in Winter" a rundown resort on the County Antrim coast emanates "a strange poetry of decay." In *Courtyards in Delft* (1981) Mahon's response to Pieter de Hooch's 1659 painting is to those very minutiae of stolid, unexciting bourgeois life that preoccupied the Flemish painters of the seventeenth century. Having described the work's details, Mahon writes: "I lived there as a boy and know the coal/Glittering in its shed, late-afternoon/Lambency informing the deal table,/The ceiling cradled in a radiant spoon."

Mahon's remote landscapes and decaying cityscapes are always described with a precision and an intensity that render them vital, alive, and often strangely beautiful. We see these characteristics throughout all of his works, particularly in such recent poems as "Derry Morning," "One of these Nights," and in "A Garage in Co. Cork" from *The Hunt by Night.* "One of these Nights" opens as

DEREK
MAHON

THE HUNT
BY NIGHT

Poetry Book Society Choice

Front cover for the 1982 book that Seamus Heaney called "Derek Mahon's most exuberant and authoritative single volume to date"

satisfaction/Of picking long butts from a wet gutter/Like daisies from a clover field in summer." The concluding image is finely judged to deepen the morbidity of a poem that could challenge many an Old Testament prophecy. It is a memento mori of an imagination painfully aware of life's brevity, of human frailty and insignificance when seen in the long vistas of time.

Mahon constantly sees the individual as a prisoner of history and history itself as an illusory progress of the species: "For this is how the centuries work — / Two steps forward, one step back" ("Derry Morning"). In "Rathlin Island" (in *The Hunt by Night*) a visit to the now peaceful site of an ancient massacre off the Belfast coast causes the speaker to reflect that "We leave here the infancy of the race,/ Unsure among the pitching surfaces/Whether the future lies before us or behind." Many of Mahon's poems are concerned with the individual's pursuit of personal freedom in an attempt to escape from all those forces—cultural, social, and historic— which inevitably help make us what we are. "The Last of the Fire Kings" (in *The Snow Party*) is a case in point. Mahon skillfully places the ancient myth of the King, who must sacrifice his life in order that the tribe may prosper, in the environment of Northern Ireland during the 1970s. The speaker asserts that "I am/Through with history— /Who lives by the sword/Dies by the sword./Last of the fine kings, I shall/Break with tradition and/Die by my own hand/Rather than perpetuate/The barbarous cycle." But the monologue ends with the admission that is impossible to evade the "barbarous cycle" of historic determinism. He must "die their creature and be thankful." The desire to be "through with history" (a phrase that recurs often in Mahon's poetry) echoes Stephen Dedalus's admission in *Ulysses* that Irish history is a nightmare from which he is trying to awake. Given the course of events in Northern Ireland since 1969 it is a wish that Mahon shares with many of his contemporaries, even those, like himself, who live abroad and are not directly involved in the day-to-day life of the province.

The barbarous nature of so much that has taken place in Belfast or Derry in recent years is only the immediate focus of a wider concern for Mahon. He ends "A Postcard from Berlin" (in *The Hunt by Night*) with a whimsical yet serious couplet addressed to Friedrich Hölderlin, "Give us a ring on your way back/And tell us what the nations lack!" At the deepest level his concern is with the nature of violence itself and its place in man's life and history. The title poem from his third major

though it were an impressionist painting in words, evoking the city of London sinisterly metamorphosed by moonlight and silence with "its squares/ Bone pale in the moonlight,/Its quiet thoroughfares/A map of desolation." Mahon's vision constantly asserts the ultimate insubstantiality of man and his carefully created artifacts when viewed in the perspective of historic time. The image of a world returned to its most primitive state is one that finds varied expression from his earliest verse to his latest. In "Entropy," "What Will Remain," and "Consolations of Philosophy" (*Lives*) he approaches the grim, despairing negations of Beckett's *Lessness*. In "Consolations of Philosophy" there is neither his characteristic wit nor irony to relieve the macabre prediction of the suffering awaiting the decomposing dead, among whom, "a few will remember with affection/Dry bread, mousetrap cheese, and the

Blue Moon

A ghost of soap in the sky,
I do my white shining
In the ~~victorious~~ dawn   *golden*
~~Who belong to another dispensation.~~

Of an alien dispensation.

for "Light Music"?

Draft for a recent poem (the author)

collection, *The Snow Party,* makes this point. This elegant lyric is based upon the travel account by the seventeenth-century Japanese haiku poet Bashō, entitled *The Narrow Road to the Deep North.* Here Mahon skillfully juxtaposes an evocative and decorous scene of ceremonial calm with an image of primitive barbarity:

> Bashō, coming
> To the city of Nagoya,
> Is asked to a snow party.
> . . . .
> Snow is falling on Nagoya
> And farther south
> On the tiles of Kyōto.
>
> Eastward, beyond Irago,
> It is falling
> Like leaves on the cold sea.
>
> Elsewhere they are burning
> Witches and heretics
> In the boiling squares.
> . . . .
> But there is silence
> In the houses of Nagoya
> And the hills of Ise.

That an old and complex civilization can contain such brutality is an irony that is delicately suggested here, especially in the seemingly casual "Elsewhere" and in sustaining the same cool tone of voice throughout the last three stanzas. Mahon has succeeded in suggesting the awful paradox that affronts the normal scale of humane values: the existence of gross inhumanity within a highly civilized culture. His achievement is that his stanzas quietly obliterate the gap in space and time that allows us to conceive of these two orders of existence as being mutually exclusive. Again in "Penhurst Place" (*Poems 1962-1978*) he evokes the home of the Sidney family and, by implication, the culture of the English Renaissance, to bring the reader to the same awareness of the interdependence of a refined civilization and imperial brute force and conquest.

The poems collected in *The Hunt by Night* reveal how consistent Mahon's interests, concerns, and preoccupations have remained since the publication of *Night Crossing.* The title poem of this volume is, like many earlier lyrics, a creatively imaginative response to a painting, in this instance one by Paolo Uccello (dated 1465). Mahon's poem re-creates all the excitement and bustle represented on the canvas, but it goes well beyond mere verbal recreation to probe the tantalizing relationship between art and life. "How to Live" and "The Earth" show his talent for taking the lines of other poets (in these instances Horace and Boris Pasternak) and rendering their thoughts and feelings in an idiom that is at once faithful to the original and to his own sensibility. "The Joycentenary Ode" is a lively and funny pastiche of the wake-talk that is both a celebration and a gentle ironic commentary on Joyce's art and life.

The qualities that most distinguish Mahon as a poet are his singularity of vision and the rich resources of technical and verbal skills that have characterized his work from his earliest poems. To read his work as a whole is to see humankind as a species lost and doomed in the vast reaches of space and cosmic time, clinging to a comforting humanity that is both pathetic and heroic; a species, moreover, who inhabit a humdrum world that sometimes radiates a strange beauty. The opening of "North Wind: Portrush" is typical:

> I shall never forget the wind
> On this benighted coast.
> It works itself into the mind
> Like the high keen of a lost
> Lear-spirit in agony
> Condemned for eternity
>
> To wander cliff and cove
> Without comfort, without love.
> It whistles off the stars
> And the existential, black
> Face of the cosmic dark:
> We crouch to roaring fires.
>
> Yet there are mornings when,
> Even in midwinter, sunlight
> Flares, and a rare stillness
> Lies upon roof and garden,
> Each object eldritch-bright,
> The sea scarred but at peace.

The formal movement of the stanzas as well as the precision and clarity of diction in controlling and articulating feeling and emotion are qualities that reveal Mahon as a poet whose individual voice carries echoes of the central tradition in English verse and whose intelligence and sensibility have been nourished on the wider reaches of European literature.

Roger McGough

(9 November 1937-   )

Edward Broadbridge
Paderup College

BOOKS: *The Mersey Sound: Penguin Modern Poets 10,* by McGough, Adrian Henri, and Brian Patten (Harmondsworth: Penguin, 1967; revised and enlarged, 1974; revised and enlarged again, 1983);

Frinck, A Day in the Life Of, and Summer with Monika (London: Joseph, 1967; New York: Ballantine, 1967);

Watchwords (London: Cape, 1969);

After the Merrymaking (London: Cape, 1971);

Out of Sequence (London: Turret Books, 1972);

Gig (London: Cape, 1973);

Sporting Relations (London: Eyre Methuen, 1974);

Clowns on the Road, by Grimms (McGough and others) (London: Eyre Methuen, 1974);

In the Glassroom (London: Cape, 1976);

Mr. Noselighter (London: Whizzard, 1977);

Summer with Monika, revised and enlarged edition (London: Whizzard/Deutsch, 1978);

Holiday on Death Row (London: Cape, 1979);

You Tell Me: Poems, by McGough and Michael Rosen (Harmondsworth: Kestrel, 1979);

Unlucky for Some (London: Turret Books, 1981);

Waving at Trains (London: Cape, 1982);

The Great Smile Robbery (London: Kestrel, 1983);

Sky in the Pie (London: Kestrel, 1983);

New Volume, by McGough, Henri, and Patten (Harmondsworth: Penguin, 1983);

The Stowaways (London: Kestrel, forthcoming 1985).

PLAY PRODUCTIONS: *Birds, Marriages, and Deaths,* London, 1964;

The Chauffeur-Driven Rolls, Liverpool, 1966;

The Commission, Liverpool, 1967;

The Puny Little Life Show, London, 1969;

Stuff, London, 1970;

Word Play, Edinburgh, 1978;

Golden Nights and Golden Days, Nottingham, Nottingham Playhouse, 1979;

Summer with Monika, Hammersmith, Lyric Theatre, 1979;

Roger McGough

Lifeswappers, Edinburgh, Edinburgh Festival, 1980;

Watchwords, Nottingham, Nottingham Playhouse, 1980;

All the Trimmings, Hammersmith, Lyric Theatre, 1980;

The Mouthtrap, by McGough and Brian Patten, Edinburgh, Edinburgh Festival, 1982;

Wind in the Willows, lyrics by McGough, Washington, D.C., 1984.

OTHER: Edward Lucie-Smith, ed., *The Liverpool Scene,* includes poems by McGough (London: Carroll, 1967);

Philip Larkin, ed., *The Oxford Book of Twentieth-Century Verse,* includes poems by McGough (Oxford: Oxford University Press, 1973);

The Puny Little Life Show and *Scaffold,* in *Open Space Plays,* edited by Charles Marowitz (Harmondsworth: Penguin, 1974);

Strictly Private, edited, with an introduction, by McGough (London: Kestrel, 1981).

Since he appeared on the Liverpool scene together with fellow poets Adrian Henri and Brian Patten in the early 1960s Roger McGough has been one of the most popular poets in Britain, both as pop poet and as popularizer of poetry. The Liverpool poets came to prominence at the same time as, and with a similar background to, the Beatles, and their best-selling poetry collection, subtitled *Penguin Modern Poets 10* (1967), carried the title *The Mersey Sound*. McGough's books have sold consistently well; all his collections have been reprinted, and *Gig* went through five printings between 1973 and 1981. On the poetry-reading circuit McGough regularly draws large audiences, the success of his work being due not least to his own performance of it. He has a wide experience of the world of popular music as a member of The Scaffold (a pop music and poetry) group, from 1964 to 1975, with whom he rose to national fame via the hit record *Lily the Pink* in 1969. He is now widely involved in theater, radio, and television productions.

McGough was born in Liverpool in 1937, the son of Mary McGarry and Roger Francis McGough, a docker: "I was born in a working-class home where, if you're a poet, it's something to be ashamed of. Sort of thing one tells one's mother and one's mother says you must get to be a teacher or something." He was educated at St. Mary's College in Crosby, near Liverpool, where he failed English literature at "O" Level at the age of fifteen. After gaining a B.A. in French and geography from Hull University in 1957 and a Certificate of Education in 1958, he taught at St. Kevin's Comprehensive School and the Mable Fletcher College, both in Liverpool, and began to give occasional readings of his poetry in local coffee bars. Partly swept along by the excitement of the city in the early 1960s, he decided to turn professional as singer and poet with The Scaffold, an antiestablishment, satirical group that had a big following on the college circuit. McGough read his poems between numbers and occasionally altered his lyrics to suit the occasion or the audience. He held a poetry fellowship at the University of Loughborough from 1973 to 1975, during which time he also toured with Grimms, an amalgam of The Scaffold and the Bonzo Dog Band, who experimented with a surprise blend of poetry, clowning, and pop music.

Since the mid-1970s McGough has spent more time and effort on the coming generation, partly through editing exciting anthologies of children's poetry and partly through his own stories and verses for children. Alongside this he has produced a steady crop of features and dramas for the BBC and a number of stage plays, one of which, *The Mouthtrap*, written in collaboration with Brian Patten, finds two poets in the dressing room during a poetry reading being visited by the Muse/Angel of Death. From 1970 to 1980 McGough was married to Thelma Monaghan. At present he lives in London.

In 1967 some of McGough's poems appeared in *The Liverpool Scene*, edited by Edward Lucie-Smith, in which the respected English critic collected various manifestations of the Liverpool muse and stressed that "essentially, the poetry now being written in Liverpool differs from other contemporary English verse by being spoken and listened to, rather than by being read." In an interview with Lucie-Smith, McGough explained that his initial inspiration came from France: "I suddenly realized that when I was reading people like Rimbaud and Baudelaire, I felt as they felt. I recognized a kindred spirit, and therefore I must be a poet, and therefore I started writing poetry." The only other literary link seems to be with Joyce and Irish verbal comedy, but McGough disowned this influence years ago: "We've got no literary or dramatic heritage. We try out what we're doing, and we test it on people, and people react, and we sort of go on from there." From this early period comes McGough's best-known poem, "Let Me Die a Youngman's Death," on the wish to die young, by violence, and not in old age: "Let me die a youngman's death/not a free-from-sin, tiptoe-in/candle-wax-and-waning death/not a curtains-drawn, by angels-borne,/'what a nice way to go' death."

Summer with Monika (1967; revised and enlarged, 1978) is McGough's attempt to lyricize a Liverpool romance in a Parisian vein. In forty-two poems of varying length and quality he celebrates his beloved with affectionate sentimentality—"we made lovesongs with our bodies/i became the words/and she put me to music"—and surrealist images of domestic bliss and bogus jealousy—"while i was polishing the bluespeckles/in a famous soappowder/i saw you fondling/the fryingpan/i distinctly/saw you fondling the frying/my fryingpan." Many of the effects for which the Liverpool poets became known are here in embryonic form: "the revaluation of the cliché," as Adrian Henri called it, in McGough's "your finger/sadly/has a familiar ring/about it"; the metamorphosis of "monika the teathings are taking over!/the cups are

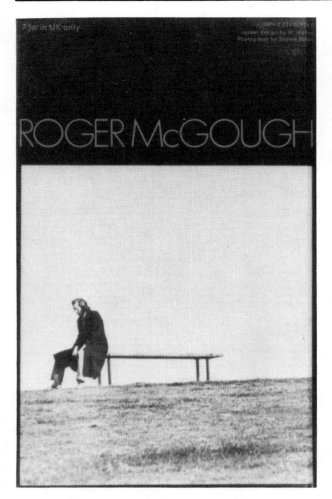

Covers for McGough's 1973 book, which includes poems that take the reader on a tour of England with his band, The Scaffold

as big as bubblecars/they throttle round the room"; the idiosyncrasy of printing together two words semantically connected, as in "the room nolonger a place for hideandseeking in/but a container that we use for eatandsleeping in"; the extensive use of the pun and the rare spoonerism; and underlying all the invitation to join the poet, the group, the movement against outside forces, be they teathings or politicians. Often the lines are loosely strung, even interchangeable, but in the eighth lyric, style, content, and technique suddenly fuse into a form and order as fluid as the subject: "i have lately learned to swim/and now feel more at home/in the ebbandflow of your slim/rhythmic tide/than in the fully-dressed/couldntcareless/restless world outside."

Watchwords (1969) gives fuller rein to these desires and sympathies. Random stimuli, often sexual, are treated expansively and lightheartedly, in the already distinctive McGough style: "she stayed

for the encores and of course very soon/seduced the whole orchestra and called the tune/oh the takings were good/but the giving divine/for now the orgasms were not only mine//But sadly the bride came before the fall/I'd settled for one though I'd wanted them all." The ego typically outwits transparently bathetic experience. Other poems move in the same direction: "Poem on being in love with two girls at the same time," "S.W.A.L.K.," and "My Busseductress," about a woman who dreams of turning her Liverpool bus into a strip joint, doing her act, collecting "fares please," and repairing upstairs with "men of her choice." The major success of the collection is "Soil," in which McGough reflects on how his childhood love of mudpies has changed to a distaste for dirt at puberty, and now to the awful reality of soil as dust: "A handful of you/Drummed on my father's/Waxworked coffin//at last it all made sense." Here the metaphor is held strictly in check, the emotion authenticated.

After the Merrymaking (1971) divides into three parts: a loose sequence of love-turned-sour poems, a set of free interior monologues by McGough, and eleven prose pieces, intended as poetry, on the "Amazing Adventures of P. C. Plod." In the first, the poet's love life remains a minefield, where escaping from one explosion only triggers another. The poetic achievement is as irregular and unstable as the emotions. Four brilliant lines—"Old scars become new wounds/when kissed overmuch/And memories longhardened/now moisten to the touch"—are immediately cheapened by: "Love is a circle/we've completed the course/Now we savour the honeymoon/before the divorce." The Plod pieces in the third part run through various tales of the stock-in-trade thick policeman. There are moments of genuine humor, as when Plod falls for Policewoman Hodges—"he felt her serge with

pleasure"—but by and large a little Plod goes a long way.

Out of Sequence (1972) appeared in a limited edition of 200 copies. With the exception of "Commonmarket Poem" (which later appeared under the title "Newsflash" in *In the Glassroom*) all the poems were reprinted in section two of *Gig* (1973). Section one is called "On the Road" and section two "At the Roadside," convenient headings for poems of action and reflection. Ironically, though, the wisest reflection takes place on the road. In eighteen poems, each with a city as its title, McGough takes the reader on a tour of England with his band, capturing the authentic, often fleeting, experience of being on the road in a chronicle of fun and futility. Show business is low business: the Birmingham hotel is "Auschwitz with H and C," the female manager a Kommandante; at Brighton "the only people who say hello/want money"; at Bradford "The occasional curry keeps the ɥɔɐɯoʇs [sic] on its

Covers for McGough's 1976 book, dedicated "to those who gaze out of windows when they should be paying attention"

toes"; and by Sheffield "Far sweeter than the stink of/death is the stink of life." The odd show goes well, but mostly the poet is "stoned" or lonely or both. But this is a self-image he controls to a calculated effect: he is the lonely clown, the Hamburg Beatle. McGough thus hammers his more depressing moments into wry comedy—"rain crackles/the flags/i pour/whiskey/over my/cornflakes//moonshine breakfast." The central poem in "At the Roadside" is "the most unforgettable character i've ever met gives advice to the young poet." Though hardly a manifesto, the fifty-odd lines add up to a view of the poet as lawbreaker and underminer: "May they [your poems] break and enter, assault and batter,//and loiter in the mind with intent.// . . . May they be damned and published."

As poetry fellow at Loughborough, a university specializing in physical education, McGough offered his gratitude in *Sporting Relations* (1974), with drawings by Terry Gilliam, formerly of Monty Python. The 600 lines cover forty-two assorted uncles, aunts, and distant relatives, all of whom excel at some sport or other. The concept is widely defined: "Angelina (blueblooded) owned a yacht/and smoked pacht/a lacht." "Uncle Len/a redundant gamekeeper/strangled cuckoos." Elmer Hoover from Vancouver goes fishing in Liverpool and catches "a shoal of slimywhite balloonthings/which he brought home in a jamjar./'Mersey cod' we told him." Back home gullible Elmer nonplusses his friends with "But you shudda seen the one that got away." The book is comedy throughout, in a tradition that stretches back through Monty Python and 1960s satire to Spike Milligan's *Goon Show* scripts for the BBC in the 1950s. Its exuberant delight in wordplay is infectious but it never pretends to be more than a joke catalogue.

In the Glassroom (1976) is "Dedicated to those who gaze out of windows when they should be paying attention"—hence the title—and contains

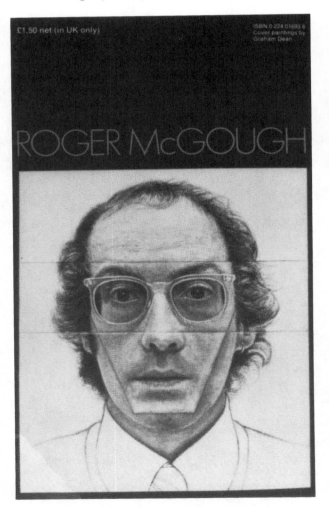

Covers for McGough's 1979 book. The title sequence is a humorous chronicle of a disintegrating marriage.

some of McGough's best poems. He begins by allowing the teacher in him to come to the fore, not least
as observer of pupil behavior. In "First Day at
School" the five-year-old wonders "What does a
lessin look like?/Sounds small and slimy./They
keep them in glassrooms./Whole rooms made out
of glass. Imagine." In "Nooligan" the tough kid, full
of bravado, brags "I'm a nooligan/dont give a toss/
in our class/I'm the boss/(well, one of them)." Both
here and in poems on football and the Liverpool
lads McGough seems to possess his subject. But the
collection also contains an equally skillful poem of
universal significance on the plight of the third
world. In "The Commission" a photographer
spends a well-earned fee on a West End dinner with
friends. Doodling on the napkin between courses
he draws a starving Asian girl and joyfully realizes
he has his next commission ready—"the one for
famine relief." The final section of the book is
"Kurt, B. P., Mungo and Me," a prose sequence
narrating the exploits of a young gang in search of
an author and an adventure. McGough cleverly
moves in and out of the action, so that when the
gang is unjustly jailed for thirty years, he turns the
judge into a bluebottle fly—Pirandello out of Milligan.

Even his serious treatments of more serious
subjects are filtered through a sharp verbal wit, like
the rhymes in "Closet Fascist," in *Holiday on Death
Row* (1979), where the executioner "enthroned
alone/in his W.C./on toilet paper/signs a decree/
deporting immigrants en masse./Salutes the mob/
then wipes his ass." One is reminded of E. E. Cummings's Uncle Sol in "out of work/divorced/usually
pissed/he aimed low in life/and/missed." The
leukemia of a thirty-year-old woman means "Her
blood is at war with itself/With each campaign more
pain,/a War of the Roses over again." The collection ends with twelve 12-line poems under the title
"Holiday on Death Row." Wife and husband battle
for survival by trying to denigrate or even eliminate
the partner. In a spare and impressionistic style
McGough depicts a fearful comedy—husband with
a rat in his jeans finds wife removing it, skinning it
alive and pulling off its head, then "Wiping blood
on pinny/she return to cakemix./Husband bury
dead rat/for another year": but the sequence ends
with "Wife/in garden, digging up rat."

Unlucky for Some (1981), which appears in its
entirety in *Waving at Trains* (1982), consists of thirteen 13-line dramatic monologues on social "losers," from the drug addict, to the alcoholic, to the
woman who would have liked children. Best of all is
the final poem on the failed actress turned prosti-

*Front cover for the 1983 collection of poems by
the Liverpool poets*

tute and now in a rest home—"I dance in here/all
the time. The girls love it./Do you like my dancing?
Round/and round. Not bad eh? For my age./I always wanted to go on stage."

The cover picture of the poet is reduced to
postage-stamp size on *Waving at Trains*, reflecting
an ego tamed and maturity gained. The style is one
of serious entertainment; rhythms and rhymes
have been tightened up. In "Noah's Arc" the
approaching flood of nuclear annihilation finds
Noah in his shelter smugly praying—"I ask the
Lord to get on with it." Typically, there is talk of
"the final absolution."

McGough is ambiguous about his status as a
performing poet. He enjoys it, feels guilty about it,
wants to be taken seriously, but at least until recently he was wary of taking up a serious stance on most

NOAH's ARC

In my fallout shelter I have enough food
For at least three months. Some books,
Scrabble, and games for the children.
Calor gas and candles. Comfortable beds
And a chemical toilet. Under lock and key
The tools necessary for a life after death.
I have carried out my instructions to the letter.

Most evenings I'm down here. Checking the stores,
Our suits, breathing apparatus. Cleaning
And polishing. My wife, bless her,
Thinks I'm obsessive - like other men
About cars or football. But deep down
She understands. I have no hobbies.
My sole interest is survival.

Every few weeks we have, what I call DD,
Or Disaster Drill. At the sound of the alarm
We each go about our separate duties:
Disconnecting services, switching off the mains,
Filling the casks with fresh water etc.
Mine is to oversee everything before finally
Shooting the dog. (This I mime in private).

                                     the days
At first, the young ones enjoyed ~~themselves.~~
~~And nights spent below. It was an adventure~~
~~To them, the days and nights spent in the shelter~~
~~Were an adventure~~. But now they're at a difficult age
And regard extinction as the boring concern
Of grown-ups. Like divorce and accountancy.
But I am firm. Daddy knows best
And one fine day they'll grow to thank me.

                            Armalite
Beneath my bunk I keep an ~~Armehite~~ rifle
Loaded and ready to use one fine day
When panicking neighbours and so called friends
Try to clamber aboard. The ones who scoff
Who ignore the signs. I have my orders:
There will be no stowaways. No gatecrashers
At my party. A party starting soon.

Draft for a poem published in Waving at Trains *(the author)*

Like

And the sooner the better. ~~A grounded astronaut~~

Astronaut ~~I grow daily more impatient~~

~~Awaiting the congressional countdown, I grow~~ *Am on tenterhooks. Each night*

I grow ~~Daily more impatient. Am on tenterhooks~~

~~Each night~~ / I ask the Lord to get on with it.

I fear sometimes he has forsaken us

We his favourite children. Meek, drilled,

And ready to inherit an earth, newly-cleansed.

I scan the headlines, watch the screen.

A doctor thrilling at each fresh tumour.

The lattest invasion, a breakdown of talks.

I pray for malignancy. The self induced

Sickness for which there is only one cure:

Radium treatment. The final absolution.

~~Our Father which art in Heaven. Amen.~~

That part of full circle we have yet to come.

Roger McGough

subjects. Only two of his volumes have been reviewed, briefly, in the *Times Literary Supplement: Gig* was panned, *Unlucky for Some* given nine descriptive lines. Academics and established poets pay little attention to him, though Philip Larkin is a fan. McGough himself rarely returns to his early poems in his readings, and rightly so. His best work lies in *Unlucky for Some* and *Waving at Trains* and, on the strength of those, in the future.

References:

Grevel Lindop, "Poetry, Rhetoric and the Mass Audience: The Case of the Liverpool Poets," in *British Poetry Since 1960—a Critical Survey,* edited by Michael Schmidt and Lindop (Oxford: Carcanet Press, 1972), pp. 93-106;

Geoffrey Thurley, *The Ironic Harvest* (London, 1974), pp. 195-197.

Medbh McGuckian
(12 August 1950-   )

Neil Corcoran
University of Sheffield

BOOKS: *Single Ladies* (Budleigh Salterton: Interim Press, 1980);
Portrait of Joanna (Belfast: Ulsterman Publications, 1980);
Trio Poetry 2, by McGuckian, Damian Gorman, and Douglas Marshall (Belfast: Blackstaff, 1981);
The Flower Master (Oxford & New York: Oxford University Press, 1982);
Venus and the Rain (Oxford & New York: Oxford University Press, 1984).

Medbh McGuckian came to prominence as a poet even before the publication of her first full-length book when, in 1979, she won the National Poetry Competition, a well-publicized media event in Britain, with her poem "The Flitting." When a pamphlet of her work, *Portrait of Joanna,* appeared in the following year, it was glowingly reviewed by the poet Anne Stevenson in the London *Times Literary Supplement:* "She is as clever (probably) as Craig Raine, as perceptive (possibly) as Elizabeth Bishop. . . . The wealth of exteriors explored by Medbh McGuckian's poems augurs the flowering of a talent which, fortunately, seems too original—too eccentric, even—to be wrongly directed by over-praise or by critical misunderstanding. She sounds, at times, like a contemporary, Irish Emily Dickinson. Flat, coy, confusing when she fails, her successes are dazzling, and her continued syntheses of looking and thinking, fascinating."

The anxiety about "over-praise" was prompted, presumably, by the National Poetry Competi-

tion award; and, in fact, the first full-length volume, *The Flower Master,* was also very warmly received when it appeared in 1982, the *Times Literary Supplement* reviewer calling it "one of the richest and most provocative collections of poetry to have appeared in recent years." In 1980 McGuckian had been given an Eric Gregory award, and after *The Flower Master,* further awards followed: a major Northern Ireland Arts Council Bursary in 1982; the Rooney Prize (Dublin), also in 1982; and the Alice Hunt Bartlett Award in 1983. Her work was also included in the influential Penguin anthology edited by Blake Morrison and Andrew Motion in 1982, *Contemporary British Poetry,* where she was made part of the editors' case for "a new confidence in the poetic imagination" in recent British poetry.

Medbh McGuckian was included in that anthology as one of a group of poets from the North of Ireland. She was born, the third of six children, into a Catholic family in Belfast in 1950. Her father was a headmaster and part-time farmer in Ballycastle, County Antrim; and her mother, who had a love of music and art, was an important early influence. During her secondary-school education at a Dominican convent, she decided "not to be a nun but a poet"; and she subsequently, like a number of well-known Northern Irish writers, read English at Queen's University, Belfast, between 1968 and 1972. She knew Seamus Heaney, who was teaching there at the time, and Michael Longley, and she also met her contemporaries Paul Muldoon, Frank Ormsby, and Ciaran Carson. The fer-

Medbh McGuckian

into something uninterpretably rich and strange. The poetry is intensely private and reserved: Anne Stevenson's "contemporary, Irish Emily Dickinson" has a real descriptive force. A characteristic strategy is to develop and elaborate an initial image, in a beautifully lucid, flowing syntax, to a point where intense physicality is weighted with a moral and emotional (in some poems, almost a "metaphysical") burden of suggestion and implication—as in "Tulips," for instance:

> Touching the tulips was a shyness
> I had had for a long time—such
> Defensive mechanisms to frustrate the rain
> . . . .
>   they exalt themselves
> To ballets of revenge, a kind
> Of twinness, an olympic way of earning,
> And are sacrificed to plot, their faces
> Lifted many times to the artistry of light—
> Its lovelessness a deeper sort
> Of illness than the womanliness
> Of tulips with their bee-dark hearts.

The initial, apparently open declarativeness of the line "Touching the tulips was a shyness" is developed to a point where it becomes very difficult to say what touching the tulips was *not,* so deeply has a whole quality of being become implicated in the touching. It is as though the initial object of Medbh McGuckian's inspiration or contemplation spreads and deepens, like a bruise or blush, under the devotedly attentive and inquisitive scrutiny of her gaze.

What the scrutiny exposes in this poem, as an abstract—but very realizedly abstract—quality inhering in the tulips, is their "womanliness." The signatures of feminine responsiveness in the poem run the risk of a preciousness ("ballets of revenge") or a reductiveness ("Defensive mechanisms") of diction; but many of McGuckian's poems strategically, if dangerously, deploy different levels of diction in close proximity. This risky procedure justifies itself when it enforces on the reader some genuine apprehension of a "womanly" sensibility in poetry without relying on the standard abstractions of any ideologically exact feminism.

The pursuit of such a vocabulary is the effort of McGuckian's work. It leads her to create an inward-turning private mythology out of such things as vegetation and the cultivation of gardens; fragments of narrative and family anecdote; a celebration of household crafts; and an interest in Oriental culture. The privacy is sometimes even more closely guarded by the use of distancing dramatic mono-

ment of native talent in Belfast at the time was a clear provocation to the development of her own gifts and, while a postgraduate in the English department of Queen's between 1972 and 1974, she began writing and publishing in local newspapers and magazines. In 1974 she started teaching English at her old convent school, and subsequently at St. Patrick's Boys' College in East Belfast. She married a teacher of geography in 1977 and began, at about that time, to write more seriously and to publish more regularly. In the same year in which she published her two pamphlets, 1980, she had a baby son; and another son followed in 1982.

Medbh McGuckian's work shares little in common with that of the Northern Irish poets who began publishing before her. It does not address itself, even obliquely, to the social and political circumstances of the North; it does not speak about "the Troubles." And yet it is, in some ways, a troubled poetry, hinting its unease in its pressurized, hothouse atmospheres, its heavy, almost narcotic rhythms, its images of domestic interiors warping

MEDBH McGUCKIAN

VENUS AND THE RAIN

Front cover for McGuckian's 1984 book. The illustration is a detail from Jan Toorop's 1882 painting The Younger Generation.

logues (although "dramatic" is quite the wrong word for the intense, studied lyricism of these poems). The mythology is in danger, sometimes, of seeming too claustrophobically hermetic; McGuckian's poems are at times too sealed and airless, overprotected—like the orchids they occasionally describe—from anything so vulgar or ordinary as interpretable "meaning." Her most resistant pieces can provoke a certain mind-numbing sense that these words, in their undoubtedly lucid syntactical organizations, could be many other words too, without much affecting the overall impression. The danger is that the rhythms and cadences do almost too much work, and that her adjectives, in particular, tend, in their vagueness and imprecision, to blur everything into a soft focus of sentimental warmth and attractiveness. What one might think of as the neo-Swinburnean is the danger McGuckian must avoid.

But at their best her poems convey a very rich sense of a womanly sensibility fruitfully discovering itself in an earned, achieved language of its own. It is a language which makes possible, above all, a marvelously realized register of desire—desire, in particular, for a privacy, a domestic interior (which is ultimately the "fictional" interior of the poem itself), made fully and properly one's own. The final stanza of the prizewinning poem "The Flitting," a poem developed, presumably, out of the experience of moving to another house, makes this clear enough, while it also apparently effortlessly releases an elaborate and ingenious metaphoric inventiveness, holding, in a gently unresolved tension, both sadness and happiness:

> I postpone my immortality for my children,
> Little rock-roses, cushioned

In long-flowering sea-thrift and metrics,
Lacking elemental memories:
I am well-earthed here as the digital clock,
Its numbers flicking into place like overgrown farthings
On a bank where once a train
Ploughed like an emperor living out a myth
Through the cambered flesh of clover and wild carrot.

Matthew Mead
(12 September 1924-   )

Wayne E. Hall
University of Cincinnati

BOOKS: *A Poem in Nine Parts* (Worcester, U.K. & Ventura, Cal.: Migrant Press, 1960);
Identities (Worcester: Migrant Press, 1964);
Kleinigkeiten (Newcastle upon Tyne: Published for *Satis* by Malcolm Rutherford, 1966);
Identities and Other Poems (London: Rapp & Carroll, 1967);
The Administration of Things (London: Anvil Press, 1970);
Penguin Modern Poets 16, by Mead, Jack Beeching, and Harry Guest (Harmondsworth: Penguin, 1970);
In the Eyes of the People (Edinburgh: Published for *Satis* by Malcolm Rutherford, 1973);
Minusland (Edinburgh: Published for *Satis* by Malcolm Rutherford, 1977);
The Midday Muse (London: Anvil, 1979).

OTHER: Johannes Bobrowski, *Shadow Land: Selected Poems of Johannes Bobrowski*, translated by Ruth and Matthew Mead (London: Donald Carroll, 1966; revised edition, London: Rapp & Carroll, 1967);
Heinz Winfried Sabais, *Generation*, translated by Ruth and Matthew Mead (Newcastle upon Tyne: Published for *Satis* by Malcolm Rutherford, 1967);
Nelly Sachs, *O the Chimneys*, translated by Ruth and Matthew Mead, Michael Hamburger, and Michael Roloff (New York: Farrar, Straus & Giroux, 1967); republished as *Selected Poems of Nelly Sachs* (London: Cape, 1968);
Sabais, *Generation and Other Poems*, translated by Ruth and Matthew Mead (Northwood, Middlesex: Anvil, 1968);
Max Hölzer, *Amfortiade and Other Poems*, translated by Ruth and Matthew Mead (Edinburgh: Published for *Satis* by Malcolm Rutherford, 1968);
Horst Bienek, *Horst Bienek*, translated by Ruth and Matthew Mead (Santa Barbara: Unicorn Press, 1969);
Elisabeth Borchers, *Elisabeth Borchers*, translated by Ruth and Matthew Mead (Santa Barbara: Unicorn Press, 1969);
Nelly Sachs, *The Seeker and Other Poems*, translated by Ruth and Matthew Mead and Michael Hamburger (New York: Farrar, Straus & Giroux, 1970);
Bobrowski and Bienek, *Selected Poems*, translated by Ruth and Matthew Mead (Harmondsworth: Penguin, 1971);
Sabais, *Mitteilungen/Communications*, translated by Ruth and Matthew Mead (Darmstadt: Eduard Roether, 1971);
Bobrowski, *From the Rivers*, translated by Ruth and Matthew Mead (London: Anvil, 1975);
Sabais, *Sozialistische Elegie/Socialist Elegy*, translated by Ruth and Matthew Mead (Darmstadt: Eduard Roether, 1975);
Sabais, *The People and the Stones*, translated by Ruth and Matthew Mead (London: Anvil Press, 1983);
Gunter Bruno Fuchs, *The Raven*, translated by Ruth and Matthew Mead (Edinburgh: Published for *Satis* by Malcolm Rutherford, 1984);
Bobrowski, *Shadow Lands*, translated by Ruth and Matthew Mead (London: Anvil Press, 1984).

From editing a small, avant-garde poetry magazine, to translating several modern German poets, to producing three skillfully wrought volumes of his own verse, Matthew Mead has pursued his literary career with an uncommonly keen dedication to poetry as an almost sacred craft. Stylistically, his work grows out of a deep awareness of the poetic tradition in English as well as of the current poetic practice in Europe and the United States, but, thematically, it encompasses an even wider range, extending from a criticism of contemporary society to a search for the ancient language of poetic myth.

Very little is known about Mead's life, in part because, as he writes, "I try to keep my person and my poems as far apart as may be. . . ." He was born in Buckinghamshire and entered the British army in his late teens. His term of service, from 1942 to 1947, included three years in India, Ceylon, and Singapore. In an article on the work of the Welsh poet Alun Lewis, killed in Burma in 1944, Mead generalized on those World War II experiences: "To serve in the Army during the last war was, for many of us, to polish, to peel, and to munch Naafi buns between 'flaps.' "

Mead's poetic career began in 1960 with the publication of a pamphlet, *A Poem in Nine Parts*, and with the appearance of *Satis*, which he edited during its three-year life. A little magazine, *Satis* existed, as Mead noted in an inaugural editorial, "to publish poems"; its contributors included Charles Bukowski, Anne Cluysenaar, Frederick Eckman, Larry Eigner, Anselm Hollo, Barriss Mills, Gael Turnbull, and Richard Weber. Much of its material was experimental and American, reflecting Mead's admiration for a "matter-of-fact romanticism" in poetry from the United States.

Satis took its name from an inscribed Roman brick in the Silchester collection of the Reading Museum. "Enough. This remark written with the finger on the surface of an unbaked brick may mean either that the brick was the last of any particular batch; or it may be an idle remark made by the workman. . . ." The magazine's explanation for its title suggested the posture of its editorial commentary and even its advertisements: offhand, distant, uninvolved. One reviewer noted the editor's "humorous, self-deprecatory stand on detachment from all creeds and doctrines in verse or politics." In explaining his stance, Mead claimed that society had become alienated from poetry and that, partly as a consequence, "We find ourselves unable to distinguish between the resultant industrial collectives except by the degree of freedom which they

allow to the individual." He thus felt himself left with a "poetic distaste" for both East and West and turned instead to poetry, a "one-man job" within societies that were becoming increasingly more specialized and commercial. David Ignatow, reviewing *A Poem in Nine Parts* at virtually the same time that these remarks were appearing in *Satis*, also noted a disillusionment with politics within Mead's poetry. Mead was instead, Ignatow felt, "in search of that rigid reality by which one ultimately must live, that which gives a sense of continuity and form." One might argue that Mead's search, to this day, remains unresolved.

As Mead recognized, *Satis* itself was inevitably, albeit ironically, caught up in the same commercial pressures for which it expressed distaste. Although 400 copies appeared of numbers 4 and 5, up from 300 for the first three issues, the fifth one was the last. "The suspension occurs for adequate reasons of love, money and lassitude . . . ," Mead wrote. That same year, 1962, he moved to Germany with Ruth Adrian, his German-born wife, whose name was always to appear alongside his in the frequent translations they published over the next twenty years.

In 1966 Ruth and Matthew Mead produced *Shadow Land*, their translations of the poetry of Johannes Bobrowski. Two more volumes of Bobrowski's work were to follow, the latest, *Shadow Lands*, a consolidated collection, coming in 1984. Bobrowski, wrote Mead, "is always a poet of the borderland where frontiers, so clearly drawn on the map, are to be seen as guesses at some ghostlier demarcation. . . . past and present are defined by no neat division, the dead speak to the living. . . ." In closely echoing the final line of "The Idea of Order at Key West," the phrase "ghostlier demarcation" points ahead to Mead's later debts to the vision of Wallace Stevens. In Bobrowski, Mead found a similar impulse to escape from biographical and historical limitations; this same feature further helps explain Mead's attraction to the other German poets whom he has translated. Horst Bienek, who was arrested on political charges in East Germany and spent several years in a Russian prison camp, writes verse that, in Mead's terms, seems "divorced from past and future." For Bobrowski, this sense of alienation from history leads to a more affirmative faith in a mythic past that still, through the details of landscape, has vital links to the present. For Bienek, alienation instead brings a sharper awareness of a painful exile and the problem of identity after the shattering experience of the prison camp; his main theme, Mead felt, is "captivity."

In Mead's other translations as well, of Nelly Sachs, Heinz Winfried Sabais, or Elisabeth Borchers, he found further examples, similar to Bienek's, of the themes of war, suffering, and isolation. The widespread devastation of Europe during World War II over and over leads these writers to a bitter disenchantment with the modern world. At a stylistic level, however, this tendency frequently distances the poems from a clear and recognizable level of shared everyday experience. With reality so harsh, the poetry begins to slip into an abstract and insulating vagueness. The problem with such work, and one which Bobrowski avoids better than the others, is a reliance on a standardized rather than a personal style. One reviewer of Mead's translations of Borchers and Bienek complained that such "shadow-poetry" could just as well be "translated by computer without too much loss." Critical reception of the Bobrowski translations, by contrast, has been much more favorable, and for Mead's own work, too, the themes and responses of Bobrowski seem to offer a more fruitful area of influence.

Mead's next major poem, *Identities*, appeared in pamphlet form in 1964. In a pattern of publication that Mead was to follow from then on, parts of this work had first appeared in little magazines, then in pamphlets, and finally in a major collected edition. The pamphlets, frequently published by Malcolm Rutherford under the old *Satis* imprint, generally came out in editions of 200 to 250 copies. With his collections, however, Mead reached a much wider audience; *Identities and Other Poems* (1967), his first major collection, continued to be distributed in America by Transatlantic Arts until the early 1980s.

Reviewers for the most part were not sure what to make of *Identities and Other Poems*. "His is a diffuse gift," remarked Michael Baldwin; "it's hard to work out just what he's up to." The reviewer for the *Times Literary Supplement* felt that he had worked it out, however, and he found it wanting. One descriptive phrase, "eclectic Common Market poetry," recalls the complaint about the "shadow-poetry" of Borchers and Bienek, and the *Times Literary Supplement* pressed the point: "one feels at times that one is reading the less successful bits in an anthology of modern German poetry. . . ." The implication was

clear: Mead's work as a translator had helped render his own writing vague, less personal, too reliant on borrowed themes and styles. Terry Eagleton felt that the polished techniques of the volume were used consciously "to put a safe distance between Mead and his attitudes, to provide a defensive cover which allows a value to be advanced, but advanced with properly self-debunking irony, avoiding anything as crude as frank commitment." Alan Brownjohn, also finding a "weakness" in Mead's poetry, noted an "unwillingness to touch down on concrete experiences or clear assertions—abstracting essences without suggesting what you are abstracting them *from*."

In some of *Identities and Other Poems*, Mead clearly does "touch down" on regions all too real and familiar. "Love for Professor Schlauch," for instance, is an ironic love poem to a literary critic overly concerned with socialist dogma. Schlauch's "purpose" is a "bore," retorts Mead, and he indignantly rejects the position that would subordinate poetry to politics. But if this collection includes poems such as "Ballade of the Spectre of Communism," it also has ones with titles such as "Chloris Periplum," "John at Machaerus," and "Sychar." Mead seems finally to reject any close contact with the world of everyday experience, preferring instead, as "Love to Professor Schlauch" goes on, to speak "the tale told true," and in a voice that is "skilful and sincere" and also "simple." Such a tale might well be concerned, not with the concretely mundane, but with the kinds of "essences" to which Brownjohn referred.

Other reviewers, more sympathetic, sought to interpret Mead's tale. Christopher Middleton found *Identities* to be immersed in the essential features of our time. Derek Porter, in *Poetry Review*, wrote that "The title-poem shatters time to bring into juxtaposition images of cruelty and of death which are outside time altogether, placing them within Mead's own legend, which is still very real." Even though such commentary recalls similar concerns in the work of Bienek and Bobrowski, with their impulse to escape from time, it still fails to explain much. "Mead's own legend," for instance, is puzzling. But for that, we may follow a lead that begins with the first issue of *Satis*, in 1960: "The clearest exposition of the purpose of poetry which the editor has read," Mead editorialized then, "is to be found in Mr. Graves' volume, 'The White Goddess.' "

Robert Graves does indeed go far toward elucidating the legends Mead is concerned with, complete with much of their abstracted essences. "The function of poetry is religious invocation of the Muse," Graves writes; "its use is the experience of mixed exaltation and horror that her presence excites." Within Graves's scheme, the muse, identified with the moon goddess, is opposed to such mythic figures as the sun god Apollo, identified with rationalism, patrilineal institutions, synthetic substitutes, the golden mean. "There is no poem in the sun!" Mead writes in "227 Idle Words Against Apollo." Instead, as in the last piece in *Identities and Other Poems,* "Nightrhyme," Mead would "See the best of earth returning/In the fitful silver light!"

In the modern world, however, one that has abandoned its ancient faith in myth, mystery, and ecstasy, poetry is no longer an honored commodity. Rationalism, science, industry, and commercialism have replaced the old values and alienated humanity from the true tales. Yet even today money will not buy truth, Graves admonishes, nor will it buy the "truth-possessed poet." Mead's social criticism thus comes to seem a part, not simply of a view of society, but of a view of the cosmos. Society stands in the way of truth. It is not that the poet has envisioned a better society that he would have replace the imperfect one before his eyes; it is rather that the present society restricts the poet's visionary dedication to the muse.

Such a vision is developed in poems such as "Three Simple Things," which Mead dedicates to his wife, Ruth, in language perfectly appropriate to describe the power of the muse, here reminiscent of the woman in Wallace Stevens's poem "The Idea of Order at Key West": "under her fingers order grew out of chaos; she established sequence and precedence; the symbols before her became coherent, interrelated." As a cotranslator of the German poets, Ruth Mead also seems to be invoked in her husband's poetic dedication to Bobrowski, "Translator to Translated":

Love
translates
as love.
Her song sung
in a strange land.

An air that kills.

The passage recalls the mixture of "exaltation and horror" that Graves attributes to the presence of the muse. Poem after poem in *Identities and Other Poems* accepts this mixed nature of the muse, whether in a hymn commemorating the seasonal passage of time, "The Autumn-Born in Autumn" ("A girl

comes to dance the year to death"), or more directly in "Three Simple Things": "Our glory is that we do not endure." Elsewhere in "Three Simple Things," Mead addresses the woman/muse in language that sums up much of the mystery, ecstasy, and dedication of Graves's mythic scheme:

I enter you blindly
as I shall enter earth
and my life is to die
          within you
and this is love.

Against such faith in the manifestation of the muse, other poems confront the barriers to her presence that have been constructed by modern civilization. The title poem of the collection, for instance, raises the same question that occupied Bienek's work: after the experience of the concentration camps, what kind of identity is left to the poet? In a lyrical passage full of natural detail, Mead seeks an answer from the woman Tatania: "Here, with your lips on mine,/Who do you say I am?" By the end of "Identities," the poet has attained some measure of success, limited and painstakingly labored to be sure, but still the ability at least to "speak with imprecision/of elusive colour. . . ." Elsewhere in the collection, in "A Poem in Nine Parts," Mead remarks that

Mine is a voice for quiet rooms,
I think that you may not hear it;
A managerial Apollo does not hear it.

But despite his doubts and his circumscribed field of influence, Mead can bring this poem, by its end, firmly back within the sphere of the White Goddess:

Mistress of fortune
    preserve our fortune,
Ruler of darkness
    prepare a death
for the flesh which sings now
makes moan and shivers silver
as the moon renews her light.

The invocation sounds a note of quiet faith; through the muse, through the woman, life will be renewed.

Three years later, in 1970, Mead published his second volume of poetry, *The Administration of Things.* In style and theme, this volume is closely allied to *Identities and Other Poems,* with several of the

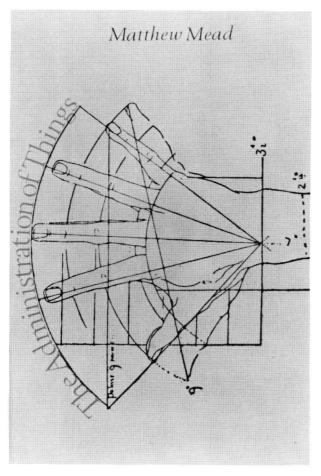

Dust jacket for Mead's 1970 book, which led Philip Hobsbaum to call him "a Poundian in a sense deeper than that of technical allegiance: an aesthete distressed by the blood and chaos of totalitarian Europe"

poems in *The Administration of Things* having appeared in the pamphlet *Kleinigkeiten* in 1966. Elements from the German translations also recur, with such lines as these, from the title poem, recalling Bobrowski:

> The silence mine, as if a dead man spoke
> Or pondered in a sunlit interval
> The dark from which he came.

The muse too remains a theme in such poems as "Echo," "A Woman of the World," and "In the Absence of the Muse." Yet, as the title of the collection suggests, Mead's concerns had perceptibly shifted into a stronger preoccupation with the progressive alienation of society from its mythic roots. In a poem on his place of residence, Bonn, entitled

"From a Provisional Capital," Mead wrote:

> A perfect frame for apathy
> Stretches as far as one can see:
> The aftermath of blood and soil,
> No KPD, no Jews in Beuel.

In its attention to the ways in which society had viciously eradicated its minority elements, whether Communists or Jews, and then settled into a dull, bureaucratic existence, like that in the suburbs of a minor German city, Mead's verse prompted commentators such as Derek Stanford, in his review for *Books and Bookmen,* to describe Mead's vision as "secular, atheistic, deterministic and pessimistic." Philip Hobsbaum sounded a similar note in summing up Mead's career through these first two collected volumes, terming him "a Poundian in a sense deeper than that of technical allegiance: an aesthete distressed by the blood and chaos of totalitarian Europe."

The term Poundian, here applied to Mead's more general thematic concerns, had frequently been used to describe his poetic style as well. Christopher Middleton, while feeling that Mead's tone was original and genuine, also noted that *Identities* had been inspired by Pound's method. Mead himself had professed allegiance to Pound as well as Graves as far back as his inaugural editorial for *Satis,* writing that "the training manuals of Mr. Pound have not been superseded. . . ." One early poem, "Render Unto Ezra," states: "If we have homes/he has instructed the architect." Some reviewers did not appreciate this influence, however, with all of its grim, staccato rhythms. A *Times Literary Supplement* reviewer felt that the Poundian "guide-lines are so solid that one trips over them," and another, John Smith, writing for *Poetry Review,* found that the influence of Pound and Eliot "is sometimes so obvious as to be devastating."

Other stylistic influences were noted as well. Hobsbaum had compared some of the writing to the Elizabethan lyrics of John Donne and the lapidary verse of Andrew Marvell. Middleton saw much more going on in Mead's early poems: working in a manner similar to that of Philip Larkin, and within the small, avant-garde group that included Ian Hamilton Finlay, Roy Fisher, Michael Shayer, Gael Turnbull, and others, Mead showed evidence of having read William Carlos Williams, Louis Zukofsky, and Charles Olson, but without having become overly dependent on them.

Mead's first two volumes, then, left some difficult problems in their wake, ones which even sympathetic readers were unable to clarify. There was the question of form: was Mead genuinely original or was he too imitative? And there was the question of content: was Mead dealing in vague obscurities or essential truths? Critics who looked toward his later work as a resolution of such tangles remained frustrated. *In the Eyes of the People,* a pamphlet published in 1973, "tends to work at several removes from anything identifiably related to experience," suggested the *Times Literary Supplement,* "and the effect is often enough excessively mannered and calculated." Looking at *The Midday Muse* (1979), Mead's third collected volume, another *Times Literary Supplement* review objected that "some of the poems seem deliberately to use language to hide what they are about."

In *The Midday Muse,* and especially in poems like "The Man with the Red Guitar," the influence of Wallace Stevens seems to have replaced that of Pound, although it is not nearly as pervasive as Pound's was earlier. On the whole, Mead has established a voice much more his own in *The Midday Muse* than in previous work. Thematically, however, the poetry seems more controlled and limited than the earlier volumes, not so much by Stevens's rhythms and tones as by his poetic vision. As in Stevens's verse, over and over here the poems tend to cast reality into deliberate and self-conscious fictions. These help to govern the violence of reality, to impose at least some order on the inhuman chaos.

Yet the assertions about human control remain unconvincing. In a poem that suggests a recurring emotional response throughout the book, "Man is the Sullen Rage of his Asphalt," Mead writes:

> The towering town
> Dwarfs us, reflected in a puddle.
> We built it, we can tear it down.

Despite the desire for a fictionalized mode of seeing, the poetry never becomes confident with its imaginative constructs. The fictions repeatedly dissolve, under the intense images of light that pervade the entire volume, into feelings of death or dismemberment. The title poem ends with "A fire, a flame, a pyre, a pall,/A charred wreck drifting west or east." In the final line of "The Man with the Red Guitar," "A course holds true from nothing into nowhere." "Three Shifts in Oblivion" leaves the reader with only a "Cold wind caressing cold stone." The true muse of the moon has finally given way to

the muse of midday, to the harsh light that reveals reality in all its horrible aspects.

The most optimistic feature to emerge from these poems is connected with Ruth Mead. She has unified Mead's career in many ways: she is a native of the country in which he has done most of his writing; she worked with him on the translations of the German poets; she is directly addressed in poems dedicated to her; and she is perhaps indirectly addressed as the woman/muse who inspires that career. Throughout much of Mead's work, whether through his use of other poets' writing in his translations, his use of other poets' styles in his original verse, or his invocation of the muse who would guide that verse, his impulse has been toward an obliteration of personality and an escape from biographical and historical time. In some poems of *The Midday Muse,* however, Ruth Mead seems to diminish the earlier distance between the person and the poems. She is no longer the muse to be invoked as much as the partner to be accompanied. In "Wasserburg," dedicated to her, Mead writes:

> We the one flesh
> We the lithe lengthening
> We of the clasp and kiss
> We the slow coming,
> Moonlight defines us
> Leaving no mark
> Lending a likeness.

The volume ends with another poem "for Ruth," the last section of "In the Eyes of the People."

> I am the shadow
> Beside you in
>   the shadow.

The shadows can occasion despair, but they can also, at rare times, allow for salvation through personal union.

In some ways, *The Midday Muse* represents a narrowing of Mead's poetic options. Its poems must fight, much harder than in his first two volumes, against a growing sense of apathy and helplessness. This tendency, coupled with a continued veil of obscurity and vagueness over the language, may well have the effect of further restricting Mead's readership and influence. He has always been "a voice for quiet rooms," consciously operating within a limited literary area; but that voice is in danger of being drowned out by "the Chancellor of Silence," to whom *The Midday Muse* is dedicated. In other

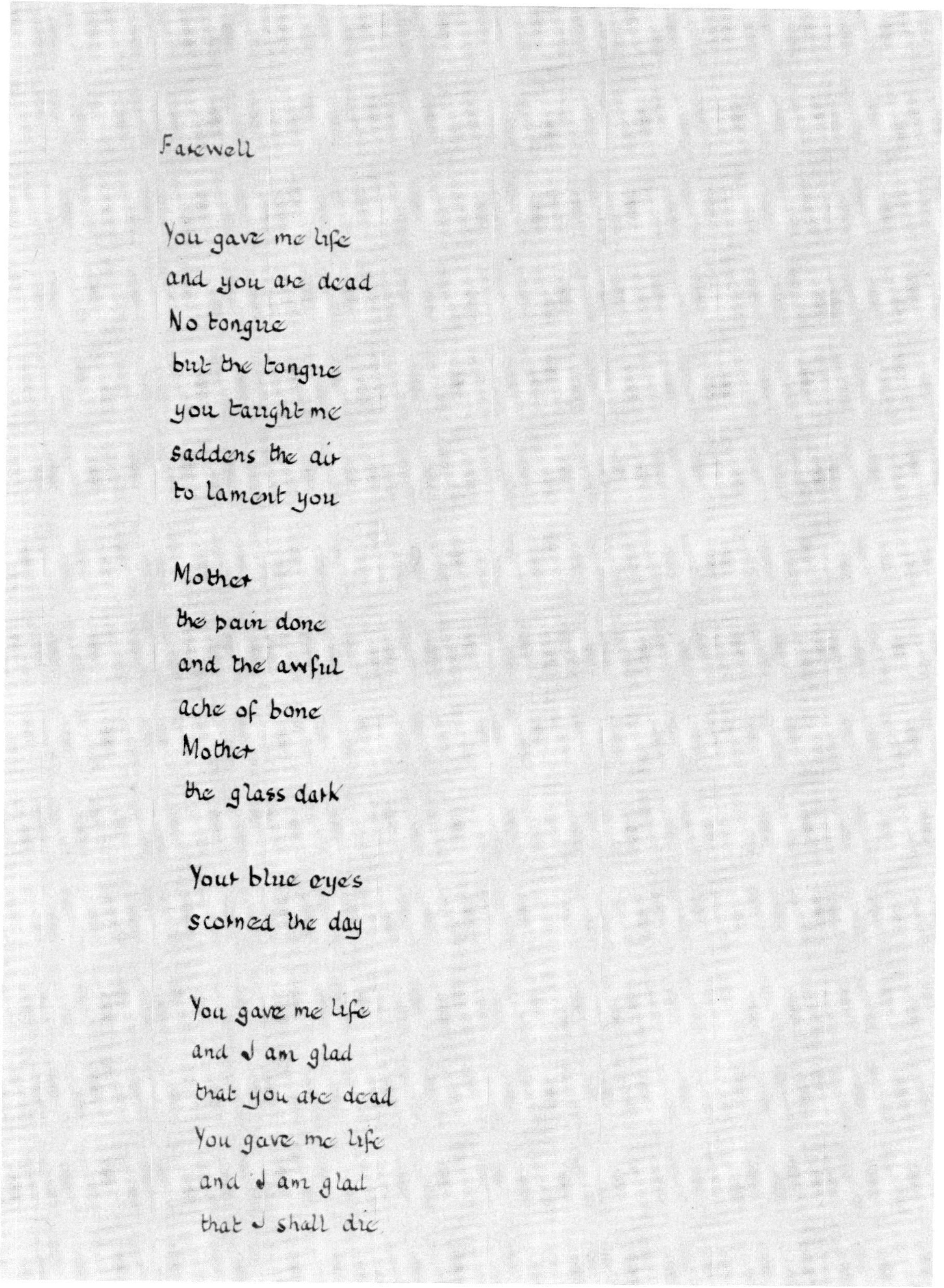

Farewell

You gave me life
and you are dead
No tongue
but the tongue
you taught me
saddens the air
to lament you

Mother
the pain done
and the awful
ache of bone
Mother
the glass dark

Your blue eyes
scorned the day

You gave me life
and I am glad
that you are dead
You gave me life
and I am glad
that I shall die

Final draft for a 1985 poem (the author)

ways, however, this volume represents a more positive development as well. The voice seems much more Mead's own, and he has also begun to discard what has so far proved to be the overly shadowy inspiration of the white goddess. Although its predominating evidence militates against any faith in human action, and thus against any further poems as well, *The Midday Muse* also contains elements of hope that do open up new avenues in Mead's career.

References:

Dick Davis, "The Poetry of Matthew Mead," *PN Review*, no. 42 (1984);

Christopher Middleton, "Englische Lyrik—heute," *Neue Deutsche Literatur*, 13 (February 1965): 156-180;

A. Kingsley Weatherhead, "Matthew Mead," in his *The British Dissonance: Essays on Ten Contemporary Poets* (Columbia & London: University of Missouri Press, 1983), pp. 56-70.

Christopher Middleton

(10 June 1926-   )

Alan Young

BOOKS: *Poems* (London: Fortune Press, 1944);

Nocturne in Eden (London: Fortune Press, 1945);

Torse 3: Poems 1949-1961 (London: Longmans, Green, 1962; New York: Harcourt, Brace & World, 1962);

Penguin Modern Poets 4, by Middleton, David Holbrook, and David Wevill (Harmondsworth: Penguin, 1963);

The Metropolitans [comedy-opera], libretto by Middleton, score by Hans Vogt (N.p.: Alkor, 1964);

Nonsequences: Selfpoems (London: Longmans, Green, 1965; New York: Norton, 1966);

Der Taschenelefant (Berlin: Verlag Neue Rabenpresse, 1969);

Our Flowers & Nice Bones (London: Fulcrum Press, 1969);

The Fossil Fish: 15 Micropoems (Providence, R.I.: Burning Deck, 1970);

Wie wir Grossmutter zum Markt bringen (Stierstadt i. Taunus: Eremiten-presse, 1970);

Briefcase History: 9 Poems (Providence, R.I.: Burning Deck, 1972);

Fractions for Another Telemachus (Knotting: Sceptre Press, 1974);

Wild Horse (Knotting: Sceptre Press, 1975);

The Lonely Suppers of W. V. Balloon (Cheadle: Carcanet Press, 1975; Boston: Godine, 1975);

Eight Elementary Inventions (Knotting: Sceptre Press, 1977);

Pataxanadu & other prose (Manchester: Carcanet Press, 1977);

Bolshevism in Art, and other expository writings (Manchester: Carcanet Press, 1978; Atlantic Highlands, N.J.: Humanities Press, 1980);

Carminalenia (Manchester: Carcanet Press, 1980);

111 Poems (Manchester: Carcanet Press, 1983; New York: Carcanet Press, 1984);

The Pursuit of the Kingfisher (Manchester: Carcanet Press, 1983; New York: Carcanet Press, 1984);

Serpentine (London: Oasis, 1985).

OTHER: Robert Walser, *The Walk and Other Stories*, translated by Middleton (London: John Calder, 1957);

Ohne Hass und Fahne, edited by Middleton and others (N.p.: Rowohlt Verlag, 1959);

Gottfried Benn, *Primal Vision*, translated by Middleton and others (New York: New Directions, 1960);

Poems and Verse Plays by Hugo von Hoffmansthal, translated by Middleton and others (New York: Pantheon, 1961);

Poet's Vocation: Selections from the Letters of Hölderlin, Rimbaud, and Hart Crane, edited and translated by Middleton and William Burford (Austin: University of Texas Press, 1962);

Modern German Poetry 1910-1960: An Anthology with Verse Translations, edited and translated by Middleton and Michael Hamburger (London: MacGibbon & Kee, 1962; New York: Grove, 1962);

Selected Poems by Günter Grass, translated by Middleton and Hamburger (London: Secker & Warburg, 1966; New York: Harcourt, Brace & World, 1966);

Courtesy of Bernard Stone,
The Turret Book Shop

German Writing Today, edited by Middleton (Baltimore: Penguin Books, 1967; Harmondsworth: Penguin Books, 1967);

Selected Poems by Georg Trakl, edited by Middleton, translated by Robert Grenier and others (London: Cape, 1968);

Walser, *Jakob von Gunten,* translated by Middleton (Austin: University of Texas Press, 1969);

Friedrich Nietzsche, *Selected Letters,* translated by Middleton (Chicago: University of Chicago Press, 1969);

Christa Wolf, *The Quest for Christa T.,* translated by Middleton (New York: Farrar, Straus & Giroux, 1970);

Selected Poems by Paul Celan, translated by Middleton and Hamburger (Harmondsworth: Penguin, 1972);

Selected Poems of Friedrich Hölderlin and Eduard Mörike, translated by Middleton (Chicago: University of Chicago Press, 1972);

Günter Grass, *Inmarypraise,* translated by Middleton (New York: Harcourt Brace Jovanovich, 1974);

Elias Canetti, *Kafka's Other Trial: The Letters to Felice,* translated by Middleton (New York: Schocken, 1974);

Grass, *In the egg, and other poems,* translated by Middleton and Hamburger (New York: Harcourt Brace Jovanovich, 1978);

Walser, *Selected Stories,* translated by Middleton (New York: Farrar, Straus & Giroux, 1982; Manchester: Carcanet Press, 1982);

Selected Poems of Goethe, edited by Middleton, translated by Middleton and others (Boston: Suhrkamp Insel, 1983).

Christopher Middleton has been an increasingly important influence on writing in English since the mid-1950s. His poems, stories, translations, and essays have demonstrated consistent refusal to disregard the more unsettling discoveries of both romanticism and high modernism. Unlike most of his contemporaries in Britain and the United States, Middleton has viewed the art and craft of writing as a hazardous, disruptive, and visionary enterprise, one in which the poet as maker undertakes to shape a language into original ways of saying and, therefore, of knowing for a shaken and uncertain world. His literary heroes and heroines are vulnerable human beings, but they do not work in confessional modes, although for him poetry at its most intense in such modes "can show what savage stuff a creative individual is made of." In his best-known essay "Reflections on a Viking Prow," which appeared in *PN Review* in 1979 and 1980, Middleton praises, instead, artificer-poets "who contend with their seas on other levels, at disparate angles, have different ways of making that stuff luminous." Such writers "all wrestle, respectfully, with arbitrariness."

As a writer who favors "disparate angles" Middleton has not feared critical hostility. Among the model artificers who have been translated by him is the Swiss novelist and short-story (or, rather, minimalist-prose) writer Robert Walser. Middleton translated stories by Walser as early as 1955, and he appears to have adopted something of Walser's attitude to the criticism of others: "Altogether, one reads Walser for his blithe difference from colleagues in any age or any condition—for his perfect and serene oddity." What has been most admirable and astonishing in Middleton's own writing is his adherence to an unfashionable poetic and his achievement within it. His work has enlarged, both actually and potentially, the scope of contemporary writing in English.

John Christopher Middleton was born in Truro, Cornwall, England, to Hubert Stanley and Dorothy May Middleton. His father, a musician and teacher, was senior lecturer in music at Cambridge University for some time. Middleton was educated at Felsted School, Essex, and, after service as a noncommissioned officer in the Royal Air Force from 1944 to 1948, at Merton College, Oxford, where he read German and French, earning a B.A. (1951) and a D.Phil. (1954). Between 1952 and 1955 he was lecturer in English at Zürich University. He married Mary Freer on 11 April 1953; they have three children, Sarah, Miranda, and Benjamin. (They were divorced in 1969.) Middleton taught for eleven years at King's College, University of London, where he was senior lecturer in German (1965-1966). In 1966 he moved to the University of Texas, Austin, where ever since he has been a professor of Germanic languages and literature. He has won several major literary awards, including the Geoffrey Faber Memorial Prize (1964) and a Guggenheim Fellowship (1974).

His earliest volumes of poetry were published by Fortune Press in 1944 and 1945, several years before he entered Oxford University. *Poems* and *Nocturne in Eden* are both juvenile work which he would not now

reckon to be any part of his achievement. In the late 1950s and 1960s he translated several books of poetry, drama, and prose, including works by Robert Walser, Hugo von Hofmansthal, Gottfried Benn, Günter Grass, and other German writers. His German contemporaries had appreciable influence on his first mature collection, *Torse 3*, which appeared in 1962. The book's title comes from one of the definitions of the word "torse" in the *Oxford English Dictionary:*

> Torse[3] [f. med. L. *torsus, -um,* for L. *tortus* twisted.] Geom. A developable surface; a surface generated by a moving straight line which at every instant is turning, in some plane or other through it, about some point or other in its length.

This definition proposes a view of poetry as continuous crafting, as an ever-changing process of original exploration. Middleton's aesthetic was to become a formalist one, but his forms are never ready-made molds. Rather, each new poem is a fresh inquiry into linguistic possibilities. The end result captures the process of this inquiry. Some of the characteristics of creative process may be presented in the poems—including, for example, the use of spontaneity, repetition, and chance to produce strange juxtapositions of word and phrase, and, sometimes, impenetrable compression as well as blind alleys or lost connections. In theory, this sense of the poem as process offers the reader an opportunity to share the poem's imaginative expeditions into new regions of language. In practice, in *Torse 3* and elsewhere, the ordinary reader may be often exasperated by the very openness of a poem's structure. Middleton's most successful poems, however, convey the wonder and mystery, the disillusionment and anguish, of human experience. Like his "artificers" he creates his poems at disparate angles to the savage and magical stuff of raw experience.

The poems of *Torse 3* were written over a period of twelve years, between 1949 and 1961, and they vary greatly in manner and achievement. Some of them echo modern writers who had become unfashionable by the 1950s, including T. S. Eliot (as in "Five Psalms of Common Man"):

> Another order of fear is chaos.
> Images of chaos variously coordinated
> by disparate imaginations accord or do not accord
> to their seasons in time enacting the indeterminations.

Dylan Thomas and the British New Apocalypse group hover around the rhythms and diction of other poems in the collection, such as "Male Torso":

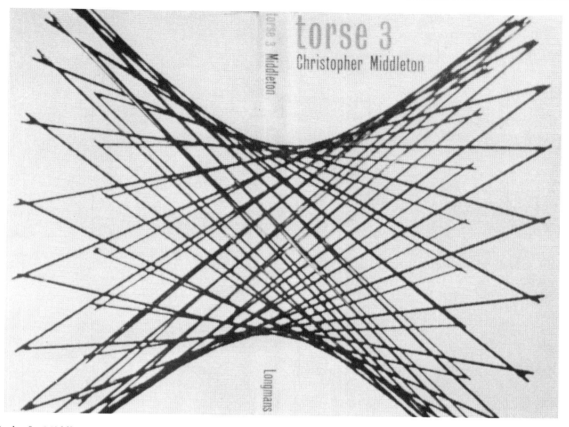

Dust jacket for Middleton's 1962 book. The title refers to the third definition of the word torse *in the* Oxford English Dictionary: *"a developable surface; a surface generated by a moving straight line which at every instant is turning, in some plane or other through it, about some point or other in its length."*

The customed eyes, before I woke, were glass;
A bleating queen whose legs were sheaths
Of hammered moon fed swill to pigs.

But there is no dominant style in *Torse 3* and despite the title and its dictionary definition no convincingly worked-through aesthetic. The collection reveals a long and troubled apprenticeship. Like his young German contemporaries (and unlike most of his British ones) he was desperately searching for a viable postmodern poetic.

The opening stanza of "Seven Hunters," the first poem in the book, tells readers not to expect those safe, rational, and limited perspectives which guided English Movement poets of the 1950s:

On skins we scaled the snow wall,
seven hunters; roped, leaning
into claws of wind; we climbed,
wisely, for no fixed point.
There was no point we knew.

Some of these poems take wise risks. "Climbing a Pebble" begins "What did it mean (I ask myself), to climb a pebble." Another, "The Lake of Zürich" (deliberately clotted in sound and diction), tries to imagine a scene as perceived by Robert Walser in his madness; it begins

Than sky, the lemon, dredged, more dark this liquid.
Fluminal violet, in a lockjaw littoral, swings
Wind-swathed, wind-cradled.

"Art Machine"—a poem based on an automatically rotating epidiascope on show at the 1960 exhibition of Brazilian art in Paris—is authentically surrealist in mode and effect:

I saw tormented women
whirl down a tall hill
a prairie lobster
polyps in a wedge and bronze
twin birds that claw their combs
then boots with sieves in black pools

The best poems in *Torse 3* hold together both distinctive voice and new poetic territory, as in "Alba after six years":

> There was a winter
>   dark fell by five
> four noses ran
>   and shouting children
> she got so quickly in a rage.

Its total indifference to the critical attitude then dominant in Britain marks *Torse 3* as an important first collection. The unevenness of its experimentation is one measure of Middleton's search for distinctive voice and vision, though there is some justice in Thom Gunn's comment in the *Yale Review*, Autumn 1963, that "the effect is less of an evolution in the writing than of a man trying on different coats."

Throughout the 1960s Middleton wrote essays which explored the more extreme modernist art movements, particularly Dadaism. "The Art of Unreason" and "Dada versus Expressionism" (both 1961), "Bolshevism in Art" (1962), and "The Rise of Primitivism" (1970)—all of which essays may be found in *Bolshevism in Art* (1978)—are studies which attempt to assess the anarcho-nihilism of Dadaism against alternative extremisms in twentieth-century art and politics. For Middleton in these essays Dada is attractive because it did not try to build fake systems of any kind for the free human spirit. As he explains in "The Art of Unreason," Dada "vindicates Dostoevsky's saying that the 'futile and fantastical element' forms part of man's very composition, compels him to resist reason, and to introduce chaos and disruption into everything for the sole purpose of asserting that men are men, not 'the keyboards of pianos.' "

Dada showed that unreason "has a positive part to play in the demolition of systems of conviction which crush man and man's spontaneity." The essential function which Middleton thus accorded to irrational spontaneity, as a guarantee of human freedom, becomes crucial to any understanding of some of the work in *Nonsequences: Selfpoems* (1965), *Our Flowers & Nice Bones* (1969), *The Fossil Fish* (1970), and *Briefcase History* (1972), as well as the collection *The Lonely Suppers of W. V. Balloon* (1975) and the poetic prose of *Pataxanadu* (1977). True art, from this viewpoint, must meet "the existential needs of man confronted with chaos in history and himself." In his essay "Dada versus Expressionism" Middleton suggests that the central question for Dadaism, as for modernism generally, was and is "an attempt to make do without revealed or traditional values in the face of chaos." There is paradox in this stance; art is simultaneously serious human activity

and part-irrational hazard, a game played against cosmic meaninglessness.

Middleton's work is not antiart (as true Dadaism wished to be). On the contrary, his poems and stories are nearly always elegantly wrought constructions (or reconstructions) of language and form. But the poetry's range is gradually extended. In *Nonsequences: Self-poems*—the volume which followed *Torse 3*—there is more sureness and control, less of a sense of merely formal or experimental exploration. Several of these poems have dreamlike resonance. The language of "House in the Street of Doves," for example, evokes surrealist-style painting: "Through/one thick white wall a window/marvelling at a street of doves." "Old Bottles" too has the genuine *frisson*:

> In my striped pyjamas,
> I was not dressed for the journey.
> I changed into padded zip
> jacket, boots, canvas trousers,
> my pockets bulged with the bottles,
> I was carrying the candles,
> and I ran and I ran.

Other poems capture the mood and method where he is nearly always at his most disturbingly successful, in the fusion of contrary experiences. In the aptly named "Disturbing the Tarantula" the images of natural beauty and natural terror are from waking experience. The poem conjures up the way in which sympathetic vibrations can echo through the whole psyche: "All things/are here, monstrous convulsed/ rose (don't anyone/dare come), sounding through/ our caves, I hear them." "Cabal of Cat and Mouse" expresses simultaneous fascination and horror at the cat's game of death with its victim. In "Generations" a son who sees his dead father's signature contemplates time, identity, and continuity:

> Never the solar track, merely
> its similitudes, a rain of dreams
> clubbing the gory hue
> into substances, these
> puzzled records of his goings-on.

Middleton's characteristic mode is active disruption of complacency in style and vision. It is painfully alive and tends to avoid unanxious states of mind. In *Our Flowers & Nice Bones* (1969) the spirit of disruption is stronger than ever before, though, once again, his poetic range is interestingly developed. "Three Microzoic Nonsonnets" employs a structure of fourteen lines, each of which contains anything from one to eight syllables. Like other poems by Middleton this sequence is carefully presented on the page:

Failing: to sit
by the knotted hands
the night through,

all
meaningless, as
the backs of words, the black
cream of moments—

And, like many of the poems and prose pieces in this collection, the sequence is not easy to follow on first reading. The spirit of fashionable "neo-modernity," the short-lived vogue which helped to produce many "concrete" and "phonic" poems during the 1960s and early 1970s, is at home here too, briefly. It appears, for example, in one V-shaped piece—"Birth of Venus"—made up entirely of *V*'s. But the notion of art as free play was by this time a basic principle in Middleton's work.

The Fossil Fish—a sequence of fifteen "micro-poems" first published in 1970—shows Middleton in a rare, totally relaxed mood. The first of these makes effective and appropriate use of semantic dislocation:

village quote idiot unquote
look a walking often takes
long at you

stops & slow hows
he come through

screwy? clutched in
his one scrotum hand the other
crumpled hugs a fingering book.

Another successfully interweaves cold geometry and warm beauty:

shorts white
at the sharp angle of
trim bronze legs
to a melon balanced
in one palm she subtends her
equilateral nose
deepening the hidden
rose of that sphere
between cone & cone.

"The Fossil Fish" was reprinted in Middleton's 1975 collection *The Lonely Suppers of W. V. Balloon*, which was the first of his books to receive much more than encouragement from British critics. Douglas Dunn, writing in *Encounter*, asserted that "he is a poet of considerable importance—an avant-garde poet we

can actually read." In *New Statesman*, another poet, Alan Brownjohn, wrote: "Middleton is easily the most intelligent and serious of our innovators, a poet with a disconcerting knack of making it new in a different way in almost every poem in a book." *The Lonely Suppers of W. V. Balloon*—with a "found" title which suggests the isolated poet on an old-fashioned quest—ranges through many countries, times, and moods, but there is throughout a consistently high level of performance. To successful use of montage ("Chanel Always Now"), surrealism ("Nine Biplanes"), and semantic shuffle ("The Fossil Fish" sequence), Middleton adds some of his most telling explorations of contrary experience. "Opoponax"—the title means "all-healing juice" in Greek—captures the essence of man's mysterious contradictions. Cruel violence and gentle good nature are invoked in images of human sacrifice and a bottle of essence of lavender: "Tenderness/And a great wet shroud/Catching the yellow blood of lavender."

Middleton's commitment to existential freedom entails absence from his poems of any formulae for human nature or any glib ideal of either individual or communal life. However, there are poems with a direct or personal emotional appeal, including "Old Woman at the County Dump," "The Pogroms in Sebastopol," and "Autobiography." The last-named ends:

As head touches pillow eyelid traps a vision
My uncertainty is the soul of the weapons system

They say my daughter they say my son
At my age you'll not find any air to breathe.

Some of the poems are versions or imitations from other languages. "Mandelstam to Gumilev 1920" is, in part, a free translation of another version (in German, by Paul Celan) of one of Mandelstam's poems. Middleton's translation is simple and direct:

There's no unmooring the same boat twice over.
Fur-shoed shadow, certain things not a soul can hear,
Or overcome—the fear we live in, thick forest.

He holds strong opinions about translation, including the view that the poet-translator can learn about new creative possibilities inherent in his own language by working from another. All his translation work suggests too that on the subject of the translator's freedom he differs from some of the great moderns (including Ezra Pound, in whom, he says, "the style is so often achieved upon forfeit of precision"). His own work proceeds from a guiding conviction that the translator should know and keep faith with the philological detail of the original text. His introduction to a recent

What tentative hand now
Carries the lamps along the sea wall, like lamps,
The young flat bottomed women?

Further revisions on Aug 29/30, over
Atlantic, on flight from N.Y. to Dallas,
finished in Dallas Airport, 30 Aug. 830.

The Ulcinj Postcards

Truly, it takes the breath away
"This "view,"
The Adriatic, opal
Unpopulated; and the dark now
Absorbing it.
: no wind,
Said Xristic, after sundown. The beach
Shrugs off its mass
Of splendid flesh:

flat-bottomed
Young women swirl along
The sea-wall, carried
Like lamps, by whom?
What hand, tentative,
Carries the young women
What tentative hand
Carries the young flat-bottomed women
Like lamps along the sea wall

Like lamps the single
bodies move,

Women with taut
Young bottoms, what
Can they be thinking of?
A major stomach, grandpaternal,
Does it only dream of filling itself?
Boys discover a place, maybe,
The jumbled shapes
Of appetition cannot hide.

Boys flit through a space, maybe,
The jumbled shapes
Of appetition cannot hide.

Here, trellised shelters,
For shadoled a small table,
Two jugs; look up, the fort, "attractive"
Turco-Venetian ruin;

And a tomb is built
Into a wall, hollow, candles "twinkle"
At the foot of
A real coffin.

Jumbled shapes of appetition
such space
As boys on tiptoe flit through

Pages from the second or third draft of a 1973 poem (the author)

What tentative hand
Carries along the sea wall, like lamps,
These young flat-bottomed women?
A major stomach, grandpaternal,

Does it only dream of filling itself?
Jumbled shapes ~~mask~~
Of apparition ~~mark own the~~ open space
As boys on tiptoe flit through.

Does it only dream of filling itself?
~~Jumbled shapes~~ All the dusky
~~shapes of~~ apparition ~~mark~~
~~Mark even~~ such space as boys on tiptoe

~~On tiptoe~~ Flit through. ~~Yet~~
Here, for studied, a small fable,
Two jugs; look up, the four, "attractive."
~~Three~~ Venetian ruin
Does it shudder a bit when filling itself?
~~Does it only~~ ~~dream when~~
All the dusky shapes
Of apparition tangle, mark even
Such space as boys on tiptoe, ~~tiptoe~~

Flit through. ~~Yet~~ Had you
Lost the thread? ~~Here~~ for studied, a fable;
Two jugs; look up, three, the four, "attractive"
Three-Venetian ruin.

volume of selected poems by Goethe (1983) indicates why he believes it to be essential that we respect the original text. It is respect for the vitalizing and liberating powers of poetry. Goethe's is a kind of lyric vision which, in our age, we have almost lost:

> Inherent in language there is a pneumatic and festive power, or a joy, which, like Aristotle's Infinite, initiates variety, as it orders development, and which links the dissimilar logics of civil liberty and art. The play of Goethe's verse-textures testifies to the latencies and activities of that power. . . .
>
> . . . the pneumatic and festive power of the word has withdrawn, it withdrew long ago, from our not-so-civilized midst, we are immobilized, and only *now* do we know it.

In its disconcerting variety of style and mood, *Pataxanadu* (1977), an extraordinary collection of minimalist poetic prose, is Middleton's most controversial collection to date. The title work consists of twenty-one short pieces, most of which take inspiration from the anarchic or nihilistic areas of European modernism, including Kafka, Dada, Alfred Jarry's pataphysics, and surrealism. Some of the pieces appeared originally in Germany. There is savage humor and bleak despair in several of these poems, as well as, often, a delighted exploration of minimalist forms. Five pieces make both amusing and exciting use of a technique of vocabulary substitution originally employed by Raymond Queneau. Middleton modifies texts by Sir Thomas Malory, Herman Melville, Sir Thomas Urquhart, Charles Doughty, and Jonathan Swift. He believes, rightly, that the original author's syntax is still audible in the transformation. In "Pataxanadu 1" it is just possible to hear Malory—and this adds to the fun:

> So Sir Landlouse rode over that brewery that was oghamic and feculent; and when he came in at middle-weight of a graven halibut
> there he saw levitating a dayblind knee that was a seditious mameluke, and that boxer licked his worship.

Several of the other pieces in the volume authentically capture the mixture of total zaniness and bitter pessimism found in European Dadaism and its artistic inheritors. Imaginative energy and versatility are evident throughout; the range of styles and techniques is astonishing. "Adelaide's Dream" is a poem of highly erotic fantasy, while "The Spaniards Arrive in Shanghai" achieves the kind of austere clarity which Ezra Pound most admired. Middleton writes effective political satire too, particularly in "The Great Duck (Paris,

June, 1968)" and "The Pocket Elephants." These satires express with near-Swiftian vigor his deep hatred of all forms of dictatorship and repressive doctrine. *Pataxanadu* is a brilliant collection. At times it exhibits overexuberance and grotesque bad taste, but it is always daring and inventive.

Carminalenia (1980) is a more restrained performance than either *The Lonely Suppers of W. V. Balloon* or *Pataxanadu*, but it is a most impressive work of art. In *Carminalenia* Middleton discards much of the neo-Dada high jinks and, with them, some of his more raucous sense of fun. These poems are often difficult to understand, partly because of increased formal compression. This difficulty remains despite two pages of author's notes which are intended also to help readers to comprehend the book's complex structure. Nevertheless this book gives, more consistently than ever before and in an individual voice, what have always been Middleton's serious artistic preoccupations.

The mystery of the poet's craft as he makes his structures over the perhaps meaningless void is explored urgently in "The World First":

> Emptiness, the emptiness in you
> Fill it, fill it with, I don't know,
> Something, not with toys, not with
>
>
> Mythologies, fill it
>
> With something, no, you can't, with solid
> Villages, or seas, bottle corks, desire.

The poem's closing lines are crammed with paradox:

> emptiness
>
> Not like this, a turning around, but to be made
> Into the holy field of apple trees
> If death itself be no more strange or final

"A Small Bronze of Licinius I" repeats the theme of meaninglessness, this time with a sideswipe at power. A bronze coin bearing the head of the emperor Licinius is incorporated into the front-cover design of the book, and as the poem describes it,

> His beard, clipped trim, looks like
> A chin strap, but
> Is broader, he meant it
> To clamp for ever to his skull
> The wreath of three spikes. Sixteen years
> A small but stylish emperor.

In A.D. 323 Licinius was overthrown and murdered by

Constantine: "Fortuna shifts/Her weight, another/Fist/Slugs flat the monstrous glory."

There are also poems of rich and simple celebration. "Night Blooming Cereus" weaves together poetical analysis (of a poem by Georg Trakl) and the emerging flower. It is a poem about emerging poetry too:

> these cups
> of nameless flowers
> had opened, once
>
> only, white, a few hours
> & heady
> through the night, inside them
>
> forty fifty filaments
> drip
> from tiny gold knobs pollen.

The volume contains many poems which show Middleton's virtuosity undiminished by the stricter controls which he has placed on his art. "Ginestra" is an evocative lyric; "Hearing Elgar Again," a moving personal poem for his mother; "The Palace of Thunder," a fine version of Apollinaire's "Le palais de tonnerre"; "Wild Horse"—a poem spun almost from nothing—is a superb *tour de force*: "Its hooves are my heartbeats/ Mine its flying sweat silken tail floats out/Into spaces which contract behind us." As should be expected there are pieces in free-ranging, more provocative style, especially the long poem "Cement Lily Fantomastikon." Three minimalist prose-poems, however, are carefully worked and fascinating.

111 poems (1983)—Middleton's selection from the five books he published between 1962 and 1980—

also includes eleven new poems. Some of these new works are relatively direct and celebratory. "Old Water Jar," for example, compresses two forms of beauty within a third, the shaping of the poem itself, yet the poem is clear and clean. Most of these new poems start from real objects, people, and places. Nostalgia is always tempered with the knowledge that memory is selective, perception only reluctantly active, as in "The Turquoise":

> For the unseen escapes,
> The remembered
> Dominion cracks, falsifies
> Desire and presence as they fly screaming
> Before us. . . .

"People in Kansas, 1910" is a meditation on an old photograph. The pain of inevitable loss is felt as keenly as ever; it is structured logically into living reality: "The sun does not shine for anyone,/The leaf arrives one breath/Only before the wind." All through Middleton's poetry is the sense of unavoidable defeat and pain, but there is also dignity and festival. He is a poet who makes our darkness luminous.

References:

Michael Schmidt, "Christopher Middleton," in his *A Reader's Guide to 50 Modern British Poets* (London: Heinemann, 1979; New York: Barnes & Noble, 1979), pp. 353-359;

Alan Young, *Dada and After: Extremist Modernism and English Literature* (Manchester: Manchester University Press, 1981; Atlantic Highlands, N.J.: Humanities Press, 1981), pp. 216-219.

Adrian Mitchell
(24 October 1932-   )

Toby Silverman Zinman
Philadelphia College of Art

SELECTED BOOKS: [Poems] Fantasy Poets No. 24 (Oxford: Fantasy Press, 1955);

If You See Me Comin' (London: Cape, 1962; New York: Macmillan, 1962);

Poems (London: Cape, 1964);

Marat/Sade, verse adaptation of Peter Weiss's play (London: Calder, 1965; New York: Atheneum, 1966);

Peace Is Milk, Peace News Poetry, no. 2 (London: Housmans, 1966);

Out Loud (London: Cape Goliard, 1968; New York: Grossman, 1968); republished, with notes, as *The Annotated Out Loud* (London: Writers & Readers Publishing Cooperative, 1976);

The Bodyguard (London: Cape, 1970; Garden City: Doubleday, 1971);

© 1984 Layle Silbert

Adrian Mitchell [signature]

Ride the Nightmare: Verse and Prose (London: Cape, 1971);

Tyger: A Celebration Based on the Life and Work of William Blake (London: Cape, 1971);

Wartime (London: Cape, 1973; Garden City: Doubleday, 1975);

Penguin Modern Poets 22, by Mitchell, John Fuller, and Peter Levi (Harmondsworth: Penguin, 1973);

Man Friday [and] *Mind Your Head* [plays] (London: Eyre Methuen, 1974);

Man Friday [novel] (London: Futura, 1975);

The Apeman Cometh (London: Cape, 1975);

For Beauty Douglas: Collected Poems 1953-1979 (London: Allison & Busby, 1982);

Nothingmas Day and Other Poems for Kids and Their Allies (London: Allison & Busby, 1984).

SELECTED PLAY PRODUCTIONS: *Marat/Sade,* verse adaptation of Peter Weiss's play, London, Aldwych Theatre, 20 August 1964; New York, Martin Beck Theatre, 27 December 1965;

US, by Peter Brook and others, with seven lyrics by Mitchell, London, Aldwych Theatre, October 1966;

Tyger, London, New Theatre, 20 July 1971;

Mind Your Head, Liverpool, Everyman Theatre, June 1973;

Man Friday, London, 1973;

The Government Inspector, adapted from Nikolai Gogol's *The Inspector General,* Nottingham, 1974;

White Suit Blues, Nottingham, Playhouse Company, August 1977;

Uppendown Money, Hertfordshire, 1978.

OTHER: Peter Brook and others, *US: The Book of the Royal Shakespeare Production US/Vietnam/US/Experiments/Politics,* includes seven lyrics by Mitchell (London: Calder & Boyars, 1968); republished as *Tell Me Lies: The Book of the Royal Shakespeare Production US/Vietnam/US/Experiments/Politics* (Indianapolis: Bobbs-Merrill, 1968);

Tim Daly, *Jump, My Brothers, Jump: Poems from Prison,* edited by Mitchell (London: Freedom Press, 1970);

Victor Jara: His Life and Songs, translated by Mitchell and Joan Jara (London: Hamilton, 1976);

Naked in Cheltenham, edited by Mitchell (Cheltenham: Gastody, 1978).

Adrian Mitchell is one of the stars of the pop poetry movement of the late 1960s and early 1970s. He is committed to poetry as an oral medium and sees himself primarily as a performer; it is, therefore, not surprising that he has devoted much energy to drama. In addition to his numerous plays, libretti, and five volumes of poetry, he has also written three novels. All these works express his idealistic socialism: his goal is not only to right the world's wrongs but also to establish contact with mass audiences. The poetry he has written over the past twenty-five years is generally characterized by easy accessibility, and it expresses the sentiments of the protest subculture of the 1960s. As Mitchell wrote in 1970, "The Lowest Common Denominator are the only audience worth bothering about."

Born in London in 1932, to James Gibb Mitchell, a scientist, and Kathleen Fabian Mitchell, a teacher, he was educated at Dauntsey's School, Wiltshire, and then did National Service in 1951-1952. In 1952 he entered Oxford, and, during his last year there, he served as literary editor of *Isis* magazine. Oxford was at that time rich with poetry and poets, and Mitchell was acquainted with Alan Brownjohn, George MacBeth, Geoffrey Hill, A. Alvarez, and Elizabeth Jennings. In 1955, at the end of his Oxford years, a pamphlet of his poems was published in the Fantasy Poets series, then edited by George MacBeth and Oscar Mellor. This slim volume contains five poems, one of which, "The Fox," is still considered among Mitchell's best and most serious works. It also anticipates his characteristic concerns. A fox speaks of the choice between battling the elemental terrors of survival in the wild and surrendering to the ease and comfort and "servile fate/Of animals who joined the heated town." The zoo, with the keeper's "grasping love" and "huntsman's face," seems to be the metaphor for all confinement within the civilized world. This bid for freedom recurs throughout Mitchell's later work in the images of the jungle, primitive man, and wild animals. His play *Man Friday* (televised in 1972) celebrates the primitive life, and in a series of poems published twenty years after "The Fox," he employs the coyly savage persona Apeman Mudgeon.

Two poems in his first volume reveal the influence of William Blake, an influence he has acknowledged throughout his career. Reading a poem which begins, as "The Child" does, "In the furnace of the womb/The ore grew thick and found its form," it is hard not to think of Blake's "The Tyger," since both words and rhythm are borrowed. The same effect is produced by "One Death," which seems to be a radically reduced version of "The Crystal Cabinet." The hints of Blake in the early work broaden later into a full-length play about Blake titled *Tyger* (produced in 1971), in which he simplifies and sentimentalizes his poetic hero.

After his Oxford years Mitchell worked as a reporter on the *Oxford Mail* for two years, and then until 1959 on the *Evening Standard*. He has also written columns and television and record reviews for publications ranging from the *Sunday Times* and the *Guardian* to *Peace News* and the *Black Dwarf*. His journalistic background surfaces in later works; for example, headlines become the vehicle for social satire in his third novel, *Wartime* (1973), and in several poems in *The Apeman Cometh* (1975).

In 1962, when Mitchell's first novel, *If You See Me Comin'*, appeared, he was known mainly through his poetry readings, which were part of the Hampstead Poets and Live New Directions movements. He was conspicuous enough for the *Times Literary Supplement* to greet the book with "special expectations." The novel is the story of Johnny Crane, a

blues singer whose occupation affords Mitchell the chance to supply the lyrics to a number of jazz songs. This interest in song lyrics persists in later volumes of poetry, particularly *Out Loud* (1968) and *The Apeman Cometh*, and in some of his plays, particularly *Mind Your Head* (1973).

Johnny Crane's mind is obsessed dually with the Korean War and the imminent hanging of a murderer. His concern with cruelty and imprisonment combines with an optimistic love-conquers-all mentality and an absolute belief in the liberating joy of singing songs. These concerns mark this book as part of the Adrian Mitchell mainstream. His poems, novels, and plays are all similar. The words change, but the antiestablishment theme continues.

The message is first distinctly heard in his first long volume of poetry, *Poems*, published in 1964. In it his obsession with war and destruction, seen as the ultimate expression of society's repressive brutality, generates the volume's strongest poems. In a 1963 interview, Mitchell had said, "I write about war, partly I suppose, because I was brought up in the war and partly because most of the nightmares I have had have been about the war. . . . when I think of the Bomb, I don't think of it as a deterrent or anything like this: I see in my mind all the pictures I have ever seen of the Bomb being tested, all the pictures I have ever dreamt of the Bomb and its effects on people." In "Fifteen Million Plastic Bags," the tone is grim, and the rhyme scheme has grisly simplicity:

> Five million bags were six feet long
> Five million were five foot five
> Five million were stamped with Mickey Mouse
> And they came in a smaller size.

Government as the agent of death and the horror of the destruction of children are recurrent subjects in *Poems*, providing titles such as "A Child is Singing," "Order Me A Transparent Coffin and Dig My Crazy Grave," and "The Dust." The "Veteran With a Head Wound" is a victim visited by memories of the horrors of war which have brought him to madness. The individual, in Mitchell's poetry, is always the victim; only institutions and governments are evil.

America is visible throughout Mitchell's work—he is half in love with the thing he hates. America is, for Mitchell, the source of jazz, the blues, and the terrible social ills that give the blues their meaning, but also, of the war in Vietnam and the powerful protest against that war. During 1963-1964 he was instructor in the Writers' Workshop at the University of Iowa, and out of his experience there comes the poem "From Rich Uneasy America To My Friend Christopher Logue," in which he writes:

> As I sit easy in the centre
> Of the U.S. of America,
> Seduced by cheeseburgers, feeling strong
> When bourbon licks my lips and tongue,
> Ears stopped with jazz or both my eyes
> Full of Mid-Western butterflies,
> You drive out of a supermarket
> With petrol bombs in a family packet
> And broadcast down your sickened nose:
> "It overflows. By Christ, it overflows."

His poems about Bessie Smith and Paul Robeson, about the war protests of a Minnesota family, about Dick Gregory and Charlie Parker, suggest that there is more to America than cheeseburgers and bourbon.

In 1966 his long (about 230 lines) antiwar poem, *Peace Is Milk,* was published as Peace News pamphlet, number two (it later reappeared in *Out Loud*). A plea for peace and love, the poem envisions a world inhabited by elephants ("us," the good guys) and flies ("them," the bad guys). This sort of broad moral dichotomy characterizes Mitchell's judgment. The poem is uneven, both in tone and quality: at its best, however, it shows a peculiar originality in its language and emotion:

> Socrates said no harm could come to a good man,
> But even Socrates
> Couldn't turn the hemlock into a banana milk-shake
> With one high-voltage charge
> From his Greek-sky eyes.
> Even Socrates, poor bugger.

Most often, however, this conversational, colloquial tone and diction dilute the poetry and the passion. Frequently the images become confused; the banana is used as a comic sort of phallic image, which makes the banana milkshake seem fairly gruesome, and the milk of peace for which the earth "screams like a baby," and on which "We all need to be breast-

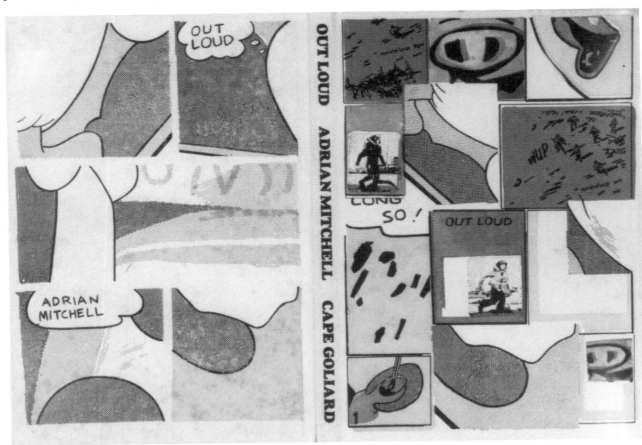

Dust jacket for Mitchell's 1968 volume of poems that Anthony Thwaite called "clear, direct, funny, warmhearted, and eloquent," but "sometimes obvious, banal, whimsical, and too genially sure of a welcome"

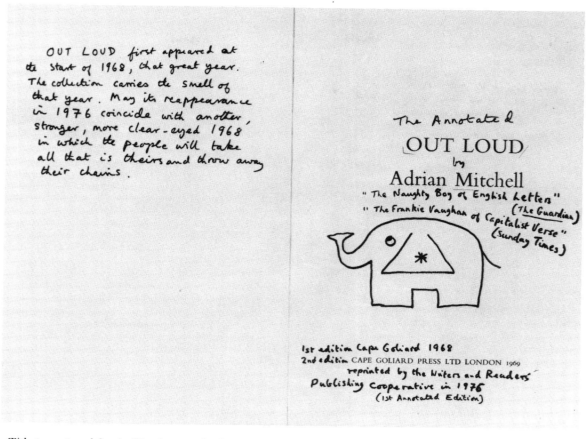

OUT LOUD first appeared at the start of 1968, that great year. The collection carries the smell of that year. May its reappearance in 1976 coincide with another, stronger, more clear-eyed 1968 in which the people will take all that is theirs and throw away their chains.

The Annotated OUT LOUD by Adrian Mitchell
"The Naughty Boy of English Letters" (The Guardian)
"The Frankie Vaughan of Capitalist Verse" (Sunday Times)

1st edition Cape Goliard 1968
2nd edition CAPE GOLIARD PRESS LTD LONDON 1969
reprinted by the Writers and Readers' Publishing Cooperative in 1976
(1st Annotated Edition)

Title page spread for the "1st Annotated Edition" of Mitchell's 1968 book, which reproduces the poet's hand-written explanations and alterations

fed" makes the line about "an Everest-sized Sophia Loren" seem startlingly vulgar. But thematically, this poem is central to Mitchell's canon.

In 1964 Mitchell wrote the verse adaptation for the English translation of Peter Weiss's *Marat/Sade,* and in 1966 he shared the P.E.N. translation prize for this work. His association with Peter Brook, who directed the celebrated stage and film productions of Weiss's play, led to Mitchell's writing seven songs for *US,* which Brook produced for the Royal Shakespeare Company. These songs appear as the first poems in *Out Loud,* and by expressing opposition to the war in Vietnam they announce the thematic concerns of the entire volume: antiwar, antibourgeoisie, antigovernment.

In a review for the *New Statesman* Anthony Thwaite pointed out that the poems in *Out Loud* "presuppose a youngish, leftist, protest-prone audience . . . a pop crowd wanting to be entertained." He went on to say that the poems have "most of the virtues and some of the vices that one would expect, given such an audience. They are clear, direct, fun-

ny, warm-hearted, and eloquent. They are also sometimes obvious, banal, whimsical, and too genially sure of a welcome. . . ."

In 1968, when *Out Loud* was published, everyone could be expected to know the topical references. But this very topicality presents problems in poetry that is supposed to have lasting value and meaning (as Mitchell must intend, since they are included in his collected poems published in 1982). Thus he had the volume republished as *The Annotated Out Loud* in 1976 with his handwritten notes —some political, some personal—reproduced in the text as an all-too-necessary gloss. Despite some of the topical references, songs such as "Zapping the Cong" are accessible on one reading, just as they are on one hearing when read aloud; they lack the density and difficulty many readers have come to expect from most twentieth-century poetry.

Mitchell stands in an antagonistic relation to society, a stance spelled out in "I Tried, I Really Tried," where "Blurred black police cars from the BBC/Circled me blaring: WASH YOURSELF

POET." Mitchell tries to achieve the wildness of his poetic heroes, Blake and Allen Ginsberg—"There are prophets like Ginsberg—grandson of William Blake" *(Peace Is Milk)*—but frequently he merely indulges in the sophomoric need to *épater le bourgeosie.* There are, however, poems of power in *Out Loud:* "To Whom It May Concern," with its refrain "Stick my legs in plaster / Tell me lies about Vietnam," was a showstopper at a poetry reading, but, as the *Times Literary Supplement* review pointed out, "What the ear then welcomed, the eye now skids over." But, then, Mitchell considers the *Times Literary Supplement* the voice of the establishment.

There are also poems of real substance in this collection. "To You" numbers the steps of a child's deforming growth within the social, educational system, which is governed by adult cruelty and rejection until "we stand, past thirty, madder than ever." The clichéd voice of the 1960s is there in the lines "We must make love / Instead of making money," but the stanza continues with what is Mitchell's strongest expression of his feelings about poetry:

> Want to spend my life building poems in which untamed
> People and animals walk around freely, lie down freely
> Make love freely
> In the deep loving carpets, stars circulating in the ceilings,
> Poems like honeymoon planetariums.

Out Loud was published while Mitchell was Granada Fellow in the Arts at the University of Lancaster where he formed a workshop which group-wrote shows, an activity begun at Bradford College of Art. This practice continued at the Sherman Theatre at Cardiff and at Dartington College of the Arts, where he "instigated" (as he prefers it) an eight-hour group show called *Mud Fair* in 1976. These residencies and fellowships have been his livelihood since his days as a reporter.

Between 1968 and 1970 a great deal of Mitchell's work was visible; there were two television documentary scripts, a stage play for children, and his second novel, *The Bodyguard.* In 1971 he returned to the U.S., this time as a Fellow at the Wesleyan University Center for the Humanities. This same year he won the Tokyo Festival Television Film Award, edited *Bards in the Wilderness* with Brian Elliott, while *Tyger* was published and his fourth volume of verse and prose, *Ride the Nightmare,* appeared.

Ride the Nightmare differs from previous volumes in that it includes some short prose pieces; likewise new is a reliance in the satirical verse on the "in" joke, but, then, Mitchell has always preached to the converted. "A Party Political Broadcast on Behalf of the Burial Party" is a whimsical warning about two lovers who are arrested in their bed for being happy:

> "Happy, milord,
> An expression common among delinquents.
> It means—irresponsible."

Found to be addicted to "Love," which is presented as "Exhibit A," and said to "remove the user's interest in money and property," they die, and Mitchell concludes the poem with the ironic catechism:

> Freedom to speak if you have nothing to say.
> Freedom from fear if you stay in your shelter.
> Freedom from want if you do what we want.
> Freedom from freedom, freedom from sanity
> And freedom finally, from life.
>
> IT IS LIKELY THAT DURING THE NEXT TEN YEARS
> YOU WILL BE CALLED UPON TO DIE FOR FREEDOM.

This tone continues in "Ode to Enoch Powell" and "A Leaflet To Be Dropped on China"; "The Oxford Hysteria of English Poetry" has some funny moments:

> After that there were about
> A thousand years of Tennyson
> Who got so bored with himself
> That he changed his name
> to Kipling at half-time.

The rare pieces in which he speaks personally can be fine, such as "My Parents," and the heated polemic and brilliant detail of "To A Russian Soldier in Prague" shows an expansion of his satiric range:

> Africa, Asia and Latin America are screaming:
> STARVATION. POVERTY. OPPRESSION.
> When they turn to America.
> They see only flames and children in the flames.
> When they turn to England
> They see an old lady in a golden wheelchair,
> Share certificates in one hand, a pistol in the other.
> When they turn to Russia
> They see —you.

This volume received harsh reviews. Alan

Peter Ling's set design for the London production of Mind Your Head *(photograph by Nobby Clark)*

Brownjohn wrote in the *New Statesman* that although *Ride the Nightmare* is "at least a continually entertaining book. . . . simply, and sadly, the poetry is not there." He goes on to say, "The brash crude-edge images . . . feel finally so *un*-moving, the arguments become labored, everything seems too firmly and fascinatedly embedded in the culture it strives to satirize." Douglas Dunn, himself a contemporary social poet, wrote a scathing indictment in *Encounter:* "usually the force of the feeling is such that qualifications or recognitions of complexity are completely missed. Naturally this leads to sentimentality on such a heroic scale that there is almost no dealing with it. There is so much lack of experience, so much exalted integrity, lying around in Mr. Mitchell's work that it is beginning to stink."

Over the next few years, Mitchell's third novel, *Wartime,* was published (a novel which goes in for some more "tory-bashing" as the *Times Literary Supplement* called it), along with a number of plays. In 1974-1975 he was resident writer at the Sherman Theatre in Cardiff, and in 1975 three of his television plays were produced. This same year *The Apeman Cometh* appeared, his last volume of new poetry

for adults to date (both subsequent books, *The Annotated Out Loud* and *For Beauty Douglas,* include only previously published work).

The Apeman Cometh contains a variety of poems, including a section of fifteen poems headed "Mainly for Kids," a major antiwar poem, "Cease-fire," dedicated to the Medical Aid Committee for Vietnam, and a passionately sympathetic song, "Victor Jara of Chile," which celebrates the Chilean folksinger and laments his death during the coup that overthrew Allende. In "The Dichotomy Between the Collapse of Civilization and Making Bread" the line "The brand name for a tribe of killer apes/is civilization" might serve as the motto for this volume. The main section of the book features the character of Apeman Mudgeon.

Besides the obvious correlation between Apeman Mudgeon's and Adrian Mitchell's initials, the fact that Apeman hunts poems in his jungle makes it clear that he is his creator's alter ego. This wish-fulfilling creature is both gentle and savage: Apeman lives the good simple life of eating and drinking, mating and sleeping, feeling "happy to be hairy," and going after poems:

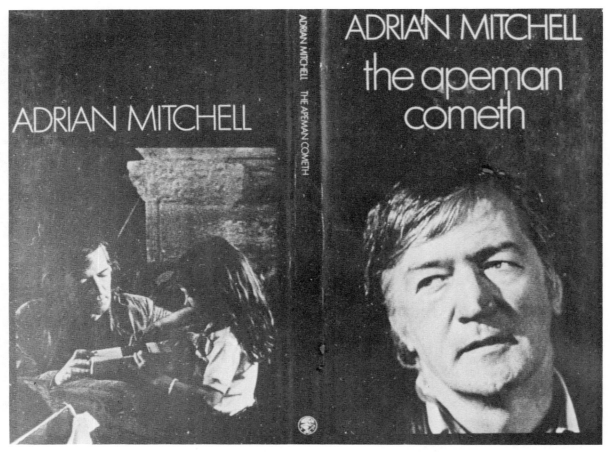

Dust jacket for Mitchell 1975 collection. The title character, Apeman Mudgeon, who hunts poems in his jungle, is cast as Mitchell's alter ego.

With fists and teeth and feet
Because he need the juices
Contained in the poem meat.

The poems are often cutely ungrammatical in this way, suggesting an uncomplicated romantic primitivism which is generally good-natured. Along the same line, Mitchell seems to insist that the writing of poetry is a natural and not a civilized occupation.

One of the book's two epigraphs is from Che Guevera: "Let me say, at the risk of seeming ridiculous, that the true revolutionary is guided by great feelings of love." Mitchell seems to see himself as the Che Guevera of poetry, but, although his political sympathies may be ardent, his aesthetic accomplishments are not strong enough to match this ardor. In a review of *The Apeman Cometh* for the *Listener* Anne Stevenson refers to him as a "rhetorical propagandist" whose "simplistic philosophy" and "very strong moral appeal—is not to adults or

to children but to troubled adolescents; his language is jazzy and full of life." Jazzy though they may be, the poems are easy experiments rather than revolutions, and nowhere does he break new poetic ground.

In 1980 and 1981 Mitchell was the Judith E. Wilson Fellow at Cambridge University. During this time three of his plays with songs were produced, and *Houdini*, an opera for which he wrote the libretto, was produced again.

For Beauty Douglas: Collected Poems 1953-1979, which appeared in 1982, takes its title from an inscription on a grave in Dimbaza, a designated black area in South Africa. Beauty Douglas, a black child who died when only a few weeks old, symbolizes for Mitchell the tragic, continuing need for protest poetry. The book is illustrated by the satiric drawings of Ralph Steadman, and the poems are arranged by theme and subject rather than chronologically.

Mitchell has recently published *Nothingmas*

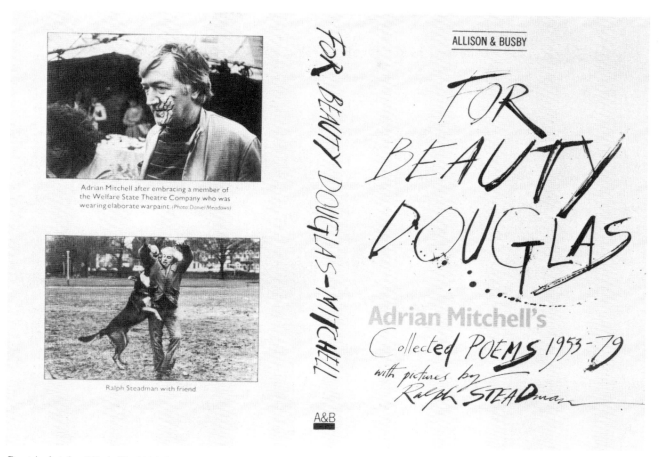

ALLISON & BUSBY

FOR BEAUTY DOUGLAS—MITCHELL

FOR BEAUTY DOUGLAS

Adrian Mitchell's Collected POEMS 1953-79 with pictures by Ralph STEADman

A&B

Adrian Mitchell after embracing a member of
the Welfare State Theatre Company who was
wearing elaborate warpaint. *(Photo: Daniel Meadows)*

Ralph Steadman with friend

*Dust jacket for Mitchell's 1982 book. Beauty Douglas, an infant buried in a designated black area in South Africa, symbolizes for
Mitchell the tragic, continuing need for protest poetry.*

Day and Other Poems for Kids and Their Allies (1984) and is currently working on a stage version of Dylan Thomas's *A Child's Christmas in Wales* and on his second version of Gogol's *The Government Inspector.* His shift from poetry to theater is clear, but the theatrical element has always been a major impulse in his career. As he himself says, his "true work" is performing. As the critical consensus indicates, Adrian Mitchell is not an important poet. His career is significant as part of a movement that made poetry popular entertainment, and that movement is now literary history.

John Montague

(28 February 1929-   )

Paul Mariani
University of Massachusetts/Amherst

BOOKS: *Forms of Exile* (Dublin: Dolmen, 1958);
The Old People (Dublin: Dolmen, 1960);
Poisoned Lands and Other Poems (London: MacGibbon & Kee, 1961; Philadelphia: Dufour, 1963; revised edition, Dublin: Dolmen/Oxford: Oxford University Press, 1977);
Three Irish Poets, by Montague, Thomas Kinsella, and Richard Murphy (Dublin: Dolmen, 1961);
Death of a Chieftain and Other Stories (London: MacGibbon & Kee, 1964; Chester Springs, Pa.: Dufour, 1967);
Old Mythologies: A Poem (N.p.: Privately printed, 1965);
All Legendary Obstacles (London: Oxford University Press, 1966; Chester Springs, Pa.: Dufour, 1966);
Patriotic Suite (Dublin: Dolmen, 1966; Chester Springs, Pa.: Dufour, 1966);
A Chosen Light (London: MacGibbon & Kee, 1967; Chicago: Swallow, 1969);
Home Again (Belfast: Festival Publications, Queen's University, 1967);
Hymn to the New Omagh Road (Dublin: Dolmen, 1968);
The Bread God (Dublin: Dolmen, 1968);
The Planter and the Gael, by Montague and John Hewitt (Belfast: Arts Council of Northern Ireland, 1970);
Tides (Dublin: Dolmen, 1970; Chicago: Swallow, 1971);
The Rough Field (Dublin: Dolmen, 1972; Winston-Salem: Wake Forest University Press, 1979);
The Cave of Night (Cork: Golden Stone Press, 1974);
Ó Riada's Farewell (Cork: Golden Stone Press, 1974);
A Slow Dance (Dublin: Dolmen/Oxford: Oxford University Press, 1975; Winston-Salem: Wake Forest University Press, 1975);
The Great Cloak (Dublin: Dolmen/Oxford: Oxford University Press/Winston Salem: Wake Forest University Press, 1978);
The Leap (Dublin: Gallery Press, 1979; Deerfield, Mass.: Deerfield Press, 1979);
Selected Poems (Toronto: Exile Editions, 1982; Win-

ston-Salem: Wake Forest University Press, 1982; Dublin: Dolmen, 1982; London: Oxford University Press, 1982);
The Dead Kingdom (Dublin: Dolmen/London: Oxford University Press/Winston-Salem: Wake Forest University Press, 1983).

RECORDING: *The Northern Muse,* by Montague and Seamus Heaney, Claddagh Records, 1968.

OTHER: "The Sentimental Prophecy: A Study of *The Deserted Village*," in *The Dolmen Miscellany of Irish Writing*, edited by Montague and Thomas Kinsella (Dublin: Dolmen, 1962), pp. 62-79;

"The Impact of International Modern Poetry on Irish Writing," in *Irish Poets in English*, edited by Sean Lucy (Cork: Mercier Press, 1972), pp. 144-158;

"Despair and Delight," in *Time Was Away: The World of Louis MacNeice*, edited by Terence Brown and Alec Reid (Dublin: Dolmen, 1974), pp. 123-127;

The Faber Book of Irish Verse, edited by Montague (London: Faber & Faber, 1974); republished as *The Book of Irish Verse: An Anthology of Irish Poetry from the Sixth Century to the Present* (New York: Macmillan, 1976);

André Frenaud, *November*, translated by Montague and Evelyn Robson (Cork: Golden Stone Press, 1977).

PERIODICAL PUBLICATIONS: "Fellow Travelling with America," *Bell*, 17 (June 1951): 25-38;

"The Tyranny of Memory: A Study of George Moore," *Bell*, 17 (August 1951): 12-24;

"Contribution to the Young Writers' Symposium," *Bell*, 17 (October 1951): 5-12;

"Tribute to William Carleton," *Bell*, 18 (April 1952): 12-20;

"American Pegasus," *Studies*, 48 (Summer 1959): 183-191;

"The Rough Field," *Spectator*, 26 April 1963, p. 531;

"Regionalism into Reconciliation: The Poetry of John Hewitt," *Poetry Ireland*, 3 (Spring 1964): 113-118;

"Under Ben Bulben," *Shenandoah*, 16 (Summer 1965): 21-25;

"The Seamless Garment and the Muse," *Agenda*, 5, no. 4-6, no. 1 (1967-1968): 27-34;

"A Primal Gaeltacht," *Irish Times*, 30 July 1970, p. 7;

"Home Again: An Ulster Diary," *Interplay*, 4 (January 1971): 37-39;

"Order in Donnybrook Fair," *Times Literary Supplement*, 17 March 1972, p. 313;

"A Note on Rhythm," *Agenda*, 10 (Autumn-Winter 1972-1973): 41;

"The War Years in Ulster 1939-1945," *Honest Ulsterman*, 64 (September 1979-January 1980): 28-37;

"Heaney and Kinsella: North and South," *Irish Times*, 1 November 1980, p. 12.

John Montague is one of the few indispensable voices coming out of Ireland today. It is probably inevitable that this Irishman of Ulster Catholic stock who has spent so much of his time in Paris should have at last settled in Cork, in a southern Irish city roughly midway between those two cultural antipodes. A poet of great sensitivity and intelligence, he has spent the last three decades trying to awaken from the nightmare of Irish history even as he has been drawn by the thin, insistent music— sound of fiddle, sound of drum—which serves as a ground bass to everything he writes. Brooklyn-born, Ulster-raised, educated in Dublin and later at Yale, Iowa, and Berkeley, an "exile" who has spent years in Paris and Celtic Normandy, a man who has translated extensively the modern French poets and traveled widely throughout Europe and India, Canada and Central America, Montague—like Joyce and Yeats before him—still feels an underlying current pulling him toward the theme that is Ireland, the land which has stung him into song. He has studied and written at length on the Anglo-Irish literary tradition and—with time—the older Irish tradition (he was, for example, editor of *The Faber Book of Irish Verse* in the early 1970s), and he has written on the Anglo-Irish figures who shaped his themes and language, among them: Oliver Goldsmith, William Carleton, William Butler Yeats, Samuel Beckett, Austin Clarke, and Patrick Kavanagh. Like one of his American masters, William Carlos Williams, Montague has listened attentively to the language of his place, the speech patterns and evasions of his Ulster neighbors, drawing on that source for his poetry. But, at some deeper, half-mythical center, he seems to have listened even more attentively to ascertain the authentic musical cadences rising out of his place. His "Farewell to Ó Riada," the Irish composer who did so much to restore the older Irish music, and his association with the Chieftains (he provided this group of musicians dedicated to restoring the older, Irish musical tradition with their name and recorded them on Claddagh records) are but two examples of this preoccupation with the older, pre-English traditions. And knowing at firsthand the murderous history of his land, Montague has made a concerted, if ambivalent, attempt at what he has called cultural miscegenation as a way out of the unyielding factionalism and provincialism that in large part defines Ulster.

For the nightmare of Irish politics is in fact Montague's birthmark as well as his birthright, as it was his Anglo-Irish literary fathers' before him. Even the "accident" of his birth is directly attributable to what the Irish euphemistically call "the Troubles," since Montague's father, James, had to leave Ulster in 1925 because of his republican activities there, such as firebranding the homes of absentee landlords. In a recent interview, for example, Montague remarked that the people who own the burned-out shell of his mother's family home in Fintona (the casualty of a 100-pound bomb exploded in the square outside the home) found old bullets—vintage 1920—stored under the floorboards in his mother's bedroom. In 1933 Montague, age four, was sent back to Ulster with his two older brothers to live with relatives, the brothers going to Fintona and John to Garvaghey in County Tyrone to live with his father's sisters, Brigid and Freda Montague. A bright student, Montague did well in the local schools at Garvaghey and Glencull and was often called upon to read aloud until, set before a crowd of older students at the age of eight, he began stammering, a nervous tic which was to remain with him, becoming in time a symbol in Montague's poetry of the crippled poet. In 1941 he won a scholarship to board at the Catholic school of St. Patrick's College in Armagh. Montague has written well of his memories of the war years in Ulster: British and American soldiers training for D-Day, the wheels of an overturned Army truck spinning as the truck sank into a bog, a German P.O.W. camp in Dungannon, food rationing, and the sirens signaling another German bombing raid.

In 1946, at the age of seventeen, Montague won a Tyrone County Scholarship to attend University College, Dublin, where he studied history and English and attended Roger McHugh's evening classes in Anglo-Irish literature. He did well in his studies, but, coming from a farm in the North, his already exacerbated sense of being the outsider was further intensified living in the capital of the Irish Free State. In the winter of 1949, just before his twentieth birthday, Montague published his first poems, winning a competition sponsored by the eminence who was to have such a profound impact on his own poetry: Austin Clarke. When Montague graduated later that year, it was with a double first in both history and English. That fall he began work on his M.A. at University College, Dublin, specializing in Anglo-Irish literature. Three years later he received his degree for his articles on George Moore and William Carleton, which had been published in the *Bell*. From the late 1940s Montague had traveled extensively throughout Western Europe, attending the American Seminar at Schloss Leopoldkron at Salzburg in the summer of 1950. In the summer of 1953 he went to the United States

for what was to become a three-year period of study. One reason he was anxious to get back to the United States was to see his father, but James Montague returned to Ulster in 1952, after twenty-seven years in exile.

The other reason Montague wanted to get to America was to get away from what he rightly perceived as the backwater of Irish letters as it existed at the time and to work with the Americans (much as Charles Tomlinson, the English poet, would do a few years later). Montague spent his first year at Yale, where he met Robert Penn Warren (a taciturn man, as Montague remembered), W. H. Auden (a nonstop talker), and Robert Lowell. He also spent much of his free time with his mother's family—the Carneys—in Brooklyn. And he also suffered a partial nervous breakdown, exacerbated—Montague believes—by the insidious pressures of the McCarthy hearings and the intensification of the cold war, as well as by the death of Dylan Thomas in a New York hospital (from overdrink) and by Montague's delayed shock over leaving Ireland.

In the summer of 1954, Montague attended the Indiana University summer school, where he came in contact with some of the New Critics, including R. P. Blackmur and William Empson, as well as Richard Wilbur and John Crowe Ransom, who helped secure Montague a part-time teaching position at the Iowa Writers' Workshop. It was at Iowa that he met W. D. Snodgrass, Robert Bly, William Dickey, as well as Louis MacNeice, John Berryman (before he was jailed for disturbing the peace), and—most important for Montague—William Carlos Williams. Here Montague also met Madeleine de Brauer, a young Frenchwoman on a Fulbright, who on 18 October 1956 became Montague's wife. After earning his M.F.A. in 1955 from Iowa for a selection of his poems, Montague spent that summer traveling through Mexico, including the pre-Columbian sites, which struck a responsive chord in him, the ancient stones of the Aztecs chiming with the dolmens of Ireland. He stayed at Tehauntepec before moving up the Pacific coast to begin work on a Ph.D. in English under Professor Thomas Parkinson at Berkeley. It was an auspicious moment to be in San Francisco, the vortex of energies which included Allen Ginsberg, Jack Kerouac, Gary Snyder, and Kenneth Rexroth even then whirling in full spin, and Montague remembers the electricity hearing Ginsberg read his just-completed *Howl* before an audience for the first (or perhaps second) time. By an extraordinary set of coincidences, then, Montague managed to be caught up in the crest of energies which American poetry was

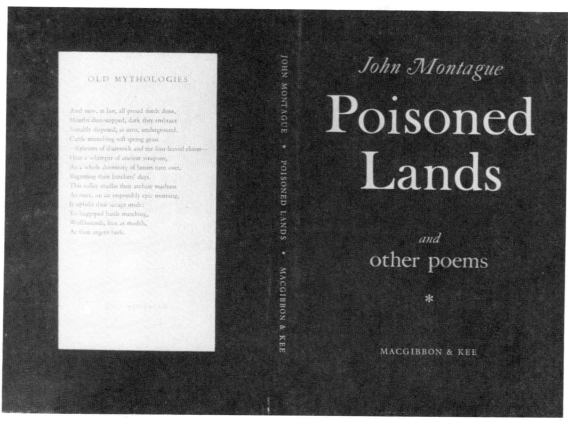

Dust jacket for Montague's 1961 book: poems written over the first ten years of his career

then experiencing, a crest which ran from Wilbur's and Lowell's brilliant, hard-edged formalities to the open-ended Blakean pronouncements of the Beats.

But Montague had been away long enough. In October he was in Normandy, France, to marry Madeleine de Brauer, and then both settled in Dublin, living at 6 Herbert Street in the Georgian section of the city. Montague went to work for Bord Failte Eireann (Ireland's tourist board) and began work on a dissertation at University College, Dublin, on the Anglo-Irish writer Oliver Goldsmith. Back in Dublin, Montague could sense a new energy in the arts, much of that centering around Liam Miller's Dolmen Press project. At Christmas 1958 Montague, just short of his thirtieth birthday, published his first book of poems with the press, a pamphlet called *Forms of Exile*. A small press affair published in Ireland in a limited edition, the book received a modicum of polite attention, including notices in the *Times Literary Supplement* and *Poetry*, before it dropped from sight. But at least it was a beginning.

In 1959, with his wife working at the French embassy in Dublin, Montague quit his job to devote as much time as he could to expanding and revising his first full-length collection of poems with an eye to publication in England and continued to write his finely crafted short stories—the best of them harking back to his Ulster days. (These were published in 1964 under the title *Death of a Chieftain and Other Stories*.) In the spring of 1961 the Montagues moved to 11, rue Daguerre in Paris, where Montague became Paris correspondent for the *Irish Times* (he saw much of De Gaulle and covered the Algerian War from Paris). Now, too, familiar figures such as Austin Clarke, Kavanagh, and Thomas Kinsella were replaced by Samuel Beckett, Jean-Paul Sartre, Eugène Ionesco, and Alberto Giacometti, presences he met frequently on the streets. Nineteen sixty-one also saw the publication of Montague's first full volume of poetry: *Poisoned Lands and Other Poems*, published by MacGibbon and Kee in London.

Poisoned Lands and Other Poems is made up of twenty-nine poems, many of them taken from his first book, and represents the fruit of ten years' work. Many of the themes which recur throughout

Montague's subsequent volumes are already present: Ireland as the hag/queen, alternately repelling and attracting the poet, the country Irishman caught in a world which is rapidly changing and that not necessarily for the better, the poet's nostalgia for the common folk who inhabit the landscape of memory (as in the evocative, Yeatsian roll call of "Like Dolmens Round My Childhood, The Old People" in the poem *The Old People,* published separately in 1960). Here, as in his short stories, Montague recalls a world which, since the end of World War II, has been vanishing at an alarming speed. Like Thomas Hardy evoking a Wessex or William Faulkner a Yoknapatawpha which had almost completely passed into history by the time they came to record these places, so Montague is at pains to portray his Ulster countryside even as he knows that the new economy (or if not that, then gelignite explosives) have wreaked havoc on that dark, sad world.

Knowing that he had been largely absent from the North for over a decade when he wrote many of his early poems, and having by then rejected the household penates of the old religion (the Sacred Heart, the Sorrowing Mother, the gilt crucifixes, the burnished wood rosaries), Montague sees himself as the Prodigal Son, in the poem of that name, returning not to relent but to witness:

> Once a year he returns: custom or the virtue
> Of remembering his family, although entering a door
> No one grudges him his absence:
> Yesterday seems perpetual,
> Even his mother smiling.

Another theme which has continued to possess Montague, and one already developed in his early poems, is that of Ireland's past greatness, often played against its tawdry, diminished presence. So, the image of a jerry-built project in Dublin, with its

> blackened rubbish dumps,
> The half-built flats, the oozing grey cement
> Of hasty walls, the white-faced children
> Deprived of sun

is followed a few pages later by the sound of Ireland's heroic dead—swish of weapon, squeal of bagpipe:

> This valley cradles their archaic madness
> As once, on an impossibly epic morning,
> It upheld their savage stride:

> To bagpiped battle marching,
> Wolfhounds, lean as models,
> At their urgent heels.

Finally, Montague provides the dialectic of his *ars poetica.* There is the need to keep returning to his roots, as in the close of "The Water Carrier," where he remembers his twice-daily trips to the spring near his home in Garvaghey for water (water for cattle, water in a white enamel pail for drinking). To drink, and like Frost, to be made whole again against all confusion:

> I sometimes come to take the water there,
> Not as return or refuge, but some pure thing,
> Some living source, half-imagined and half-real

> Pulses in the fictive water that I feel.

Montague spent the spring semesters of 1964 and 1965 teaching again at Berkeley, where he met Robert Duncan, Louis Simpson, Thom Gunn, and other Bay Area poets. He also witnessed at first-hand the growing opposition to the Vietnam War. Back in Ireland he continued his work as literary director for Claddagh Records (between 1962 and 1975, for example, he was responsible for arranging recordings for Clarke, Kavanagh, Kinsella, Robert Graves, Hugh MacDiarmid, and Seamus Heaney). In the spring semesters of 1967 and 1968 he taught again, this time closer to home, at University College, Dublin, and when Valentin Iremonger became too ill to continue work as editor of the *Faber Book of Irish Verse,* Montague assumed responsibility for that as well, in time producing an extraordinary gathering of Irish voices, many in brilliant translations from the Gaelic by poets who had themselves been shaped by choice and by memory by that long and rich tradition. In the meantime, MacGibbon and Kee published Montague's second full-length book, *A Chosen Light* (1967).

Unlike so many second collections of poetry, *A Chosen Light* shows that its author had grown, in significant ways, into a new mastery of his craft. The title refers, presumably, not only to the quiet, monastic light Montague evoked earlier in his meditation on the hermit tradition, a light still visible in the stones themselves along the Dingle Peninsula, but also to the light which he sees streaming through the windows of his studio at 11, rue Daguerre, before traffic disturbs the world again. It is a meditative light he wishes to evoke, "soft and luminously exact," what a painter would call a "chosen light." In another poem in the volume

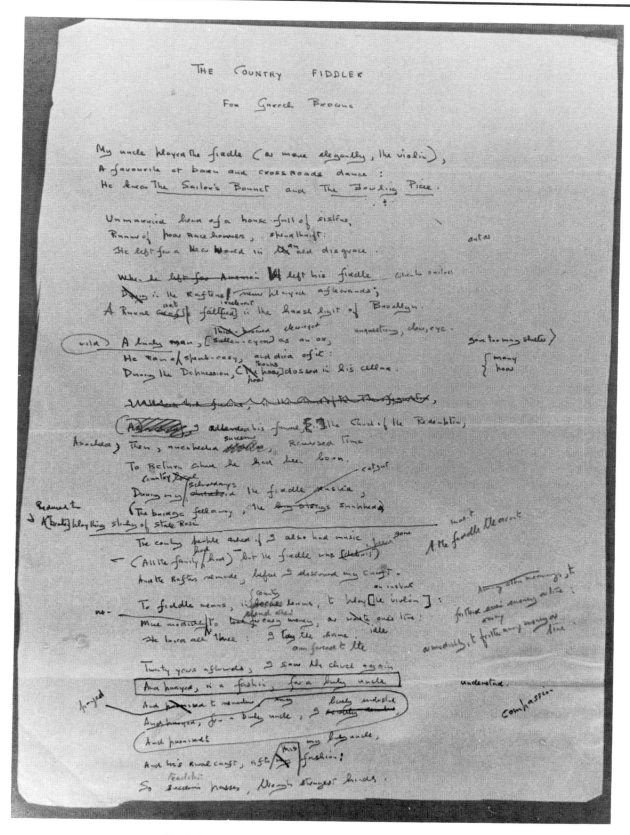

Draft for a poem published in A Chosen Light *(the author)*

called, tellingly, "A Bright Day," Montague speaks of his need for a radically denotative language, "a slow exactness//Which recreates experience/By ritualizing its details." These are details seen with the precise eye of a Charles Tomlinson or a William Carlos Williams (honored, not incidentally, as the master who recognized Montague when he embraced him as a poet—the ritual laying on of hands—at the Iowa Writers' Workshop in 1955).

A Chosen Light is divided into four sections. The first, "All Legendary Obstacles," focuses on the theme of sexuality: the priapic and narcissistic as well as the Calvinistic and Jansenistic manner in which his Ulster neighbors so readily condemned what they secretly yearned after: sexuality and its expression among the young. Montague remembers here the bittersweet memory of walking with a young Irish woman whom he could not touch though his whole body yearned to, remembers too the difficult struggle he had consequently as he learned how to live with his wife, the private pain of marital discord, the failing attempt to understand his wife's own past with its cultural divide, the dense underbrush of silence growing between them, and a return at the close of the sequence to Montague's own more familiar roots as he tries once again to understand how that boy in all his awkward sensuality and delayed springtime had become this angry husband.

If the first section centers on French landscapes, the second section—"The Country Fiddler"—recalls again Montague's Ulster youth. "The Country Fiddler" remembers his godfather and namesake who, like Montague's own father, had had to exile himself in Brooklyn, where he "ran a wild speakeasy, and died of it"—that is, of drink. He remembers also the old fiddle his uncle used to play, and which he left behind to have it fall apart. But when the old man died, the younger promised to play that old music once more in his own fashion, through the instrument of his poems: "So succession passes, through strangest hands." In poems such as "Hill Field," "The Road's End," "Witness," and "Clear the Way," Montague records the passing of his childhood world in the name of something called progress, and he mourns that passage. It is not the tractors which are the enemy, he will tell you, for they can do the work more effectively and far more easily than horses. The real problem is, rather, with the new factory farms and huge combines, which are rapidly destroying the organic balance of the very soil they work. Traveling out on the Dingle Peninsula, where Gaelic is still spoken in an unbroken line of succession, Montague stops to ask

directions at a cottage and is greeted in the old tongue by a woman, and something deep and powerful stirs in him: a world nearly lost now, "obscured in sea/mist," where the old stones of the faithful "held into the Atlantic for a thousand years."

"The Cage" focuses subtly and sometimes indirectly on the sense of human limitation, the realization Montague experiences at the midpoint of his life: that the old generation is passing away, which means that his will be next. This sequence begins with a short elegy for a fellow poet and friend, Theodore Roethke, and ends with memories of his father, who died in November 1959. In between it obliquely laments the deterioration of his marriage and the unsettling sense of an impending apocalypse of sorts when Montague recalls the frightened faces in Paris when De Gaulle narrowly escaped being assassinated by extremists in the French army for his handling of the Algerian War, and then recalls two P.O.W. camps: the first in Ulster, where German prisoners—though living exposed to the eyes of curious villagers—were treated humanely; the second a memory of the camp at Rudshofen, with its "crematorium for Jews and Gypsies." Something new and terrifying, he feels, has entered the world of political expediency in our time: the final solutions of the superpowers.

To counter that apocalyptic vision, however, Montague chooses another light in the final section of the book, called "Beyond the Liss." Here he opts not for a Christian vision but rather for an Orphic one: pagan and older than the moral order of his father's fathers. Remembering the young in one another's arms at the yearly festival at Mullingar in 1964, when Pope John lay dying, Montague sings out, in a parody of Yeats's poem: "*Puritan Ireland's dead and gone,/A myth of O'Connor and O'Faolain.*" And in "Beyond the Liss," Sean the hunchback hears "an errant music,/Clear, strange, beautiful," and is invited into "the world of ideal/Movement" where "all/Act not as they are/But might wish to be." Having achieved that "perfect music," however, something in the hunchback seeks to destroy the freely offered gift, and soon Sean finds himself back in the real world again, a hunchback once more. It is a wonderful parable of the power of the poem to transform the poet who is often—Montague suggests, pointing to himself—his own worst enemy. In poem after poem Montague hears that thin scrannel music in the hills, "the wail of tin/whistle" climbing "against fiddle, and/the *bodhran*" beginning its beat, until all is lost once more.

In 1970 Montague published his third full-

Front cover for the book Montague called "a temporary exhaustion of an obsession"

length book of poems, *Tides.* Four years earlier, the engraver S. W. Hayter had asked Montague to provide him with poems to go with a series of engravings on the sea which he had recently completed. Out of that meditation on the recurrence of the sea's rhythms came not only Montague's "Sea Changes," the last of the book's five movements, but the central image which informs the entire book. *Tides,* Montague has written, is the record of "a temporary exhaustion of an obsession," beginning and ending "with the sound of water rising/falling." The poems here are more naked and vulnerable than those Montague had allowed himself to write earlier. And they are darker, more fiercely deterministic than his earlier poems. Like fish, like the very seaweed and the rocks themselves, he insists, we are caught in life's groundswell, pulled by life's needs to make love, to generate, to die. Life is a dream, the last poem reminds us, where we are enmeshed in our own minds, pulled this way and that on the currents of time and history, where

> we all turn
> turn and thresh
> and disappear.

As with all of Montague's work, these poems are autobiographical. But where he had often seemed to stand outside his poems, commenting on the course of events as from the shoreline, here Montague becomes one more object moved by the same instincts as all other organisms. In the opening sequence, "The Wild Dog Rose," Montague dreams on helplessly as he watches a woman butchered on an operating table. And then, in the following poems, he admits the open battle that life with his wife has become. And yet, as if to intensify the guilt he feels, he finds himself, after quarreling with her all through the night, being pulled inexorably by the tide of his wife's body to make love to her. Montague shifts then to tell the story of an old woman from Garvaghey, the village *Cailleach,* the old hag who, at seventy, had to fight off a drunken laborer who, one night in desperate loneliness, found himself pulled by inexplicable needs to her cottage, where he tried to make love to her before crashing to the floor in a drunken stupor. Then Montague brilliantly juxtaposes this story with a strong translation of "The Hag of Beare," an Irish ballad of the ninth century. Unlike the old woman whom Montague had known who had kept close watch over her virginity all her life, the hag of Beare has known many men in her life (and will invite Christ in if he should come knocking too). But now even she can only wait for the one end—the flood tide of death as her "aging blood/Slows to final ebb."

In the next section, "The Pale Light," Montague returns again to the theme of love, to the experience of the Dark Lady Death. Now the images become even more terrible, as women are identified with Medusa and with death, and he confesses now to his fears that the woman will destroy him and all he has so carefully worked for. Again, after arguing all night, he and the woman come together toward dawn, but this time his seed "hisses" into her "maw-like womb," the hiss transforming itself into "the whimper of death being born." In the prose poem "The Huntsman's Apology," Montague seems to answer the Dark Lady's special delivery letter with his own poem, telling her that their relation is over: "You think I am brutal and without pity but at least I execute cleanly because, like any true killer, I wish to spare the victim."

By contrast, the third section, "Life Class," celebrates the woman who now gives him a new sense of life. "A Dream of July" celebrates this other woman's "abundant body," the "spike/Of each small nipple/A wild strawberry." It is probably no accident that the poem is shaped like a phallus. Recalling Yeats and the Cave of Porphyro, the speaker admits that he too has been lured, pulled, swayed to forget his pain and to live again in the other woman's love. Even at forty, he has come to see,

> the pale-faced
> imperious virgin
> who rules our best
> dreams still strides
> the night,

and we follow on the tide of our own longings.

In "The Northern Gate," Montague salutes the tidal draw of his artistic fathers, naming two Irish exiles who—like himself—elected to spend so many years in Paris: Joyce and Beckett. Having saluted them, he himself returns to Ulster and to the last days of his father, drawn by the old household pieties and by the place names that brought his father home to die:

> Beragh, Carrickmore
>
> Pomerroy, Fintona—
> placenames that sigh
> like a pressed melodeon
> across this forgotten
> Northern landscape.

Shortly after his father's death in 1959 Montague began his long meditation on Ulster and especially the country village where he was raised: Gavarghey. The word comes from the Gaelic *Garbh acaidh* which, translated as "The Rough Field," provides the title for the book that most critics feel gives Montague his strongest claim to recognition as a major voice in contemporary poetry. From the three blank verse sonnets which open *The Rough Field* (1972), written on a return trip home in the summer of 1960, until the book's publication by Dolmen Press twelve years later, Montague worked slowly and painstakingly on his eighty-page epic. He remembers reading a prize poem in the assembly rooms of the Presbyterian church in Belfast, "a drab Victorian building in the heart of the city," and of hearing "the rumble of drums" outside as Orangemen prepared for their annual parade on 12 July, a date recalling the final defeat of the Catholics at the Boyne in 1690. "Bumping down towards Tyrone a few days later by bus," he says, "I

Front cover for Montague's long meditation on Ulster

had a kind of vision, in the medieval sense, of my home area, the unhappiness of its historical destiny. . . . I managed to draft the opening and the close, but soon realised that I did not have the technique for so varied a task. . . . Although as the Ulster crisis broke [in 1969], I felt as if I had been stirring a witch's cauldron, I never thought of the poem as tethered to any particular set of events. . . . Experience of agitations in Paris [1968] and Berkeley [1965] taught me that the violence of disputing factions is more than a local phenomenon. But one must start from home—so the poem begins where I began myself, with a Catholic family in Gavarghey, in the county of Tyrone, in the province of Ulster."

Many of the poems published in Montague's first three collections of poetry as well as in earlier pamphlets find their way naturally into *The Rough Field,* his most sustained, ambitious, and perhaps most satisfying volume to date. From *Tides* Montague has taken "The Wild Dog Rose" and "Omagh Hospital," from *A Chosen Light* he has taken "The Country Fiddler," "The Road's End," "The Cage," and "The Siege of Mullingar," and from *Poisoned Lands* the prize poem he read in Belfast in 1960 at the start of his Ulster meditation: "Like Dolmens Round My Childhood, the Old People." In its clarity of diction *The Rough Field* recalls late Yeats and Williams; in its lyrical and narrative unfolding and even in some of its particulars, it seems to owe something to Hart Crane's *The Bridge* (1930). The poem is divided into ten sections and an epilogue, beginning with Montague's return to Gavarghey and ending with the poet's leaving the North and with it that bitter, strife-ridden world of his youth which—he has come to see—is already gone.

Between that arrival and return, the poem provides, first, a meditation on the passing of Brigid Montague (1876-1966), the aunt who raised the poet after his return to Ireland in 1933, a woman whose blend of Catholic pieties (the Little Flower devotions, the rosary, the crucifix on the wall) and Irish superstitions (the dead who walk the houses, the wail of the banshee) so deeply shaped the poet's own psyche. This meditation leads in turn to a section called *The Bread God* (published separately in 1968), in which Montague's eighty-year-old Jesuit uncle, self-exiled to Australia when Montague's father and uncle were dispersed to Brooklyn, realistically recalls the Ulster Catholicism of his own youth, pious women praying at the one Sunday Mass while the menfolk stayed home. This voice is contrasted with the stridency and dementia of the radical Protestant pamphlets of the Ian Paisley sort denouncing Catholics and in particular the "idolatry" of communion. Against this vision of sectarian hatred Montague evokes the tenacity of his own Catholic forebears, the Tague clan, who, under pain of imprisonment, attended the outlawed Mass covertly in the hilly countryside throughout much of the seventeenth and eighteenth centuries. "A Severed Head" laments the defeat of the Ulster O'Neills in Queen Elizabeth's time and the subsequent forcible suppression of the Irish tongue by the British rulers that followed. And yet Montague knows that the old tongue exists still in the "lawless" English of the Irish and Scots place names which remain his Ulster heritage:

And what of stone-age Sess Kill Green
Tullycorker and Tullyglush?
Names twining braid Scots and Irish,
like Fall Brae, springing native
As a whitethorn bush?

"The Fault" is a meditation honoring Montague's Republican father and admitting that the old music which could so stir his father into burning out one of the local absentee landlords has also stirred the son to take action in his poems: "This bitterness/ I inherit from my father, . . . /the vomit surge/of race hatred" for the English who scattered "his household gods, used/his people/as servants, flushed his women/like game." In the sixth section, "A Good Night," the poet joins old friends at "The Last Sheaf," a local pub, for "the usual/Grotesque, half animal evening so/Common in Ireland." Afterward, in the light that comes early to this place in summer, the poet staggers drunkenly through the countryside of his boyhood, reliving some of those early pastoral scenes before he is finally surprised by "a clump/of bullocks." They have already been bought at auction by the English, and he is pulled up short, remembering who still rules here, and understands why such drunken nights, where nostalgia gives way to oblivion, are still so common in Ireland. In the morning light he sees another modern dance hall for the young going up and realizes bitterly that this music with its promise of sexual energy and its come-hither illusion of change will no doubt "house more hopes than any/verse of mine."

Hymn to the New Omagh Road (published separately in 1968)—section seven—continues with the theme of "progress" by providing a sardonic balance sheet of gains and losses now that a new highway has cut away much of the ancient countryside. *Patriotic Suite* (published separately in 1966) evokes again that "weaving" strain of melancholy that so haunts Montague's poems and for which he salutes Seán Ó Riada, who did so much to revive the ancient Irish music. Here in rapid succession Montague recalls various strains in the Irish National Movement: the Easter 1916 Rising, the transformation of Irish culture into twentieth-century norms, the mixed blessings of "provincial Catholicism," and the hopeful return of a new, less restrained attitude toward sexuality among the young. Still, throughout this section, it is the note of deep melancholy which pervades Montague's world which we hear as counterbass, everything

wound in a native music
curlew echoing tin whistle
to eye-swimming melancholy

is that our offering?

The ninth section, "A New Siege," Montague

calls a historical meditation for Bernadette Devlin, the Ulster Catholic M.P. whose actions—including imprisonment—highlighted Catholic resistance to the political and economic status quo in Northern Ireland when civil strife broke out again in 1969 (even as Montague's poems had forewarned it would). Montague read this poem outside Armagh Jail in June 1970 at a rally there as a way of protesting the manner in which Ulster Catholics were being treated. Even the order of the poem he had been working on for so long, he admits, threatens to fall apart in the presence of so much pain, his music "invaded/by cries, protestations/a people's pain." Finally, he sees the rough field which has informed his poem and has indeed *become* his poem (that is, its own, raw field of action), has exploded into "crossing patterns/weaving towards/a new order/a new anarchy/always different/always the same."

Montague ends *The Rough Field* with "The Wild Dog Rose," which becomes now a symbol of the pathology of intense loneliness which is the music he has heard all his life in Ireland and which he has evoked again and again throughout his poems. It is this repression of all that is good in itself, the refusal to acknowledge simple human needs and human desires which, Montague laments, has turned in on itself and led in Ireland to violence against others and against oneself. Whatever the cherished myth of "man at home/in a rural setting" may have meant, a myth which has haunted Montague himself as much as anyone, and despite his continued circling in *The Rough Field*, he knows by poem's end that he can never go home again.

A Slow Dance (1975) returns to the lyric impulse which had informed *Tides*. But where the earlier book had incorporated the rise and fall of water as its all-embracing motif, here Montague uses the sound of that ghostly music he keeps hearing—a music older than Christian Ireland, a plangency which his poems embody even as the late Seán Ó Riada (who died in Cork in 1971) restored that music in his Irish compositions. It is a music as old as Ireland, Montague suggests, and in fact it is nothing less than the tearful music of the human condition itself. All we can do is to try and dance to its slow, stately, implacable rhythms. So the book opens nakedly to take the reader further back than Montague had gone before. By an act of the imagination, we are set dancing in a plodding pattern akin to the old Irish jigs:

Start a slow
dance, lifting

a foot, planting
a heel to celebrate

greenness, rain
spatter on skin,
the humid pull
of the earth.

That Montague is after something older than St. Patrick's message—something closer to Robert Graves's White Goddess myth—becomes clear in the litany of praise Montague now sings, not to the Blessed Virgin, but to the ancient hill mother (Mons Veneris), the goddess of pleasure and fertility.

The second section focuses on a cold, harsh, yet fertile nature, which is also part of the slow dance of life and death. Life is filled with losses, the poet knows, and yet he will "still affirm/That nothing dies, that even from/Such bitter failure memory grows," grows into song. And though his childhood landscape is nearly gone, "effaced,/a quick stubble of pine recovering most," still there remains "that restless whispering/you never get away/from," so that the poet goes on "combing and stroking/the landscape" until once more it gleams.

In the third section, the midpoint of the book, Montague turns to the unavoidable cave of night. This is his vision of the apocalypse, "the high/vapour trails of the last destroyers"—SAC and Illyusin bombers?—seen in a dream juxtaposed with a monster closer to his soil: Cromm Cruaich, Ireland's own Moloch, come to demand more blood sacrifices. At night in a hotel in Belfast, the poet tries to protect the woman he is with from the Bosch-like horror exploding all about him. A child is buried by children while "jungleclad troops/ransack the Falls" and a "warm bomb" explodes in the middle of the "last evacuees" who are trying to sing a consoling hymn even as their limbs are blown off. What image for it, the poet wonders, but the squeal of a pig he once saw slaughtered, its cry so terrible, so "Piercing & absolute,/only high heaven ignores it."

After this terrifying nightmare at the heart of the book—Montague's version of a meditation in time of civil war—he returns to the warm memory of the familiar dead. There is a comic and sad ballad recalling his parents' stormy life together in Brooklyn and his own conception as a way of reconciling them. But "Mother Cat," the poem which follows, focuses on the newborn kitten who is trying to suck from its mother's breasts and who fails; by its placement especially it suggests Montague's own deepest sense of estrangement from his mother, who had let him fend for himself as best he could. In "A Graveyard in Queens," Montague takes his mother's sister, his aunt Eileen, to visit the cemetery in Queens, New York, where his namesake, the country fiddler, lies buried. Again he stares at his name on the gravestone and again he hears the ghostly fiddle "filter through/American earth/the slow pride of a lament." And in "All Souls" the poet evokes not the great Yeatsian presences, but only his own more human family, who have no other life now but what he, one among the living, can offer, remembering as he toasts them that his own knuckles are "branched with bone," and that he must some day join their company.

Finally, in the moving last section of the book, his extended lament for Ó Riada, Montague joins his own singing with this fellow singer's, a voice now stilled forever by the interposition of death. That music, he realizes, while it sang of Ireland's defeats, at the same time "redeemed" the sad time with "the curlew sorrow" of the visionary song. And yet the music goes deeper even than that, the poet sees now, for it is the music of the world's sorrow,

a lament so total
it mourns no one
but the globe itself
turning in the endless halls. . . .

During the spring of 1968 Montague was in Paris where the student-worker demonstrations were then in full force, and it was here that he met Evelyn Robson, the woman he would marry in 1972, after his divorce from Madeleine Montague that same year. Offered a position in the English department at University College, Cork (in part through the intercession of Ó Riada), Montague set up home here with his young wife, first at Roche's Point and then on Grattan Hill, where they still live at least part of the year. On 15 August 1973 their first child, Oonagh (Una) was born. It is with this theme of modern love, the breakup of his first marriage and the building of a new relationship, that Montague's next book, *The Great Cloak* (1978), is concerned. Montague had already treated this subject in the second and third sections of *Tides*, but there he had done so somewhat tentatively and obliquely, insisting on his own privacy. Now, however, he speaks openly, nakedly. Then he was still caught in the deadly crosscurrents of two relationships. Now, with the passage of time, he can

Front cover for the poems that concern the breakup of Montague's first marriage and the building of a new relationship

look at the larger pattern which his own love has woven.

The Great Cloak is divided into three sections: "Search," "Separation," and "Anchor," and Montague has provided a "Plot" headnote which is as candid in its revelation of motives as anything he has written: "These poems should not only be read separately. A married man seeks comfort elsewhere, as his marriage breaks down. But he discovers that libertinism does not relieve his solitude. So the first section of the book ends with a slight affair which turns serious, the second with the despairing voices of disintegrating marriage, the third with a new and growing relationship to which he pledges himself." Though *The Great Cloak* was not published until 1978, internal evidence suggests that the poems themselves were completed by 1974, before, that is, Montague moved with his wife and baby to

Grattan Hill. The lovers in "The Search" are peculiarly unrealized, insubstantial wisps, as if Montague did not wish to flesh out what might after all be only passing, if intense, relationships. His second wife, for example, is not named until after she is married and carrying Montague's child, an event which occurs only in the book's last pages. At first the other women exist, as is often the case with such affairs, more as a condition by which the poet hopes to find solace in his "separate self/while profound night/like a black swan/goes pluming past." And yet, in spite of himself, the poet is tugged back repeatedly to them as if by a golden hook. One of the most honest poems in this searingly honest sequence is "Closed Circuit," in which the poet sees his woman making love to another man. Here is a precise image of the dynamics of promiscuity and of how one may be entrapped in love's tormenting net:

> her petal mouth
> raised to absorb
> his probing kiss
> and hears her small voice
> cry animal cries.

Othello himself thought no greener thoughts.

The second section provides an extended look at the final breakup of Montague's first marriage, and everywhere we hear the hurt cry of desolation and the yawning realization of loss. In several painful poems, Montague allows his first wife to speak. And in one of these, "She Dreams," one of the major reasons for the breakup of the marriage is hinted at: the fact that, after ten years, the marriage is still childless. "I came to where the eggs lay in the grass," she cries:

> I watched them for a long time, warming them
> With my swollen eyes. One after another
> They chipped and scraggy heads appeared;
> The embryos of our unborn children.

Knowing now—both of them—that the marriage is over, the poet returns to the Georgian Dublin street where he and his wife had lived those first few years of their marriage when it all seemed to work for the best. If now he could only reverse time and raise up the dead who were his neighbors then, the boisterous Brendan Behan among them, including the pony and the donkey too who grazed across the way ... but time will not relent. What is done is done, past recovering.

The third section, "Anchor," returns momen-tarily to *Tides* before Montague evokes the old landscapes of Ireland (his own version of Eden) and this new Adam and Eve growing into one another in intimacy, as they learn to share each others' inner lives, wrestle with the serpent of discord, and then come together again:

> Honeycomb of reconciliation:
> thigh melting into thigh,
> mouth into mouth, breast
> turning against ribcage.

The poet celebrates: "we make love as though/this small house were/a paradigm of the universe."

And then his Eve is pregnant and then, at forty-four, Montague has his firstborn, a daughter: Oonagh. In the book's last two poems Montague addresses his old wife and his new, attempting to reconcile himself finally with the first, chillingly evoked in the foghorn he hears, "a friendly signal in distress," before he turns then to celebrate his new beginning. But that new beginning is also evoked ambiguously in the image of the Atlantic's shifting edge, quiet for the moment, but also capable of some unexpected and terrible groundswell. Yet, for the moment at least, the poet sighs, exhausted with his obsessions:

> So fate relents.
> Hushed and calm,
> safe and secret,
> on the edge is best.

Since 1972 Montague has continued to teach at University College, Cork, while spending long periods in France and in North America. "Outside my window," he told an interviewer in 1979, "there is a boat which goes to London. Over the hill is an airport with planes departing for Paris." Since 1974 he has taught variously at Buffalo, Toronto, the University of Vermont, and the Sorbonne. In 1979 he traveled extensively through Northern India. In the same year he became the first president of Poetry Ireland and (in December) saw the birth of his second child, another daughter, Sybille. He and his wife, a translator in her own right, published a book of French poetry in translation in 1977. In May of 1981 Montague opened the International Poetry Festival in Toronto, and in the following year his *Selected Poems* was published.

In 1983 a new book of poems, *The Dead Kingdom,* was published in Ireland, England, and the United States, the first new volume, really, since *The Great Cloak,* a book which covers close to a decade's new work. *The Dead Kingdom* is "a strange book, begun on a train back to Cork, after my mother died," Montague said in July 1982. (In that sense it is the twin to *The Rough Field,* which began on a bus trip back to Gavarghey fourteen years earlier.) "How it will appear finally," he added, "is difficult because another, less autobiographical, urge kept adding distancing poems (how many mothers have died? countries been sick?) to enlarge the framework. . . . It is not especially Irish, but invokes many archetypes; mythical and maternal." As with his earlier work, at least since *Tides,* Montague's *The Dead Kingdom* is a five-part sequence, a journey once again into the poet's difficult beginnings in Brooklyn and Ulster, a world which is for him now indeed a dead kingdom. "*Northwards,* annually," the first poem begins wearily and sadly, "a journeying back,/ the salmon's leap/ & pull to the source." By now, the poet has come to understand, the pattern into the past has been long established. Sartre speaks of Faulkner's sense of time as a receding of perspective, as if one were to stand on the platform of the last car of a passenger train and watch the tracks converging in the far distance. And so one feels it is with Montague, for whom the look homeward is the only authentic view left. That, and of course the death waiting at some miserable junction up ahead, as it waited for his parents.

Montague has said that *The Dead Kingdom* is "darker than any of my [other] works," as any book which takes us into the world of the dead must necessarily be, a weary journey north again to see and hear the same insanities about righteousness while Protestants and Catholics die for battles and causes now 300 years old. The cumulative sense one is left with after finishing this book is one of sadness. The Montague one finds here is vulnerable, naked, more naked than he has let himself be before, for he has tapped into truths about his past which threaten to leave him homeless for good. There are many strains here interwoven to make up a complex music, but under them all is the same sad, elusive scrannel cry that is Ireland. That is the background for the two figures most clearly evoked here: a dead father and a dead mother.

In earlier volumes Montague had portrayed his father, the failed Republican lost in a Brooklyn boardinghouse for twenty years—the years of the Depression, the war years and their aftermath— while his youngest grew up with his sisters back in Garvaghey. And then: to return home, a broken old man with his few possessions roped into a suitcase, back to the woman he had not seen for twenty years, a cracked tenor, a singer of Irish ditties, glancing

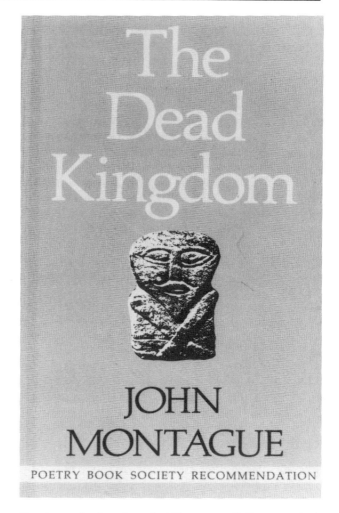

Front cover for the volume that Montague calls "a strange book, begun on a train back to Cork, after my mother died"

awkwardly at his now old wife, a few years of twilight remaining before his last trip to the cancer ward and death. This father will seem all the more familiar, of course, since several of the poems Montague includes here were first published in his earlier volumes.

But it is Montague's mother who is fleshed out for the first time in what are undoubtedly the finest and most disturbing poems in *The Dead Kingdom.* It is as if, in gauging the distance he had come since his own unhappy childhood, when his unhappy mother refused to nurse him and he was shunted about the Brooklyn neighborhood to be cared for by whoever would have him, that he is finally able to admit what Robert Lowell came to admit about himself only as he approached sixty: that he was after all, an unwanted child. If the midsections of this volume seem to be a shrinking away from the terrible absence he has been seeking, a soothing over of the original wound with the evasive balm of myth and poetry, a convocation of the world's ills offered instead, the reader will understand. It is no accident that the book begins and ends with the presence of Montague's wife and unborn child (thus establishing the "present moment" as 1973), for it is from them—from their "flowering presence"—that he will gather the strength to plunge into what his poetry will turn into the "flowering absence" of that difficult, motherless past, where he may

> learn something of that time
>
> Of confusion, poverty, absence.
> Year by year, I track it down
> intent for a hint of evidence,
> seeking to manage the pain—
> how a mother gave away her son.

There is a bittersweet image in "The Locket," where Montague remembers himself as a young man bicycling the seven miles from the Montague farm at Garvaghey to his mother's home in the bare, wintry crossroad town of Fintona and trying to make his mother notice him, as he courts her like any young man his belle, replacing his absent father until, leaving, he is told not to come back because, like his father, he always leaves her just as she grows fond of him once more. Snuff-taker, brandy-imbiber, incurable romantic remembering her own youth when she knocked the tall hat off an English bobby, a Republican whose brothers were incarcerated for Republican activities, she has grown old and silent, and will carry that silence with her into death. And it is only after her death that her rejected son, who sings of her now, learns that the same woman who refused to nurse him kept an old photo of him from his youth in Brooklyn in a locket around her neck. It is a small enough consolation.

By book's end, Montague has once again turned south, as he did in *The Rough Field*, away from the Dead Kingdom which sits in his heart and which will probably continue to haunt him for the rest of his life. It is back then to his second wife, Evelyn, who has wept for the woman she will never meet and who carries within her a daughter who will grow up to look like that dead woman. It is all in the past, now, Montague says, as he addresses his wife by name: "I place my hopes/beside yours, Evelyn," acknowledging her with candor and simplicity, hopes which are like "frail rope-ladders/ across fuming oblivion."

In the next few years we can expect another selection of short stories to add to *Death of a Chieftain*. And, now that Seamus Heaney's selected prose has been published, we can at least hope to have Montague's own lucid and informed prose published to stand beside Heaney's. As for the poems, the complementary impulse toward light has asserted itself in Montague's most recent work. The new poems he has been writing, he explains slyly, "are about nature and babies and water: eternal sureties." Montague continues to write poetry which is distinctive and which bodes well for the health and central importance of Irish poetry in international letters in the last part of the twentieth century. His is a poetry which gains by being read in the aggregate and in the individual books of poems rather than the *Selected Poems* (which Montague himself compiled) because Montague's is a winding, subtle music which—like the classical Irish music that is its shadow—keeps returning on itself until its pride of line etches itself on the mind. It is a poetry which has successfully fused Austin Clarke's chiming assonantal melodies (the Irish play of sound wedded to the English language) with Yeats's middle and late austerities of syntax and thought. Already a number of critics have called him a major voice in Irish literature, a judgment which rings true in his case. And though he has, perhaps, a smaller following than his younger contemporary, Seamus Heaney, Montague's voice is distinctive, irreplaceable, and a necessary complement to Heaney's austerities. Moreover Montague is fifty-six, and, if he follows the patterns of longevity and late flowering manifested in Yeats, Clarke, and Kavanagh, then—as solid as his achievement to date has been—we have yet to see the full-blown achievement of this extraordinary and very human poet.

Interviews:

"D'une Conversation du 4.iv.72 avec Serge Faucherau," *Les Lettres Nouvelles*, 73 (March 1973): 234-238;

Adrian Frazer, "Global Regionalism: Interview with John Montague," *Literary Review*, 22 (Winter 1979): 153-174;

Timothy Kearney, "Beyond the Planter and the Gael: An Interview with John Hewitt and John Montague," *Crane Bag*, 4, no. 2 (1980): 85-92;

Stephen Arkin, "An Interview with John Montague: Deaths in the Summer," *New England Review and Bread Loaf Quarterly*, 5 (Autumn-Winter 1982): 214-241.

References:

James Brophy, "John Montague's Restive Salley-switch," in *Modern Irish Literature: Essays in Honor of William York Tindall,* edited by R. J. Porter and J. D. Brophy (New York: Iona College Press/Twayne, 1972), pp. 153-169;

Terence Brown, "John Montague: Circling to Return," in his *Northern Voices: Poets from Ulster* (Dublin: Gill & Macmillan, 1975), pp. 149-170;

John Wilson Foster, "The Landscape of Planter and Gael in the Poetry of John Montague," *Canadian Journal of Irish Studies,* 1 (November 1975): 17-33;

Donald Hall, "The Nation of Poets," *Parnassus,* 6 (Fall-Winter 1977): 145-160;

Seamus Heaney, "The Sense of Place," in his *Preoccupations: Selected Prose 1968-1978* (London: Faber & Faber, 1980), pp. 131-149;

Frank Kersnowski, *John Montague* (Lewisburg, Pa.: Bucknell University Press, 1975);

Benedict Kiely, "John Montague: Dancer in a Rough Field," *Hollins Critic,* 15 (December 1978): 1-14;

Edna Longley, "Searching the Darkness: Richard Murphy, Thomas Kinsella, John Montague and James Simmons," in *Two Decades of Irish Writing: A Critical Survey,* edited by Douglas Dunn (Cheadle, Cheshire: Carcanet, 1975), pp. 118-153;

Derek Mahon, "Poetry in Northern Ireland," *Twentieth Century Studies,* 4 (November 1970): 89-93;

Paul Mariani, "Fretwork in Stone Tracery," *Parnassus,* 8 (Fall-Winter 1979): 249-259;

Harry Marten, "Memory Defying Cruelty: The Poetry of John Montague," *New England Review and Bread Loaf Quarterly,* 5 (Autumn-Winter 1982): 242-265;

Honor O'Connor, "The Early Poetry of John Montague," *Etudes Irlandaises,* new series 2 (December 1977): 63-72;

Sydney B. Poger, "Crane and Montague: 'The Pattern History Weaves,'" *Eire-Ireland,* 16 (Winter 1981): 114-124;

Thomas D. Redshaw, "John Montague's *The Rough Field:* Topos and Texne," *Studies,* 63 (Spring 1974): 31-46;

M. L. Rosenthal, *The New Poets: American and British Poetry Since World War II* (New York & London: Oxford University Press, 1967), pp. 297-306.

The author is grateful for the assistance of Mark Waelder, who allowed him to use his forthcoming selection of John Montague's prose, and his bibliography, for the preparation of this entry.

Andrew Motion

(26 October 1952-   )

Robyn L. Marsack

BOOKS: *Inland* (Burford, Oxfordshire: Cygnet Press, 1976);

The Pleasure Steamers [single poem] (Oxford: Sycamore Press, 1978);

The Pleasure Steamers (Manchester: Carcanet Press, 1978);

The Poetry of Edward Thomas (London & Boston: Routledge & Kegan Paul, 1980);

Independence (Edinburgh: Salamander Press, 1981);

Philip Larkin (London & New York: Methuen, 1982);

Secret Narratives (Edinburgh: Salamander Press, 1983);

Dangerous Play: poems 1974-1984 (Edinburgh: Salamander Press & Penguin Books, 1984).

OTHER: *The Penguin Book of Contemporary British Poetry,* edited by Motion and Blake Morrison (Harmondsworth: Penguin, 1982);

"Skating: Memories of Childhood," *Poetry Review,* 73 (September 1983): 28-39.

From the appearance of his first full-length book, *The Pleasure Steamers* (1978), Andrew Motion has been counted among the most gifted poets of his generation. The award of the much-publicized

Arvon/Observer Poetry Prize in 1981 (for "The Letter," included in *Secret Narratives*), and his editorship with Blake Morrison of a controversial anthology, *The Penguin Book of Contemporary British Poetry*, in 1982 have kept his name before the reading public. Yet his poetry—like its author—is characterized by elusiveness and reticence, a withholding of information.

Nevertheless, Motion has provided a memoir of his childhood and youth that gives insight into the experiences and background on which some of the poetry draws. Andrew Peter Motion was born in London in 1952, the elder of two sons of a brewer. The family moved when he was small to "a dark Victorian warren called Little Brewers, which was apt . . . near unspoilt country, and we led what I suppose was a typical landed life. It was extremely horsey." He presents this life—in the intervals from boarding school, first at Maidwell, then Radley College near Oxford (1965-1970)—as a haze of contentment, in which the central figure is his beautiful, slightly mysterious mother. At Radley he "started to be quite good at some things—especially English, which consisted largely of writing essays . . . and reading First World War poets." It was in his last year at school that his mother was injured in a riding accident, which confined her to a hospital until her death ten years later. Poems about this immobile, mute existence, his father's constancy, and his own visits, form the third section of *The Pleasure Steamers* (1978).

Motion went up to University College, Oxford, where he obtained a first-class B.A. (with honors) in English, and then stayed to work on a B.Litt. thesis on Edward Thomas, under the supervision of John Fuller. Fuller has been described by another poet, James Fenton—perhaps tongue-in-cheek—as "our secret guru"; a "decisive influence" on a number of young writers. Fuller has written shrewdly about Auden, and his own elegance, range, and stylistic panache owe something to Auden's example. Wit and inventiveness are not qualities associated with Motion's work, but love of the craft is surely something reinforced by Fuller's example, as is the instinct not to occupy center stage in poems. In 1975 Motion won the Newdigate prize, (won by Fuller in 1960); it has been offered in Oxford every year since 1806, for a poem of not more than 300 lines on a set subject. The theme chosen was "the tides," and Motion's poem *Inland* (1976)—about an inundated village—is in many ways a paradigm of his work. An extended sequence, it is spoken in the first person but not in propria persona, employing historically verifiable

Andrew Motion on the way to accept the John Llewellyn Rhys Memorial Prize for his 1984 book

details, brooding over a particular patch of pastoral England. On reading through Motion's poetry, it is striking that the constant element is water: here the fens, in other poems the sea; drenched landscapes in general. Since *Inland* the voices have become more individuated; the settings often refer to Britain's recent imperial past (a noticeable trend in contemporary fiction and poetry); the evocation of period and place is sparer and sharper. The emotional register of his poetry remains a steady dwelling on loss and isolation, an undermining of security and identity, embodied in this early sequence by the forced migration of a whole village.

Other strong influences on Motion's poetic practice are Edward Thomas and Philip Larkin, whom he came to know when he was a lecturer in English in 1976-1980 at the University of Hull, where Larkin is the librarian. In his books about these poets, Motion emphasizes not their accepted insular virtues but their ability to synthesize modernism and the prevailing orthodoxies: that of the Georgians in Thomas's case, of the Movement in Larkin's. Blake Morrison remarked of the "typical" younger poet of the 1970s that "having read Pound and Eliot at a fairly early stage of his development, he does not feel the pressure to react extremely [to modernism], whether in idolatry or repudiation. . . ." Motion is "typical" in this sense (and in the sense of the general sociological pattern Morrison outlines), and proposes a "specifically English line" with which he associated Larkin: Wordsworth, Tennyson, Hardy, Edward Thomas, A. E. Housman, and Auden, all of them writing in the "language such as men do use." Both Thomas and Larkin are deceptively low-keyed in their tone, "disarmingly so," as Motion points out in his persuasive defense of Thomas's achievement. It is the natural key for him too, particularly noticeable at the close of his poems, with their falling cadences: "all your unfinished lives/fading through dark summers,/entering my head as dust" ("In the Attic"); "with only the moon to show us/the lives we found, and cannot keep" ("Past Midnight"); "who talking/each other to sleep at last heard only/their luminous silence we could not survive" ("Inside and Out"). Like Thomas's, his sentences tend toward the conditional; like Larkin's, his words are often negatively prefixed.

By these means, Motion can achieve a delicacy and tenderness that allow the private and public to intersect without diminishing either, as in "Inside and Out," which is at once a love poem—rare enough in his books, though more have appeared in journals—and an elegy for the dead of World War I. For generations schooled in that literature, and in Great Britain, where that war still dominates in the imagination beyond any previous or subsequent wars, to mention the names is enough: "Vimy, Arras, Bapaume"—Arras where Edward Thomas was shot in 1917. More than that, the countryside itself has been reshaped by the war, and Motion finds the image for this enduring reminder: "the wind, tracing a ridge/of lost lines over the fields, always raising the same delicate spray of graves." The precision of his vocabulary here evidences his deep absorption of the literary experience, the nouns apt to the wind's tousling grass or corn but martial in their meaning too. The ridge and the lines of the land are momentarily exposed as the wind passes, then disappear; they call to mind the lines of men who defended each ridge of that contested ground, now all lost to view, now dead.

A later war shadows "The Pleasure Steamers" (also published separately as a pamphlet by Fuller's Sycamore Press in 1978): one of the boats is called *Mapledurham*, "one/my father saw, lying offshore/in 1940, from France." Here again Motion is calling on legendary history, the vessels of every description that set out to evacuate the soldiers stranded in France. In his memoir, he recalls his father's disappearing "most weekends to 'play soldiers,' as my mother said. He had joined the Territorial Army after the war, and eventually commanded the Essex Yeomanry. Kit [his brother] and I were very proud of that." The personal pride is obliquely present in Motion's poetry, intimately connected with a feeling

for his country that is difficult to pin down, but certainly there. He says of the "English line" of poets: "they are all centrally concerned with the relationship between themselves and their towns or landscapes, and habitually express a sense of communion with their surroundings in exalted or even semi-mystical terms. They are all, that is to say, intensely patriotic poets, though not all of them need the presence of war to crystallize their feelings. . . ." The poems in *The Pleasure Steamers* often lack these poets' particularity, the felt knowledge of specific landscape. His debts to Larkin and Thomas are discernible—as in the third section of "Letter to an Exile" and in "Wistman's Wood." Yet for a first collection the assurance is remarkable, and was much remarked upon.

The coexistence of public with private loss is the theme of Motion's second collection, aptly entitled *Independence* (1981); more sophisticated, allusive and touching. He had left Hull in 1980 to live in

Front cover for Motion's first full-length book, which earned him a reputation as one of the most gifted poets of his generation

Oxford again, and had become editor of *Poetry Review*, the Poetry Society's quarterly journal, whose format he greatly improved. Interviewing James Fenton for *Poetry Review*, Motion asked whether narrative was "a way of drawing on strong personal feelings but at the same time freeing yourself from them." Fenton demurred, though it is clearly what Motion believes. In the introduction to *The Penguin Book of Contemporary British Poetry*, the editors maintain that the "new spirit" of British poetry often takes the form of "a renewed interest in narrative . . . antipathetic to the production of a candidly personal poetry." Partly this is a reaction to the 1962 Penguin anthology, *The New Poetry* (edited by A. Alvarez), with its fashionable emphasis on "confessional" poetry.

The "story" of *Independence*—published in an elegant edition by the new Salamander Press, founded by Tom Fenton and drawing on the Oxford circle of poets—is a long retrospective, in which the narrator recalls his youth in India, his courtship and marriage in 1947, the year of Indian independence, his wife's death after a miscarriage, and his eventual retreat to her father's house on the gray English coast. The poem is, in effect, "a hole / in the misted silvery glass" of memory, the image that opens and closes it. And as Alan Ross remarked in his approving notice in the *London Magazine,* it is "a tombstone inscription brought to life, and without ever resorting to overt political statement it movingly resumes themes and incidents that have occupied English writers on India long before Kipling." The technique is cinematic, both in the vividness of individual scenes and in the quick cut of recollection from one to the next. Motion's considerable achievement in the poem is his fleshing out of the word "independence," on a personal and national scale, and in the unobtrusive paralleling of events so that the pregnancy takes place not only at the time of the "birth of a nation," but when the country was split into India and Pakistan; there are two kinds of birth-giving and pain. Both involve incomprehension, separations, and grief; the husband who broods over his absence at the time of his wife's miscarriage, wondering whether things might have gone differently, has affinities with those who engendered the deed of partition, apparently the only possible course but carried through in blood. These births, which were awaited with a liberating sense of potential, result instead in diminished possibilities. The newly married couple and their coming child seem sealed off from the larger events: the narrator says "We slept outside that summer, / two wide-eyed effigies hand in hand /

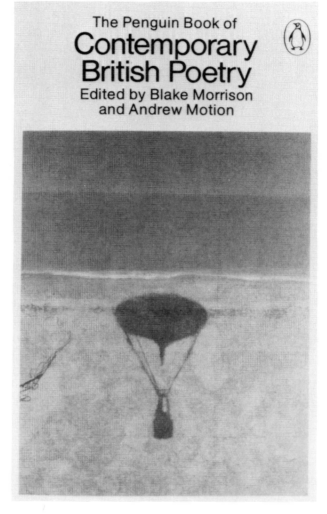

Front cover for the controversial anthology whose editors assert that "a shift of sensibility has taken place very recently in British poetry"

on the cool veranda, our hearts racing"—and the literary echo is of Larkin's "An Arundel Tomb." The narrator's confusion about the future, his regret and nostalgia for life out there, is in miniature the reaction of England to her long involvement with the subcontinent, the sense of displacement when the separation was arranged. "Interdependence" is the poem's actual theme, treated with passion and compassion.

Motion's shorter poems from this period are collected in *Secret Narratives* (1983). In the same year Motion moved to London, and relinquished his editorship of *Poetry Review* for the post of poetry editor for the publishing firm of Chatto and Windus. The title of his collection fits snugly into the trends he and Morrison identified in their Penguin anthology. Many critics felt that their introduction was tendentious in its desire to impose a coherent aesthetic on post-1960s poetry, but anthologies are often a means of validating preferences and practice. Certainly Motion's poems show a reluctance to "point the moral of, or conclude too neatly, what [they] choose to transcribe." The first poem, "Open Secrets," declares what it is: there are two stanzas in quotation marks, with a third beginning "Just now, prolonging my journey home to you, I killed/an hour where my road lay over a moor, and made this up." "Killed" is daring, as there has been a slaughter in the preceding stanza. The ending is a poetic variation on Motion's question to Fenton:

> He was never
> myself, this boy, but I know if I tell you his story
> you'll think we are one and the same: both of us hiding
> in fictions which say what we cannot admit to
> ourselves.

The inadmissible may be partly an energy that needs violent outlets, a verbal equivalent of physical directness. There is more energy in this collection than previously. In *Poetry Review* Claude Rawson compared "Wooding" from *Secret Narratives* with the elegaic poems in *The Pleasure Steamers:* the loss is the same in both books, but dramatized in "Wooding." A father and two sons can be seen from the windows of an old people's home; they "suddenly seem engaged in some adventure, half cloak-and-dagger, half schoolboy yarn." And in "The House Through," a woman haunts her home and husband: the poem is in her voice and instead of the tentative, introspective register of the anniversary poems in *The Pleasure Steamers,* Motion assumes her identity and can powerfully create the sensation of the insubstantial encountering substance:

> Here at the door I am
> identical with its thin paint.
> Then one step and darkness
> falls in a furious storm

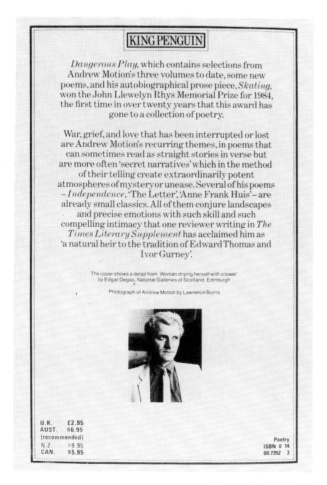

Covers for Motion's highly acclaimed 1984 book

of grains, splinters, rings
until daylight appears again,
and the hall, and his voice
outside in the garden singing.

Another woman composes letters to the deluded former owner of her new house—he has perhaps murdered his wife and is in an asylum—"telling myself it was/kindness, and might even turn into love" ("Writing"). Auden's dictum that poetry makes nothing happen may be right, but Motion recognizes the seductive facility with which words can be used, irresponsibly, dangerously, and pitifully.

His range in this collection has been intriguingly extended. There is the literary account—advertised as such, "it was straight out of Conrad"—of "The Great Man": one does not recognize this version of Schweitzer until the startling detail, "He was flat/for most of a fugue. . . ." "Anne Frank Huis," on the other hand, is a description in first person, as though deferring to a directness the subject demands. Sometimes "narrative" is only anecdote and not telling enough; and the coincidence of a domestic act—moving house—with a public event—the arrival in England of wounded soldiers from the Falklands—is too obviously manipulated. But the element of risk-taking is vitalizing. The longer stretch seems to suit Motion best, as in "Bath-

ing at Glymenopoulo," which shows how the accumulation of small details can compose a significant whole, how nostalgia can be validated, how betrayal and the very messy facts of death can be openly narrated yet work on the imagination by what is implied too. This recreation of a World War I incident gives us Motion's maturing accomplishment at its finest.

Having had a new selection of poems published in 1984, Motion is now working on a commissioned biography of the Lambert family—George, Constant, and Kit. The biography is another aspect of Motion's fascination with re-creating other lives, trying out other voices; the title of the well-received collection, *Dangerous Play*, which won the John Llewelyn Rhys Memorial Prize for 1984, affirms his pleasure in the craft of poetry, balancing between what is fantastic and what is, devastatingly, true.

Reference:

Blake Morrison, "Young Poets in the 1970s," *British Poetry Since 1970: a critical survey,* edited by Peter Jones and Michael Schmidt (Manchester: Carcanet Press, 1980), pp. 141-156.

Papers:

The library at University of Hull has a manuscript notebook, wih drafts of poems included in *The Pleasure Steamers.*

Paul Muldoon
(20 June 1951-   )

Lester I. Conner
Chestnut Hill College

SELECTED BOOKS: *New Weather* (London: Faber & Faber, 1973);
Mules (London: Faber & Faber, 1977; Winston-Salem: Wake Forest University Press, 1977);
Immram (Dublin: Gallery Press, 1980);
Why Brownlee Left (London & Boston: Faber & Faber, 1980; Winston-Salem: Wake Forest University Press, 1981);
Out of Siberia (Deerfield, Mass.: Deerfield Press/Dublin: Gallery Press, 1982);
Quoof (London: Faber & Faber, 1983; Chapel Hill: University of North Carolina Press, 1983);
The Wishbone (Dublin: Gallery Press, 1984).

Paul Muldoon is generally associated with Seamus Heaney, Michael Longley, Derek Mahon, and James Simmons. These poets, who emerged in Northern Ireland over a short span of time and achieved, in varying degrees, international recognition, constitute an outbreak of rich and varied talent from one small area such as has not been seen in Ireland since Yeats and the Celtic Renaissance.

Of this group, Muldoon is the youngest and perhaps the most discernibly individual. Edna Longley, an Irish critic, calls him "the most conspicuously *sui generis* of contemporary Ulster poets." Derek Mahon has said that, unlike the other poets

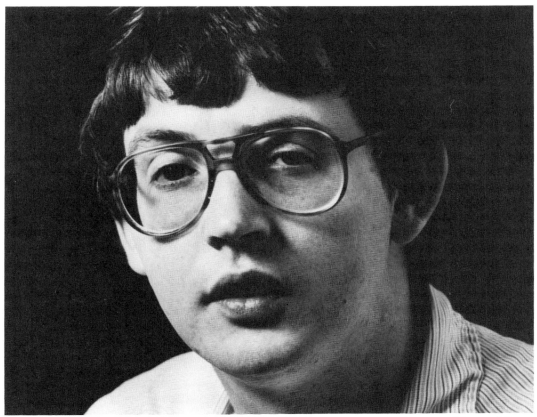

Courtesy of Bernard Stone,
The Turret Book Shop

with whom he is associated, Muldoon has seemed to go in two directions at once: back to the Irish mythological roots with the others and forward to metaphysical worlds of his own devising. These two worlds come together in his poetry and, as they are intertwined, seem not divergent at all.

Muldoon was born in County Armagh, Northern Ireland, in 1951, and brought up in the townland of Collegelands, near a village called The Moy, where his mother, Brigid, was a schoolteacher and his father, Patrick, a laborer involved also in market gardening. Both his parents were Catholic, and Muldoon was raised in that religion. He went to the grammar school St. Patrick's College, in Armagh, where he learned the Irish language as well as Irish literature and song. At St. Patrick's he also studied English literature, which he eagerly absorbed. It was then that he began to write poetry, at first in Irish, but he soon switched to writing in English because of his better command and control of the language.

From St. Patrick's he went to Queen's University in Belfast, where his tutor was Seamus Heaney, and here he joined Heaney, Michael Longley, critic Michael Allen, and other young poets who met weekly and discussed their new poems. Muldoon has said, "It was very important for me, since a writer must be a good critic of his work. There was no sloppiness in the group, everyone was quite outspoken. It was a very healthy kind of society, and I use the word 'society' to describe the group. It was scarcely a group at all, even though it's become a critical convenience to see them as presenting a united front to the world: you have only to read them to be aware of the variety. They're not united by any kind of manifesto."

Muldoon, though he has traveled extensively in Europe and America, lives in Belfast where he is a producer for BBC—Northern Ireland. He is much in demand for public readings of his poetry throughout Ireland, in England, and in America. His "Talks" shows take him everywhere in Ireland for interviews and tapings. A typical show consisted of his interviews with the staff of the Yeats International Summer School in Sligo, but the shows are endlessly various. The themes of his poetry, too, he says, deal with "everything and anything. Home, abroad. Sex and death."

In his first book of poems, *New Weather* (1973), the varied themes are held together through sensual, deeply sexual imagery: the "necessary heat." This book of poems and those that follow also form a kind of *Bildungsroman* or portrait of the artist as the boy that was and the man that evolves: "how I am, here and now, in Ireland and the world," or, as he writes in "Wind and Tree":

In the way that most of the wind
Happens where there are trees,

Most of the world is centred

About ourselves.

From the first poem, "The Electric Orchard," to the last one, "The Year of Sloes, for Ishi," the landscapes shift, change colors, change focus from cutting-edge sharp to mist-filled impressionistic.

As Edna Longley writes, "Generally in his poetry Ulster landscapes, troubled or not, tend to dissolve into something rich and strange." The poet acknowledges that such landscapes are finally moral or psychological: "Physically verifiable, I hope, even if I haven't always 'experienced' them, but finally only backdrops for what is psychologically verifiable, for what's going on in the foreground. The Moy, for example, is all about a state of mind. It's my New England, or Yoknapatawpha, or wherever. Somewhere you think you are before you realize you're nowhere." His employment of this sort of moral landscape, as well as his interest in poems as voyage or quest, suggest the possibility of W. H. Auden as a strong influence. But to him Muldoon adds other, stronger influences: "I read Auden certainly, early on. And particularly early Auden. It's possible that I learned something from him about those psychological landscapes. But I guess it comes more from Robert Frost or Edward Thomas, my main men. I suppose that I became excited early on about the possibility of writing a poem about the aftermath of apple-picking—something I did plenty of—which wasn't about

apple-picking at all. . . . I decided to take, in so far as one can, the road not taken."

William Butler Yeats was a more subtle influence. Yeats disdained poetry employed as journalism and believed that true poetry could come forth only when the public event had been transformed by the private, poetic conscience. The better modern Irish poetry that deals with that country's troubles usually follows Yeats's concept, as do the poems in Muldoon's second volume of poetry, *Mules* (1977). Muldoon, using voices as richly ironic as the one in "Lunch with Pancho Villa" and as enigmatic as the voice in the title poem, thus writes his "war" poems. In the first, his imaginary Pancho Villa is made to say:

Look, son. Just look around you.
People are getting themselves killed
Left, right and centre
While you do what? Write rondeaux.
There's more to living in this country
Than stars and horses, pigs and trees,
Not that you'd guess it from your poems.
Do you never listen to the news?
You want to get down to something true,
Something a little nearer home.

In "Mules," not without its particular irony, he wonders at the results of mating mares and jackasses: "Should they not have the best of both worlds?" The two worlds are, of course, open to wide interpretation, embracing many contrasts. The animals figure in both Celtic mythology and Christian account. They may also contrast North and South, Protestant and Catholic, art and nature.

The poems of this volume, however, seem removed from political troubles and are concerned with interpreting the pains of growing up, as in "Cass and Me," "How to Play Championship Tennis," and "De Secretis Mulierum." The poems also have the sense of quest—not merely a quest for answers, certainly not for a Holy Grail, but the quest for one's self, particularly as the play of language records and is essential to the self. The first-person speaker in these poems is not so important as where the words take the individual. As Muldoon writes, "The 'I' isn't so important . . . not at all important, in fact. The important thing is the language and what the language will do if you give it a free hand. Words alone are certain good, as the man said." The free hand does not mean any loss of control, but Muldoon does give much away, making a reader feel the importance even before understanding arrives. He is not obscure, but he is spare and economical with his words.

If the test of a good poet is growth, Muldoon's third book of poems, *Why Brownlee Left* (1980), passes. Though many themes and some techniques continue, the poetry is more mature, more experimental in form and texture, and richer in irony and wit. The story of an artist's young life continues, from the incredible wit of the first poem to the astounding achievement of the last, "Immram," a kind of personal myth. Whether taking off into new and previously unexplored landscapes or remaining at home in more familiar Irish ones, the poems are more haunting, somewhat more troubled and troubling, "wondering if you'd bring me through/To a world where everything stands/For itself . . . ," but not doing so.

An important episode in this book is the chronicle of the end of a love and marriage—autobiographical in only its essential outlines—and the effort to piece together what happened. Muldoon was married and divorced but prefers not to discuss his marriage beyond what may be implied in the poetry. The episode is joined to poems of childhood and youth and to the speculative quest poems by the title poem, "Why Brownlee Left," a brilliant sonnet that asserts, "Why Brownlee left, and where he went,/Is a mystery even now." At the end of the poem an abandoned team of horses and a brown meadow unploughed stand as in the landscape of a Dutch painting. The protagonist is the past, the future, the land, the abandoned man and wife:

*Cover for Muldoon's 1980 book, winner of a
Geoffrey Faber Memorial Prize*

> By noon Brownlee was famous;
> They had found all abandoned, with
> The last rig unbroken, his pair of black
> Horses, like man and wife,
> Shifting their weight from foot to
> Foot, and gazing into the future.

The future contains the past, and the past may begin in myth and legend, archetypal beginnings, and in the mists of early history. From such a past into a surreal, futuristic dream world, Muldoon takes his longest, most unusual poem, "Immram." Based upon and indebted to Whitely Stokes's translation of "Immram Mael Duin," the account of a medieval voyage-quest of the heroic figure Mael Duin, whose name is an early form of Muldoon, Paul Muldoon's poem is to the medieval account as Joyce's *Ulysses* is to Homer's *Odyssey*.

Muldoon has talked at length about this poem. "Immram" means "voyage tale," and the medieval story tells of the hero's voyage to avenge the death

of his father. After many strange adventures, he arrives before an old hermit who tells him to turn the other cheek. In Muldoon's version, the adventures are contemporary and even hallucinatory. In writing the poem, Muldoon was aware of Swift's accounts of voyages and of Tennyson's version of Mael Duin, and Byron's travels as well. And in giving the poem something of the sense and style of a thriller, Muldoon acknowledges a debt to Raymond Chandler.

The events of the original poem are twisted and turned and made to underscore a concept of layers of perception that Muldoon explores in many poems. The poem is also an exercise in the futility of trying to control and direct the events. At the end of the poem, the old hermit of the original, now a Howard Hughes figure at the top of the hotel, wanting only his Baskin-Robbins banana-nut ice cream, dismisses the protagonist: " 'I forgive you,' he croaked. 'And I forget.' " It is the quickening and deepening of the layers of perception that finally make *Why Brownlee Left* (for which he won the Geoffrey Faber Memorial Prize) a remarkable book of poems, an accomplishment in advance of Muldoon's earlier work.

Muldoon's next volume of poetry was published in 1983 under the title *Quoof*. In an early draft, the collection was called "The Sightseers," suggesting a considerable poetic ambiguity. Then for a time Muldoon considered calling the book "Last Poems," no doubt to suggest other ambiguities, among them the end of events or phases of life, the poet's trade or skill, or the idea of "the wisdom before the event." The poet's final title, *Quoof,* was his family's word for a hot-water bottle. Each title suggests something different about how the poems should be read. Perception, ways of perceiving the old and the new, is still a foremost consideration throughout the book.

Muldoon also changed epigraphs before the book was published, but it is important for the reader to be aware of both. The first, proposed, epigraph was from Aldous Huxley's *The Doors of Perception:* "I saw no landscapes, no enormous spaces, no magical growth and metamorphosis of buildings, nothing remotely like a drama or a parable. The other world to which mescalin admitted me was not the world of visions; it existed out there in what I could see with my eyes open." The epigraph actually used in *Quoof* is from Knud Rasmussen's *The Netsilik Eskimos:* "But the old foster-mother was a great shaman and, when they had been left alone, and all her neighbors had gone their way, she turned herself into the form of a man and married her adoptive daughter. With a willow branch she made herself a penis so that she might be like a man, but her own genitals she took out and made magic over them and turned them into wood, she made them big and made a sledge of them. Then she wanted a dog, and that she made out of a lump of snow she had used for wiping her end; it became a white dog with a black head; it became white because the snow was white, but it got the black head because there was shit on one end of the lump of snow. Such a great shaman was she that she herself became a man, she made a sledge and a dog for hunting at the breathing-holes." Perception, imagination, magic, and high wit dominate this superb collection, which was a choice of the Poetry Book Society.

The opening poem, "Gathering Mushrooms," begins the perception of family and growing up, and the images of concrete wall, dung, and soiled gray blanket suggest troubled Ireland and the need to "lie down . . . and wait." The mushroom continues as an image into the last poem of the book, contributing to the unity of the collection. The speaker in poems such as "Trance" and "The Right Arm" is three years old, waiting for Santa Claus or reaching into a jar of sweets. Waiting and reaching become contrasting themes throughout. "The Mirror," though adapted from the Irish of Michael Davitt, is, nevertheless, an elegy for the poet's father, written before Patrick Muldoon died in February 1985. Wisdom before the event depicts the central endeavor of the poems, whether the event be death, or peace, or the impact of art.

The reader of these poems notes an increase in experimentation with stanzaic forms—sonnets are frequent, as are two-, three-, and four-line stanzas. In all, twenty-seven of the twenty-eight poems are relatively short, all of them building to the great long poem, "The More a Man Has the More a Man Wants," that ends the collection, covering twenty-five of the book's sixty-four pages.

Like his previous long poem, "Immram," "The More a Man Has the More a Man Wants" is a quest poem, hallucinatory and real. The poem, full of scintillating wit, makes quantum leaps about the world but focuses upon the pursuit and capture of Gallogly in the North of Ireland. Since Gallogly is a kind of Everyman—he is otherwise known as Gollogly, Golightly, Ingoldsby, and English—the poem works as a kind of morality play. The words of the rejected epigraph of Huxley are here worked into the lines of the poem, and sexual reference and references to dung and at stool, and slop bucket, recall the present epigraph. Themes that always preoccupy Muldoon are very evident in this book of poems: personal history (real and imagined), Ireland, voyage and quest, love and death, experiment and experience. None of Paul Muldoon's poems takes the reader "to a world where everything stands/For itself . . . ," but they depict the world that Muldoon sees with his eyes wide open.

Twelve poems written since the publication of *Quoof* have been gathered together in a slim volume entitled *The Wishbone* (1984). Much animal imagery is seen in these poems, and bones are also prevalent. Themes of life and death and the contrast between past and present dominate the poems. When these are combined with poems now being written, to form the next collection, they will mark the continuing progress and excellence of this important twentieth-century voice.

Interview:

John Haffenden, *Viewpoints: Poets in Conversation* (London: Faber & Faber, 1980), pp. 130-142.

Reference:

Edna Longley, "Stars and Horses, Pigs and Trees," *The Crane Bag*, 3 (1979): 54-70.

Richard Murphy
(6 August 1927-   )

Maurice Harmon
University College, Dublin

BOOKS: *The Archaeology of Love* (Glenageary: Dolmen, 1955);

Sailing to an Island [single poem] (Dublin: Dolmen, 1955);

The Woman of the House (Dublin: Dolmen, 1959);

The Last Galway Hooker (Dublin: Dolmen, 1961);

Sailing to an Island (London: Faber & Faber, 1963; New York: Random House, 1963);

Penguin Modern Poets 7, by Murphy, Jon Silkin, and Nathaniel Tarn (Harmondsworth: Penguin, 1965);

The Battle of Aughrim and The God Who Eats Corn (London: Faber & Faber, 1968; New York: Knopf, 1968);

N-Trances (Sydney: Solomoth Press, 1971);

High Island (London: Faber & Faber, 1974);

High Island: New and Selected Poems (New York & London: Harper & Row, 1974);

Selected Poems (London: Faber & Faber, 1979).

OTHER: Maurice Harmon, ed., *Richard Murphy: Poet of Two Traditions: Interdisciplinary Studies*, includes material by Murphy (Portmarnock: Wolfhound, 1978).

Richard Murphy is one of a small number of Irish poets who came to international recognition in the gradual revival of Irish literature that took place in the 1950s and 1960s. His contemporaries included Thomas Kinsella and John Montague; his predecessors Austin Clarke and Patrick Kavanagh. What made his work different from theirs were the themes of ancestry, history, and place that characterized it from the beginning, its neomodernist form and its urbanity of manner. Richard Murphy had the distinction, quite unusual in the new generation of writers, of having been born into the

Photo by Stephen Moreton; courtesy of Bernard Stone, The Turret Book Shop

Protestant-Irish Ascendancy class, of having been educated mainly in England, and of feeling a need to reach across the sectarian, social, and cultural divisions of Irish life so that he could find imaginative enrichment among the "native" Irish of the countryside. The search for that harmony of separate and different elements in his background has been a constant feature of his work. He has defined a place for himself that is composed of the sophistication of his British education (a respect for intelligence, urbanity, and tact) and of the wildness and natural beauty of the landscape of western Ireland, its way of life, its people, its animals. As a descendant of a diminished class he has needed to find a place for himself; as an exile from the professions of the diplomacy, church, and military careers that had characterized his family, he has had to find skills of a profession that has its own proud standards. He began with words and they have served him well.

The son of Elizabeth Mary Ormsby and William Lindsay Murphy, he was born on the family estate of Milford House, County Galway, and spent the first several years of his life alternating between the west of Ireland and Ceylon, where his father was for a time Mayor of Colombo. Winning a competition for voice in 1937, he entered Canterbury Cathedral choir, where he was a chorister and studied harmony and the composition of anthems and magnificats. After the fall of Dunkirk he was taken back to the seclusion of Connemara, where he enjoyed a more carefree life, and his interest turned from music to poetry. In 1941 he won a Milner scholarship to King's School, Canterbury, then housed for safety in Wales. From there he went to Wellington College, a school with military traditions. As a boy he had daydreams about battles and might have followed in the family tradition of an army career, but at Wellington he became a pacifist, something of a loner, and began to write poetry. In 1944 he won a scholarship to Magdalen College, Oxford, where he studied English literature under C. S. Lewis and Anglo-Saxon under J. A. W. Bennett. In 1946 he rented his first cottage in Connemara. At this period of his life the conflict between the pressures and responsibilities of academic life, a professional career, and his growing interest in the freedom to express himself and to live in close harmony with nature was particularly strong. He left Oxford in 1946 for half a term, and sought the beauty and peace of Connemara, but he completed his B.A. in 1948 and was granted an M.A. in 1955. Despite occasional visits abroad, to London where he visited places associated with T. S. Eliot's *The Waste Land* (1922), to the Bahamas, where his father was governor, to Crete, or to Paris,

his heart was in Connemara. The pattern of his adult life has been composed of visits abroad, often as visiting poet at universities in England or America, sometimes to give readings of his own work, and long periods in the west of Ireland, particularly in the village of Cleggan, where he eventually built his home.

His first collection of poems, *The Archaeology of Love* (1955), is a handful of short lyrics set in various places associated with his recent travels. Several describe the beauty of particular places in Crete, Greece, Connemara, and London. But the main theme of the collection is his love for Patricia Avis, whom he met while he was a student at the University of Paris in the summer of 1954. In the following spring they visited Brittany, where he wrote "Girl at the Seaside" and "Auction," and in 1955 they went to Greece and Crete, where he wrote "To a Cretan Monk" and "Archaeology of Love." They married in May 1955 and went to live at Quay House, Rossroe, Connemara, where the philosopher Ludwig Wittgenstein had lived in 1949. (Murphy had rented Quay House in 1951 and had found some of Wittgenstein's letters in the turf shed.) "The Philosopher and the Birds" identifies the poet and the philosopher in that both had given up academic life for the life of Connemara. "Living with Animals" from the same collection is a joyful description of a harmonious relationship between man and nature.

Between the publication of *The Archaeology of Love* and his next collection, *Sailing to an Island* (1963), Richard Murphy's life had taken more definite directions. The happiness of his marriage and the birth of his daughter, Emily, in 1956, gave way to tragedy with the death of his wife's sister-in-law, the sudden death of her brother, and his divorce in 1959. Also, in 1958 his grandmother Lucy Mary Ormsby died. Murphy was already working on *The Woman of the House,* his tribute to her, which was broadcast on the BBC Third Programme in 1959 and published in a small limited edition by Dolmen Press, Dublin. In the summer of this year he sought a more active kind of life to counteract his sense of failure after the divorce. He bought a boat called the *Ave Maria,* and the long poem "The Cleggan Disaster" began to take shape.

Sailing to an Island contains a number of poems from the first collection and three poems which had been published as individual works—*Sailing to an Island* (1955), *The Woman of the House* (1959), and *The Last Galway Hooker* (1961). In the years immediately following his settling in Connemara he wanted to bring together the two sides of his experiences, the English schooling that had trained his mind and the Irish way of life that was more physical and emotional. That attempt is visible in the major poems of the collection, those about the sea and those about ancestors and their houses. Of the sea poems, three are of particular importance—*Sailing to an Island, The Last Galway Hooker,* and *The Woman of the House.*

    Sailing to an Island, a descriptive narrative, is based on a journey that he and his brother made in 1954, when they tried to sail to Clare Island, where the legendary pirate queen, Grace O'Malley, had lived in the seventeenth century. But, as the poem relates, their journey became a nightmare of storm and danger until they sought and found shelter in the harbor of Inishbofin. The quest for the island of myth was replaced by the discovery of a real world, and Murphy has never since deviated from reality.

    The Last Galway Hooker is an account of the life of a sailing boat, a hooker, that Murphy bought in 1959. The narrative leads to the moment of purchase, and much of it deals with the boat's earlier life. This chronological account is in effect a definition of ancestry: the boat's experiences and attributes may be seen to be part of what Murphy buys. The poem also testifies to his respect for the well-made, whether it be a boat, a house, or a poem. He admires craft, skill, and the materials used whether they be wood, stone, or words. The poem concludes with a proud naming of the craftsmen brought together to renew the hooker—"Her skilful sail-maker,/Her inherited boatwright, her dream-tacking steersman"—and with his prayer to be worthy of ownership.

    There is an Anglo-Saxon quality about Murphy's poems of the sea. Men pit themselves against the elements, as the poet describes the moods of the ocean and extols the virtues of good seamanship. *The Last Galway Hooker* even has a four-stressed line with a long caesura, which is the characteristic line of Anglo-Saxon poetry. "The Cleggan Disaster" is a descriptive narrative of an event that took place in 1927. It deals with survival, not death, relating the courage and the skill of one man, Pat Concannon, who knew how to survive a terrible storm in which many lives were lost.

    Poems of the sea are derived from one side of Murphy's instinctive life, poems about ancestral figures and their ways of life emerge from the other side. The tact and civility of his work, inherited through his class and education, are evident in *The Woman of the House.* In part a portrait of faded gentility, it also reflects a life of unfulfilled potential

that reached across the divide between Big House and peasant holding through acts of charity and benevolence. The poem is a tender tribute to his grandmother's goodness and her lively personality, and its conclusion acknowledges the responsibility of heritage:

> Through our inheritance all things have come,
> The form, the means, all by our family;
> The good of being alive was given through them,
> We ourselves limit that legacy.

Just as the spacious world of the Irish eighteenth century, embodied in the great houses and the life-style of the nobility, shrank to his grandmother's circumscribed life, so his has diminished to what he can make of what he has inherited. He recognizes that the more relaxed ways of nineteenth-century aristocracy have disappeared:

> Time can never relax like this again,
> She in her phaeton looking for folklore,
> He writing sermons in the library
> Till lunch, then fishing all the afternoon.

Other poems in the collection—"Auction" and "Epitaph on a Fir-Tree"—are briefer acknowledgments of the same truth.

    Apart from these and a few poems from *The Archaeology of Love,* the collection has a number of lyrics—a fine portrait of Theodore Roethke, who visited Cleggan in 1960, and a few poems that fore-shadow directions subsequently taken by Murphy, such as "Droit De Seigneur," which anticipates material in *The Battle of Aughrim* (1968) and "The Drowning of a Novice," which has the compactness of poems of disaster in *High Island* (1974).

    In fact, *Sailing to an Island,* which went through three printings and then into a paperback edition, is a volume of considerable worth, its merits enduring the passing of time. The descriptive narratives of the sea and the simpler lyrics with their neomodernist clarity of syntax and simplicity of style define Murphy's aims and demonstrate the arrival of a poet with a distinctly personal vision and idiom. The theme of ancestry which many of the poems reveal is even more central to his next major work, the long historical meditation called *The Battle of Aughrim* which was first broadcast by the BBC in 1968.

    The Battle of Aughrim was first conceived as a descriptive poem. Murphy had just begun to work on it in 1962 when Ted Hughes and Sylvia Plath

Dust jacket for Murphy's 1967 poem in several voices that was written originally as a radio script

came to visit him at Cleggan. Hughes recommended dramatic monologues instead, and Murphy accepted the idea. In the *Irish Times* (17 May 1973) Murphy called the poem an attempt

> to get clear a division in my mind between England and Ireland—between an almost entirely English education, an English mind and Irish feeling. I tried to reconcile these two by focussing on the battle (in which my ancestors fought on both sides), finding out all I could: what it was really about; putting in different points of view, the errors and atrocities on which myths are made, and drawing up an evaluation of what the religious conflict meant, what it meant in the past and how the past is still influencing us.
>
> It did, for me, reconcile the Irish, Catholic and Protestant. The equation was drawn up and there it is.

In retrospect the poem may be seen as an act of self-liberation from the conflicts within Murphy's own mind, a necessary exorcism of the burdens of history.

The fact that the poem was prepared as a radio script and that it is written in several voices is important. The effects of contrasting, distinctive voices, whose attitudes and accents are indicative of ethnic, religious, political, and cultural values, are central. The poem assumes some familiarity with the historical battle fought in 1691. On one side was the Irish army fighting in the name of King James II and in the Catholic interest; on the other was the English army fighting in the names of King William and Queen Mary and in the Protestant interest. The site of the battle was almost the center of Ireland, and in Murphy's imaginative interpretation it was the event from which much of modern Irish history came, including his own heritage. His ancestors on one side were given 70,000 acres of land in the west of Ireland, diminished by his time to 300. It was a sectarian conflict; its end result was the collapse of Gaelic Ireland and the triumph of eighteenth-century Anglo-Irish aristocracy. Not until the emergence of Daniel O'Connell in the early years of the nineteenth century did Catholic Ireland rally again. The legacy of Aughrim was class and religious division, endemic violence that erupted yet again in the North as Murphy was completing his poem.

Historical meditation is an exploration of the self within the historical process. In Murphy's case it is an attempt to achieve a balance between plantation demesne and peasant holding, between the cold isolation of the aristocracy and the warm community of the people, between English rationality and Irish feeling. These are Murphy's polarities, the antinomies within which he moves and has his being. It is not a question of giving up one for the other, but of combining the Ascendancy's best qualities of order, reason, urbanity, and benevolence with Irish passion, wildness, and close contact with nature.

The poem is a complex act of understanding expressed in a variety of tones and rhythms and through a shifting scenario of people, events, times, and places. Based on contemporary accounts and documents, local history, and folklore and on direct investigation of the landscape, Murphy's poem establishes a poetic truth from many separate details. His intelligent, objective manner gives the poem a sense of order and proportion, a multi-layered perspective within each of its four parts.

The book also contains "The God Who Eats Corn," a long poem about his father, William Lind-

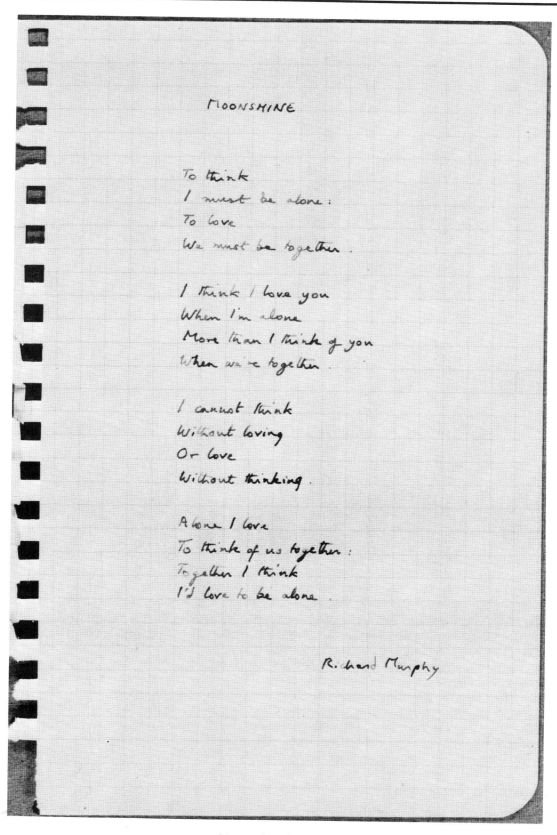

MOONSHINE

To think
I must be alone:
To love
We must be together.

I think I love you
When I'm alone
More than I think of you
When we're together.

I cannot think
Without loving
Or love
Without thinking.

Alone I love
To think of us together:
Together I think
I'd love to be alone.

Richard Murphy

Manuscript (the author)

say Murphy, who retired from the British Colonial Service as governor of the Bahamas and in 1950 settled on virgin land in Southern Rhodesia, where he established a farm and later a school for African children. Murphy stayed there for three months in 1960. The poem which grew out of this visit is about the evils as well as the foolishness of colonialism. While he can be indulgent about his father's paternalistic outlook, he is critical of the racialism on which the colonial system is based: "The white man rides; the black man is his horse."

These two long poems helped to liberate the poet from his ancestral conflict. Almost at once he began to write a more personal kind of poetry which was collected in *High Island* (1974). High Island itself is a small island off the Connemara coast from Cleggan, which he bought in 1969 and on which he stayed for brief periods in the following summer. There are three separate complementary worlds in this collection: Ceylon with its strange exotic culture, where the lonely child lives in the colonial compound; the world of Irish tinkers or itinerants, which is outside of the settled community, close to nature and untameable; the island world, itself composed of two islands—High and Omey—and the coastline; here the poet's persona exists and finds images for a complex relationship with its varied life, the people, the creatures of sea and air, the sense of the past. The poems are celebrations of his imaginative possession, bearing witness to life and revelatory of personal feeling. The freeing of the poet's voice may be seen in the opening poem, "Seals at High Island," which is charged with the movements of mammals and water and orchestrated in appreciative enjoyment of rhythm and the music of words:

Swayed by the thrust and backfall of the tide,
A dappled grey bull and a brindled cow
Copulate in the green water of a cove,
I watch from a cliff-top, trying not to move.
Sometimes they sink and merge into black shoals,
Then rise for air, his muzzle on her neck
Their winged feet intertwined as a fishtail.

A similar delight in the movements and life of creatures is present in poems about storm petrels.

The Ceylon poems capture the frightening aspects of a foreign culture as experienced by the child for whom the father is remote and uncomforting. They are complemented by the poems about Irish itinerants, particularly in the case of two poems—"The Writing Lesson," which is about the

child in Ceylon, and "The Reading Lesson," in which the poet tries in turn to teach an itinerant boy. Richard Murphy's relationship with the itinerants has been practical. In 1966 he became keenly aware of their plight, existing by the roadside in tents and caravans, and he tried to teach an itinerant boy to read, but the boy ran off to the roads when the summer came. In 1973 he accepted responsibility for an itinerant family in danger of being dispersed and got a home for them in Cleggan. He was particularly sensitive to the fact that whereas his family had been given thousands of acres of Irish land, the itinerants had no land.

Another feature of many of the poems in *High Island* is their compressed narrative element. Material that could be used by novelists is here reduced to a minimalist statement. One of the book's finest poems is the sea narrative "Pat Cloherty's Version of *The Maisie*," a swift vernacular account of a shipwreck that combines the idiom of oral narrative with Murphy's neomodernist style. The difference between the sea narratives of *Sailing to an Island*, with their undulating rhythms and evocative images, and this stark talk is a measure of the development in Murphy's work. The poetry of *High Island*, while restrained and formal, is a poetry of metaphor and simile, of connotative power and of varying rhythms.

In fact the strength of Richard Murphy's poetry is based on his sense of form. He writes slowly and carefully, and his work has developed in clear directions. He has sought and found a space within which to write, an area that enables him to bring together in fruitful relationship the two sides of his heritage. His intelligent and painstaking investigation of the past, notably in *The Battle of Aughrim*, has resulted in a different kind of lyric poetry, less inhibited, more personal, in which the possibilities of language find expression with greater range and flexibility. The well-crafted quality of his work, which at times seems to be a limitation, seems in recent years to give it an abiding power of clarity, order, and coherence. While Murphy's poetry does not challenge the reader with linguistic daring or complex structures, it provides a satisfying sense of sureness of craft. The evidence of recent work in periodicals is of a poet who continues to enjoy mastering form, particularly the sonnet, while at the same time becoming freer in the expression of personal feeling. In 1980 he settled into a new house in Killiney, County Dublin, and the poems now respond to the landmarks and monuments of the new shoreline.

Eiléan Ní Chuilleanáin
(28 November 1942-   )

Joseph Browne
West Chester University

BOOKS: *Acts and Monuments* (Dublin: Gallery Books, 1972);
Site of Ambush (Dublin: Gallery Books, 1975);
The Second Voyage (Dublin: Gallery Books, 1977; Winston-Salem: Wake Forest University Press, 1977);
Cork (Dublin: Gallery Books, 1977);
The Rose-Geranium (Dublin: Gallery Books, 1981).

OTHER: "Death and Engines," in *Choice*, edited by Desmond Egan & Michael Hartnett (Dublin: Goldsmith Press, 1973);
"Gaelic Ireland Rediscovered: Courtly and Country Poetry," in *Irish Poets In English*, edited by Sean Lucy (Cork & Dublin: Mercier Press, 1973);
"Drawing Lines," *Cyphers*, 10 (Spring 1979): 47-51;
"Love and Friendship," in *The Pleasures of Gaelic Poetry*, edited by Sean Mac Reamoinn (London: Allen Lane, 1982);
Irish Women: Image and Achievement, edited by Ní Chuilleanáin (Dublin: Arlen House Ltd., 1985).

In "Love and Friendship," her essay on Gaelic love poetry composed between the fourteenth and early-eighteenth century, Eiléan Ní Chuilleanáin explained and lauded the "mystery" of those poems in that they "expose just as much as the poet permits — they have a reticence, a quality of anonymity that gives them half their strength." She might, coincidentally, have been speaking of her own poetry although "reticence" and "anonymity" do not always or necessarily afford a strength, but often lend an obliquity to her poetry's intensely imagined, private, and frequently mysterious world. Sixteen years prior to this essay, in the poem "Ars Poetica," one of the four poems for which she won the *Irish Times* Poetry Award in 1966, Ní Chuilleanáin declared that "a poem is/singular and exclusive as a man's death." In her five books of poetry published to date, she has employed a most distinct sensibility, which encompasses history, legend, mythology, the past and present to create a dynamic, albeit "singular and exclusive," universe.

Born in Cork City, Ireland, Eiléan Ní Chuilleanáin was the first of three children born to Eilis Dillon, novelist and author of children's fiction, and Cormac Ó' Chuilleanáin, professor of Irish at University College, Cork. She has identified "almost equally" with both parents, with her father "as an academic, a man of strong self-control and critical sensibilities," and with her mother "as a creative person." She was "consciously very happy as a child," and the "strong aesthetic experiences" of her childhood have remained with her and are "at the centre of everything" she does and writes. Growing up in "a big official house in the University" with her parents who "were intellectuals and had a few bohemian friends" made her "feel very alien and very confident" that she "didn't have to live the life of people" she saw around her. In a life she has described as "academic, urban and feminine," Ní Chuilleanáin was educated at Ursuline Convent, Cork, and University College, Cork, where she earned a B.A. in English and history in 1962 and an M.A. in English in 1964. From 1964 to 1966 she did research at Oxford for a B.Litt. (1969) in Elizabethan prose, concentrating in the field of religious writing. She wrote a thesis on Thomas Nashe, but spent most of her time reading sermons. The poetry of the English Renaissance has remained especially important to her, providing alternate ways of using language and imagery, while poetry in Irish, Latin, French, and Italian also offers her "alternate rhythms and perspectives." She acknowledges William Butler Yeats, Constantine Cavafy, Sir Philip Sydney, and Richard Crashaw as having played special roles in the formation of her work. Her sensitivity to language and its resources was evident when as a schoolgirl she translated "pages and pages of French novels into English, totally preoccupied by prose style and her choice of words. . . ."

In 1966, in addition to winning the *Irish Times* Poetry Award, Ní Chuilleanáin was appointed to a lectureship in English at Trinity College, Dublin, where she now teaches exclusively in the renaissance area. Since returning from Oxford to Ireland she has also diligently promoted Irish poetry through weekly poetry readings arranged primarily to encourage and publicize younger Irish poets. In 1972 she organized an exhibition entitled "Irish Poetry Now," which represented poetry since the death of Yeats. Most significant, however, was her founding in 1975, along with Pearse Hutchinson, Macdara Woods, and Leland Bardwell, of the literary magazine *Cyphers* which has accomplished their goal of becoming "part of the tradition of Irish poetry with international, especially European connections." It has also become the most distinguished literary magazine in the Republic of Ireland. In 1978 she married Macdara Woods, a poet and co-editor of *Cyphers*. They have one child, Niall, born in 1983.

In "Early Recollections," a poem she considers her "most directly autobiographical one," Ní Chuilleanáin candidly proclaimed, "I know how things begin to happen/But never expect an end." If we are to understand her work then we must, she warns, understand that her childhood gave "hope and no warnings." Earlier in the same poem she had

asked, "If I produce paralysis in verse/where anger would be more suitable,/Could it be because my education/Left out the sight of death?" Such lines anticipated a critical response from Hayden Murphy (in *Hibernia*, 18 March 1973) which found her first book of poems, *Acts and Monuments* (1972), deficient in "fire and spirit" and hampered by "paralytic politeness." However, what has been misconstrued as "paralytic politeness" may actually be a unique blend of intentional and unintentional mystery, anonymity, and reticence. Just as she had praised the Gaelic love poems for their reticence and anonymity, Ní Chuilleanáin commends the poetry of her Irish contemporary Medbh McGuckian, because it is "authentically mysterious in the way a poet has a right to be, revealing with deliberation what she chooses and convincing us that the mystery of the poem corresponds to a mystery in human existence" (*Cyphers*, Summer 1981). Thus, in her own poetry, it is more a problem of the reader being convinced that a poem's specific mystery reflects the general mystery of humanity than it is a problem of politeness. When combined with her evaluation of McGuckian, two comments from her essay on recent poetry in Northern Ireland, "Drawing Lines" (*Cyphers*, Spring 1979) effect a helpful approach to Ní Chuilleanáin's own poetry: that when a poem succeeds it "creates its own meagre, mysterious context, its present moment in which it exists fully"; and that "To think about what a poem is you need to consider the nature of the poet's self which in turn must be part of the content." Thus, the intentional mystery of her poems results from what she believes is her "right" as a poet to manifest as much of her unique vision of the world in the poem's context as she chooses, while the unintentional mystery, or what John W. Foster (in *Eire-Ireland*, Winter 1978) has called her poems' inadequate "intrinsic sense of . . . persona," results from a problem with her "self." In a particularly honest and objective self-appraisal Ní Chuilleanáin sees that her " 'self' problem has been mainly in the area of articulating my feminine identity. My early poems concealed this behind various asexual masks. To say 'I' in a poem is hard for me." Although this "self" or "I" problem has admittedly remained unsolved, she does explain that "many more female figures appear in my more recent poetry—many of them are not myself but I can include myself among them." In spite of her partial emergence from behind previous masks, many of Ní Chuilleanáin's poems remain elusive for even the most persistent and sensitive reader. Nevertheless, her poetry's

Eiléan Ní Chuilleanáin (photograph © Michael Barron; courtesy of Bernard Stone, The Turret Book Shop)

claim, "The past is the present, isn't it? It is the future too."

The concluding lines to the title poem of *Acts and Monuments* illustrate a meaningful present as existing only in terms of the past, "like the waterline the sky/Lids and defines the element/Where no unformed capricious cry/Can sound without its monument." In Ní Chuilleanáin's world people and objects have meaning, identity, and relevance only when, like the trees discussed earlier in "Acts and Monuments," they are rooted in time and space and, as such, achieve the form and permanence of monuments. Unless all things exist as such, they are only "unformed" and "capricious." To understand life in general or a specific person, artifact, or natural object, we must, as argued in such poems as "Evidence," "Exhumation," and "Family," gather up what time, age, and the earth provide. We must, therefore, "disinter gently/the historical ages and layers of love." We must, as Ní Chuilleanáin herself has done, remain "interested in layers and levels." Like Yeats's Michael Robartes, Ní Chuilleanáin has "kissed a stone/And after that arranged it in a song. . . ." She has, through her awareness of the stone's significance, seen the past in the present and then verbalized her awareness in a song—her poems.

Just as water surrounds and traverses a large part of Ní Chuilleanáin's native city of Cork, so too is it omnipresent in her poems. In poem after poem water is juxtaposed antithetically with "the historical sense" or "simultaneous order" to instill conflict and create a dialectic structure. The poem "Family" succinctly declares, "Water has no memory/And you drown in it like a kind of absence"; whereas "Earth remembers/Facts about your relations/. . . and every stone recalls its quarry and the axe." When she was writing these early poems Ní Chuilleanáin "was in love with a man who loved the sea," and to this day the sea represents "travel and isolation"—elements which she believes are also "spurs to the writing of poetry." A poem which manifestly encompasses the dominant qualities and thematic bases of these early poems is "The Second Voyage." Here Odysseus, the traveler, is at sea, isolated and surrounded by waves, longing for "warm/Silent valleys" where he can plant his oar as a "gatepost or a hitching-post"; the sea, however, imprisons him, and he can only imagine life on land while "His face grew damp with tears that tasted/Like his own sweat or the insults of the sea." Odysseus is so thoroughly realized as a human being that the poem becomes brilliantly immediate and harmonious in

creative vigor, thematic depth, and technical range are consistently and sufficiently evident to authenticate its artistic worth.

Appropriately, in view of her undergraduate concentration in English and history, Ní Chuilleanáin's first collection, *Acts and Monuments,* illustrates both in its title and its thirty-four poems, all written between 1966 and 1972, a striking verbalization of what T. S. Eliot called "the historical sense." For Eliot, this sense "involves a perception, not only of the pastness of the past, but of its presence. . . ." Such a sense compels the poet to write of the present, but with a concurrent feeling for the past through which the poet composes "a simultaneous order." Thoroughly imbued with such a historical sense, Ní Chuilleanáin's poems, like Mary in Eugene O'Neill's *Long Day's Journey Into Night,* prothe poet's blending of subject, theme, language, structure, and personal vision.

Although acts of being and becoming predominate in *Acts and Monuments*, the death of Ní Chuilleanáin's father and the suicide of a friend in 1970 prompted her to articulate an eschatology in several of its poems, most notably "Death and Engines." A short time after its original appearance, the poem reappeared in the anthology of Irish poetry *Choice* (1973), where the poets prefaced their poems with explanations. Ní Chuilleanáin wrote, "I needed a poem to express my fear of death and to communicate with other people so that if I died that would not be an entirely isolated moment." Always conscious of her isolation and her upbringing which taught her never to "expect an end," Ní Chuilleanáin paradoxically maintains these qualities as major factors in her poetry's creativity, while at the same time trying to eliminate them because of their painful, traumatic results. This paradox, however, creates a sense of shared humanity which encourages the reader to pursue each poem's essential meaning and vision in spite of its seemingly private or exclusive nature.

The twenty-two poems written between 1972 and 1975 which compose her second collection, *Site of Ambush* (1975), sustain and elaborate upon the subjects and themes of *Acts and Monuments*. The opening poem, "The Lady's Tower," is strategically placed because in it Ní Chuilleanáin believes she has succeeded in "partly solving the female 'I' problem." The poem's persona dwells, Yeats-like, in a tower by "a sliding flooded stream." Existing in a private, isolated world, the "I" of the poem is, nevertheless, intimately caught up in and conscious of herself and the natural world around her. At night she ascends the high tower which "leans / Back to the cliff" and sleeps in a bed "made / Even with a sycamore root...." Unlike earlier poems, which were often obscured by a vague or incompletely realized persona that excluded the reader, "The Lady's Tower" is an entirety because its persona and her world complement and complete one another, thereby engaging the reader in their existence. In "The Ropesellers" Ní Chuilleanáin's historical sense is also more definitively articulated and objectively realized. Just as "The ropes are searching backward" and "twine with the earliest roots of trees / Coiling around rocks ...," so too do people carry "burdens ... that weigh like childhood." Each of us is held by "A knot binding us to the first day...."

"Site of Ambush," the long title poem of the collection, is partly about her "father's experience

Front wrapper for Ní Chuilleanáin's second volume of poetry, twenty-two poems that sustain and elaborate upon the themes and subjects of her previous book

in the Black and Tan War" and "partly a meditation on time and ... bereavement." Both her parents were involved in the Black and Tan War—her father as a Republican participant and her mother as the child of participants. "Black and Tan" was the name given by the Irish to the makeshift English army sent to Ireland in the early 1920s to fight the Irish Republican Army. "Concerned with Irish historical identity" primarily because of her parents' involvement in that war, Ní Chuilleanáin takes a specific time, place, and incident, and weaves them inextricably into a universal skein of time, place, and human existence, a skein effectively symbolized by the spider in the poem's concluding lines who "swayed on the end of his thread / A pendulum."

The Second Voyage (1977), published simultaneously in Ireland and the United States, contains thirty-seven poems from the previous two collections plus four new poems: "Barrack Street," "A Gentleman's Bedroom," "Night Journeys," and "Seamus Murphy, Died 2nd October, 1975." The first two poems are also in *Cork* (1977), while all four reappear in *The Rose-Geranium* (1981). They are all obviously important to her, but in 1984, when queried about what poems she considered most successful in realizing her artistic goals, Ní Chuilleanáin listed "Seamus Murphy" first. The poem serves as a paradigm of her poetic art in all its aspects. While the narrator strolls through a graveyard on a "coiled" path, she reflects that "In time they all come around/Again . . ."; that is, the types of human beings who lie buried there, and "as always you are facing the past. . . ." Familiar symbols abound: a ladder, the spider, a stone, an old clockface; and all of them merge organically and flow effortlessly within the poem's thematic structure.

The poems in *Cork* (1977) were commissioned to go with Brian Lalor's drawings of Cork City and were published a few months after *The Second Voyage*. Ní Chuilleanáin is unsure as to whether "the poems go very well on their own," but they do, however, provide a chance for her "to get away from mythology and into the world of human artifacts." Ironically, it is when she deals with the natural world in her personal, imaginative fashion that Ní Chuilleanáin is at her best. When her poems deal with other people and "human artifacts," particularly as drawn by someone else, as in *Cork*, her art loses much of its distinctive appeal and merit. The more successfully she surrounds and imbues Lalor's drawings in *Cork* with her own unique poetic values and technique, the more artistically successful the poems. The more she deliberately writes to the "human artifacts," the less vital, lucid, and assured is her expression; thus, the natural world of "Géarsmacht na mBradán" ("The Harsh Discipline of the Salmon") evinces a spontaneity and imaginative enthusiasm while "A Gentleman's Bedroom" appears flat and uninspired.

The Rose-Geranium (1981) consists of "Night Journeys," ten poems from *Cork*, "Seamus Murphy," "The Last Glimpse of Erin," "He Hangs in Shades the Orange Bright," "March 18th 1977," and "The Rose-Geranium," which is a sequence of eighteen poems written in the late 1970s. Looking back at *The Rose-Geranium*, Ní Chuilleanáin explained that it gave her "a chance to revise *Cork* and cut it, to include a group of short, domestic, directly personal poems, and in the title-sequence to explore human relationships obliquely in a way" that she "needed space to deal with." A sequence under-

standably appeals to her sense of progression and continuity, and the poems in each of her collections are most profitably read sequentially as a concatenation of statements and observations. The tone and theme of "The Rose-Geranium" are trenchantly stated in the opening stanza, "She learned again so soon/How the body is subdued/To all the laws that rule/The acorn's fall and the erosion of tall cliffs." The themes of time, change, aging, and death which previously had been simply characteristics of mythology, legend, history, and the natural world, that is, of the world outside her, are now observed as an intimate part of her own being and of her relations with others. A sense of trepidation, almost of desperation, permeates these poems, driving the narrator to exclaim, "I seek for depths as planets fly from the sun/What holds me in life is flowing from me and I flow/Falling, out of true." Many of the poems appear as images of specific

Front wrapper for Ní Chuilleanáin's fourth volume of poetry, comprising two sequences: "Cork," written in response to a series of drawings, and "The Rose-Geranium," which "depicts a human landscape"

people and special scenes which the narrator strives to etch in her memory because she is suddenly alarmed by their vulnerability to "the laws that rule." In an essay on "Gaelic Ireland Rediscovered: Courtly and Country Poetry," Ní Chuilleanáin noted the "immediacy" and "agonizing freshness" of that poetry; her words seem written for "The Rose-Geranium."

Since publishing *The Rose-Geranium* Ní Chuilleanáin has written seven or eight poems which she believes "are weighty and individual," but which

"came slowly." In her more than one hundred published poems, however, she has, like the Gaelic poetry she so admires, provided us with a body of work "full of suggestions and fascinating patterns."

References:
Siobhan McSweeney, "The Poets' Picture of Education," *Crane Bag,* 7, no. 2 (1983): 134-142;
Hayden Murphy, "Coincidence of Poets," *Hibernia* (18 March 1973): 18;
"Poetry Award," *Irish Times,* 12 February 1966, p. 7.

Desmond O'Grady
(27 August 1935-   )

William S. Waddell, Jr.
St. John Fisher College

BOOKS: *Chords and Orchestrations* (Limerick: Echo Press, 1956);
Reilly (London: Phoenix Press, 1961);
Professor Kelleher and the Charles River (Cambridge, Mass.: Carthage Press, 1964);
Separazioni (Rome: Edizioni Europei, 1965);
The Dark Edge of Europe (London: MacGibbon & Kee, 1967);
The Dying Gaul (London: MacGibbon & Kee, 1968);
Off Licence [English versions of Irish, Armenian, and Italian poems] (Dublin: Dolmen Press, 1968);
Hellas (Dublin: New Writers' Press, 1971);
Separations (Dublin: Goldsmith Press, 1973);
Stations (Cairo: American University in Cairo Press, 1976);
The Gododdin/A Version [from the Welsh of Aneirin] (Dublin: Dolmen Press, 1977);
Sing Me Creation (Dublin: Gallery Press, 1977);
A Limerick Rake: Versions from the Irish (Dublin: Gallery Press, 1978);
The Headgear of the Tribe: New and Selected Poems, edited by Peter Fallon (London: Brian & O'Keeffe, 1978; Dublin: Gallery Press, 1979);
His Skaldcrane's Nest (Dublin: Gallery Press, 1979);
Grecian Glances: Versions from the Classical Anthology (Cambridge, Mass.: Inkling Press, 1981).

PERIODICAL PUBLICATIONS: "Ezra Pound: A Personal Memoir," *Agenda,* 17-18 (Autumn-Winter-Spring 1979/1980): 285-299;
"The Burden of the Past and Modern Irish Poetry," *Proceedings of the Harvard Celtic Colloquium,* 1 (1981): 169-176.

Desmond O'Grady has enjoyed for more than twenty-five years a productive international career as a poet and educator. He has been one of a group of Irish poets who, after Denis Devlin and Patrick Kavanagh, have worked to bring Irish poetry out of the shadow of Yeats. Among this number, O'Grady occupies a chronological pivot point: he is some six or seven years younger than Richard Murphy, Thomas Kinsella, and John Montague; some four or five years older than Seamus Heaney, Michael Longley, and Derek Mahon. O'Grady's strategy in creating his own voice and his own subject has been to unite his concerns as a contemporary Irishman with a larger perspective in both space and time. He has lived, studied, and taught in America, on the Continent, and even in the Near East, writing poetry that he sees not as exclusively Irish, but "in the European mainstream." O'Grady, nonetheless, has never abandoned Ireland or his identity as an Irishman, or more precisely as a Celt: "I am aware of what it means to be a Celt, not like an Irishman but to belong to a particular people." The Celtic identity gives O'Grady access to centuries of history and legend and to a continent's worth of geography: "From the southern Russian steppe to the boglands

Desmond O'Grady (photograph © Jerry Bauer)

of the west of Ireland is the territory and sovereignty of the Celt, and that includes the Arab world. I have no interest in anywhere else." His poems explore the connections among a relatively few individuals' present, a whole people's past, and a poet's sense of present and past intermingled. The best of his poems are sustained by a sharp eye for detail and a fine and subtle rhythmic sense.

The son of Joseph Leonard and Elizabeth Ann Bourke O'Grady, Desmond James Bernard O'Grady was born in Limerick, Ireland, and educated there in the Irish national schools and the Jesuits' Sacred Heart College until he was fifteen. During his childhood he also received a considerable noncanonical education from his uncle Feathereye Mykie Bourke, young O'Grady's first storyteller and guardian of the oral tradition. In 1950, O'Grady left Limerick for the Cistercian College in Roscrea, County Tipperary. He further developed his interest in poetry—reading Ezra Pound, T. S. Eliot, and other moderns—and began writing his own verse while studying with the Cistercians. After 1954, he attended lectures, especially Kavanagh's, at University College, Dublin, but never took a degree. Several of the poets he studied influenced

O'Grady's early poetry, especially John Keats, Gerard Manley Hopkins, and Dylan Thomas, but other influences were to last throughout his career—most vitally those of Pound, Pablo Picasso, and James Joyce: "Ezra Pound together with Pablo Picasso opened up the worlds of literature and art to me as a youth in the west of Ireland. Somehow I fused the two in my method and matter . . . and controlled it with jesuitical Joycean architectonics." Throughout his career, O'Grady has sought to create and maintain intricate relations within and among his books, the ideal being to see "each part of each work in relation to the whole work and each subsequent work in relation to past work done and future work planned."

Evidence of his intention appears even in his first volume, *Chords and Orchestrations,* published in Limerick in 1956. The book is framed by two seven-part poems whose titles explicitly extend the musical reference of the book's title. O'Grady was just twenty-one when *Chords and Orchestrations* appeared, and it should be no surprise that the work is immature. The themes are conventional—nostalgia for the lost innocence of childhood, romantic isolation for the man of poetic temperament—and the language derivative—mostly from Keats, Hopkins, and Thomas. O'Grady's own foreword to the book marks it as an apprenticeship volume, and he has never reprinted any of its poems. The final poem, however, the sonnet sequence "Theme for Seven Instruments," displays a high degree of technical facility. O'Grady tries multiple variations of conventional sonnet form and mixes anapests generously into the iambic base to create a supple, musical rhythm.

O'Grady began his career as a teacher before publishing his first book of poetry. He started at the Berlitz School in Paris when he was just nineteen. He taught, wrote, and enjoyed the heady atmosphere of the city. In Paris O'Grady met Olga Jwaideh, another person to whom the French capital was a new and strange city, and the young man from Limerick and the young woman from Baghdad were married in 1957. Though the marriage was brief, they do have a daughter, Deirdre. Before his marriage, in 1956, O'Grady left his job at Berlitz and exchanged the worldly milieu of Paris for the isolation of a Cistercian monastery on Caldey Island, off the coast of Wales. He stayed on the island during the winter of 1956-1957, planning the "Reilly" sequence for his second book. In a statement for *Contemporary Authors,* O'Grady credits the Cistercian abbot, Eugene Boylan, whom he had met originally at Roscrea, with forming the poet's "attitude to routine and artistic discipline."

O'Grady returned to teaching in 1957, when he accepted a post at the British Institute in Rome. He lived in Rome until 1962, teaching at the British Institute and later at St. George's English School. During his stay in Rome, O'Grady became ever more active in international literary and artistic circles, but no experience had greater impact on his career than his meeting and subsequent friendship with one of his most important teachers, Ezra Pound. He had read Pound's work at Roscrea under Thomas Cole and corresponded with him from Caldey Island and Rome while Pound was still confined in St. Elizabeths Hospital in Washington, D.C. That correspondence had put him in touch with Olga Rudge and others of Pound's friends in Italy. When the elder poet was released to return to Europe, O'Grady was among the welcoming party, and they formed a close association that lasted until Pound's death. Pound's influence is apparent in O'Grady's poetry, especially in his approach to translation, his international perspective, and his belief that the archetypal is reflected in individual experience. But Pound's influence was also personal. In a memoir published in *Agenda* in 1979, O'Grady wrote, "Pound's physical presence gave you a spiritual strength, a kind of poetic grace and courage to take on the dragons of the sacred way in the sacred wood daily." In this creative atmosphere O'Grady wrote and revised his second volume.

Reilly (1961) contains his first thoroughly mature work. The book begins with sixteen individual lyrics and closes with the sequence of twenty-four poems that gives the book its title, a more ambitious "orchestration" than any in the first volume. The poems in both sections of *Reilly* develop the poet's sense of isolation, even exile, but the nostalgia that rings false in *Chords and Orchestrations* is almost completely absent, replaced by anger and bitter satire. The "Reilly" sequence follows a deliberately Joycean structure. O'Grady has called it "one poem in twenty-four parts, one for each hour of the day beginning in the night's phantasmagoria . . . involving the narrative conscious, the dream subconscious and the racial conscious of the proto Celt." Its three sections are titled "Reilly Dead," "Reilly Born," and "Reilly Living," but the cyclical nature of the structural scheme and the poems themselves undermine the optimism suggested by these titles. "Reilly Dead" certainly begins the sequence in the inferno, presenting a series of exaggerated, Gothic tales of families beset by desertion, violence, hatred, madness, and death. The poet-persona appears in "Reilly Born" as an exile, evolving in the section's

first two poems a statement of the goal of poetry—to rebuild "what has been destroyed"—and the means of such rebuilding—a "severe mind" and a cold, clear-sighted eye worthy of Yeats's fisherman to probe the world as it is. But the dominant theme of the rest of "Reilly Born" is uncertainty and the sense that whatever order and wisdom experience has won cannot be passed on, even to Reilly's own child. The poems of the last section, "Reilly Living," only deepen the feeling of doubt. The first three—"Reilly's Bath" and "Afternoon," both first-rate, and "The Decision"—are dominated by an atmosphere of lassitude bordering on despair. In another poem, Reilly's neighbors, "hungry as knives, / . . . wait with the patience of buried bones" to "haunt and hunt him down," and O'Grady ends the volume with "Reilly Overheard Mumbling to Himself in the Night," a poet's apology for his failure to make himself understood, a last wish only to feel "More quietly at our ease among the tins and cans, / The broken bricks and beaten walls that made us real." The persona's achievement, even his sense of possibility, has been inexorably reduced. Thus Reilly, O'Grady's first extended persona, shares with the Dying Gaul and his other later personae an essentially tragic destiny.

O'Grady's own destiny took him, shortly after the publication of *Reilly*, to Cambridge, Massachusetts, where he taught for a year at West Roxbury Latin School and became a teaching fellow at Harvard, finishing an M.A. in Celtic studies in 1964. During his stay in the United States, O'Grady met the woman who became his second wife, Florence Tamburro; they have a son, Leonardo, born 15 March 1967. In 1964 O'Grady published *Professor Kelleher and the Charles River*, a tribute to John V. Kelleher, his mentor at Harvard. Following his departure from Cambridge, O'Grady returned to Ireland with his new family before taking a position as senior English master at the Overseas School of Rome, a post he retained until 1974, his longest stint at a single school. In 1965, he brought out in Rome a volume called *Separazioni*, with Italian translations of the poems on facing pages. But neither his turn to more formal academic training and increased academic responsibility nor the slim volumes of 1964 and 1965 indicated waning interest in poetry. O'Grady's formal study of Celtic history and literature proved a strong influence on his poetry. Celtic history gave him a tradition and mythology to frame and support the observations of his own experience, finally making history for O'Grady a palimpsest, a layered transparency, much as it had been for his friend Ezra Pound.

Celtic verse fused heroic and elegiac elements to provide the melancholy tone that came to dominate O'Grady's poems of his own life and times, replacing the anger that surfaces in *Reilly.*

In 1967, O'Grady published in London a major collection of new and selected poems entitled *The Dark Edge of Europe.* The book's structure offers a recapitulation of O'Grady's career: pushed to the dark edge of Europe, he draws himself up before departure, a "scattering," followed by a return to Ireland and things Irish seen from a new perspective after absence. *The Dark Edge of Europe* is the summation of O'Grady's early work, which, as the poet himself wrote for *Contemporary Poets,* "dealt with the experience of growing up on the west coast of Ireland, with the leaving . . . for the cities of the Continent and America and the need to connect my life there with the one I had left." The book was well-received—Julian Symons, for example, praised the book in the *New Statesman* for precise observation of character and scene—and is still regarded by many as O'Grady's finest volume. *The Dark Edge of Europe* derives its strength partly from O'Grady's turn in many of its poems to a directly personal poetry, versions of experience unmediated by a persona or romantic posing. The restrained and lovely title poem is an excellent example. It begins in present observation of a peasant family ending their day's labor, backtracks to memories of "Four countries and four loves/ . . . and no one of them/Quite understood or really concluded," then returns to the twilight present to close with one of O'Grady's explicit leave-takings: "Somewhere out in the dark pall/Over Europe I leave my loves for dead." Less successful is "The Scattering," a fairly derivative modernist work recalling Pound's *Hugh Selwyn Mauberley* (1920) or Eliot's *The Waste Land* (1922) in both manner and theme. O'Grady actually quotes Pound's poem briefly.

The most interesting sections of *The Dark Edge of Europe* are "Separations" and "Land and Sea," both for the poems themselves and for the fact that their successes and failures are characteristic of much of O'Grady's later poetry. Here and elsewhere, O'Grady seems masterful when his language is measured and restrained, when the words reinforce both subject and emotion. When verbal excess, on the other hand, causes the words to usurp the place of subject and emotion, the poems become like fireworks—sudden, dazzling, but instantaneously gone. The "Separations" section contains both the most solid successes and the noblest failures. The poems collected there swing back and

forth between large abstractions and closely observed, concrete detail, between apocalypse and the realm of daily life. Sometimes the contrasting manners are set side by side in adjacent poems; more often O'Grady attempts to mix the two, modulating between them, finding a trace of the grand mysteries in everyday events. In *Professor Kelleher and the Charles River,* the transition is severely strained. O'Grady overpowers the richness of the setting, forcing the metamorphosis of poet and professor into Dionysian and Apollonian archetypes— creating "some new order" through "their ageless struggle"—by borrowing the rhetoric of Yeats's "The Second Coming." The result is bombast. He shows a surer hand in "While Visiting Clonfert Cathedral," one of the volume's best poems. There the poet does not press the natural contrasts between the age and majesty of the eleventh-century cathedral and the "girl herding the pair/of her children home" along the same road, between the centuries of loss and separation embodied in the churchyard and the powerful individual sense of another's "absence" he has come to the cathedral to escape. Without excess pressure, these contrasts and others in the poem reflect and refract each other, building a more satisfying complexity of vision, a livelier sense of all times' simultaneity. The envoi to "While Visiting Clonfert Cathedral" uses a voyage metaphor to crystallize O'Grady's fascination in this poem and many others:

> The securer mind sinks a fresh foundation for the hesitant
> blind heart's dependence: the past is present, the present
> past and the heart strives daily, like some winged merman,
> to navigate the most relevant, personal course between them.

O'Grady followed *The Dark Edge of Europe* the very next year with *The Dying Gaul* (1968), a long poem he has described as a "breakthrough" for him, "cubist in structure . . . in the manner of Joyce's *Ulysses* and Eliot's *Waste Land.*" The series of thirty-three lyrics attempts to meld personal history with legend and literary sources in order to create a meta-history inhabited by mythical heroes. When *The Dying Gaul* appeared, critics found it finally less compelling than *The Dark Edge of Europe.* The reviewer for the *Times Literary Supplement,* for example, thought the individual parts insufficiently unified and damaged rather than deepened by the historical references. At its best, however, *The Dying*

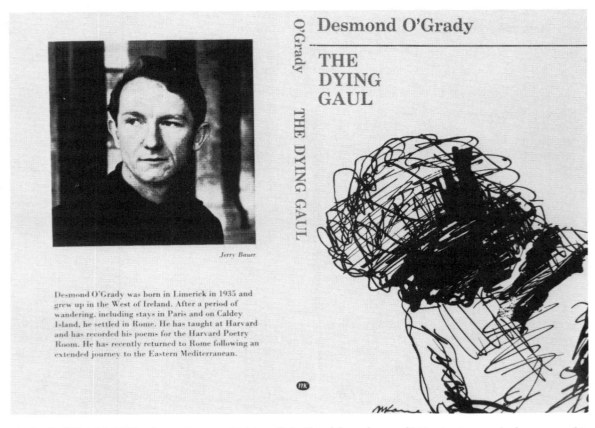

Dust jacket for O'Grady's 1968 volume of poetry, which he called a "breakthrough . . . cubist in structure . . . in the manner of Joyce's Ulysses *and* Eliot's Waste Land"

Gaul provides a rich if not startlingly original mix of elements that mankind's imagination has used to elevate our experience. The volume is difficult, but is held together in its complexity by the narrative line and the explicit literary and mythological background. O'Grady begins with three epigraphs, evoking the long, though non-Celtic, literary heritage of the West. The two excerpts from the *Oresteia* and one from *Hamlet* introduce also the theme which runs throughout *The Dying Gaul* of tragedy involving kingship and kinship, succession, treachery, vengeance, and destiny. O'Grady speaks in the first poem of the "chosen child·. . . . the marked man," and the final poem ends, "Man,/ avenged, declares:/I am my father's son." In addition to specific literary allusions, he has filled *The Dying Gaul* with elements of religious ritual, the seasonal cycles of the earth and its fecundity, human mortality, heroism, and regeneration, the motif of voyaging, and the duty of history and art to record triumphs and tragedies with honor and care. In poem 32, he writes, "Though speech be spectral/

word becomes deed,/deed word": vows and promises are kept, and the acts in turn become the stuff of heroic legend, keeping alive a heritage. *The Dying Gaul* is a self-portrait, as O'Grady has said, because the poet speaks directly in several of the lyrics, and speaks both as poet-historian and as the most recent successor to the heroic protagonist. This dual perspective is more self-dramatizing than self-aggrandizing, allowing the poet to share in the tragedy of mankind's "ageless struggle, condemned to lose."

O'Grady had begun shortly after his return to Rome in 1965 to spend the summer vacations between terms at the Overseas School on the Greek island of Paros. He once told John Liddy in an interview for the *Stony Thursday Book* that he settled on Paros by a chance that had the effect of fate. On a Turkish ship, bound for Patmos, where legend says Saint John wrote his gospel, he debarked during a stop at Paros and found the island so congenial that he decided not to continue his journey. In Greece, far across the continent from his native Ireland,

O'Grady found an island kinship and a sense of balance: "There is a connection between the dark edge of Europe I came from and the enlightening edge of Europe I settled for as counterpoint." The Cycladic setting dominates his poems of the 1970s. The sense of relation to and affection for Greece and the friends he found there informs *Hellas*, the pamphlet O'Grady published in 1971. It contains a three-part poem in response—"because of the shock, the sudden/rage of our disappointment"—to the military coup that took place in Greece in April 1967. Confronted by this cruel betrayal of the Greek past, which recalls to him "the despaired history/of my own country," O'Grady finds solace in the things that cannot change—the sun, the sea, the Greek landscape, and the rhythms of the country's peasant culture—and in the art that can endure—Homer and Callimachus from the ancient past, George Seferis from the present. As one would expect, he mixes these elements with personal memories of individual friends and their hospitality. Thus *Hellas* treats the particular political occasion of the poem with the characteristic O'Grady blend of comparative history and personal experience.

In fact, O'Grady included *Hellas* in his next volume, *Separations*, published in Dublin in 1973. The title obviously suggests continuity of themes already begun in the poet's work, but the book also employs elements of style that had received less emphasis in his recent poems, notably some relatively strict—though never rigid—metrical forms and more frequent rhyme. "Three Poems for Children" opens with Swiftian tetrameter couplets and continues, rhymed and regular, in quatrains. Such regular rhythm is found again in only one other poem, but perhaps one third in all make good use of rhyme. The full inventive range of O'Grady's play with rhyme, both full and half, is well displayed in "Limerick Town." *Separations* is divided into two sections, "People" and "Places," though all but one of the poems in "Places" is also inscribed to a person. The poems take up separations in age, in time, in space, or in all three together, dealing with the separation usually by recalling particular times of presence. These are consistently, sometimes intensely personal poems, resembling those in the "Separations" section of *The Dark Edge of Europe,* content to describe events from the poet's own experience, remembered in sometimes striking detail. The volume pays tribute, individually and collectively, to O'Grady's circle of elected friends, a community to replace the "soured towns" his earlier speakers had left behind. The inclusion of poems to

mentors and other elders and poems to children invokes the theme of succession and tradition within that community. *Separations* is quieter and more initially accessible than *The Dying Gaul,* but unlike that volume, is likely to seem less rather than more interesting in repeated readings.

For O'Grady, 1974 brought a change analogous to his departure for America twelve years earlier. He decided to leave his post at the Overseas School in Rome and began the next winter a series of temporary teaching positions that would take him once again away from Europe (except for his return to Paros each summer), this time to the Islamic world. From February 1975 until June 1976 O'Grady was visiting poet in residence at the American University in Cairo. The next academic year he spent at Tabriz University in Iran, as visiting professor of English literature, and from 1978 to 1980 he held a similar post back in Egypt at the University of Alexandria. The years of the late 1970s—and the poet's early forties—were a time of extraordi-

Front cover for Hellas *(1971), O'Grady's three-part poem written in response to the Greek military coup of 1967*

nary productivity for O'Grady. From 1976 to 1979, he published three volumes of original poems, two books of translations, and another collection of his work.

This burst of energy began, somewhat inauspiciously, with *Stations* (1976), published in an edition of 250 by the American University in Cairo. This small volume contains only fourteen poems and very few that show O'Grady in top form. Some display an extravagant diction so concerned with sound that it pushes syntax to the limits of intelligibility, creating once again the impression that the poet is straining for effects. He is more successful when he does not press the point, as, for example, in "Village Carpenter." In that poem, O'Grady manages an understated confrontation with mortality via the short tale of his new nodding acquaintance with the local coffin builder. A sense of a crisis passed informs the book's opening poems, especially "Sunrise." The first three poems—"Spring," "Sunrise," and "Morning"—all suggest obvious new beginnings, but these hopeful perspectives give way in the latter half of the book to autumn settings and bleak landscapes.

Sing Me Creation (1977), which began O'Grady's longstanding association with Ireland's Gallery Press, is actually, like *The Dying Gaul,* a single, multipart poem. O'Grady has given the volume both prologue and epilogue and has designed the opening and closing sections with a certain symmetry of language and subject, enhancing the unity and closure of the sequence. The narrative unity of *Sing Me Creation* lies in the life of the poet himself, for O'Grady's personal experience provides the occasions for the poems, a later self-consciousness their substance. In the prologue, he introduces his protagonist in familiar terms as a traveler, who "went a long journey":

> His purpose: praise, search,
> his appointed pain
> in the countries of the world
> that house his image.
>
> Weary, worn from his labours,
> he returned and told
> what he'd seen and learned
> to help kill the winter.

Some of these words come almost directly from *The Dying Gaul;* in fact O'Grady quotes himself for a line or two several times in *Sing Me Creation* (and elsewhere, too, a technique that makes explicit certain connections between poems and volumes). The

book moves through familiar thematic territory: the mystery of the poetic vocation; the life of the voyager, the quester; the complexity and power of contact, relations—inherited, discovered, forsaken, renewed. Though the second and third of these themes support more individual poems, the first dominates the book as a whole. O'Grady has taken his title from the story of the discovery of the uncanny poetic ability of Caedmon, the unlettered cowherd whose first poem celebrated God's creation. O'Grady's book takes the creation of a life, of a poet's life and work, as analogous to the creation of a world. O'Grady's point of view is saved from hubris because he speaks always as a storyteller and never as a prophet and because he remains humble before some experiences, such as love and fatherhood. He gives voice, moreover, to considerable self-doubt and uncertainty through rhetorical questions, a stylistic device which assumes significance for the first time in *Sing Me Creation.* Nearly all of the poems in this volume contain a fine line or two, but a majority do not sustain the same tension and energy through the whole poem. A lack of variety in manner and length helps to establish the unity of the volume but makes for a rather monotonous rhythm for reading straight through. O'Grady achieves the most success in the book's longer poems, where moods and thoughts can build, as in "The Voyage," "Landfall," "Gestation," and "Darkness and Light."

In 1978, eleven years after *The Dark Edge of Europe,* O'Grady brought out a second "retrospective" entitled *The Headgear of the Tribe.* The Gallery Press edition contains a foreword by publisher Peter Fallon which serves as a good introduction to O'Grady's poetry. Poems from the first half of O'Grady's career dominate the collection, which includes substantial selections from *Reilly* (restoring to *Reilly* several poems that had been absorbed into *The Dark Edge of Europe*) and *The Dark Edge of Europe,* and reprints *The Dying Gaul* complete. The selections from O'Grady's publications in the 1970s are smaller. *The Headgear of the Tribe* is not entirely backward-looking, however. It closes with two poems from *His Skaldcrane's Nest,* which would appear in 1979, and three from "The Suras of the Wandering Celt," which looms as O'Grady's epic. "Basically," he has said recently, "everything I write of original verse from now on will find its place somewhere, sometime in the Suras." Even the three poems printed in *The Headgear of the Tribe* suggest the epic scope of the work through their interest in the clothing, art, and ritual customs of the ancient Celtic tribes, as well as the economic necessity that impelled them west and the diplomatic skill that gained them a foothold in Europe. "The Suras of the Wandering Celt" represents a logical end of O'Grady's voyaging, geographical and mythological, back to his origins: he has crossed Europe to the east to meet his ancient ancestors and join them in their original trek to the west. *The Headgear of the Tribe* ends with the promise of these richly textured poems.

"The Suras of the Wandering Celt" has yet to be published, but O'Grady's next volume, *His Skaldcrane's Nest* (1979), is full of rich and beautiful poetry of a different kind. *His Skaldcrane's Nest* deals exclusively in contemporary settings; its poems speak with a measured voice grounded in subtle rhythms, gentle but not at all weak. It may be O'Grady's best collection. In poem after poem he listens with an ear for the soft sounds—goat bells, vine leaves scraping on terrace flagstones, a distant boat motor thudding like a lover's heart—writes with an instinct for the perfect word, saying of the old gods, for example, Greek or Irish, "They still guide us./Their very souls still remember./Their strength soaks our air." The book's title, obscure as it is, points toward its dominant theme. A "skaldcrane" is not a bird, despite the "crane" and the similarity to "scaldcrow." "Skald" was the word for "poet" in old Norwegian and Icelandic dialects. From a similarly archaic perspective, "crane" might be short for "cranium," hence skull or head. "His skaldcrane's nest" thus suggests a sheltered home, a haven, for the wearied head—and mind—of the wandering sailor-poet, and certainly the dominant mood and theme in the poems are reconciliation: with self and others, with Ireland and Greece, with mortality and desire. O'Grady expresses his resolution in the opening poem, "Easter":

> Begin again with cone and square,
> leave winter with last year. Describe
> what's palpable—straight, unadorned, clear;
> order, form on the sensuous; to make
> a thing of balance, serenity, devoid
> destruction, that gives delight and hurts not.

But that balance and serenity are never achieved by driving out feeling. On the contrary, these poems are full of genuine feeling—nothing shrill and forced, no empty dramatic gesture, but a presence of love, compassion, grief that is sturdy and solid. O'Grady crafted these poems in a language that is never far from the colloquial, which often breaks in very effectively, as in the last lines of "Crisis '74," where the speaker and a woman friend are con-

fronted by her son's awkward question:

> My own son must,
> by now, have said the same some other where.
> We big-fish adults, flounder and gulp air.
> We know it's actions, not fast words, that count.
> We say so every time, promise, then disappoint.

In "Son," O'Grady uses a mock-heroic detail to make both the scene and the emotion real without mockery:

> I have watched you,
> brazen as brass,
> blond as sovereigns,
> upstart of beauty
> who once, gallavanter,
> galloped bareback the sows
> squealing wild from the sty—
> eager grip on their earlugs.

Several of the poems in *His Skaldcrane's Nest* are elegies for friends, some famous—Robert Lowell, John Berryman, Pablo Neruda—some unknown. Through a practiced art of anecdote, O'Grady succeeds wonderfully well in invoking his friends' presence, usually for a hearty salute rather than a sad farewell. In the volume's last poem, reconciled to his own mortality, he imagines his own funeral and bids farewell also with a salute:

> I have been happy in this hospitable harbour,
> this scrummaged village below my broken mountain.
> Friends of our homely cafe drink deep for me this
>   night.
> I wish you all long life.

This last poem from *His Skaldcrane's Nest* is actually a free adaptation from Turkish poet Nazim Hikmet. Throughout his career, O'Grady has practiced translation as a complement to his original poetry. As a native Irish speaker from childhood, he began translating Irish poetry first, during his stay on Caldey Island. He has since made translations also from Italian, Armenian, Russian, Greek, Welsh, and Arabic. O'Grady has published three substantial volumes and one chapbook of translations. His attitude toward translation draws heavily on Ezra Pound's: on Pound's famous dictum, for example, that a country's literature should be translated once every fifty years because of the shifting meanings of language, and his conviction that a good translation must be creative, a poem in its own right. In a short essay following his rendering of the

Welsh epic *The Gododdin*, O'Grady writes, "My purpose here is to give a 'reading' of the poem—my own reading, something of what Ezra Pound intends when he talks of his 'Homage to Sextus Propertius.'" O'Grady calls his reworkings of other poets variously "translations," "transubstantiations," or "versions," roughly according to their accuracy in a scholarly sense. Besides reflecting his international perspective, translation offers O'Grady an apt union of his interests as poet and teacher: a chance to practice disciplined attention to language and tone and a chance to make available in English the work of poets he thinks should be read.

In the fall of 1980, O'Grady returned to Harvard to study once again with John Kelleher, and in 1982 he earned his doctorate in Celtic languages and literature and comparative literature. He spent the latter half of 1982 traveling in Europe, returning to Ireland near the end of the year to prepare several books for publication, including two volumes of new poems and two of selected translations. As of February 1985 none of these books had appeared. Beyond these projects, O'Grady continues to work on "The Suras of the Wandering Celt," a volume of selected essays, a book of prose memoirs, and a translation from Arabic of the pre-Islamic Golden Odes. His poetry doubtless will continue its concern with the themes of exploration and return, origin and destiny, developed through multiple forms in the alliterative, near colloquial idiom that he has made more and more his own. O'Grady retains his concern with the interrelatedness of his works, describing his art in metaphors that express the complexity and continuity of the design: "The totality of the oeuvre is like a large stained-glass window or several related [windows], or a complex carpet page of an illuminated Celtic ms. like the Book of Kells. . . . All is deliberate in art and all that's related to its making. . . . All appears cyclical. Hence architectonic composition. . . . A circle (or line and every line straight or not is a segment of a circle) is composed of points, every point an . . . epigram [which] builds to an epiphany, to an episode to an epic or complete circle."

Reference:

Stony Thursday Book (Limerick, Ireland), no. 6 (1978).

Tom Paulin
(25 January 1949-)

John Haffenden
Sheffield University

BOOKS: *Thomas Hardy: The Poetry of Perception* (London: Macmillan, 1975; Totowa, N.J.: Rowman & Littlefield, 1975);
A State of Justice (London: Faber & Faber, 1977);
Personal Column (Belfast: Ulsterman Publications, 1978);
The Strange Museum (London: Faber & Faber, 1980);
The Book of Juniper (Newcastle upon Tyne: Bloodaxe, 1981);
Liberty Tree (London: Faber & Faber, 1983);
A New Look at the Language Question (London: Faber & Faber, 1983);
Ireland and the English Crisis (Newcastle upon Tyne: Bloodaxe, 1984);
The Riot Act (London: Faber & Faber, forthcoming 1985)

PLAY PRODUCTION: *The Riot Act*, Belfast, Lyric Theatre, 1984.

OTHER: "A Necessary Provincialism: Brian Moore, Maurice Leitch, Florence Mary McDowell," in *Two Decades of Irish Writing: A Critical Survey*, edited by Douglas Dunn (Manchester: Carcanet, 1975; Chester Springs, Pa.: Dufour, 1975);
"'Letters from Iceland': Going North," in *The 1930s: A Challenge to Orthodoxy*, edited by John Lucas (Hassocks: Harvester, 1978).

PERIODICAL PUBLICATIONS:
POETRY
"The Argument at Great Tew," *Irish University Review*, 13 (Spring 1983): 83-87.

NONFICTION

"Tom Paulin writes . . . ," *Poetry Book Society Bulletin*, 92 (Spring 1977);

"Living out of London—VII," *London Magazine*, 19 (April/May 1979): 83-88;

"Tom Paulin writes. . . ," *Poetry Book Society Bulletin*, 104 (Spring 1980);

"Viewpoint," *Times Literary Supplement*, 21 March 1980, p. 320;

"A Naked Emperor?" [on John Ashbery], *Poetry Review*, 74 (September 1984): 32-33.

Tom Paulin is one of the most intelligent and accomplished poets to have emerged from the North of Ireland in recent years. The authority of his political imagination won immediate recognition in the mid-1970s (*A State of Justice* was a choice of the Poetry Book Society), and since then his artistic range has steadily expanded, enabling him not only to redeem the banality of civic life but also to envision a new order which marries his exact historic sense with the joy of artistic formalism.

Though actually born in Leeds, England, Paulin grew up after 1953 in Belfast, where he attended Rosetta Primary School and Annadale Grammar School. His father is a school headmaster, and a liberal. "In the early and mid 1960s—which is as far back as my political memory can go—the North of Ireland had a placid stagnant atmosphere," the poet has written. "In those days I used to read Russian novels and various revolutionary texts, and I'd sometimes see Belfast through dim images of St. Petersburg . . . the capital of a remote province that dozed under a dull and corrupt oligarchy." His maternal grandparents, strenuous Ulster Scots, emigrated from Glasgow to Belfast in 1912, the grandfather to be manager of an ice and cold-storage firm and an elder of the Presbyterian church, the grandmother to be a cook in the army set up by Lord Carson to fight the British army— "in order to keep Ulster British." The family tradition of Calvinist authoritarianism fascinates and repels Paulin; so do the contradictions of Ulster Protestantism: "It's a culture which could have dignity, and it had it once—I mean that strain of radical Presbyterianism, free-thinking Presbyterianism, which more or less went underground after 1798. I pretty well despise official Protestant culture, and can't now understand how people can simultaneously wave the Union Jack and yet hate the English, as many Protestants do."

Paulin belonged to a Trotskyite organization while at school: "I felt disaffected from my background, the whole Unionist culture—not that my

parents voted Unionist—and I read Orwell in the absorbed way one does at that age. There's a sense, particularly in Irish culture, of deliberate—in fact doctrinaire—disloyalty. I grew up in a culture that was officially Loyalist, but I came to see that it was a rotten society: I left it not for political reasons but simply because I wanted to get away from the claustrophobia of that society."

After taking a B.A. with first-class honors in English at Hull University, he spent two years in research at Lincoln College, Oxford, achieving a B.Litt. in 1973. Since 1972 he has been a lecturer in English at the University of Nottingham—"on the border between the civil lawns of the south and the brick mills of the authentic north," as he has described it: "the England which begins at the river Trent, that great hyperborean tundra of mills, mines and factories which dreams itself as the territory of fierce, passionate, authentic feeling. For some reason, that northern part of England never seems quite English, and I don't think it did to Lawrence—he sought parallels for it in other countries, other cultures, different ways of feeling." The crumbling city of Nottingham quickened his imagination, and there he began to write poems catechizing the "steel polities" he had observed in Ulster.

Paulin's first volume of poetry, *A State of Justice* (1977), bears a title which, he has explained, "partly refers to the Old Testament God of retributive justice—a concept which has always been embodied socially, culturally and politically in the North of Ireland. Justice is terrifying, both as an idea and in practice—when it's institutionalized it can seem to reproduce the cruel state of nature it's supposed to supersede." The poems scrutinize and diagnose the derelict spirit of Ulster. "States"—with its fiercely spitting fricatives, and the devastating internal rhyme (Waste/state/nature)—intransigently pronounces:

> Any state, built on such a nature,
> Is a metal convenience, its paint
> Cheapened by the price of lives
> Spent in a public service.

Paulin repudiates an "official god" which subordinates people to repressive system. Tyranny begets communal sterility, which is reflected in the accurate and sometimes clearly conceptual drabness of the poet's indictments. Soldiers are described in "Practical Values," for example, in terms of blank authoritarianism:

> Their massed, exact designs are so complete;
> Anonymous and identical, they're shaped
> By murderous authorities, built like barracks.
> Servile and vicious in their uniforms,
> In their skins of sleeked metal, these bodies trade.

At the time of writing these bitterly rational descriptions and analyses, Paulin had committed himself to what Thomas Hardy called "a certain provincialism of feeling." However unaccommodating the place of his imagination, it had to be registered with unflinching regard. The poems answered above all to Paulin's own observation that "we should recognize the authority of Belfast's permanent suffering—an authority which is not external but which we are part of and so owe a responsibility to and for." They spoke equally to a Marxian sense of necessary participation in the historical process, and in Paulin's case that process matched his paradoxical sense of hostile fidelity to the colonial locality.

Reckoning with what is bleak and actual in Ulster, in a spirit not of rejection but of gritty endurance, Paulin decries any attempt to subtract self from society—whether it is by solipsism or hedonism. To move outside history is to represent a metaphor for cultural narcissism and collusion. "In a Northern Landscape" rehearses the spurious ethos of a pastoral idyll, which may seem beguiling but is in fact reactionary because asocial:

> Their isolation is almost visible:
> Blue light on snow or sour milk in a cheese-cloth
> Resembles their mysterious element.
> They pickle herrings he catches, eat sauerkraut
> And make love on cold concrete in the afternoons;
> Eaters of yoghurt, they enjoy austere pleasures.
> . . . .
> Like oppressed orphans who have won a fierce
> privacy.

The view that poetry should be "responsible" and "relevant" Paulin found sustained by Lionel Trilling's *Sincerity and Authenticity* (1972) and Richard Sennett's *The Fall of Public Man* (1977), which he described as "two devastating critiques of that ethic of authenticity which pervades European culture. It sets intimate personal feeling above impersonal social relations and codes of behaviour, and its intense narcissism—to give one example—finds an extreme contemporary expression in Ingmar Bergman's dreary accounts of desperate affairs on isolated Nordic islands." This exacting sense of the primacy of civil and social contracts informs even the last poem of *A State of Justice*, "Also an Evasion," which censures a figure who fusses with the entries in his journal: "they're just a pottering/ About the time I own," and a means of failing to register "The cries of children in gardens/Softing like white songs/That'll never reach these glazed boards." That fine cadence and brilliantly piquant set of puns ironically expose the speaker's indifference to the clamorous needs of the children at his door.

The best achieved poems of the book carry imaginative weight beyond preformulated assertion or rational strictures; as in "Bradley the Last Idealist" and "Settlers," they suggest narrative or potent metaphor. "*Fin de Siècle*" evokes the class divide between a "linen girl" who inhabits a large house with a "silver pond"—she is a chimera only to be attained by overleaping social contingencies—and a man who both represents and is tied to political reality:

The beeches in this green demesne,
The dovecote by the summer-house,
Will never tell how when a culture sends
A hopeless man to love a drifting girl,
Then never lets them touch or kiss,
Its selfish flowers have begun to stink.

As Paulin explained in an interview, "what I was getting at is the way history strives towards a social ideal—a good and just society—and never achieves the ideal. Roughly, the man is history and the girl is the ideal. She is too pure because her ideal consciousness is detached from the practical world."

Although Paulin's poetry of the mid-1970s brings into ambivalent focus a spiritually null and apparently intractable social reality, it does intimate imaginative redemption. "Newness" and "The Hyperboreans" afford a more tenderly perceived purposiveness, reviewing dour actuality as an envisioned order. So does "A New Society":

Just watching this—the laid-out streets, the mixers
Churning cement, the new bricks rising on their
    foundations—
Makes me want to believe in some undoctrinaire
Statement of what should be. A factual idealism.

The poem ends with intelligent irony by apprehending "an unremarkable privacy,/A vegetable silence there for the taking," but as a whole it is uncomfortably deliberative. Paulin's trenchant sense of responsibility left him suspicious of vision and transcendence, and a number of the early poems manage only to give form to fact, composing but not quite rescuing the social burden.

However, by the end of the 1970s Paulin found that his imagination and political commitment need not be bound by the given historical order. Being far less disposed to shoulder a static parochialism, he posited a developing state—a full cultural identity which should be republican and nonsectarian. As he explained in the introduction to his collection of essays, *Ireland and the English Crisis* (1984), "Until about 1980 I . . . believed what most Ulster Protestants still believe—that Northern Ireland was, and ought to remain, permanently wedded to Great Britain. Although I had always hated Ulster Unionism very bitterly and supported the Civil Rights movement from the beginning, I believed that social rights and greater social justice could be achieved within the context of the United Kingdom. . . . With this change of mood went a rejection of that attitude held by many people— men mostly—who belong to the sixties generation.

It is a deeply earnest attitude which identifies with a form of hyperborean and Lawrentian provincialism, and it is hostile to the idea of institutions, formality, opera, educated southern accents, and the necessary insincerities of good manners. Although I shall always remain what Henry Joy McCracken called 'a northern,' I no longer feel, either in Ireland or England, any hostility towards a southern insouciance. It seems wrong to hug too close that 'provincialism of feeling' which Hardy recommended."

This development gives overall design and internal tension to *The Strange Museum* (1980). While several of the poems still incisively analyze what is made "fixed and dull" by a tyrannous institution, the poet's imagination has become more challenging, his language more energetic—formal and tender, mixing *gravitas* with *civilitas*. The "public uniform" ("Surveillances") and "factual establishments" ("Before History") he still records with

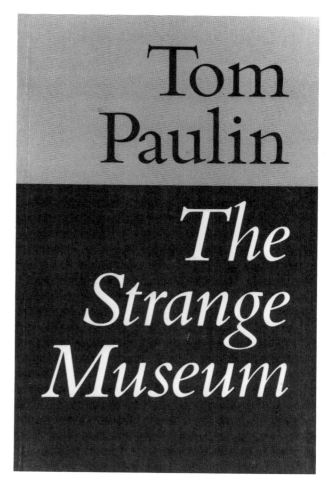

Front cover for Paulin's 1980 volume of poetry, his second collection to be recommended by the Poetry Book Society

anger, but the citizens with a redeeming reverence, as in "An Authorized Fear":

> I look into faces, see grief in strangers,
> But not the thing I fear. So I watch them there,
>
> Spending tears and wasting their allotted time,
> Mourners who stand weeping in a lost garden.

Other fine poems engage a Chekhovian tact in characterizing figures who are displaced and unfulfilled. "Anastasia McLaughlin" recovers late-Victorian Belfast society, and a diminishing nostalgic delicacy is poignantly commemorated in "The Harbour in the Evening":

> Victorian childhoods
> Where little stick figures go flickering
> Along the roads? Such eagerness that used to be.

In his critical study *Thomas Hardy: The Poetry of Perception* (1975), Paulin had vigorously argued against the servile limitations of an empirical epistemology. Although Hardy was an agnostic positivist, his poems were not subservient to observed facts, Paulin stressed, but at their best transformed observations into visionary presences. While not eschewing his political identity, Paulin's own metaphorical narratives in *The Strange Museum* likewise gain access to the transfusing valuation of imaginative vision. "Trotsky in Finland" focuses on Trotsky's own ironic recognition that even he once savored a moment out of history: he "consumes" the "bourgeois moment" in which an actress "admires her face / Bloomed in the smooth lake," before resuming the path of his destiny. "An orthodox Marxist," Paulin explained elsewhere, "would argue that to seek such moments of pure being within political reality is to perforate history with an escapist concept of bourgeois leisure; however a glance at the extraordinary closing paragraphs of Chapter 13 of Trotsky's autobiography will show that even the most dedicated revolutionary could turn from politics to a numinous stillness" (*Encounter,* May 1979).

In a review of *The Strange Museum* for the *Times Literary Supplement* (4 April 1980), John Bayley correctly pointed out that, like Seamus Heaney (to whom he is in many ways dissimilar), Paulin is both sardonic and graceful in his poetry. That graciousness is fully achieved in "The Idea in History," a poem which "plots" an evolutionary shape from Schopenhauerian purity—

> Out of soft starfish
> The first eye opened
> To a pure shrill light

—toward the unambiguous achievement of civil order:

> Surfacing like a white fish,
> A consciousness is forming.
> It travels from bland minsters
>
> To snowcem estates, ideal
> Under mountains that were wet,
> Bare, until the builders came.

Paulin no longer finds that the historical consciousness is a grueling and stagnant burden, to be faced in a spirit of grim memorial dedication, but that it offers opportunities for formal celebration. While some poems of *The Strange Museum* assimilate Ulster to the lessons of "a dank *mitteleuropa,*" others describe a new order, with self-delight and formal freedom. In practical political terms it may be that Paulin is envisioning a state that is little more than a platonic ideal, but he validates the ideal by grace of imaginative expression. As he explained with canny irony, "Some writers are compulsive mnemonists who dream of strolling in the gardens of forgetfulness."

"The Garden of Self-Delight" misgivingly appeals to a Mediterranean aestheticism, "Saying art is for itself / and prays to mirrors in the sand, / Its own mirrors of burnt sand / where the smooth forms look pure," in the inalienable knowledge—as he phrases it in another poem, "The Other Voice"—that "The fear of necessity / Is an absolute narrative." With even less sense of compromise, however, "Man with Hookah" shares the relaxed experience of Indian culture:

> those smiling couples with their long noses
> And oval eyes
> Swim playfully inside a graceful love.

John Bayley remarked that "the poems in this volume have . . . begun to take themselves seriously, and with markedly debilitating effect." But his comment that Paulin had given himself over to a facile seriousness, with pointed commentary and predictably loaded images, neglects the shaping tension and plotting of the whole book. Neil Corcoran in the *PN Review* (1980) exercised better judgment in describing "the fine analytical passion" of the ways in which Paulin contrives the "oppositions and confrontations" of his poems—including poetry and political fact, "tender absenteeism" and exacting civility. "But Paulin's essential quality," Corcoran properly remarked, "is a kind of Marvellian compaction of an uninsistent personal cadence with a generous, clear-eyed, unsentimental public responsibility. . . ." Although Paulin has commonly found himself pressed, out of bitterness or frustration, to make overt and even assertive statements in some poems, he is equally alive to the temptation of "careless aestheticism." It is the great achievement of *The Strange Museum* to test and mediate between those tendencies of his imagination.

The title poem embodies in little the shape of the volume as a whole, which Paulin has said he "spent a long, agonizing time revising and shaping. . . . From the first poem to the last there's meant to be a kind of parabola—where do you find the living form that expresses the spirit?" The first stanzas of "The Strange Museum" describe the past as a "patriarch's monument" in which the speaker may have been "some servile spirit . . . locked in a fierce doctrine of justification": his recourse, as Paulin described it in *Viewpoints*, is to escape history

"into the banal pleasantries of suburbia which it's a mistake to undervalue":

> There was the rickety fizz of starlings
> trying to sing, and a grey tenderness.
> I was happy then, knowing the days had changed
> and that you would come back here, to this room.
> You were the season, beyond weather, the first fresh-
>   ness.

The tripping excitement at the beginning of these lines formally gives place to the ceremonious measures of love. That kind of conclusion is echoed in the liturgical character of the final lines of "A Lyric Afterwards": "there is this great kindness everywhere:/now in the grace of the world and always." Paulin had certainly reached the stage of being able to compose "ideas as spirit developing and expressing itself in form."

In a remarkable article published in the "Viewpoint" column of the *Times Literary Supplement* (21 March 1980), Paulin denounced "the present fierce trivialization of both political thinking and

Front cover for Paulin's 1983 volume of poetry, described by the publisher as a collaboration with artist Noel O'Connor

aesthetic judgment." Citing Trotsky's "Class and Art," on the one hand, he argued against the cruel error of subordinating art to ideology, since the rhetoric of confrontation can only lead to slogans and barbarous activism. Equally "if you enforce an absolute separation between art and politics, art will become over-exquisite, privatized and insouciant. . . ." The burden of his argument is that art and politics are faces of one coin, and to split them is a form of debasement that amounts to the abolition of both. "Committed art and hard-line politics are identical twins, just as a bored flaccid political climate accompanies, or is implied by, an exclusive aestheticism."

The identification of art and politics is pursued in Paulin's most recent volume of poetry, *Liberty Tree* (1983), which is both trenchant in its attacks on the civic disease of Ulster Protestantism and more sprightly in embracing a visionary ideal. Whereas *A State of Justice* could sometimes be crude in depicting contemporary servility, using a simple rhetoric of statement, the poems of *Liberty Tree* are more sophisticated and resourceful. They are both mature in the use of visionary imagination and fierce in their satirical bite, as well as being sometimes strategically clownish. In "Manichean Geography I" Paulin finds painfully comic and often confounding analogues for the gross mentality generated by colonial imposition:

> Seeding like brisk parachutes,
> The ancestral spirits will fall
> From the pod of an airship,
>
> And the chosen people will serve
> Themselves with orange jube-jubes
> In a brand-new discount warehouse.

In " 'What Kind of Formation are the B Specials?,' " the censor's stamp—"magenta and military"—in post-Solidarity Poland brings into adroit focus "a strange/shivering translation/where the kingdom of letters/is like the postal system/of a frozen state." In the Ulster village of "Desertmartin" he sees another chilling likeness:

> Masculine Islam, the rule of the Just,
> Egyptian sand dunes and geometry,
> A theology of rifle-butts and executions:
> These are the places where the spirit dies.
> And now, in Desertmartin's sandy light,
> I see a culture of twigs and bird-shit
> Waving a gaudy flag it loves and curses.

Reviewing *Liberty Tree* for the *Times Literary Supple-*

ment (2 September 1983), Michael O'Neill found "disfiguring contempt" in the last three lines quoted, but Paulin is characterizing the complex contradictions of the so-called "loyalty" of Official Ulster Unionism, which embraces a terrible paradox that validates his comparison with Islamic Revivalism: it is certainly "a form of shock-tactics" (as Stephen Romer called it in *PN Review*, 1984), a one-sided and explosive convocation. Paulin explained his purposes in *Viewpoints:* "By taking a historical event and translating it into imaginative terms or drawing imaginative parallels with it, you're suddenly transforming it perhaps into the world of myth—certainly into the realm of what is fictive. And by doing that you are actually punching a hole in the historical process and opening up an imaginative view of it."

Certain other poems are obscure and indeterminate, exploiting Ulster dialect (and some neologisms) to affirm a sense of cultural identity. Paulin has written that "it is perfectly possible to draw on, say, French and Irish without being aligned with a particular concept of society. For creative writers this can adumbrate a pure civility which should not be pressed into the service of history or politics." But he is not unaware that linguistic exclusion has another obvious effect: to vex or defy the English reader who has no immediate access to dialect introduced at such density. Many instances nonetheless produce poetry of rich metaphorical implication, as in "Martello," an account of Ulster Unionists:

> Lymphatic and nettly, like jellyfish
> crowding in a duskiss tide,
> their images slop against the eyes;
> and what dory monsters glup to the surface,
> each like a plated turd with a pilot-light.

The comic voice which is by turns vehement and warm is very much part of Paulin's progressively capacious sense of imaginative freedom, his deepening attention to contemplation and vision. In the dialogue included in "And Where Do You Stand on the National Question?," Paulin's poetic voice relishes "this local stir in us all"—"a word's relish,/the clitoral tick of an accent,/wee lick of spit or lovejuice"—and declares (with a subversive allusion to Henry James):

> "I want a form that's classic and secular,
> the risen *République*,
> a new song for a new constitution—
> wouldn't you rather have that
> than stay loose, baggy and British?"

TOM PAULIN
Ireland and the English Crisis

In these brilliantly argued essays on English and Irish literature, Tom Paulin shows how writers react to political struggles and cultural change – from Joyce in colonial Ireland and Auden in England in the Thirties to today's Belfast poet or Derry dramatist. The keynote of this controversial book is the phrase *'writing to the moment'*. And like Samuel Richardson – whose motto this was – Tom Paulin is writing *in* the instant, about the present, and for the current age.

Switching from hard-hitting attack to equally fierce defence, Tom Paulin tackles the present crisis in English studies. In a now notorious discussion of structuralism in education, he routs those radical critics and "semioticians" who would reduce literature to "texts", and who analyse Shakespeare and soap operas under the same heading of "ecriture". This exemplary incisive essay confronts critical fashions like "deconstruction" and exposes their destructive limitations.

Tom Paulin is outspoken and uncompromising in pursuit of social justice and artistic freedom and integrity. This collection includes his famous polemic against Conor Cruise O'Brien, as well as his careful, rigorous account of Ian Paisley's writings and pronouncements. In these and in other essays he establishes a historical and cultural perspective, exploring first the "Englishness" of D.H. Lawrence, John le Carre, and the expatriate Henry James, then the "Anglo–Irishness" of Oscar Wilde, William Trevor and Louis MacNeice.

These forceful essays will contribute to a tradition of critical independence. They will combat what Tom Paulin calls the 'terminal self-disgust' with which much contemporary literary criticism is afflicted.

Tom Paulin lectures in English at the University of Nottingham, and in 1983–84 is a visiting lecturer at the University of Virginia at Charlottesville. A leading Irish poet, he has published three books of poems, *A State of Justice* (1977), *The Strange Museum* (1980), and *Liberty Tree* (1983), all from Faber, as well as a collaboration with the artist Noel Connor, *The Book of Juniper* (from Bloodaxe – see page 25). His critical study *Thomas Hardy: the Poetry of Perception* was published by Macmillan in 1975.

216 x 138mm. 208 pages. Autumn 1983.
£8.95 cloth 906427 63 0.
£4.50 paper 906427 64 9.

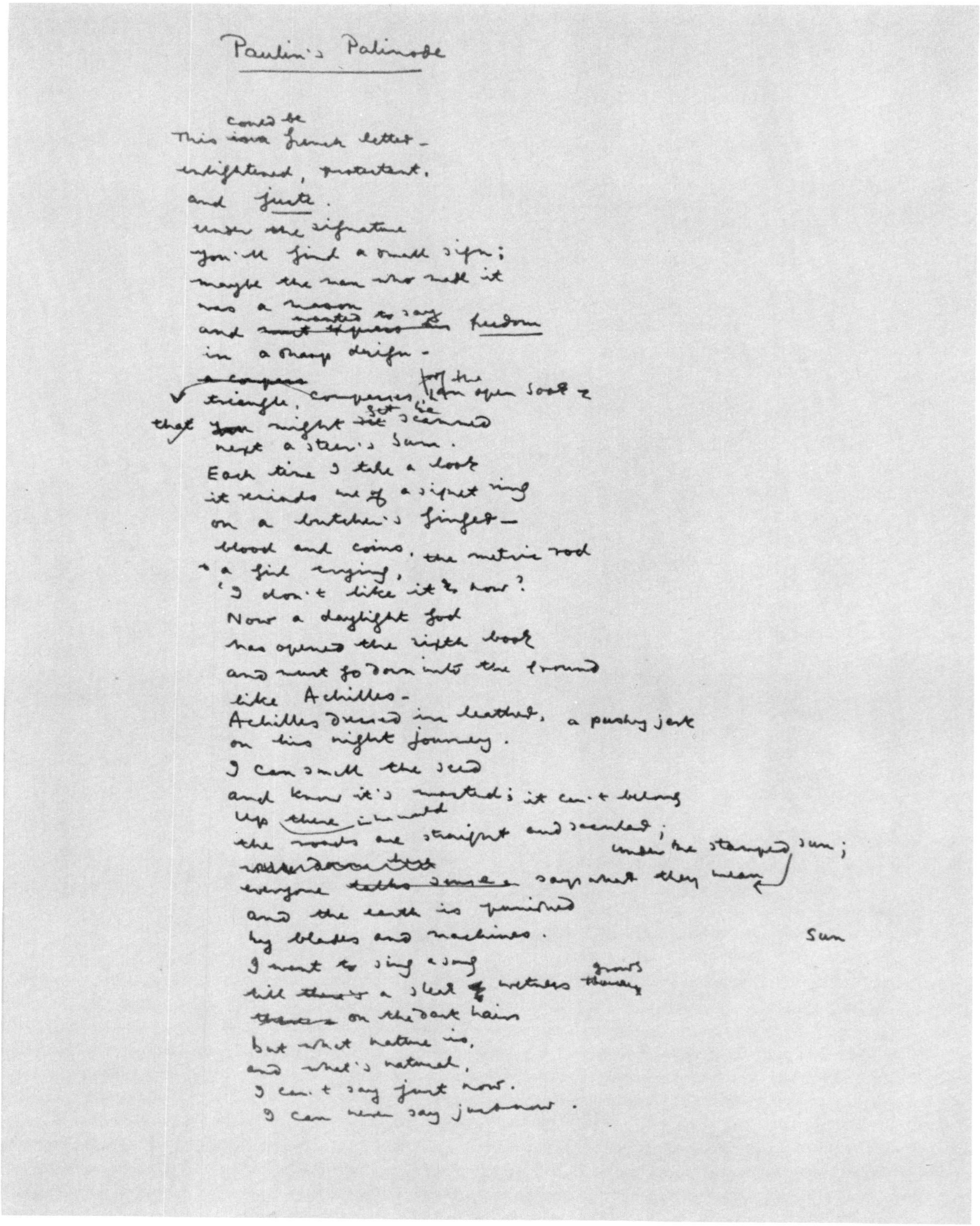

Paulin's Palinode

Draft for a recent poem (the author)

That note of formal declaration is sustained in other poems, including "A Nation, Yet Again," which proposes—with "a delicate, a tough, new style"—to conciliate northern exigencies with southern pleasures. As Paulin keenly pointed out in an uncollected review of *The Faber Book of Poems and Places* (*Times Literary Supplement,* 16 January 1981), there are "points of intersection between history and the floating present, or between temporal experience in a place and the visions that transcend it." The principal sequence of *Liberty Tree,* "The Book of Juniper," an emblematic lyric of exceptional grace and craft—"a miniature epic/of the boreal forest"—invokes a dream of the ideal:

> that sweet
> equal republic
> where the juniper
> talks to the oak,
> the thistle,
> the bandaged elm,
> and the jolly, jolly chestnut.

Moving with sinuous, two-stressed lines, "The Book of Juniper" carries a stately prophecy, binding aesthetic formality with political implication. The poem is certainly more than a fond platonic fancy, for its achievement is to exemplify the civil grace it proposes.

Tom Paulin's earliest work recorded a dulled social reality with laconic and unenergizing rigor, but within a decade he has advanced into imaginative freedom—and without suspending his strict sense of the identity of art and politics. With a developing but disciplined hedonism, perhaps partly encouraged by the examples set by Craig Raine and Christopher Reid, Paulin is making of himself what he has called James Joyce: a politicized aesthete.

His poetry has received the Eric Gregory Award (1976) and the Somerset Maugham Award (1978), and he was joint winner, with Paul Mul-

doon, of the 1982 Geoffrey Faber Memorial Award. For the academic year 1983-1984 he was a Fulbright Scholar at the University of Virginia. His future work seems likely to include more extended narrative poems and translations; he is currently compiling *The Faber Book of Political Verse,* and he has already produced *The Riot Act* (forthcoming from Faber & Faber in 1985), an idiomatic version of Sophocles' *Antigone* which reveals a precise application for the play in the modern tragedy of Northern Ireland. The *Times Literary Supplement* review of the theater production (19 October 1984) acclaimed it as a "powerful version." Paulin's prospects should make it increasingly and happily appropriate to match him with his own description of Joyce: "Joyce is both *flâneur* and rebel, aesthete and revolutionary, and his gay, joyous, libertarian vision is remarkable for its ruthlessly ironic intelligence and for a pure delight in style and surface. He is a deeply European figure dreaming of an impossible country. . . ."

Interviews:

P. R. King, "Tom Paulin," *Nine Contemporary Poets: A Critical Introduction* (London: Methuen, 1979), pp. 228-235;

John Haffenden, "Tom Paulin," *Viewpoints: Poets in Conversation* (London: Faber & Faber, 1981), pp. 157-173.

References:

John Bayley, "In the uniform of the disarmed," *Times Literary Supplement,* 4 April 1980, p. 384;

Neil Corcoran, "Stillness into history," *PN Review,* 7, no. 4 (1980): 55-56;

Michael O'Neill, "Cultural Imaginings," *Poetry Review,* 72 (June 1982): 68-69;

Claude Rawson, "Telling Stories," *Poetry Review,* 73 (September 1983): 59-61;

Stephen Romer, "Spicing the bitter," *PN Review,* 10, no. 5 (1984): 53-54.

Tom Pickard
(1 January 1946-   )

Ken Smith

SELECTED BOOKS: *High on the Walls* (London: Fulcrum Press, 1967; New York: Horizon, 1968);
The Order of Chance (London: Fulcrum Press, 1971);
Guttersnipe (San Francisco: City Lights, 1971);
Dancing Under Fire (Philadelphia: Middle Earth Books, 1973);
Hero Dust: New and Selected Poems (London: Allison & Busby, 1979; New York: Schocken, 1979);
OK Tree (Durham: Pig Press, 1980);
Jarrow March (London: Allison & Busby, 1981; New York: Schocken, 1981);
Custom and Exile (London: Allison & Busby, forthcoming 1985; New York: Schocken, forthcoming 1985).

TELEVISION: *Squire,* BBC 2, 1974;
The Jarrow March, BBC 3, 1976.

RADIO: *Great Day of His Wrath,* BBC Radio 3, circa 1975.

Tom Pickard is a poet and prose writer, and in more recent years an author of plays and documentaries for radio, film, and television. This later work, based in personal interpretation of careful research and interview techniques, bears a close relation to his poetry, both as an enlargement of his earlier work and as source and renewal of his poetry. Over the years, as he has moved outward intellectually and geographically from the confines of his early experience, he has articulated the voices of his region and his class and its culture. Moving from the North East of England to London, and from London to Warsaw, Tom Pickard's work has expanded with his vision into an authentic voice of experience closely felt and sharply drawn.

Born in Newcastle upon Tyne in 1946, he was adopted by a great-aunt and uncle, and grew up on Tyneside, an heir to working-class and Northumbrian attitudes deepened in defiance of a history of long poverty, unemployment, and class conflict. The North East of England, long a deprived area, finds its roots in the old kingdom of North Humberland, and its historic discontinuities in the Industrial Revolution and the struggles of the last two centuries. It is a landscape represented often by absence—by closed shipyards and coal pits, by strikes and wrecked communities. Such a history is one of uprooting, of internal exile and urban blight, and of resentment at the richer South. It is also a landscape of open country, moorland, and dramatic coastline, much of it scarred by mining, where country and city confront each other, often sullenly. By tradition the Geordie is fiercely independent, loyal to his class and dialect, the bearer of a pride that has often proved self-defeating; his is also the history of the sellout, of the elected representative toadying to his masters:

> councillor elected by my father
> he said you wore a workers cap
>   called everybody marra
> but the word I heard was slave
>
>   bloodfluke in the brain of an ant
>   that gold chain was scraped
> from the lungs of pit men
>
>   your gown is a union leader
> gutted and reversed.

The experience of struggle has, nevertheless, traditionally produced a class solidarity. There are surviving traditions of song and dance, the music of pipes and colliery bands that continues despite closures and sentimentalities. The Geordie tongue is a quick singing speech full of humor and lyricism, harsh to the "southron's" ear yet tender in content. Like all dialect, it nurtures those who speak it while it may be used to exclude outsiders. A vigorous dialect of English, it retains the inventiveness and coinings of the old Germanic and Scandinavian languages that have produced it, and a large vocabulary of its own.

Born to such speech, Tom Pickard's work demonstrated early its robustness, adapting its properties of song and storytelling. His early work found its beginnings in street song and ballad, wit and bawdy and sharp observations and protest. His poems are often epigrammatic, making use of assonance and the music of his native tongue and turning all into an individual style.

In an article, "Serving my time to a trade" (*Paideuma,* volume 9, number 1), Pickard describes himself in 1963 and in the years that followed. He had left school at fourteen and without further formal education undertook his own study, entering the commonality of urban experiences: work of any sort when work was to be found, and always the return to the dole office as a statistic in the "bank of human capital." He had already begun to write. With others he founded a magazine (*Eruption*), a bookshop (Ultima Thule), and, in a medieval tower on the Newcastle city wall, the Mordern Tower reading series that was to become an international poetry center. Through such outlets Pickard began to establish contact with a larger world, with poets Jonathan Williams, Allen Ginsberg, Basil Bunting. At that time Bunting was living and working in Newcastle. He and his poetry had sunk into an obscurity assigned him by fashion and the English literary establishment. Bunting was to encourage Pickard, and indeed Pickard was to encourage Bunting through mutual criticism and support. Through the Mordern Tower there was a platform for readings and an ethos in which to write. Recognition, slow to come and intermittent when it did so, arrived as a Northern Arts grant in 1965 and Arts Council of Great Britain awards in 1969 and 1973. And in America there were wider horizons beckoning: "By some route I came across the Beat movement and first got a sniff of the Americans, discovering a punchy, taut and tender language. Following through some of the Beat's major sources I came to e. e. cummings, Whitman, Pound. . . ."

In 1967 Fulcrum Press published *High on the Walls,* confirming Pickard's growing reputation, much of it underground, as a poet. "Few poems, but new and lasting, their maker very young," Bunting wrote in his preface to the book. "Tradition and fashion have no power over a man who has escaped education, with fresh eyes, fresh voice, and skill to keep the line compact and musical." Yet there are continuities of the past into the present—analogies of industrial and domestic life with writing itself ("a trade"), the survivals of the old life of penury, labor, defiance, servility, of men "proud to be humbled by their superiors," of "The thudding industrial hammer/is not much harder than the men it has made." And in "Nenthead," describing the pathos of a worked-out lead mine, can be found echoes of the music and alliteration of an older poetry—

> where the crag crumbles
> and the murmer turns
> the stone to sand.

"Sometimes men make sounds as birds do—just to sing," Robert Creeley has said of Pickard's work. In later years Pickard was to write songs for Alan White and Alan Hull of Lindisfarne, and to work with Alan Price, late of The Animals. His abilities as a singer and a teller of stories continued to produce a poetry intended for the voice, sung or spoken, but aloud.

By the late 1960s he was married to Connie Davidson, an associate in the Mordern Tower. There were two children. The marriage was later dissolved. Pickard was beginning to outgrow the North East, traveling to London and America. With *The Order of Chance* (1971) the elements of his earlier work began to deepen into the landscape of dream and nightmare. The song became the chant, as in "New Body":

Dust jacket for Pickard's 1971 book, in which the urban setting of his earlier poems deepens into a landscape of dream and nightmare

As you expected thunder
I was calm

As you expected blood
I was stone

As you expected shape
I was air

And the poetry began encountering the commercial world of London, exploring division and loss—"the space between us," growing more confident in its expression of an erotic, often savage, innocence. The book's title is expressive of the discovery of an order made from circumstance and discovery. As Desmond Graham has said, "his is a poetry of what the moment invents, however brief, and the art is that of timing."

Such a poetry runs the risk of being overlooked as incidental, fragmentary, imagistic. Pickard's sources in Ezra Pound and Louis Zukofsky would deny this; "Throughout Pickard's work form itself is a political act," Graham further remarks. With Pickard defiance of the existing norms and forms of literature take their counterpart in resistance to the prescribed orders of society and politics. Always he has gone on to invent and adapt form, to "say it in your own words."

Experiments with prose narrative and the picaresque led to *Guttersnipe* (1971), and with dramatic form to the semiautobiographical television play *Squire* (1974). In 1973 Pickard moved to London, and there followed a variety of scripts and documentaries for radio and television, most notably *The Jarrow March* (1976), a celebration of the march of the unemployed from the North of London in 1936. Among the "southrons" he was awarded a C. Day Lewis Fellowship by the Greater London Arts Association (1976-1977), and from 1979 to 1980 he was creative writer in residence at the University of Warwick. Other work has included scripts and stories for children, and a BBC Radio 3 commissioned documentary on the nineteenth-century arsonist of York Minster,

Jonathan Martin, *Great Day of His Wrath.*

All this work is to be considered as a whole, and the divisions imposed by genre to some degree artificial. Much of his work reappears as poetry (*The Jarrow March,* for instance), drafted and reworked. The title poem from *The Order of Chance,* extensively reworked and expanded, became *Dancing Under Fire* (1973). There is an ecstatic quality to this poem, its title to be taken literally and metaphorically. It reshapes experience: love, oppression, individuality, the past predicating the present: "father you built the lines I travel on/my direction was laid by your sweat and death." Eric Mottram points to the poem's combining of "a variety of prosodic forms with experience of dream, the writings of Jung and the felt life of Newcastle and the North East, day to day life known by a working class man with a developed literary education." The poem's inner narrative of Marta, the war-wounded veteran, draws backward to origins in children's rhymes, forward into chant. As Mottram explains, "New forms convey the myth and ritual of folk and tribal poetry."

The poem was to appear in *Hero Dust* (1979), a collection of new and selected poems. Here the horizons of Pickard's work have widened to embrace England, America, and Eastern Europe. In 1976 he traveled to Warsaw and there met Joanna Voit, a Polish artist. They were married in 1978 and have a son, sharing their lives between Warsaw and London. Love, tenderness, travel, the alienations imposed by frontiers, inform these poems more and more, and with *Hero Dust* Pickard can be said to have matured into a poet of the heart and all its passions:

a city in your smile
   a continent on this tongue
an ocean on those lips

A further collection of poems, *Custom and Exile,* remixing the erotic and the political preoccupations of Pickard's work with poems set in America and Poland, is to appear in 1985.

Peter Porter
(16 February 1929-   )

Thomas Dilworth
University of Windsor

BOOKS: *Once Bitten, Twice Bitten* (Northwood: Scorpion Press, 1961);

Penguin Modern Poets 2, by Porter, Kingsley Amis, and Dom Moraes (Harmondsworth: Penguin, 1962);

Poems Ancient and Modern (Lowestoft, Suffolk: Scorpion Press, 1964; New York: Walker, 1964);

Words Without Music (Oxford: Sycamore Press, 1968);

Solemn Adultery at Breakfast Creek: An Australian Ballad, words by Porter and music by Michael Jesset (London: Keepsake Press, 1968);

A Porter Folio: New Poems (Lowestoft, Suffolk: Scorpion Press, 1969);

The Last of England (London & New York: Oxford University Press, 1970);

Epigrams by Martial (London: Poem-of-the-Month Club, 1971);

After Martial (London & New York: Oxford University Press, 1972);

Preaching to the Converted (London & New York: Oxford University Press, 1972);

Jonah (London: Secker & Warburg, 1973);

A Share of the Market (Belfast: Ulsterman, 1973);

Roloff Beny in Italy, by Porter and Anthony Thwaite (London: Secker & Warburg, 1974);

Peter Porter Reads from His Own Work [book and record] (St. Lucis: University of Queensland Press, 1974);

Living in a Calm Country (London & New York: Oxford University Press, 1975);

The Lady and the Unicorn (London: Secker & Warburg, 1975);

The Cost of Seriousness (London & New York: Oxford University Press, 1978);

The Très Riches Heurs (Richmond, Surrey: Keepsake Press, 1978);

English Subtitles (London & New York: Oxford University Press, 1981);

Collected Poems (London & New York: Oxford University Press, 1983).

RADIO: *The Siege of Munster,* BBC, 1971;
The Children's Crusade, BBC, 1973;

All He Brought Back From the Dream, BBC, 1978.

OTHER: *A Choice of Pope's Verse,* edited by Porter (London: Faber & Faber, 1971);

New Poems, 1971-1972: A P. E. N. Anthology of Contemporary Poetry, edited by Porter (London: Hutchison, 1972);

The English Poets: From Chaucer to Edward Thomas, edited by Porter and Anthony Thwaite (London: Secker & Warburg, 1974);

New Poetry 1, edited by Porter and Charles Osborne (London: Arts Council, 1975).

Peter Porter is a poet of unrest. Because this unrest is often moral and sometimes metaphysical, his writing has a prophetic quality rare in contemporary poetry. In the first decade of his career, Porter was a Hamlet raging at the world, seeing dishonesty in sex, emptiness in materialism. According to Alan Brownjohn, this Porter wrote "some of the most ruefully and brutally witty poems" of the 1960s. More than a social satirist, however, Porter is also what Douglas Dunn calls "a tragedian who can't stop laughing." The tragic aspect emerged most clearly during the second decade of Porter's career, when his primary concern was "the tactless misery of self." In the poems of this period passion gives way to resignation, satire to meditation. As before, the language is rich and forceful, but these poems exhibit a mature agility within conventional forms. His craftsmanship, his ironic tone, and his epigrammatic wit may qualify him to be W. H. Auden's successor, as John Lucas claims he is, but Porter's sensibility has an existential edge sharper than Auden's, and Porter has developed a voice distinctively his own. On the basis of his later poetry, several critics, David Selzer among them, would endorse John Lucas's statement that Porter is "one of the best poets now writing."

In person, Porter is gentle, mild-mannered, self-deprecating, and pessimistic. He is also, according to George MacBeth, "a loyal, generous friend." Until about the mid-1960s, Porter was what he himself calls an "unhelpful socialist." Now his social

Evening Standard *Collection,*
BBC Hulton Picture Library

objective is to conform in his own life to the mores of an ideal civilized community. Possibly for this reason he likes, and keeps, cats. He once favored Vienna, perhaps as a reflection of his ideal community; now he prefers Lesina in Italy. However cosmopolitan his cultural affinities, though, the indelible stain of his litmus years is Australian. He himself thinks the reader can hear Australia in the cadences of his verse, particularly in its "dying falls," but Porter's manner and techniques are, as A. D. Hope puts it, "very much those of contemporary English poets rather than contemporary Australian ones." In other words, Porter's forms are usually closed and restricting rather than open and loose in the Australian (and North American) mode.

Porter was born into a fifth-generation Australian family which, on his father's side, had lived in Brisbane since the 1860s. His father, William, was in the wholesale cotton-goods warehousing business. His mother, Marion, was a nurse. On both sides, his family background is urban and mercantile. Porter grew up on the south side of Brisbane, and childhood holidays were spent in Sydney. His regional identity is urban, therefore, and alien to the prevailing pastoral mythos of Australian poetry. Only recently, on a visit, did he see a kangaroo in the wild.

Since childhood, he has had a strong sense of "living a beleaguered existence." An only child, he and his parents were, during the Depression, poor though culturally middle class. His family life ended in his ninth year, in 1938, when his mother died. He was then sent to boarding schools. His father never remarried.

Porter received his formal education at a Church of England grammar school in Brisbane and at Toowomba Grammar School. He could not afford to attend university. At Toowomba he began to read the poets who would influence his own poetry: Shakespeare most of all, and Donne, Rochester, Pope, Smart, Byron, Browning. At nineteen, he read Auden's *The Age of Anxiety* (1947) and, as he puts it, "the scales fell from my eyes." Later influences, not as strong as Auden's, would include English madrigal writers and William Empson.

Instead of attending university, he went to work—as a newspaper reporter in 1947-1948 and subsequently in "the rag trade" or clothing industry. At the age of twenty-two, in 1951, he immigrated to England, where he worked until 1953 as a clerk. Because of difficulty earning a living, he returned for ten months to Brisbane in 1954. There, and again in London later, he continued to work as a clerk. In 1956 he worked as a bookseller—a job he in some ways enjoyed but which paid badly, and in 1959 he began to work in advertising as a copywriter. He disliked this work, but it paid well and gave him spare time to read, to study languages, and to write. He remained in advertising for ten years. In 1961 Porter married Janice Henry, a nurse. The following year, their daughter Katherine was born, and a second daughter, Jane, arrived in 1965. The financial responsibilities of raising a family may partly explain Porter's persevering in advertising. At any rate, in the context of his uncongenial employment, his early poetry takes on additional, autobiographical significance.

Porter's first collection, *Once Bitten, Twice Bitten* (1961), is powerful in its imagery and, with slight modulation, bitter in tone. Some poems reflect his Australian childhood, but most are set in London, and these concern lust, death, and materialism. Always the primary, underlying subject is the speaking self. In the bitter satires spoken in the first person, Porter is often selective, presenting only the most negative aspect of his target, so that even when the reader also disapproves of the object of his

anger, he feels there must be an undisclosed, subjective explanation for its intensity. Porter implies his awareness of this hidden dimension in "John Marston Advises Anger," spoken by a modern equivalent to Marston's renaissance malcontent. But whether or not a subjective source is always deliberately implied, the satiric impact is limited because the internal wound is unacknowledged and its precise nature withheld. Even so, these poems, like the rantings of John Osborne's angry young man, rivet the reader's attention. (Porter saw the first performance of *Look Back in Anger* at the Royal Court Theatre in 1956.) By contrast to the first-person satires, subjectivity is up front in what Porter calls his "near dramatic" monologues. And in these monologues, subjectivity usually finds poetic justification in objective circumstance. One of the best of these monologues is "Annotations on Auschwitz"—a powerfully prophetic poem, which combines subjectivity with history in a way that makes profound sense of its concluding nonsense statement, that "all poultry eaters are psychopaths." Another impressive monologue, "Conversations of Death," conflates lust, commercialism, and madness in a way that implies their metaphorical equivalence. In both of these poems, Porter's method is that of the metaphysical poets, who risk incomprehensibility so that the reader can find for himself an underlying meaning. Other particularly fine poems in *Once Bitten, Twice Bitten* are "Metamorphosis," "Tobias and the Angel," "Beast and the Beauty," and "The Picture of Nobody."

In this first collection, Porter is sometimes technically clumsy. The failure to justify emotion is, of course, a failure in technique. In addition, the requirements of prosody frequently distort his language, forcing him to be cryptic or to relinquish grammatical sense, as when he uses adjectives for nouns ("Private abounds in verities"). In order to rhyme especially, he distorts natural syntax. Sometimes rhyming trivializes a poem, though with some poems it serves to place the tongue in cheek. Too many lines go dead ("He happens upon himself who wants to feel"), but in retrospect the images generally remain fresh—in spite of their conventional surrealism, which Porter himself calls "that trademark of the 'sixties." When the poet contemplates an H-bomb explosion, for example, he sees "light without shadow" and says we "will cry for tears—our own eyes." There are echoes of early Eliot, and of Auden, but these are not obtrusive. Moreover, in the best of these poems, which are usually written in free verse, Porter already has a voice distinctively his own. It is a voice full of neurotic compulsion that carries the reader headlong, sometimes arousing in him the speaker's own repressed panic at being caught in a "bright locked world." This is the poetry of entrapment.

In *Poems Ancient and Modern* (1964) the satirical emphasis is on lust and greed at the expense of love. Porter implies that such perversion of values is perennial by mixing speaking personae from the present and the past. The temporal parallel occurs within poems in his first collection, but here past and present divide to occupy separate poems and give to the entire collection an interesting tension. While Porter thinks that in this book he breaks "out of anal forms into Audenish historicism," he seems also to move through territory somewhere between Browning's *Men and Women* (1855) and Eliot's *The Waste Land* (1922). Generally the historical personae effectively displace the poet, but in a few instances the personae are merely camouflage. An example is "An Anthropologist's Confession," in which a Victorian scientist represses his own sexuality by having a native killed for rape. Here the poet-moralist is clearly and clumsily visible. In "Happening at Sordid Creek," which structurally mimics Ambrose Bierce's "An Occurrence at Owl Creek Bridge," an office worker wakes from an erotic daydream to awareness of mortality ("I was a sieve/that held water"). It is a fine poem, but the word "Sordid" in the title insists on directing the reader's response in a way that is false to the poem. The moral didact is not present, however, in "How to Get a Girlfriend," "The Great Poet Comes Here in Winter," and other fine poems of lyric association.

An outstanding aspect of this collection is its sequences, the best of which is "Punic Problems"— a series of seven fragments spoken by Carthaginians at the time of the wars with Rome. As in St. John Perse's *Anabase* (1924), an ancient civilization is made immediately present. The same effect is apparent throughout this collection which, as a whole, brings social consciousness to a sense of the contemporaneity of ancient city life.

Another aspect of this book that distinguishes it from the first collection is Porter's use of the epigrammatic statement. Such statements are present in earlier poems, but now they constitute entire poems in a staccato of news flashes. For example, "Sydney Cove, 1788" is twenty-five separate statements in thirty-three lines. The autonomy of each statement gives the poem a sense of inclusiveness that makes its brief chronicle seem comprehensive. The fracturing of continuity also approximates a sense of delirium under the hot Australian sun.

"The World of Simon Raven" is another poem that owes its power to the short statement. These, and many other poems whose sentences are not short, are written in a new, energized line most clearly seen in a fine 204-line poem entitled "Blucher's Prospect." The tautness and compression of the verse minimizes moral judgment, and when judgment occurs, gives it punch (high financiers "eat/ Death, buy up meaning"). Often these poems display epigrammatic wit (to a developer, "trees are/ growing on money"). Forceful images do not dominate the poems, as they do in the first book, but original images still appear, as when dawn is called "the bruise of light." In another fine poem, "The Sins of the Father," epigrammatic conciseness, moral judgment, irony, and historical consciousness all contribute to a lyrical awareness of the process of aging. In its diversity of aspects, this poem is the entire book in microcosm.

Porter's next collection, *A Porter Folio* (1969), is, as the title implies, diverse in style, tone, and subject, but death and disapproval of Christianity dominate the collection. Porter's antireligious view colors much of his early poetry, but in this book, especially, God is his whipping boy. Like that Russian Hamlet, Ivan Karamazov, Porter holds God responsible for death and suffering as though they were moral evils. In "After the Temptation," he criticizes a presumptuous nonchalance which he finds to be present in the accounts of the temptation of Jesus. But the implication that this flaw characterizes the whole of the New Testament, or the whole of Christianity, does not seem intellectually sound. Here and in many of the other poems of complaint, moreover, the evil of the subject is exaggerated, as is the tone of the speaker. Such heightening creates a conflict in the reader, for if the tone engages, the distortion of subject alienates. The difficulty is that, as Porter himself puts it, the public voice of his poetry often "approximates the argumentative voice rather than the speech-making voice." His rhetorical posture presumes a reader ready to argue, and on his terms. For readers not so inclined, these poems are not entirely successful.

But many poems in this collection do completely engage the reader. There are fantasies that interiorize objective place and social situation to express their psychological and imaginative contexts with an economy not possible within the conventions of realism. Sometimes Porter plays for the fun of it. There is an unusual, pure lyricism in "Three Poems for Music," which is reminiscent of Yeats, and a more characteristic, analytical lyricism in "My Late T'ang Phase," "The Thirteen Couplets," and a brilliant poem, "Fantasia on a Line of Stefan George." In these inward explorations Porter was finding the mode and tone of what would be the best of his later poems. Here the speaker is most of the poem's content; the reader can roughly equate the speaker with Porter, who once admitted, "One doesn't want the poet to be in his poems the sort of chap he actually is in life, but, by and large, I think in my poems I probably am." Now, however, he achieves a union of intellect and heart that is missing in much of the verse in the earlier collections. In the last of "The Three Dreams," for example, the poet becomes the love poem he writes: "If the ink lasts/this poem will get me finished." And he concludes,

> You're making me on the page
> and smile at the pun.
>
> 'I was born of an act of love
> and now I shall never change.'

Aesthesis is its own heaven, but always in this book the poet comes "back to the wound." The collection ends with "The Porter Song Book," a rapid montage of images and situations focusing on loneliness, death, madness, and boredom. In the last of these sixteen fragments, the montage becomes kaleidoscopic ("LSD   Head of Seth/   Dry ice burn   garden dig   world without   end in   death"), and encompasses the thematic diversity of the collection.

Porter considers *A Porter Folio* his "most discursive book, wasteful but the most free of stylistic hang-ups." While the language of its poems is sometimes, as in the earlier books, manic and cynical, at times now the language is loosely colloquial. Sometimes it is so loose that the poem falls apart, but in so carefully guarded a poet this relaxation is a positive sign. It begins a transition to the less complex and less introverted of Porter's later styles.

A Porter Folio was delayed in publication so that he was able to include in it poems written in 1968 while he was still working at his advertising job. That year he was fired, and he then began working as a free-lance writer, an occupation which, he says, "remains respectable and indigent at the same time." Since 1970, he has also been visiting lecturer at various English and Australian universities, and has received occasional grants.

The poems in his fourth collection, *The Last of England* (1970), are much like those in earlier books, but they also contain an explicitly autobiographical element. In what sometimes reads like an

updating of *The Waste Land,* Porter claims that today classical and Gothic cultures are reduced to cinematic pap, and that everywhere beneath chic surfaces lie banality, aimlessness, and despair. The book's unifying concept and metaphor is contemporary Western man as consumer: instead of living, he merely uses up life. Porter's personal alternative is to be "a consumer of art" because Bach's cantatas, for example, are "things of spirit." As he seems only to half-realize, however, aestheticism is merely refined hedonism, and for a latter-day humanist, however misanthropic, "spirit" means something other than it did for Bach. Even the high culture of the aesthete is largely, therefore, a flight from despair which merely serves, en route, to mix memory and desire. The fashionable void that is modern culture, and which resides as well in the aestheticism of the poet, finds its metaphor in death. Our epitaph will read: "Here they belong/Who died so young although they lived so long." Poems such as "On This Day I Complete My Fortieth Year" disclose a personal interiority to complement the empty surfaces of the satirical poems. Self-disclosure lies at the heart of the collection, in the "Sanatized Sonnets," which have been widely praised by reviewers. For the first time, Porter reveals the subjective dimension underlying his satire. "The irascible poet/with weak eyes" who accuses others "of being merely/imitations of the perfect/collection of monsters/in his heart" differs from Porter only in thinking the others are not themselves genuinely monstrous. The inclusion of the poet's self somewhat mitigates the arrogance in some of the exclusively satirical poems in this collection.

Porter's language here varies from the loosely colloquial, which is funny and clear, to the elliptical and cryptic. His occasional obscurity is defensive— as the poet, "inside his armoured need," fully realizes. But the difficulty seems unnecessary, and here and in his later work it has probably lost Porter a great many readers. Rhyme now no longer distorts syntax, but it sometimes introduces distractingly haphazard imagery which contributes to obfuscation. As Alan Brownjohn put it, the "more intimate ruminative poems are among the best" in this book. They unite the man who suffers with the poet who creates, and if the former wears a suit of armor, at least he has his visor up.

In *After Martial* (1972), the discipline of translation frees Porter, temporarily, from defensive complexity. He relaxes into his Roman alter ego— an epigrammatic poet who, in his early twenties, left his native land (Spain) for his culture's capital city. Porter recreates forty-seven of Martial's epi-

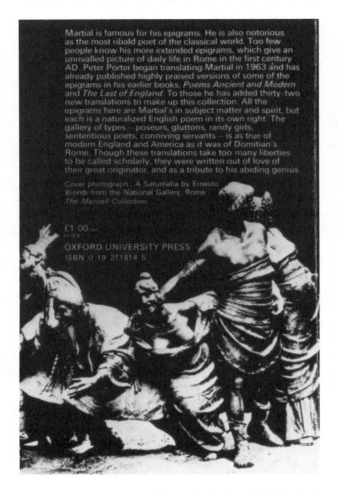

Covers for Porter's 1972 book, "recreations" of forty-seven Latin epigrams

grams, mostly lesser-known ones. In his introduction, which should be a *vade mecum* for translators of poetry, Porter says he concentrates on the *effect* of the poem in Latin, and declares his primary loyalty to "the poem in English." Four of these translations—"recreations" might be a better word—first appear in *Poems Ancient and Modern;* and *After Martial* does extend that collection's expression of the universality of urban life throughout history. Particularly by his extensive use of anachronism, Porter makes Martial's world contemporary with our own. But there is a fundamental shift in mode here. In Porter's early work, description is incidental to satire. Now, in his "collaboration" with Martial, satire grows out of description, and only a few of the satires are moral. Mostly they reflect social biases. Martial casts barbs at frigid women, men with handicapped girl friends, fat and ugly women, cuckolds, and sexual deviants. The poems project the faults, therefore, as well as the virtues of the Martial perso-

na as an embodiment of his society. That is why, like any gossip, he generates intimacy with his audience, which includes the reader. The sense of Martial as a person dominates the book and unifies its variety of form, tone, and subject matter. Mostly he is ironically witty and, consequently, at a distance from his subject, but he can also be tenderly intimate, as in a beautiful and moving elegy for one of his slaves, a little girl dead at the age of five:

> And monumental earth
> draw back eternal weight from her
> small bones;
>   don't be severe and tread
> on her with gravity: she never did on you.

The pun intensifies the pathos. In the final poems, Martial retires to rural Spain, and celebrates it in pastoral antithesis to urban Rome, in which he has taken a less-approving delight. There is also a moving celebration of friendship. These later poems disclose a generosity and warmth that help explain why the irony of the previous poems in this book is always playful, never bitter. These translations have been praised by reviewers, including Michael Wood, who thinks them "full of wisdom and common sense," but they have not been praised enough. This book is literary magic and, for Porter, a watershed in his development as a poet. He will never be the same after having been Martial.

The reader can sense the change in *Preaching to the Converted* (1972), which Porter himself considers his best book. In this collection, satire is rooted in description, which is weighted with personal feeling. And tone has changed from antagonism to disappointment. This is no longer poetry of statement, of finished conclusions, of verdicts. Thinking, as a process, is restored and, for the reader, the tone is more immediate. Satire persists, broadening its scope from popular culture to fashionable highbrow "Hardly Art"—like the music of John Cage—and the ecological consciousness and natural food

Front cover for the book that Porter considers his best

of suburban romanticism. But in this book Porter's emphasis shifts from satire to elegy. Death haunts nearly every poem, yet the language remains witty. (Sex for "the Over Forties" is a matter of "trying to keep it up with the Joneses.") There are three weak poems and about thirteen that are first-rate. Among these latter are "Evolution," about Jerusalem as an image of personal and social renewal; "An Open and Shut Case," about a sexual encounter, apparently in a dream, which frees one from "the owners of the world"; and "On the Train Between Wellington and Shrewsbury," in which people become increasingly uncomfortable in the presence of a professional pig slaughterer. Rhymed poems sometimes limp, but they usually work, and "Between Two Texts" may be his best poem in rhyme so far. John Lucas, who sees in some of the poems "a knowingness which is merely slick," is certainly right about several of the final "Postcard Poems" being "too slight a joke to earn their keep . . . witty but essentially trivial." In many of the longer poems, however, Porter finds what seems his most congenial form—a poem in free verse of about forty or fifty relatively long lines, varying in rhythm but never far from pentameter. In this fluid form, which allows for thorough elaboration of thought, he writes with complete assurance. It is also the form of many of his best poems in later books. His language now is rich in texture, varied in sound. He is able to relax, and the result is a new magnanimity; this Hamlet has finally reached the end of act four. He still feels existential unease ("ordinary gestures of time working on faces the watermark of hell"), but there is also, if only in drunkenness, an intimation of "a shape to the world, more real/than time, more absolute than music."

Living in a Calm Country (1975) consolidates the gains made in *Preaching to the Converted* and is, in retrospect, the most accessible of Porter's books. The dominant themes are beauty—in art, landscape, and personality—and the paradoxical effect of death, which enhances the importance of beauty by rendering it impermanent. The calm country of the book's title is the self, "calm as a cup." The book is unified as none of Porter's others are, because all of its poems begin in what might be called composition of place. They are meditations proceeding by indirection, in which objects in places evoke dramatic situations and emotional responses. The freedom of the poet's mind in motion generates tonal immediacy for the reader, while place tends to neutralize or objectify the poet's feelings. Place may be the English or Australian countryside, a tidal

Front cover for Porter's 1975 collection, unified by the poet's perception of himself, "Living in a calm country which is me"

"Exit, Pursued by a Bear," is a brilliant four pages of rhyming couplets measuring the commercial world of modern theater against the greatness of Shakespeare. In this poem, satire mixes with qualified celebration. Shakespeare is the "Great Enigma of each generation," but also a man who cared too little about his youngest daughter to educate her to literacy.

Porter still sometimes distorts his poetry to meet the formal requirements of meter and rhyme (for example, in "Studies From Lempriere"), but generally poetic impulse thrives as well in conventional forms as in the longer free-verse poems. Always satire is matched by a depth of feeling and an affection for people that is not evident in the earlier collections. The reviewer for *Choice* noted that in this book Porter has not "fully come to terms with his own experience," but most other readers, such as Douglas Dunn and Russell Davies, have been unqualified in their praise. If he had written nothing else, *Living in a Calm Country* would make Porter an important poet.

In December 1974, after these poems had been written, Peter Porter's wife died at the age of forty-one. She is the "S. J. H." to whom the collection is dedicated. Her death broke Porter's strongest attachment to England, leaving him more than ever uprooted. Although most of his friends and contacts are in England, he feels now that he could be equally at home anywhere in the English speaking world. After his wife's death, he went with his daughters in 1975 to Sydney for five months. He returned to England because his daughters are Londoners and prefer England, though he himself has several times considered returning to Sydney to live.

Porter's next book, *The Cost of Seriousness* (1978), has as its dominant themes art and the suffering of the artist. The cost referred to in the title is pain. The best poems—they are the best Porter has ever written—are elegies for his wife. In "The Easiest Room in Hell" the attic room of her childhood symbolizes the poet's empty self, and in "An Angel in Blythburgh Church" the poet looks at the carved face of an angel, wants to pray, but then remembers his sick wife

> Staring for hours up to the ceiling where
> Nothing is projected—death the only angel
> To shield her from despair.

In "An Exequy" his grief becomes the more poignant for the restraint imposed upon its expression by rhyming couplets. In another of these poems,

pool, an empty home, a tearoom, a painting, or the heaven of the gods. Time, always approximately the same, is celebrated in "Ode to Afternoon." The poet is middle-aged, and repeatedly alludes to the later Eliot, that other poet of afternoon. Some poems originated in a visit to Australia in March and April of 1974, after an absence of twenty years. The visit, at the invitation of the Adelaide Festival, was for Porter a return to roots. One of the poems that commemorates it is "An Australian Garden"— an interplay of light, memory, and mythic imagination which has been much praised by reviewers. The "Baroque Quatrains dedicated to James Fenton" are minor masterpieces—mixing high, sometimes precious style with refreshingly crude language, and evoking a baroque world set not in landscape but within architecture. The book's finale,

"The Delegate," the dead wife speaks from the metaphorical hell of nonexistence. This poem receives the most praise from reviewers but seems marred by the banality of its central pronouncement that *"we are condemned only for our lack of talent."* There is also something disconcerting about using one's dead wife as a speaking persona. But these elegies are all direct and very moving. In them Porter breaks into new territory of the heart, expressing a strength of feeling which is otherwise missing in his later poetry and which is, unlike the strong feeling of the early poems, entirely justified by its occasion.

The other poems in the book are not as moving or impressive. One of the cleverest of these lesser poems is "Three Transportations," which records Gertrude Stein's imagined reaction to Australia. Many of these poems are haunted, such as "The Picture of Nobody," which captures the nostalgia of photograph albums. Porter's writing continues to

Front cover for Porter's 1978 book, poems shaped by the death of his wife in December 1974

move away from London to continental Europe and from satire to discursive meditation. In the process, as John Fuller complains, Porter tends increasingly to wear his culture on his sleeve. In one poem alone, he refers to Horace, Catullus, Baudelaire, Neruda, Auden, Rameau, Beethoven, Meredith, Lope de Vega, Goethe, Schiller, and Donne. Such cultural boasting is characteristic of the less direct of Porter's later poems and is really a highbrow variant of the earlier, satirical naming of names to evoke a "Condé Nast world." The poet is approving now, solemn and reflective, but the paraphernalia of high culture, when not fully integrated into one's imagination over a long period of time, can only be worn, like fancy dress, in a way that smacks of dandyism. There are, furthermore, a few poems in *The Cost of Seriousness* that are weaker than any in the previous collection. His meditation on Melozzo's painting of the Annunciation concludes: "blessed is the virgin/ Who shall be the mother of death." The language is flat; the effect, naive. Despite its faults, however, many reviewers, such as John Fuller and Anne Stevenson, regard *The Cost of Seriousness* as Porter's best book so far. Undoubtedly, in the elegies for his wife, it contains his best poems.

The poems in this collection that are set in Italy reflect five visits there, none longer than three weeks, between 1971 and 1976. Since then he has visited Italy at least once a year.

His next book, *English Subtitles* (1981), concerns the relationship of imagination to life. Its dominant theme is that the imagining of something better makes the actual worse. In "Garden of Earthly Delights," for example, the city as "concrete garden" evokes the pastoral myths it denies. And in "Story that Should Have Happened," the England of imagination stirs anticipation which the real England disappoints. (John Lucas claims this is the best poem of its kind ever written.) We are back in "the Land of Afternoon," through which flows the river of Ecclesiastes. For the poet now, even aesthetic experience is an inadequate refuge from discontent, which is caused partly by something within himself. The most personal revelation of this discontent is an impressive autobiographical poem called "What I Have Written I Have Written," in which Porter admits his lifelong possession of "the little stone of unhappiness." The poem's title quotes Pontius Pilate, and so links up with a poem entitled "The Unlucky Christ," in which Porter sees himself as "chosen . . . to be acquainted with grief." Christ overcame death, but in a world where we weary of each other "to escape unhappiness," death is the least of our sufferings. These poems, which feel the

Front cover for Porter's 1981 book, in which, he has said, he is "entering a new phase, becoming more cryptic and yet more anecdotal at once"

serrated cutting edge of time, are impressive, and there are others as direct and of the same high quality.

There are also poems of indirection, in which Porter displays a new deftness. In them, feeling is aroused without being given a clear conceptual counterpart. Denotative sense is only suggested, glimpsed without being fixed in sight; these poems haunt the mind. They are usually successful and intriguing (see, for example, "The American Articulate"), but they can misfire and remain merely obscure, as in these lines from "Occam's Razor":

> What the gods mean by words
> goes the long way round or takes on flesh
> in dreams for the vistas of nicknames.

A few of these poems—"About on the Serchio," among them—resemble those of the later Mallarmé—not so precious, much more forceful, but communicating almost nothing. They do not fully break out of the poet's subjectivity. Or maybe Porter is carrying to its extreme his own cocktail-party dictum: "Don't try to say what you mean, try to say something a little more interesting than you mean." In any case, these poems may account for Laurence Lerner's being "often puzzled, usually impressed, but only occasionally delighted" with this collection. But on the whole, the poems in this book are remarkably good. As John Lucas writes, "It is a volume of great power and beauty, with all Porter's gifts on show, and very few weaknesses." Porter himself feels that in this collection he is "entering a new phase, becoming more cryptic and yet more anecdotal at once."

Despite his reputation as an intellectual poet, and his Audenesque propensity for rhetorical statement, Porter is primarily a poet of feeling. The appeal of the early satirical poems is, after all, largely their passion. Moreover, the major fault of these early poems is that, even when their passion is justified by its object, they lack philosophical foundation, for Porter is a humanist aware of the bankruptcy of humanism. This fault is intellectual. Porter's rage in these poems is nevertheless near to prophecy, which, unlike satire, requires no moral consensus. Yet even prophecy presupposes a basis surer than the prophet's anger, so that Porter's is a voice crying in its own wilderness. The enduring effect of disproportionate emotion in the early poems is to register dissociated sensibility—the disjunction of feeling and thought—which is endemic to modern civilization. In the later poems, Porter heals this dissociation, for himself at least, by withdrawing from social criticism to a more meditative, personal poetry. The shift is registered in the change in his style from what Douglas Dunn calls "energetically sub-Augustan" to what he later calls "simplified baroque." The synchronization of thought and feeling in the later poems restores intellectual integrity, but as a consequence the early strength of feeling is rarely present. Porter's true subject is the self, and in the later poems he speaks with greater candor about himself. But he continues to work up the texture of his verse into a formal, rhetorical medium, an obvious artifact. In the process, his poetry sometimes becomes needlessly obscure, raising a chorus of complaint. Damian Grant writes, for instance, that he cannot "see why Peter Porter's very public themes—death, love and sex, art—require him to take refuge behind

Peter Porter

occasional mistakes, it also explains his current technical virtuosity, which is unsurpassed by any poet of his generation. But we read him primarily because in most of his poems he tells us important truths about our civilization and ourselves.

Because he is not, in national origin, an "English poet" and not, in subject matter or style, an Australian poet, Porter's achievement is sometimes neglected by academic critics, who tend to think in nationalist categories. But of the poets writing in England (and Ireland) today, Peter Porter is one of the best.

Interviews:

Peter Orr, *The Poet Speaks* (London: Routledge & Kegan Paul, 1966), pp. 179-184;

Philip Martin, "Peter Porter," *Quadrant,* 18 (January/February 1974): 9-14;

"Country Poetry and Town Poetry: A Debate with Les Murray," includes an interview with Porter by Don Anderson, *Australian Literary Studies,* 9 (May 1979): 39-48.

References:

Roger Garfitt, "Peter Porter," in *British Poetry Since 1960: A Critical Anthology,* edited by Michael Schmidt and Grevel Lindop (Oxford: Carcanet Press, 1972), pp. 49-57;

Max Richards, "The Citizenship of Peter Porter," *Australian Literary Studies* (May 1978): 351-359.

Papers:

The Australian National Library, Canberra, has drafts for *Once Bitten, Twice Bitten* and drafts for all of Porter's poems written in the 1970s, that is, those included in *Living in a Calm Country, The Cost of Seriousness,* and *English Subtitles.* The Lockwood Memorial Library, at the State University of New York at Buffalo, has a few drafts for poems included in *Once Bitten, Twice Bitten.* The Indiana University Library has most of the drafts for *A Porter Folio* and some for *The Last of England.* The British Museum contains most of the manuscripts for *Poems Ancient and Modern* and the poems included in *Penguin Modern Poets 2.* The University of Reading Library contains most of the manuscripts for *Last of England* and all the manuscripts for *Preaching to the Converted.*

obsessive embedded allusion, clotted syntax, and other defensive gestures that make his poems so inhospitable to the reader." The reason Porter takes refuge is not his themes but their relationship to himself. He has not yet found his own middle way between the excesses of confessional poetry and the public self-consciousness to which his habit of irony testifies. A fault perhaps more irritating is his increasing tendency to cultural dilettantism, which is a form of protective coloration that ultimately results in disguised light verse. But Porter himself— feeling and thinking (in that order)—is near the center of his best poetry, which is most of what he writes now, and what makes the high quality of his recent poems more admirable is that Porter takes chances. He is a technical adventurer, always exploring forms and modes, and experimenting with the textures of language. If that accounts for his

J. H. Prynne

(24 June 1936-   )

Michael Grant
University of Kent at Canterbury

BOOKS: *Force of Circumstance and Other Poems* (London: Routledge & Kegan Paul, 1962);

Kitchen Poems (London: Cape Goliard, 1968; New York: Grossman, 1968);

Day Light Songs (Pampisford, Cambridgeshire: R. Books, 1968);

Aristeas (London: Ferry Press, 1968);

The White Stones (Lincoln: Grosseteste Press, 1969);

Fire Lizard (Barnet, Hertfordshire: Blacksuede Boot Press, 1970);

Brass (London: Ferry Press, 1971);

Into the Day (Cambridge: Privately printed, 1972);

A Night Square (London: Albion Village Press, 1973);

Wound Response (Cambridge: Street Editions, 1974);

High Pink on Chrome (Cambridge: Privately printed, 1975);

News of Warring Clans (London: Trigram Press, 1977);

Down where changed (London: Ferry Press, 1979);

Poems (Edinburgh & London: Agneau 2, 1982);

The Oval Window (Cambridge: Privately printed, 1983).

OTHER: Veronica Forrest-Thomson, *On the Periphery*, includes a memoir by Prynne (Cambridge: Street Editions, 1976).

PERIODICAL PUBLICATION: "Charles Olson, *Maximus Poems IV, V, VI*," *Io*, no. 16 (Winter 1972-1973): 89-92.

When the poetry of Jeremy Prynne began to appear in England during the 1960s, it secured for itself a reputation and influence among independent and avant-garde poets that was not matched by its reception in the established centers of literary decision-making, the London weeklies and academic reviews. To the literary establishment Prynne's poetry seemed willfully hermetic, bound by an aesthetic formalism derived from the obscure reveries of Charles Olson and the American projectivists. On the other hand, for those who were attempting to establish in England, for the first time

since the modernists, a coherent and enduring practice of poetry, Prynne's writing was and remains exemplary in its procedures and address. But the publication of *Poems* in 1982, essentially the collected works, may mark the beginning of a wider recognition of the texts.

Jeremy Halvard Prynne was born on 24 June 1936. After an education in the English primary and secondary system, followed by a period of two-year service in the British army, Prynne was enrolled as an undergraduate at Jesus College, Cambridge, from 1957 to 1960. He graduated with a first in the second part of the English Tripos, and took up an appointment as Frank Knox Fellow at Harvard during the academic year 1960-1961. He returned to England as a research student at Cambridge, and in 1962 was appointed to a fellowship at Gonville and Caius College, where he has remained since. He was married in 1969 and has a daughter and a son.

Prynne's first collection of poems, *Force of Circumstance,* appeared in 1962. Published by Routledge and Kegan Paul, and omitted from *Poems* (1982), it was the only publication of Prynne's work by an established British publishing firm. This collection, influenced though it is by the formal concerns of Donald Davie and the approach to landscape of Charles Tomlinson, constitutes an attempt to move beyond these positions, which at that time represented the most serious attention to poetry easily available in the English poetic milieu. The poems in some instances move beyond meaning toward a foregrounding of the poetic process, so that what is said also implies the position from which the statement is made. Poems such as "Surface Measures" move from a depiction of the concept of the human, as seen in the image of ladders or as "vertical music," to an evocation of the "latent matrix above/This brilliant music" which is continuous with the sea and "the land where oranges grow." By the use of paradox, the "latent" matrix that is "above" the brilliant music, apprehended by children in the "ignorance" of their dance, points to a real beyond everyday reality, an above that is also below, to which the poet and the child have comparable access. The poet's active role in this process can be seen in the high degree of self-consciousness he displays regarding his artifice: his syntactic coherences are strongly marked and his diction foregrounds itself as a play between concretion and abstraction. Thus the poet is established, as the enunciator, in the position of truth, a position reinforced by irony and judgment. "I" is, of course, the vertical letter. The contradictions in this position, between the claim to truth and the displacing effects of the language of that claim, were to provide a tension sustained over much of the later work.

Six years were to pass before another volume, *Kitchen Poems,* appeared in 1968. During this period, Prynne's poetic interest had moved from the poets (predominantly British) who had influenced his earlier methods to the work of the American projectivists, Charles Olson, Robert Duncan, Robert Creeley, as well as to the work of Jack Spicer and Robin Blaser. Prynne acted as a major channel for British access to the American poetry of the postmodernist period, both personally as a teacher and friend of younger poets, and by the example of his poetry, which was appearing in fugitive publications in England, such as the *English Intelligencer.* Prynne's reputation during the 1960s and earlier part of the 1970s was high among independent poets in Britain, and the publication of his work from 1968 onward did nothing to diminish his standing. The accomplishment of its language, the beauty of its music, and the seemingly hermetic quality of its significances, all combined to give an almost mythic quality of luminous opacity to the writing. Prynne's readership, though small, constituted most of the poets in England who were to produce, during this period (and after), experimental work of significance and interest. There can be no doubt that Prynne's example liberated English poets into a genuinely new conception of poetry, the structure of his language itself giving courage to those who would break with the empiricist conventions of the mainstream, whether the pinched observations of Larkin or the violent music of Hughes.

In *Kitchen Poems,* Prynne took up, at the level of the name, the relations between language and the real. Expanding and enriching the significance of this inquiry was the practice and theory of Olson and the projectivists. It is into the gap that opens between the name and what is named, between sign and referent, that deception and trickery penetrate. Names can return us to things, to the world of

which they are themselves a part, only insofar as we are prepared to trust to the very trickery that has deceived us and to recognize in the absence, the lack, of language an unveiling, a bringing into presence. In the language of poetry speaks that which speaks nowhere else. Poetry is a calling by name of that by which poetry is spoken. Prynne writes, in "Sketch for a Financial Theory of the Self": "the *names,*/do you not/see, are just/the tricks we/trust, which/we choose." Tradition, custom, is the richest expression of trust we have, its most profound expression the mysteries of liturgy, ritual, that enact and sustain the deep analogies between language and the real. For us, now in a world in which that trust has been broken, a world of monetary exchange, of the ego centered upon consumption and profit, it is our condition that "what *I am* is a special case of/what *we want....*" Language, reduced to demand, closes in upon the needs of the ego. But paradoxically, for Prynne, such needs return us to the elemental clarity of certain facts, to the physical-

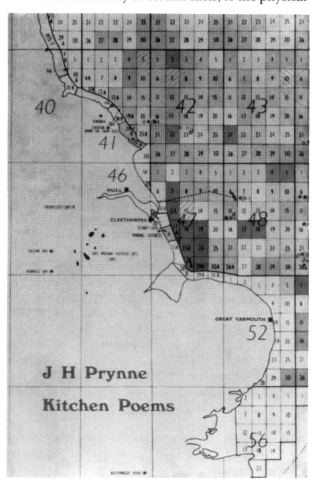

Dust jacket for Prynne's 1968 volume of poems that examine the relations between language and reality

ity of the body, and opens to language anew the experience of the real:

> The purity is a question of
> names. We are here to utter them. This is
> a prayer. I have it now between my
> teeth and my eyes, on my forehead. Know
> the names. It is as simple as the purity
> of sentiment: it is as simple
> as that.

Echoing, and displacing T. S. Eliot's "You are here to kneel / Where prayer has been valid," Prynne insists upon the significance of present experience, that the name be apprehended in the same instant as the thing in a moment of inaugural freshness, primacy, in simplicity, in the purity of sentiment. These moments of apprehension come about in the course of ordinary events insofar as an imaginative bracketing off of distraction isolates an individual event in the continuum, revealing an immanent transcendence of self across object, object across self, so that the true self coheres with the true object, the ground of what is, of being. The self enters upon discretion, upon the transcendence of a love made immanent in its objects, as Prynne explains at the end of "A Gold Ring Called Reluctance":

> I am interested instead in
> discretion: what I love and also the spread
> of indifferent qualities. Dust, objects of use
> broken by wear, by simply slowing too much
> to be retrieved as agents. Scrap; the old ones,
> the dead who sit daily at the feast. Each
> time I hesitate I think of them, loving what
> I know. The ground on which we pass,
> moving our feet, less excited by travel.

Prynne locates, as an experience of daily life, the truth, as he sees it, of what is perhaps the major stream of Anglo-American modernism, that which began with the imagist insistence on the primacy of the image as what participates in what it represents. This possibility of a poetry of the real, of the ground, reinforced as it was for Prynne by his reading of Edmund Husserl and Martin Heidegger, found exemplary manifestation in the poetry of William Carlos Williams and Olson (hitherto at best neglected, at worst scorned, in an England that took Auden's poetry to be the measure of major status). Prynne's poetic procedures enabled his work to turn back upon the economic, political, and social realities of English life in a way that was without precedent. Prynne elaborated one of the basic tech-

niques of modernist poetry to create an effect of the real. In "A Gold Ring Called Reluctance" the lines at the end of the poem pull back from the world of social and political circulation, to effect a collision between name and referent, so forming the "concrete detail." The surrounding context, the social meaning, is banished to create an illusion of direct reference to the real. This meaning, banished from the level of denotation, returns at the level of connotation. "Reality" re-enters as a connotative meaning, so that the dust, object, scrap, at the very moment they are claimed to denote reality directly, do nothing other than signify it silently. The objects say "we are reality." The category reality is indicated and not its contingent contents. The lost meaning returns as the verbal object of a metalanguage, and so signifies the real, the truth, the ground. This whole operation in turn becomes a connotator of love, of *agape*, the feast of love, in which time is overcome by means of a transfiguration. The dead return among the living (the reference to Eliot's *Little Gidding* is hard to avoid), and the present moment and the present presence (ground beneath our feet) are gathered up into a catholicity in which it is possible to speak truly of "we."

Prynne's poetry, by misrecognizing a semiotic effect for truth, repeats and endorses an ideology of return to a lost wholeness, an Edenic origin, which underlies a considerable part of the modernism associated with Pound, Williams, and Olson. In the Americans, this sense of wholeness issues forth in myths either of the local, as with Williams, or of the prelapsarian, as with Olson and Pound. Prynne, though more circumspect in this connection, also elaborates myths at the level of structure, at the same time as he attempts to locate this structure more precisely within the givenness of individual experience.

In *Day Light Songs* (1968) Prynne worked through formal problems of syntax and subject position that his poetic procedures rendered inescapable, problems fundamentally of self and other and their articulation in a spatial field. The poems are small, dismembered in their line units, and, in their concern with breath, with song, may be related to the Elizabethans, such as Thomas Campion, and to Louis Zukofsky, who had taken up Pound's concern with the romance tradition of song and related it to an ontology of language. Prynne aligned himself with this work and carried further than his predecessors a recognition of language as the dwelling place of being.

It was *The White Stones*, published in 1969, that gave definitive voice to his concerns of this period.

As "The Holy City" makes clear, the sense of language as both the substance and the form of truth made possible a poetry of luminosity and confidence, in which the conflict underlying this alignment of interests was repressed:

> There's no mystic moment involved just
> > that we are
> > is how, each
> > severally, we're
> > carried into
> the wind which makes no decision and is
> a tide, not taken. I saw it
> > and love is
> > when, how &
> > because we
> > do: you
> could call it Ierusalem or feel it
> as you walk, even quite jauntily, over the grass.

The breaking of the lines, of the continuity of meaning, becomes the mark of scrupulosity, and at the same time locates the subject of the enunciation, the one who speaks, in the field of language. The language of this poem, by effects of syntax, breaks with the referent, and emphasizes the particles of language, "how," "when," "&," "do," and so on. Particles, single words, even phonemes, are brought into high relief as elements in their own right, in order to identify them as the utterances of one origin, the real, given in *this* act, this speaking of and in the real. The act of speaking and what is uttered are to be identified. From the point of view of the reader, the poem's address is to begin in trust and to end in communion. In other words, the poem attempts to locate the reader in the field of the real (field of the poem also) as that is given by the end, the community of the Holy City, the *eschaton*, "Ierusalem." What is is, and "Ierusalem," the Blakean hope, is realized.

Since verbal trust in our culture is impossible, being eroded by semantic trickery and deceit, the poem itself is offered as the site of a utopia, which the act of reading confirms. Reading aligns the subject of the statement, the "I" of "I saw it," with the subject of the enunciation, the I who utters, and with that Other, the reader, of whom the poem makes its demand, a demand for love. Not only does the poem demand of the Other, it puts the Other in the position of making a like demand of the poem, of the real. Thus the reader is brought to close the radical gap opened by language. The play between referent, meaning, and word drops away. The meaning is identified with the infinitude of

things (and Prynne's poems have a cosmic reach) so that the word returns from the real as such. That is, it returns as the real.

Prynne has, thus, over three volumes, recapitulated the Hegelian project of making consciousness real to itself. It is this project that underlies not only a great deal of romantic verse (Prynne's interest in Friedrich Hölderlin, Georg Trakl, and Paul Celan is marked) but also the dominant tradition of Anglo-American modernism, from the imagists on through the poetry of Olson. The return to romanticism has characterized American postmodernism, as Olson's refusal of Joyce and Eliot indicates, and Prynne's work must be seen in relation to this tendency.

However, since language does not stay in place, word splitting endlessly away from meaning, the poetry of truth, of the real, has always to be repeated. The end is always already a new beginning. In the volumes that followed *The White Stones*, Prynne engaged upon a rigorous investigation of the possibilities opened up for him by the earlier work.

Brass, published in 1971, indicates the direction Prynne took. "L'Extase de M. Poher" is a sustained and delirious denunciation of the bureaucratic, scientific discourses of technological man. Out of the conflict of these discourses an extraordinary verbal surface is constructed, composed of multifarious idioms, each of which, as it collides with the other, is given as designated by a single sign, "rubbish." Throughout the larger part of the text, this one sign governs what could be an almost infinite number of significances. "Rubbish" is not bound to any single concept, but can range across the discourses of the modern world. One discourse is interchangeable with any other. In the last few lines, however, there is a crossing over, a chiasmus, which in another context Prynne called the "twist-point." "Rubbish" is that which gives onto the "essential," "the/most intricate presence in/our culture." "Rubbish" alters its status: from being a single sign in the larger field of the poem, it becomes all those signs (actual objects in the real) that can signify the essence of things. In other words, there is a triggering effect, whereby the verbal entity "rubbish" shifts its status in respect of the real, the change in status being the mark or connotator of the poem's access to and participation in the ground beyond it. Prynne's poetry aims at effecting a disappearance of the ego in an encompassing subjectivity that communicates without intermediary with the essence. Thus the poem conceives of itself as a "model question," a question both to and of the model that turns the subject, the reader, and opens him to his own access to being.

If Prynne's earlier poetry connoted the real by emphasizing the processes of meaning rather that meaning itself—a technique traditional to the moderns—his later work has proved more radical in method. Now the forms of language are experienced as participating in the forms or underlying orders of the real itself, a participation understood as a coinherence of inner and outer effected by syntactic reversals, such as chiasmus, correlated with verbal play. A poem from *Into the Day* (1972) cross stitches the letters *a* and *u* in "lack" and "luck" so as to interweave them across the literal passage of the poem's "not succeeding":

> Lack spreads like snow
> back by the path to the iron pipe
> flaking and not succeeding.
> And over this luck comes, the bird
> making shadows like fortune,
> like heat and light, on the wing.
> Lack warms, it is the conduit
> of starlight through the shut window,
> lack of love hot now, luck cool
> by turn, the bird it likes.

By means of such techniques, Prynne was also able to incorporate parody and archaism, as with "The *Plant Time Manifold* Transcripts" published in *Wound Response* (1974). This text is a parodic evocation of the language of scientific research, which is at its conclusion played across an archaic diction, a device which, though no less constructed than the scientific discourse, permits the effects of turning and displacement to work on the mind of the reader.

In later volumes, such as *High Pink on Chrome* (1975) and *News of Warring Clans* (1977), the poems present a series of petrified landscapes in which the reader is brought to recognize himself. As each of the poems turns back on the reader, it brings him to recognize that he himself produces these images of stasis, of death. It is indeed as though the problem of trust could only be resolved in death, in that everything in the poem is both there for the reader and is at the same time that which puts the reader in his place, in his relation to the poem and to the world. Thus the binding in of the reader to the language and of the language to the real is worked through in an ever-tightening circulation of subject positions.

The later poetry is engaged precisely with these problems. The poetry of *News of Warring Clans,* for example, is both an opening to and a disavowal of the lack, the play, of desire. The text holds back somewhat from need, by demanding, and offering, the real: that which it does not have and which cannot be possessed or given. The real is embodied in the poem as love, love identified with death, the "ace" (in the hole, end and beginning).

> This is the ace
> of all desire,
> fed by the smoke
> and flame of this
> exhausted fire.

And yet these lines suggest, despite their closure, the ash of an obliteration which generates, beyond the demand for love, the force of pure loss, experienced as such even though its formulation here strives to disavow it. Loss represents intrusion within language's closure upon itself. It is the force of loss to point out within language the opening of language to what is elsewhere.

The effect of lack can be recognized in other poems. The intrusion of loss is afforded explicit recognition in a poem from *Down where changed* (1979), a title that itself seems to offer some expectation of fissure:

> If the day glow is mean
> and spoiled by recognition
> as a battery hen, you must know
>
> how the voice sways out of time
> into double image, neither one true
> a way not seen and not unseen
>
> within its bent retort
> we feed on flattery of the absent
> its epic fear of indifference
>
> all over again and then
> that's it, the whole procession
> reshuffles into line.

Here, Prynne opposes the dialectic of absence, its "epic fear of indifference," its "bent retort" the very structure of much of the preceding poetry, to the neither one nor the other of the double image. And yet the poem, having set up the play of difference in the opening lines, returns to the security of recollection as the term of an embittered dismissal. Likewise, the final poem of the collection (and of *Poems*) reiterates the same pattern:

What do you say then
well yes and no
about four times a day
sick and nonplussed
by the thought of less
you say stuff it.

The poem confronts "it," that which is "less" than the "yes and no" of the dialectic of presence and absence of ontology. The poem can extend "it" only the flatness of a demotic denial. Nonetheless, the very contrast of idioms in the language splits the poem away from the conclusion it seeks to effect: "stuff it." The subject receives from what is other even the message he emits.

It must ultimately be emphasized that it was the aim of Prynne's project to endorse an aesthetics of reflection. His use of chiasmus was recuperated as an incarnational aesthetics of mimesis, whereby the high was embodied in the low, the low in the high. The figure of such an aesthetics is paradox, implying circularity and closure. By effectively foreclosing the play of word over word, Prynne was able to reify the structure of his poetry, and make it both subject and object of its own processes. Instead of being viewed as an effect of signification, the poems become things—real entities—in their own right. In this sense of the poem as thing he followed the mainstream of Anglo-American modernism.

Prynne's writing is, undoubtedly, the most audacious of postwar English poetry. In vindicating the tradition from which it emerges, his writing erases that tradition. The attempt to present poetry as what exemplifies a universal and aesthetic mode of cognition, as a direct glimpse of the truth, subverts itself, allowing itself to be read in the terms of a specific practice of writing. By taking language to the limits set by its own assumptions of the poetic, Prynne's work effects the recognition of those assumptions for what they are: misrecognitions, ideologies. By opening onto an elsewhere, an excess, a beyond, Prynne's work, in spite of itself, has explored the conditions for the language that speaks always too early, or too late.

Prynne's most recent book, *The Oval Window* (1983), takes these issues further. Combining the syntactic flexibility of the earlier writing with the poetic density of the later, *The Oval Window* confirms that the poetry of Jeremy Prynne is that of a major English poet.

References:
Peter Ackroyd, *Notes for a New Culture* (London: Vision Press, 1976), pp. 129ff.;

Elizabeth Cook, "Prynne's Principia," *London Review of Books*, 4 (16 September-6 October 1982): 15-16;

Donald Davie, *Thomas Hardy and British Poetry* (London: Routledge & Kegan Paul, 1973), pp. 105, 113-116, 118-121, 128-129, 146, 178-180;

Veronica Forrest-Thomson, *Poetic Artifice: a theory of twentieth century poetry* (Manchester: Manchester University Press, 1978), pp. 47-51, 139-146;

Douglas Oliver, "J. H. Prynne's 'Of Movement Towards a Natural Place,'" *Grosseteste Review*, 12 (1979): 93-102;

Nigel Wheale, "Expense: J. H. Prynne's *The White Stones*," *Grosseteste Review*, 12 (1979): 103-118.

Craig Raine

(3 December 1944-   )

Michael Hulse

BOOKS: *The Onion, Memory* (Oxford: Oxford University Press, 1978);
A Martian Sends a Postcard Home (Oxford: Oxford University Press, 1979);
A Free Translation (Edinburgh: Salamander Press, 1981);
Rich (London: Faber & Faber, 1984).

OTHER: *Poetry Introduction 4,* includes poems by Raine (London: Faber & Faber, 1978);
Blake Morrison and Andrew Motion, eds., *The Penguin Book of Contemporary British Poetry,* includes poems by Raine (Harmondsworth: Penguin, 1982).

The effective impact of Craig Raine on contemporary British poetry may be dated roughly from summer 1977, when his poem "Flying to Belfast, 1977" took first prize in the Cheltenham Festival Poetry Competition and Raine began an eighteen-month stint as book editor for the *New Review.* The following year "Mother Dressmaking" also won the Cheltenham first prize; his first collection of poems was published; and "A Martian Sends a Postcard Home" shared the *New Statesman*'s Prudence Farmer Award for the best poem published in its pages during 1978. Raine was to win this award again in 1980 with "Laying a Lawn," while "In the Mortuary" took second prize in the 1978 National Poetry Competition: both of these poems were included in *A Martian Sends a Postcard Home* (1979), his second book, which has to date been reprinted five times and has given a name to that Martian school of which Raine is considered the founding father. If the poet has been fortunate with prizes, his work, though still surrounded by controversy, has widely been recognized as inventive, exciting, and original, and the influential arbiters as well as the poetry-reading public have rated him highly. The nature of poetry in Britain has been profoundly changed by Raine, and already, after less than a decade, it is clear that his impact must be assessed both in terms of its intrinsic value and with a view to its larger influence.

Craig Raine

The son of Norman Edward and Olive Marie Raine, Craig Raine was born into a working-class family in 1944 in Shildon, County Durham. His father, in the poet's words, "mastered a variety of trades—painter, decorator, plumber, electrician, and glazier," and before World War II was for some time a featherweight boxer, who in 1937 "fought against Germany and beat the Olympic Games winner, Otto Kästner. Ribbentrop presented the cup. The fight was apparently a tremendous bloodbath." Disabled since the war, Norman Raine is apparently both a fascinating raconteur and "a practising spiritualist and a faith-healer." Craig Raine's mother emerges from the poet's description as less colorful but intense, intelligent, and as Raine says "Lawrentian," bent on her children's doing well, and it is she rather than the poet's father who on occasion finds her way into the poetry. In Raine's childhood she "took in sewing," and the boy's close observation of his mother's work finds expression in "Mother Dressmaking":

> She takes
> a prehistoric triangle of chalk
>
> and leaves a margin for the seams.
> Her scissors move through the material
>
> like a swimmer doing the crawl,
> among the archipelago of tissue paper.

Another poem in *A Martian Sends a Postcard Home*, "Listen with Mother," draws on his upbringing in his mother's Roman Catholic faith:

> Sixpence safe in my glove, a clean handkerchief,
> and the Sacred Heart spiky as a cactus
>
> on the front of my Missal, I tiptoed
> and genuflected like a little Quasimodo,
>
> crippled by embarrassment—late again . . .
> The snore of Latin, the radiator's vertebrae,
>
> an altar boy's baseball boots under his cassock—
> it all comes back, vivid and meaningless.

But Raine feels that he "wasn't a religious boy" and the poem too goes on to say, "I never liked God"; and indeed, the moral core present in the poet's work can never be reduced to the more simplistic of religious solutions.

Craig Raine attended Barnard Castle, an Anglican public school, and went on to Oxford in 1963, where he read for an honors degree in English language and literature at Exeter College. By this time he was writing his first poetry—a schoolmaster described early attempts as "pimply Dylan Thomas"—and also enjoyed his studies, finding the Oxford atmosphere agreeable: "Oxford taught me not exactly scepticism but an argumentative open-ness," Raine has said, adding: "I really have a free-floating acceptance of possibilities; I don't think anything is unthinkable." If Oxford suited his cast of mind, Raine also found in the city a home (he still lives there) and a source of subject matter, par-

ticularly in "The Window Cleaner," "Houses in North Oxford," "Danse Macabre," and "Jew the Obscure"—all in *The Onion, Memory* (1978). From 1966 to 1968 he read for a further degree, a B. Phil. in nineteenth- and twentieth-century studies, and, after teaching part-time for a year, then spent two years (1969-1971) reading for a D. Phil. at Exeter College. His subject for his thesis was "The connection between Coleridge's philosophy and his criticism in *Biographia Literaria*," but it has remained uncompleted. After a one-year appointment lecturing at Exeter College, during which time, on 27 April 1972, he married Ann Pasternak Slater, Raine resumed reading for his thesis, but in 1973 again abandoned it, turning to free-lance journalism. The first of his weightier literary journalism, essays on Samuel Taylor Coleridge, Charles Dickens, Siegfried Sassoon, Wallace Stevens, and T. S. Eliot, dates from this period; but the call of the university (and perhaps of a steadier income) was strong, and from 1974 to 1979 he was again a lecturer at Oxford, variously in Lincoln, Exeter, and Christ Church colleges. During this same time his children were born: Nina on 15 November 1975, Isaac on 29 June 1979. The birth of Nina, as Raine has attested, affected him strongly, and his daughter appears in two poems in *A Martian Sends a Postcard Home*, "Pretty Baa Lamb" and "Laying a Lawn," which have mortality and the miracle of life as their subject. "Few things," the poet has written, "bring mortality so vividly close as holding a perfect, vulnerable scrap of flesh in your arms." Meanwhile, Raine was book editor for the *New Review* from June 1977 to December 1978, and in 1979 he once again quit academic security to spend a year as coeditor of *Quarto* (to December 1980), followed by six months as poetry editor for the *New Statesman* in 1981. Raine has also broadcast for the BBC and has given frequent readings of his work, and since October 1981, he has been poetry editor with Faber and Faber in London, the firm that now publishes Raine's own poetry.

If this account suggests that there is an autobiographical element in Craig Raine's poetry, it should be stressed that his work is in no way confessional or solipsistic, and indeed the first-person singular is relatively fixed on the external world of objects and phenomena, which he views wittily and even jokingly but at the same time with a serious intensity reminiscent of Rainer Maria Rilke or the French symbolists. To his contemplation he brings a Joycean inventiveness and a near-metaphysical ethic which is akin to Donne, though the more

Dust jacket for Raine's first volume of poems, called by Martin Amis "one of the most arresting debuts for a decade"

These lines might be Raine's manifesto. "Shallots," in *A Martian Sends a Postcard Home*, adds the observation "that images provide/a kind of sustenance,/alms for every beggared sense—" and again the words contain a vindication of Raine's method. Raine's poetry might be described as constantly examining whether seeing *is* believing, and it adds to the trusting labors of the miniaturist the wider ironies of the philosopher. The reader should also be aware that Raine's affinities are demonstrably with the great modernists: with Joyce, Stevens, and Eliot and the imagists, though with the line of wit as well, from John Donne to Samuel Johnson.

Yet beyond abstract considerations, the heart of Raine's poetry is not in any theorizing or manifesto but in the witty angle from which he looks at the everyday, as in these descriptions of animals: "Dolphins darn the sea."; "Mosquitoes drift with

Dust jacket for the volume that gave the Martian school of poets their name

explicit statements Raine has made on aesthetics sometimes lead in other directions as well. Of particular interest is the poem "An Enquiry into Two Inches of Ivory," in *The Onion, Memory*, an overmodest allusion to Jane Austen's reference, in a letter of 16 December 1816, to "The little bit (two inches wide) of ivory on which I work with so fine a brush, as produces little effect after much labour." This poem includes the following passage:

> Esse is percipi—Berkeley knew
> the gentle irony of objects, how
> they told amusing lies and drew laughter,
> if only we believed our eyes.

> Daily things. Objects
> in the museum of ordinary art.

paraplegic legs."; a horse's "puffy mouth is like a boxing glove"; and

> a glinting beetle on its back
> struggled like an orchestra

with Beethoven.

Three distinct but related poems, "Karma," "Shallots," and "Dandelions," are exercises in the conceit, considering gardens and vegetation in terms of a system of imagery drawn from Hindu mythology and Indian life: dead dandelions are "like Hare Krishna pilgrims"; bulging dustbins are "each an avatar of generosity"; and

> the magnolia dances motionless,
> like a deity with many arms. Bells

bloom on her upturned finger tips.

"Yellow Pages," the justly celebrated opening section of *The Onion, Memory*, consists of a number of Joycean close-ups, including those of a butcher ("His striped apron/gets as dirty as the mattress in a brothel . . ."), a barber ("His scissors scandalmonger round the ears"), a gardener ("Up and down the lawn he walks with cycling hands/that tremble on the mower's stethoscope."), and a grocer ("His cheesewire is a sundial selling by the hour."). "A Martian Sends a Postcard Home," perhaps Raine's best-known poem, has an imagined alien taking a semicomprehending look at our everyday world and getting it amusingly wrong, as in his view of cars:

> Model T is a room with the lock inside—
> a key is turned to free the world

> for movement, so quick there is a film
> to watch for anything missed.

Raine has an inventive eye and a fertile imagination, as well as a strong sense of humor. Undoubtedly his things are daily things, his gentle irony lives between lies and laughter, and his images, ultimately life-affirming by virtue of their palpable fascination with the fabric of daily living, certainly provide a kind of sustenance. Nevertheless, the reception of Raine's first two collections was by no means uniformly positive. A broad spectrum of reviewers found Raine too flashy, too much a dandy, too unserious and flippant, too unfeeling. To such accusations Raine has replied: "Currently

we have a very crude view of what constitutes feeling; there's a terrible dead orthodoxy about what poets are allowed to feel." In saying this, Raine speaks as an influential mover in a current British reaction against the postconfessional cult of the self. "The equation (fashionable in the 60's) between sincerity and what Joyce called, as he repudiated it, 'a scrupulous meanness' of style now seems narrowly prescriptive," Raine has written, and he adds, "Wit is not incompatible with seriousness." Feeling in Raine's poetry emerges through images—suggesting Raine's affinity with Eliot, perhaps—and it is useful to accept the healthy corrective this method offers to a restrictive view of emotion in poetry. The extent to which this corrective has already been accepted in Britain is a measure of Raine's success in creating the taste by which he is to be understood.

Yet, beyond the question of whether moral seriousness can be expressed through a jeu d'esprit, there perhaps remain some doubts when the reader considers Raine's subject matter. Shallots and dandelions and a Martian's quaint incomprehension may be a novel way of testing Ezra Pound's equation of technique and sincerity, but these subjects are not a centrally human thematic material; and it is reassuring to see that Raine tackles the major human concerns, death and love, mystery and misunderstanding, hope and despair, with deference and sensitivity. "Anno Domini," a ten-part sequence on the life of Christ, is not finally successful, but "Laying a Lawn," "Listen with Mother," and "Flying to Belfast, 1977," with their interpretations of childhood, mortality, and the happy menace in marriage, show that Raine can make moving poetry out of essential experience. "In the Dark" tells the tragic story of a girl, who, after two suicide attempts, kills her unwanted child, and in this poem Raine's imagery, far from being flashy, has a serious moral function and a structural necessity in the narrative:

> God danced on his cross
> at the foot of her bed

> like Nijinsky having a heart attack . . .

This poem and "In the Kalahari Desert," both from his second collection, mark Raine's movement toward narrative in poetry, a development which has been continued in the pamphlet *A Free Translation* (1981) and in *Rich* (1984), which includes the poems from the pamphlet.

The most striking feature of *Rich* is its con-

A FREE TRANSLATION

Craig Raine

*Front wrapper for Raine's third volume of poetry. The cover
drawing is by Henri Matisse.*

firmation of the personal and autobiographical vein
in the poet: "Inca" and "A Walk in the Country"
join the earlier "Laying a Lawn" as celebrations of
the childhood frailty of his daughter; "A Hungry
Fighter" and "Plain Song" depict his father as boxer
and faith healer, while his mother appears in "Plain
Song" and "The Season in Scarborough 1923," and
a number of poems persuasively treat of love and
sex. Though at times these poems can be too sentimental, or have that inconsequentiality which is
the mark of the private in a public place, Raine
nevertheless achieves both humanity and precision;
"In Modern Dress," for example, watches his son in
the garden, "a full-length Hilliard/in miniature
hose/and padded pants," and goes on:

So many expeditions
to learn the history
of this little world:

I watch him grub

in the vegetable patch
and ponder the potato

in its natural state
for the very first time . . .

The Elizabethan imagery which unifies this poem,
and which in the description of Raine's son as "Sir
Walter Raleigh" at first seems forced and merely
visual in character, here is wholly apt, and it is a sign
of the dexterity of Raine's wit that it cuts two ways:
the child resembles an explorer, down to his first
discovery of a potato, but the explorer, we are reminded, and indeed the human race, has resembled
a child in its slowness to grasp the facts of the world.
"In Modern Dress" has a mainspring of fatherly
love, but in the course of the poem Raine offers
comments which are relevant to the experience of
humanity as a whole; it is a mark of the maturity of
his wit that in doing this he is wholly without pon-
derousness or pretension.

Rich is linked to Craig Raine's earlier work,
then, through the personal content of many of its
poems and also through a lengthy prose memoir
which forms the second of its three parts, "A Silver
Plate," in which Raine gives a vivid account of his
father and of his own family background to the age
of sixteen. It is linked also in the inventive ingenuity
of its images: we read of an "usherette/by Salvador
Dali/with a drawer in her midriff/full of ice
cream," and of "eggshells/cracked on the kitchen
table/like an umpire's snail/of cricketers' caps." But
in two respects Raine has gone beyond *The Onion,
Memory* and *A Martian Sends a Postcard Home*: he has
heightened the narrative element in his work, and
he is indulging a fancy for language play. A Joycean
linguistic zest was apparent in "The Corporation
Gardener's Prologue" in the first book, but now a
more systematic concern with frontiers of language
is apparent, in various ways, in "Gauguin," "The
Sylko Bandit," and "Purge." And narrative, a mode
widely adopted in even very short British lyrics of
the 1980s, provides the drive for half the poems in
Rich, notably "The Man Who Invented Pain" and
"The Gift."

Craig Raine remains an influential and initiat-
ing mover in a shift of direction everywhere visible
in British poetry today, and is regularly a focus of
public attention: in April 1983 his poem "Arsehole"
(adapted from Rimbaud) provoked controversy
when it was published in the *New Statesman*, and in
October 1984 press coverage followed Raine on his
round-Britain tour with Seamus Heaney. Unques-
tionably he is the most important of a group of

younger poets, including Christopher Reid, David Sweetman, and others, who have collectively been labeled the Martian poets or the Metaphor Men. It may be that the Martian tag is a misrepresentation, as Peter Conrad has pointed out. Raine's work is very much of this world, indeed his passion is all for the domestic and ordinary, however he transforms it. Metaphoric he certainly is, and perhaps neo-Elizabethan would be the most apposite description of his faith in wit. Just as one accepts the seriousness of Donne or Joyce through a barrage of invention, so too one must recognize that Raine's agile wit is an inseparable part of his devotion to the real world. If his apparent confidence and faith in a real world have a sentimental naiveté about them, they also make possible an energy which has been absent in too much recent British poetry. His future development must be of great interest to anyone seriously concerned with the future of the poetic imagination.

Interview:

John Haffenden, *Poets in Conversation* (London: Faber & Faber, 1981).

References:

Michael Hulse, "Alms for every beggared sense: Craig Raine's aesthetic in context," *Critical Quarterly,* 23 (Winter 1981): 13-21;

Blake Morrison, "Young Poets in the 1970s," in *British Poetry since 1970,* edited by Peter Jones and Michael Schmidt (Manchester: Carcanet Press, 1980), pp. 154-156;

John Osborne, "The Incredulous Eye: Craig Raine and Postmodernist Aesthetics," *Stone Ferry Review,* no. 2 (Winter 1978): 51-65.

Tom Raworth
(19 July 1938-   )

Kit Robinson

SELECTED BOOKS: *The Minicab War,* by Raworth, Anselm Hollo, and Gregory Corso (London: Matrix, 1961);

The Relation Ship (London: Goliard, 1966; London & New York: Cape Goliard/Grossman, 1969);

Continuation (London: Goliard, 1966);

Haiku, by Raworth, Hollo, and John Esam (London: Trigram, 1968);

The Big Green Day (London: Trigram, 1968);

Betrayal (London: Trigram, 1969);

A Serial Biography (London: Fulcrum, 1969; Berkeley: Turtle Island, 1977);

Lion Lion (London: Trigram, 1970);

Penguin Modern Poets 19, by Raworth, John Ashbery, and Lee Harwood (Harmondsworth: Penguin, 1971);

Moving (London & New York: Cape Goliard/Grossman, 1971);

Act (London: Trigram, 1973);

Pleasant Butter (Northampton & Paris: Blue Pig/Sand Project, 1973);

Back To Nature (Bexleyheath, U.K.: Joe Dimaggio, 1973);

Ace (London: Goliard, 1974; Berkeley: The Figures, 1977);

Bolivia, Another End of Ace (Kent, U.K.: Secret Books, 1974);

That More Simple Natural Time Tone Distortion (Storrs: University of Connecticut Library, 1975);

Cloister (Northampton & Paris: Blue Pig/Sand Project, 1975);

Common Sense (Healdsburg, Cal.: Zephyrus Image, 1976);

The Mask (Berkeley: Poltroon, 1976);

Logbook (Berkeley: Poltroon, 1977);

Sky Tails (Cambridge, U.K.: Lobby, 1978);

Four Door Guide (Cambridge, U.K.: Street Editions, 1979);

Nicht Wahr, Rosie? (Berkeley: Poltroon, 1980);

Writing (Berkeley: The Figures, 1982);

Tottering State, Selected and New Poems 1963-1983 (Great Barrington, Mass.: The Figures, 1984).

RECORDING: *Little Trace Remains of Emmett Miller,* Stream Records, 1969.

OTHER: *Weapon Man* (broadside poem) (London: Goliard, 1965);

From the Hungarian (translations, with Val Raworth) (mimeo, Bowling Green, Ohio, 1973; Healdsburg, Cal.: Zephyrus Image, forthcoming).

PERIODICAL PUBLICATIONS: "Journal," *New World Journal* (Spring 1979): 126-134; "Heavy Light," *Heretic,* no. 1 (1981); "Catacoustics," *This,* no. 12 (1983).

Tom Raworth stands out as perhaps the most elusive—and at the same time the most sensitive to contemporary realities—of postwar poets in Britain. English critic Eric Mottram has called him "the best we have," and his reputation in America, particularly among those who also read recent American poetry, is unequaled by any of his fellow countrymen. The poetry and prose of Tom Raworth is marked by a razor-sharp attention to detail and mercurial mental shifts. When he reads his poetry, his delivery is the fastest in the business, but what is remarkable is the range of expression he gets without slowing the pace. His collaborations with artists and printers make his books some of the loveliest, and oddest, to be found.

Thomas Moore Raworth's parents were Roman Catholic, his Irish mother by birth, his father by conversion. When Tom was two his father left to serve in World War II and did not return until the boy was seven. "I can remember learning to read at 4," Raworth writes, "Clearly, because the teacher (Miss Firth) was showing my mother what I could do with a book that must have been something like 'Ivor the Engine'; because I got stuck at the end of a sentence and she said, 'It's what your father's in,' and I said, 'Army.' The word was 'signals' . . . he was a radio operator with the XIV Army in India, Ceylon and Burma." Tom grew up in a semidetached house on the border between North West Kent and London and went free to grammar school after the labour government's education act, but he left at sixteen out of boredom. Along with his parent's religion and musical taste, he rejected their belief in the desirability of a university education. So he went to work, first as a clerk in an insurance company, then booking films into cinemas, packing costume jewelry, shipping cans of fruit, selling expensive china (where he met Jayne Mansfield), laboring on a construction site (building Erith Power Station), and, by 1956, at age eighteen, after failing the army medical exam and having a hole in his heart sewn up, typing lists of drugs in the basement office of a pharmaceuticals company. There

Joanna Voit

he and another employee began to write a secret-agent novel, circulating the manuscript through the company's internal mail system (parts of it are published in *A Serial Biography,* 1969).

The milieu in which Tom Raworth came of age may shed light on the almost fastidious precision of his writing, its latent nastiness and diffident charm. Jeff Nuttall has related "the cool" in Raworth's work to his early identification with the youth culture of the "Teds." "It is the cool," he writes, "which is the articulation of pride and arrogance that the young English working class formulated for themselves in the 1950's. It is the cool of the drape suit and the blue suede shoes. . . . Teddy boys cultivated an elaborate etiquette, an incredible pitch of vanity."

In his youth Raworth frequented all-night jazz clubs and played piano in a short-lived jazz combo. Adopting the style and dress of the Teddy boys, he lived a life replete with violent interludes. As he records in *A Serial Biography* (1969), "I learned to always strike the first blow when the tension mounts . . . once that's done, to never relax the pressure."

Raworth recalls of his marriage, during the late 1950s, "Val and I met in an elevator and got married." Geoffrey Moorhouse's 1963 article in the *Guardian* profiles the young poet at twenty-five, still uncertain about his writing, but already underway as a publisher printing his own magazine, *Outburst,* on a secondhand treadle press. At that time he and his wife had two children, with another on the way, and Moorhouse noted, "At the moment the family is going through a small financial crisis . . . and Raworth is taking pills to hold down his appetite to the need for breakfast and nothing more than the odd cup of tea and biscuits each day."

At this time he began making contact with poets: Michael Horowitz and other jazz poets of the London subbeat scene, as well as Andrew Crozier, Anselm Hollo, Piero Heliczer, and David Ball. In addition to *Outburst,* which included work by Americans Robert Creeley, Ed Dorn, Charles Olson, Philip Whalen, LeRoi Jones, Larry Eigner, and Gregory Corso, he published three small books under the imprint of Matrix Press: Dorn's *From Gloucester Out,* Heliczer's *& I Dreamed I Shot Arrows in My Amazon Bra,* and Hollo's *History.* In 1965, he and Barry Hall began Goliard Press, publishing books by Ron Padgett, Tom Clark, Charles Olson, and J. H. Prynne. Hall and Raworth also set type for Asa Beneviste's Trigram Press, and Stuart Montgomery's Fulcrum Press, including Basil Bunting's *Briggflats* (1966). In 1967, they were approached by the publishing house of Jonathan Cape, to whom they had been recommended by poet Nathaniel Tarn as a "good small poetry" section. Hall accepted the offer and so began Cape Goliard Press, which was to publish Olson's *The Maximus Poems* (1970). Raworth, foreseeing an imminent loss of autonomy, withdrew. At that time he was offered, through Donald Davie and Ed Dorn, who had both been teaching at the University of Essex, a place there to continue his education. (Davie had been impressed with Raworth's first collection of poetry, *The Relation Ship,* 1966.) The family moved to Colchester. That summer Raworth did his first public reading, for Tom Pickard, at Morden Tower, Newcastle. In 1969, when Cape Goliard reprinted *The Relation Ship,* it won the Alice Hunt Bartlett prize, then Britain's major poetry award.

The poems in *The Relation Ship* are condensed instants in the language of daily life, marking quick shifts of attention. They register specific, isolated points of view extended, or distended, in time, recording momentary distractions, sound interference, sudden memory, views through glass, mirrors, funny and awkward social complications, frustration at failure to push past immediate conditions, and refusal to pretend more. The poem "Anniversary" begins, "the train runs, trying to reach the end of the darkness," and ends, "the six of

us move in the night/each carrying a different colored torch." The writing appears as a train—landscape rushes past; the subject: isolate individuals in the dark, moving in relation, creating abstract patterns. There is a tribute to the American gangster film and by extension to American writing in "I Mean," where Raworth's quote from Sam Fuller's screenplay for *Pickup on South Street* (1953)—

> jean peters to widmark "how'd
> you get to be this way?
> how'd i get this way? things
> happen, that's all. . . ."

—might stand as a description of the making of the poems as well. They are notations of events occurring in real time without explanatory padding, and the tone switches quickly to bespeak love, song, spleen, wit, vulnerability, and rage. A sequence of journal poems entitled "Six Days," written in Paris (some time between 1962 and 1966) in the tiny garret room of Raworth's friend David Ball, it is a running account, in long lines, of perception and desire, a witty romance set in the remains of European modernism, with French, British, and American language ironically juxtaposed. Following this sequence is an additional poem, "The Wall," written after Raworth went to work as an international telephone operator. It is a "tired poem . . . written after working 12 or 14 hours . . . trying to get what was happening, what I'd been thinking about sitting there facing those flickering lights . . . talking to people in German and French . . . playing records . . . playing with the machinery. . . ." Later, "A Pressed Flower" was added, a domestic poem celebrating the birth of a child, and ending, again, with the image of a telephone:

> at the other end of the line i say
> there is no answer   but the room there
> is filled with people looking at the phone

The poem is both the record of a mind's activity (subject) and an enigmatic artifact (object), both clear and opaque. After the event it resists comprehension, like a telephone no one can answer.

In *The Big Green Day* (1968), its title taken from a line in Ted Berrigan's *The Sonnets* (1967), increased clarity of focus is brought to bear on the poem as a miniature, packed with detail stripped of context. The opener, "Who Is Hannibal's Descendant Leading His Elephants Against the Tanks?" is a beautiful condensation of faceted images—horse, flower, and woman. That woman is "all the women i

Dust jacket for Raworth's 1968 collection of poems. The title is from a line in Ted Berrigan's Sonnets.

meant," and to her the book is dedicated. The titles and voices take on the sounds of old movies or the tendentious whine of British colonialism as in "North African Breakdown": and nothing works in this damn country./no, it's not a bit like home." That uncomfortable territory, where beads of sweat form on the stiff British upper lip, is not the only world now that the sun has in fact set on the British Empire. It is equally a space of the imagination where simple things become difficult because literally anything can happen: "i would be eight people and then the difficulties vanish/only as one i contain the complications." This predicament launches the next poem, "You've Ruined My Evening/ You've Ruined My Life," a quasi sestina in a light-hearted, lyric mode, which has as its subject the stripping away of the borders of the self. The entire book has a zippy, rambunctious tone, alternately alert and dopey, insouciant and self-effacing. There is a shift away from the painstaking measure of daily life made in *The Relation Ship*, to a conceptualization of the poem as art object, a gift to be shared among friends.

As George Butterick has pointed out, "In Tom Raworth's poetry there is a reluctance to sort, and so distort, language from experience. It is an agreement the poet has with himself, to let things stand, to accept the persistent fall of experience." The poems pledge allegiance to raw detail, stripped of narrative or rhetorical backing, and turned on imagination's lathe. Thus, judgment is often referred to perception, as in "Collapsible": "behind the calm famous faces knowledge of what crimes/ rain on one window showing the wind's direction." In "Don't Follow My Toes" fatuous imperialist bombast ("yes, the italians were always underfoot") is followed by stone-cold depth perception ("it is noon, it is summer, and birds fly through the shadows of the empty station"). The specific felt instant is always prior to, and given credence over, the idea which "lasts" ("nothing lasts").

A Serial Biography began as correspondence with Ed Dorn, but, when Stuart Montgomery saw some of the letters in Tom Clark and Andrew Crozier's magazine, the *Park*, he suggested a larger Fulcrum Press edition, and Raworth added sections to form the book. Arranged achronologically, the paragraphs each deal with a different period in the poet's life. Subjects include thoughts in a sensory deprivation chamber, scenes from childhood, fragments from his early collaborative secret-agent novel, courtship and seduction, nights on the jazz scene, married life, and imaginary days on the job. The author's persona, rendered through both the first and third person as well as through various proper names, is not so much a character as a shifting locus for sensation and cognition. The realities disclosed are splintered and interstitial. As Ed Dorn has written of *A Serial Biography*, "One of the basic honesties of this writing is the constant attention to the multiplicity of location perception can take: faced with any reality we are no longer of one piece. . . . The scattering is a realism."

Lion Lion (1970) was written in 1968, when Raworth traveled to Spain, where he studied Spanish at the University of Granada as part of his University of Essex degree program. Revolution was in the air, there as elsewhere in Europe. The specific nature of Raworth's political involvement is not known. It is doubtful he took a leadership role, but perhaps his status as a foreign student was enough to cast suspicion on him. He made his exit, by plane from Malaga, just ahead of a rumored deportation order. *Lion Lion* is a set of witty, elusive verses, undercutting their own connotations at breakneck speed. The title poem begins where *The Relation Ship* left off, with the obdurate inscrutability of the message "found." The poet is not being deliberately obscure, nor holding back secret meanings. His verse is enigmatic precisely because the words are written down as they occur to him. Further, in "South America," the possibility of error takes on new value—"as in the progress of art the aim is finally/to make rules the next generation can break more cleverly"—so that, by breaking with convention, mistakes may render improved results ("he sees he has written pain for paint and it works better"). Raworth appears here as a combination inventor and escape artist, whose vocation is to devise airtight security systems from which he must then proceed to spring himself.

Logbook (1977), ephemeral prose written in Colchester in 1970, extends the prose fragmentation of *A Serial Biography* to the form of the book itself. Its first page, numbered 106, begins, "would have explained it." Then the "message in a bottle" motif is introduced: "The third day of our voyage was perilous. Multitudinous seas incarnadine. But the small craft that came out to meet us contained us and went sailing into the sunset, carrying only ten pages of my logbook (106, 291, 298, 301, 345, 356, 372, 399, 444 and 453), slightly charred by the slow

Front cover for Raworth's 1970 collection of poems, with a slide of Raworth by Angela Duthie

still silent instant." In fact, these are the only pages included in the book, each beginning and ending in mid-sentence. The sea-voyage theme, as in the nineteenth-century adventure novels of Jules Verne or Robert Louis Stevenson, suggests its obverse, the cozy, bourgeois domesticity by which the individual is secured from imagination's perilous seas (a boat is a room). But the violent swiveling and physical rupture of Raworth's prose, with the explosion of the image bank depicted in Frances Butler's illustrations, signals the obsolescence of western cultural icons, a space where, by a kind of Doppler effect, objects only get further away, a world in which "all books are dead & we live where the edges overlap."

Moving (1971) pursues the record/object problem entered in *The Relation Ship* and this time treats it as a kind of game. One section, "Stag Skull Mounted," is a notebook poem with entries labeled with time and date. Toward the end there is a reduction of the journal to a series of reflexive, one-word entries—such as "word," "poem"—ending with "this trick doesn't work." The project becomes one of tracking the poetic impulse, a game of recording in real time. And as soon as this game has defined and refined its own rules, the poet quits.

The next book, *Act* (1973), is in sections: A revision game with changes drawn in and printed over in purple ink, short poems, and prose notations proposing Raworth's first extensive published

JUICE

how many of them
we need
for protection
from society's
divisions
everything
tagged for preservation
~~but now we see~~
~~more~~
~~below~~ in blue moonlight
ice glistens
in snowprints
crackles
carrying wet coal
in an old iron casserole
"i didn't imagine
you couldn't have"
looking away
to reality
long shadows
from scattered stones
hours of nothing
for one small gleam
huffing

how many
of them
we need
for protection

but we see more
below blue moonlight
ice glistens

Revised typescripts (the author)

JUICE

polishing

shielding my eyes

from its palpable glow
                this
to stamp the image

hopping black across the sky

thought after thought

that link alone

flesh to invisible bone

remembering

imagining

reasoning

whang

through the right hemisphere

there

only   is only

is silence   silence

filled with sound

flagstones

disappearing

into night

as water

at a loose end

this drifts along

press button

for date

describing

a moving image

'lots of collectors'

'art's running out'

babies aware

thoughts on poetics. The theme is sounded in these verse lines:

> for god's
> sake
> stay open
> to your time
>
> what's done
> is
>
>   *
>
> nothing
>
> lasts
>
>   *
>
> we
>   are
>   now.

The notations sketch the rude outlines of a radical constructivism: "the true direction is always a glancing off—there must be an out—all truth is not *contained* in the language: it *builds* the language." Against a picture of language as a container, a generalizing circumscription of knowledge, Raworth proposes that the truth, true seeing, generates language in increments which work as tools to further sharpen the perceptions. In this view, reality is not static, but dynamic. The immediate record of cognition is itself an act and creates change.

The insistence on invention and the present makes Raworth severely skeptical of theory, including his own:

> the critics almost invariably concentrate on
> what should be subliminal—they spread the
> jam so thin it loses its taste—using the past to
> hold you in their present. . . .
>
> i confess: i have become an explainer
> i have fallen onto description's other side.

Through American painter Jim Dine, Raworth met American poet Kenneth Koch and subsequently was invited to read in New York. From there he traveled by Greyhound to Iowa City, where Anselm Hollo was teaching in the University of Iowa creative writing program. More trips followed, including visits to San Francisco and Toronto. From 1972 to 1977, he stayed, with his family, in America, where he taught at Bowling Green, lived in Mexico City, taught again in Chicago and in Austin, and finally moved to San Francisco. When he returned to England it was to take up as poet-in-residence at King's College, Cambridge, where the Raworths have continued to reside.

If art is a game of making and breaking rules, such that mistakes may render improved results by violating pre-established definitions, then "Every act/re-alines your boundaries" ("Homily," from *Act*). Raworth's sense of himself as a poet has extended beyond the boundaries of English poetry. "There's an English insular sense that I sometimes feel oppressed by," he has said, "That I don't see any point in. . . . I don't really see any reason in terms like English poet." His forays into European and Latin and North American language and life make his work international.

The art of poetry exercises the ear and the eye, and Raworth's work keeps both at play. The forms of his books have themselves been made subjects for experiment, as in the case of *Common Sense* (1976), printed with illustrations by Michael Myers, on a small spiral-ring dime-store notebook; *Logbook* (1977), a pseudojournal with lavish double-page psychotropic images by Frances Butler; and *Writing* (1982), printed on pages fourteen inches wide with seven narrow columns per double-page spread. Musically, the poems manifest a keen ear for rhythmic change and a rare ability to "play it by ear." Raworth has been said to sit at the piano playing random notes as he reads, or whistle snatches of tunes between tapping out lines at the typewriter.

Raworth's sense of the poem as record of an immediate ongoing present may reflect the poetics of Gertrude Stein, William Carlos Williams, Ezra Pound, and Charles Olson, but Raworth eschews specific influences, wary of situations where literature perpetuates itself out of reading; and to keep free of such disturbance, he seems to have steered his own course round the masters. Of his own process he has said, "My method is the essence of simplicity. I write down fragments of language passing through my mind that interest me enough after thought has played with them for me to imagine I might like to read them. What form that documentation takes doesn't interest me as an intention, but only as the most accurate impression of the journey of interest." In the collection *Nicht Wahr, Rosie?* (1980), Raworth supplies notes to the poem "El Barco del Abismo," revealing the genesis of each line. What is significant in this unpacking of the materials of the poem is the privacy of the notes. They are details as mysterious in themselves as the lines they apparently occasioned. In a 1972 interview Raworth stated, "I really have no sense of questing for knowledge. At all. My idea is to go the other way, you know. And to be completely empty and then see what sounds. . . . Boredom, trust and fun are the key words somehow. . . ." Boredom occurs as a limit. Attention shifts radically whenever ideas sounded in the writing point toward an endless exposition of the already known. Trust enables the writer to step into linguistic space and to accept those events which occur singularly there, without recourse to precedent or outside authority. Fun is obviously of the essence throughout. The author's enjoyment of the writing activity comes across as an intense, and sometimes a perverse glee.

In the poem "Shoes," from *The Big Green Day,* a series of elements—shoes, leather, cows, milk, baby, child—are linked in a ring. The series is not simply a conceit but a result of the brain's firing across language circuits ignited by feeling. The process of association at play is exposed in *A Serial Biography:* "It became impossible for him to stop playing the game. You're not normal she told him. I've never been a garage. The visitors looked at him puzzled. And how could he explain to them the chain: normal norman norman norman mailer norman mailer the deer park deer park dear park dear expensive a dear park park a car park a dear car park a garidge at claridge's garage." The links in the chain here presented are usually left out in the poem. The lines then occur as poles defining mental space. In *The Mask* (1976), one of Raworth's more minimal works, ephemeral entries, some smaller than one word, are separated by five-pointed stars. In *That More Simple Natural Time Tone Distortion* (1975) and *Ace* (1974), which sports a red star on its blue cover, the asterisks are gone and the problem of large structure is entered. Raworth's solution is to let the lines roll in series, leaving readers to form sequence and division where and as they may.

Ace is an exploration of discontinuous language in continuous time. The language of the poem is composed of bits (short lines) which, by virtue of a polyvalent syntax, can point forward and/or back. There is no punctuation. Meaning is dependent on where the mind locates its attention within the continuum and how it groups the particles. Each language event (line) qualifies what has come immediately before and violates any totalization prior to it. Time destroys fixed ideas. *Ace* represents a kind of realism, not by pretense of verisimilitude but by thinking in flux. Thus, meaning is never static. This mode is expanded in *Writing* (1982),

Drawing of Raworth by Barry Flanagan

where the poet states, "with such/limited information/many connective/gestures/remain unseen/both beginning/and end/being necessary/to between." *Ace, Writing,* "Catacoustics," and "West Wind" exist in a continual between.

In *Writing* the large structure, simply a sequence of quickly hinging short lines separated occasionally by stanza breaks, is open enough to allow virtually anything into the poem. There is a "work within a work" motif, introduced by quotation marks, such as "page one the title/'CREDULITY,' " or,

> i sleep
> but not before writing
> "A BEHAVIORIST VIEW OF CHANGE."

Brief perceptions, jokes, or meditations are embedded in the ongoing writing. Various themes run through like multicolored threads. The poem evinces a principled restlessness with given ideas: "how vain our comfy knowledge" and "o for more works of reference." There are bits of story and turns of phrase from Welsh legend, drawn from reading and conversation with Valarie Raworth, who is Welsh. The archaic material is deployed in alphabetical wordplay. "Any *interpretation* by any reader will do." The book is dedicated "to the moles and to the bats." It is a kind of soundgram, locating reader and writer in space by "making natural/ forms of thought."

Tom Raworth appeared in the summer of 1981 at the Julia Morgan Center in Berkeley, California, to read from his work. In addition to reading several of his early books in their entirety, he also read the whole of *Writing,* a poem of roughly 2500 short lines. He kept up an astonishing speed with no loss of precision or variation of expression. But, to keep things interesting for himself, because he had just read *Writing* several days previously in San Francisco, he chose to read the whole long poem backward, line by line. Given the autonomy of the lines and rapid disjunction, this may have made as much sense as starting from the beginning. While many syntactic connections were obviously lost, others became possible for the first time.

Given his disdain for the predictable, it is hard to guess where Tom Raworth's writing will lead. But it is reasonable to think that he will continue to work in the short line, large structure mode of his most recent poems, possibly extending that out into an epic-length work. And the adventurous prose may find subject matter well suited to its dispersive qualities in the upcoming final decades of the twentieth century. As each work presents the poet with a limit, his powers of invention, and violation, are bound to be tested.

Interviews:

"Raymond Gardner interviews the poet, Tom Raworth," *Guardian,* 8 March 1971;

"Tom Raworth—An Interview, Conducted by Barry Alpert, Spencer, Indiana, February 11, 1972," *Vort,* no. 1 (1972): 29-46.

References:

William Corbett, "Harwood/Walker & Raworth," *Poetics Journal,* no. 2 (September 1982): 57-60;

Ed Dorn, "On Tom Raworth," *Vort,* no. 1 (1972): 56-57;

Curtis Faville, "Reflections on Raworth," *Daily Iowan,* 6 November 1970;

Rod Mengham, "Raworth," L=A=N=G=U=A=G=E, no. 6 (December 1978);

Geoffrey Moorhouse, "The Outburster," *Guardian,* 14 October 1963, p. 7;

Jeff Nuttall, "The Singing Ted," *Poetry Information,* nos. 9-10 (1974): 23-30;

Geoffrey Ward, "On Tom Raworth, " *Perfect Bound* (Winter 1976-77): 14-19;

Lewis Warsh, "On Tom Raworth's *A Serial Biography,*" *Poetry Information* (1975): 15-16.

Papers:

The Wilbur Cross Library at the University of Connecticut, Storrs, has a collection of Raworth's papers.

Peter Reading

(27 July 1946-   )

Alan Jenkins

BOOKS: *Water and Waste* (Walton-on-Thames: Outposts Publications, 1970);

For the Municipality's Elderly (London: Secker & Warburg, 1974);

The Prison Cell and Barrel Mystery (London: Secker & Warburg, 1976);

Nothing for Anyone (London: Secker & Warburg, 1977);

Fiction (London: Secker & Warburg, 1979);

Tom o'Bedlam's Beauties (London: Secker & Warburg, 1981);

Diplopic (London: Secker & Warburg, 1983);

5 × 5 × 5 × 5 × 5, by Reading and David Butler (Sunderland: Ceolfrith Press, 1983);

C (London: Secker & Warburg, 1984).

Peter Reading is one of the most inventive, idiosyncratic, and challenging of English poets under the age of forty. The son of Wilfred Reading, an electrical engineer, and Mary Catt Reading, he was born in Liverpool, and educated at the Alsop High School and Liverpool College of Art, where he trained as a painter and earned a B.A. degree in 1967 (it would be tempting to trace "painterly" con-

Photo by Perian Wilde,
courtesy of Secker & Warburg

cerns in his verse, but these are largely absent; the provincial art-college background is often drawn upon, however). He taught for a short time at a large comprehensive school in Liverpool before returning in 1968 to his former college as a lecturer in the department of art history. Since 1970 he has lived in Shropshire and done a variety of jobs of a menial nature at an animal feed mill; from 1981 to 1983 he held a fellowship at Sunderland Polytechnic. Reading married Diana Gilbert on 5 October 1968, and they have one child, a daughter born in 1977. He received a Cholmondeley Award for Poetry in 1978 and the first Dylan Thomas Award in 1983, for *Diplopic* (1983). His interests include

wine, ornithology, and mycology (all of which surface from time to time in his work); characteristically, in a letter supplying the above information he noted, "I need hardly add that I am an atheist and a carnivore."

Most of the twenty-two poems in Reading's 1970 pamphlet, *Water and Waste,* were included in *For the Municipality's Elderly,* his first full-length collection, which appeared four years later. One or two of the earlier pieces that were dropped, however, repay the attention of anyone who comes to Reading's work with the longer view in mind. "Dead Horse," for example, looks bracingly at the theme of consolation, but offers little itself:

Not to be born is best, said Sophocles,
(the second-best is an abysmal bore)
a view which he would re-assert, I'm sure,
hearing the second-rate asthmatic wheeze
of this ephemeral trite Audenese. . . .

These lines are not, certainly, great verse, but the stringency, the stoicism, the spectacularly depressed tone of voice, though all a little too easily won, give a foretaste of Reading's distinctiveness and power, while the traces of a very English "social" sprightliness hovering around this maudlin look at the worst foreshadow some much more memorable utterances. Another piece of "ephemeral trite Audenese" from this quirky voice in its earliest venturings, a stanza in a similar meter from "Letter in Winter," a poem included in the 1974 book, adumbrates a complete social attitude, knowing, detached, almost Olympian, infinitely unimpressed (something like the Auden, in fact, of mid-to-late career):

We are awaiting yet another Christmas,
giving a last chance to a disproved theory;
above the streets the tawdry clowns grow tired,
impassive plastic faces losing patience,
regretting like tired gods what they have sired
—unctuous uncontrolled and unrequired,
a world fatigued and overweight and weary.

It is a note that did not satisfy Reading for long; most of *For the Municipality's Elderly* crosses it successfully with something far less smooth, less fluent. The somber diction, dignified movement, and "rough edges" of the poems in that book, the mix of Latinate constructions and a syllabic approximation to quantitative meter, with heavy alliterative stress (deriving from Middle English poems such as *Piers Plowman*, but most likely via Auden), all combine to give them an air of considerable *gravitas*, a whiff of something ancient and serious, while the poems' subjects are local, contemporary, domestic, and personal. Or rather, the *voice* of the poems is contemporary, their occasions local and personal; for the overriding theme of the collection (and Reading's books are very much "wholes," unities in which poems reflect or contradict or counterpoint each other, cross-refer and echo backward and forward throughout), its obsession almost, is time: the passing of time and the passing away of human lives and achievements.

Along with the world-weary "Letter in Winter," there are also in *For the Municipality's Elderly* a "Spring Letter," a "New Year Letter," and an "Eas-

ter Letter"; seasonal change, natural cycles of growth and decay, like decaying man-made artifacts, body forth constant reminders of mortality. Not only mortality, but also transience, littleness, anonymity, the great black blank; the need to leave some trace, as in "Plague Graves":

I suppose we secretly hope for some permanent
monument left of us, some recognition
by those coming after. No chance;

and "Brabyns Park":

Scrub and unlevel rubble occupy
where the hall stood. The one real monument,
it seems to me, is that they occupied
it once themselves.

Bricks are "crisp, friable, flaking"; there are "brown flakes/of mummy" and "papyrus husks" on the linoleum; the year goes by, and all points to doom and darkness; the densely rendered detail of decline is riven occasionally by shafts of different light, as time and human generations are telescoped to bring the remote past very close indeed.

Occasionally the flat insistence on "devious thinking" which wrests a wry consolation from despair can seem forced, overstated, or simply too flat. The real consolations come when an amused self-consciousness turns the expected on its head (as when the speaker of "St. James's," for example, carried by force of habit into a church, finds himself thinking of Philip Larkin and John Betjeman, and descends into the chancel "not from interest but a sense/of having to have a sense of history"), or when Reading's language, warily on the lookout for signs of life, takes on a life—exorbitant, anarchic—of its own.

The Prison Cell and Barrel Mystery (1976) is a book about love, but love that comes or is acknowledged too late—when each of the lovers is already married to someone else. It has its prologue in "Juncture" from *For the Municipality's Elderly* ("So strange to see you, whom I loved/ten years ago . . . whereas you never loved me/while I loved you, you might love me/after I had ceased to love you") but refracts this central anecdote or situation through a dazzling variety of moods, forms, and voices. In *The Prison Cell and Barrel Mystery* Reading's technical resourcefulness comes into its own, his irony deepens and sharpens, and a characteristic mordant note enters his poetry. The elegiac tone of the first collection is replaced by sardonic wit, and the book's tragicomic burden disperses itself among brief vignettes and terse dramatic monologues that present, obliquely and economically, complex emotional realities. These can be absurd or harrowing, or both: "Nocturne" transcribes the simultaneous dreams of a couple, each dreaming of the other's death; "Correspondence," the letters of a quartet who are in and out of each other's homes, and beds, with comical speed and insouciance; "Ménage à Trois," a farcical incident from the lives of "the psychologist's mistress and the/psychologist's wife and the psychologist," as observed by an outsider ("we may be mad, Michael, but GOD, IT'S REAL") and relayed to the poet.

Marriages failed or staled, adulteries or potential adulteries, emotional or sexual dissatisfactions abound. Liverpool, where Reading was born (and which in *For the Municipality's Elderly* was "that city . . . of smoke and pimpled dummies and debris"), reappears, in one of its aspects at least—its dividedness. A ferry plies between Liverpool and Birkenhead:

> This *Kwickie Service*
> (I think I have never seen you so sad)
> draws me towards the river to cross
> from your side of the ferry to mine.

The book also contains the first of many Reading technical tours de force, the poem "Trio," which in lines of three syllables, in three columns of print across each page (each column representing a different "voice" so that each page contains the separate, concurrent, or sequential thoughts and utterances of three people), tells the story of a visit made by a man to a woman whom he once loved, whose present life is not happy, and of his wife at home thinking of the intended visit. There is compassion, and bitterness, beneath these "Life's Little Ironies," as one poem calls them in a Hardyesque phrase. Only in the still more Hardyesque "Duologues," which render the dialect speech of bucolic types discoursing on life, love, loss, and death, does a trace of cruelty or condescension make itself heard. "Ménage à Trois," the last piece in the collection, actually ends with "Michael" thinking

> meanwhile I must tell
> my friend Peter Reading about it—he'll
> probably find it terribly funny.

The lines acknowledge and preempt a charge that elsewhere Reading definitely courts: the charge of callousness, of mocking the afflicted. Reading is a poet of shock tactics, but as his books have grown more shocking—their fascination with grotesque or appalling undersides of life more detailed and insistent—an overall shape and tendency has become discernible as well, the deadpan tones drawing less ambivalently and playfully on the potential ambivalence and playfulness of surface irony, to point at deeper ironies, to speak the unspeakable.

Nothing for Anyone (1977) seems the most uncertain and "undirected" of Reading's books; "teasing and provocative," says the dust jacket: "deceptively off-hand," the poems show "an alert and original mind at work." While these statements are certainly true, they do not prevent the reader's wanting, or expecting, something more from Reading. There are poems here, again, about marriage, about death, and about traveling in France (a subject approached with a new expansiveness) —including a hilarious piece which purports to be a poem *trouvé*, a transcription of a set of camping-site rules from Provence; a nineteenth-century mini-tragedy told through the entries in a lady's album; and an eighteenth-century recipe or prescription for a poultice against cancer. The book shows Reading at his most formally ingenious and adventurous, but its inventiveness and technical sophistication seem unfocused. Its oddness—both in the writing and in the "oddities" which it picks up—is appealing but also a little pleased with itself.

Despite the title, which recognizes and mocks both the idea and the fact of variety, miscellany ("something for everyone," runs the cliché), the book makes a few desultory gestures toward the recurrences and recapitulations that are so effective in other volumes (in two or three poems, for example, it picks up with amused distaste the very notion of recapitulation, caricatures it as inane repetition, then drops it), but they *are* desultory. One funny poem here, though, is picked up again in a later book. "10 × 10 × 10" introduces the reader—in ten stanzas, each of ten lines, each line of ten syllables—to "Donald"—a fictitious character, two of whose ludicrous scrapes the poem details with relish. There are even 2.6 lines' worth of (or twenty-six) asterisks in place of syllables when he is knocked unconscious toward the end. "Donald" turns up again on the first page of Reading's next book, *Fiction* (1979).

This "Donald," a fictitious novelist, creates a character called "Don," who writes poetry under the nom de plume of "Peter Reading." Don, or "Peter Reading," in Donald's novel sues the real Peter Reading for having written "a fiction about a poet/who wrote verse concerning a novelist/called

Also by
Peter Reading
For the Municipality's Elderly
"I was impressed at the end. The language is alive, though dense; the feeling real."
Peter Porter, **Observer**

"Mr Reading has already a distinctive style . . . His poems have an attractive
modesty and in aiming for small effects frequently succeed."
Dannie Abse, **Times Literary Supplement**

The Prison Cell and Barrel Mystery
"An elegant fashion that is all his own. The poems are almost all about emotional
near-misses, people who 'fell in love / each with the other . . .', but not, regrettably,
concurrently': a part of Larkin-land, but drier, the vegetation sparser, the air fiercer
and more healthy."
Martin Dodsworth, **Guardian**

Nothing for Anyone
"*Nothing for Anyone* is Peter Reading's third book of verse and the best so far . . . an
oasis of intellect and wit . . . the poems are quite remarkably good."
Gavin Ewart, **Times Literary Supplement**

"Peter Reading uses his sharp wit and technical agility to shape urbane jokes in
entertaining verse forms . . . Delight in the trivial and more bizarre aspects of
everyday life is combined with a real compassion for human ills."
Shirley Toulson, **British Book News**

Fiction
"Start with a paradox – 'verse is not fiction – ask any librarian' – then make your first
poem ('Fiction') one about a fictitious novelist Donald, who writes about 'don', who
writes poetry under the name of 'Peter Reading', and you have cleared a space, even
if only a mental space, in which to be Peter Reading, witty, ferociously smiling,
carefully not expecting too much. He has the sort of brilliance that fascinates as well
as repels."
Martin Dodsworth, **Guardian**

"Peter Reading is a clever and inventive poet . . . The very title of the book, *Fiction*, is
one of the many jokes in a sophisticated collection."
Robert Greacen, **British Book News**

**Published by
Secker & Warburg**

Peter Reading

Tom o'Bedlam's Beauties

SECKER & WARBURG

**Peter Reading
Tom o'Bedlam's
Beauties**

poems

Dust jacket for Reading's 1981 collection of poems, which was recommended by the Poetry Book Society. The title, taken literally from the Old Herefordshire name for a variety of eating apple, refers to the forms of madness that are the subjects of Reading's poems.

'Donald' whose book 'Fiction' deals with 'Don'/(a poet who writes satirical verse). . . ." Mirror on mirror mirrored is all the show—so far. This fantastical play on the postmodernist obsession with "reflexivity" and authorial self-consciousness serves a serious purpose as well. "Even one's self is wholly fictitious," the poem ends, and the volume gets into its stride with a series of satirical portraits, which may or may not be the inventions of the poet "Don," or the novelist "Donald," or "Peter Reading," or not inventions at all. The reader might consider the opening piece another evasive stratagem, a way of ducking responsibility for some of the more grotesque imaginings that follow; rather, it frees the poet and his words from the burden of literalness and casts a harshly ironic light on his freedom, which is a freedom thus to "play" with others' lives or deaths—even invented lives, invented deaths.

Donald comes and goes throughout the book, and is, according to the spoof "Notes" appended to the volume, the witness of an event that similarly comes and goes, with rather more violence: the deaths of a farmer and an unspecified number of cows (followed by the suicide of the train engineer) in a collision on a railway crossing. There are some satirical swipes at municipal complacency (with regard, in particular, to the arts) and at artists' (or sham-artists') complacency; another 10 × 10 × 10 poem, "Inter-City," a funny-sinister, mad anecdote about Donald on a train (presumably the one from which he witnessed the accident); "Opinions of the Press," a splendid piece of self-examination constructed from reviewers' opinions of Reading's earlier books; prose poems; and another tour de force, the poem "5"—five pages this time, each page devoted to the five senses, each sense having five lines of five syllables each—which evokes a man's death, a childhood memory and an erotic memory interrupting the sensations of his last, hospitalized hours. Reading in this book seems finally and unequivocally to have "found his voice"—economical, witty, *very* mordant.

That voice continues into his next book, *Tom o'Bedlam's Beauties* (1981). The "beauties" in the collection are apples, but also, of course, inmates of the lunatic asylum. Opening with a riddle in Anglo-

Saxon style whose solution is a straitjacket, the first part of the book details the variety of ways in which people end up in one, or in a padded cell. The second part, "Some of Their Efforts" (the note of condescension is just right), sketches a few of the human documents—the human voices, the human tales of pain and breakdown—behind the findings of the invented "Glibber and Crass" on "The therapeutic value of Poetry practised amongst the mentally disturbed." The personae of this tragicomedy range from the simpleminded, through the victims of "stress," to the suicidally depressed. The point about them is not so much that they are mad, but that they have such good reasons to be so; some, like the vivid Brigadier Peregrine Fashpoint-Shellingem or the narrator of "Artemus' Wardrobe" ("A Bedlamite, got luce without is droors!/The most embarrassust I ever been") are simply out of place in the world at large; most are genial eccentrics, harmless except to themselves. The villains are those who seduce and betray, exploit, torment, and mock them (whether innocent schoolboys or malevolent dispatch clerks); the poet's designs cannot, of course, be entirely free from suspicion in this regard, and he knows it.

Some of the same personae crop up in more than one poem; events in one piece are looked at in another from a different point of view. The book's unity derives not so much from these linkages but from the muted sadness, pity, and anger that play over the vignettes, the exactness of suffering conveyed. One or two pieces, tending to a clichéd neatness or oversimplification, or to facile grotesquerie, are unsatisfactory; but for the most part the poems are persuasive, unsettling, and memorable. Among them are two of the strongest single poems Reading has written, the historical dramatic monologues "Hardship Aboard American Sloop the Peggy, 1765" ("That night my fenfes quit me—/'tis said they have not returned") and "Phrenfy," both of which employ *f* where the eighteenth-century printer would have used a swash *s* (which looks like an *f*). The book is a brilliant, scathing achievement.

The epigraph to his 1983 book, *Diplopic* (double vision), is one of the funniest ever invented, and also tells something about the poems that follow:

Optician, I am having Double Visions
to see one thing from two sides. Only
give me a Spectacle and I am delighted.

—*English Phrases for Malay Visitors*
(Vest-Pocket Editions, 1950)

In the book's "double visions" a given incident or anecdote is recounted twice, once from "the inside," in the voice or voices of the protagonists or at least of a concerned observer, and again in a tone of scrupulous detachment, a style that is either "scientifically" or insanely emotionless. It is possible to see this particular creative tension at work in Reading's poetry from the start; *Tom o'Bedlam's Beauties* makes it explicit, and it is both theme and structure in *Diplopic*. The poems come in pairs, one half of each pair varying in form from an extended pastiche of Henry Wadsworth Longfellow's *Hiawatha* (1855) to a minimalist free-verse fragment, the other half always a sonnet, regular or otherwise. The overall tone darkens yet further, the incidents are more grotesque or horrible: tragedy (small, personal, "insignificant") cuts deeper and far more often across the grain of "black humor." Commiserations are offered in one poem to a bereaved woman, and in the next it is revealed that her blind ten-year-old daughter has wandered, bewildered, onto a live electric-railway track. A humiliated, psychopathic lover's speech disintegrates in a frenzy of choreophrasia as he disembowels his girlfriend—in the accompanying sonnet, her corpse is mistaken for "a plastic dummy from a boutique/(boots, long white thighs, pants pulled right down, a sack/over the head and torso) dumped among bins/and tumps of fetid garbage. . . . "; delinquents attempt a gratuitous massacre of kittiwakes and effect the particularly vicious mugging of an old lady, with a good deal of torture thrown in (Reading has his revenge on one of the thugs later, mangling his arm in a piece of agricultural machinery—readers should not be soothed by the echo of Robert Frost).

The variety of forms, and of forms of suffering, is impressive and disturbing. The reader remembers the wry "give me a Spectacle" in the epigraph; and there *is* in the book an element of put-down, of the black-comedian's easy scoring off his targets. (Innocent and/or frigid girls, for example, are not by any means fair game, yet they are given a very hard time here.) The poet quotes Graham Greene—"There is a splinter of ice/in the heart of a writer"—and continues: "I savour/the respective merits of one/kind of mayhem over another . . . ," but of course the effect is far from simple.

Perhaps there is too little of this kind of complexity in *5 × 5 × 5 × 5 × 5* (1983), a pamphlet produced in collaboration with the artist David Butler: an ingenious and often extremely funny or touching work, it is also a worrisome one. Five sections—with five poems to a section, five stanzas to a poem, five lines to a stanza, five syllables to a line—

sketch in five characters , "regulars" in a pub, their destinies—variously unhappy, sometimes brutal— and conversations interwoven over the pints of beer. Their misadventures may be trivial or terminal. One, returning home drunk, incurs merely the wrath of his wife. Another, a pathetic and harmless would-be intellectual, is beaten up by skinheads in the lavatory. A hopeless and hapless has-been ventriloquist, who entertains no one, ends in the same lavatory "weeping, and weeping." A loutish, witless rugby player is killed off, while playing, in a fantasy of the poet's, then revived by the combined efforts of "Author and Surgeon" a few pages later on.

Author and surgeon are far less effective in Reading's 1984 book, *C,* which is all about dying horribly. A lot of $5 \times 5 \times 5 \times 5 \times 5$ teeters on the edge of caricature (a lot of ordinary life does the same thing). As in the less successful black-comedy poems of *Diplopic,* there is a feeling that the poet-comedian's inventions are being punished for being less sophisticated or imaginative than he would wish, and, as a corollary, that his redemptive strokes—implied pity, or the implied "It was only a joke!"—flirt with the facile, patronizing or sentimental. *C* (the big one, cancer, the subject of the book, and, as Roman numeral, its organizing principle: "Incongruously I plan/100 100-word units," the epigraph announces) focuses such doubts more sharply than before, and refutes them.

The "100-word units"—they are for the most part prose, and to call them prose poems would be a travesty of everything Reading is trying to do— probe our horror and dread of painful death through analytically precise notation of the medical facts, which are very nasty indeed; "you might lend the issue added poignancy/by being distanced," suggests one of the poems in *Diplopic. C,* though on occasion courting this kind of inverted sentimentality, goes far beyond it, and beyond knowingness, by drowning all possibility of distance or poignancy in a welter of feces, blood, and vomit, or in a chorus of the agonized, bitter voices of the dying. Reading balances an appalled descriptive clarity in dealing with physical realities against extreme, almost mad sophistication in handling the gruesome ironies of helplessness—the helplessness of the dying and the helplessness of their helpers.

The poet is helpless himself, or at least his "hero," the "Master of the 100 100-word units," is. Verse ("unvindicable") is one of the book's first casualties, and is only used wherever it is most grimly inappropriate—or even more grimly appropriate (a thirteen-line sonnet for unlucky people, catalectic or truncated tetrameters for a mastec-

tomy, "Quasi sham tétramètre, sub-Corneille, sub-Racine,/is too grand, is too weak, for this slow tragedy,/screaming 'Please, get me well! Dear sweet God, make me well!' "). The voice of the "stoical" poet is interspersed with others': a hysterical bereaved wife, a coolly despairing consultant, a paleontologist (whom Reading's readers have encountered before, in *Diplopic* and $5 \times 5 \times 5 \times 5 \times 5$), the tramp or gypsy Tucker, also known as "Char" or "Mort," who has—literally—the last laugh. These characters are revolved before the reader in linked episodes, the narrative threads crossing most strikingly in the "same vertical column" of an acrostic verse, representing five floors of a hospital—and all moving toward the same end. "All planted, at the time of going to press. Some feared oblivion; most feared pain."

The paleontologist makes repeated attempts to establish the insignificance of human life, suffering, and death in the vast perspectives of geological time (a Reading leitmotif); the Master's domestic and erotic memories counter him with an unbearable sense of impending loss. Both the former's insane passion for scholarly data and the latter's Vergilian noble-suicide fantasy sound a bit desperate by the end, with their cancers well advanced and things getting *pretty* nasty. Abject misery and rage— the rage of the dying against the living—is counterpointed by the rigorous neutrality of the medical dictionary and the nursing handbook. A note of understandable strain recurs: "Why write it? Why ever write any of it? Poetry all weak lies, games." and this often comes accompanied by some fairly hard puns: "Terminal verse. Rain-pits 700000000 years old in Precambrian rock; a species evolved 696000000 years after that: a handful of stresses and punctuation: ars only as long as vita: pentameters, like colons, inadequate." A good deal of the book may seem outrageous, even pitiless, in its particular stylizations of outrage and pity. It is Reading's most uncompromising book, but also, in its focus on the mortality of "Poor frail dear frightened little vulnerable creatures" (not just the poet and the paleontologist, but the folksinger, the Head of Fine Art, Tucker's "erstwhile leman," the lady from Azalea Terrace: "Us *all*"), his most humane. There may always be those, of course, whose first question would be: But is it poetry? To answer them there is the last-but-two "unit," containing a page from a notepad found, the poet imagines, on his body after his dreamed-up suicide (he is in fact too weak, by now, to move from the bed): "No. Something more prosy/for this job. . . ./ . . . ./But some structure still?/Why? Dignity?" The very last words are more affirmative: "My wife patiently washes my faece-besmirched pyjamas, for *prosaic* love."

Reading's early work did not attract a great deal of critical attention or understanding (his second book, for example, was impatiently dismissed by D. M. Thomas). The three most recent collections have deservedly been far better treated in this respect, and, during the last year or so, Reading's writing has also provoked considerable interest—not all of it of the most helpful kind—outside literary-critical circles. He became, briefly, something of a controversial figure after the poem "Cub," a dramatic monologue voiced by a cub reporter who witnesses a violent incident in Lebanon, was printed in the *Times Literary Supplement* for 23 March 1984. The poem was badly misunderstood; the most common misreading took it to be an anti-Semitic statement. It was virulently attacked as such, and fiercely defended as the ironic, antiwar poem it in fact is in the letters columns of both the *Times Literary Supplement* and the *Times.* Reviewers and poets, though better informed and usually more appreciative of Reading's originality, have also expressed doubts, however. Gavin Ewart, an admirer of Reading's work and undoubtedly an influence on it, pointed, while reviewing *Diplopic,* to the element of overstatement or cruelty in one or two pieces; Grevel Lindop, in an otherwise laudatory review of *Tom o'Bedlam's Beauties,* remarked of some of the poems that "their very pursuit of 'fun' and 'flexibility' [the qualities, according to a poem by Reading in that book, that Gavin Ewart points us toward, in life and poetry] threatens to diminish their humanity and lead them into the realm of the whimsical and self-admiring." This uncertainty about tone was most succinctly put by Edna Longley, in the course of her account of *Fiction;* she saw, in what were admittedly "good jokes," a "defensive strategy" taking shape.

Longley found some of the reasons for this in the general cultural "climate," but there are more personal ones as well. It is certainly true that the typical Reading poem of recent years is a triple or quadruple take, irony reinforcing irony and undercut by further irony; that such undercutting is, to the English ear, a time-honored preemptive move; and that Reading, as he sets down, with a wry laugh, the rueful exactions of his scholarly and curious mind on the uglier truths of loss, ageing, pain, misadventure, misery, disease, and death, can lay himself open to accusations of "inhumanity" or

heartlessness. And that "defensive strategy" can suggest, not only ironic self-awareness but something closer to self-disgust. Reading acknowledged all this in an interview given to the present writer and published in *Poetry Review* (April 1985). Here he spoke of his admiration for Samuel Beckett, Francis Bacon, and Evelyn Waugh (all artists with a sharp eye for, and complex responsiveness to, the grotesque), noted his own "supercilious" ear and eye for the speech and behavior of others, and, more important, discussed some of the preoccupations that inform his writing: "Art has always struck me most when it was to do with coping with things, often hard things, things that are difficult to take. . . . We all have a lack of sympathy, or we wouldn't be able to tick over. We're spared real grief by the impersonality of most affairs. . . . There seems to be nothing but health-giving sanity in dealing with any issue that comes your way. . . . There's a completely literal justification for my being, if you like, heartless and all that. I don't really think there's anything *to* us, we're organisms, and that's O.K. . . . When people are insulted by their gods being insulted, this is baffling and shocking to me, a simple man who is insulted hugely, in the normal course of events. What horrifies me, really, and comes as a surprise, is that people continue to be bothered by such things, and that dangerous, violent, horrible, malevolent theisms thrive, more to the point. . . . I hope I'm not essentially gloomy, that is to say regretful. But I feel total impotence."

That he has continued to make from this feeling his clever, dark, funny, and despairing books, his "comedy of terrors" as George Szirtes has called them, testifies not merely to the persistence of a vision but also to an intellectual fertility and range, an imaginative boldness and linguistic vitality that are rare in contemporary British poetry. As Mick Imlah, editor of *Poetry Review,* has put it, his poems have "fascinated many readers and upset or repelled a vociferous few." In a *Times Literary Supplement* symposium (27 April 1984) on the question "Which poet or poets have had the greatest effect on your idea of poetic form, and the forms in which you write," Reading answered, "Auden, for . . . the idea that 'Blessed be all metrical rules/that forbid automatic responses,/force us to have second thoughts, free from the fetters of self.'" The prolific Reading looks set to go on shocking or teasing readers—fascinated, upset, or repelled—out of their automatic responses for some time to come.

Peter Redgrove

(2 January 1932-   )

Lawrence R. Ries
Skidmore College

SELECTED BOOKS: *The Collector and Other Poems* (London: Routledge & Kegan Paul, 1960);

The Nature of Cold Weather and Other Poems (London: Routledge & Kegan Paul, 1961);

At the White Monument and Other Poems (London: Routledge & Kegan Paul, 1963);

The Sermon: A Prose Poem (London: Poet & Printer, 1966);

The Force and Other Poems (London: Routledge & Kegan Paul, 1966);

Penguin Modern Poets 11, by Redgrove, D. M. Thomas, and D. M. Black (Harmondsworth: Penguin, 1968);

Work in Progress MDMLXVIII (London: Poet & Printer, 1968);

The Mother, the Daughter, and the Sighing Bridge (Oxford: Sycamore Press, 1970);

Love's Journeys (Cardiff: Second Aeon, 1971);

Three Pieces for Voices (Woodford Green: Poet & Printer, 1972);

Dr. Faust's Sea-Spiral Spirit and Other Poems (London & Boston: Routledge, 1972);

In the Country of the Skin [radio play] (Rushden, Northamptonshire: Sceptre Press, 1973);

In the Country of the Skin [novel] (London: Routledge & Kegan Paul, 1973);

The Hermaphrodite Album, by Redgrove and Penelope Shuttle (London: Fuller D'Arch Smith, 1973);

The Terrors of Dr. Treviles, by Redgrove and Shuttle (London: Routledge & Kegan Paul, 1974);

Sons of My Skin: Selected Poems 1954-1974, edited by Marie Peel (London & Boston: Routledge & Kegan Paul, 1975);

The Glass Cottage: A Nautical Romance, by Redgrove and Shuttle (London: Routledge & Kegan Paul, 1976);

From Every Chink of the Ark and Other New Poems (London & Boston: Routledge & Kegan Paul, 1977);

Ten Poems (London: Words Press, 1977);

Miss Carstairs Dressed for Blooding and Other Plays (London: Boyars, 1977);

The Wise Wound: Menstruation and Everywoman, by Redgrove and Shuttle (London: Gollancz, 1978); republished as *The Wise Wound: Eve's Curse and Everywoman* (New York: Marek, 1978);

The Weddings at Nether Powers and Other New Poems (London & Boston: Routledge & Kegan Paul, 1979);

The God of Glass (London: Routledge & Kegan Paul, 1979);

The Sleep of the Great Hypnotist (London: Routledge & Kegan Paul, 1979);

The Beekeepers (London: Routledge & Kegan Paul, 1980);

The Apple-Broadcast and Other New Poems (London & Boston: Routledge & Kegan Paul, 1981);

The Facilitators, Or, Madam Hole-in-the-Day (London: Routledge & Kegan Paul, 1982);

The Working of Water (N.p.: Taxus, 1984);

The Man Named East (London: Routledge & Kegan Paul, 1985).

PLAY PRODUCTION: *The Hypnotist*, Plymouth, 1978.

TELEVISION: *Mr. Waterman*, BBC TV, 1961;
The Sermon: A Prose Poem, BBC TV, 1964;
Leap in the Dark; Jack Be Nimble, BBC2 TV, 1980.

RADIO: *The Nature of Cold Weather*, BBC Radio 3, 1961;
The White Monument, BBC Radio 3, 1963;
The Anniversary, 1964;
The Case, BBC Radio 3, 1965;
Double Bill, BBC Radio 3, 1965;
The Son of My Skin, BBC Radio 3, 1973;
In the Country of the Skin: A Radio Dramatization, BBC Radio 3, 1973;
The Holy Sinner, adapted from a novel by Thomas Mann, BBC, 1975;
Dance the Putrefact, by Redgrove with music by Anthony Smith-Masters, 1975;
The God of Glass, BBC Radio 3, 1977;
Martyr of the Hives, BBC Radio 4, 1980;
Florent and the Tuxedo Millions, BBC Radio 3, 1982;

Photo © Edward Lucie-Smith,
Courtesy of Bernard Stone,
The Turret Book Shop

The Sin-Doctor, BBC Radio 3, 1983;
Dracula in White, BBC Radio 4, 1983;
Scientists of the Strange, BBC Radio 3, 1984.

OTHER: *Poet's Playground 1963,* edited by Redgrove (Leeds: Schools Sports Association, 1963);
Universities Poetry 7, edited by Redgrove (Keele: Universities Poetry Management Committee, 1965);
New Poems 1967: A P.E.N. Anthology, edited by Redgrove, John Fuller, and Harold Pinter (London: Hutchinson, 1967);
New Poetry 5, edited by Redgrove and Jon Silkin (London: Hutchinson, 1979);
Cornwall in Verse, edited by Redgrove (London: Secker & Warburg, 1983).

Peter Redgrove was one of the original members of that clique of poets who began meeting under the direction first of Philip Hobsbaum in the 1950s and later of Edward Lucie-Smith. The

Group, as they were called, were not held together by a strict and unified poetic; they did, however, share a need for intellectual camaraderie where they could read and discuss their works in progress. Redgrove was able to use the Group as a sounding board, although his growth as a writer remained unrestricted by this interaction. The development of his language into a vibrant concretism, rich in sound and imagery, is probably the Group's most enduring legacy in his poetry. For while this early association occurred at a time when critics were too eagerly assigning the British poets to unnecessary categories, Redgrove was able to create his own unique voice without becoming dependent upon a superimposed poetic doctrine.

His closest association, both intellectually and aesthetically, was with Ted Hughes, a contemporary who also did not easily fit into the standard categories. Hughes was his friend at Cambridge, and in their poetry they share an awed and celebratory testimony to raw nature. The force of their world is exuberant but unsympathetic to human needs, and man's consciousness must give way or integrate itself into the amoral universe. Redgrove's basic subject is the tension between the impulses toward the rational by the human conscience and the anarchic powers of nature, whether these instincts be found in the internal or external world. Over the years, Redgrove's poetry has moved from a straightforward, strongly imagistic approach, to a personal, self-interrogative exploration, and finally to surrealistic, symbolist investigations in verse and in prose. Always underlying these changes in style and form remains his search for the organic unity of being in which the mind can somehow be reintegrated with the amoral, elemental drives of the natural world.

Redgrove was born in Kingston, Surrey, and educated at Taunton School, Somerset, and at Queens College, Cambridge, where he read natural sciences. His knowledge of the natural world becomes central to his poetry because he approaches that world with an analytical eye, an eye trained by chemical research. His emphasis on organic unity is not the effect of a romantic pantheism, but results from his exploration of organic matter. From 1954 to 1961 he spent time as a scientific journalist and editor, while trying to horde time for his writing in the early morning hours. In 1961 he spent a year at Buffalo University as visiting poet, and in 1962, he was appointed Gregory Fellow in Poetry at Leeds University and remained there until 1965. During this time he married and had three children, but the fellowship at Leeds helped free him from the mid-

dle-class mores that up to that time had set the rhythm of his everyday life. He learned to set aside artificial strictures, whether they were the business suits he had worn or the fidelity he had practiced within his marriage of thirteen years. Mirroring the change in his life, his poetry lost much of its formalistic structure and became more dependent on the internal, personal eye. He and Barbara Redgrove were divorced, and in 1969 he began to live with Penelope Shuttle, with whom he has collaborated on much of his later work. They have had one daughter, born in 1976, and were married in December 1980. From 1966 to 1983 Redgrove held the position of author and senior lecturer in complementary studies at the Falmouth School of Art in Cornwall, with the exception of the 1974-1975 academic year when he was visiting professor at Colgate University.

The Collector and Other Poems (1960) was hailed as a robust, fresh volume of verse whose voice was distinctive and impressive. Reviewers for the *Times Literary Supplement* and the *New Statesman* noted Redgrove's similarity to Hughes in theme, but there is little or no sense of derivation or imitation. What the reader senses in this volume is a poet who has a keen awareness of the force of life and a gift for observation that allows him to put this energy on display. His poems are about the small areas of life that need the measure of a sharp eye to give them proper respect: cutting grass, stepping on a beetle, being stung by an insect. The energy of these poems is always rather ruthless, violent, and apparently meaningless or insignificant. The poet is a "collector" of observations, and what he observes he is frequently unable to understand in human terms. This first volume of poetry is a series of mythical, philosophical questionings that Redgrove returns to throughout his career.

Little time passed between the publication of *The Collector and Other Poems* and the appearance of his second volume, *The Nature of Cold Weather and Other Poems* (1961). Reviewing the book for *London Magazine*, George MacBeth immediately proclaimed that "Peter Redgrove is perhaps the most prolific young writer of repute since Auden." However, his ability to produce a substantial body of poetry in a short time did not guarantee literary success. This volume is an extension of the first, and in it Redgrove often pushes his powers of observation to extremes. His concern is to show rational man in relationship to uncontrollable nature. In the title poem, there are two voices: unfeeling nature, and encrusted man, who has been cut off from his responsive nature. The photographic eye is still at work, but Redgrove often burdens the reader with too much detail. At times the reader is buried beneath an avalanche of words and must attempt to make his way clear on his own. While the poet is certainly entitled to make demands upon his audience, too often these poems do not justify the author's proliferation of impacted detail. The nature poems are especially weighted down. On the other hand, Redgrove makes some new discoveries about the human world in this volume, and he becomes a more compassionate poet. He sheds his shrillness and pretension in "Disguise," which tells of a despondent, overweight man trapped in his own flesh. "Mr. Waterman" is a prose poem that humorously and touchingly describes how the water in the family pond assumes various forms and guises and rivals a middle-class working man for the favors of his wife: "I dread the time (for it will come) when I shall arrive home unexpectedly early, and hear a sudden scuffle-away in the waste-pipes, and find my wife ('just out of the shower, dear') with that moist look in her eyes, drying her hair." Whether Redgrove is describing nature itself ("The crested waves skip into the bay/Like small birds flocking, claws flicking") or his relationship with the natural world ("The rockery outside knuckles my mouth in prayer"), these poems have texture and substance. The reader can quickly distinguish the significant from the unimportant. One of the gravest temptations to Redgrove is to begin admiring his own cleverness at image making and to forget his audience.

His third volume in four years appeared in 1963 and was titled *At the White Monument and Other Poems*. As one might expect from such a prolific writer, the poems mainly repeat earlier themes and techniques. His thought still centers on the domestic scene in its tension with the natural world, and his language is original and provocative. But these poems must be judged on the relation of language to thought, on the ability of metaphor to explore meaning. This is clearly where this volume fails. Redgrove becomes so excited by what he is able to do with the language that he forgets, it seems, where his poetry is going, and for this reason many of the short poems seem incomplete. The verbal excitement has taken all the play away from the meaning, and poems in which the fecund imagination at first promises lush riches become finally the emptiness of mirage. In his first volume, Redgrove was frequently able to enhance the trivial by ornamenting it with language. Too often in this third volume he suffocates or irritates his audience by sleight-of-hand tricks that distract rather than

enlighten. One reviewer (*Times Literary Supplement*, 12 December 1963) noted his rich imagination but thought the "merely verbal excitement" led too frequently to boredom. The *New Statesman* (6 December 1963) admired his wide-ranging vocabulary, but thought the concept of the poem was too frequently suffocated by an excess of detail.

In *The Force and Other Poems* (1966) Redgrove still has his feet well planted in the mire, but with each examination of the natural world he tends to turn inward. The force he speaks of is the force of Dylan Thomas and D. H. Lawrence, the force that is both creator and destroyer. In poem after poem he attempts to understand how man has harnessed, resisted, or made his peace with such forces. He draws upon his scientific background and with that knowledge tries to convince the reader of the strange spirituality of the universe. A small poem, "Directive," opens with the admonition: "Attend to the outer world." Although he still delights in verbal fireworks, he is frequently able to subjugate language to theme and drive home his point, as in "Directive":

The World attend you
Like a friendship, in three clear notes
Out of a bird's open throat.

His message is hammered home again and again: man must accommodate himself to the forces of the universe and exist in some mutually supportive system with nature. Redgrove has not by any means abandoned his delight in linguistic battering and verbal play. But he is able to generate a great deal of poetic zeal in order to celebrate the joyful energy that seethes with the universe. John Fuller (*London Magazine*, March 1967) admired his ability to recreate this power through his poems: "No other poet shows life so intensely in terms of its basic forces." The reviewer for the *Times Literary Supplement* (23 February 1967), on the other hand, thought the energy of his poetry was rather directionless, and as a result, reading Redgrove's poetry, he said, was likely to leave the reader not only frustrated but physically fatigued.

After *The Force and Other Poems*, Redgrove's poetry begins to turn more and more inward. Before his next major volume of poetry, *Dr. Faust's Sea-Spiral Spirit and Other Poems* (1972), he published several small pamphlets in which he began to experiment with style and theme. One of these, which he called simply *Work in Progress MDMLXVIII* (1968), so impressed Gavin Ewart that he remarked, "The very quality of his imagination is entirely different from anybody else's." In *Love's Journeys* (1971), his poetry has become so subjective that the reader rarely recognizes the terrain of the poem. Much of the poetry is constructed of pure dream material and remains largely inaccessible. But there is an unmistakable sense that Redgrove is carefully exploring new ground, more for himself than for an audience, but hoping that some may find these surreal landscapes as exciting as he obviously does.

Many of the poems in *Work in Progress* and *Love's Journeys* are included in *Dr. Faust's Sea-Spiral Spirit and Other Poems*. Seemingly involved in almost a last desperate attempt to hold onto the physical world before being sucked into the vortex of the psyche, he produced a number of poems that return to the world of "mountainous sand-dunes," "granite, the great rock," "the wide flat waters." There are poems of heightened physical descriptions, such as "Minerals of Cornwall, Stones of Cornwall":

> Tissues of the earth, in their proper place,
> Quartz tinged with the rose, the deep quick,
> Scrap of tissue of the slow heart of the earth,
> Throbbing the light I look at it with,
> Pumps slowly, most slowly, the deep organ of the earth.

These descriptions reinforce Redgrove's reputation for a fertile imagination wedded to keen observation. What emerges is a sense of awe and wonder at the organic unity of nature, but without much distinction or variation between the observations. This lack of emotional shift or variation of tension produces a numbing effect, locking the reader out of the poet's exhilaration. When human sensibility is admitted to the world of the poem, its presence serves mainly as a point of reference; rarely does the focus of the poem become the human relationship. While similar criticisms may be made of the poetry of Gerard Manley Hopkins and Robinson Jeffers, their poems are ultimately mirrors which illuminate areas of the human condition. Redgrove, on the other hand, employs the human perspective to heighten his wonderment of the physical world.

Critics often paired Redgrove with Ted Hughes at this time, seeing in the poetry of both men an avoidance of human affairs and a somewhat sacrilegious attachment to the inhuman. The reviewer for *Stand* applied Samuel Johnson's statement on Milton: "The want of human interest is felt throughout." The poems of *Love's Journeys*, which

deal more directly with human relationships, were seen as being so subjective that few readers would be able to accompany the poet on these journeys (*Poetry Review,* Summer 1971).

By this time, the poet had extended his vision of the natural world to the point of repetition, so a change was obviously due. Redgrove admits to some rather severe changes in his personal life at this time. His three-year fellowship at Leeds finally freed him from the structures of working in an office, wearing suits, and other "unnecessary and obsessional formalism," as Redgrove calls it. For the first time he felt responsible only to himself and began to examine other structures within his life. For thirteen years he had been in a marriage which was governed by the "tribal values" of faithfulness and restriction. After he was able to leave his office job, he found that he was able to shed conventional middle-class views, and he came to a fresh understanding of the issues of feminism. His embracing of feminism culminated in his collaboration with Penelope Shuttle on *The Wise Wound,* work that proved to be a major influence on his later poetry. Their collaboration presaged a change of style in his poetry from the formal and deliberate to a softer, more relaxed tone. Accompanying this change in style is an attempt to deal more vigorously and honestly with interior reality.

In a 1975 interview, Redgrove talked extensively about an experience he had when he entered the army at eighteen and decided shortly thereafter to fake a loss of memory in order to be released. He was examined by an army psychiatrist and diagnosed as "incipient schizophrenic," for which he was exposed to a new treatment, insulin shock therapy, in which all the sugar was drained from his blood until he went into convulsions and ultimately into a coma. At that point he was brought back to equilibrium gradually. He went through this therapy many times. Redgrove explains, "And the myth of it is that you die and are reborn. And that's exactly what happened. I remember being taken to pieces and being put together again."

In the mid-1970s, Redgrove seemed ready to deal with this experience and to try to understand its meaning. He was also living with Penelope Shuttle, and much of his future writing would be done in conjunction with her. A third important factor is that the works of Norman O. Brown and other symbolic psychologists became a central focus for his intellectual life. He had undergone Freudian analysis and had trained as a Jungian analyst with Dr. John Layard. Since 1969 he had been practicing analytical psychology as a lay analyst. It is little won-

Peter Redgrove (photograph by Nicholas Elder)

der that Redgrove moves from the poetry of natural wonder to the poetry of natural religion. He explains, "For myself, all the things that official religion ought to be about is in poetry. . . . What poetry is about is what is commonly called sacred."

In 1973 and 1974, Redgrove brought out two poetical novels, *In the Country of the Skin* and *The Terrors of Dr. Treviles,* both of which have their loci in the spiritual psyche. *In the Country of the Skin,* which won the *Guardian* Fiction Prize, explores the duality of nature through a series of spiritual, intellectual, and erotic discoveries. The central character, Jonas, discovers a magical persona, Silas, that exists within him. For Jonas to live in a world where poetry and sexuality are allowed to exist, the erotic and creative concerns of Silas must be satisfied. This journey to psychic freedom is not concerned with external events. As Redgrove explains, "in an erotic state of mind you are living in a state somewhere between dream and waking, where the imaginative becomes literally true. This is the theme of *In the Country of the Skin.*"

The Terrors of Dr. Treviles, which was co-authored with Penelope Shuttle, is an attempt to explore and outline a philosophy, "almost an explanatory novel," for Redgrove says he felt a responsibility to those of temperaments different from his. In this work, the rational powers of the

world are pitted against the magical psychologist, Dr. Treviles, who embodies the good qualities of the world: mystical religion, art, biology, emotion. The story of Dr. Treviles's struggle to freedom is told in spritely prose, but like many novels of ideas the story is dull and plodding.

In 1975, an edition of Redgrove's selected poetry from the past twenty years appeared under the title *Sons of My Skin.* Edited and given a somewhat overindulgent introduction by Marie Peel, it provides a good retrospective of the poet's work and allows the reader to trace his development from the early affirmation of the life force to the later intellectual and symbolist rebelliousness against consciousness. The early poems underscore the fact that Redgrove produced good, original nature poetry in which he strives for a sensuous understanding of life. A vigorous, dynamic vision wedded to a fresh descriptive use of language keeps his poetry from becoming idle glances at nature. However, when read as a group, the poems tend to congeal because of the density of image and language. The same style that allows the poet to approach the world with fresh vision also in part separates the poet and his subject from his audience.

The second half of *Sons of My Skin* demonstrates clearly the change in Redgrove's poetic vision. The natural and human worlds are left behind for a more mystical, surreal one. The irony of these poems is that in their rebellion against consciousness they carefully avoid any relation to the natural structures that Redgrove has always held in awe, while they reach toward a self-conscious surrealism. The necessity to achieve some higher realism finally represents an abandonment of the natural world.

The poems in *The Hermaphrodite Album* (1973), again coauthored with Penelope Shuttle, continue the thematic and stylistic directions of his recent poetry as well as of the two novels. Redgrove and Shuttle began with poetry that each wrote from the individual psyche, but as the volume evolves the poets act and react to the poems of the other so that the distinct imaginings gradually begin to merge and change into each other. The effect is a highly subjective poetry that too often is exciting only to the authors. Both subject and style deny entrance to most readers. Redgrove explains that "the poems are supposed to be experienced as in a light trance" (*Hudson Review,* Autumn 1975). A serious problem in this volume is one to which Redgrove has always been prone: his stylistic persiflage is such that he is tempted to write phrase after involuted phrase without much accumulation of meaning. The ob-

Dust jacket for Redgrove's first novel, winner of the Guardian *Fiction Prize*

vious parallels with the surrealists of the 1930s are acknowledged by Redgrove. In attempting to characterize the poems in this volume, he says, "They're surrealistic in the sense that they explore a world whose boundaries shift and change and transform. And they're surrealistic in the sense that they draw on this kind of dreamlike life, or a world in which the limitations *are* only subjective." When the limitations are this subjective, the poet has left unfulfilled, at least in part, his portion of the poetic contract. A review in the *Times Literary Supplement* ended tersely, "The collection is a sad abuse of proven talent."

Two more recent collections of poetry, *From Every Chink of the Ark and Other New Poems* (1977) and *The Weddings at Nether Powers and Other New Poems* (1979), continue this voyage into the unconscious. Both volumes are attempts to wed his fascination with the irrational with his original wonder at the natural. Many of these concerns run parallel to Hughes's thematic development, but while Hughes

was becoming more intrigued with the immediacy of detail (in *Gaudete*), Redgrove was moving into a more complicated use of language in order to examine the structures behind the phenomena.

From Every Chink of the Ark is a celebration of life, in whatever form it might be found. And it is found mainly in either primitive or mystical experiences. As in his fiction, he uses magic and fantasy as vehicles to transcend the rational. This world is pursued in long, unpunctuated poems that make great demands upon the reader, and the circle is drawn so tightly that there is little room in this imaginative world except for the initiated. It is the ordinary world that is shut out, and with it is excluded the potential for a shared perspective. A volume such as this tends to intensify the alignment of critics. The *New Review* said that Redgrove is "no longer willing to be answerable for his voyeuristic derangements," while the *London Magazine* saw this poetry as "Fantasy run amok in unpunctuated confusion." Anne Stevenson, writing in the *Times Liter-*

An old town's narrow streets on a clear day. A muddy walk to penetrate the green secrets of the world. Consequently the lights played about the altar again. I had xxxxx brou ht them wit me out of the green orld.

It had showered, and as I walked out into the air through wet clothes, as thou h the invisible clouds of water-vapour spiralling through the green ledges and boughs were gases of touch and a more closely linked vision. The net of jewels appeared in the spider-web, the dumpling shuddering in her Taj ahal, the spider in her star-shaped clothes . he boson full of invisible violets. In te verbena voyages of the dowager dowser she veered towards my vapours. There were angels with big sleeves reading inte annelid church, and the xxxxxxx weir fell quiet as the tide rose. Of these, spider, net of jewels, stone xxxxxx angels with bibles in a quiet church, dowser greeting me because I was wet from the rain (she had never noticed me before; which was te mystery sufficient to make li the play about the altar once again.

FROM THE LIFE OF A DOWSER-2

An old town's narrow streets
On a clear day. A muddy walk
Penetrates the green secrets.

In consequence the lights play
About the altar again. I brought them with me
Out of the earth-green world.

It has showered, and I was feeling
The world out through wet clothes
As though my skin were tripled,

As though the viewless clouds of water
Spiralling through the green ledges of boughs,
The vapour boiling off me like a field

In sunshine, my other flesh, my invisible
Astrals, were touching all the branches,
My vapours twining with the tree-dews

And their balsams, computing out of me
Gases of touch and linked vision.
The net of jewels started up in the spider-web,

That dumpling shuddered in her Taj Mahal,
The spider in her star-shaped clothes.
I saw the matronly dowser abroad,

She walked out in the rain as I did;
I shared the ecstasy of the dowsers.
The approach of dowsing resembles rheumatism,

The full clarity is like that spider-water,
Electrical, shining inwardly

Her bosom was full of invisible violets,
In her verbena voyages she veered
Towards my vapours, by which we merged and loved.

Thus the angels with their blowing sleeves,
Settled to their reading in the annelid nave,
And the weir outside fell silent

As the tide rose and we came home:
Nets of jewels, stone angels
Handling bibles in a quiet church,

Dowser-greeting; now the lights ran
And skittered round the sacred cup and candles.

An old town's narrow streets
On a clear day. A muddy walk
Penetrates the green secrets.

In consequence the lights play
About the altar again, which I had brought
With me out of the earth-green world

Dressed in its russet and olive.
It ad showered, and I was feeling
The world out trough wet clothes

As though my skin were tripled
As though the viewless clouds of water
Spiralling through the green ledges and boughs

The vapour boiling off me like a field
In sunshine, my other body, my invisible
Astrals were touching all the branches

My vapours twined with the tree-dews
With their balsams compulating
Gases of touch and linked vision.

The net of jewels started up in the spider-web
That dumpling shuddering inher Taj Mahal,
The spider in her star-shaped clothes.

I saw the matronly dowser abroad.
She walked out in the rain as I did
I share the ecstasy of the dowsers

The approach of dowsing is like rheumatism
The full clarity is like electrical water
Shining inits filaments and loaded circuits

Her bosom was full of invisible violets
In her verbena voyages she veered
Towards my vapours by which we loved

There were angels with big sleeves
Settled to their reading inthe annelid nave
And the weir outside fell silent

As the tide rose and they came home.
Net of jewels, stone angels
With bibles in a quiet church.

Dowser-greeting; now the lights ran
And skitt red round the sacred cup and candles

Two drafts and the published version of a poem by Redgrove (the author)

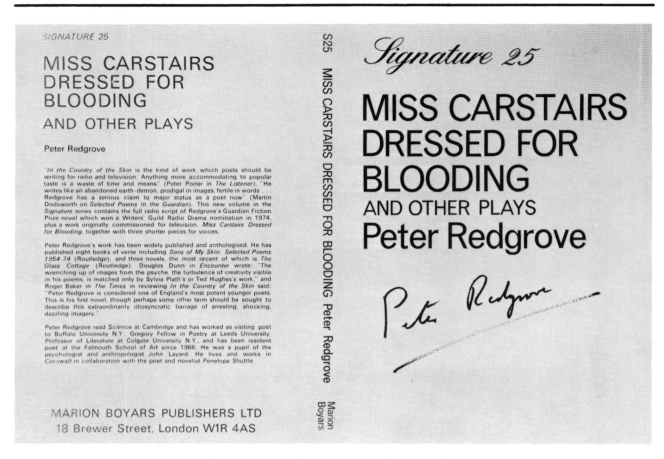

Dust jacket for Redgrove's second collection of plays

ary Supplement, after acknowledging that "his expression can be difficult and clumsy," proclaimed that "his feeling for the deepest, most mystical levels of existence is unparalleled in modern poetry."

The Weddings at Nether Powers continued to provoke this debate, although here the poet seems more in control of the fantasy world than in the previous volume. His imagery, especially the consistent use of water, works as a unifying element that allows the reader greater access to the poet's vision. The poet himself is identified with water as the source of all life, whether great or small. This force also imbues nature with a vital holiness, and water is posited against the world of stone, the world of petrification. Cloud and thunder are portents of energy and restoration; they open up a magical, fecund, transcendent reality where "the toad sprouts feathers, every wart a gem."

The imagery of these poems frequently works in opposition to the long, involuted style that still carries over from the earlier volume. This style is a

reflection of his commitment to surrealism, a surrealism that works better in his shorter poems. The imagery is reminiscent of nineteenth-century French symbolism, which also found shorter forms more accommodating for wedding the precise to the imprecise. Too much reflection can sometimes be a burden to a writer; Redgrove stands closer to the glory of the world when he does not intellectualize his response. The more he tries to elaborate upon his response, the more his language tends to get between his subject and his audience.

If *The Hermaphrodite Album* can be seen as Redgrove's least communicative work in his surrealistic style, *The Apple-Broadcast and Other New Poems* (1981) represents his most effective work in this style. He has grown more proficient in adapting his basic subject, the natural world, to his later concerns with various levels of consciousness. This growth is a welcome, encouraging sign that he has become neither static nor stale. One of the recurring images of this volume is the baking of bread, which is equated with the activity of the poet. Both are seen as acts of daily renewal, not stone-etched, eternal gestures.

More important, Redgrove returns to what he has done best poetically, to reinterpreting the physical world and its energies. His vision is more mature, but there is no great need to blur it with complicated linguistic gestures. "At the Street Party" crisply, simply extends his vision of the water that has permeated all his poetry: "Water makes her way, accustomed/Into all places, through mire as an eel,/Through the air as a hawk." *The Apple-Broadcast,* although a difficult volume of poetry, displays a great sense of play and invention, as well as the poet's real gift for storytelling.

Redgrove has gone through several transformations during the nearly thirty years he has been writing and publishing poetry. He began as an explorer of nature, but with a curiosity overlaid by scientific training. His awe of the natural world

gradually led him inward, where he brought his investigative powers to the recesses of the psyche. While this middle period was obviously a fertile one for Redgrove's imagination, his poetry became more obscure and difficult, almost an abandonment of the world in which he began to write. Perhaps because of the nature of his interests, he turned more to the poetic novel as the means to explore his themes. But gradually he is moving back toward his beginnings, fortunately not in a repetitive or regressive way. Rather he brings to the natural world the wisdom and vision that his journeys through the world of the fantastic have provided him. Through this dialectic, Redgrove has created his own particular role in the poetry of fantasy. In assessing the manner in which Redgrove has staked out his imaginative claim on the world, Philip Hobsbaum has declared, "Peter Redgrove is the most imaginative and vital poet of the last thirty years."

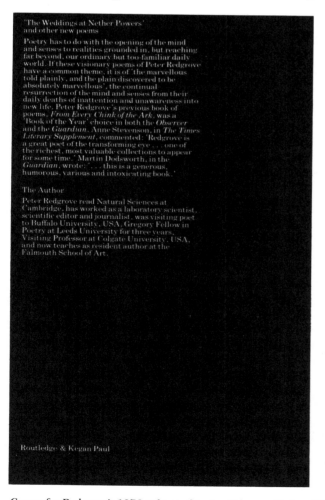

Covers for Redgrove's 1979 volume of poetry, "pleasurable proof," wrote one reviewer, "that Redgrove remains one of the most energetic and original of living English poets"

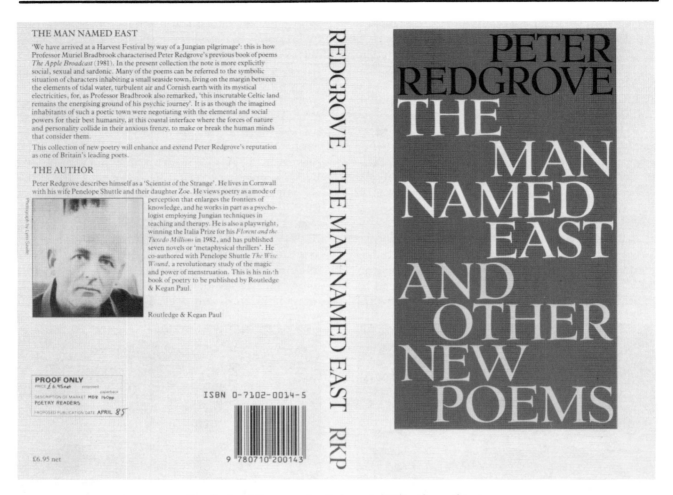

THE MAN NAMED EAST

'We have arrived at a Harvest Festival by way of a Jungian pilgrimage': this is how Professor Muriel Bradbrook characterised Peter Redgrove's previous book of poems *The Apple Broadcast* (1981). In the present collection the note is more explicitly social, sexual and sardonic. Many of the poems can be referred to the symbolic situation of characters inhabiting a small seaside town, living on the margin between the elements of tidal water, turbulent air and Cornish earth with its mystical electricities, for, as Professor Bradbrook also remarked, 'this inscrutable Celtic land remains the energising ground of his psychic journey'. It is as though the imagined inhabitants of such a poetic town were negotiating with the elemental and social powers for their best humanity, at this coastal interface where the forces of nature and personality collide in their anxious frenzy, to make or break the human minds that consider them.

This collection of new poetry will enhance and extend Peter Redgrove's reputation as one of Britain's leading poets.

THE AUTHOR

Peter Redgrove describes himself as a 'Scientist of the Strange'. He lives in Cornwall with his wife Penelope Shuttle and their daughter Zoe. He views poetry as a mode of perception that enlarges the frontiers of knowledge, and he works in part as a psychologist employing Jungian techniques in teaching and therapy. He is also a playwright, winning the Italia Prize for his *Florent and the Tuxedo Millions* in 1982, and has published seven novels or 'metaphysical thrillers'. He co-authored with Penelope Shuttle *The Wise Wound*, a revolutionary study of the magic and power of menstruation. This is his ninth book of poetry to be published by Routledge & Kegan Paul.

Routledge & Kegan Paul

PROOF ONLY

£6.95 net

ISBN 0-7102-0014-5

Proof copy of the covers for Redgrove's 1985 volume of poetry

References:

Douglas Dunn, "Ways of Booming," *Encounter*, 45 (September 1975): 76-80;

Roger Garfitt, "The Group," in *British Poetry Since 1960*, edited by Michael Schmidt and Grevel Lindop (Oxford: Carcanet Press, 1972), pp. 13-69;

Philip Hobsbaum, "Poetry of Barbarism," in his *Tradition and Experiment in English Poetry* (London: Macmillan, 1979), pp. 308-330;

Jed Rasula and Mike Erwin, "Interview with Peter Redgrove," *Hudson Review*, 28 (Autumn 1975): 377-401;

M. L. Rosenthal, *The New Poets: American and British Poetry Since World War II* (New York: Oxford University Press, 1967);

Anne Stevenson, "The Voice of the Green Man," *Times Literary Supplement*, 18 November 1977, p. 1355.

Papers:

The Humanities Research Center in Austin, Texas, and Brotherton Library, University of Leeds, have collections of Redgrove's papers.

Christopher Reid

(13 May 1949-   )

Michael Hulse

BOOKS: *Arcadia* (Oxford: Oxford University Press, 1979);
Pea Soup (Oxford & New York: Oxford University Press, 1982);
Katerina Brac (London: Faber & Faber, forthcoming 1985).

In 1978 and again in 1980 Christopher Reid shared with Craig Raine the Prudence Farmer Award, a poetry prize given each year for the best poem or poems to have appeared in the pages of the *New Statesman* during the previous twelve months. The coupling of the names was symptomatic: it has been somewhat difficult for Christopher Reid to be acknowledged and assessed as a poet in his own right, for the tendency among British critics has been to see him as little more than Craig Raine's righthand man in the Martian school. There is some reason for viewing these poets in tandem, not least their shared Oxford background and publisher, and there is also justice in considering Reid the less substantial talent, but it is evident too that Christopher Reid's poetry has characteristics and strengths which are distinctly his own.

Christopher John Reid was born in Hong Kong, the son of James Theodore and Alice Margaret Reid (née Dedear): his father worked until his retirement for the Shell Oil Company. Christopher Reid, as is frequently the case with expatriate British children, spent his life from school age in boarding and public schools in England, first at Kingswood House, Epsom (1956-1962), and then at Tonbridge School (1962-1967). His early life in Hong Kong does not appear in his poetry, which is more strongly resistant to the autobiographical than Raine's work, nor do recollections of his school career or of subsequent studies at Oxford (Exeter College, 1968-1971) play any part in his poems. After graduating in 1971, Christopher Reid worked at various times as a part-time librarian in the Ashmolean Classics Library, an actor, a filing-clerk, a flyman in the Victoria Palace Theatre, and as what he describes as a "nanny/tutor." That none of this experience has made any impression upon his creative work suggests that resistance to the

Christopher Reid (photograph by Mark Lumley)

autobiographical is almost a phobia. As Reid himself puts it, "I am quite happy to be shrouded in mystery so far as my private life is concerned."

This aversion to the presence in the poetic writings of an autobiographical persona is more pronounced in Reid than in any of those poets—John Fuller, Craig Raine, David Sweetman—with whose names his own might reasonably be associated; and Reid is nothing if not consistent. For example, when reviewing Sylvia Plath's *Collected Poems* in the *Observer* (1 November 1981) Reid makes it clear that he shares that English reluctance to approve extremes of the ego: "her work attracts aficionados not so much of poetry as of personality: connoisseurs of morbid states of mind; feminists keen to see their grievances projected in dramatic form; those who are thrilled by the idea of suicide; soul-mate egotists and the like." It has been a feature of the new cult of man-about-town wit and dandyish urbanity in British poetry to reject the ethic of confessionalism and prefer not to show a private face in a public place, and Christopher Reid is perhaps the most resolute of these public wits.

Thus the poems in his first collection, *Arcadia* (1979), take a big band, gardens, a pigeon, a horse-jumping meet at Windsor, a rugby match, a games arcade, a weight lifter, a butcher, indeed anything and anyone but Reid himself as their subjects. The results are certainly readable and inventive, with a

> squiggly hookah,
> fendered in levers, wheezing the blues;

those three hypodermics pumping in a row;
men groaning and swooning. . . .

In this poem "Strange Vibes," the big band which is the subject is not even mentioned specifically: in Reid as in Richard Wilbur, John Fuller, or Craig Raine there is much of the riddlemaker, with a gentle smile on his lips and a deep zest for new angles of perception.

In 1978 Christopher Reid won an Eric Gregory Award from the Society of Authors for the typescript of *Arcadia,* and it is important to remember that at that date—the year marked Raine's first book publication—the Martian emphasis on simile and metaphor was still new and could make a strong impact. *Arcadia* appeared in 1979, the year in which Craig Raine's second volume, *A Martian Sends a Postcard Home,* gave a label to the new movement of wit and imagination, and Reid's work was manifest-

Covers for Reid's first book, a Poetry Book Society recommendation and winner of the Somerset Maugham Award and the Hawthornden Prize

The opening poems in *Pea Soup*, Christopher Reid's second collection, dwell on domestic themes, but there follow pieces in which the poet explores more exotic territory — foreign and fictitious lands — in his meditation on the 'next-to-nothingness' of human life. Readers of his previous book, *Arcadia*, may detect a new, more sombre note in this one, and yet the comic spirit and enjoyment of metaphor still prevail. *Pea Soup* ends with a handful of love poems, addressed to the poet's wife.

Christopher Reid received both a Somerset Maugham Award and the distinguished Hawthornden Prize for *Arcadia*.

'After reading *Arcadia* you feel that the world is a stranger, richer, more various place than you'd supposed, a feeling which it takes commitment of a kind to produce.'
Blake Morrison in the *New Statesman*

'*Arcadia* sparkles with fresh insights . . . There's an appealing boyishness, and a Proustian flavouring . . . a bright debut.'
John Carey in the *Sunday Times*

'This is the kind of originality one would run a hundred miles to find.'
Gavin Ewart in *Quarto*

Cover illustration: The Nightingale's Banquet.
Attributed to Ryūryūkyo Shinsai (1764?-1820).

OXFORD UNIVERSITY PRESS
£4.50 net in UK   ISBN 0 19 211952 4

PEA SOUP
CHRISTOPHER REID

Covers for Reid's second volume of poetry, which received mixed reviews

ly of the same cast as Raine's. Reid's "smutty pigeon on a parapet/pecks for crumbs like a sewing-machine." In his games arcade "the one-armed bandits kept saluting,/or sounded off in spates of shooting" and "visiting generals looked impressed/ by the medals that swivel on a manly chest." The weight lifter "carries his pregnant belly/in the hammock of his leotard/like a melon wedged in a shopping-bag. . . ." Ginger-root is "arthritic" and chilies are "red leather winklepickers." The most mundane of activities can find a place in a sequence labeled "The Haiku adapted for Home Use," as in these lines on clipping one's nails: "A clipper rounds the cape./Something drops overboard—/of a crescent shape."

Like Raine in his poems unified by Indian or Hindu imagery, Reid too takes over from the metaphysical poets the knack of basing a series of

perceptions on a single conceit, as in "From an Idea by Toulouse-Lautrec" with its unifying religious imagery. "Most of my poems," wrote Reid in the *Poetry Book Society Bulletin* when *Arcadia* was a recommendation, "began with enjoyment—a delight, say, in something perceived—and the poem will have lost everything unless that initial enjoyment is conveyed by the finished work." Indeed, the pleasure principle is central to Reid's poetry, though his work is by no means naive. On the contrary, it is often complex both intellectually and allusively, as in "The Life of the Mind," a curious poem (arguably the finest in *Arcadia*), which appears to allegorize the passage of an idea through the mind.

In 1979 the moment was right for Christopher Reid's urbane poetry of wit, his air of relaxation in the cultural museum, and *Arcadia* brought him a Somerset Maugham Award (1980) and the

Hawthornden Prize (1981). There were those who dismissed his image-making fancy as a trivialization of poetry, but on the whole critical and popular response to his work was positive. This was not the case when his second collection, *Pea Soup,* was published in 1982. John Lucas in the *New Statesman* suggested that "like the Imagist moment, the Martian moment was important in re-directing our attention to matters that had gone out of the news; but perhaps it is time we went back to calling a fly a fly," and he added that "a poet of Reid's talents should begin to test himself on more rebarbative material than he has so far shown himself willing to attempt." Similar complaints, though often tactfully embedded in enthusiasm for Reid's untiring inventiveness, could be heard from the majority of reviewers of that second volume.

The reason for this change of mood, or diminishment of receptivity, lies in the strikingly unusual tone and manner that Raine and Reid both adopted at the end of the 1970s. It made its impact by being so obviously different, but once the reading public had become used to the new approach, it was easy for further work in that style to appear self-parodying. In the early 1980s Raine appeared to be moving toward a more relaxed, narrative mode, but the Reid of *Pea Soup* appears unaware of any need for development. In various poems Reid's exclamations at finding himself in a "playground of impromptu metaphors," that life "reads like a rebus" and is governed by "certain arcane laws," or that "everything was bogus," encouraged the belief that Reid was entering a phase of self-parody: the success of the Martian mode, with its new angles of perception, was related to its not insistently drawing attention to the freshness or bizarreness of its approach.

Yet, it must be admitted that those points in which Reid is plainly Craig Raine's superior—the ingenuousness of his playful aesthetic and the fertility of his metaphysical investigations—remain strongly present in *Pea Soup,* while there are also signs that a more personal note may be entering his work. In *Arcadia* only the wedding poem, "A Valve against Fornication," reads as if it might be autobiographical, but in *Pea Soup* there are a number of attractive love poems addressed to his wife, actress Lucinda Gane, whom Reid married on 7 July 1979. "Bravura Passage," a catalogue of grimy Thamesside observations, ends with a comparison of a motor launch "abounding in chutzpah" with "you/ and your adventurous beauty/in the midst of things," while in "At the Wrong Door" the poet misses his wife after her bath and pauses "to think how somewhere else/you may be standing, naked, lonely,/amid a downfall of dampish towels." And in one of the volume's most attractive pieces, "Kawai's Trilby," about an experience in a hotel room during Reid's Japanese travels at the end of the decade, he writes with a simple directness he had not previously been able to command:

> Maudlin without you, in a world
> lacking all reciprocity,
> I watched the emblems as they twirled,
> the brand-names blinking, and briefly
> felt the dull fear of a lost child.
>
> An apprehension of Japan,
> vertiginous and mad! I knew
> the swimminess of Limbo then,
> its throb of silence, and missed you
> to make sense of the things I'd seen.

Christopher Reid works in London as a freelance journalist. In the autumn of 1985 a new collection, *Katerina Brac,* will be published by Faber and Faber, now also the publisher of Craig Raine, who is their poetry editor.

John Riley

(10 October 1937-27 October 1978)

Tim Longville

BOOKS: *Ancient and Modern* (Lincoln: Grosseteste, 1967);

Common Objects 1962-1964, by Riley and Tim Longville (Lincoln: Grosseteste, 1967);

The Civil War, by Riley and Longville (Lincoln: Grosseteste, 1967);

A Legend of St. Anthony, by Riley and Longville (Lincoln: Grosseteste, 1967);

What Reason Was: Poems 1967-1969 (Lincoln: Grosseteste, 1970);

Correspondences (London: The Human Constitution, 1970);

The Lou Poems, by Riley and Longville (Lincoln: Grosseteste, 1971);

Ways of Approaching (Pensnett: Grosseteste, 1973);

Prose Pieces (Pensnett: Grosseteste, 1974);

That Is Today (Newcastle upon Tyne: Pig Press, 1978);

A Meeting (Alvechurch: Stingy Artist, 1978);

Collected Works (Wirksworth: Grosseteste, 1981).

TRANSLATIONS: *In the Arms of the Gods, Versions of Hölderlin,* volume 1, translated by Riley and Tim Longville (Lincoln: Grosseteste, 1967);

What I Own, Versions of Hölderlin, volume 2 (Pensnett: Grosseteste, 1973);

Mandelshtam's Octets (Pensnett: Grosseteste, 1976);

Mandelshtam: The Stalin Ode Sequence (Melbourne: Rigmarole Of The Hours, 1979).

John Riley

John Riley's poetry is one of the most interesting and substantial achievements from the whole range of experimental writing produced in England during the last twenty years. Owing little to and largely ignored by the literary establishment, Riley's work expresses an admiration for the intentions and techniques of Americans such as Ezra Pound, George Oppen, and Charles Olson (for whom he wrote a fine memorial poem), and a passionately unacademic interest in a range of foreign poetry, including French and German (he translated Friedrich Hölderlin extensively), but focusing finally on the Russian poetry of the twentieth century, from which he translated work by writers such as Boris Pasternak, Anna Akhmatova, Vladislav Khodasevich, and, particularly, Osip Mandelshtam. Underlying such cosmopolitan elements is a spiritual concern so deep-rooted that it led him increasingly to view social and political matters (indeed, finally, to view everything) as intelligible only in the light of an essentially religious perspective (which led him in 1977 to become in fact what he had long been in effect, a member of the Orthodox church), and an altogether uncozy form of localism which had little in common with most recent English writing about place. Out of these elements he fashioned, in the last ten years of his life, a poetry both profoundly his own yet full of absorbed influences, entirely English yet in many obvious ways quite un-English, savagely serious yet often and disturbingly comic, at once restlessly experimental yet rooted in tradition.

John Riley was born into a working-class family with a strong Methodist tradition, in Leeds, Yorkshire. He went to school in that city and remained proudly a Yorkshireman all his life. After national service in the air force, during which he spent time in Germany and learned Russian, he read English at Cambridge from 1958 to 1961. For several years after graduating he made his living from teaching in schools in or near Cambridge and then at Bicester, near Oxford. It was during this period that he first began to write poems which were recognizably his own, that his first books were published, and that he was involved in the establishment of Grosseteste Press and *Grosseteste Review,* two connections he maintained for the rest of his life.

Riley's first separate collection, *Ancient and Modern* (1967), is divided into two halves, separated by a bridging poem which indicates the continuities as well as the differences in the two parts. The poems in the first part are mostly short, songlike (several have the word song in their titles) notations of particular moments and experiences. Clipped and broken but exact, the style owes much to the tone of Pound reinterpreted through such American poems of the early 1960s as Robert Creeley's, as in "January 1966":

> if there's time
> > I'll plant a tree
>
> there where that blackbird is, a
> > sycamore
> > for speed
>
> against the black wall

Though even in the first part there are poems which venture further, the second section is by far more ambitious. These are poems in which the idea of experience and the idea of perceiving self recording that experience are subjected to an examination that increasingly casts doubt on apparent certainties. One of the sustaining maneuvers throughout Riley's poetry is the way in which a superficially magisterial voice, announcing what is known, is encroached on and called into question as the poem develops, to end, characteristically, in a state of still-unsettled though subdued doubt. In these poems, our experience of and in this world is valued mostly for its mental intensity. In poems

Front wrapper for Riley's first volume of poetry. The photograph is by the poet.

such as "Views of Where One Is" there is "a constant movement/From mechanical habit consciousness//Distantly, distantly, on the horizon." But in "This Time of Year" a placid, admiring recorder undercuts that high ideal:

> I stop to admire
> The sky through an arch of branches
> And thinking to go higher
> Am caught in this gesture of pleasure

Likewise, the last poem in the book, whose simple, lyrical title "Love Poem" is ironically examined through the spiky argumentativeness of the piece itself, raises questioning eyebrows at, though remaining in anguish attached to, the whole notion of the lover-artist-recorder, whether of persons or places; it ends bleakly and abruptly: "—Not that anything has to be improved./Simply that everything must be done away with."

What Reason Was (1970) is a sustained attempt

to deal with the questions raised by the later poems of *Ancient and Modern* and to find an adequate aesthetic form for a position in which questions can become answers and unrest a solution—or, as "The World Itself, The Long Poem Foundered" puts it:

> How to trace longing beyond sight,
> Removed beyond sensible reaching? And to give it
>   voice?
> . . . .
> A stillness encompassing movement.
> With enormous beauty still to answer to.
>
> Blackness seeps through the closed door, douses
>   the lamp.
> It is a longing for the same world, and a different
>   world.

The unity of the book—its relentless probing of related issues—is one of its most remarkable features. All of Riley's books are unified, not random collections, but in *What Reason Was* the wholeness is

Front wrapper for Riley's 1970 collection of poems written between 1967 and 1969

perhaps most immediately and richly apparent, the argument, from piece to piece and within each individual piece, most urgently pursued. It is worth remembering that this is the achievement of a man in his early thirties.

A kind of narrative framework is created around the progress and eventual collapse of a relationship. Although these are anything but anecdotally autobiographical poems, there are several immediately available and finely achieved lyrics of a more or less straightforward sort, such as the last poem of the twelve-part "A Sequence" beginning,

> I'm tired of this word love it's over-
> Worked, let's forget it
> And rest in it, and what a day for it

Rhythm and emotion are knit into a single sensuous whole. Poems in the second half of this book (the division is as real as in *Ancient and Modern*) blend this sensuous richness with a speed and freedom of intellectual movement. Through images of Byzantium recalling Yeats but ranging far from his spirit, Riley explores the achievement of love, the achievement of art, and the longing for more permanence than either can afford. The argument looks toward sensual experience as a solution, though he often denies the possibility of it. Ironically, these poems can sing while denying the possibility of singing, and they achieve real permanence while refusing to admit that art can achieve it. The most extreme example is perhaps the last poem in the book, "Poem on These Poems," in which human love, divine love, the work of art, the losses inherent in all, are danced between—"Love, love, the great love, or the unexpected,/My God my love I cannot see or sing"—until the poem ends unexpectedly at ease and singing, though resolved only in its lack of resolution:

> It is cold beyond the reaches of our air,
> Our slow time; its trappings are gold and silver.
> And poetry a voice, a voiceless eye
> A dream from which I do not hope to wake. Love,
> We find ourselves at the foot of the tree. We have
>   always been there.

At the end of the 1960s, Riley gave up teaching. A brief period in Cornwall provided the immediate stimulus for a number of poems, and its landscape became a part of the backdrop of his work for a number of years. Then he returned to Leeds, where he remained for the rest of his life, except for a brief but important visit in the summer of 1973 to Istanbul, the city which became increasingly important in his poems and which he insisted on calling by its older name, Constantinople. His life in Leeds was devoted to his writing. In 1973 he was married and in 1977 received into the Orthodox church.

His next collection of poems, *Ways of Approaching* (1973), is both more varied and more ambitious than *What Reason Was* and a less complete though more exacting achievement. Some individual lyrics are among his finest, but the most characteristic pieces in the book, those which give it its tone, are the longer ones—"Prelude," "Report, Unfinished," "Czargrad." Here, set patterns of thinking, perceiving, and writing are more than ever splintered in an increasingly ruthless, even desperate attempt to make the work of art render back to us what Riley sees as the true face of our deepest life. The ending of "Prelude" exemplifies this vision:

at the limit of the known, enlightened—unen-
    lightened

how many other paths unwalked and this
I've walked on twice before with a shiver of the new
each time to the limit, almost, of the known:

a punctuated silence, third time one tree
a mass of green from ground to sky gathers light,
a figure seen a long way off could be, un-

named, the centre of the world and in between
this known and this unknown, the exclusive, the
    vague,
in these gaps we gather guilt and love, and die:

imperceptibly the woods the sounds that come
from isolated farms scatter curlews
over unknown land, what I know of myself
what I know of this world and others.

What he was trying to create is perhaps best summed up in a phrase from "Report, Unfinished": "something beyond/a wreck or an edifice." The word "Unfinished" in the title of this poem is integral, not accidental: there could be no real end to a work so committed to process as achievement in itself, to *Ways of Approaching*—an equally unaccidental title—as the only point of arrival.

The most sustained and remarkable of these longer poems is "Czargrad," which occupied his attention for some years. The first three of this poem's four parts were published in *Ways of Approaching*, but the finished whole appeared only

after his death, in the *Collected Works*. "Czargrad" represents his most intense and conscious attempt to bring together all of his concerns in one major work. Czargrad, the Byzantine holy city, serves as an image for what it is possible to achieve at the highest and most complex levels of human creativity; but the form and mood of the poem differ from the hieratic hymn praising the fixed, permanent "artifice of eternity" that Yeats celebrated. Indeed, the most obvious first impression of the piece is of impermanence: it changes in tone and rhythm, from place to place, from time to time, from theme to theme; and that impression is a real reflection of the poem's intention: because for Riley Czargrad, real though it is as a place and vivid though it is in the poem, both as it is now and as it was in the past, is not finally a place but a possibility—a state of the spirit—in which all the highest human powers are fully used. The poem creates and records for us, at the same moment, a flow chart of the flickering movements of that spirit. In time and space, the poem can move from the poet's room in Leeds in the 1970s, to Byzantium in the tenth century, to the Italy of Monteverdi, to nineteenth-century Cornwall. A virtuoso (but not at all exhibitionist) range of rhythms and images includes passages of despair at the collapse of "The City" as a community of the spirit and moments of limpid, untroubled lyricism. Passages of broken feeling and groping syntax—

birds off across November fields   mist
startling confidence tricks   a heron   slim wrists
the people one meets   what's to be done
with love
spread wider   identity   you
are invited we never
knew each other   hardly
for the years and circumstances begin life
naked   phenomena   dark, evenings, mornings

—are counterbalanced by episodes which embody the ecstatic stillness of complete contemplation, in which the recreation of the city of the spirit is a glimpsed possibility:

stillness in the house, delight still
ascent and descent still possible, labour of precision
the crows' thick wings pass overhead; life intensified, held now
as albatross wings are a part of the wind
....
    a concentration of attention such
deep well of love
        bright cloud is

<pre>
fixed
        that love
                        is never fulfilled
    but the ways
                    of approaching
                                        endless
</pre>

The movement of the poem is not linear. It does not record a progress. Circling and swirling and returning on itself, stammering, repeating, and hesitating, but fierce in its integrity, it refuses to claim or say more than it truly may; moments of illumination are followed often by inarticulation or despair. When the poem ends, after four hundred lines, it does so almost tonelessly, fading away in exact notations reminiscent of the poetry with which Riley's career had begun, a lyrical quietism returning purified and strengthened, more exact and more complete:

<pre>
        and that the sun sets
    blood-red sated with its own weight
    below the bleached fields
    that all that is done
    all day the drone of a harvester
    next field
</pre>

Ways of Approaching was followed almost immediately by *Prose Pieces* (1974), just as *What Reason Was* had been accompanied by another prose work, *Correspondences* (1970). In each case, the book of poems and the book of prose are closely related. *Prose Pieces,* in fact, mixes prose and poetry (it includes a number of poems not available elsewhere). This collection explores preoccupations similar to those of *Ways of Approaching;* its methods involve equally radical dislocations of sense, whose results are simultaneously strange and convincing. Riley's prose, like that of Hölderlin, Mandelshtam, and Pasternak, is the prose of a poet, but, like theirs, it is (as well as a commentary on its author's poems) an achievement in its own right.

Only one other small volume of poems, *That Is Today* (1978), appeared during Riley's lifetime. *A Meeting* (1978) is a selection of poems from the long work in prose and poetry "Between Strangers," which was unfinished at the time of his death. The selection was made by Riley but the book was published posthumously. The *Collected Works* of 1981 includes several poems from his last years which had not appeared in book form (as well as a considerable number of earlier poems, some of which

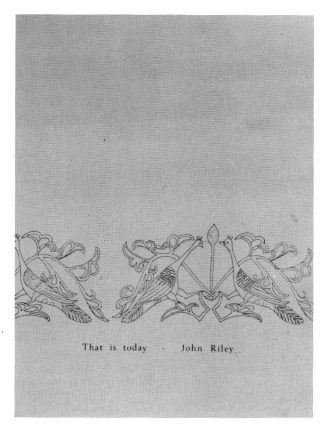

Covers for the last volume of Riley's poetry published before he was beaten to death by muggers in 1978

John Riley and Australian poet Kris Helmensley

had only appeared in magazines, and some of
which had never before been published, many of
real interest and value). The poems from *That Is
Today* and the uncollected poems from the last
period may be considered as one group, with a
number of common characteristics. Generally,
there is a return to poems of a more obviously
lyrical length and feeling, though the complexity of
form and tone retains what Riley had learned in
writing the longer pieces in *Ways of Approaching*.
These are brief but precise enactments (rather than
notations) of shifts of feeling in moments of illumination; the language and rhythm change rapidly
and allusively; the poems show no clear beginnings
or endings but a daring line-by-line openness of
feeling and form. Riley's last completed individual
poem (there are later poems forming part of "Between Strangers") is untitled; as for many of these
last pieces, titles seem to have come to be seen as tags
too rigid for poems which so assiduously attempt to
escape the preformed. This last poem conveys
much of the hesitant, highly charged, abstract lyricism of this final period:

quiet birds fly
sky spread over all
nothing sweeter in sickness
than the smell of evening
half-powers held
in the luminous and grass
in now half-light
rather more than grass
the unstill the unstill
checked

at the boundary of mind's reach
at the edge of heart's sensing
violence of colour
and the wind rising

On the night of 27 October 1978, while walking home after an evening in the local pub which
figures in much of his late writing, particularly in
"Between Strangers," Riley was attacked and killed
by muggers. He was just forty-one.

In a career of no more than fifteen years, what
he had achieved was remarkable, both in variety
and quality. There are the deeply personal transla-

tions, particularly from Mandelshtam and Hölderlin. There are the radically experimental combinations of poetry and prose. Above all, there is a concentrated collection of poetry, in which hardly one trivial or routine piece disrupts the successive explorations of more and more complex states with more and more daring and accomplished technical means. Whatever its weaknesses and limitations—and Riley himself was never satisfied with his work and habitually looked forward in hope rather than backward in satisfaction—this is surely a body of work which will form a permanent addition to poetry in English. His poem to Rilke, from *Ways of Approaching,* finely summarizes his own achievement:

I have brought it to my heart to be a still point
Of praise for the powers which move towards me as I
To them, through the dimensions a tree opens up,

Or a window, or a mirror. Creatures fell
Silent, then returned my stare.
Or a window, or a mirror. The shock of re-

Turning to myself after a long journey,
With music, has made me cry, cry out—angels
And history through the heart's attention grow
    transparent.

References:

Richard Caddel, Jeremy Hooker, Yann Lovelock, and David McDuff, "Four Views of John Riley," *Poetry Review,* 71, no. 1 (June 1981): 46-60;

Roger Garfitt, "The heart's attention," *Times Literary Supplement,* 25 December 1981, p. 1507;

Tim Longville, ed., *For John Riley* (Wirksworth: Grosseteste, 1979);

Douglas Oliver, "John Riley," *PN Review,* 20 (June 1981): 39-41.

Carol Rumens
(10 December 1944-   )

John Press

BOOKS: *A Strange Girl in Bright Colours* (London: Quartet Books, 1973);

A Necklace of Mirrors (Belfast: Ulsterman Publications, 1979);

Unplayed Music (London: Secker & Warburg, 1981);

Scenes from the Gingerbread House (Newcastle upon Tyne: Bloodaxe Books, 1982);

Star Whisper (London: Secker & Warburg, 1983);

Direct Dialling (London: Chatto & Windus/Hogarth Press, 1985).

OTHER: *Making for the Open: The Chatto Book of Post-Feminist Poetry,* edited by Rumens (London: Chatto & Windus/Hogarth Press, 1985).

Every decade from the 1930s to the 1960s saw the formation of poetic groups or movements that, for a while, appeared to dominate the poetic scene. After "the poets of the thirties" came the Apocalyptics of the 1940s, who were succeeded by the Movement of the 1950s and the Group of the 1960s. English (as distinct from Northern Irish) poets broke the pattern after 1970, declining to forge such alliances, perhaps because they did not hold in common the kind of religious, political, or aesthetic beliefs that might have bound them together. Of the generation who attained poetic maturity in the 1970s without the consciousness of belonging to a group, Carol Rumens is among the most talented.

Carol-Ann Lumley, daughter of Wilfred Arthur Lumley and Marjorie May Mills Lumley, was born at Lewisham, South London, on 10 December 1944 and spent her early childhood nearby at Forest Hill, where she attended St. Winifrede's Convent School. In 1956 the family moved to Croydon, Surrey, where she received her secondary education at Coloma Convent Grammar School. She entered Bedford College, University of London, in 1964 to study philosophy. Her poem "College Fauna" records the next sequence of events: "I set out for Philosophy/and left clutching Marriage." On 30 July 1965 at Croydon she became the wife of David Edward Rumens. They have two daughters: Kelsey, born on 6 November 1966, and

Carol Rumens (photograph by Sabina White)

Rebecca, born on 19 April 1968.

Although she wrote poems prolifically in her early years, only a few fragments remain. It was as a prose writer that she first achieved publication at the age of sixteen in the *Croydon Advertiser,* for which she reviewed concerts given by many leading British and foreign orchestras at Fairfield Halls, Croydon. During the years that she remained at home when the children were small, Carol Rumens carried on writing. After the publication in 1973 of *A Strange Girl in Bright Colours* she began to work in publishing and then as a copywriter in advertising. She continued to write poems throughout the 1970s: the appearance of two pamphlets and two books of verse between 1978 and 1983 won her a reputation.

The poems in *A Strange Girl in Bright Colours* (1973) are neither better nor worse than most of the work by young poets that appeared in the little periodicals of the late 1960s and early 1970s. They are fluent, pleasant meditations on a variety of related themes—childhood, puberty, love, marriage, childbirth—but they lack artistic force and control. Two poems at the end of the book reach a higher

level of accomplishment: "Ovulen 50," a bitter attack on the birth-control pill, and "Houses by Day," in which the narrator reflects how "The trauma of marriage swallowed me" and sardonically acknowledges that "my role is to wait/for the key in the lock, to serve the first clean kiss/and light up at a flick of my clitoris."

A note in this first volume remarks that the author is "interested in most forms of liberation, particularly women's and children's." The dozen poems that make up *A Necklace of Mirrors* (1979) are all concerned with the suffering of women in various epochs. It is indeed the endurance of suffering that lends unity to the lives of the women, real and imaginary, who are evoked in these poems—including Sappho, Li Ju-Chen, a sixteenth-century witch, Charlotte Brontë, the Sybil at Cumae, Anna Akhmatova. Although this pamphlet marks an advance on Rumens's first volume, the strong, generous emotion that suffuses the poems has not attained the authority of mature poetic achievement. But the very last line of the book, in the poem called "Coming of Age," is prophetic: "The first fruit blooms, the voice comes clear and human."

Unplayed Music (1981) registers a steady increase in poetic skill and imaginative force. Although it includes three poems from *A Necklace of Mirrors,* the rest of the poems appear to have been written between 1978 and 1981. As before, many of the poems explore various aspects of family life and feminine experience, notably "Before These Wars," a tender evocation of the poet's father and mother bathing in the sea during the unclouded early days of their marriage. Two poems demonstrate the poet's ability to survey with calm sadness facets of mortality and decay. "The Girl in the Cathedral" meditates on the contrast between Susannah Starr, aged ten, and the ecclesiastical dignitaries who, like her, lie entombed in the cathedral, while "The Light of Reason" describes a tatty old reference library crowded with dusty out-of-date tomes. The volume's title poem has a line that prefigures a rhetorical device Rumens often employs in her later poetry: "Oh night of ice and Schnapps, moonshine and stars." This kind of irony, laced with plangent rhetoric, is a heady brew that she takes considerable pleasure in concocting. In 1981 her best poems were still to come, but *Unplayed Music* signals the arrival of a poet who has discovered an individual view of the world and fashioned a style of her own.

Scenes from the Gingerbread House (1982), a sequence of nine short poems written in 1979, recalls the author's childhood to the age of eleven,

Covers for the sequence of nine short poems about the poet's childhood to age eleven

when she left the "gingerbread house," the name she gives to the red-brick Edwardian house in Forest Hill, where she and her parents lived with her grandparents, who owned it. It was a house of grief, haunted by the ghost of her grandparents' child who had died in a hospital at the age of six months, and by the living specter of their mentally retarded daughter. Rumens evokes with unfailing skill the hidden menace of the gingerbread house, where her parents were trapped like Hansel and Gretel. One day, when she stood with her father on the pier at Folkestone, she caught a glimpse of France, "A smear of cloud where water/fainted into blue air." It is typical of her artistry that she does not overplay the symbolism of that distant view, with its promise of liberation.

Star Whisper (1983) is Rumens's most complex and ambitious book. Though the first section contains poems on a variety of topics, the dominant note is exile, a sense of loss, with particular reference to Eastern Europe. The more-unified middle section, while ostensibly concerned with the flora

and fauna of Regent's Park, London, refers directly or obliquely to aspects of love and marriage. The poems in the third section also contemplate the web of family and sexual love. Thus related themes recur throughout the volume, giving it a unity that is musical rather than logical.

The title poem, "Star Whisper," is a meditation on a passage from Alexander Polovtsoff's translation of *Wyna: Adventures in Eastern Siberia* (1938) by General D. Gourko that is used as the first of the book's two epigraphs: "In my ears I heard all the time a sound as a trickle of corn, produced by the freezing of one's own breath into hoar-frost; this music was locally called 'star whisper' and only occurred when the thermometer was below—68°C." This strange music—"It's what the stars confess when all is silence/—Not to the telescopes, but to the snow"—is contrasted with life in the West, where, unlike the inhabitants of Siberia, "you can breathe a hundred times a minute" and yet not know the significance of being alive. Of the other poems in this first section inspired wholly or in part

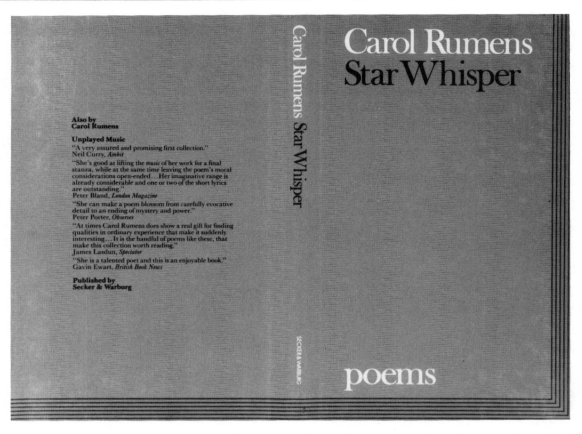

Dust jacket for Rumens's most ambitious collection of poetry. The title is from a passage in D. Gourko's Adventures in Eastern Siberia:
*"In my ears I heard all the time a sound as a trickle of corn, produced by the freezing of one's own breath into hoar-frost; this music was
locally called 'star whisper' and only occurred when the thermometer was below −68°C."*

by themes of suffering and loss, the most accomplished is "Lines on the Shortest Day, to Heroes Old and New," a poem whose epigraph is drawn from John Donne's "A Nocturnal Upon St. Lucy's Day, Being the Shortest Day." Although its stanzaic pattern is not based on Donne's poem, the poem sparkles with metaphysical wit and glows with an ardent romanticism that both excoriates the West and looks contemptuously at "the state with its new breed of tsars." It ends with an invocation to St. Lucy, a stanza that begins: "Be Patron, then, upon this darkest day/Of every fierce refusal to betray."

Other poems in this section are concerned with domestic losses. The most moving is "An Easter Garland," inspired by the poet's memories of her father, who, when he was a sick man, mowed the lawn for his "work-shy" daughter. In the final stanza Carol Rumens celebrates her sense of her father's presence after his death in imagery taken from the gospel story of the Resurrection:

In the lonely garden of the page,
something has happened to your silence.
The stone cloud has rolled off.
. . . .
and I, though stupid with regret,
would not be far wrong
if I took you for the gardener.

These lines are an example of the way in which she raises the emotional and musical intensity of a poem as it reaches its climax.

The second section of *Star Whisper* is made up of the sequence "Regent's Park Crossings," which is prefaced by the Prince Regent's comment on seeing John Nash's plans: "It will quite eclipse Napoleon," and by Napoleon's observation that love was once "the whole concern of everyone's life. That is always the fate of leisured societies." Only the first of the seventeen poems in the sequence "Grand Designs" evokes the world of the Prince Regent, of "footmen and maids abandoned in the grass." The remaining poems are set firmly in the contemporary park, where lovers work out their relationships against a background of flowers, trees, shrubs, water, grass, and clouds. The progression of the sequence is one of mood and imagery rather than narrative, as it moves from May to the imminent fall of snow and the coming of darkness. Nor is love a source of delight. "Dark Path" records the loss of love: the "unlucky white May tree," the green path, the Queen Anne's lace, and the lake are dark, dead, or ghostly. The black swans in their "listless epithalamium" offer no more than a bleak comfort: "Better, they'd say, an unadoring pair/than one in love, alone."

Despite the intelligence and sophistication of "Regent's Park Crossings," the sequence lacks the steady coherence of *Scenes from the Gingerbread House*. The poems in the third section of the book are considerably weightier and more emotionally satisfying, particularly those that explore the nature of love. "Cherchez l'Ail" contains a line heavily charged with regret: "Tides turn, the damaged love-boat drifts away"; and "Double Exposure," a poem about a failed marriage, is a long, muted cry of pain. It is, however, not a moan of self-pity: the poet loses neither intellectual nor emotional control, observing with fine exactness the domestic interiors of a London suburb and the sleazy cosmopolitanism of the metropolitan streets in lines such as "Greek music pours from windows dark/as wounds in scabby tenements." There are other poems that show the poet's ability to assimilate into her art the hardness of the neon-lit city, as well as more tender poems about children and herself as a child.

Direct Dialling (1985) contains nineteen poems, some of which rank among Rumens's most ambitious and weighty compositions. She is much concerned with human suffering, especially in Eastern Europe, and in "Outside Oswiecim" she contemplates the horror of the holocaust:

They wanted us corpses and they wanted us

grave-diggers, they wanted us music, machines, textiles.
They kicked us as we fell. How human they were.

The predominant tone of this volume is one of somber grief, the movement of the verse reflecting the poet's emotional state. Rumens has almost completely abandoned rhyme and the glittering images that made *Star Whisper* such a delightful collection. While acknowledging her seriousness and social awareness, one may still feel that *Direct Dialling* represents a departure from, rather than an advance on, her two previous volumes; and it is reassuring to find here two poems, "Time Trouble" and "Circe," that display her old acuteness and elegance.

Reviewers have found much to praise in the poems of Carol Rumens. There is general agreement about the vivid quality of her images, the sensuous elegance of her language, the effortless power of her best work, and her ability to bring a poem to an end on a note that combines musical resonance with mystery. She has received an impressive number of prizes and awards: the 1981 Prudence Farmer Award for "An Easter Garland," judged to be the best poem of the year published in the *New Statesman;* the Poetry Society's 1981 choice of *Unplayed Music* as the Alice Hunt Bartlett Prize for the most promising volume by a newcomer; the selection of *Star Whisper* as the Poetry Book Society's Choice for Summer 1983; a Cholmondeley Award for poetry given in 1984 by the Society of Authors. She has been a selector for the Poetry Book Society, sits on its board, was elected a Fellow of the Royal Society of Literature in 1984, and is the current writer in residence at the University of Kent, Canterbury.

It is not easy to forecast the direction in which she is likely to move in the years ahead. Perhaps she will continue to explore themes that have already begun to preoccupy her—feminism, the nature of exile, the loss of human rights in Eastern Europe. Such themes are likely to give her a wealth of material on which to meditate until the end of the century and beyond.

Michael Schmidt
(2 March 1947-)

Robert B. Shaw
Mount Holyoke College

BOOKS: *Black Buildings* (Oxford: Carcanet Press, 1969);
Bedlam and the Oakwood (Oxford: Carcanet Press, 1970);
Desert of the Lions (Oxford: Carcanet Press, 1972);
It Was My Tree (London: Anvil Press, 1972);
My Brother Gloucester (Manchester: Carcanet Press, 1976);
A Change of Affairs (London: Anvil Press, 1978);
An Introduction to Fifty Modern British Poets (London: Pan, 1979); republished as *A Reader's Guide to Fifty Modern British Poets* (London: Heinemann/New York: Barnes & Noble, 1979);
An Introduction to Fifty British Poets, 1300-1900 (London: Pan, 1979); republished as *A Reader's Guide to Fifty British Poets, 1300-1900* (London: Heinemann/New York: Barnes & Noble, 1979);
The Colonist (London: Muller, 1980); republished as *Green Island* (New York: Vanguard, 1982);
Choosing a Guest: New and Selected Poems (London: Anvil Press, 1983).

OTHER: *British Poetry Since 1960,* edited by Schmidt and Grevel Lindop (Oxford: Carcanet Press, 1972);
Flower and Song: Poems of the Aztec Peoples, translated, with an introduction, by Schmidt and Edward Kissam (London: Anvil Press, 1977);
British Poetry Since 1970, edited by Schmidt and Peter Jones (Manchester: Carcanet Press, 1980; New York: Persea, 1980).

Michael Schmidt's career as a poet has advanced side by side with his career as a publisher. Even if he were not a prolific writer, his position as head of Carcanet Press and editor of *PN Review* would be enough to assure his high standing in the world of British letters.

Michael Norton Schmidt was born to American parents in Mexico City in 1947. His father, Carl Bernhardt Schmidt, was in his fifties when this last of his children was born. A versatile and enterprising man, Carl Schmidt had risen to captain in the U.S. Army in World War I and was an aviator before going into business. Both professionally and personally he was interested in agriculture; he introduced the Fuerte avocado to the United States. In Mexico he made a prosperous living in the oil business. Michael Schmidt's mother, Elizabeth Norton Hill Schmidt, was younger than her husband. Born in Georgia, she had traveled in Chile and Peru before marrying and settling in Mexico.

Apart from three years on his father's avocado ranch in California, Schmidt's early childhood was spent in Mexico, where he grew up in the comfortable surroundings of the expatriate business community which he was later to evoke in his novel *The Colonist* (1980). He was indulged in his numerous hobbies as a boy and became in due course a gardener, an ornithologist, a collector of Indian artifacts, and, most important, a writer. By the time he was nine he had a large library, a typewriter, and a rhyming dictionary. Beginning at age twelve he was sent abroad for schooling, first to the United States (The Hill School) and later to England (Christ's Hospital, an inspiring place for a young writer, as its alumni include Samuel Taylor Coleridge and Charles Lamb).

Admitted to Harvard in 1966, Schmidt intrigued his classmates with his unusual background, his habit of serving tea every afternoon, and his equally disciplined habit of writing a poem every day. His experience at Christ's Hospital had disposed him to prefer the English educational system, and after a single year at Harvard he transferred to Wadham College, Oxford, where he was to complete his B.A. in 1969. During his Oxford career his involvement in literature deepened. He contributed to and helped to edit the undergraduate magazine *Carcanet,* whose name he adopted for the Carcanet Press, which he founded in his last year at Oxford.

Schmidt's remarkable progress as a publisher has tended to overshadow his writing career. Carcanet Press began modestly in Schmidt's lodgings outside of Oxford, with the publication of a number of small poetry pamphlets. By 1972 it had a greatly expanded list and had moved, with Schmidt, to Manchester, where he had accepted an appointment as special lecturer in poetry at the university. Manchester is not a place noted for its literary associations; as Schmidt likes to point out, it is where Marx met Engels and Rolls met Royce. Nevertheless, in its quarters in the monumental, mid-Victorian Corn Exchange Buildings the enterprise has flourished, fueled by its founder's indefatigable energy.

The prime achievement of Carcanet has been its maintenance of a broad and varied poetry list—almost the only list open to first collections in the worst days of the recession-ridden 1970s. Aside from bringing new indigenous work before the public, the press has published many American poets, both older and younger, who had previously had little or no English audience, including Delmore Schwartz, Allen Tate, Yvor Winters, John Ashbery, and Robert Pinsky. Carcanet has always been ready to engage in what Schmidt terms "rediscoveries": its editions of neglected or previously unpublished works of H. D. (Hilda Doolittle) being especially noteworthy in this regard. The press's attention has not been limited to the English language; translations have figured in its list with increasing frequency. Schmidt has also been keen to publish what he calls "context work"—prose writings of poets, or works of an interpretive nature. It is not unusual today for English writers to consider Carcanet the primary publisher of poetry in Britain.

The year of Schmidt's move to Manchester, 1972, was also the year he founded the magazine *PN Review,* which he continues to edit. (Until 1984 C. H. Sisson and Donald Davie were listed as editors together with Schmidt.) A literary journal of the highest seriousness, it has prompted comparison with T. S. Eliot's *Criterion* or Edgell Rickword's *Calendar of Modern Letters.* Although the stated editorial positions reflect what Schmidt calls a "radical conservatism," the magazine, like the Carcanet list, impresses the reader with its range and capaciousness. By juxtaposing learned, thoughtful essays on writers of the past with incisive reviews of current ones, the magazine broadens in a most salutary way our conception of the literary situation in which the contemporary poet pursues his craft.

In 1979 Schmidt married the writer Claire Harman, who has recently edited the *Collected Poems* (1982) of Sylvia Townsend Warner. The Schmidts have a son, Charles Bernhardt, and a daughter, Isabel Claire. He continues to live, write, teach, and conduct business in Manchester.

Schmidt's writing career began with two small booklets, *Black Buildings* (1969) and *It Was My Tree* (published in 1972 but containing poems written as far back as 1968). These are the work of a promising apprentice. Although none of the poems is fashioned with the authority Schmidt has achieved in later work, some give early notice of his gift for the arresting phrase. To a dog hit by a car and dying, "The road is one long bruise." Swarming bees form "a livid glove on the tree." This penchant for summary images, often ones of disturbing import, is further displayed in his first full-length collection, *Bedlam and the Oakwood* (1970).

This book also contains its quota of apprentice work. Many of the poems are essentially literary anecdotes, including vignettes drawn from the lives and writings of Jonathan Swift, Samuel Johnson, Arthur Rimbaud, and Rabindranath Tagore. He serves as a graceful raconteur and a humane critic, but as a rule has little that is unexpected to say on these subjects. The ironic relations between the human frailties of artists and the enduring qualities of their works offer too many opportunities for easy moralizing, and the poems seem formulaic in the judgments they impose or imply. More promising are the pieces drawn from the poet's life and travels in Mexico: for instance, "The New Volcano," "At Nautla," "Cotopaxi," and "Convento del Carmen: Mummies." One is not likely to forget the rendering in this last poem of a convent's "mummy-room":

> A mother superior in sack-cloth, who appears
> to have been corpulent has fallen forwards,
> her face rests against the glass.
> . . . .
> Choiring still, dead mouths hang always open
> in an O as lips dry back on bone.

Sheer force of description carries the poem to success here, as in some of the other Mexican scenes. In this book there is not much of an attempt to enhance the meanings of poems by manipulations of rhythm and meter. One feels that the poet's structural efforts have been directed chiefly toward the arrangement of images, rather than toward the shaping of lines or stanzas as units of sound. The unrhymed verse maintains its close affinities to prose so determinedly that it sometimes dilutes the intensity of even the more impressive images. There is often a certain lopsidedness in the development of a young poet's craft; in Schmidt's case the powers of the ear lagged behind, or were perhaps impeded by, those of a restless and penetrating eye.

    In Schmidt's second collection, *Desert of the Lions* (1972), there is a more evident cohesion of the various creative faculties. Lines and stanzas are not as likely to seem arbitrarily or awkwardly shaped, appearing instead as essential and organic units of the larger structures. The book's subject matter indicates that the poet has come to realize where his imagination is most at home; Mexican themes and settings are more prominent than in the preceding volume. Schmidt makes the most of the enlarged and ambivalent point of view which his expatriate upbringing had provided. One of the sections of Mexican poems is called "Native Tourist"—a convenient phrase suggesting the balance of intimacy and otherness in the poet's outlook. Nearly all of Schmidt's Mexican poems have politics for impetus, if one construes "politics" with adequate breadth. He has said that the main themes of all his writing are guilt and power. In the Mexican context such concerns are bound to preoccupy a poet versed in the brutal history of the Spanish conquest, and haunted by the tremendous disparities of wealth

Dust jacket for Schmidt's 1972 collection, dedicated to American poet Elizabeth Bishop, whose influence is apparent in many of the book's poems

and poverty which the nation today exhibits. The poems naturally risk degenerating to propaganda, but Schmidt for the most part manages to avoid this common pitfall with considerable tact. His carefully judged strategy is to let the social message emerge as if spontaneously from precise renderings of scene. In "Bird Vendor" the description of the hunchback selling his caged songsters may strike us at first as a somewhat grotesque exploitation of local color. It is only upon weighing the import of some of the details that the vendor, who "wears a priest's black shirt" and feeds his birds on buckshot to make them sit still, emerges as a symbol of social oppression. Nor is it finally that simple, for the vendor himself is shackled by the system he represents: "he will not grow wings even/as we remember him/a cage among wire cages."

    Some of Schmidt's exactness of description

recalls the poetry of Elizabeth Bishop, and the affinity is not accidental: *Desert of the Lions* is dedicated to her. Schmidt seems indebted to Bishop not only for a descriptive technique but for the flexible stance he adopts. The poems which came out of Bishop's life in Brazil must have provided him with many hints for handling tone and perspective. Her poems too, view a culture not the poet's own with a mingling of knowledgeable sympathy and critical distance.

In a poem such as " 'Indian Pipes' are Flowers," Schmidt penetrates layer after layer of the tragic strata of the past:

> Indians who could not say the Creed
> were brought for instruction, with them
> their mild gods of furrow, maize—
> exorcized, and only the birds knew.
> Indian bones were buried always outside
> consecrated ground, not deep.

Now that the inquisitorial monks in their turn have vanished, the landscape itself seems to memorialize the antagonism of conflicting cultures: the "pink Indian-pipes" confront the ruined monastery, "tall above catacombs, black,/moss-grown with absent bells." "Minute red poppies . . . like bloodseed" spring from soil on which too much blood has been shed. Other poems which effectively evoke such haunted spots are "Desert of the Lions" and "Alone, and in a Lonely Place." The book includes several memorable poems focusing on animals. Again, Elizabeth Bishop may have provided the cue for some of these. But Schmidt adapts such subjects to his overriding concerns; his studies of beasts are usually a means for further pursuing his meditations on power and victimization. In "Trap" a fox caught by one paw "felt only that its tendons/tugged it to stay put in the bad dream/of human faces"; in "Scorpion," the poisonous insect, captured and dropped among the "sharp red pincers" of an anthill "twitches/its tail to a nicety and twice/stings itself—to death." Such accounts may be read as miniature allegories of the human struggles dealt with elsewhere in the book more directly.

The poet's own choice as the best of his books of poetry is *My Brother Gloucester* (1976). The title is quoted from *Richard III*, the passage in which Clarence, before his murder, recalls his dream of drowning. Imagery drawn from the deeps of the sea recurs throughout the book, and the deeps of the earth appear also. In Schmidt's earlier work, as we have seen, going beneath the surface was likely to mean searching the historical past, looking for

the roots of injustice. Here the import of such imagery is harder to define. The divers in "The Diving Bell," the volume's final and summary poem, drop to a "dayless world/with no history but the living//relics"—that is, the ancient forms of life now extinct at shallower levels. Time is suspended much as the diving bell is on its cable. When the divers' lamps switch on, it is only to give the speaker a glimpse of a realm in which oppression and darkness are the norms.

> Under tons of water the fish bear
> all movement in a gradual agony.
> This is the depth from which death raises them.
>
> Colour that never was before
> glows with a crude, wounded brilliance.

The poem ends by comparing the exploration of the divers to those of Darwin and Dante—a pairing that comes to seem more apt the more one considers it. The dive is a quest for knowledge of nature—"the unknown fossil worlds//that live in us"—and experiencing it provides the divers with knowledge of their own depths as well, our moral nature, which to most of us is territory not wholly charted. The last lines of the poem—"We will go home and sketch/a chart we know is real and unbelievable"—show that the poet does not underestimate the hindrances either to his search or to his making known his findings.

"The Diving Bell" suggests that the poet is ready to turn toward a more introspective, perhaps even confessional mode of writing. Yet the images here, and in other poems of descent such as "The Crypt" and "Cave Pool," are deployed with poise and caution; even as they hint at efforts to plumb psychic and spiritual depths, they retain their objective status as elements of scenes carefully appraised. In "The Crypt" the visitor to a burial chamber which "underlies/the market-gardens like a tuber" communes both with the tenants of its "shadow avenues" and with himself. He notices "sharp crippled blooms of limestone" and "the pale-fingered spiders [that] move like hair/between the bedrooms of the dead" even as he finally reflects: "The crypt resolves whatever ghosts we bring./We surface to unportioned solitude." Observation and introspection are held delicately in balance. Equally poised and enigmatic, "Cave Pool" can be read simply as naturalistic description of "the blind cavefish that move in a blind shoal" or as a parable of the poet's creative act, of the mysteries of its origins and ends. The fish are attracted to the spelunker's lamp even without seeing it; they congregate "dazed with sensation" until the visitor speaks:

> and they, not frightened, but because the spell
> breaks at the echo in the stone,
> hardly flex their bodies and file out
>
> as messengers with news of light and sound
> into the earth. Our torches cannot follow:
> one by one they pass down corridors
> that vein beneath our feet, our continent,
> to the darker heart that makes
> pulse-echo of this penetrable dark.

Here the fish are bearers of the poet's word; they have virtually become words sent forth with their "news of light and sound" to pay tribute to the invisible source and echo of all human utterance.

Schmidt has said that he believes "Words," which appears in *My Brother Gloucester,* to be his best single poem. Based on some lines of Hugo von Hofmannsthal's, it is an address to a child and can be seen as a succinct restatement of the first part of Wordsworth's Immortality Ode. The child's growth into adulthood is a growth away from unity with nature. The acquisition of language separates the child from the world that was the undisputed possession of preverbal consciousness.

> —We are men because we are alone:
>
> we touch and speak, but silence follows words
> the way a shadow does, the hand draws back.
> The curtain blows and there is no one there.
>
> What removed you to this solitude,
> into this common light, this common twilight?
> It is that word, twilight, that called you down—
>
> a word the wind has handed on to us
> undeciphered, and it might be love—
> rich with a honey pressed from hollow combs.

This poem brings a calm, melancholy lyricism to its treatment of the familiar romantic theme of the loss and compensation that attend any process of growth. It is intriguing to find such a skeptical view of language emerging in this particular volume. For this book is, as a whole, more technically assured than its predecessors. It may be that it is superior accomplishment in the use of words which alerts a writer to the limited reach of language, its agonizing incapacity to express a vision piercing the "common twilight" of our shared experience. This is a

dangerous theme for poets to dwell upon; understandably, it can sap their enterprise of its native hue of resolution. As if in evasion of such a destiny, Schmidt in his next collection moved into a notably different mode.

The title of *A Change of Affairs* (1978) refers as much to an alteration in style throughout the book as to the content of the narrative sequence of the same name. The publisher's claim is that "this is [Schmidt's] first collection as an English poet. The American models are no longer apparent." It is true that one can easily detect the tones of certain English poets filtered through Schmidt's new voice. Philip Larkin is audible here and there, Geoffrey Hill, a bit, C. H. Sisson, quite a bit. But one could find American precedents as well in Yvor Winters and his school. It makes more sense to designate style according to its inherent qualities rather than its supposed nationalistic affinities. It is evident that Schmidt in writing this book subjected his style to a radical chastening; the word "austere" is probably the handiest to describe it. The most noticeable change pertains to imagery. After steadily developing a talent for fielding intense images and making them vehicles of argument, Schmidt now elects to make his images as unshowy as possible, and to cut down on their number. Considered statement, tightly wrought syntax, now bear the burden of discourse. At the same time, the verse technique has become more consciously traditional. For the first time there is a significant recourse to rhyme; the line lengths within a poem tend now to be regularized, and lines are fashioned with a strong regular beat and are often end-stopped. For many poems the standard line length is a parsimonious dimeter or trimeter. To one familiar with Schmidt's earlier work the narrow columns of type may give the impression of having been ruthlessly squeezed.

One wonders if this move toward a drier, more impersonal style was in some sense a precautionary measure which the poet felt his new subject matter might require. For as Schmidt's style has grown more calculated and aloof, his subjects have grown more intimate. Aside from some interesting revisions of Bible stories in its first section, the book is largely concerned with the experience of love, and more often with a love that is frustrated than one that is fulfilled. "A Change of Affairs," the lengthy narrative sequence at the center of the book, calibrates minutely the fluctuations of emotion throughout an eventually doomed love affair. The psychological insights are frequently impressive; Schmidt has a tragic sense of the gulf between romantic passion and its physical transmission which might remind us of Yeats's sad musings on the perpetual virginity of the soul:

Our bodies act the heart
But only casually—
A kind of squandering
That will put nothing by
For when they move apart
Yet turn on the same bed
Irritable, alone;
They misplay the role
And will not be beguiled
By any words we use
To lie back quietly.
They have accustomed us
To intermittent love.
I am prepared to go
Until you take my hand.

The style throughout the sequence is measured, thoughtful, and discreet, but finally too abstract to sustain attention over the space of twenty-five pages. There is no attempt at realistic description of the lovers or their surroundings, and Schmidt's failure to evoke any tangible settings or individualized traits of personality in the poem seems to be a crucial flaw. It leaves the action and characters curiously insubstantial, and our admiration for the poem's rhetorical poise does not greatly compensate for our disappointment at its lack of compelling human interest. Schmidt's new style shows to best advantage in taut lyrics of disaffection such as "Choice," "Piano," "Vows," and "The Thread" in which the solitary lover, unaccustomed to sewing buttons, stabs his finger:

Here I sit, a finger at my lips,
I hear nothing, close my eyes, see nothing;
Your scent is gone now even from the bed.
I taste only myself, a modest salt.

Perhaps a blending of this new flavor with some of the headier vintages Schmidt was earlier wont to serve is what is needed. If he could somehow combine the descriptive vigor of his earlier books with the structural control that distinguishes his latest, he could well surpass the finest poems he has written, early or late.

Perhaps this book's turn toward abstraction is a regrettable effect of the poet's deracination. By the time it was published Schmidt had been a resident in England a dozen years; as he readily acknowledges, the place has never stimulated his imagination as the scenes of his childhood and adolescence have done. The Mexican settings which supply such particularity to his earlier poems are ones he has returned to most recently in prose rather than verse. *The Colonist* (1980) is a sensitive and adept first novel set in Mexico. Brief and intense, its plot dramatizes in microcosm the confrontation of the commercial exploiters and the natives they exploit. As in E. M. Forster's *A Passage to India* (1924), the novelist follows the struggle of the individual spirit to fight free of the artificial bounds imposed by national status and social caste. Schmidt intends to follow this impressive debut with further fiction.

Choosing a Guest: New and Selected Poems (1983) provides a convenient overview of Schmidt's development as a poet. The selection of poems from earlier volumes is carefully representative, but could perhaps have been more generous: there are, in particular, a number of strong poems from *My*

Front cover for Schmidt's 1983 collection, which demonstrates his continuing gift for austere but intense statement

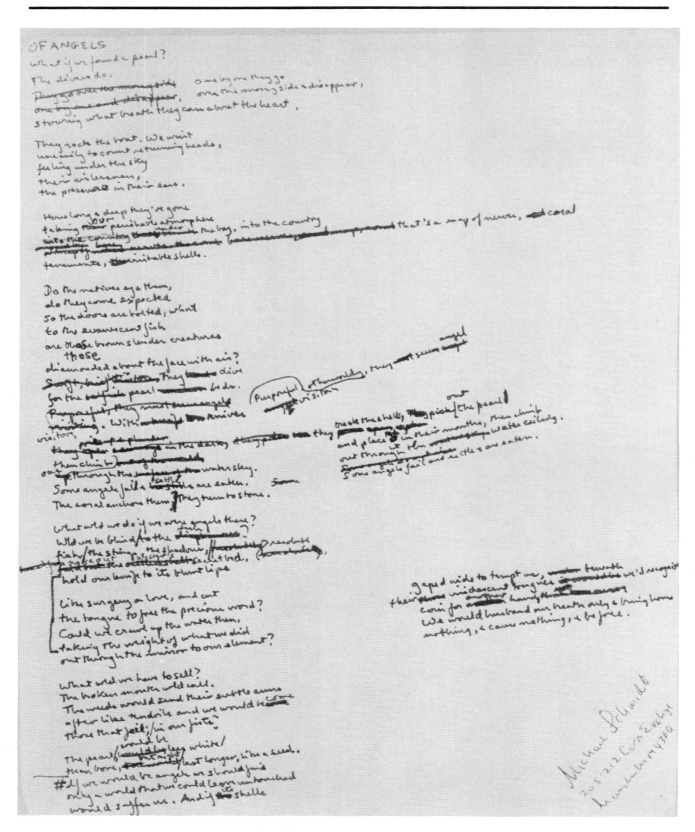

Draft for a recent poem (the author)

Brother Gloucester and *A Change of Affairs* which are as deserving of inclusion as those which the poet has chosen. The section of new poems exhibits no surprising departures from the style of *A Change of Affairs.* The same strengths, the same deliberate limitations are evident. The poet continues to refine his gift for austere but intense statement; some of these new poems, such as "A Phrase of Dryden's Virgil," seem powerful not despite, but because of, their extreme brevity.

An accomplished poet, a promising novelist, a critic, editor, and publisher of discernment and conviction, Schmidt in his late thirties is a fully fledged man of letters. His influence on the culture of his adopted country, already considerable, seems destined to increase.

Peter Scupham
(24 February 1933-   )

Neil Powell

BOOKS: *The Small Containers* (Manchester: Phoenix, 1972);
The Snowing Globe (Manchester: Morten, 1972);
The Gift (Richmond: Keepsake Press, 1973);
Prehistories (London: Oxford University Press, 1975);
The Hinterland (Oxford: Oxford University Press, 1977);
Summer Palaces (Oxford: Oxford University Press, 1980);
Winter Quarters (Oxford: Oxford University Press, 1983).

OTHER: Eric W. White, ed., *Poetry Book Society: The First 25 Years,* includes material by Scupham (London: Poetry Book Society, 1979).

Peter Scupham is among the most distinguished poets to have emerged in England during the 1970s. Even in a period not easily categorized by literary groupings, his is a strikingly individual talent: partly because he began to write relatively late (he was never that vain and vulnerable creature, the *young* poet); partly because his concerns have, as we shall see, more to do with history and continuity than with the ephemeral present; and partly because his fondness for timeless formal structures owes little to contemporary fashions.

John Peter Scupham was born in Liverpool, to John and Dorothy Clark Scupham, but spent his childhood in Cambridgeshire. He was educated at The Perse School, Cambridge; at St. George's, Harpenden; and, after national service, at Emmanuel College, Cambridge, where he read English, graduating with honors in 1957. His father was an educationist who became controller of BBC Educational Broadcasting; this background may have something to do with the son's dislike of his schooldays and distrust of education in general. Nevertheless, after teaching at a grammar school in Lincolnshire from 1957 to 1961, Peter Scupham became a successful and highly original teacher of English at St. Christopher School, Letchworth. He married Carola Nance Braunholtz on 10 August 1957. The younger two of their four children are currently undergraduates at Oxford and London universities; he lives in Hitchin, where he runs a fine small press (The Mandeville Press) and writes, as he has said, "in a room where the most disparate objects, an Etruscan bronze, a grey felt mouse, a microscope, a sixteenth century bible, live in a chosen harmony. . . . The room contains the centuries, and I feel acutely ill-at-ease in places where *now* is the only dimension visible; life is a texture where past and present become each other."

His first collection of poems was a pamphlet entitled *The Small Containers,* published in 1972. Most of its contents eventually found their way into subsequent book-length volumes, but the two introductions—one in prose, one in verse—have not been reprinted. In the verse introduction, a self-portrait called "Man on the Edge," he characterizes himself as follows:

He laughs much, with what could nearly be innocence,
Tickling himself with feathers of nonsense;

His words all lean sideways, blown by his eloquence.

He likes gappy-grin gargoyles, girls and cheap wine,
Pegs nodding like blue-tits on the washing-line,
Badly smashed-up people who are getting on fine.

He dislikes wasp-traps, pills and Education,
Considering blah blah what is good for the nation,
Lukewarm bathwater driptap conversation.

The somewhat forced jauntiness—a strategy against despair, it seems—is a recurrent tone in the early collections *The Small Containers* and *The Snowing Globe;* the preference for the actual over the abstract, the admiration for survivors, and the irritated dislike of jargon and wet moralizing are characteristics which have endured throughout his work to date. In the other prose introduction Scupham adopted Stephen Spender's distinction and hoped to be a "transparent" poet like Auden rather than an "opaque" one like Dylan Thomas: he has not always avoided opacity, but the poems in *The Small Containers* are at least transparent in their clear announcement of their concerns. The "repertoire" (Scupham's own word, and a revealing one, from "Small Pets") is ostensibly domestic: heirlooms, children drawing, playing; visits to doctor, eye clinic. But the poems ritualize their subjects: the "Small Pets" are accorded "gay funeral"; a college reunion becomes a "Wake" and a "Lying in State"; the eye clinic is compared to Purgatory. Despair is only headed off by a kind of determined playacting in which the various resonances of "play" and "act" seem valid. In "Arena," the last poem of *The Small Containers,* and one which oddly does not reappear in the major collections until *The Hinterland* (1977), the poet contemplates puppets and asks his son:

> "How do they work,
> Giles?"
> "By magic." Then, corrective, the quick codicil:
> "By string."

And though Scupham casts his vote for magic, he knows that poems too work by string.

His subsequent work can be seen as a series of attempts to explore the tensions between magic and string, "nearly" innocence and experience. His first full-length collection, *The Snowing Globe* (1972), is especially interesting for its refinement of the rather crude prototypes in *The Small Containers*. The "Man on the Edge" style, a catalogue of bits and pieces related more by magic than by logic, is jauntily indulged in poems such as "Good Morning" and "Lessons in Survival," which may be more serious and defensive than the playful language chooses to admit, and developed in "Address Unknown," where a similar technique abruptly becomes surprisingly moving:

> My house is clipped lightly to an old hillside,
> Held against cloud and shine by the wills of others,
> Tacked up with sticky grit and threads of power.
>
> Its teeth are set on edge by a guitar trembling;
> Each thought unpeels a slim skin from the paintwork.
> House, I have stuffed you with such lovely nonsense:
>
> All these sweet things: Clare's Poems, Roman glass-
>   ware,
> A peacock's feather, a handful of weird children,
> A second-hand cat with one pad missing, missing.

Such lines indicate a characteristic strength: the ability to invest domestic subjects with an elegiac dignity untainted by either pretentiousness or bathos. *The Snowing Globe* is rich in exact, startling images: a frog "Falls through water like a chipped pebble"; hours "Detonate ... like mad bird scarers"; and

> The rambling bee, obtuse and hairy,
> Unzips with his dull purr
> The studious air.

The love poems are perhaps less successful. It is as if Scupham, having found a style "where past and present become each other," effectively reaching across the time scale imposed by human mortality, has trouble in adopting a more conversational tone. In some early poems he is tempted by a compensatory brashness, in others by a mannered elegance

which does not quite come off, as a Mozartian tone lurches into Palm Court: "I am most taken by this demure mood, lady:/The gentle voice with which you ease the air." This, and much of the group of love poems collected as *The Gift* (1973), teeters on the brink of self-parody: the implied rejection of a quotidian norm brings with it dangers of apparent insincerity, ventriloquism.

Prehistories (1975) finds Scupham challenging his mannerisms, writing with increased assurance. His elegiac tone has gained in weight and naturalness:

> At the close of a long summer, slow green fires
> Consume the wandering fly and the poppy's mem-
>   brane.
> Life dwindles to a vigorous wreckage of bleached
>   grass.

As before, the finest effects come from the juxtaposition of familiar details and startling image:

> Beyond the dented churns, the huddled farmyard,
> Look, a green and lackadaisical finger
> Reveals a hair-line fracture in the land.

Here, in the opening stanza of "Public Footpath To," the signpost as a "green and lackadaisical finger" leads the reader firmly into both poem and landscape with the right combination of lightness and descriptive accuracy. The same kind of motif reappears later ("a church tower makes her slight invitation"), and throughout the poem one has the sense of the landscape doing the work, taking the initiative, until overpowered by the concluding image of "one self-sufficient tractor/Dragging the sullen landscape down to earth"—an image equally effective in its literal truthfulness and in its confident note of resolution.

The greater geographical openness is accompanied by a firmer historical awareness and the two merge in the geological themes and images which recur through the book, though most explicitly in "Excavations"—eleven poems which explore the relationships between places, their pasts, and the authorial present—and in the title sequence: "deepening" seems the right word for this development, in more than one sense. "Ghosts are a poet's working capital," says Scupham in "Prehistories," though this line seems too facile a formula to describe his enterprise, typical of the poet's tendency to form striking epigrammatic lines from half-truths, his "nearly" innocence at work again. The

Drafts for a poem published in Prehistories *(the author)*

25

29/10/72

Public Footpath To

Yes, you can go down there, if you so fancy.
Look, a green and lackadaisical finger
Reveals a hair-line fracture in the land.

Your car manhandled to the tussocked roadside,
The dented churns and jumbled farmyard skirted,
Push past the late blackberries, dull and sour.

cold
~~Where~~ mud glints, beaten to a pale rivulet,
Button your coat against the coming season;
Wince at the whiplash of a trailing stem.

                              absorbed
Pause, lost, the thread ~~broken~~ by knitted ploughland;
Stooping, unpick that crumpled fabric, palming
A broken tile, a freckled knob of bone.

Feel the cold rising from damp skins of leaf-mould,
The swell of ~~(the)~~ ground magpies are working over,
The weight of that wood grasping the far hill.

Such slim capillaries, such seams and crinkles,
Overflown by clouds, nodded at by thistles,
Sealed by the impress of lost summer girls

And men whose ways were set by dawn and sunset,
Offer a sense of flowers, endurances.
Time has stopped dead in these forgotten tracks.

where
~~The~~ rank, disordered trees and sniffling grasses
Huddle and fuss among the wind's ~~rough~~twitchings.
A crumbled mouth yawns at the dim hedge-foot.

                    - tower *makes her slight*
Though a ~~far~~ church ~~extends an~~ invitation,
Horizons after
~~Something delivers here~~ as the bruised air thickens.
Let the past keep her right of way, while you
           reading
           back in familiar ground
Are sensible, going over old ground again,
Of labouring barns, ~~far~~ self-sufficient tractors
~~Pulling~~ ~~recalcitrant~~ landscape ~~into shape.~~
Dragging the ~~stubborn~~   *back to earth*
                sullen

513

most intriguing part of this sequence seems to be
the enigmatic first poem, which begins:

> Adrowse, my pen trailed on, and a voice spoke:
> "Now, you must read us 'Belknap.'" My book was
>   open.
>
> I saw their faces; there were three of them,
> Each with a certain brightness in her eyes.
>
> I would read "Belknap." Then a gardener's shears
> Snipped fatefully my running thread of discourse.
>
> And in my indices, no poem upon which
> I could confer this honorary title.

As a reflexive—self-generating, self-analyzing—
poem, this is at once truthful and magical, a long
way from "Man on the Edge."

"If poetry is concerned with knowledge,"
Scupham wrote in that first introduction, "Auden is
surely right when he calls it a game as well." He has
been a formalist, game player as well as role player,
from the start, fond of regular metrical forms and
(in some of the early poems especially) strict rhyme
schemes such as terza rima. The formal interest is
most strikingly evident in the complex "Hungarian"
sonnet sequence—fifteen interlocking rhymed
sonnets, each last line becoming its successor's first
line, the fourteen first/last lines comprising the fifteenth sonnet—which gives its title to Scupham's
third full-length collection, *The Hinterland* (1977).
Introducing the book to members of the Poetry
Book Society, Scupham explained that the sequence was "written in a state of absorbed puzzle-
ment over four or five days: one of those occasions
rare, but compelling gratitude. Images from the
sequence had teased me for years, but I had
ploughed them under, knowing I had no proper
home for them. The sequence moves backwards
and forwards from the years 1914-1918, a meditation on complexities of creation and destruction."
The significant words are "ploughed them under"
and "meditation": "The Hinterland," moving back
to World War I from the summer of 1975 (images
of the hot August and of Dutch elm disease recur in
the sequence), has a peculiar density of matured,
mingled imagery blended with a privately ruminative tone. This mixture is both characteristic and
problematical: at worst it leads to a degree of opacity undesired, and possibly unsuspected, by the
poet. *The Hinterland* as a collection, however,
broadens Scupham's range to include a new relaxed

humor and a pared-down lucidity. The humor
emerges in "Marginalia" and in "Answers to Corre-
spondents" (subtitled "Girls' Own, 1881") in which
Scupham brilliantly versifies the agony columns of a
nineteenth-century girls' magazine:

> Constant Reader, if, as you hint, they are improper,
>   We still do not see how to alter your cat's eyes;
> Marinella, your efforts to remove tattoo-marks
>   Are wasted. Wear longer sleeves. We do not
>   advise
> Cutting or burning. Smut, we could never think it
>   A waste of time to make you better, and wise.

The twentieth century, on the other hand, comes
off badly, damned with veiled but devastating bitterness in "An Age." The lucidity, allied to the recurrent past/present theme, is well exemplified by
"Minsden":

> The chapel bears this press of trees,
> Leading old windows, topping out
> Some roof above the fallen roof,
> Bustling their heavy green about
> The shrouded flint. A pallid breeze
> Picks at the twigs and faded stuff,
> Fussing the tangled floor: dust blurs
> Lost village and lost villagers.

And towards the end of the book come poems in
which this elegiac clarity is finely synthesized with
Scupham's habitual linguistic richness—notably
two unrhymed sonnets, "As The Rain Falls" and
(another churchyard poem) "The Doves":

> Rough marble lets fly her cold scintillae.
> What were you for, who lie here in accord
> With the erosions of this further season?
> Light shivers from drubbed grass; then the stillness,
> And the doves, as doves do, mourn, mourn.

Summer Palaces (1980) opens with a sequence
of poems about theater in which a kind of opacity
returns: a defensive reaching-out for handy mythologies seems to head off the gritty practicalities
of dramatic production, and the reader only gradually becomes aware, as Scupham always is, of "the
darkness gathered in the wings." There is a lot of
offstage darkness in *Summer Palaces*, as indeed there
is in T. S. Eliot's "Journey of the Magi," to which the
title of the book and the first stanza of the title poem
directly allude:

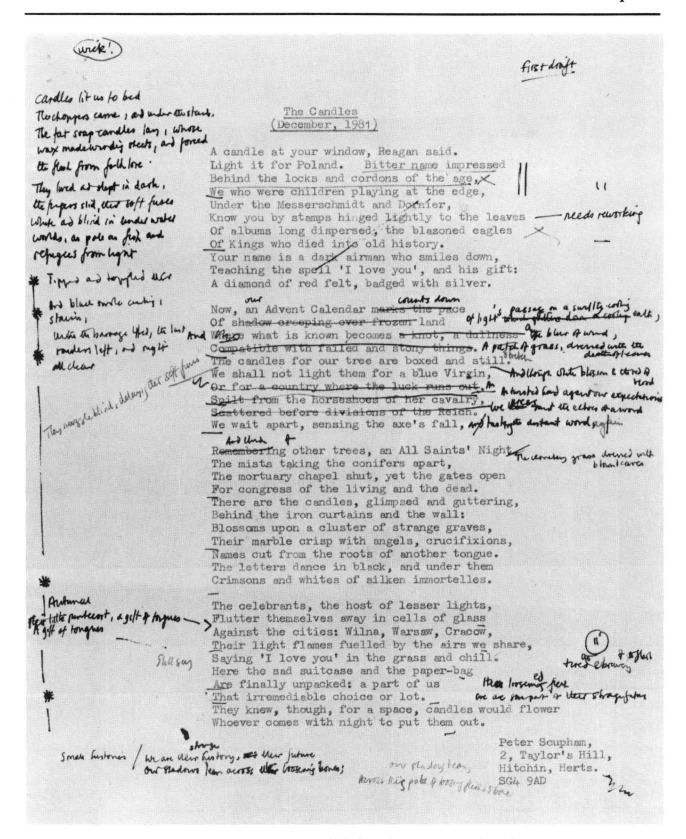

Intermediate draft for a poem published in Winter Quarters *(the author)*

How shall we build our summer palaces?
Will the girls bring us sherbert, and our gardens
Brown to the filigree of Chinese lanterns?

Even if the question seems to invite the answer "No," there are other childish rewards to be had; the poem is the last of a sequence called "A Cambridgeshire Childhood." However, at the end of the poem, the offstage darkness makes its appearance, with a fine premonition of age:

The night lies warm upon a wall of shadows.
We lie as naked in our drifting beds
As the close moon, staining us with silver.

"A Cambridgeshire Childhood" is altogether an attractive sequence, demonstrating qualities of exact observation ("War Zone") and quizzical humor ("Cam").

There are four sequences in *Summer Palaces*— the two already mentioned, "Megaliths and Water" and "Natura"—but it is the odd, separate, and distinctive poems which provide best evidence of Scupham's increasing diversity: the elegy "H. J. B."; "The Waiting Room," another lucid poem about death; "South Cadbury," which embraces a world from kestrels to beer cans; "The Gatehouse," an acute fusion of past and present; "Horace Moule at Fordington," where a familiar literary-biographical mode is treated with clarity and restraint; and "High Summer," almost a pendant to "The Hinterland." "Natura" contains some of his most vivid writing about plants:

A push of wheat softens the sprawling field,
The bones' complexion, gentled into green,

Ghosting a crop whose plaits and bunches thicken
To summer, working slowly with the grain.

The vitality of those lines and the delighted joke which concludes them are typical of "Natura"— darkness at least temporarily banished.

Since Scupham's interest in historical continuities and his delight in formal poetic structures are unfashionable, it is no surprise to find that his books have been given a rough ride by some fashionable reviewers. Paradoxically, his refusal to write aggressively controversial poems has been the cause of some aggressive controversy; while the technical virtuosity of "The Hinterland" prompted Craig Raine in the *Observer* to compare the sequence to "a constriction suit" and Colin Falck in the *New Review* to associate himself with "Readers who suspect that this may be the kind of foolery that gets poetry a bad name." Other reviewers have complained, with more justice, that some poems are marred by overornate or unnecessarily recondite language. Nevertheless, Scupham evidently enjoys the support of some leading magazine editors, a distinguished publisher, and a loyal readership. His concern with poetic craftsmanship should enable him to outlast many flimsier and more modish writers. But perhaps his greatest asset is that deep cultural-historical taproot, so unusual and so welcome at a time when English poetry can seem to be a rather shallow-rooted plant.

Penelope Shuttle

(12 May 1947-)

Caroline L. Cherry
Eastern College

BOOKS: *An Excusable Vengeance*, published with *Infatuation*, by Carol Burns, and *The Road*, by J. A. Dooley (London: Calder & Boyars, 1967);

Nostalgia Neurosis and Other Poems (Aylesford, U.K.: St. Albert's Press, 1968);

All the Usual Hours of Sleeping (London: Calder & Boyars, 1969);

Branch (Rushden, U.K.: Sceptre Press, 1971);

Wailing Monkey Embracing a Tree (London: Calder & Boyars, 1973; Boston: Boyars, 1980);

Midwinter Mandala (New Malden, Surrey, U.K.: Headland Publications, 1973);

The Hermaphrodite Album, by Shuttle and Peter Redgrove (London: Fuller d'Arch Smith, 1973);

Moon Meal (Rushden, Northamptonshire, U.K.: Sceptre Press, 1973);

The Terrors of Dr. Treviles: A Romance, by Shuttle and Redgrove (London: Routledge & Kegan Paul, 1974);

Photographs of Persephone (London: Quarto Press, 1974);

Autumn Piano and Other Poems (Liverpool: Rondo Publications, 1974);

The Songbook of the Snow (Ilkley, U.K.: Janus Press, 1974);

Webs on Fire (London: Gallery Press, 1975);

The Dream (Knotting, Bedfordshire, U.K.: Sceptre Press, 1975);

The Glass Cottage: A Nautical Romance, by Shuttle and Redgrove (London: Routledge & Kegan Paul, 1976);

Four American Sketches (Knotting, Bedfordshire, U.K.: Sceptre Press, 1976);

Rainsplitter in the Zodiac Garden (London: Boyars, 1977; Nantucket, Mass.: Longship Press, 1978);

The Wise Wound: Menstruation and Everywoman, by Shuttle and Redgrove (London: Gollancz, 1978); republished as *The Wise Wound: Eve's Curse and Everywoman* (New York: Marek, 1978);

The Mirror of the Giant: A Ghost Story (London: Boyars, 1980; Boston: Boyars, 1980);

Hills Harris (Oxford) Ltd.

Prognostica (Knotting, Bedfordshire, U.K.: Booth, 1980);

The Orchard Upstairs (Oxford: Oxford University Press, 1980);

The Child-Stealer (Oxford: Oxford University Press 1983).

Penelope Shuttle, like many of the poets who emerged during the late 1960s and 1970s, is concerned with charting the landscape of inner experience and intimate relationships. More particularly, she is drawn to the intersection between the powerful rhythms of women's bodily experience and their imaginative, creative, relational lives. A novelist and author of radio plays as well as a poet, Shuttle often brings a proselike directness to her poems and a poetic resonance and intensity to her prose. Although she terms herself a "feminist radical Social Democrat" in politics and speaks of her desire to provide "validation for the psyche of women unclouded by patriarchal requirements," her poetry is neither exclusively feminist nor overtly political; rather, she seeks to evoke both masculine and feminine aspects of herself and of her reader, to confront the emotional with the intellectual. She has been linked in Blake Morrison and Andrew Motion's *The Penguin Book of Contemporary Poetry* (1982) with the younger generation of British poets who show "a new confidence in the poetic imagination."

A member of the postwar generation, Penelope Diane Shuttle was born near London in Staines, Middlesex. The daughter of Jack Frederick Shuttle, a business executive, and Joan Lipscombe Shuttle, a housewife, she attended Staines Grammar School, a private preparatory school, and Matthew Arnold County Secondary School, a modern girls' school. She found little support in formal education for her intense immersion in literature and her precocious gift for writing; she was publishing poetry by the age of fourteen and had completed her first novel by seventeen. Instead of attending a university, she worked at a series of temporary secretarial jobs in the greater London area to support her writing. She had published two novels and a brief collection of poetry by the age of twenty-two, but the strain of writing, working, and living in "my feverish generation" led to bouts of anorexia nervosa, agoraphobia, and, at the age of nineteen, a nervous breakdown.

Her ability to make poetry out of distress is reflected in her first brief collection of ten poems, *Nostalgia Neurosis and Other Poems* (1968), published in a limited edition of five hundred copies. Addressing "all those young men/of nineteen fourteen," she writes in the title poem, "All I know is that pain/is no new doctrine, boys./But our interpretations change." But there is healing, too, a process caught in "Winter Jasmine" in finely observed images of nature and love that return in later poems: "In favour/of the sun,/their yellowness/is a sharp lemon,/interrupting winter/with a legend/of spring/hidden within each womb." Jim Burns, reviewing this pamphlet, spoke of "an attractive directness in the way she uses language." Shuttle's work received early recognition, winning Arts Council Awards in 1969 and again in 1972.

A major transition in her life occurred in 1969 when she met poet and novelist Peter Redgrove. She left her job in Somerset to live with Redgrove in Falmouth, Cornwall, where Redgrove has been resident author at the Falmouth School of Art since 1966 and where they continue to live. The relationship has had a decisive effect on the work of both authors and has resulted in several collaborations; they speak of their union as "a kind of circulation of energies." Residence in Falmouth was also influential. Shuttle had always felt "an affinity with the West Country," and in Cornwall she nourished her interest in local archaeology and folklore, her responsiveness to landscape, and her sensitivity to the effects of weather and the rhythm of the seasons, all reflected in her poetry.

A number of the themes and images which mark Shuttle's later work were focused and nurtured in an event that occurred early in 1971. At this time, Shuttle reports that she was suffering "near-suicidal menstrual distress." Using Jungian techniques derived from Dr. John Layard, his analyst-teacher, Redgrove enabled Shuttle to translate her depression into images and dreams which they analyzed. This therapy, extending over several months, alleviated the symptoms, deepened their understanding and appreciation of bodily processes, enhanced Shuttle's creative abilities, and led to further research over the course of several years.

The immediate literary fruit of their collaboration was *The Hermaphrodite Album* (1973), a collection of poems and prose poems which they characterize, in a phrase translated from Goethe, as the work "of a composite being." Containing the poem sequence "Witch Skin," for which Shuttle received the Greenwood Prize for poetry in 1972, this volume displays a medieval sense of an animated nature alive with dark forces, expressed in an eccentric blend of Christian and folklore images: "Downstairs/the gentlewoman moos/prehistoric mice/gobble the falcon/the gun-dog and the war-horse elope. . . ." The critical reaction to this volume was not uniformly favorable; the *Times Literary Supplement* termed it "a sad abuse of proven talent" which threatens "to drown the reader in a flood of surrealist/symbolist rhetoric." Nevertheless, there is power in the brooding mystery of some of these poems, and a mapping of territory to be more masterfully explored in later work: the creative and destructive blood, the womb, the branch both bare and flowering, ice, rain, and glass. Robert Nye wrote, "Those who look to poetry for spiritual nourishment will find food here."

Meanwhile, Shuttle continued to receive

attention with several pamphlet collections of poetry published during this period: *Midwinter Mandala* (1973), which one critic termed "a fine bunch of startling poems"; *Photographs of Persephone* (1974); *Autumn Piano and Other Poems* (1974); *The Songbook of the Snow* (1974); and *Webs on Fire* (1975). There is a sense of creative expectancy and transition in many of the poems, reflected in "The Death of the Hyacinth" in *Autumn Piano,* in which she waits for "some new thing without bitterness,/which I will record and which will change me,/send me on new journeys/amid the web-worlds of the beckoning room."

In 1974 Shuttle was awarded the E. C. Gregory Award for Poetry. She continued to publish poetry in magazines, in the P.E.N. *New Poems* anthologies for 1973-1974, 1974-1975, and 1976-1977, in the Arts Council Anthology of New Poetry, and as broadsheets. Her work was also broadcast on BBC Radio and recorded for the poetry room at Harvard University.

The highly poetic, surrealistic novels Shuttle wrote during this period, both by herself and with Peter Redgrove, attracted significant critical interest. Robert Nye called Shuttle's *Wailing Monkey Embracing a Tree* (1973) a "highly original piece of work," and Victoria Glendenning wrote in regard to *Rainsplitter in the Zodiac Garden* (1977) that "Penelope Shuttle is an uncompromising explorer, digging away in the moist rabbit-hole of the subconscious, hoping we can follow her." Peter Ackroyd characterized Shuttle's *The Mirror of the Giant* (1980) as "a convincing sexual fable in which the stones have learned to speak of their loneliness." *The Terrors of Dr. Treviles: A Romance* (1974), by Shuttle and Redgrove, drew the comment from Marie Peel that "all these ideas open the gates of the mind with a fine flourish" and praise for "the ease and power, the light and shade, the visual beauty and exactness of the presentation and writing throughout." Gay Clifford characterized *The Glass Cottage: A Nautical Romance* (1976), by Shuttle and Redgrove, as "like a prose poem . . . concerned with a mythopoeic sort of ordering that sees existence as non-finite—not limited by chronology, or geography, or even death."

Shuttle's and Redgrove's daughter, Zoe Teresa Redgrove, was born in December 1976; her care consumed a good deal of Shuttle's energies in the years immediately following, but produced a corresponding enrichment of experience and invigoration of style.

The research on menstruation begun in 1971 resulted in the publication in 1978 of Shuttle and

Redgrove's *The Wise Wound,* a serious and thorough examination of the psychological, biological, sociological, imaginative, and mythic/religious ramifications of the monthly cycle, which, they point out, affects men and children as well as women and which, properly understood, is a blessing and not a curse. *Psychology Today* asserted that the book "could bring about a major change in our understanding of the sexes." Drawing on authors as diverse as C. J. Jung and R. D. Laing, Joseph Campbell and Robert Graves, Katharina Dalton and William Masters, this book explicates many of the themes and symbols that dominate the creative work of Shuttle and Redgrove: images of cervix and womb, blood and moon, the Grail, and Lilith, the child stealer. Their best-selling book, *The Wise Wound* has received widespread attention and was reprinted as a Penguin paperback in 1980.

Front cover for Shuttle's first full-length collection of poetry. Though some reviewers found the imagery obsessive, Anne Stevenson admired Shuttle's attempts "to reveal symbolically a landscape of consciousness."

Draft.   15. Jan 8 5.

new

It was
The dream of a day of pets,
  of silver carnivores tame as cats from siam,
     went   day
as the dreamer ~~going~~ into the world
of his dream, saying,
  a son is a pearl in the palm
And the snakes ~~that~~ sighed,
you must tell us how you dream,
  how do you do it?
but he concealed his secret, like a shame,
  as he ran past the confiscated houses of the losers

The tiny river whose door is open
shelters him,
but a river can't keep secrets,
the colour of the sky is a river's open secret
  ~~& so is the lake's name, water - star~~
     the river
but ~~it~~ was his smiling friend, the ~~for river~~,
and ~~the observ~~ er was happy to be lost
as a child without rules
or an explorer ~~us~~ getting the water he wants

~~Lot the day dreamed the~~ red ~~leaves~~ ~~cmy out~~

~~For the day dreamed~~ The trees are the day-dreamer's pets,
the birds are his sex, lifted into skies secret as any
             our planet
light makes a soothing house for him,
the windows are not made of grief, the roof is not sad,

                                  summers
the rooms are white ~~too~~ , ~~chalked chairs~~
~~and~~   without rain   (storm)

And the last shout of the dreamer
as he dreams, earning his living,
is his way of not weeping . Jan 15 - 85.

In December 1980 Shuttle and Redgrove were married, and in the same year Oxford University Press published Shuttle's first full-length collection of poetry, *The Orchard Upstairs*. These poems show a firmer hand and greater artistic command than do Shuttle's earlier works, playing against each other in a contrapuntal interweaving of ideas. Several of the poems are meditative, evoking the ghostly traces of transient experience: in "The Dancer," she speaks of the dancer's "frail geography barely remembered except as a swift erasure of shadows." Others exude a joyous energy, a sense of rebirth and renewal: in "Three Lunulae, Truro Museum," "The women of the lunulae/threw no barbaric shadows/yet a vivid dance/lit up their bones." Central to the volume are the complex bodily rhythms of womanhood; Shuttle places common female experiences, caught in poems with titles such as "Period," "The Conceiving," "Expectant Mother," "First Foetal Movements of My Daughter," against the background of the need for psychic order and the imaginative and real desire for a child. The outer world may be threatening and potentially destructive, but it is brought into equilibrium with the inward powers of creation. The despair of failed conception is answered with hope: "No sooner has the month's answer come,/been feared, hated and then accepted,/danced with, adored,/than the fallow hesitations of myself/are audible again,/I hear the new question and its invitation." Ultimately, these poems suggest an acceptance of process, a recognition of what it means to be a woman. The balance between the creative and destructive forces is achieved most powerfully in "The Orchard Upstairs," a poem ripe with possibilities. The final lines fall with a calm certainty:

> In the morning, the sun cools itself
> against the orchard mirror
> I sit on the window ledge
> and below me the lawn is calm green water,
> a lake of old love.

Some of Shuttle's images have been criticized as too literal or obsessive; Laurence Lerner says that the "scarlet imagery soon palls, and there are times when her concern with bodily processes seems to parody itself." But Anne Stevenson, in an appreciative review for the *Times Literary Supplement*, understands that when the author "undertakes to reveal symbolically a landscape of consciousness, she lays

Front cover for Shuttle's 1983 collection of poetry. The title refers to Lilith, the demon who preys on children and pregnant women.

herself open to critical abuse."

The Orchard Upstairs was followed three years later by *The Child-Stealer* (1983), also published by Oxford University Press. Here Shuttle speaks in a somewhat different voice, more consciously poetic, more distanced and reflective, less personal and turbulent. There is a sense of chronological progress in many of the poems; the child is born, and the poet uses her both to reflect experience and to help decipher it. Characteristic of this volume are poems of process, growth, and acceptance, such as "Mother and Child," "The Children," and "The Flower-Press": "Deeper and deeper you draw me into life,/you make the dead come alive again/by sensing how even the shadow of a flower/may be perfect, and so suffice." Shuttle preserves the distinction between inner and outer landscapes in "Indoors and Outdoors": "Indoors, the snow is afraid of me./Outdoors, I fear the calamity of cold,/unignitable enemy. . . . Winter inherits the outdoors./Indoors the fires are making themselves at home."

Fleur Adcock noted the "plainer, more prosaic style" in these poems and observed that "Shuttle has always been an uneven poet, because an instinctive one. She would have done better to rely on her instinct, which was accompanied by a fairly sound poetic ear, than to attempt modes for which her talent is not suited." Other reviewers were more favorable; Michael O'Neill remarked that "*The Child-Stealer* is certainly good enough to make one interested to see what this poet will do next."

It is clear that Penelope Shuttle is still developing, creatively interacting with biological and familial changes in her own life as she strives to articulate her experiences in language that will provide a guide and a mirror for her readers: an unashamed exploration of female nature for women, and a means of accessing the power and wisdom of the unknown for men.

James Simmons
(14 February 1933-   )

James J. Murphy
Villanova University

BOOKS: *Aikin Mata,* by Simmons and Tony Harrison (Ibadan: Oxford University Press, 1966);
Ballad of a Marriage (Belfast: Festival Publications, Queen's University, 1966);
Late But In Earnest (London: Bodley Head, 1967);
Ten Poems (Belfast: Festival Publications, Queen's University, 1968);
In the Wilderness (London: Bodley Head, 1969);
Songs for Derry (Portrush: Ulsterman Publications, 1969);
No Ties (Portrush: Ulsterman Publications, 1970);
Energy to Burn (London: Bodley Head, 1971);
No Land Is Waste, Dr. Eliot (Richmond, Surrey: Keepsake Press, 1973);
The Long Summer Still to Come (Belfast: Blackstaff Press, 1973);
West Strand Visions (Belfast: Blackstaff Press, 1974);
Memorials of a Tour in Yorkshire (Belfast: Ulsterman Publications, 1975);
Judy Garland and the Cold War (Belfast: Blackstaff Press, 1976);
The Selected James Simmons, edited by Edna Longley (Belfast: Blackstaff Press, 1978);
Constantly Singing (Belfast: Blackstaff Press, 1980);
Sean O'Casey (London: Macmillan, 1984);
From the Irish (Belfast: Blackstaff, 1985).

PLAY PRODUCTIONS: *Aikin Mata,* by Simmons and Tony Harrison, Zaria, Nigeria, Ahmadu Bello University, 1965;
An Exercise in Dying, Lancaster Festival, 1970;
Black Eye, Belfast Festival, 1975;
The Death of Herakles, Belfast Festival, 1978;
Doily McCartney's Africa, Edinburgh Festival, 1981.

OTHER: *Out on the Edge,* edited by Simmons and A. R. Mortimer (Leeds: Leeds University Department of English, 1958);
New Poems from Ulster, edited by Simmons (Coleraine: New University of Ulster, 1971);
Ten Irish Poets, edited by Simmons (Manchester: Carcanet Press, 1974);
Soundings 3, edited by Simmons (Belfast: Blackstaff Press, 1976).

To outsiders it may appear that the world of Northern Ireland since the late 1960s has been one of destruction, of darkness without light. As tragic as the history of this province has been, however, the same period has witnessed an explosion of intense poetic activity of the highest order. Since his founding of the *Honest Ulsterman* in 1968, James Simmons—poet, musician, critic—has been at the heart of this resurgence of the creative life of Northern Ireland. His work, however, has not been a response to the province's political life, but rather an attempt to account for his own life. In the midst of public turmoil, private lives go on, with their tragedies more deeply felt, their joys calling forth man's need to raise his voice in celebration.

James Simmons (courtesy of Bernard Stone, The Turret Book Shop)

James Simmons was born in Londonderry, Northern Ireland, on 14 February 1933, the Valentine's Day connection appropriate to one who would make his poetic career largely an exploration of love's complexities. His early schooling at Foyle College, Londonderry, and subsequently at Campbell College, Belfast, left him restless under the strictures of formal education. In fact, he describes himself as "very badly educated." This statement is misleading, however, for much of Simmons's youthful interest was in music and song, and much of his study was directed to those areas. He finished school in 1949 with little desire to pursue a university education and, at age eighteen, left for England, hoping to find some success as a writer or performer, two careers which have remained inseparably connected for him. For several years, he held various temporary jobs and was even involved in an unsuccessful attempt to sail around the world. These were years of important growth for Simmons

as he read and learned his craft, especially through songwriting. As he says, when he began to write seriously, he "knew more about popular songs than poetry."

Having failed to launch a show-business career, he returned to Northern Ireland to work as a barman in Portrush, County Antrim, still convinced that a life of poetry and song was his future. Events then combined to direct him to his goal. In 1956 his marriage to Laura Stinson brought some temporary stability into his life and became an important source of inspiration for one of his major subjects—the joys and trials of marital love. Second, the distinguished critic Bonamy Dobree offered Simmons a scholarship at Leeds University. His wife helped to pay their expenses, and Simmons was free to devote full energies to literary study and to grow as a poet in the company of Tony Harrison, Geoffrey Hill, Wole Soyinka, Tom Blackburn, and G. W. Ireland. In 1957-1958 he rose to the editorship of *Poetry and Audience* at Leeds. He received his B.A. degree with honors in 1958 and returned to Ireland to teach at the Friends' School in Lisburn. His efforts at poetry and songwriting began to receive recognition as he appeared performing his work on radio and television and in 1961, he received the Eric Gregory Award for poetry. He spent the years 1963-1966 teaching at Ahmadu Bello University in Nigeria. There he wrote and published, in 1966, his first play, *Aikin Mata*, in association with Tony Harrison. During this period, his poetry began to find a wider audience through publication of his work in such respected magazines as *New Statesman* and the *Spectator* and, in 1966, Festival Publications of Belfast released his first poetry pamphlet, *Ballad of a Marriage*.

Simmons returned from Africa in 1967. The difficulties of a year's unemployment and the increasing tensions of life in Northern Ireland were eased somewhat by the publication in that same year of *Late But In Earnest*, his first full-length volume of poetry. After a rather long and convoluted journey, he had arrived as a poet.

The volume was, as he puts it, "a little late, so there is no juvenilia." This feeling of a late beginning contributes to the volume's note of lost youth, of the passage of time. As a poet and as a man, he is attuned to the dangers of diminishing powers, of missed opportunities, of the changing roles that age brings. As he writes in "Written, Directed by and Starring...,"

It's hard to start upon this middle phase

when my first period never reached the screen,
and there's no end now to my new screen-plays,
they just go on from scene to scene.

At age thirty-four, he sees himself as already in the "middle phase" of his life, while only beginning his first phase as a professional poet. This conflict permeates the poems. As the title indicates, he is "late but in earnest." "Me and the World" suggests the general concern of the volume, the poet's relationship with the world seen in the image of a girl friend: "I live with photographs/for the world, my girl, is away mostly." The metaphoric equation of girl friend and world captures the spirit of the relationship. Girl friends are mysterious, tempting, flighty and, all too often, absent, but a girl friend's smile can momentarily fill the world with wonder. These are the moments Simmons cherishes, when the world and its lover are on speaking terms. Then, even "the crippled houses respond/to the continual miracle of sun and dust." Such incandescent moments are precious precisely because they are so fleeting. Girl friends are elusive, and, for all the joy of shared moments, there is the fear that the joys of love are doomed to pass. Thus the defensive conclusion to the poem: "My smile is genuine, though when she laughs/I don't forget my jar to warm the bed, my photographs."

This fear that the powers of love diminish is found again in "For John Clare," when Simmons writes, "I/who loved Illona Massey at fourteen/with a great love am now a has-been." That romantic love is the province of younger men also suggests that marital love, like middle age, lacks the power of enchantment. In "Lot's Wife," torn by "all she left," Lot's wife takes her eyes off her husband and looks elsewhere, with tragic result. As Lot discovers, the loving response is no longer there:

At last Lot drew his wagon to a halt;
dog-tired but glad, he groped his way inside,
looking for pleasure in his sleeping bride,
kissed her, and on her cold cheek tasted salt.

Although not always smooth, the love that does not diminish is that of parent and child. "Late But In Earnest" may contain no juvenilia, but some of its most touching moments are in Simmons's treatment of the relationship with his mother and grandmother. In "Ode to my Grandmother," his own balancing of life's contraries is attributed to her:

I celebrate the equilibrist skill
my granny had.
Being rare—an integrated character—
to grief she never came
nor swayed far,
treading, happy and sad,
a taut line to death.

The volume may have been "late" by his estimate, but throughout it indicates a poet whose study of his craft has paid dividends. The sense of structure is especially strong. Here is a first volume, liberal in spirit, but firmly rooted in a traditional sense of rhyme and form. His own comment on this aspect of the volume is that "I suppose I have something in common with the Movement, the pleasure in traditional quatrains that early Donald Davie, Larkin and Amis have, also some Auden influence."

The success of his first volume helped propel Simmons into a leadership position in the Northern Ireland poetic movement. Sensing the need, amid the province's increasing turmoil, of an outlet for poets and intellectuals to express themselves freely, in 1968 he founded the *Honest Ulsterman*. Had James Simmons never written another poem, this effort alone should insure him a place in Ireland's poetic history. The journal has been, from its inception, a major forum for Irish writers. Many of the writers whose works found an audience there—Seamus Heaney, Derek Mahon, Brendan Kennelly—are now leading voices in Irish cultural life. Simmons's prefatory editorial to the first issue indicates clearly that the magazine's subtitle, "a magazine of revolution," should not be seen mainly in the light of the turbulent politics of Northern Ireland, but as a plea for a revolution in man's understanding of himself. From this understanding, all else should flow. His words speak for themselves: "It is a literary magazine; but literature starts and finishes with men talking to men, and the most important thing for a man talking to men is to be honest. . . . Each man is the principal actor and audience in his own life. . . . Political progress from now on will not depend on our allegiance to leaders, ideas, and systems, but in each individual's allegiance to himself. . . . the real reforms, the real revolutions must be in ourselves. . . . Living is not a science, it is an art." Simmons edited the magazine for two years before passing the leadership on to Michael Foley and Frank Ormsby.

In 1968 Simmons took a position at the New University of Ulster at Coleraine, teaching drama and Anglo-Irish literature, a position he has held since. In 1969 *In the Wilderness* was published. It is, as he puts it, "riddled with Lear and Jesus. I have always had at the back of my mind a mainstream from Shakespeare." In the major poems of the volume the reader is brought into Simmons's own wilderness with Lear, Cordelia, France, Gloucester, and Shakespeare himself. The world of camping and the solitary journey dominate; the loneliness of the soul is the poet's great teacher. The world is now a wilderness, not a girl friend whose smile brings light. In the title poem, Simmons explains, "A teacher in the wilderness alone/learns to make bread and sermons out of stone." In many of the poems, the soul is brought, like Lear's, to a condition of being "alone/with birds, stones,/water and air." Clearly, the purgative nature of Lear's suffering is a consolation to Simmons. The intimate connection of tragedy and joy in the poems recalls the spirit of William Butler Yeats in "Lapis Lazuli." Life's struggles produce poetry since "The shaken mind finds metaphors/in winds that shake the great outdoors" ("Outward Bound"). The poet is "Under duress trying to sing/in tune . . . the storm/ endured, we hope to come to harm/at home, with better dignity/or style or courage."

Simmons's own marital struggles are made to parallel the family turmoils in *King Lear*. In "At Cordelia's Grave" the Duke of France provides an analogy for Simmons's own increasing alienation in marriage, as he eloquently laments his wife's attentions, like those of Lot's wife, always flowing elsewhere: "I thought she was so glad/to be rescued from her mad/fathers and sisters." The breakup of order in one's personal life is touchingly expressed by Gloucester in "A Speech for Gloucester," "I was not aware/order was failing everywhere." It remains for the Fool to remind the reader that such pains as these can bring healing. Throughout, Shakespeare's Fool seems to know that Lear's tragedy is but an extreme example of the tragedies through which all men must make their way. Simmons suggests we must come through retaining our sense of life's joys. We must, as his "sore, ageing clown" tells us in "Circumnavigators," "fare forward." Simmons's ability to use the Lear material in this ultimately positive sense is best seen in "To My Grandmother, while reading *King Lear*." Earlier she was his "equilibrist," perhaps like Lear's Fool, not immune to pain and death, but with a knowledge and perspective to balance both and retain the smile so important to Simmons. Her story, less dramatic than Lear's, is by that very reason more universal. He writes,

This happier story has no madness
and no ingratitude, no storm,
only its own bearable sadness
here where it is still warm.

The life of the average man, unlike Lear's, brings "bearable" sadnesses and, more important, it brings causes for song, as Simmons reminds the reader in "Join Me in Celebrating." An "unhoped for gift," the birth of a child, transforms the world. All sorrow drops away for the moment and he proclaims:

I wouldn't change my condition
for freedom, cash, applause,
rebirth of young ambition
or faith in Santa Claus.

Simmons continued to combine his teaching,

Front cover for the book that led one reviewer to call Simmons "Perhaps the greatest new poet now living in the North of Ireland"

songwriting, and poetry careers, and in 1971 *Energy to Burn* was published. He feels it contains "some of the best love poems, the mixture of daily reality and passionate form." Reviewing it for the *Toronto Globe*, Anthony Cronin called Simmons, "Perhaps the greatest new poet now living in the North of Ireland." Throughout, he speaks directly about himself and the increasing tensions in his personal life. The title comes from "One of the Boys," in which an earlier theme is echoed, "Now middle-aged, I know,/and do not hide the truth." It is the truth of being "tired, tired/and incapacitated," left only with memories "of nights in cars/with energy to burn." As he describes the volume himself, "It establishes the breaking marriage theme, but Christ is in there too. Burning turns up throughout the book." The world of girl-friend romance is forgotten when one can "regret even the childish vows/we giggled in the face of Heaven." This capriciousness has degenerated badly:

> For this philosophy I burn.
> I am sick of love and my wife leaves
> to consult a solicitor, to turn
> my house into a den of thieves.

In "Roots," one of his favorite poems, he cynically recounts his own courtship and marriage, "Her soul was lost, though marriage saved her honour." His personal life is laid bare in the "Marital Sonnets," the volume's centerpiece. The sonnets combine present pain with memories of where marriages begin; tenderness mingles with resentment. "When I was twenty-four I was so lonely/I married her to keep me company/and learnt to value solitude the hard way." Driven further into himself, the married poet "had limited success/constructing poems from unhappiness." More realistic about love than Shakespeare, he can tell the reader, "Let's call this love, that alters when it finds/alteration, the marriage of two minds."

Extramarital relationships are, of course, one possible escape. A number of poems treat this subject quite openly, but Simmons leaves one feeling that, while mutual infidelity may lessen guilt, it does not relieve pain. The need for permanence outlasts the deceptive fulfillments of temporary sexual relationships. "This way adulteries end. A famished kiss/before we dress at the half hour/and separate. We have time but no desire./. . . The great storm runs its course." At age forty, he finds the smiles of girl friends are no longer enough. In fact, many of the volume's concerns can be traced to Simmons's concern about age. He still has "energy to burn"

and yet he worries, as in "Sonnet for the Class of '58," that "Perhaps never, or only when drunk, does life/seem as it once seemed, a war to be won."

Simmons does not apologize for his honest language or his blunt treatment of sensitive subjects. In the satiric "Censorship," the small-minded bookseller who objects to the poet's work is comically forced to proclaim Simmons's own poetic faith, "It's true. It's urgent. What else could I say?" Academic criticism of his work is not immune either when, in "For the Centenary," he satirizes scholars who "slouch towards the university presses."

In 1973 *The Long Summer Still to Come* was published by the Blackstaff Press. The change to an Irish publisher was significant to him. He says, "Changing from the Bodley Head was part of realizing how much Ireland was home." Although his earlier volumes, his songwriting, and his teaching had brought him recognition, the volume is not generally triumphant in spirit. With some notable exceptions, most of the poems are painfully purgative expressions of the estranged husband-father. There is an anger and a cynicism in many of the poems that seems at first out of spirit with his earlier desire to celebrate.

Actually, the music is still there, but it is drawing on different models, as jazz and the blues provide a new note to Simmons's style. Structurally, the poems open out, achieving a freedom for the longer meditative pieces. The volume is largely his jazz expression of self, freedom of lifestyle embracing freedom of poetic style. At other times he echoes his earlier use of Lear, stressing the paradox that life's pains can produce a profound music. Like Louis Armstrong, the poet declares in the opening poem, "Didn't He Ramble," "I look into my heart and blow." He makes no apologies for his style: "Profundity without the po-face/of court and bourgeois modes. This I could use/to live and die with. Jazz. Blues." Simmons's sense of the intimate relationship of poetry and music is evident in his comment that "my songs try to include as much matter as poetry and my poems try to be as clear and luminous as songs." His tribute to Blind Willie Blake's music expresses his feeling that in the purest music one finds "the word of life." There is, as in his own best work, "Tough reasonableness and lyric grace/together, in poor man's dialect."

Within this jazz framework, Simmons expresses his own world and the pain of the larger world of Northern Ireland's problem. As he puts it, "the troubles begin to intrude." In scarred, argumentative Ulster, can the poet find any listener who will hear only music? His countrymen are pictured as "half-living, dull, scared." The poet cannot live where the only voices heard are those of the "boring idealists," where public voices bring only "vicious applause"/: "For me to live my exhausted country/ must suffer artificial respiration." In the midst of this despair, warmed by a rare day of full sun, the poet can only hope. "I wait to learn my place,/ imagine true applause, remote/as the sun kissing my face./Then comfortably scratch my bum./The long summer still to come."

This link of the private and the public worlds is found in several of the poems. In both arenas, as he tells us in "Marriage," "life is naturally messy." But, as pervasive as the province's turbulence can be, a man's private concerns have more immediate reality. In "Ulster Today," newspapers contain horrific accounts of "the tragedy and the betrayals." The frequency of violence makes it seem almost irrelevant, "Whereas/the silly reviews in *The Irish Times*/have driven me mad." Clearly, the recognition of the importance of the individual experience over political abstractions has literary as well as political implications. There is understandable frustration with literary theorists in "To Certain Communist Friends": "Christ didn't take the nail and fetters/to get on well with men of letters." Correspondingly, honesty to oneself remains the highest achievement.

The following year, 1974, *West Strand Visions* appeared. A number of the poems develop images introduced in the title piece, where the poet looks from his window over scenes on the strand below. In fantasies, he is released into flight. The gulls become "engaging bi-planes/locked in each other's sights and strategies." A man watching children in the surf "is me,/estranged from mystery,/. . . shouting in apparent ecstasy/a pane of glass and fifty years away." The flight image reappears in "Flight," where the poet feels wings sprout on his back "to lift me off these stones into the sky." In "To a Dead Birdman," he speaks of a skydiver: "In free fall from the skies/he conquered pain."

The strand images of the title poem are also related to the use of sea journey and island images in "Robinson Crusoe" and "On Circe's Island." "On Circe's Island" is a virtuoso performance, a nine-part poem of varied stanzaic structures and tight rhymes. Away from home like Odysseus, Simmons finds a temporary peace, not with Circe but with solitude. In "that ruined hot-house, the solitude," he learns that "Responsibility must be particular,/ not to every creature under the sun,/not universal love, but cleaving to one."

One of the strongest works is "Claudy," perhaps the finest indicator of Simmons's success at uniting his poetic and songwriting gifts. His ballad makes the reader feel the terrible loss of decent lives when a car bomb wrecks the village of Claudy. He opens with images of ordinary lives on an ordinary day—people opening doors, crossing streets, "straightening things." Then, "An explosion too loud for your ear drums to bear,/and young children squealing like pigs in the square,/and all faces chalk white and streaked with bright red,/and the glass and the dust and the terrible dead." According to Oliver Edwards, " 'Claudy' steps straight into the succession of the Great Irish Ballads. It is important that ballads like 'Claudy,' his stark account of the bombing of that tragic village should never be forgotten."

Throughout the mid-1970s, Simmons continued his university teaching and traveled extensively, performing his work in Canada, the United States, France, and Germany. In 1976, he was the featured subject of an edition of *Omnibus* on BBC. Also in that year *Judy Garland and the Cold War* was published. He describes it briefly as "very much about art and artists, including poets." One such artist is the title figure, Judy Garland, who "spent a lifetime/trying to fly/over the rainbow/way up high/without mechanical aids." With "her private life a mess," she was publicly adored. Like Simmons, her art was song; like him, she worked for an audience blind to itself. Her pains ran deep, and still she sang, one of Simmons's own recurring needs. He concludes that poem, "Oh, sing on Judy,/ in the gramophones/on altars in how many/million homes,/the promised rainbow." To Simmons, Jesus himself calls us to music and surely he knew about pain. In "Dickie Wills Said: Variations," "As Jesus said, 'Stuff the applause,/we're here because we're here because/the rat race has gotta swing./So let's see everybody dancing.' "

Throughout his career, Simmons has reasserted his belief in the richness of ordinary life and his impatience with literary abstractions. This belief is especially apparent in the poems from *No Land Is Waste, Dr. Eliot*, which had been published separately in 1973. He describes these poems as "an achievement taking on the modern movement, but also quite autobiographical." T. S. Eliot's London is no wasteland full of hollow men. Clerks, typists, barmen populate the poems, as Simmons mockingly invites "Stearns" to come with him and meet the real people he never sees in his upper room. Here he would see his typists "turning their lunch hours in the heart of town/to sensuous gaiety." And "Oh Stearns, come round to meet the boys tonight,/to see the hollow men get full and fight." Eliot is "the pompous swine," and Simmons's man "not hollow, he's a mate of mine."

In 1977, Simmons's marriage ended in divorce. That same year he received the Cholmondeley Award for Poetry, and, in 1978, the Blackstaff Press released *The Selected James Simmons,* which received the recommendation of the Poetry Book Society. In this same period, he founded his own record company, Poor Genius Records, which has released two LP's, *Love in the Post* and *Resistance Cabaret,* and a single of his "Ballad of Claudy."

His most recent volume, *Constantly Singing,* was published in 1980 and has also received the recommendation of the Poetry Book Society. It is divided into four parts: "Natural Forces," "Intimations," "Of a Marriage," and "Last Things." He comments, "My impulse is to celebrate, and the first section in this book is unashamedly lyrical about the

THE SELECTED
JAMES SIMMONS
Edited by
EDNA LONGLEY

Front cover for the collection of some of the poems that led P. J. Kavanagh to describe Simmons as "quite outstanding, a kind of MacNeice with the Anglo-Irish gloves removed"

delights of new love and new energies in middle age." Throughout, Simmons plays with the theme expressed in his title. In the ten-part opening poem, "Meditations in Time of Divorce," the newly liberated husband adjusts to waking up alone: "Nevertheless he feels potential/not loss. Like St. Patrick he rises/reciting . . . constantly singing, not/putting a sour face on it." He finds comfort in rediscovering an earlier sense of family by visiting his father's grave and planting flowers: "All smiles, in solitude, constantly singing/he can relish the graveyard tap running/the black clay off his hands coldly." To his mother, he is "her prodigal son rejoining the family."

"Cloncha" is a tenderly lyrical account of his sharing with a new love the joys of the Irish countryside. They are "exploring delightedly/as lovers do." There is a special delicacy to many of the images, a new intensity of lyricism: "In petal and bloom of benweed/gorse and dandelion/bright yellow intensified." Rural Ireland inspires a sequence of such images, as Simmons allows the details to carry the point. The lovers share "pale water agile on slatey beds/of mountain streams, rain/on hotel windows, the pale gold/of whiskies set on the wine-dark/wood of country bar counters." A feeling of peace pervades the poem, the poet emphasizing that "The years from war to war/must be worth living for." This sense of peace clearly dominates in the private as well as the public sphere. He concludes, "I sing of natural forces,/marriages, divorces."

The "Marriage" poems, together with the earlier "Marital Sonnets," confirm Simmons's place as one of the most important voices on the subject of modern marriage. Images of geography and explorations recall John Donne's love poems, but the prevailing attitude is harsher. Marriage seems the enemy of love. "We stayed together out of shame/and habit, and the children came." The "Of A Marriage" section ends with a poem called "Divorce." It is no easier, it seems, to live like "a free republic" than to live with "an imperial power." In words that reach far beyond the question of marriage, he concludes, "I'm only saying it's hard work/to live, to govern right."

In Northern Ireland, this idea of governing right cannot be separated from the violence in the public world. Of the volume's concern with this turmoil, in poems such as "Coleraine, 1977," Simmons comments, "There is also the political stalemate of Northern Ireland in which suffering and frustration are the worse because there seems to be no cause and no leader to give meaning, to direct

CONSTANTLY
SINGING

James
Simmons

POETRY BOOK SOCIETY RECOMMENDATION

Front cover for Simmons's 1980 book. The title is taken from a line in Sean O'Casey's Juno and the Paycock: *"An' constantly singin', no less, when he ought always to be on his knees offerin' up a Novena for a job."*

effort. Neither the arts nor the educational establishments, to which the protagonist directs his energies publicly, seem effective."

Despite this recognition of the troubles of Ul-

ster, the spirit of celebration dominates. It may be that, after birth "like exiles we roam," but moments of wonderful richness console us as we wander "the long way home/with no sense of direction." The accumulated force of Simmons's work emphasizes not pain, but the joys of new love, the miracle of birth, the blessings of the sun in a wet land, the consolation and exhilaration of music, the inherent instinct to "fare forward." Memories may often include pain and loss, but at the end of this volume in "Olive & Davy," he remembers warmly his aunt and uncle, "an old story/from the common stock." In the "Last Poems" section there is even a blessing for a wedding: "May all the world's lovers,/all husbands and wives,/get lost in forever/for once in their lives" ("The Work of the Penis").

Remarried in 1981 to Imelda Foyle, Simmons continues to live and teach in Northern Ireland. His critical energies have been directed most recently to Sean O'Casey, and his book on the dramatist was published in 1984 by Macmillan as part of the Modern Dramatists Series. In his poetic life, he will no doubt remain "constantly singing." In his lifelong emphasis on the need to celebrate, he joins that tradition expressed by Yeats's "Dialogue of Self and Soul," "We must laugh and we must sing,/We are blest by everything,/Everything we look upon is blest."

References:

Terence Brown, "Four New Voices: Poets of the Present," in his *Northern Voices* (Totowa, N.J.: Rowman & Littlefield, 1975);

R. T. Chapman, "Talking to James Simmons," *Confrontations,* 10 (Spring 1975): 70-79;

Edna Longley, Introduction to *The Selected James Simmons* (Belfast: Blackstaff Press, 1978).

Iain Crichton Smith
(Iain Mac A'Ghobhainn)
(1 January 1928-   )

Stan Smith
Dundee University

BOOKS: *The Long River* (Edinburgh: Macdonald, 1955);

New Poets 1959, by Smith, Karen Gershon, and Christopher Levenson (London: Eyre & Spottiswoode, 1959);

Burn is Aran, as Iain Mac A'Ghobhainn (Glasgow: Gairm, 1960);

Thistles and Roses (London: Eyre & Spottiswoode, 1961);

Deer on the High Hills: A Poem (Edinburgh: Giles Gordon, 1962);

An Dubh is an Gorm, as Iain Mac A'Ghobhainn (Aberdeen: Aberdeen University, 1963);

The Law and the Grace (London: Eyre & Spottiswoode, 1965);

Biobuill is Sanasan Reice (Glasgow: Gairm, 1965);

An Coileach, as Iain Mac A'Ghobhainn (Glasgow: An Comunn Gaidhealach, 1966);

A'Chuirt, as Iain Mac A'Ghobhainn (Glasgow: An Comunn Gaidhealach, 1966);

The Golden Lyric: An Essay on the Poetry of Hugh MacDiarmid (Preston: Akros, 1967);

Three Regional Voices, by Smith, Michael Longley, and Barry Tebb (London: Poet & Printer, 1968);

At Helensburgh (Belfast: Festival Publications, Queen's University, 1968);

Consider the Lilies (London: Gollancz, 1968); republished as *The Alien Light* (Boston: Houghton Mifflin, 1969);

The Last Summer (London: Gollancz, 1969);

From Bourgeois Land (London: Gollancz, 1969);

Iain Am Measg nan Reultan, as Iain Mac A'Ghobhainn (Glasgow: Gairm, 1970);

Maighstirean is Ministearan, as Iain Mac A'Ghobhainn (Inverness: Club Leabhar, 1970);

Selected Poems (London: Gollancz, 1970; Chester Springs, Pa.: Dufour, 1970);

Survival Without Error and Other Stories (London: Gollancz, 1970);

My Last Duchess (London: Gollancz, 1971);

Penguin Modern Poets 21, by Smith, George Mackay Brown, and Norman MacCaig (Harmondsworth: Penguin, 1972);

Love Poems and Elegies (London: Gollancz, 1972);

Hamlet in Autumn (Edinburgh: Macdonald, 1972);

The Black and the Red (London: Gollancz, 1973);

An t-Adhar Ameireaganach, as Iain Mac A'Ghobhainn (Inverness: Club Leabhar, 1973);

Rabhdan is Rudan, as Iain Mac A'Ghobhainn (Glasgow: Gairm, 1973);

Eadar Fealla-dhà is Glaschu (Glasgow: University of Glasgow Celtic Department, 1974);

Goodbye, Mr Dixon (London: Gollancz, 1974);

Orpheus and Other Poems (Preston: Akros, 1974);

Poems for Donalda (Belfast: Ulsterman, 1974);
The Notebooks of Robinson Crusoe and Other Poems
(London: Gollancz, 1975);
The Permanent Island (Edinburgh: Macdonald,
1975);
An t-Aonaran, as Iain Mac A'Ghobhainn (Glasgow:
University of Glasgow Celtic Department,
1976);
The Village (Inverness: Club Leabhar, 1976);
In the Middle (London: Gollancz, 1977);
The Hermit and Other Stories (London: Gollancz,
1977);
An End to Autumn (London: Gollancz, 1978);
River, River: Poems for Children (Edinburgh: Mac-
donald, 1978);
Na h-Ainmhidhean, as Iain Mac A'Ghobhainn (Aber-
feldy: Clo Chaillean, 1979);
On the Island (London: Gollancz, 1979);
Am Bruadaraiche, as Iain Mac A'Ghobhainn (N.p.:
Acair, 1980);
Selected Poems 1955-1980, edited by Robin Fulton
(Edinburgh: Macdonald, 1981);
Murdo and Other Stories (London: Gollancz, 1981);
A Field Full of Folk (London: Gollancz, 1982);
The Search (London: Gollancz, 1983);
The Exiles (Manchester: Carcanet, 1984);
Mr. Trill in Hades (London: Gollancz, 1984);
Selected Poems (Manchester: Carcanet, 1985).

PLAY PRODUCTIONS: *An Coileach*, Glasgow,
1966;
A' Chuirt, Glasgow, 1966;
A Kind of Play, Mull, 1975;
Two by the Sea, Mull, 1975;
The Happily Married Couple, Mull, 1975.

OTHER: "Modern Scottish Gaelic Poetry," in *Scot-
tish Gaelic Studies*, edited by John Macdonald
(Aberdeen: University of Aberdeen, 1953);
Duncan Ban Macintyre, *Ben Dorain*, translated by
Smith (Preston: Akros, 1969);
Sorley Maclean, *Poems to Eimhir*, translated by Smith
(London & Newcastle upon Tyne: Gollancz/
Northern House, 1971);
"Between Sea and Moor," in *As I Remember*, edited
by Maurice Lindsay (London: Hale, 1979).

With more than forty volumes of poetry and
prose to his name, in English and Gaelic, Iain Crichton Smith is increasingly acknowledged as the elder
statesman of modern Scottish letters and Scotland's
most distinguished living poet. In 1978 he was
awarded the Queen's Jubilee Medal and in 1980 the
Order of the British Empire. He is a Fellow of the

Royal Society of Literature, and received honorary
doctorates from Dundee University in 1983 and
Glasgow University in 1984. He has received many
awards: Scottish Arts Council Awards (1966, 1968,
1974, and 1977); the SAC Prize (1978); a BBC
award for television drama, a Book Council award,
and a P.E.N. award (all in 1970); a Silver Pen Award
(1971); and two Poetry Book Society recommendations (1972 and 1975). Yet in some ways this recognition is more formal than felt. The Scottish literary
establishment has never really taken him to its
heart, and his work has sometimes received only
grudging praise in his own country. It is too rigor-
ously intellectual, too finely disciplined in its feelings, too unflinching in its loyalty to the modernist
inheritance, too cosmopolitan, therefore, in its pure
and lucid English, its refined and sinewy Gaelic,
even when dealing with the most ostensibly parochial of subjects, to appeal to a society he has himself
consistently indicted for its venality, its cult of the
average, the mediocre, and the indifferent, and its
ersatz emotionalism.

"Chinese Poem," in *The Notebooks of Robinson
Crusoe* (1975), draws an analogy between himself,
writing from the Highlands to a friend in Edinburgh, and those sad poets of frontier exile translated by Arthur Waley, to ask: "When shall our land
consider itself safe/from the assurance of the third
rate mind?" It is a pertinent question for any Scot to
ask, but particularly so for one whose whole literary
career, while drawing on the widest of literary and
intellectual sources, has shown unswerving devotion not only to the idea of Scotland but also to the
minute particularities of Scottish provincial life. No
one more than Crichton Smith has cast a discrimi-
nating and dispassionate eye on the cozy and self-
satisfied intimacies of that life; no one has a sharper
sense of its petty absurdities and small tyrannies;
and no one a more caustic anger at squandered
opportunities and lost principles. He has consistently spoken up for the strenuous demands of the
intellect and the puritan conscience, urged the pursuit of an "Excellence!/'costing not less than everything'" on a people who would rather be "the in-
trepid hunters of golf balls" ("The White Air of
March").

Crichton Smith's ability to bring a double vision to bear on contemporary Scottish life has its
roots in his double cultural patrimony. The son of
John and Christina Campbell Smith, he was born
on New Year's Day 1928 in the small village of
Bayble, on the island of Lewis in the Outer Hebrides. He records in his autobiographical memoir
"Between Sea and Moor" that he naturally spoke

Gaelic at home and in the village, and equally naturally spoke English in the town of Stornoway, where he went to school. The two worlds coexisted, and his character was formed at their interface, just as the dual call of sea and moor—the faraway and remote versus the close and intimate—have coexisted throughout his work.

Stornoway ("seven miles and a whole world away. . . . Could Babylon have been a more lustrous city?") first introduced him to a larger world, its cinema allowing him a vicarious "dazzle of heroism," as his reading opened him to "that other world of cowboys and detectives in their lonely romantic settings." A "very isolated child," often kept home from school by a widowed mother whose husband, a sailor, had died of tuberculosis (then endemic to the island), Crichton Smith compensated for the anxious solicitude which "suffocated" him by voracious reading. Suffering attacks of bronchitis or asthma, "In the long summer days I would lie in bed listening to the sounds that went on outside the house, in a dream of longing for some other world that wasn't this one, a world inhabited as much by English public schoolboys as by my own friends." A class photograph of the time shows "a child whose eyes are heavy and almost dim with fright, staring into a world which he finds threatening"—a weakness later converted into strength in the fastidious "aristocratic" persona that brings the defamiliarizing gaze of the stranger to bear on the familiar and commonplace.

His first volume, *The Long River* (1955), contains poems about Lewis which he could write only after he had left that enclosed, insulated world, having received a bursary to study English at Aberdeen University in 1945. In his memoir he speaks of how for the first time, there, he "felt free on the anonymous streets and because I was young . . . found my solitude exhilarating." This first book shows the early influence of W. H. Auden, whom he had read eagerly as a teenager, in its tight rhymes and clipped utterance. Likewise Audenesque is the wish, denied as it is spoken, in "On Helensburgh Sea-Front"—"Let me abolish from my verse/the 'I' and 'me' the 'my' and 'mine.' " Occasionally it echoes Dylan Thomas. Already, however, in a cold, hostile universe, "Turning on the icy wheel/Of image without substance," singing "to placate a lost ghost" and to forge a persona "hard and virgin" like the clouds, it is to Hugh MacDiarmid that he mainly turns for models, calling MacDiarmid "a tenant of the most perilous places" to whom he dedicates "these plain though ardent lines."

Like MacDiarmid, he is preoccupied with

what his memoir calls "our own obdurate world," whether, as in "Bricks," the resistant, undemonstrative materiality of things, or the unknowable strangeness of other people. "Anchored Yachts on a Stormy Day" sees a correspondence between people and things in this honed northern world: "almost (so one would think) about to break/but never breaking quite," as "a demon gaiety tightens their dull weight." This antithesis runs through his work, apparent even in the titles of such volumes as *Thistles and Roses* (1961) and *The Law and the Grace* (1965). His memoir speaks of "searching for a wider world of ideas which I could only get through books, a freedom which I imagined as existing elsewhere." In the exacting standards of literary modernism, which MacDiarmid had shown could be applied to a parochial Scottish culture, Crichton Smith found that otherness he sought, rooted in the actual.

Reviewing *The Long River* in 1955, Laurence Graham struck a characteristic and much-repeated note in criticism of Crichton Smith: "Perhaps he will some day discover the more positive virtues of his islands and his people and with that discovery will come the one vital thing still lacking in his verse, warmth and community." Responding to charges of intellectual coldness and aloofness in an interview in *Scottish International* (September 1971), Crichton Smith spoke with a considered dignity: "I do tend to be analytic. I don't know whether this is a bad thing or not. When one talks about the heart, I begin to get very suspicious because I think that a lot of Scottish poetry has, in fact, in the past suffered from too much emphasis on what might be called the heart. . . . I think myself that I would prefer to be an analytical poet, a questioning poet, rather than a poet of the heart considered simply. But on the other hand I think that I agree with you in . . . the idea of a lack of joy. I think this is true and I think I would be false to myself in importing into my poetry something which is difficult to get."

In the same interview he speaks of often feeling "ashamed of Scotland" as a country unable to produce anything excellent. Here and in a later interview (*Seven Poets*, 1981) he links this deficiency to "a lack of professionalism" worthy of MacDiarmid, and Celtic Football Club (a sly allusion to the famous Catholic team from a man with a Free Church Presbyterian background), and contrasts it with the situation of Irish poets, who are "very lucky, in a sense, because they have to deal with real things." Among these "real things," the earlier interview makes clear, is a "people [who] believe intensely in what they are doing, and they are willing even to destroy their own property . . . , to burn their own houses in favor of a particular ideal." (He is thinking, he indicates, of the current violence in Ulster.) Even his own verse seems to be shouted into an empty room and gets back only a "hollow echo." But, in the second interview, he cites with approval MacDiarmid's view "that the Scottish poet must assume the burden of his people's doom" and that "the Scottish people can never learn. . . ." That he could say this so shortly after the Scottish National party had won a large number of seats in the 1970 general election testifies to Crichton Smith's long-sightedness on the national question. As it turned out, the party's show of strength was brief.

Already in *The Long River* he had praised togetherness: "for at the end we come/in spite of wildness and scorn/to anchor in some cold place/unless we create a home," concluding, in an echo of Auden, "for nothing is done alone." More recently, he has written of "my concern with the idea of community, and also a developing concern of mine with the idea of exile. The two ideas are not unrelated." Precisely how they are related is disclosed in an anecdote he tells in the 1981 interview. Leaving Lewis for the first time at the age of seventeen to attend the university, his first experience of a kind of exile, he stepped off the train in Aberdeen to be confronted by a blind beggar: "I thought, 'This is impossible. You can't have this.' On the island of Lewis you could never have beggars. In the village where I grew up, if there was someone who was poor, he or she would be looked after, and I thought there was something extraordinary about this, that someone could so openly, so publicly admit to being so vulnerable, to put a cap on the pavement and look for pennies." His "feeling for vulnerable people," which runs through his work, has a double edge. He may stress its sources in "a closely knit community . . . if you twitched one part of the village organism, the rest . . . twitched." But a major part of the shock lies in the beggar's voluntary self-exposure, his surrender of that proud independence which is the most positive item in the Calvinist legacy. It touched a raw nerve because he and his brothers were raised on a £1-a-week widow's pension: in a different kind of society, this could have been his own fate.

There is scarcely a volume of his which does not contain at least one poem called "Old Woman." In "Between Sea and Moor" he confesses to "a certain pessimism . . . to do with growing up among an ageing population, so that I seem to know more about the old than I do about the young." But this distinction is too simple. In *Thistles and Roses* (1961)

the indignity and pathos of age lie in the helpless dependence of the "Old Woman." The poet's own helplessness before such scenes moves him not only to anger but to shame: "imprisoned in my pity and my shame/that men and women having suffered time/should sit in such a place, in such a state. . . ." In an early poem, "For My Mother," such a mood is linked to a set of moral attitudes which transcend age. He speaks of his mother's poverty and of his guilt at thinking of her "gutting herring/ (at seventeen) on a hard Lowestoft quay" while he at the same age had the privilege of a university education. (In "Between Sea and Moor" he speaks of her as "an inconceivable girl in a world so different from mine," and of feeling "guilty as if I had condemned her to that life.")

"A Young Highland Girl Studying Poetry" in *Thistles and Roses* shares the same passion. The girl's frown of concentration as she struggles with an alien literary culture is compared to a more usual form of labor for "her kind," with a cunning metaphor:

Poetry drives its lines into her forehead
like an angled plough across a bare field.
I've seen her kind before, of the live and dead
who bore humped creels when the beating winds were
    wild.

Nor did they know much poetry but were skilful
at healing children, bringing lambs to birth.
The earth they lived from did not make them soulful.
The foreign rose abated at their mouth.

The irony here fuels anger at the economic and social forces which exclude such women, young and old, not only from poetry but from the "foreign rose" amid the field of thistles. "Yet they were dancers too," he goes on, and had a right to that richness and grace more refined souls assumed as their birthright. The young woman, as much as the old, figures as the victim of exploitation in these poems, and also as a figure of contrary grace (in poems such as "Schoolgirl on Speech-day in the Open Air," the two sonnet sequences "Love Songs of a Puritan" and "Girl with Orange Sunshade," and "By Ferry to the Island").

He graduated in 1949 from Aberdeen University with an M.A. honors degree in English. As a schoolteacher all his working life, in Clydebank, Glasgow (1952-1955), and the small town of Oban in the Highlands (1955-1977), Crichton Smith will have witnessed many such encounters between pupil, the uncomprehending victim, and a domi-

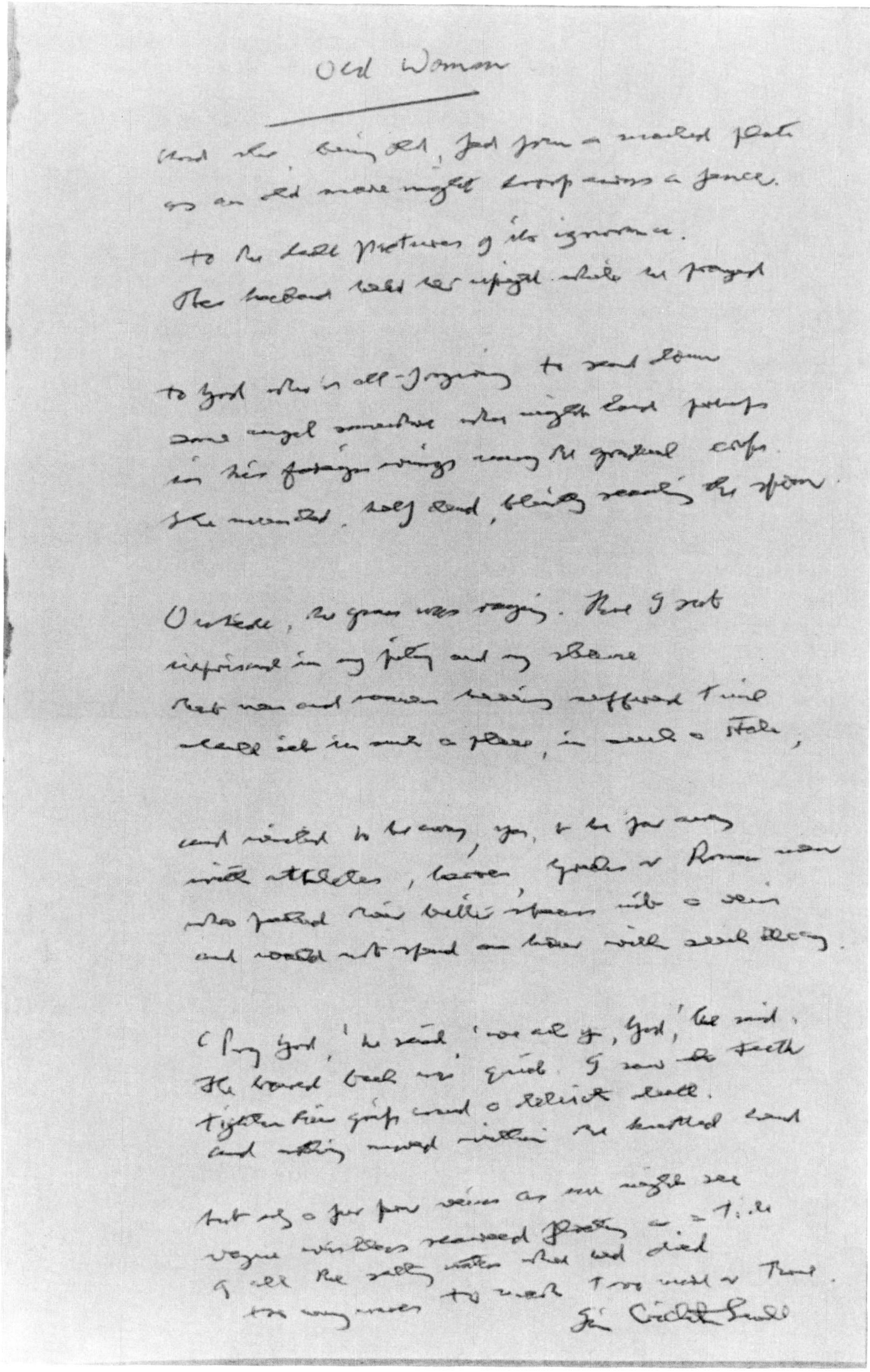

Old Woman

And she, being old, fed from a mashed plate
as an old mare might droop across a fence
to the dull pastures of its ignorance.
Her husband held her upright while he prayed

to God who is all-forgiving to send down
some angel somewhere who might land perhaps
in his foreign wings among the gradual crops.
She munched, half-dead, blindly seeking the spoon.

Outside, the grass was raging. There I sat
imprisoned in my pity and my shame
that men and women having suffered time
should sit in such a place, in such a state,

and wished to be away, yes, to be far away
with athletes, lovers, Greeks or Roman men
who jousted their bright spears into a vein
and would not spend an hour with such decay.

'Pray God,' he said, 'we ask you, God,' he said.
The bowed back was quiet. I saw the teeth
tighten their grip around a delicate death.
And nothing moved within the knotted head

but only a few poor veins as one might see
vague wishless seaweed floating on a tide
of all the salty waters where we died
too many miles [illegible]

Iain Crichton Smith

Manuscript for a poem published in Thistles and Roses *(the author)* nant but alien culture. Perhaps the two years national service as a sergeant in the Education Corps (1950-1952) after his teacher training at Jordanhill College (1949-1950) alerted him to the larger lessons of the classroom as mental barracks. "Studies in Power" records his own sense of being a stranger amid "the appalling ardour," meeting beset by motion and countermotion. He fears that his poems are only "cardboard coins" beside the real currency of power. It is only the "harder language" of "a vase in bloom/gathering light about it clearly clearly/in adult daylight not by moon obscurely," filling the room "with its bare constant self" that rescues him from "terror." "Lilac, Snow and Shadow" likewise moves from the lyric "simplicities of a complex air" to confront that seductive "sensuous music" of destruction beloved of all the power brokers, focused in the gory details of an Elizabethan beheading. "A Note on Puritans" examines with both admiration and distaste the "singleness and loss of grace" that conscripts men to systems of belief and power, where they are prepared to burn and be burned for "truths [that] can make men brutish." Although such men display "great courage," it is not to be compared, as the last poem of the volume makes clear, with that "rare courage, not oppressive" of one who has the humility to see "the fractured failure of the best we are" and find "in spontaneous gestures a fixed fate."

This grace note was developed in *The Law and the Grace* (1965). It is there, first of all, in those poems about the thistles and occasional roses of schoolteaching; in, for example, "Schoolroom," "Encounter in a School Corridor," and "Rythm" [*sic*], which explores with quiet compunction the world as seen through the eyes of a barely literate schoolkid only interested in football—"They dunno how it is. I smack the ball/right through the goals. But they dunno how the words/get muddled in my head, get tired somehow." But the poem which most develops out of the classroom a fraught sense of the power relations that underlie and deform a culture is "Schoolteacher," which draws a constructive analogy between the teacher and the subject she teaches, to reveal how far education is a process of reproducing relations of power and submission. She is a "Roman lady, in [a] distant gown." The poet begs her to build some roads, color the map of Europe, but she is adamant in her class position, which is also her position in class: "How the empires fade/is wild barbarians at 4 o'clock."

Elucidating this volume, Crichton Smith has written: "*The Law and the Grace* [is] a key poetry book since . . . I made the analogy of The Law (in reli-

gion) as corresponding to metrical forms etc in poetry and the Grace (in religion) corresponding to 'inspiration' in poetry. My ideal poem would be one in which Grace is fighting to emerge by a fight with metre, law, boundaries. This in turn associated with community and the misfit, . . . fighting against restrictions of community, limiting yet freeing." The *Scottish International* interview provides a more philosophical dimension, incidentally illuminating "Schoolteacher" in terms which point toward Nietzsche's Apollo and Dionysus (Nietzsche is spoken of as one of those who "are willing to test themselves to their own limits intensely"): "ideas of music, grace and harmony etc. are typically Celtic ideas, and I feel that poetry always oscillates between . . . the ideas of harmony . . . and the ideas of barbarism. . . . In the early poetry that I wrote the ideas of harmony and classical music . . . can be considered as . . . the metre of the poetry, . . . and Roman and Greek ideas of barbarism can be considered as the kind of things that operate . . . to destroy the metre. . . . Actually, the kind of poetry that I would have liked to write [is one] where there would be metrical ideas of harmony and music, which at the same time would be under siege by a kind of barbaric emotional power, which would almost destroy the metrical harmony, but would not be able to accomplish it." In that same interview, the poet insists that he is intellectually a free thinker, but concedes that emotionally he may remain "stained" by the religion he rejects, so that "it is probably true that I am Calvinistic, without theological allegiance."

Inevitably, perhaps, the "theological" rigor is concentrated in the guilt-inducing figure in another poem titled "Old Woman," whose "set mouth/forgives no-one, not even God's justice/perpetually drowning law with grace." Yet the poet's vision opens up a perspective of sociological charity onto this theological self-righteousness, bringing the grace of a humanistic understanding to bear on the law of absolutist values:

Your cold eyes
watched your drunken husband come
unsteadily from Sodom home.

Your grained hands
dandled full and sinful cradles.
You built for your children stone walls.

Without patronizing, the poet evinces both enormous respect and overwhelming sadness for the life fulfilled through self-denial, through that "unforgiving" dedication to a remote ideal, "while the free daffodils/wave in the valleys and on the hills/the deer look down with their instinctive skills."

This last observation goes to the heart of that fine sequence *Deer on the High Hills,* first published separately in 1962. There, Crichton Smith is concerned with the strangeness of a reality stripped of its magic, disenchanted, writing—in cadences which often echo Wallace Stevens—of a world where "There is no metaphor. The stone is stony./ The deer step out in isolated air./We move at random on an innocent journey." Here, however, he is preoccupied with the power that single ideas can have over one-track minds, as in "Lenin," "that troubling man/'who never read a book for pleasure alone.' " Lenin is "The germ inside the sealed train," whom it would be easy to admire for his "ruthless" single-mindedness and his contempt for the "unsymmetrical," "endlessly various, real human/world which is no new era, shining dawn," but whom the poet refuses to romanticize any more than he will endorse the Calvinist extremism he can understand.

Such figures of power as Lenin and Napoleon fascinate Crichton Smith. In *The Golden Lyric: An Essay on the Poetry of Hugh MacDiarmid* (1967) he speaks of "the patience of Lenin—the patience of stones—and a kind of ruthlessness." He can see why it should appeal to the Communist MacDiarmid, for in his poetry one finds a note encountered elsewhere perhaps only in the fascist-leaning "exclusiveness" of Yeats: "the progress of MacDiarmid is from the human to a poetry of landscape and stones and language. It is the aristocratic lonely voice . . . that convinces." Yet, one should not expect from a poet "a purely logical mind (however much an artist may be betrayed into hankerings after this)." For "Any thinking person who has thought long and deeply—or even felt long and deeply—must realise that no one dogma is sufficient to interpret for us the meaning of the universe," and MacDiarmid's Leninist posturings are in fact a reflection of the very sensibility he reacted against: the "colossal pride and ignorance" of "the self-satisfied Scotsman."

From Bourgeois Land (1969) has its Lenin poem outrageously suggesting that the Scottish petit bourgeois might actually welcome the apocalypse he brings in a convulsion of relief that it is all finally over. There is also an admiration for the "competent," even reassuring quality of "that terrible blunt voice" with its contempt for art and anything of the spirit, so that "My hands applaud my death. . . . / My pale fists tighten as I play at golf." But the most outrageous collocation of *From Bourgeois Land* is that

between contemporary Scotland and Nazi Germany, through the figure of Eichmann, "a clerkly scrupulous man/who takes a pride in neatness," simply "doing his job" in the opening poem of the volume. Such unquestioning efficiency in the prosecution of inhuman goals, the "accountancy of murder," is more than a mere failure of the man's imagination, and cannot be comprehended even by the most strenuous efforts of the poet's own. It is no more forgivable than the plague; yet it is all finally, in the last words of the poem, an expression of the "bourgeois soul." In a subsequent poem, which opens with an affectionate evocation of "My Scottish towns with Town Halls and with courts," this unobtrusive ubiquity of the Law leads on to a horrifying vision in which "from such quiet places furies start./Gauleiters pace by curtained windows. . . . /Mad bank clerks bubble with a strange new world," and waiters, aesthetes, "Stout fleshy matrons" and schoolmistresses, butcher and errand boy and scholar all indulge in an orgy of violence in which, as it closes, "Desire has seized at last the virgin Act./And distant Belsen smokes in the calm air."

Crichton Smith opts in this volume for what Frederic Lindsay has called "a passion of condemnation unqualified by more typical strategies of ambivalence." Among its targets are the leaden platitudes of the small-town bigwig ("To speak the truth is more than bad taste./It is a treachery to the provost"), the vulgarity of the popular press (In "Dido and Aeneas" their story is treated as a headline "romance"), the cant of the church in "forgiving" Robert Burns his sins, the fatuities of poetry readings, and the lawyer who admires in nature a God "with an eye for the small print" and "a language more obscure/than even a lawyer's." Set against all these degenerate forms of language is the language associated with love ("Let your eyes flash a clear unbourgeois honour") and with poets who may "stutter awkwardly when asked to speak" but who are nevertheless "immune to bribery, . . . / and trained to justice by implacable love." A secular theology of grace—of love not abolishing but fulfilling the Law, converting *lex* to *jus*—runs through the volume, and its final poem, an Audenesque address to children, urges them to seek such fulfillment not in small-minded bureaucratic systems but rather in loving "the Disordered Man who sings like a river/whose form is Love, whose country is Forever."

But it is "Hamlet," taking up the volume's recurring image of faces distorted in the reflections in spoons and presenting a jaundiced hero sick of

"Bad jokes and speeches," which points toward the themes of *Hamlet in Autumn* (1972). This volume has its Lenin poem too: "Russian Poem," a sequence which evokes that Chekhovian Russia where "Ennui covers the land," where every sensitive soul imagines himself Hamlet, and "Something is bound to happen." That "something" is Lenin, providing simple answers to complex questions, so that it seems that "Reality" has "come at last": "He has simplified the world like an assassin./Where his barrel points is where evil is." This ennui, "How Often I Feel Like You" suggests, is the terror of a land which feels "something is happening everywhere but here," which fears "God has forgotten us" and cries "Help us, let something happen, even death." Hamlet is only one recurring figure of this motif, in a volume which, for all its somber tones, is astonishingly rich in its range of image, allusion, incident, and character. Over all, however, presides the memento mori of a death's head: in "Films" "the promenaders/parade in green, their skulls as white as snow"; in "Finis Not Tragedy" a "skull-faced secretary" stands smiling as papers are torn into pieces. As in "Oedipus and Others," "Death [is] everywhere" and the sonnet sequence "Carol and *Hamlet*," ostensibly about a schoolgirl studying Shakespeare for her examinations, tells the reader "That's why Hamlet always talks of death." "Dear Hamlet" goes further, claiming that, while "So little sufficed" Claudius, "you, you needed more. That more was death." It is the skull of Yorick which presides over this volume, decentering all the heroes and villains with his macabre grin. Even that fine sequence which celebrates the honor and dignity of John Maclean, "Headmaster, and Classical and Gaelic Scholar," who knew "that what protects us from the animals/is language healthy as a healthy pulse," extends the elegiac mode from the individual not just to a landscape but to a whole civilization entering its autumnal decline.

The other volume published in 1972, *Love Poems and Elegies,* explains the deepening of the funereal tone in a dust-jacket note: "The poems . . . sprang directly from the death of my mother. They lead to reflections on death, on the Highlands, and on particular moments which appeared significant." His 1971 interview concluded on the same note: "everything I have ever done is really eventually coming to this question. What is death? What is a dead person, and in the end what is the value of writing when one is confronted by a dead person?"

Many of the elegies are reminiscences of his mother from his childhood and beyond. In "You Lived in Glasgow" he recalls the 1930s, reflecting

"The past's an experience that we cannot share," but nevertheless he moves about "a cleaner city" than his mother briefly inhabited, looking for "a ghost within a close who speaks/in Highland Gaelic." "In Your Long Skirts" contemplates a sepia photograph of her in 1908, with long-dead girl friends among the fish barrels, "all gazing/to a sun that's off the edge and is made of salt"—already contemplating, it would seem, that death he has now confronted. "You Told Me Once" goes into the circumstances of that death—lack of oxygen ("I tried/to fit the mask against your restless face/in the bumpy ambulance")—in a way which explains a powerful and harrowing leitmotif of the volume: death in the cold airless solitude of outer space, the fragile life-support system of ship and space suit gone. "The Space-Ship" makes this leitmotif explicit:

> I think of you and then I think of this
> picture of an astronaut lacking air,
> dying of lack of it in the depths of space,
> his face kneading and working under glass.

But the image is carried over into the love poems too, as in the anxiety of "The Dream":

> I'm drifting towards you, we are great moon bears
> hulking in light. And then you drift away.
> Hiking my oxygen I follow you.
> And then I am alone. The space-ship's gone.
> You're at the window, white face peering out.
> The taxis stream in rain past a green star.

This use of the same image in both a love poem and a poem about death is what he calls in *The Golden Lyric* a "dialectical movement," veering between one extreme and another; but it is typical of Crichton Smith that he should not only balance his book by juxtaposing love poems and elegies but should also weave a common imagery into the two modes. The love poems are short, taciturn, strangely hesitant to speak with the kind of forthrightness which characterizes his satires and even his elegies, as if loss were easier to utter than fulfillment or expectation. At their best they have the reticence and the sadness of elegy—a poignant mingling of tones carried over in *Orpheus and Other Poems* (1974), with its explicit linking of love and bereavement in the long, half-narrative title poem. Here the poet who can move stones by his music cannot win back his lost bride from the underworld. Hades tells him that "by her absence your music is more clear/barer and purer," "Our return/is not permissible to an earlier way," and "If you will learn to love you must go forward." In the final section, he returns to a worldly hell which is a city much like Glasgow, to be loved "not as in a dream/but on this smoky field of green and orange"—an explicit enough allusion, for Scottish readers, to the tribal colors of Catholic and Protestant, Celtic and Rangers.

Returning in order to go forward is a theme of many of the poems. "Island Poems" look back to explore the churchyard, beach, and people of Islay for tokens of a joy which survive death, finding in "the grave flesh" a "harvest" which, in the words of a seventy-year-old islander speaking of his wife, "entrances me more each day." In his own love for his companion on the trip the poet finds a similar captivating entrance developing an implicit pun on the earlier verb, as they leave the island: "we shall be ready to enter/by that harsher newer door."

The love poems of this volume, though still turning on the thought of death, have a new vivacity and directness, and a sharp carnal tang. The tone continues in *The Notebooks of Robinson Crusoe* (1975). In the last poem Crusoe, about to leave the island of the spirit where he has spent thirty years in solitude, accompanied only by the flesh's ignorant, inarticulate Friday and sustained only by abstract lusts and dreamings, considers with some trepidation the new world he is entering: "on a day when the ordinary becomes priceless, the common pots and pans reveal their human lineage." It ends with Crusoe's finding—"as the sailors weave about me their human erotic legends"—"rich merchandise for my new dream," as he "emerge [s] from the world of sparse iron into the vast cinema of sensation."

This transit is revealed in the intervening poems in an access of colloquial vigor and shrewd topical reference. In "Housman" the "Queen of the air and darkness" is redefined as an Oxfam lady. "Party" begins, "I put my hand under your bum. You're drunk. . . . /At 2 a.m. everyone thinks of sex," and poems such as "The Three," "He and She," "In the Glen," and "Letter" explore, partly through dialogue and partly through correspondence, the lineaments of modern marriage and adultery, in London as in the Highlands. In its dramatic monologues and narratives ("Faustus Speaks," "Incident"), its vignettes of contemporary life and its evocation of the lives of others ("The Workmen," "My Uncle"), this volume reflects even in its title the turn toward "That element of honour and of risk,/aere perennis, the quotidian" ("The Interview")—the sort of turn Robert Lowell took in *Notebook* (1970). Crichton Smith first singled out Lowell in *The Golden Lyric*, discussing "A Quaker

Graveyard," which influenced several of his maritime elegies. He has expressed "tremendous admiration for Lowell's poetry in the seventies and my sense of his problem of having to break out of strong metrical forms towards a free verse (mirroring perhaps a shedding of his New England armour towards a more fluid diurnal movement)." "On the Fact that Karl Marx Wrote Love Poems when he was Young" reveals that seeking the quotidian is not an abandonment of the historic vision. It may be that "love is/what moves the factories and the other stars," but, like Lowell, whose *Notebook* in rewriting became *History* (1973), he insists on "roses being political and waving/in the breeze of history, steadily bereaving. . . ."

In 1977 Iain Crichton Smith married, retired from schoolteaching to take up full-time writing, and brought out *In the Middle*. The title poem reveals that he is not concerned, like Dante or Eliot, with being "in the middle way" ("In the Surgery" and "Evening" recognize that he is well past that point); rather it is being "pig in the middle," with arms pulling from left and right, that disturbs him. One pull comes from that scholar who figures in several poems. He is distressed that the world is changing: "My study is invaded by men with rotten teeth/with wooden legs, bad gums, and politics./ They asked me why Jane Austen lived after all" ("The Scholar"). In "The Whirligigs of Time" terrorists and revolutionaries, who are the contrary pull on the poet, enter the scholar's study and execute him in the name of change. "The Old School Books" records this shift of values, which has rendered the confident patriarchal authority of the books' statements obsolete. Coming to terms with supersession is the theme of many of the poems. "The Elite" thinks of how dinosaurs, as "the rain came down," "got on with being dinosaurs," without worrying whether they were in decline. Life gets on with the business of creating more life, as "In the Surgery" indicates:

> There's no cure for it.
> The new children are taught their alphabet,
> and the new mothers enjoy their miracles.
> What is in the water but more water?
> If you close your eyes, you hear the endless footsteps.

Other poems evoke a "Purple Bucket" which is not in use, or imagine "In other places all sorts of things are going on," or wonder "When the house is quiet/ and my glasses lie on the chair/and the TV is off/ who am I?" The poems, that is, explore the multiplicity of absence as well as presence. What runs through this and many poems is that "endless river" which, "In Our Safe House," he rejoins in going back to bed, the same river which carried his "Lady of Shalott" to the "reality" which killed her, and in which "My Child" dabbled and "The Ducks" swim. In "Rainy Day" it has become a second Flood and "the raw sunset/at the end of waters." Crichton Smith writes of poems such as these (and of "The Cry," "The Scream," "The Horror"): "Reading them, I find that what they seem to be about is the strangeness and the eeriness of reality. I had wanted to write about simple things, the traffic of day to day, but found that overwhelming these was a cry or scream of mortality. Now and again, the world of the scholar and the 'elitist' enters, but with diminishing force. It is as if these poems—perhaps too simple—were telling me of the horror which closes Conrad's *Heart of Darkness* but that in the end—as in the last poem—we must celebrate change which is the source of the horror."

"None is the Same as Another," the poem referred to, stands "in the middle," giving equal weight to two, opposed options—that the proposition of the title is both "matter for crying/since never again will you see/that one, once gone," and that it is "not/a matter for crying," ending with an almost joyous acceptance: "Stranger, I take your hand,/O changing stranger."

"We Poets" had taken a complementary position—that, despite the "uniquely different" languages they speak and the different countries they celebrate, poets "all over the world" inhabit "the same city," starting "from different premises/ . . . see the same landscapes." Crichton Smith's Gaelic poems explore the doubleness of his own seeing in similar terms. "Shall Gaelic Die?," translated by Crichton Smith from his own Gaelic, asserts: "He who loses his language loses his world" and asks: "When the Highlands loses its language, will there be a Highlands, said I, with my two coats, losing, perhaps, the two." This insistence on plurality, the resistance to the homogenizing, centralizing force of bourgeois culture, is of a piece with his hatred for the single-mindedness of Lenin and all the other power brokers—here, it is intimately linked with General Wade, building roads into the Highlands to extend the power of the British state.

The English reader is fortunate in that Crichton Smith has translated his two major collections of Gaelic poetry, as well as the work of major contemporaries such as Sorley Maclean and Gaelic verse from the sixteenth century onward. *Biobuill is Sanasan Reice* (1965)—"Bibles and Advertisements"—and *Eadar Fealla-dhà is Glaschu* (1974)—"Between

Comedy and Glasgow"—can be found in pellucid translation in *The Permanent Island* (1975). Though the first is full of the rain, bleak moors, and seas of a small parish, of old women and other figures of endurance, it vibrates, too, with a global awareness, speaking of Hiroshima, Belsen, and Guernica, balancing Calvin with Freud, linking "Bayble and Athens, isn't the compass strange and strict?," and reminding the reader, as he does in his memoir, that island people are of necessity sailors, and that such a vocation takes them to the ends of the earth. As "The Island" makes clear, islands of the spirit are not immune to wars that sweep the globe: Malta and Crete and Singapore all saw violence, "And even on Lewis and Islay the aeroplanes of our time will burst, and angels and devils from the clouds descending through desperation or hope." In the second volume he more subtly counterpoises the parochial and the universal, writing haiku in Gaelic,

Iain Crichton Smith
Selected Poems 1955-1980

Front cover for the collection that led one reviewer to express "a sense of shame at being in the presence of what is superior to oneself"

speaking of Beethoven at a *ceilidh* (a Gaelic hootenanny), juxtaposing the world of the "long Sundays/ . . . without TV or radio" with a world which goes out when the television is switched off.

Crichton Smith's most powerful volume of prose, *Consider the Lilies* (1968), is a novel about the Highland Clearances. Discussing "Bibles and Advertisements" in 1971 he indicated that a new clearance was under way in the Highlands, with the population hemorrhage due to lack of work, the incursion of television and of a new enemy more insidious than General Wade: the tourist. The Highlander, he says, has "a heritage of defeat" and of "spiritual guilt." Tourism reduces people to "becoming servants to other people, . . . to the outsiders." But it is the "passiveness" of the Highlander before this erosion and dependency which terrifies him most. Whereas Lewis was "a classless society," Argyll, where he now lives, seems to be a slave to the materialism of "the Bed and Breakfast routine" described in "By the Sea" (first published in *Scottish Poetry 3*, 1968). As "Dunoon and the Holy Loch" in this same sequence makes clear, such ostensible backwaters of cultural and economic decline in fact lie right at the heart of a global system of power and destruction. Kenneth MacKellar may sing from the domed pier, but out in the loch lurk United States submarines carrying "missiles like sugar rocks . . . incised/with Alabaman Homer," and the "thin pale girls/who wear at evening their Woolworth pearls" gaze from the railings "at the world's end." That punning conclusion sums up the double vision of Iain Crichton Smith, discerning, in the pull between the near and the remote, those larger relations of power which may, in the end, engulf the most secluded parish.

With the publication of *Selected Poems 1955-1980* (1981), the time has come to take stock of Crichton Smith's reputation. Reviewing the collection in *PN Review,* Dennis Keene was, at first, cautiously convoluted in his response: "I imagine it would still be thought of as eccentric to maintain that he was a major poet, and yet the evidence of these poems makes such a claim at least not unreasonable." By the end of his review, however, he has grasped the thistle, and come to make that claim: "Reading these poems provides what only the genuine article gives, a sense of shame at being in the presence of what is superior to oneself, and then the feeling of being released by absorption into something so good that it makes one's small self cease to matter." The years to come will confirm the justice and the concentricity of that assessment.

Interviews:

Lorn Macintyre, "Poet in Bourgeois Land: Interview with Iain Crichton Smith," *Scottish International Review* (September 1971);

"Iain Crichton Smith," in *Seven Poets*, edited by Christopher Carrell (Glasgow: Third Eye, 1981).

References:

J. H. Alexander, "The English Poetry of Iain Crichton Smith," in *Literature of the North*, edited by David Hewitt and Michael Spiller (Aberdeen: Aberdeen University Press, 1983), pp. 189-203;

Robin Fulton, *Contemporary Scottish Poetry: Individuals and Contexts* (Edinburgh: Macdonald, 1974), pp. 43-66;

Frederic Lindsay, "Disputed Angels: the Poetry of Iain Crichton Smith," *Akros*, 12 (December 1977): 15-26;

Edwin Morgan, "The Raging and the Grace: Some Notes on the Poetry of Iain Crichton Smith," in his *Essays* (Cheadle: Carcanet, 1974), pp. 222-231.

Ken Smith
(4 December 1938-   )

Roger Garfitt

BOOKS: *Eleven Poems* (Leeds: Northern House, 1964);

The Pity (London: Cape, 1967);

Academic Board, Poems (Harpford, Devon: Peeks Press, 1968);

Frontwards in a Backwards Movie (Todmorden, Yorks: Arc & Throstle, 1969);

Work, distances/poems (Chicago: Swallow, 1972);

The Wild Rose (Memphis: Stinktree, 1973);

Hawk Wolf (Knotting: Sceptre, 1974);

Wasichi (London: Aloes Books, 1975);

Anus Mundi (Ware, Mass.: Four Zoas, 1976);

Blue's Rocket (Exeter, Devon: Warts & All, 1976);

Island Called Henry the Navigator (Glen Ellen, Mich.: Cat's Pyjamas, 1976);

Tristan Crazy (Newcastle upon Tyne: Bloodaxe Books, 1978);

Tales of the Hunter (Boston: Night House, 1979);

the joined-up writing (London: X Press, 1980);

What I'm doing now (London: Oasis Books, 1980);

Between the Dancers (London: Circle Press, 1980);

Fox Running (London: Rolling Moss Press, 1980);

Grainy pictures of the rain (Lonoke, Ark.: Truedog Press, 1981);

Abel Baker Charlie Delta Epic Sonnets (Newcastle upon Tyne: Bloodaxe Books, 1981);

Burned Books (Newcastle upon Tyne: Bloodaxe Books, 1981);

The Poet Reclining: Selected Poems 1962-1980 (Newcastle upon Tyne: Bloodaxe Books, 1982);

Terra (Newcastle upon Tyne: Bloodaxe Books, forthcoming 1986);

A Book of Chinese Whispers (Newcastle upon Tyne: Bloodaxe Books, forthcoming 1986).

Ken Smith is a poet and prose writer and a former editor of *Stand* and *South West Review*. From 1969 to 1973 he lived in the United States, and he continued to be better known in America until the publication of his selected poems, *The Poet Reclining*, in 1982 reestablished his reputation in England. *The Poet Reclining* is a testament to Smith's integrity and endurance. A major imaginative enterprise "in the American grain," it had to be sustained against the grain of contemporary English poetry.

Kenneth John Smith was born in Yorkshire, the son of a farm laborer, John Smith, and Millicent Sitch Smith. Harsh conditions and an unyielding temper ensured that his father never kept a job for long. The first of the wanderer figures that haunt Smith's poetry were his own family, moving on at the end of harvest:

> a darker blur on the stubble,
> a fragment in time gone, we left
> not a mark, not a footprint.

The isolation of this life meant that he grew up "talking to myself and inventing mates," which is where "the habit of inventing people and dialogue, stories and fictions" began.

Solitude intensified when he moved to the city at the age of thirteen. The horizon shrank, the world became small and hostile. His conversation with himself became silent and turned to writing. His father had saved enough to buy a grocer's shop in Hull, an independence with which he rapidly became embittered. He prospered and bought a second shop, which Smith ran when he left school. But there were continual violent arguments, in which Smith had to defend his mother. It was a situation Smith was locked into until, at the age of nineteen, conscription released him.

In the Air Force he became a typist, and assuaged his boredom by reading widely and completing his university entrance qualifications. He was demobilized in the spring of 1960 and returned to Hull, where he married Ann Minnis, a secretary, on 1 August. In the autumn they moved to Leeds where he read English at the university. Leeds had become an important literary center. The school of English included Wilson Knight, Douglas Jefferson, and Geoffrey Hill, who was then teaching contemporary poetry. Jon Silkin had just completed two years as Gregory Fellow in Poetry and was now an English undergraduate himself. His successors as Gregory Fellow were William Price Turner and Peter Redgrove. Literary activity centered on the weekly magazine *Poetry and Audience,* of which Smith became assistant editor. Through *Poetry and*

Ken Smith with one of the webs he makes as a hobby (photograph by Claire McNamee)

Audience he met Silkin and in 1963 he became a coeditor of *Stand,* an association that lasted until 1969.

For a few months after graduating with a B.A. in 1963 he edited, reviewed, and wrote full-time. But his daughter Nicole had been born in 1961 and the pressure of supporting a family soon forced him into teaching, first at a school in Dewsbury (1963-1964), then at Dewsbury and Batley Technical and Art College (1964-1965). His son Danny was born in 1965 and his daughter Kate in 1966. In 1965 he moved south, to teach complementary studies at Exeter College of Art. The teaching proved complementary for him too. His own education had been literary and linear: from the art students he learned to think laterally, by image and association, and acquired a much sharper visual sense. It was a development that was to prove crucial to his poetry.

His first pamphlet, *Eleven Poems,* was published in 1964 and his first collection, *The Pity,* in 1967. *The Pity* was very well reviewed. P. J. Kavanagh wrote in the *Guardian,* "Anyone who despairs of contemporary verse should be led by the hand to this book." The most arresting poem is the title poem, which incorporates the lines Mao Tse-tung wrote in prison when his pregnant wife was garroted in the next cell:

> I cut my hands on the cords at the strangling post
> but no blood spilled from my veins;
> instead of blood I watched and saw the pity run out of
> me.

Writing in Mao's voice, Smith gives a restrained and sensitive account of that moment of inner revolution when "Compassion . . . takes the hawk's wing, diving."

In one sense Smith's poetry was released as soon as he was free from study. He wrote "The Pity" and "Family Group" in the week that he graduated. In another sense the poems still felt like studies, the results of conscious writing strategies. Despite the achievement of *The Pity,* he felt the need to break his habits of mind, to break free from his cultural inheritance: "Part of being English is that we entertain really only a few footholds on the imagination." In 1969 he moved to America, where he took up a post as writer in residence at Slippery Rock State College in Pennsylvania. Once outside England he felt free "to take much bigger risks . . . to follow out ridiculous ideas. . . . I could invent much more, push a particular image in ways that in English poetry would be regarded as luxurious."

He learned from the work of American poets: James Wright, Robert Bly, David Ignatow, William Stafford, and the Alaskan poems of John Haines. He learned still more, perhaps, from oral and primitive poetry, in which there was a revival of interest in America at that time. His second collection, *Work, distances/poems* (1972), includes "Ghost songs," "Ghost dances," and an adaptation, "From the Nahua": but particular borrowings are important only as indications of a deeper influence on his poetic language that persisted on his return to England. When he walks beside a playing field in Exeter and writes of

> accepting my birthday.
>
> How the shadows move in
> at such news and are strange
> in the light. This feather
> left for his marker my brother
>
> the crow had dropped by the goalpost
> seems a dead man's finger
> keeping his page
> in the unfinished biography,

he is reentering, if only for the space of a metaphor, a universe that is a unity, where the poet can discern his own myth taking shape in correspondences, reflections, foreshadowings. Poetry ceases to be what it so often is in England, an art of framed observations: it becomes the spelling out of a selfhood, "a language to speak to myself." The practice of the poet becomes a matter

> of silence
> and waiting, how to forget,
> how sleep, to see and not notice
> the moment the mind
> takes to its channel, its
> leaping and threading and listening,
> the business of dreams, visions,
> and distant barely perceptible sounds
> —how they effect
> what is brought to the world's gate.

One sequence is literally "the business of dreams." "The Eli poems" sprang, as Smith describes in a prose passage, "the door," from insistent dreams of a landscape through which two figures moved, Eli, a lodging house keeper, and Kate, a mill girl he had got with child. The first poem, "Eli's poem," was dreamed complete as a poem on a page in a book and typed out immediately on waking. The final

poem, "Half songs, 1790," came from a waking dream a year later, a daylight glimpse of Kate that was like "a going and a showing at the same time."

More often Smith works from a kind of personal archaeology. The sequence "the clearing" came from exploring an actual clearing (set in "Minnesota perhaps" but in fact in Massachusetts) and sifting through the settler's abandoned house. Once again a prose passage, *"Concerning the clearing,"* gives the genesis of the poems. Into this reconstructed history, the sense of "poverty rising out of the ground," he weaves elements of his own mythology. The hawk of "Hawk Vision," who in a moment of liberation "diving/somehow upward" vanished, now returns "hungry,/weary, wrong-muscled,/grey bird of my death." The fusion of personal myth with documentary material is Smith's way of relating his own life to the unity of lives, of reaffirming that he is "a cry among cries."

"Tales of Urias the shape-shifter," an intermittent sequence, began to take shape in Yorkshire beside Colden Water, a moorland stream that became a mill stream in the Industrial Revolution. One root of the poem is a local belief, recorded by Elizabeth Gaskell, that "there were little people, there were spirits here . . . until the machinery came." Another root is Smith's own sense of

> something very surly and crushed that for the sake of a metaphor . . . for the sake of a fiction you could say was the spirit of that water . . . My sense of the world is not much in common with my time . . . The universe is articulate, it is trying to speak, we are one of the agencies by which it speaks,
>
> part of how the world thinks
> so through us the blank
> stuff of space knows itself.
>
> But we're not the only agency.

Here again Smith's poetry forms part of an older tradition. "The kingdom" of which he writes is the kingdom of William Blake's grain of sand, of Thomas Traherne's Orient and immortal wheat. "The other world" appears when we give proper attention to this world:

> Describing the buds of the sycamore
> coming out boxed each 4 to unfold
> is to be in the other world
> listening in this one.

Three years at Slippery Rock were followed by

a year as poet in residence to the College of the Holy Cross and Clark University in Worcester, Massachusetts. *Work, distances/poems,* which had been rejected by three English publishers, was published by Swallow Press in Chicago and was well-received in America. Ralph J. Mills, writing in the *Chicago Sun-Times,* welcomed Smith as "a poet of formidable range and strength." Smith returned to England in 1973 but has continued to travel extensively in America and to have his work published in America.

There is no stylistic or thematic division between *Work, distances* and *The Poet Reclining* as there is between *Work, distances* and *The Pity,* and the above discussion of Smith's work ranges freely between them. But ten years separate the two volumes, ten years in which Smith became virtually an underground poet in England, He received an Arts Council Bursary in 1975 and from 1977 to 1979 he was the founder editor of *South West Review.* But his own work surfaced only in pamphlets. From 1976 to 1978 he was Yorkshire Arts Fellow at Leeds University, commuting from Exeter, where his wife Ann held a secretarial post. Immediately after the Leeds Fellowship was over, the marriage broke up.

Smith moved to London and into the experiences of his long poem *Fox Running* (1980), a brilliant recreation of a man under stress encountering the city. Rapid, compulsive rhythms create flicker pictures of the Underground and the seedier districts, in which Fox glimpses his double, the shadow he could so easily become:

> Faces
> mentioning defeat saying
> bankruptcy desertion failure redundancy
> lost bottle. Their light
> that had gone or never lit
> or they burned now on the lamp oil
> of necessity the pure oil
> of ageing euphoria.

All that separates them is the survival instinct, what-

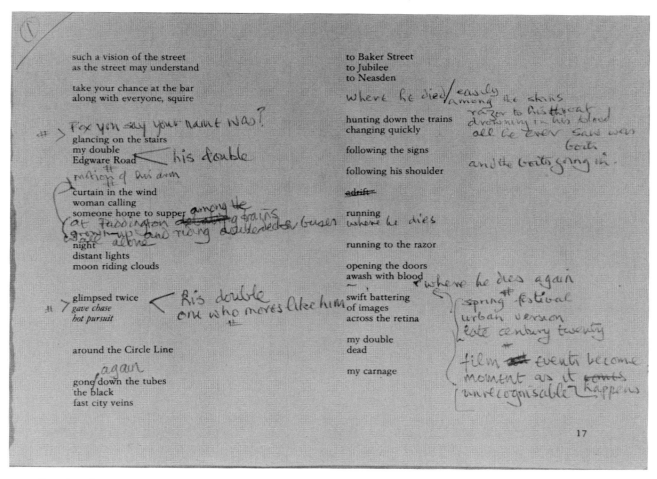

Tearsheet from a 1981 issue of Rolling Moss *with Smith's holograph revisions of his poem* Fox Running *(the author)*

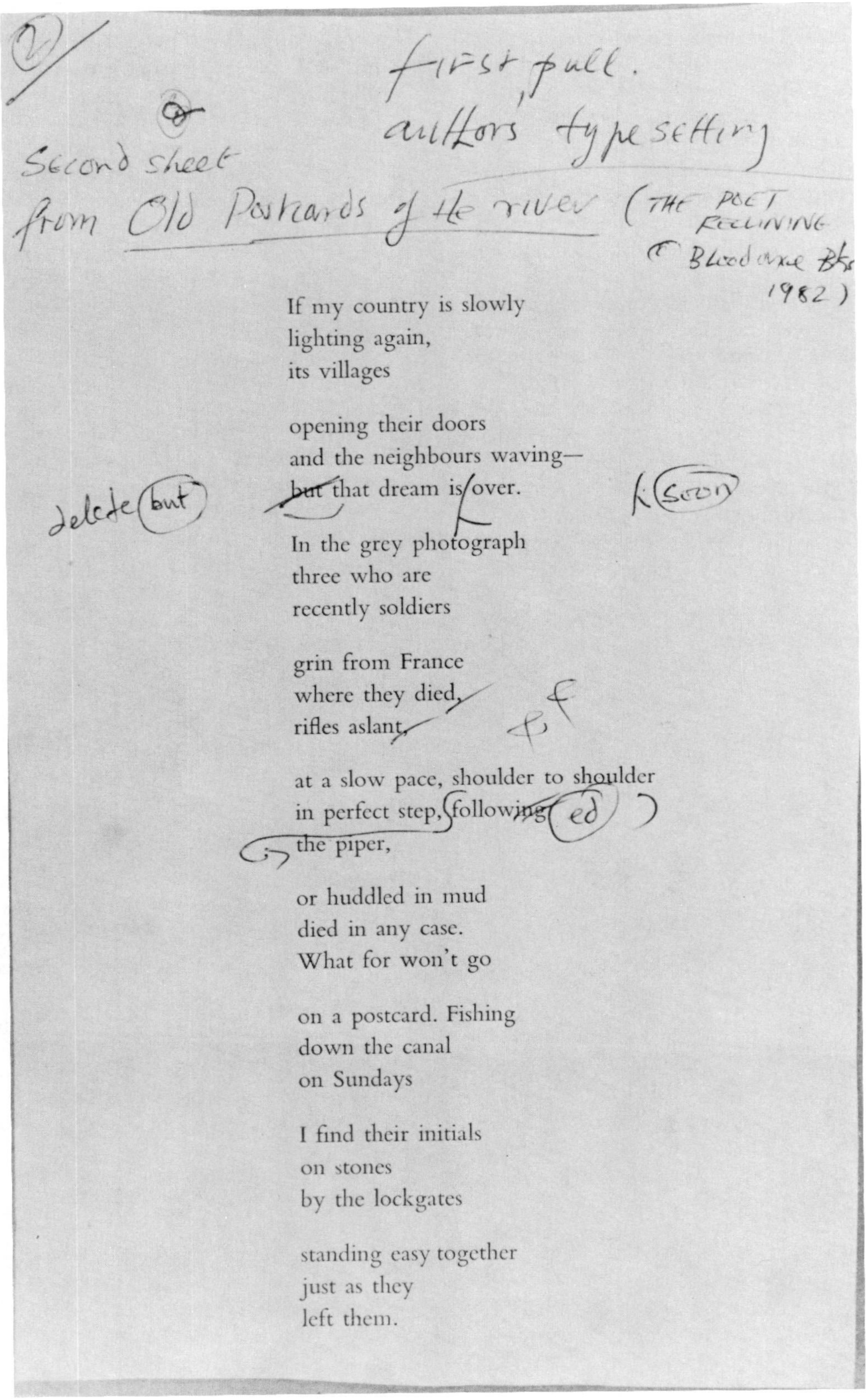

② /

first pull.
authors' typesetting

Second sheet
from Old Postcards of the river (THE POET
RECLINING
© Bloodaxe Bks
1982)

If my country is slowly
lighting again,
its villages

opening their doors
and the neighbours waving—
but that dream is over.

delete (but)   k (scott)

In the grey photograph
three who are
recently soldiers

grin from France
where they died,
rifles aslant,   & f

at a slow pace, shoulder to shoulder
in perfect step, following (ed))
the piper,

or huddled in mud
died in any case.
What for won't go

on a postcard. Fishing
down the canal
on Sundays

I find their initials
on stones
by the lockgates

standing easy together
just as they
left them.

Revised proof. The type was set by Smith (the author).

ever it is in Fox that "speaks/from the lengthening floor/of his blood his conviction/*not me not me Jack.*" Smith finished up as a live-in barman in an Irish pub in Kilburn. As a poet he survived, in the words of Jeff Nuttall's *Guardian* review, by "taking heartbreak in both hands and using it like bricks and mortar to build art. . . . *Fox Running* is an astonishing leap in compositional scope."

Through the University of Antioch in London Smith met the American writer Judi Benson and made a new home with her and her son Todd. From 1979 to 1981 he was writer in residence at Kingston Polytechnic. He now lives in London's East End. *Fox Running* was published by Smith's own press and then republished in 1981 by Bloodaxe, who went on to publish his selected poems, *The Poet Reclining* (1982). The volume was widely acclaimed, even critics such as Peter Porter, who would be hostile to the element of projective verse in Smith's poetics, being forced into "a new respect for his powers."

His forthcoming collection *Terra* includes two new sequences, "Hawkwood" and "The London Poems." "Hawkwood" is based on the figure of Sir John Hawkwood, a fourteenth-century condottiere, whose career enabled Smith "to write about war and aggression and masculinity . . . under this metaphor of the wanderer." The poems are like "late night work Hawkwood might have done . . . a closed book I'm opening." "The London Poems" are all short, twelve-line poems, "sonnets without the concluding couplet," his interest being partly formal, to see how much he could pack into three four-line stanzas.

At the same time as *Terra,* Bloodaxe will publish *A Book of Chinese Whispers,* a collection of prose pieces. Smith's prose is closely akin to his poetry. Some ideas simply develop into prose: "the stories are really very convoluted metaphors." Because there is a limited market for experimental fiction, the prose pieces have so far only appeared in five pamphlets. *A Book of Chinese Whispers* will collect these pamphlets together with more recent prose. It should add another dimension to the work of a poet who sees his development as a long "learning to let be . . . to let a set of images or patterns or obsessions form itself into shape."

Jon Stallworthy

(18 January 1935-)

Margaret B. McDowell
University of Iowa

BOOKS: *The Earthly Paradise* (Oxford: Privately printed, 1958);

The Astronomy of Love (London: Oxford University Press, 1961);

Between the Lines: Yeats's Poetry in the Making (Oxford: Clarendon Press, 1963);

Out of Bounds (London: Oxford University Press, 1963);

The Almond Tree (London: Turret Books, 1967);

A Day in the City (Exeter: Exeter Books, 1967);

Vision and Revision in Yeats's Last Poems (Oxford: Clarendon Press, 1969);

Root and Branch (London: Chatto & Windus/Hogarth Press, 1969; New York: Oxford University Press, 1969);

Positives (Dublin: Dolmen Press, 1969);

A Dinner of Herbs (Exeter: Rougemont Press, 1970);

Hand in Hand (London: Chatto & Windus/Hogarth Press, 1974; New York: Oxford University Press, 1974);

The Apple Barrel: Selected Poems 1955-63 (London: Oxford University Press, 1974);

Wilfred Owen: A Biography (London: Chatto & Windus/Oxford University Press, 1974; New York: Oxford University Press, 1975);

Poets of the First World War (London: Oxford University Press, 1974);

A Familiar Tree (London: Chatto & Windus/Oxford University Press, 1978; New York: Oxford University Press, 1978).

OTHER: *Yeats: Last Poems. A Casebook,* edited by Stallworthy (London: Macmillan, 1968; Nashville: Aurora, 1970);

Five Centuries of Polish Poetry, revised edition, translated by Stallworthy, Jerzy Peterkiewicz, and

*Photo by Fay Godwin;
courtesy of Bernard Stone,
The Turret Book Shop*

Burns Singer (London: Oxford University Press, 1970);

Alexander Blok, *The Twelve and Other Poems,* translated by Stallworthy and Peter France (London: Eyre & Spottiswoode, 1970; New York: Oxford University Press, 1970);

New Poems 1970-1971, edited by Stallworthy, Seamus Heaney, and Alan Brownjohn (London: Hutchinson, 1971);

The Penguin Book of Love Poetry, edited by Stallworthy (Harmondsworth: Penguin, 1973); republished as *A Book of Love Poetry* (New York: Oxford University Press, 1974);

Boris Pasternak, *Selected Poems,* translated by Stallworthy and France (London: Allen Lane, 1982);

The Complete Poems and Fragments of Wilfred Owen, edited by Stallworthy (London: Hogarth Press, 1983);

The Oxford Book of War Poetry, edited by Stallworthy (London & New York: Oxford University Press, 1984);

The Poems of Wilfred Owen, edited by Stallworthy (London: Chatto & Windus, 1985).

Jon Stallworthy has attained considerable recognition for his poetry. His work published after 1969, when compared with most of the poems in his first two collections (written between 1956 and 1963), demonstrates a steady development in his mastery of his art, as well as a broadening of theme and a greater willingness to communicate personal feeling. In addition to his poetry, Stallworthy's achievements as editor, translator, critic, scholar, and teacher are significant and have contributed to his development as a poet. His scholarly interests lie mainly in the investigation of the development of creative processes. Most noteworthy are his studies of W. B. Yeats, *Between the Lines: Yeats's Poetry in the Making* (1963) and *Vision and Revision in Yeats's Last Poems* (1969), his biography, *Wilfred Owen* (1974), and his edition of *The Complete Poems and Fragments of Wilfred Owen* (1983). With Jerzy Peterkiewicz and Burns Singer he translated poetry from the Polish language (*Five Centuries of Polish Poetry*, 1970), and with Peter France, he translated Alexander Blok's *The Twelve and Other Poems* (1970) and Boris Pasternak's *Selected Poems* (1982).

Jon Howie Stallworthy's parents, Sir John Arthur Stallworthy, a surgeon and medical writer specializing in obstetrics and gynecology, and Margaret Wright Howie Stallworthy, were third-generation New Zealanders who married in 1934 and went to England for what they believed would be a temporary stay. (In *A Familiar Tree* Jon Stallworthy describes his great-great-grandfather's leaving his home near Oxford in the early nineteenth century to become a missionary in the Marquesas.) World War II prevented their return home, and in 1939 Dr. Stallworthy assumed the position of area director of obstetrics and gynecology for the Oxford United Hospitals and remained in that post for twenty-eight years, until he became Nuffield Professor of Obstetrics at Oxford University. Thus, the poet, born in London in January 1935, was educated in England, where, he has commented, his New Zealand heritage made him feel an outsider at Dragon School, Oxford (1940-1948), and later at Rugby School, Warwickshire (1948-1953). Entering the army in 1953, he became a lieutenant in the Oxfordshire and Buckinghamshire Light Infantry, seconded to the Royal West African Frontier Force, and in 1954-1955 served for fifteen months in Nigeria. Upon his return to England, he entered Magdalen College, Oxford, where he received a B.A. in 1958 and a B.Litt. in 1961. He won the Roger Newdigate Prize for English Verse at Oxford in 1958 for *The Earthly Paradise*, having been second in the Newdigate competition the previous year.

On 25 June 1960 Stallworthy married Gillian Waldock; they now have three children. In 1959 he began working with book publishers, first as an editor for Oxford University Press in London (1959-1971), then as an editor for the Clarendon Press at Oxford (1974-1977), and later as deputy academic publisher of the Oxford University Press at Oxford (1974-1977). In 1971-1972 he was a visiting fellow at All Souls College, Oxford. He presently holds the John Wendell Anderson Professorship in English literature at Cornell University in Ithaca, New York, a position that took him to the United States in 1977.

Stallworthy's first two collections, *The Astronomy of Love* (1961) and *Out of Bounds* (1963), include a few failures, some excellent poems, and many reasonably successful ones which suggest a young writer's attempts to vary his techniques and subject matter. The faults are those frequently found in early poems—some clumsiness in versification, an overloading of lines with images which call attention to themselves and which interfere with communication of idea and feeling, the presence in love poetry of occasional lines that verge on coyness, the occasional flat statement of sentiment, and an imitative rather than an original and individual voice. These first volumes, however, show an interest in an exploration of verse technique and a greater breadth of subject than reviewers credited them with at the time of their publication.

Typically, in both of these books Stallworthy chooses an octosyllabic line, easily and frequently varying the length, and he employs both exact rhyme and half rhyme at ends of lines. When he experiments with other patterns, as he does often in the second volume and in the first half of *Root and Branch* (1969), he tends to lose naturalness and control of the meter. In the predominantly octosyllabic poems, he attains a particular grace by preventing the ends of sentences and ends of lines from coinciding, thus softening the end rhyme and minimizing the natural pause at these points to facilitate the smoother flow of the poem.

Even in *The Astronomy of Love*, Stallworthy does attempt, however, to use many varying patterns of versification, sometimes indeed for the sheer pleasure of playing with words and rhythms, as in the light-hearted rondo "La Ronde" and the intricately patterned "Romance," where the poet asks why a man such as he, who dreams of fairy-tale princesses and of heroic women that are shipwrecked or about to be burned at the stake, should have fallen in love with the woman he now addresses, who is wearing a commonplace hat and carrying a basket.

In an enthusiastic review for the *Critical Quarterly*, poet Robin Skelton called *The Astronomy of Love* a book replete with wit and passion rendered in a clear and assured voice, and remarked on Stallworthy's unusual gift: an ability to create a memorable line—sometimes an epigrammatic one—which is "at once simple and deeply disturbing." Even in his least unified poems, Stallworthy has fashioned such lines. Though James Dickey, writing for the *Sewanee Review*, was the book's severest critic, even he noted Stallworthy's technical facility ("He moves very gracefully down the lines of a poem, regardless of what they are saying"), and added, "He is gentle and humorous and intelligent."

Early critics of Stallworthy focused on his somewhat imitative and derivative love poems and failed to note the wide range of subject matter in his first two volumes, which also include poems on childhood memories (particularly of violence or death), the raising of Lazarus, sword dancers, Yeats's unrequited love for Maud Gonne, Toulouse-Lautrec, a witch, cowboys, a circus clown, a circus disaster, and the Trojan horse.

Stallworthy himself realized that, unlike some other poets of his generation, he did not address political and social issues of consequence. In his defensive "Letter to a Friend" (*The Astronomy of Love*) he admits that he has failed to decry rape, murder, and war, but he urges his friend to accept his poems "woven out of love's loose ends," and to recall that "cloud, star, leaf, and water's dance/are facts of life, and worth your glance." He asserts that his goal as poet is not just a realistic transcription of contemporary experience but the creation of an imaginative perspective as well: he would hope "to make/in the sloganed wall the people pass/a window—not a looking-glass." (Even in later poems where he concerns himself with violence, suffering, and war, he feels that his goal remains the creation of a heightened imaginative understanding or vision, which would enable the reader to see "fields beyond the smoke." He does not simply mirror despondency or catastrophe but places such aspects of experience in perspective and explores their implications or origins.)

This commitment to the imagination is evident in other poems in *The Astronomy of Love*. For example, "Epstein's Lazarus" presents the miracle as negative and violent, allowing the reader to look from a "new window" on the biblical event and on Jacob Epstein's sculpture of the risen Lazarus. He graphically presents the violence which Lazarus must have felt when he was dragged from the tomb, as an agony far greater than that his mother had felt when he was "wrested" from her womb. "Wrenched" back to life as the penalty for his mother's love for him, Lazarus stands as a living corpse, suffering and shocked not so much by death as by life. When Stallworthy exploits the eeriness of ghost legend, he more importantly interprets Epstein's rendition of the risen Lazarus by suggesting Lazarus's thoughts and feelings. Harsh diction forces the reader to view Lazarus as victim, and Lazarus, rather than Christ, becomes the central figure. Christ appears in the poem only as hands that drag the corpse from the tomb.

The romantic title poem in *The Astronomy of Love* is closely followed by an antiromantic poem, "The Common Breath." In their obsessive urge to escape loneliness the man and woman in this poem engage in compulsive but meaningless sex—even breathing as one and hoping to cast one shadow. In bleak daylight, the cynical lover knows that, should he read of his mistress's death, he would lose only enough of their "common breath" to interfere with his whistling for one day.

A loose pastiche of images seems to fragment "Poem upon the Quincentenary of Magdalen College," but these images—separately considered—produce startling lines. Through them, one faintly hears the dirge for the inexorable passing of time, a dirge that the poet cannot hear as he meditates alone in the chapel at night upon the stone carvings on the walls—fiddlers and dancers, restless and disconsolate because no one comes to mourn with them for "the dying of five hundred Junes." The organ, bells, and psalmist all are silent, but at dawn a blackbird "in the last tail coat" whistles the requiem for the ancient past of the college.

In *Out of Bounds* (1963) Stallworthy further establishes what readers such as James Dickey failed to see in the more imitative poems of the first book, the province of experience that is unique to the individual poet and that Dickey referred to as "the place where poetry must be made, the place of one's own (and owned) reality." In "First Blood," a poem with autobiographical authenticity, the horror felt by two boys at their botched shooting of a squirrel results in a frantic effort to "Finish him off"— "Four shots point blank/to dull his eyes, a fifth to stop/the shiver in his clotted flank." The simplicity of the quatrains, which reflect the boys' fragmented conversation, makes the directness of the poet's retrospective comment at the close more memorable in its acknowledgement of the guilt and humiliation which he shares with the boys: "we, like dishonored soldiers, ran/the gauntlet of a darkening wood."

The same simplicity and directness characterize the pastoral poem "Letter to My Sisters." Near the close, one is aware of some rhetorical artifice in Stallworthy's advice to his twin sisters, but in the first several stanzas of this poem, one can fault nothing other than a few romantic archaisms. The girls lazily enjoy the countryside and the pleasure of eating good food by the lake, hearing only "cowbells and churchbell and the kiss/of scythes in tilting pastures." Sleeping until nine, they have croissants beside the quiet lake and, at ten, walk to the village "for the long hot loaves and cheese/to be eaten as you lie/halfway to a Renaissance sky. . . ." Homely details make rural paradise seem almost a reality.

In "From W. B. Yeats to his Friend Maud Gonne" Stallworthy employs a modified sonnet form, with uneven rhyming of couplets. Though the poet understands Yeats's passion and his reticence, he fails to understand Maud Gonne's rejection of him. He cannot see why the heart of the woman so often given to outgoing sympathy "for anarchists and peasants and sick birds,/could not be crowbarred open by such words/as break the heart of time. . . ." The simple pathos of this poem is striking.

In *Root and Branch* (1969) Stallworthy demonstrates a more mature artistry, revealing a range of interests, including international issues and historical events. Though his subjects and themes have become more complex, his assured control of tech-

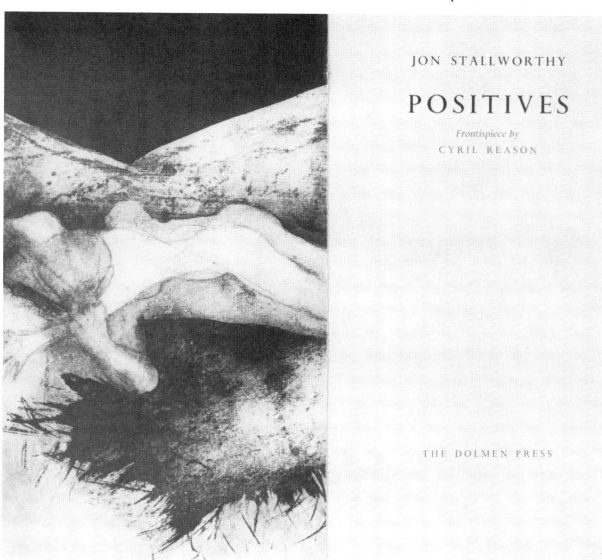

Frontispiece and title page for the 1969 limited edition of five poems by Stallworthy. The frontispiece, which was first published in the Oxford Illustrated Old Testament, *is an illustration for chapter six of the Song of Solomon.*

nique makes his poetry appear simple. The first poem, "True Confession," suggests a new directness and candor, as the poet recognizes from experience that truth—unlike what his teachers told him as a child—is a dangerous commodity, but one that must be sought at any cost. He is ready to be done with "lies of friendship, lies of love,/expedient hypocrisies," so that with such pretenses cast aside, he can be truly himself: "shield gone and visor, glove/struck off—here I unsheathe my pen." While he wryly warns that "Poets are liars" and that he may regress, Stallworthy clearly tells the truth as he discerns it about wars, army bases in other countries, commercial exploitation, man's loss of contact with nature, and the undramatic pain of love denied or denigrated. In several poems he searches for truth in the commonplace object (stone; thistle; the thumb's pressure on leather, wood, and stone; the bread upon a plain board; and carcasses of hogs hung at a market). Other poems show a preoccupation with communication (telephones, letters, telegrams, roads, construction workers' signals, news coverage of war, poets' protest of war, doctors' pronouncements, neon signs in Nepal, a jukebox replacing an ancient prayer wheel, and newspaper records of deaths and births proving that "Blood is not blood when it is ink").

Another group concentrates on family tradition and the possible connections that can exist between generations. In "Two Hands" and "A Letter From Berlin, 1938," for instance, he explores the differences between himself and his father, as well as the characteristics they possess in common; and in *The Almond Tree* (published separately in 1967) and "The Fall of a Sparrow" he probes the anguish of his relationship between himself and his newborn retarded son.

In "Two Hands" he watches his father, as the surgeon dozes over medical journals after performing thirteen operations in one day, and contrasts accomplishments wrought by his father's hands with those of his own hands, which do not save lives but play indecisively with a pencil. The emphasis is on admiration and compassion for the fatigued father more than on self-effacement. "A Letter from Berlin, 1938" is a versification of a story that his father told him about after observing a demonstration by a famous surgeon of "the perfect vaginal hysterectomy." Deeply impressed by the deftness of the surgery, which permitted almost no bleeding, the father wrote: "It was like a concert, watching those hands unlock the music from their score." After the performance, he learned by accident that

the patient had died on the operating table and that the surgeon typically broke the unwritten rule that, if the patient dies, the operation ceases. The poet, holding the yellowed letter in his hand, feels it make "a ritual wound" in his palm, which opened to a trench "filled/not with snow only, east of Buchenwald." Thus, linking the incident with Nazi sadism, he shares thirty years later the experience not only of his father but of his father's generation.

In *The Almond Tree* Stallworthy recaptures the exhilaration of driving through the London streets to the hospital for the birth of his first child, the subsequent shock of hearing that the child has Downs Syndrome (a shock he symbolizes as a bullet—the "first death"), and his numb sense of being brought back to life by the almond tree in blossom. The beauty of its broken buds sailing away in the wind comfort him as his child in a numbered crib seems to him now placed in a small boat to sail away from him. Through the detachment resulting from sudden and overwhelming tragedy, he feels, looking down from the window high in the hospital, like a pilot whose plane has been shot down and who is looking earthward from beneath his parachute canopy. Later he sees the hospital as a huge ship where charts are confused and voyages misdirected.

"The Fall of a Sparrow" presents the new parents struggling all night to understand the unreasonable fate of their child: "If not the hand of chance/dicing with chromosomes,/what strategy of Providence/cost our sparrow his five wits?" Stallworthy rejects his "comforters" with their speculation that this child's birth will inspire the father to write intensely felt poetry: "Does Providence sell a sparrow for a song?" At dawn the crib shakes and "the fallen sun/rises for father and mother."

Two fine longer poems at the end of *Root and Branch* repeat a few images in varying combinations, with varying meanings. Their changing implications produce subtle irony and even paradox. "Elm End," the second prizewinner in the 1965 Guinness Poetry Competition, suggests the imminent death of an old man. Rows of giant elms planted on his estate over generations, each elm marking the birth of a baby in the family, will be felled after his death as the estate is sold and divided. Heavily falling snow makes the elms into a beautiful arching "vault." Falling on the gate it covers the broken parts of stone cherubs emasculated by village boys, and it muffles all sound. In the pervasive silence of the poem the rusty bell cannot ring, and the servants seem like elusive ghosts. In the second section, the poet moves indoors to the man's room, where in the dying man's mind the snow becomes the sheets on his bed, which his claw-like fingers clutch, as he has held fast to snowy acres of his land. Above him, the griffin carved on the massive headboard clutches in his claws a scroll, on which is written "Hold fast." Carved at the order of the dying man's grandmother's grandmother when her husband was marching to Waterloo and Napoleon, the griffin warns against forgetting the perspective of history. This mythological figure, traditionally the guard of hidden treasures, is mindful of the passage of the years, and sees not the hollow trunks of the trees but their long roots under the snow. The only sound is the old man's breathing, which echoes the wind in the chimney. He will not hear the only other sound in the poem, because he is dead when "the bulldozer roars/at its kill." The strength and beauty of the old ways diminish as the man dies and the trees are felled.

With a similar manipulation of imagery but in a lighter mood, "March Morning, N.W. 3" celebrates the return of spring to London. The poem vividly presents contrasting aspects of London through the symbols suggesting such dichotomies as death and resurrection, decay and blossoming, winter and spring, fatigue and renewal of the spirit, death-bringing materialism and life-enhancing cosmic changes. Construction cranes are in the park as the poet wakens and opens the window; later, the huge cranes, destroying and rebuilding, hoist men and materials into the spring air. Daffodils in the park are linked with the daffodil-yellow helmets of construction workers. The trees in the graveyard "hoist" the energy derived from the "distilled dead" for nourishment and the dead are given a kind of new life in the green leaves. In contrast to these buried dead, half-dead commuters ride the "underground" and need also to be "hoisted" into the fresh air for revival. Fountains begin to flow from green mouths that have been sealed all winter, not with ice but with city soot.

In Stallworthy's fourth volume, the narrative sequence *Hand in Hand* (1974), many of the poems celebrate joy, love, and life. It became the Poetry Book Society Recommendation for 1974, the same year that Stallworthy won the Duff Cooper Memorial Award. In "Elegy for a Mis-Spent Youth," with retrospective amusement and bemused nostalgia, he recalls an evening with his "spirited friend," the whiskey bottle, and he whimsically arranges the lines to form typographically the outline of the bottle. "After 'La Desserte,' " "Pour Commencer," "A

Question of Form and Content," "Breakfast in Bed," and "Personal Column" are brief love poems revealing in common a lightness of tone. Mostly playful exercises, they present from a perspective of bemused detachment the varieties possible in sexual attraction and often suggest its transitory nature. Despair and heartbreak, love under duress, and tragic passion are absent from these poems. Celebrating unmistakably the joys of physical desire, the poems are forthright rather than erotic. They, like the poems in *The Astronomy of Love*, lack tension.

Nevertheless, too few love poems anywhere begin as convincingly as Stallworthy's brief "Breakfast in Bed": "Lying in late;/two croissants, warm/

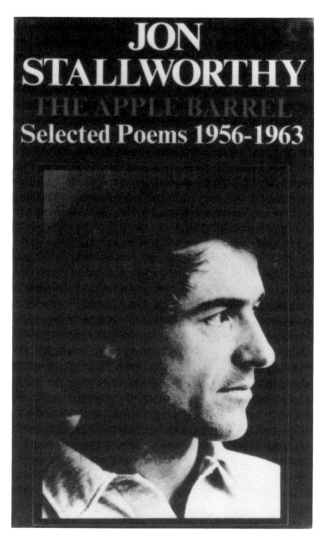

Front cover for Stallworthy's 1974 selection of early poems "that seem worth their place in the apple barrel." The title page subtitle is Selected Poems 1955-63.

Dust jacket for Stallworthy's 1978 book, which grew out of his discovery in 1973 that his great-grandfather was the son of a missionary to the Marquesas

in each other's arms . . . ," or as curiously as does "A Question of Form and Content": "I owe you an apology,/love, my love, for here you are/in a school anthology. . . ." In the first two stanzas of "Walking Against the Wind," also a most effective poem, he depicts the warm love of a young man and woman on a cold night in London as they feed each other hot chestnuts. Later the poet, walking in the cold wind, lets the lovers "shelter in my mind/at midnight," and hopes they will never know the coldest, and possibly the least expected, wind on earth— that which blows "nightly between those/whom God hath joined together/to have and not to hold."

Among the best of the poems in the volume are those on family relationships. In "Mother and Child" the poet reminds the mother, settled back into her "dune of pillows," of the night when she conceived her child, comparing the event to a current of a river rising in her, "lifting inland/the unknown here, at the tide's return,/made known, breathing under your hand." The newborn infant

does not remain abstract but in the last lines of the brief poem vigorously—almost violently—sucks at the breasts that are not yet filled with milk. Besides "At Bedtime" (in which the poet reads a story his son will never be able to understand) and "The Almond Tree Revisited," the poem "This Morning" depicts the variety of emotion possible in the family's daily life, as one morning the poet and his little daughter discover that spring has come as they "take each other to school." While he ponders what he must write that night for his daughter's eventual understanding ("they, you will learn, have nothing, that/have nothing to lose."), she promises to pick him flowers, make him cakes, and "swing in the sun all afternoon." *Hand in Hand* has a vitality, a plenitude of emotion, a variety of mood, and a range of subject that exceeds the earlier volumes, but it does not in any single poem rival the best of the poems in *Root and Branch.*

In *A Familiar Tree* (1978) Stallworthy creates a family history which covers two and a half centuries, from 1738 to 1977. In an interview with Patricia Haberstroh he described the historical research that informs this verse cycle. One day in 1973 he noticed his father's copy of *Early Northern Wairo* (1916), a local history written by his great-grandfather, John Stallworthy, who had been an advocate of prohibition in New Zealand while a member of Parliament for Kaipara. For the first time, Stallworthy discovered that his great-great-grandfather, George, had been a missionary who left England for the Marquesas in 1833 and had died in Samoa in 1859. To his amazement he also discovered that George Stallworthy had been born in 1809 in Preston Bissett, a village that was a mere fifteen miles from his own home. Moreover, in the churchyard of Preston Bissett's thirteenth-century Church of St. John Baptist, he found the stones of seven Stallworthy ancestors who had died between 1742 and 1810. This discovery determined the four-part structure of the book: England (1738-1833); the Marquesas (1833-1859); New Zealand (1872-1934); and England again (1934-1977). To write *A Familiar Tree* he consulted the parish register, where curates had recorded baptisms, marriages, and deaths for the years 1650-1830, and he employed material on the missionary ventures in the Marquesas that he found at the London library of the School of Oriental and African Studies—including news clippings about George Stallworthy's leaving Preston Bissett, his obituary, and copies of the sermons he had delivered in London.

This windfall of material, joined with Stallworthy's fascination with family relationships and historical perspective, made writing *A Family Tree* irresistible. As a New Zealander in England he had as a child felt like a stranger; but on a trip to New Zealand he had observed that people there perceived him as a stranger. In "Identity Parade: before the shaving mirror, 1959" (first published in *Root and Branch*), he sees himself as a series of separate identities, a stranger even to himself, the product of generations who are strangers to him. He supposes that someday he will be yet another stranger who observes and judges the self he is now and all his earlier selves. Yet there is psychological and genetic continuity in human life, as is implied in the book's epigraph from Leo Tolstoy's *War and Peace:* "The movement of humanity, arising as it does from innumerable arbitrary human wills, is continuous. To understand the laws of this continuous movement is the aim of history. . . . we must leave aside kings, ministers, and generals, and study the common, infinitesimally small elements by which the masses are moved."

The chronological sequence begins with the birth of one John Stallworthy in 1738. This poem is followed by one about the death of his father, John, in 1744. The rest of the poems in the section trace succeeding generations up to the point when, on 16 October 1833, George Stallworthy sails from Gravesend to serve as a missionary in the Marquesas, where he lives among cannibals, experiencing the trials of a hurricane, a plague of caterpillars, and the deaths of his first wife and several of their children. After his death in 1859, his wife leaves with four children to return to England, but on the voyage three children die in less than a week. Her one remaining son, John (the author of the *Early Northern Wairo*), lives to adulthood, establishing several thriving Victorian businesses in New Zealand—in lumber, paper, printing, and journalism—and becoming a Member of the New Parliament. His sons fight for the King in Europe in World War I, and are then given free (though very poor) land by the government when they return to New Zealand. In 1934 Jon Stallworthy's own father and mother arrive in England to study. The final section begins with Dr. Stallworthy's letters to New Zealand of late 1939, in which he expresses his disappointment at being prevented by the outbreak of war from returning home for Christmas and his fear that the need for doctors will keep them in England. The last two poems in the book are for Nicolas, the poet's younger son, to whom Stallworthy dedicates the book. In the last poem Stallworthy calls the book a modern "Mirror for a Prince," and tells Nicolas to pack it with his toys as he and his parents depart to live in the United States in 1977.

All of the book's poems are independent entities, but there are subtle relationships among the poems, and they are unified by the family chronology. Stallworthy characteristically moves out from the facts of the lives of his ancestors to a consideration of the historical circumstances in which they found themselves and which helped to form them, recreating history in terms of art, much as a historical novelist would.

The voices reflected in the poems and the verse forms through which they speak vary dramatically—versified wills, petitions against enclosure, letters written on shipboard, lullabies, the lonely meditations of widows, dialogues between an earnest missionary and the warriors whom he would convert, and journal entries describing the hardships in a primitive land. Despite such variety, Stallworthy also employs unifying devices which allow the poems to be seen as components of a long narrative poem. For example, the book opens with "At

```
                    ONE DAY

        The last morning as an immortal
        passed into the last afternoon
        and when the bedside lamp was lit
        you told me: Grandmother has died.
        Died?
                    She has gone to Heaven.
                                        When
        will she be back?
                            We don't come back.
        We?
                    Everyone goes to Heaven.
        Will you go?
                        One day.
                                    Black lightning
        scissored the wall, and the floor
        fell away in a down-draught
        of terror -
                    I had forgotten
        that sheer shaft, the vertigo,
until   the manic echo, till  the day
        (your grandson fell) in the well, and  standing astride
        Astride his darkness, I threw him
        the line you lowered, to me there.  wondering
        When were you ever at my side
        as now, my dear, my phantom limb?
```

Revised Friday 9 Oct. 1981

until the day your grandson fell
to your death and, standing astride
his darkness, I threw him

Revised typescript (the author)

the Church of St. John Baptist, Preston Bissett, May 1974," a friendly letter to "Dear John" from his "own house," and it closes with "Envoi, June 1977," a letter to the poet's son Nicolas—two poems in seven-line stanzas, which create a frame for the rest of the poems. The women speak in poems composed of six-line stanzas, contributing to the sense that all the women are one woman—a gentle, patient, devoted helpmate, and mother. Easily merging into the characters' words and thoughts throughout the poems are echoes of the King James Bible that rise silently in the subconscious mind, particularly in moments of stress. Imagery in poem after poem centers on birds, trees and acorns, seedtime and harvest. Death is spoken of as "planting." The lullaby in "Mother and Son, 1738" refers to pregnancy in terms of seed and growth:

the cradle will rock   Sown
in me   grown in me   known
to me always

The seeds planted in the ground by the farmers at Preston Bissett in the first section parallel the seeds of the gospel planted in the hearts of "the heathen" in the second section. Departures and arrivals, births and deaths, the vanishing of the birds and their return—these are the impressive patterns that move beneath the poems and draw them together.

Stallworthy has said that in writing *A Familiar Tree* he may have been influenced by his long study of Yeats and by his admiration for Robert Lowell's *Life Studies* and Alexander Blok's *The Twelve*. The many voices that appear in this poem, the combination of documents and personal speech, and the adept shifting among many forms of versification all suggest parallels between *A Familiar Tree* and the works of Yeats, Lowell, and Blok. Yet more significant, *A Familiar Tree* is a strongly original work.

Though Stallworthy's promise was apparent in the 1950s, his reputation as poet, biographer, and scholar grew substantially in both Britain and America in the mid-1970s. Since his appointment to the John Wendell Anderson Professorship of English Literature at Cornell University, Stallworthy has devoted himself to literary biography and to the study of Wilfred Owen's manuscripts, and has published no volumes of poetry since 1978. *Wilfred Owen: A Biography* (1974), which Graham Greene described as "surely one of the finest biographies of our time," earned for Stallworthy the W. H. Smith Literary Award for nonfiction (1975) and the E. M. Forester Award of the American Academy of Arts and Letters (1976). Scholars have also praised Stallworthy's monumental *The Complete Poems and Fragments of Wilfred Owen* (1983) for its exhaustive analyses of manuscripts, its comprehensive scope, its attention to detail, and its brilliant readings of the poems.

Stallworthy's interests in writing biography and criticism remain, nevertheless, primarily those of a poet and creative artist. In his discursive prose he is preoccupied with the mysteries of creative expression and growth, with the workings of the imagination, with the ability of the artist to project his vision, and with the relationship between the poet's art and his life. He himself commented that all his writing was subservient to his creative work as poet: "I count myself a maker and such other things as I have made with words—studies of Yeats 'at work,' translations of poems by Blok and Pasternak—have been made with one purpose in view: to learn how to make better poems."

Anne Stevenson
(3 January 1933-   )

J. E. Chamberlin
University of Toronto

BOOKS: *Living in America* (Ann Arbor, Mich.: Generation Press, 1965);

Elizabeth Bishop (New York: Twayne, 1966; London: Collins, 1967);

Reversals (Middletown, Conn.: Wesleyan University Press, 1969);

Travelling Behind Glass: Selected Poems 1963-1973 (London & New York: Oxford University Press, 1974);

Correspondences: A Family History in Letters (Middletown, Conn.: Wesleyan University Press, 1974; Oxford: Oxford University Press, 1974);

Enough of Green (Oxford & New York: Oxford University Press, 1977);

Sonnets for Five Seasons (Herefordshire: Five Seasons Press, 1979);

Green Mountain, Black Mountain (Boston: Rowan Tree Press, 1982);

Minute by Glass Minute (Oxford & New York: Oxford University Press, 1982);

Black Grate Poems (Oxford: Inky Parrot Press, 1985).

OTHER: Blake Morrison and Andrew Motion, eds., *The Penguin Book of Contemporary British Poetry*, includes poems by Stevenson (Harmondsworth: Penguin, 1982);

"The Music of the House: Scenes from Childhood," *Poetry Review*, 72 (September 1982): 5-10.

Anne Stevenson

Anne Stevenson is one of the few contemporary poets whose writing incorporates most of the preoccupations of postmodernist poetry. She has a woman writer's necessary ambivalence about the language available to her, about the heritage which she must recognize, and about the obligations to others which either sustain or subvert her imagination. She has a fine sense of the complicated differences between American and British poetry, and she embodies the traditions of both in a poetry that achieves definition because of its allegiances, and distinction because of its intense and relentless individuality. She defies the riddling invitations of much twentieth-century verse by writing a poetry which begins rather than ends in song, a verse of subtle musical sensibility which still holds its own in the company of those zealous tropes, metonymy and metaphor. And she has been part of a wide circle of contemporary poetry and has developed her own voice in the company of such figures in the evolution of contemporary poetic discourse as Donald Hall, Philip Hobsbaum, and Andrew Motion.

Anne Stevenson was born in 1933 of American parents in Cambridge, England. Her father—Charles Leslie Stevenson—had gone to Cambridge to study English a few years earlier, after taking a degree at Yale. In a timely way he read I. A.

Richards's *Principles of Literary Criticism* (1924) on the boat, and turned to philosophy instead, studying with Richards, G. E. Moore, and Ludwig Wittgenstein. The family returned to America in the summer of 1933, and Anne grew up in Cambridge, Massachusetts, and New Haven, Connecticut. Her father was an exceptionally good pianist, and the Stevenson children grew up surrounded by music. Anne played the piano, learned the cello with her father, and went to the University of Michigan Music School expecting to make music a career. The Stevenson family had moved to Ann Arbor when her father took a position teaching philosophy at the University of Michigan; Ann Arbor and Wilmington, Vermont, where the Stevensons had a summer house, were the places where Anne set down roots. But pulling up roots has obviously been a part of her life as well. She left a career in music to read Italian and French at the university, though she did not leave music behind; and she left Ann Arbor (after earning a B.A. in 1954) to go to Cambridge, England, and to marry, though she did not leave Michigan behind. Furthermore, her mother—Louise Destler Stevenson—and particular times and places from her past have continued to haunt her poetry, and to inspire it.

Her marriage (to an Englishman with whom she had grown up in New Haven during the war) brought a daughter, and difficulties. In 1960 she returned to Michigan to study with the poet Donald Hall, receiving an M.A. in 1962. It was at this point that she began to take her own writing seriously; and one of the results was her first book, *Living in America* (1965), published under the auspices of the undergraduate journal *Generation* by the University of Michigan.

Living in America shows something of Stevenson's musical ear, with its slanting rhymes, murmuring rhythms, and subtle use of run-on lines as figurations of disintegration as well as transformation. There is an instinct for parody here: the tone of T. S. Eliot's early poems, with the rhythmic imitation turned in Stevenson's case against the 1930s and 1940s instead of the 1890s. And there is the mockery, as well as the music, of William Butler Yeats, whose influence Stevenson is quick to acknowledge; in these poems, the gaiety which she thinks about never quite subsumes the bitterness which she feels. Finally, a poem such as "The Grey Land" illustrates what will become two of Stevenson's characteristic devices:

> I must have been there,
> and you—and you,

> for we were the very landscape
> we walked through.

There is the distinctively American inheritance of what Wallace Stevens called "Theory": "I am what is around me./Women understand this." And there is the repeated word or phrase—the nervous echo, the insistent double, the recollecting mirror: "and you—and you." In Stevenson's later work, this doubling develops into something between a persistent motif and a personal signature.

Stevenson taught briefly before remarrying, in 1961, to Mark Elvin, a scholar and teacher of Chinese history, who was at Harvard for the year on leave from a position in Cambridge, England. They returned to Cambridge in 1962, shortly after her mother died of cancer; then moved to Glasgow in 1966 where they had two sons. Stevenson had been writing during this period, and in 1969 *Reversals* was published by Wesleyan University Press.

Reflections and reversals preoccupy the poems in this volume. The repetitions of the first poem, "In the House," are insistent: "these keys are my keys, this door my door"; " 'mother, mother', they wail . . . and yet when I bend to them/It is like kissing a photograph"; "here there are vases and reflections of vases/on the tables; and gardens,/and reflections in the windows of the gardens." In "The Takeover" the women flit "from mirror to mirror," and the poet ambiguously confesses, "I don't know/what I would want to replace them if they should go." With what to replace them? or whether?—"replace" is left to hover uncertainly. "The Suburb" is conditioned with photographs and mirrors, and with a specifically verbal repetition as well: "No time, no time . . . carefully, carefully . . . 'please, please!' " There is a vulnerability which is imaged both in the doubtful voice and in the complementary visions of thresholds and horizons, but it is a vulnerability which tends to form itself into apology rather than fear. The title poem develops a fugal uncertainty from a nice conjunction of landscape, horizon, and sky; and categories—always, usually, sometimes, less, and more—suggest the possibilities of now and enough. The poems move between America and England, and from the metaphysical ("The spirit is too blunt an instrument/to have made this baby") to the urgent ("Come with me. Look. The city."). And the poems are balanced between the imperatives of discovery and invention, as "the images flow and reverse" or "as an eye holds rock . . . in precise inversion." In a sense, for Stevenson seeing takes priority over saying, and mirroring over making. In "Utah" there is "lightning, but no rain"—printed as "lighting" in the original edition, and corrected later—in a wasteland scene which ignores the thunder, and what the thunder says.

During the period in which the poems in *Reversals* were being written, Stevenson was also writing a critical commentary on the poetry of Elizabeth Bishop, at the suggestion of Donald Hall. It was published in 1966 by Twayne in their United States Authors series. There is something of Bishop's casual immediacy in Stevenson's verse, and she shares Bishop's idiosyncratic commitment to the necessary indeterminancy of an act of poetic "translation," a sense that the poet's messages are always incomplete, and that bringing together what remains to be said and what remains when silence falls is the obligation of the reader that cooperates in the poetic process. On the whole, Stevenson's book on Bishop is best taken on its own terms, as an analytical introduction to the work of a poet whose instinctive awareness transcends any particular poetical fashion. But Elizabeth Bishop remains an important presence for Anne Stevenson.

Between 1970 and 1973, Stevenson had written *Correspondences: A Family History in Letters,* which was published by Wesleyan University Press in the United States and by Oxford University Press in England in 1974. It is a family history, with the imaginative facts of the poet's heritage transformed into a chronicle of Puritan consciousness and of the self-consciousness of women living in times of spiritual and material obsession, times in which the clarities of industry and thrift took precedence over the mysteries of grace and mercy. It consists of a series of poems, each taking the form and fiction of a letter, connected by newspaper clippings and journal entries which belong within the fiction, and spanning the period from the 1820s to the 1960s. For Stevenson, the poem is an act of witness, a confession of her history and her beliefs. There is fear in it, a Coleridgean fear:

> What am I to think, father?
> What is Our Heavenly Father if
> such dreams are of his making?

And there is a grim humor, the product of a view in which God and Mammon are still negotiating: praise God and keep your powder dry; Yankee common sense and idealism. There is a kind of key to the poem: Kay Boyd is Anne Stevenson; her mother is Ruth Arbeiter, the worker and the stranger in Judah, sick for home amid the alien corn . . . though that role is very much the daughter's too, as she moves from asylum to exile. And Professor Arbeiter, Ruth's husband and Kay's father, is a complex presence. But this scheme by no means exhausts the poem's startling effects and compelling power; as in a letter written by the recently divorced daughter to her mother from the Good Samaritan Hospital in New York, describing how she wandered

> like a schoolgirl from
> museum to museum . . .
> . . . .
> At the end, in the end
> to the Cloisters.
> You took me there often as a child,
> you remember? Your small puzzled
> prudish fat daughter!
>
> But weirdly, mother, weirdly,
> this time it was just as before.
> Just as hallowed and hushed and mysterious.
> Just as drenched in its greyness and gentleness.
> As if I'd been waiting there somewhere . . .
> some part of me waiting in childhood,
> expecting myself to come back.

Travelling Behind Glass appeared in 1974 simultaneously with *Correspondences.* Together the two books marked her first publications in England, by Oxford University Press, which has published all of her subsequent major books. *Travelling Behind Glass* consists of poems written between 1963 and 1973, with selections from her two previous volumes, and a dozen new poems. The title poem, which is the most ambitious and the most successful, begins in a meditative mode, with a denial of metaphor ("Caves are not mouths./Stones are not breasts") and ends with an affirmation, which is also a confession ("But I have forgotten what/home it was I came for./My body's a cave and my/two breasts are stones"). The energy of the poem derives from a sense of isolation, what Walter Pater once called "experience [which] is ringed round for each one of us by that thick wall of personality through which no real voice has ever pierced on its way to us, or from us to that which we can only conjecture to be without," a kind of solipsism which leads to a "strange, perpetual weaving and unweaving of ourselves." In Stevenson's poem, it is the glass which dreams of a volcanic disintegration into space, while the traveler drives

> alone and alive
> on the oily circumference,
> peering at the twittering abyss,

l'abîme des oiseaux,
until the glass shatters (loud iridescence)
into its stars, and the stars
scatter, flashing like kingfishers,
into the emptiness.

This passage might be read as merely a clever ambivalence—"Am I swallowing the road or/am I what the road swallows?" asks Stevenson's traveler—except that the poem is about women, and the experience they share, or can never share. It comes as close as any contemporary poem to providing an image of a search for a way of making contact without losing control—or of losing control by making contact.

This period was both personally troubled and imaginatively productive for Stevenson. She left her husband for a time, and extended her acquaintance among other poets, of different generations. The most important among these were Philip Hobs-

baum, who was a significant presence in her life during the writing of *Correspondences;* and Andrew Motion, who suggested the title for her next book, *Enough of Green,* and has continued to share with her a sense of the possibilities of contemporary poetry.

The next few years were not only times of wider association but also of considerably greater independence. Stevenson was Compton Fellow of Creative Writing at Dundee University from 1973 to 1975, and while there she wrote most of the poems which appeared in *Enough of Green,* published in 1977 by Oxford University Press. It is a complicated collection of poems, but one in which she achieves her own voice more distinctively and more consistently than in her previous books. Some of its elements develop a relentless authority, especially those repeated phrases, with effects from the magical (" 'You, you,' he murmurs, dark purple in his voice") to the melancholy ("I know the price and

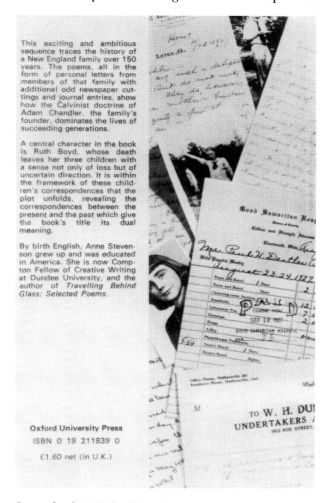

Covers for the British edition of Stevenson's 1974 series of epistolary poems, which trace the history of a New England family from the 1820s to the 1960s

Anne Stevenson grew up in America, lives in England, and is spiritually at home in Scotland. What the *Times Literary Supplement* cited as a 'fresh authentic brand of realistic observation' in her earlier poetry has deepened and hardened in this new collection. The dramatic style of her epistolary poem, *Correspondences*, is still in evidence, but the realism has become more abstract as the poems have become more intense, or more compassionately ironic.

Many of the poems in *Enough of Green* were written while Miss Stevenson was Fellow in Writing at Dundee University (1973-75), living in a cottage on the Tay estuary. Their setting is Scottish; their language is the American English of a writer who has made a strength of an outsider's distinct vision. Scotland in these poems is not so much a particular country as a human landscape in which the poet, painfully yet robustly, is determined to survive.

Anne Stevenson is presently the Arts Council Fellow in Writing at Bulmershe College, Reading. She is the author of two American collections as well as of *Travelling Behind Glass* and *Correspondences* (O.U.P. 1974), books which have established her reputation in this country as 'a poet with an impressive capacity to reflect intelligently on what she sees'.

Cover photograph: Camera Press

OXFORD UNIVERSITY PRESS

£2.25 net in UK   ISBN 0 19 211874 9

Covers for Stevenson's 1977 collection. The title, which also appears in the book as the first line of "Colours," was suggested by Andrew Motion.

still I pay it, pay it"). There are repeated sound patterns, both simple ("I want to break it into panes/ like new ice on a pond; then pay it/pain by pain to your account") and more complex:

> Nothing they put on
> will equal these lines of cold branches,
> the willows in bunches,
> birches like lightning,
> transparent in brown spinneys, beeches.

In poems such as "Ruin" these elements are finely combined, as in the final stanza:

> Beneath choke-cherry, broadfern
> bramble and mullein,
> boulders they'll build from,
> bedrooms they'll lie in.

The book is more effectively organized than her previous work, and it has a new confidence, an assured nonchalance:

> You know it by the northern look of the shore,
> by the salt-worried faces,
> by an absence of trees, an abundance of lighthouses.
> It's a serious ocean.

There is also a greater use of abstractions around which to turn the concrete and the particular, and more of a commitment to those things which, like Keats's Grecian urn, "shalt remain, in midst of other woe/Than ours, a friend to man." Behind this commitment lies a sense of ambivalence about the poet's "sheet anchors," as Coleridge used to call the few people and places and beliefs which gave him some stability, some point of reference.

Stevenson has the wanderer's uneasy doom: she is both escaping and questing, and perhaps also returned home; she is moving from some beginning, and to some end, and can never be sure which. As Kay Boyd, the poet's spectre, says of herself in *Correspondences*, "she lives a long way from Eden. The tug back/is allegiance to innocence which is not there." That of course does not get rid of the allegiance, which binds like any law.

Stevenson has become a Christian in the past few years, and this has intensified her attention to luminous particulars. The sound of Hopkins comes through in some of her recent poems; and so does a new spiritual dimension—a language of grace, a grammar of assent.

After leaving Dundee, Stevenson taught at Lady Margaret Hall, Oxford (1975-1977), and Bulmershe College, Reading (1977-1978). In 1978 she met the poet Michael Farley, and together they started The Poetry Bookshop in Hay-on-Wye on the Welsh border. The bookshop was a remarkable, but financially unsuccessful venture; but the period was productive for Stevenson, and in Hay she wrote most of the poems in *Minute by Glass Minute*, published in 1982 by Oxford University Press. It contains a sonnet sequence, *Sonnets for Five Seasons*, which was originally published in 1979 by the Five Seasons Press in Herefordshire, and a long poem, *Green Mountain, Black Mountain*, which was published in 1982 by Rowan Tree Press in Boston. *Green Mountain, Black Mountain* shuttles between meditation and confession, even as it moves from the New World, the Green Mountains of Vermont, to the Old World, the Black Mountains of Wales, and back again. It is organized as an elegy for the poet's parents, and Stevenson acknowledges her inspiration in a note at the end of the 1982 edition:

> My father, Charles Stevenson, was a pianist before he was a philosopher, and I remember him so much more clearly as a musician than as an academic that I have tried to write this poem as the *cantata* I would have written for him had I been able to write music. I have felt the sections to be arias, recitatives, chorales, following an introductory incantation; but it would be an unnecessary affectation, I think, to label them as such. . . .
>
> Section III is dedicated to my mother, Louise Destler Stevenson, to whom I owe more than I can express. A spirit of sensibility, generosity and intelligence, she was a greater human being than she was a writer, and with her death almost all of her was lost. In the final section, the chant of the thrush

imitates the various tunes of the British Song Thrush; blackbirds in Britain are lowvoiced, melancholy, exquisite.

The final lines read:

> In dread of my shadow on the Green Mountain,
> Gratitude for this April of the Black Mountain,
> As the grass fountains out of its packed roots,
> And a thrush repeats the repertoire of his threats:
>
> > I hate it, I hate it, I hate it.
> > Go away. Go away.
> > I will not, I will not, I will not.
> > Come again. Come again.
>
> Swifts twist on the syllables of the wind currents.
>
> Blackbirds are the cellos of the deep farms.

Like the blackbird, the thrush may be British, but it is also American, Whitman's hermit thrush, the caroler of death when lilacs last in the dooryard bloomed.

Minute by Glass Minute has other fine poems, among them "Swifts," in which the swifts return as "spring comes little, a little," and Hopkins and Dylan Thomas affirm their Welsh presence:

> Sure enough, bolt nocks bow to carry one sky-scyther
> Two hundred miles an hour across fullblown windfields.
>
> . . . .
>   . . . And so
> We have swifts, though in reality not parables but
> Bolts in the world's need, swift
> Swifts, not in punishment, not in ecstacy, simply
>
> Sleepers over oceans in the mill of the world's breathing.
> The grace to say they live in another firmament.
> A way to say the miracle will not occur,
> And watch the miracle.

In an account written for the *Poetry Book Society Bulletin*, Stevenson recalls writing the opening poem, "Buzzard and Alder," from a line of which the title of the book is taken, explaining that she wrote it "immediately and without revision after a singular experience. Walking by the River Wye in the sudden brightness of a November noon, I chanced to see a buzzard descend and settle into an almost leafless alder tree which stood some distance away. The slant, brilliant sunlight struck river, bird, tree and recent rain, so that their dazzle momen-

MINUTE BY GLASS MINUTE

ANNE STEVENSON

*Front cover for Stevenson's 1982 book. The title reflects
Stevenson's sense of "the fragile order and interdependence . . .
not only of human life but of all animal and plant life on earth."*

goes, 'tis like the Distance / On the look of Death—":
Buzzard, hunched in disuse before it shatters winter, wheeling after food. Alder, silently glazing us, the dead.

The verbal range of these new poems of Stevenson's is greater than in her earlier work, while she continues to explore the possibilities of iteration, of echoes and repetitions, of mirrorings and recognitions. A rather different sense of fear, even of dread, permeates some of the poems, balanced by a new instinct for the sacramental promise of scrupulous description, and a Wordsworthian confidence in the blessings of "a something given." "Between," the middle sonnet in *Sonnets for Five Seasons,* gives an indication of her achievement. Other contemporary poets—Charles Tomlinson, for instance—might share her ability to effect this kind of flowering grace and casual paradox, but the wonderful note—"of now, of now, of now"—is Stevenson's alone, as is its echoing music.

> The wet and weight of this half-born English winter
> is not the weather of those fragmentary half-true
> 　willows
> that break in the glass of the canal behind our rudder
> as water arrives in our wake—a travelling arrow
> of now, of now, of now. Leaves of the water
> furl back from our prow, and as the pinnate narrow
> seam of where we are drives through the mirror
> of where we have to be, alder and willow
> double crookedly, reverse, assume a power
> to bud out tentatively in gold and yellow, so
> it looks as if what should be end of summer—
> seeds, dead nettles, berries, naked boughs—
> is really the anxious clouding of first spring.
> . . . "Real" is what water is imagining.

tarily blinded me. The image of bird and tree, however, stood out against this blindness in a tremulous white after-image, so that for a second or two, I felt that I had been struck dead and was watching the world recede from me like a tiny spinning globe—or spider's web—of thinnest glass. The experience was too brief for speech, yet the sense of having seen into the fragile order and interdependence of things—not only of human life but of all animal and plant life on earth—remained with me like a kind of revelation." The poem itself, like many of Stevenson's, is held together both by the hesitant spell which it casts and by its equally hesitant rhymes, with their vowel and consonantal indecision. It is also held together by that "certain slant of light / Winter afternoons" that Emily Dickinson wrote about: "When it comes, the Landscape listens—/ Shadows—hold their breath—/ When it

In 1981-1982, Anne Stevenson was Northern Arts Literary Fellow at the Universities of Newcastle and Durham, and during this time her work appeared regularly in periodicals. She has done some reviewing—prose has always had an important place in her writing—and she has taken the opportunity to comment on the work of contemporary poets whom she admires, such as Peter Redgrove. Affinities between Redgrove and Stevenson are not apparent so much in their verse as in their unusual generosity of spirit. And in the insular world of British poetry, their acquaintance is natural, since Redgrove originally comes out of a Cambridge gathering that included Hobsbaum (to whom Redgrove passed on the editorship of *Delta)* and other poets who were brought together in the 1960s as The Group. The unique and anomalous character of Stevenson's poetic stature has been

Anne Stevenson (courtesy of Bernard Stone, The Turret Book Shop)

confirmed by her being represented (along with nineteen other poets) in *The Penguin Book of Contemporary British Poetry* (1982), edited by Blake Morrison and Andrew Motion.

A long and lyrical autobiographical essay by Anne Stevenson, "The Music of the House: Scenes from Childhood," published in *Poetry Review* in September 1982, provides an account of some moments in her life in a way that illuminates her sensibility now as much as her life then. For Stevenson is still inclined toward a backward glance more often even than most poets, for whom Mnemosyne must always be the privileged muse. There is a fearsomely antinomian quality about Stevenson's poetry: she will not and can not "own them now, without knowing"; but neither can nor will she accept her past. As the West Indian poet Derek Walcott has asked, "where else to row but backward?" Wordsworth would have understood. So will Anne Stevenson.

D. M. Thomas
(27 January 1935-   )

Karen Dorn

See also the article on Thomas in *DLB Yearbook: 1982.*

SELECTED BOOKS: *Penguin Modern Poets II,* by Thomas, D. M. Black, and Peter Redgrove (Harmondsworth: Penguin, 1968);
Two Voices (London: Cape Goliard, 1968; New York: Viking, 1968);
Logan Stone (London: Cape Goliard, 1971; New York: Viking, 1971);
The Shaft (Gillingham, Kent: Arx, 1973);
Love and Other Deaths: Poems (London: Elek, 1975);
The Rock (Knotting: Sceptre Press, 1975);
The Honeymoon Voyage (London: Secker & Warburg, 1978);
The Flute-Player (New York: Dutton, 1978; London: Gollancz, 1979);
The Devil and the Floral Dance (London: Robson, 1978);
Birthstone (London: Gollancz, 1980; New York: Viking, 1984);
Dreaming in Bronze (London: Secker & Warburg, 1981);
The White Hotel (London: Gollancz, 1981; New York: Viking, 1981);
News from the Front, by Thomas and Sylvia Kantaris (Todmorden: Ark, 1983);
Ararat (London: Gollancz, 1983; New York: Viking, 1983);
Selected Poems (London: Secker & Warburg, 1983; New York: Viking, 1983);
Swallow (London: Gollancz, 1984; New York: Viking, 1984).

OTHER: Introduction to *Work in Progress,* by Peter Redgrove (London: Poet & Printer, 1968);
The Granite Kingdom, Poems of Cornwall: An Anthology, edited by Thomas (Truro: Bradford Barton, 1970);
Poetry in Crosslight, edited by Thomas (London: Longman, 1975);
Anna Akhmatova, *Requiem and Poem without a Hero,* translated by Thomas (Athens: Ohio University Press, 1976; London: Elek, 1976);
John Harris, *Songs from the Earth,* edited by Thomas (Padstow: Lodenek, 1977);

D. M. Thomas (photograph © Jerry Bauer)

Akhmatova, *Way of All the Earth,* translated by Thomas (London: Secker & Warburg, 1979);
"On Literary Celebrity," *New York Times Magazine,* 13 June 1982, pp. 24-38;
Alexander Pushkin, *The Bronze Horseman and Other Poems,* translated by Thomas (London: Secker & Warburg, 1982; New York: Viking, 1982);
Yevgeny Yevtushenko, *A Dove in Santiago,* translated by Thomas (London: Secker & Warburg, 1982; New York: Atheneum, 1982).

D. M. Thomas is widely known for his novel *The White Hotel,* which quickly rose to the top of the best-seller lists after its American publication in the spring of 1981. Yet, he is also an accomplished poet. In his poetry, as well as in his novels, he has developed a style that is a powerful evocation of the imaginative life.

A native of Carnkai, near Redruth, Cornwall, Donald Michael Thomas grew up in what he considered a "distinctive landscape with a spirit," and as part of a Methodist chapel-going family with a strong interest in America. An ancestor had lived briefly in New York, and his parents, Harold Redvers and Amy Thomas, had spent ten years in California, where his father, a plasterer, had built a house. The Cornish sea coast and abandoned tin mines of Thomas's childhood have been transformed into what he calls the "inner landscape" of his writing.

When he was fourteen, Thomas went with his parents to Australia, where his recently married older sister, Lois, was living. They remained there for two years, during which time Thomas attended University High School in Melbourne.

During his two years of compulsory national service—at a time when Churchill was concerned about the shortage of Russian-speaking interrogators in the event of a third world war—Thomas underwent a course in Russian. Though he did not do well at the final examination—he was passed for low-level interrogation after further study—his knowledge of Russian developed into a consuming interest in Russian literature. He has published two highly regarded translations of the poetry of Anna Akhmatova—*Requiem and Poem without a Hero* (1976) and *Way of All the Earth* (1979)—and his translations of Alexander Pushkin's *Bronze Horseman* and Yevgeny Yevtushenko's *A Dove in Santiago* appeared in 1982. A portrait of Akhmatova, painted in the Russian realist style of the 1920s, hangs in his study in Hereford, near the Welsh border, where he now lives.

D. M. Thomas studied English at New College, Oxford, where he gained a first-class undergraduate degree in 1958 and an M.A. in 1961. He later said his favorite poets at that time were William Butler Yeats, Robert Frost, and Emily Dickinson—and it was at Oxford that he began his own career as a poet. Quite by chance on an afternoon walk he came upon the scene of an accident: the white face of a girl covered with a red coat was the compelling image that led to his first poem. Though the poem was never published, he showed it to his tutor, John Bayley, who predicted that he would be a late developer. His recent career has seemed a fulfillment of that prediction, for after a decade of writing poetry he has written five novels. He still regards himself as a poet who also writes novels, and many readers have admired the com-

plex web of images that gives each novel its distinctively poetic tone and structure. Indeed, Thomas's initial experience in Oxford—the compelling image of the girl—illustrates the importance of the germinal image in his more recent work. He has said that he can "only get to grips with a novel when there is some kind of *symbol* at work.... I'm not really interested in exploring motivation. I need an image that is capable of expanding, and then individual words, enriched by association with that central image."

Thomas has been married twice and has three children. For fifteen years he taught English at Hereford College of Education and was head of the English department at the time the college was closed in 1978.

As a young writer Thomas admired the "imaginative vision" of science fiction, and *Penguin Modern Poets II* (1968) includes a selection of his early poems based on the science-fiction myths of Ray Bradbury, Arthur C. Clarke, Tom Godwin, Damon Knight, and James H. Schmitz. Thomas soon abandoned the conventions of science-fiction writing, which he thought did not allow for the "concreteness" he wanted in his poetry.

His later volumes of poems include experimental pieces built up from a phantasmagoria of details and images drawn from contemporary life. The title poem in *Two Voices* (1968) combines prose and poetry, science fiction, and scenes from travels in the American Southwest. He is interested in the interplay between dreams and waking, of inner consciousness and the outer world. The various voices and levels of diction create a kaleidoscope of images, but in the concluding poem of *Two Voices*, "Requiem for Aberfan," Thomas achieves a similar effect through a new simplicity. "Requiem for Aberfan" is a sequence of ten poems on the deaths of 116 children and twenty-eight adults that occurred when a landslide overwhelmed the school in the coal-mining village of Aberfan. Using contemporary accounts from a book by Tony Austin and a BBC television documentary, especially the reports of siblings' dreams and parents' reactions to the tragedy, Thomas juxtaposes his poems to the original prose passages to suggest the living presence of the dead.

In *Logan Stone* (1971) Thomas continued to experiment with juxtapositions of literary styles and images. The most ambitious poem in the volume, "Computer 70: Dreams and Love Poems," combines prose and verse to portray a couple's sexual life amid the shaping images of fantasy, dreams, and the television screen: Chappaquidick, the Boston strangler, the moon landing, the assassination of President Kennedy, and atrocities reported from the war in Vietnam. Even the simplest sections are heavily embellished:

> Ophelia in your party dress
> the automobile's skirts of steel,
> heavy with their drink,
> have pulled you to an unmelodious
> and evil lay.

Thomas has described his early poetry as "over-elaborate" and "too intellectual, too cerebral." The compression of viewpoints and images in "Two Voices" and "Computer 70" had no successor in his subsequent volumes of poetry, and he may be said to have found a new mode of expression in his narrative prose. During his last years at Hereford College he began work on his first novel, *Birthstone* (the second novel to be published). Drawing upon local Cornish characters and Thomas's fascination with America, the novel depicts the adventures of an American couple—mother and son—who return to Cornwall with a Welsh guide in search of their ancestry. The construction of the plot began as a game with a Welsh friend, who exchanged episodes with Thomas as a way of keeping in touch. They chose Cornwall as the setting and decided that the woman guide would be Welsh. Thomas was intrigued with the Cornish stone Men-an-Tol and suggested that they start "with someone crawling through that. And as you obviously have to have more than one person in a novel, we developed three main characters—the American couple and the woman. At that stage I didn't know the character was going to be a split personality." The characters grow older and younger as the magical stone takes its effect. The varied sexual activity was regarded by some readers as pornographic and led one reviewer, Alan Hollinghurst, to describe the novel as "immensely unlikable."

In contrast with the method of composition in which essential elements are discovered en route, Thomas's poetry began increasingly to spring from a central controlling image. An autobiographical sequence, *The Shaft* (1973), took its main image from the reopening of the Cornish tin mines by international combines. Thomas saw the shaft in the poem "as one and many, like the persona: who is variously a foreign mining engineer, myself, my father, dead miners related to me."

The next two volumes of poetry, *Love and Other Deaths* (1975) and *The Honeymoon Voyage* (1978), employ a variety of poetic forms to explore two themes that increasingly dominate Thomas's work—the theme of death and loss and the theme of sexual attraction in its erotic and destructive aspects. In *Love and Other Deaths,* "Lilith-prints" is a sexual-creation sequence in which all historical development is imagined as a stemming from the sexual activity of Lilith, Eve's apocryphal rival, and the volume includes a series of erotic poems written in response to the ancient Chinese book of divination, *I Ching.* "Sonoran Poems" explores the bond between brutality and lust through the kidnapping of a diplomat by extremists. The poems of death and loss are the most impressive: "Cecie," about the death of a beloved maiden aunt, "Rest-Home: Visiting Hour," about his dying father, "The Journey" and "Rubble," about his frail and dying mother, are all poems of steady tone and well-observed detail.

Thomas returns to these themes in *The Honeymoon Voyage* with "Diary of a Myth-Boy," based on a Brazilian tribal myth, "Ninemaidens," inspired by a Cornish stone circle, and "Weddings," after Catallus LXII. His most accomplished poem is the title poem, on the death of his mother. For readers of his earlier poetry, the detail is familiar: the Cornish coast, the seas and harsh storms, his parents' journey to California, family photographs. These details are transformed by the central image of the voyage, at once a journey to death ("We have felt lost before,/I tell your mother as the dead/Ship's engines nose through the silent/Mist . . . "), and a reliving of a honeymoon trip to America. The final stanza—the persona is the poet's dead father—is a resolution of the images of harsh climate and stormy journey:

> Trust me, I tell her, for
> The last time I returned I led
> You, little more than a child when
> We parted, to a city
> So wonderful it took away your speech . . .
> And she trusts me, while her grief spills
> Naturally with the honeymoon snow.

Readers who have followed Thomas's development as a poet—the increasingly controlled poetic form and simpler evocative images—see in his work as a translator of Anna Akhmatova the galvanizing experience for his own writing. *Requiem and Poem without a Hero* (1976) was published while he was still teaching at Hereford College. By that time the future of the college was in jeopardy because of a series of political decisions that had led first to the expansion and then the closing of the institution. Thomas was embittered by the waste and futility—the new library stands empty and the residence halls have been converted into a school for the blind. Following the closing Thomas returned to Oxford to do research in the problems of verse translation. His second translation of Anna Akhmatova's poetry, *Way of All the Earth,* was published in 1979. In his introduction he draws attention to her fidelity to "the clear, familiar, material world," and he sees in his earlier translation "*Requiem*" her response to the Stalinist terror, not a relentless piling-on of detail, as in Solzhenitsyn's *Gulag Archipelago,* but rather an intensity of understatement: the life of one woman standing in the endless queue outside a Leningrad prison." According to Thomas, Akhmatova "achieves universality, through an exquisiteness of style that is at the same time anonymous and transparent. . . ."

Anna Akhmatova's life and poetry have become the inspiration for Thomas's own work. The image of her alone in her bare room in Leningrad is the model for the character Elena in *The Flute-Player* (1978), whom Hollinghurst called "an angelic whore of artistic inspiration, a symbol of the unexpressible instinct towards art." From her bare room she keeps alive a generation of persecuted artists in the midst of a chaotic totalitarian city. Thomas has described the novel as a "microcosm of the twentieth century but also in another way of all centuries—writers throughout the centuries and indeed women throughout time." *The Flute-Player,* written virtually in one draft, was conceived in response to a fantasy competition conducted by Gollancz Press. Thomas won the Gollancz Prize in 1978, though he considers the novel not an escape from reality, as in science fiction, but an escape into reality (the fantasy label was not included on the American edition). That same year Thomas was given the Cholmondeley Award for Poetry. In 1980 *Birthstone,* the first novel he wrote, was published and he was awarded an Arts Council Award for Literature. He was still relatively unknown until the publication in 1981 of *The White Hotel,* an immensely moving and powerful novel that, in Margaret Drabble's words, completely changed the habit of novel writing.

The critical reception of *The White Hotel* was extraordinary. First published by Gollancz in England in January 1981, the novel received cautious and contradictory reviews. (The *Spectator* announced the appearance of a major author while the *New Statesman* decried the book as a muddle of pornography and violence.) Later, in March 1981, Viking Press brought out the American edition, and in reaction to the tremendous American response, Penguin published a paperback edition in England

that went straight to the top of the best-seller lists, won the Cheltenham Prize, and narrowly missed the McConnell Booker Prize for Fiction in 1981. On the strength of the book's critical reception, Thomas was invited as a visiting lecturer to American University in Washington, D.C., early in 1982. After little more than a week he resigned and returned to England to escape from what he has described as the confining image of the "successor author." He returned briefly in the spring for a promotion tour.

The story of *The White Hotel* is revealed through a variety of literary forms: letters of correspondence, poetry, analytical prose, and prose narrative. The themes of love and death in Thomas's earlier poetry reappear in the story of Lisa Erdman, a Viennese soprano who undergoes psychoanalysis with Sigmund Freud as a treatment for hysteria. There are six sections of the novel, prefaced by an imaginary correspondence between Freud and his colleagues about an erotic poem written by a female patient, Lisa, whose case history Freud plans to write. The first section, the poem itself, which describes the sexual fantasies of the patient during a stay at the white hotel, is followed by a prose-narrative account of the same fantasy. Then in what is regarded as the strongest section of the novel, an imaginative reconstruction of a case history based on Freud's own studies of Fräulein Anna O. and "Dora," Thomas's character Freud analyzes the autoerotic paradise of the poem. In the fourth section Lisa has recovered and resumed her career, remarrying and moving to Kiev with her Russian husband, also a singer, whose first wife Lisa had understudied. After her husband's disappearance in the Stalinist purges, Lisa and her stepson are murdered in Babi Yar, in a brutal parody of her earlier symptoms of hysteria. In the final section, a dream coda, Lisa is reunited with her friends and family in the new paradise of Palestine. Thomas was interested by the suggestion of one reviewer that *The White Hotel* was a paradigm of Thomas's own career as a poet, and Thomas recalled that he was "aware that in some ways the changes of style were some kind of mental development—the very primitive thing with the poetry, then the expansion of it in the prose, analytical, and so on. Becoming more and more realistic, until the last episode which then drifts away into a kind of mysticism."

Thomas's imaginative treatment of contemporary issues—female sexuality, psychoanalysis, and the Holocaust—led to the enthusiastic reception of the novel in America. Readers have been fascinated by the construction of the book, which

Dust jacket for Thomas's 1983 selection of poems written over a span of twenty years. In his preface he explains that "all my poems take issue with love and death."

began, according to Thomas, with a poem about Freud and Jung, "Vienna. Zürich. Constance," written five years earlier (and included in *The Honeymoon Voyage*). In the poem a young man and woman, aspects of Freud and Jung, travel on different trains for a rendezvous, though they never actually meet. Thomas then wrote "The Woman to Sigmund Freud," which he incorporated in the poem of *The White Hotel*, but not until he read Anatoli Kuznetsov's *Babi Yar* did he realize that the poems were the beginning of a novel that would end in Babi Yar. The psychological element of the story came from Thomas's observation that Freud's Jewish patients had symptoms that Freud traced to their childhood experience, "whereas in fact it could just as easily have been an awareness of the terror that was approaching. . . . That seemed to be a very exciting idea to work on. . . ."

The White Hotel has led in turn to new poems. Thomas's latest volume, *Dreaming in Bronze* (1981), includes "Peter Kürten to the Witnesses," based on the German murderer who appears as a character

in the novel; "The Wolf-Man," one of Freud's most famous case histories; and a sequence of letters in verse, imagined to have been exchanged between Freud and three colleagues, in which their inner compulsions leading to the suicide of one colleague are given definition through the imagery of wild animals. "Two Women, Made by the Selfsame Hand" is a narrative poem about a couple tempted by two different figurines in a craftshop—an erotic nymph and a madonna and child. The nature of their relationship, according to Thomas, is reflected in their different tastes.

Thomas's *Selected Poems* was published early in 1983 soon after his fourth novel, *Ararat,* and was followed by his fifth novel, *Swallow,* in 1984. The narrator of *Ararat* is a Soviet poet who entertains a casual mistress with a tale on the theme of Mount Ararat. The image of the sacred mountain on the border between the East and the West embodies Thomas's interest in the divisions within the outer world and the life of the imagination. In a 1982 BBC radio talk, Thomas recalled Boris Pasternak's remark in *Dr. Zhivago* that the artist is always meditating on death and thus always creating new life. Thomas's sonnet "Still Life," in *Dreaming in Bronze*, reproduces this movement from death toward creation.

Interviews:

David Wingrove, "Different Voices," *London Magazine*, new series 21 (February 1982): 27-43;

Jean Ross, Interview with Thomas, *Contemporary Authors* (forthcoming).

References:

A. Alvarez, Review of *The White Hotel*, *New York Review of Books*, 28 (19 November 1981): 16;

Tim Dooley, "The suffering objects of desire," *Times Literary Supplement*, 22 January 1982, p. 90;

Anne Duchêne, Review of *The White Hotel*, *Times Literary Supplement*, 16 January 1981, p. 50;

Paul Gray, "Beyond Pleasure and Pain," *Time*, 117 (16 March 1981): 88;

Alan Hollinghurst [On the poems and novels of the author of *The White Hotel*], *London Review of Books* (3 December 1981): 14;

Peter Prescott, "The Selling of a Novel," *Newsweek*, 99 (15 March 1982): 70;

John Updike, Review of *The Flute-Player*, *New York Review of Books*, 28 (14 December 1981): 203.

Anthony Thwaite
(23 June 1930-)

Christopher Levenson
Carleton University

BOOKS: [Poems] Fantasy Poets, no. 17 (Oxford: Fantasy Press, 1953);

Poems (Tokyo: Privately printed, 1957);

Home Truths (Hessle, Yorkshire: Marvell Press, 1957);

Essays on Contemporary English Poetry: Hopkins to the Present Day (Tokyo: Kenkyusha, 1957); revised as *Contemporary English Poetry: An Introduction* (London: Heinemann, 1959; Chester Springs, Pa.: Dufour, 1961);

The Owl in the Tree (London & New York: Oxford University Press, 1963);

The Stones of Emptiness: Poems 1963-1966 (London: Oxford University Press, 1967);

Japan in Colour, by Thwaite and Roloff Beny (London: Thames & Hudson, 1967; New York: McGraw-Hill, 1967);

The Deserts of Hesperides: An Experience of Libya (London: Secker & Warburg, 1969; New York: Roy, 1969);

Penguin Modern Poets 18, by Thwaite, A. Alvarez, and Roy Fuller (Harmondsworth: Penguin, 1970);

Points (London: Turret Books, 1972);

Inscriptions: Poems 1967-72 (London & New York: Oxford University Press, 1973);

Poetry Today 1960-1973 (Harlow: Longman, 1973);

Jack (Hitchin: Cellar Press, 1973);

New Confessions (London & New York: Oxford University Press, 1974);

In Italy, by Thwaite, Beny, and Peter Porter (London: Thames & Hudson, 1974);

Beyond the Inhabited World: Roman Britain (London: Deutsch, 1976; New York: Seabury Press, 1977);

A Portion for Foxes (Oxford & New York: Oxford University Press, 1977);

Twentieth Century English Poetry (London: Heinemann, 1978; New York: Barnes & Noble, 1978);

Victorian Voices (Oxford: Oxford University Press, 1980);

Telling Tales (Avon: Gruffyground, 1983);

Poems 1953-1983 (London: Secker & Warburg, 1984);

Six Centuries of Verse (London: Thames & Hudson/ Methuen, 1984).

OTHER: *New Poems 1961*, edited by Thwaite, Hilary Corke, and William Plomer (London: Hutchinson, 1961);

The Penguin Book of Japanese Verse, edited and translated by Thwaite and Geoffrey Bownas (Harmondsworth: Penguin, 1964);

The English Poets: From Chaucer to Edward Thomas,
   edited by Thwaite and Peter Porter (London:
   Secker & Warburg, 1974).

If there is in England today an heir apparent
to the title of reigning man of letters, the mantle of
John Lehmann or Stephen Spender, his name is
probably Anthony Thwaite. While there are others
who have produced a more obviously major body of
work in poetry, or who have excelled in a number of
genres, there is none who has combined both the
scope and seriousness of Thwaite's own poetry with
his breadth of experience and authority as an editor. Uniting urbanity with wide interests and sympathies, Thwaite, in his major concerns and in the
course his life has taken over the past twenty-five
years, takes on a representative quality.

Although born in Chester, Anthony Thwaite
attaches more significance to the fact that both sides
of his family come from Yorkshire as far back as
they can be traced. This, as Thwaite says, is quite
far, for his father, Hartley Thwaite, was an amateur
genealogist, interested in local history. On his
father's side these ancestors were solidly North Riding tenant farmers; his mother, Alice Mallinson
Thwaite, was descended from coal miners and pub-
licans in the West Riding. Although the young
Anthony did live in parts of Yorkshire—including
Leeds and Sheffield—and the adult poet referred
to himself in a 1980 *London Magazine* article as a
"Norfolk-resident Yorkshireman," in fact, because
his father in his job at Lloyd's Bank was frequently
being promoted to posts in different parts of the
country, he spent "a wandering childhood."

His furthest wandering was one to which
many wartime English children were subjected:
Anthony Thwaite spent the crucial years between
the ages of ten and fourteen as an evacuee in the
United States, staying with an aunt and uncle.
Attending public schools in Virginia and Washington, D.C., Thwaite felt held back educationally, and
after his return to England in 1944 he felt a need to
catch up. He did not take his School Certificate until
the age of seventeen and did not arrive at Christ
Church, Oxford, after his national service, until the
age of twenty-two.

For one so obviously attached in his poetry to
many aspects of the English countryside, it is interesting to hear Thwaite declare that since he has
lived in so many places both as child and adult he
does not really feel that he belongs anywhere in
England in particular—unless it be at his present
home, a converted Mill House dating back to the
sixteenth century, and situated just outside Nor-

Courtesy of Bernard Stone,
The Turret Book Shop

wich, where he has lived since 1973 and wants to
stay for the rest of his life.

Two aspects of Thwaite's life, the beginnings
of his poetry and his passion for archaeology, were
encouraged by the fact that he attended Kingswood
School, near Bath, a school that had been founded
by John Wesley in 1748 for the sons of his itinerant
preachers. Being the son of a Methodist preacher,
Thwaite's father went there free and thought so
highly of the place that he sent Anthony at his own
expense. Here at the age of seventeen Thwaite became the so-called senior secretary of the Archeo-
logical Society. In fact as late as 1951, while with the
army in Libya, Thwaite was still intending to be a
professional archaeologist. His interest in poetry
had started when he was about fourteen, "because
the English master one day read out in class an
Anglo-Saxon riddle in translation. I was taken with
this. It seemed to be an exciting way of using

words. . . . I think the riddle element, this business of solving something has always appealed to me in poetry." He began writing copious pastiches, unconsciously, of Rupert Brooke, T. S. Eliot, Dylan Thomas, and George Barker, and performing the role of Poet, "letting my hair grow, wearing filthy corduroys, and affecting a turtle-neck sweater of a type I had seen Dylan Thomas wearing in a *Picture Post* photo."

In some ways Thwaite's literary career can be seen in terms of a sequence of expansions and contractions, explorations followed by consolidation. To begin with at least he seemed to belong with that postwar diaspora of British literati who, thanks to agencies such as the British Council, have spent periods abroad, teaching English language or literature. Apart from his two years in Libya and Japan, Thwaite listed (in a 1980 article) Germany, Iraq, Yugoslavia, Greece, India, Pakistan, and the Soviet Union as countries where he has lectured, and most of his books contain a balance of both foreign and native elements. His first full-time job, after receiving his B.A. in 1955, was teaching English at Tokyo University (1955-1957), already something of a tradition for British poets (for example, William Empson, G. S. Fraser, and D. J. Enright have also taught in Japan). For Thwaite the time spent in Japan, just after his marriage on 4 August 1955 to Ann Harrop (who later, as Ann Thwaite, made a name for herself as a biographer and an author of children's books) was a period of twofold discovery, both of a new country and of a new marriage. Thwaite's attachment to both has endured: the marriage has survived into its thirtieth year—it helps, Thwaite feels, that his wife is also a writer— while the poet has made it his business to keep abreast of what was happening in Japanese literature, at least in translation, a fact reflected by his editorship, with Geoffrey Bownas, of *The Penguin Book of Japanese Verse* in 1964.

Thwaite's first full-length book of poetry, *Home Truths* (1957), is distinguished from his subsequent volumes by shorter lines and more obviously lyric stanza forms. A closer look reveals a use of mythological subject matter that has no overt personal relevance: like Pope's early pastorals they seem to be exercises in an approved manner. In common with many poems written at that time by such Oxford poets as Jonathan Price and George MacBeth, whose work appeared in the Fantasy Press pamphlets and student anthologies, these poems are characterized by an offhand knowingness that tends to the aphoristic. Even without such labels as "Explanation for Some" or "Advice on

Parting," the tone tends to be expository, generalizing, and impersonal:

> Choice governs nothing but the act's delay
> And choice of will confuses what we choose.
> The hardest acts are those whose products stay
> Constant, the hardest words those which we say
> And think we wholly mean. When we refuse
>
> The palpable truth of love's first avatar
> We give the act of choice an active lie.

The influence of William Empson—whose *Collected Poems* appeared in 1955—can also be postulated behind the facade at least of logical argument that relies on a conversational manner and the frequent use of such interjections as "perhaps," "of course," "you say," or "then," this quasi-forensic tautness being only enhanced by strict rhyme and stanza form. Allied to such *savoir faire* is the kind of bravado that one associates with the early work of Thom Gunn, then a major influence at both ancient universities. Thus in "Samson to Delilah" we read:

> You tore the pillow when you raised your head,
> Leaving a tuft of hair; stood up and said
> "Only by lust will you be comforted."

Nevertheless, Thwaite exhibits fluency in the sheer manipulation of the iambic line and the five- or six-line stanza with end rhymes. As Thwaite himself acknowledged, "I find a six line stanza in iambic pentameters terribly easy to do. . . ." Unlike his subsequent verse, almost none of these poems starts from a concretely evoked place or situation, and their characteristic openings read more like theorems: "Sharing two lives, these two believe/ What both hold is a third indeed." Nor do the poems grow more specific as one reads on, and instead of defining details, at once specific and representative, terms like "such weak trust," "meaning," "absence," and "blank sound" seem to aim at the resonance of instant mythology. This lapidary quality, combined often with an almost Augustan balance, gives Thwaite an eloquent—but illusory— command over abstraction: in at least two poems, "The Fallen City" and "Death of a Rat," it is almost impossible to tell which is the actual situation and which the metaphor. In short, both the preferred subject matter and its treatment may be termed "literary" at this stage, a charge that, to do him justice, Thwaite levels at himself (or at least at his male persona) in "The Dream" when "she" comments,

You see me as a well of memory
From which you draw the irrigating flood
To nourish elegies: you brood on me,
Narcissus in a former ecstasy.

Yet Thwaite even in this volume has a deftness of touch that goes beyond glibness and precocious wisdom. What one sees emerging toward the end of the volume, in poems such as "Three Kinds," "Home Truths" (which states a preference for the "unromantic," unheroic comforts of home), "Not so Simple" and "At the Noh," is the poet-as-himself, writing out of obviously personal situations rather than hiding behind literary archetypes, and preferring the admission of ignorance or inadequacy in the face of foreign complexity to the assumption of knowledge that characterized the earlier poems. In "The Poet at Lake Nojiri" a new kind of irony takes over, reminiscent of D. J. Enright in the way it juxtaposes, without added emphasis, the incongruities of calm landscape and hidden violence.

The culmination of this volume, both personally and poetically, comes in the two final poems, "To My Unborn Child" and "Child Crying." For Thwaite the experience of parenthood reinforced the sense of strangeness that he had found in a very different culture and underlined the "unique design" of the individual human. The final poem, especially, returns to the poet's earlier discontent with language, as he cradles the crying child:

No language blocks her way,
Oblique, loaded with tact.
Hunger and pain are real,
And in her blindness, they
Are all she sees; the fact
Is what you cannot say.

The direction of the book as a whole, then, is toward a focusing, a moving inward to particular times and places, a direction that is to be developed to its limit, at least in terms of domestic themes, in Thwaite's second book, *The Owl in the Tree*. By the time this was published in 1963, he was already something of a force in London literary circles, but in 1966 he claimed that "what I am writing myself and what I am reading as an editor can be put into different compartments and the one doesn't influence the other." Certainly any restrictively literary quality to his work is absent in *The Owl in the Tree*. Rather, the poet presents himself as the man-in-the-street, a guise already popularized by Larkin in the 1950s in pieces such as "Poetry of Departures." Such a change brought with it a greater freedom of

vocabulary, the deliberately folksy vagueness of "a sort of shelf," "rather smudgy black," and the at times self-consciously casual, even slangy tones of "throw most of the clobber away," "hoarding a load of crap," and "one told of where to get/the best crumpet," together with the trick of incorporating snatches of (usually overheard) conversation.

As with Larkin these "popular" elements coexist with stanza forms of considerable intricacy, though Thwaite rarely if ever attains the memorable cadence that at times puts Larkin in the company of William Butler Yeats or Theodore Roethke. What Thwaite does develop in this volume, what is to become a permanent facet of his art, is the ingeniously elaborate rhyme scheme in long stanzas, often ten lines or more:

On Sunday afternoons
In winter, snow in the air,
People sit thick as birds
In the station buffet-bar.
They know one another.
Some exchange a few words
But mostly they sit and stare
At the urns and the rock buns.

Even with full rhymes, the distances between first and eighth, second and seventh lines is great enough that the general effect is of orderliness rather than specifically rhyme. For as Thwaite remarked to Peter Orr, "what I have to say does on the whole fall into some kind of received form, especially the iambic pentameter, with some kind of rhyme scheme." This kind of framework, he felt, gave his verse an edge it might otherwise lack.

Virtually all the poems in *The Owl in the Tree* deal with everyday experience and are written as if they derive from specific incidents and settings; but whereas some, such as "Mr Cooper," "Public Bar," "Incident," or "County Hotel, Edinburgh," concern encounters with strangers—"Two nights in Manchester: nothing much to do,/One of them I spent partly in a pub"—others, no less detailed, could be termed domestic, involving the poet's immediate family: "Lit by the small night light you lie/And look through swollen eyes at me."

If travel broadens the mind, it does so by increasing one's sense of relativity. Perhaps because of his two years as a foreigner in Japan's very different society, Thwaite has a built-in perspective in poems such as "Public Bar" that enables him to transcend his fellow-drinkers' limited experience and in a stranger see, as they cannot, "what his credentials are." Thwaite's humane insights and his firm grasp of local detail are complementary in "Mr Cooper," where he discovers the words "Mr Cooper—dead" on a jeweler's card left in a men's urinal at a pub, as also in "Incident," where he allows himself to give in to a hard-luck story told him by an elderly, out-of work woman in a railway compartment; for if these poems carry conviction as insights into the human condition it is because they are so minutely corroborated by such details as place names and overheard conversations.

The same holds for a class of poems represented by "Sunday Afternoons" (in a station buffet bar with "Not many waiting for trains/Or waiting for anything/Except for the time to pass") or by "County Hotel, Edinburgh," with its portrait of a permanent winter resident, seventy-year-old Miss Minnes aloof in the lounge before the two-bar electric fire: these atmospheres, predominantly of desolation, lost opportunities, and resignation, are presented without comment, as vignettes. Simply to call the remainder of the poems in this volume domestic would be misleading. Several, it is true, reflect the infancy of his first two daughters, but none is a mere paean to parenthood. On the contrary, while some poems, such as "Night Thoughts" and "The Hedge," express dissatisfaction with "the routine we so despise,/the nagging sense of grudge," many details of his established, middle-class suburban life and the protective home environment seem presented primarily to emphasize the opposite, the dangers outside. At first such disruptions of domestic tranquillity are internal, like the cry heard in a nightmare and remembered all through the next day. In "Disturbances" (which employs an Audenesque trimeter line, though with a Yeatsian use of the refrain) it is a matter of momentary glimpses and intuitions:

> Only, sometimes at night
> Or running downhill for a train,
> I suddenly catch sight
> Of a world not named and plain
> And without hedges or walls:
> A jungle of noises, fears,
> No lucid intervals,
> No calm exteriors.
> *An owl calls from a tree.*

Gradually, however, as the book progresses—and in this volume, as in most subsequent volumes, there is a real sense of sequence—the dangers become more objective and external, culminating in poems about cruelty and death that are by no means contained by the term "domestic" but encompass

massacre, atomic warfare, and the violence that the poet recognizes within himself. These poems project a world that is potentially and, elsewhere, actually, far less calm than their ordered meditations suggest. Even poems that do celebrate domestic happiness, such as "A sense of property," occasioned by Thwaite's looking in on his sleeping daughter, end with a sense of the incalculability of the future: superimposed upon the present scene he "sees" his daughter at age twenty. In this case, however, the final stress falls on positive aspects, the permanence of inherited family traits and relationships as contrasted with mere acquisitions which "cloy and cling." Elsewhere, as in "Sick Child" with its premonitions of death or in "White Snow," which treats the small child's growing awareness and its interrelatedness with language, the more experienced adult can foresee, as in the final couplet of "White Snow": "The snow melted, the trees green,/Sure words for hurts not suffered yet, nor seen."

What emerges then, toward the end of what is very much a transitional volume, is an increasing awareness of the darker side of human nature: as the growing, humanizing process is confronted by the certainty of future pain, and the security of church and "ritual piety" by disillusion and hard reality, so too the security of home is confronted by the threat of total annihilation. "In the Shadow" counterpoises quite explicitly the safety of the nursery with the "one fiercer enemy/[who] lurks among blind alternatives/In conference rooms or in the sky:/Passion and skill to end even history. . . ."

That word "history" is crucial for Thwaite. No poet of talent can for long evade his true distinctiveness, and part of Thwaite's, as the reader begins to discover in this volume, is his curiosity about, and concern for, the past and his own connections with it. As he remarks in the first poem, "Things," "What I really want is things/To tell me what I have been." At about the same time, Thwaite was commenting in an interview, "I write poems to preserve things . . . things that have happened to me and made me think about them." The recurring element here is the personal relevance. The obvious relationship to his archaeological interests he made quite explicit in the Summer 1977 issue of the *Poetry Book Society Bulletin:* "I have a notion that for me the making of poems is both a commemoration (a moment captured) and an excavation (the archeologist manqué side of me digging into something buried and bringing it to light)." Probably the most significant formulation came in a conversation with the present writer: "a sense of inheritance has been my theme." The concept of inheritance is vital because it presupposes the value of the past not simply as a repository of documents or artifacts but as an extension of ourselves, a mirror in which we can see more clearly aspects of our present selves. Such a view has increasingly led Thwaite to identify himself with particular figures in the past.

Thus, although some of the later poems in *The Owl in the Tree*, such as "At Enoshima" and "The Barrow," reveal Thwaite's archaeological interests, while others such as "House for Sale" express his curiosity about other lives, *The Stones of Emptiness*, which appeared in 1967 and contains poems written from 1963 to 1966, is still quite startling in the thoroughness with which it turns away from domestic themes. Clearly a decisive factor was Thwaite's own turning away from London to go to Benghazi, where he was an assistant professor of English literature at the University of Libya in 1965-1967.

The book makes a fine—and very English— start with "Leavings," whose virtuoso manipulation of consonants echoes the intensely tactile details of detritus, raw material for future archaeologists:

>   Trash, husk, and rust,
> Grass sickled, scythed, and mown, hedge-clippings,
>   leaves,
> . . . .
> Humus of twigs and insects, skeletons
> Of petals.

Similar qualities are found also in such poems as "At Pagham Harbour" and "At Dunwich," both concerned with drowned coastal settlements and permeated by a sense of the sea reclaiming its own. The increasing attention to "humble" details such as "the birds' frail tracks/The scribbled spoors of crabs, and scattered rocks" is matched by a refusal to elevate his subject matter through imagery: "You can see, at low tide,/A mound of masonry/Chewed like a damp bun." Thwaite is at his best in poems such as "The Pond" that successfully evoke the gross superfluity of nature as children fish weeds and minnows from a pond, only to have them die:

> The nostrils snuff its rank bouquet—how warm,
> How lavish, foul and indiscriminate, fat
> With insolent appetite and thirst, so that
> The stomach almost heaves to see it swarm.

What strikes one here, apart from the lushness itself, is the way the poem verges on epigram. Pointed up by the *abba* rhymed quatrains, this quali-

ty is especially apparent in the too-pat concluding stanza:

>   while the children bend
> To spoon the corpses out, matter-of-fact,
> Absorbed: as if creation's prodigal act
> Shrank to this empty jam-jar in the end.

This dexterity is nothing new for Thwaite, whose metrical elegance lends itself to epigram. Indeed it is possible that Thwaite's main formal tension is between writing long meditative poems and sequences and concentrating on self-contained shorter poems. As he commented to Peter Orr in 1962, "I'm not very good at extended schematic writing. . . . most of my poems really do take just one thought, one anecdote or one concept and explore that pretty briefly and, I hope, deeply." In this volume, "Lesson," one of Thwaite's most effective poems, beautifully exemplifies the epigrammatic method, a consummate blending of form and content. It is powerful because in the old beasts trained to lead the younger ones to the slaughterhouse it has chosen exactly the right structural simile. At other times— "Street Scene: Benghazi" or "County Hotel, Edinburgh" (from the previous volume)— the result is a vignette, an aperçu, or, in the case of poems such as "Habit" and "Dust," poems of definition, almost in the seventeenth-century sense, "characters." With his admiration of the articulate and his skilled techniques, Thwaite can, as Roy Fuller has observed, "make a passable poem through an exercise of intellectual will," and this sort of poem occasionally appears both in *The Stones of Emptiness* and in subsequent volumes.

Most of this book is comprised of poems based on his Libyan experience "of the past, change, ruin, continuity, survival," but despite Thwaite's archaeological enthusiasms, the recurrent stress is on such negative feelings as absence, the sense of noninvolvement (as in "The Watchers" and "Ceremonies"), and the imponderable quality of a past that can be known only through artifacts. Thus the overwhelming impression is of the kind of resignation and indifference that permeates poems such as "Butterflies in the Desert":

> Thrown together like leaves but in a land
> Where no leaves fall and trees wither to scrub,
> Raised like the dust but fleshed as no dust is,
> They impale themselves like martyrs on the glass.

This impression is not diminished by devices of ironic juxtaposition of contemporary and ancient

Thus in "At Asqefar" finding a German soldier's helmet evokes parallels between the North African campaign of World War II and the Trojan War, while in "Distances" British soldiers carve their names in places mentioned by Cato, Lucan, or "Ophellas of Cyrene, Ptolemy's Prefect." The poet's attitude sometimes seems ambivalent: in "Cleaning a Coin" he writes of "a rendering down of the last/ Twenty-five centuries/To a scoured chip of bleached bronze." Yet what he refers to as "this close-focused telescope, History" can be dismissed in "Ali ben Shufti" as a fraud suitable only for foreigners. This well-managed dramatic monologue allows Thwaite to make fun of his own activities through the voice of the Libyan dealer for whom the past "means nothing to me but this:/A time when things were made to keep me alive" and "for fifty piastres I give you a past to belong to."

Theoretically more positive is Thwaite's first attempt at a poem sequence, "The Letters of Synesius," twelve verse letters from the fourth-century Bishop of Ptolemais. Whether written, as claimed by Peter Porter, "in a finely controlled free verse" or a freer than usual blank verse, this extended use of the persona unites the sensibilities of the ancient and modern worlds:

> The ephebes have trouble
> In mastering the Christian calendar,
> The Latin alphabet. Teach us, they cry,
> And go on strike. For the Franks, the wine is cheap
> But when you walk on the beach at the city's edge
> The smashed Heineken bottles shine like grass:
> Expensive mosaic. . . .

Thwaite's brief preface says that Synesius was Greek by ancestry, Roman by citizenship, but considered himself Libyan, and it seems that the issue of intercultural relations is central to the poem. Yet, the persona, despite the surprise effects of deliberate anachronisms such as oil drums and Landrovers, does not generate enough excitement to carry the poem, which lapses at times into world-weary commentary. Contributing to these lapses is the increasing use of scholarly or technical terms such as "ephebes," "ghaffirs," "hispid," and "syllabary" in this sequence, or "finials," "cruck," "scrim," and "usufruct" in *Inscriptions* (1973). One wonders whether Philip Larkin's churchgoing persona, who wonders about the "pyx" and "rood loft" as though they were alien things, would feel at home with Thwaite's vocabulary, which, although it embraces at one end the language of the contemporary gutter, at the other takes many technical terms from

archaeology and the law, and in general manner (as much a matter of syntax and sentence structure as of vocabulary) is often erudite and exacting in areas that are hardly common knowledge.

It is difficult not to feel about *The Stones of Emptiness*, highly praised though it was, a sense of restlessness and dissatisfaction, as if the poet could not decide what posture, what kind of language, and even what kind of verse form he ultimately wanted to adopt. "Personal Effects," about the poet's inability to travel light, gracefully admits the literal predicament:

> Odd that a man with so much need of roots
> Restlessly plucks them up, weighing a ton,
> And finds that burdened travel somehow suits
> His nature and his situation.

One begins to wonder whether Thwaite is not also too well-equipped intellectually and in terms of background knowledge for the kind of poetic traveling we find here and in *Inscriptions*. Although the use of the persona, as in "The Letters of Synesius," was to prove of continuing importance, it seems accompanied by an increasing tendency to long lines and often an excess of picturesque details that tend to slow the syntax. Poems such as "The Watchers" with its short, involved, two-beat line become ever rarer in their use of more overtly lyric forms.

The year 1972 formed something of a watershed in Thwaite's domestic life. Shortly after he and his wife had purchased the Mill House at Tharston, what Thwaite terms the "sulphurous atmosphere" at the *New Statesman*, where he was literary editor under Richard Crossman, "burst into flames, Crossman was sacked. . . ." A new editor was chosen, and Thwaite found himself without a full-time job. The chance to live year round in the country and to work as a free-lance writer was thus thrust upon him, and taken.

Not that this change of habitat and life-style leaves any immediate trace in his writing. *Inscriptions* (1973), in any case, gathers up the poems of the five preceding years, and the volume on which he was then working, *New Confessions* (1974), could not, by reason of its setting, make much direct reference to rural Norfolk; this occurs first in *A Portion for Foxes* (1977).

One of the main features of *Inscriptions*, in fact, is the further move toward the devices of the monologue and the persona poem, whether what is impersonated is a great historical figure such as

*Front cover for Thwaite's 1974 sequence of poetry and prose
passages that grew out of his fascination with Saint Augustine
of Hippo*

expectations of the circus and the poet's own more
experienced and, in this event, justified misgivings:
where the adult sees seediness and cruelty to animals, the child "twirls and dances in her happiness."
To be sure, the book does contain some attractive
vignettes of types, such as "Bureaucrat in Retirement," or "The Collector," even if, in terms of pithi-
ness, these inevitably suffer in comparison with Auden's work in the same subgenre, together with
what one might term "footnote" poems, the contemporary equivalent of the eighteenth-century
occasional poem. Thus "Entry" is provoked by an
entry in a parish registry of a child born in the
bullrushes in 1778 of "a woman out of her mind"
and christened Moses Ozier, while "Note on the
Blue Notebook" speculates on what was contained
in the thirty or so missing pages removed from a
dead poet's notebook, and on the reasons for their
removal.

The implied reproach—of a certain connois-
seurlike attitude to aspects of life removed from the
poet's intense personal experience—is not offset by
his sheltering, in "The Antiquarian" for instance,
behind a mild self-irony that in the form of face-
tious longwindedness is reminiscent of T. S. Eliot at
his most tentative:

> To reconstruct an afternoon in an antique time
> Out of a broken dish, some oyster shells
> And an ashy discoloration of the otherwise ochreous
>   soil—
> This is an occupation for philosophers
> With more than a taste for language-problems.
> It has no value beyond itself. Not even
> The scrupulous cataloguing of shape, disposition,
>   provenance
> Will alleviate the strong smell of futility rising
> Like a cloud of midges: the site-notebook
> Is, like what it records, a disjected and maybe random
> Commentary without conclusions.

The cloud of midges, while out of keeping with the
abstract tone of the rest of the passage, does at least
provide some poetic relief.

A return after the first third of the book to
English settings results in a number of poems, such
as "The Foresters Arms," "At Dunkeswell Abbey,"
and "Reformation," that slip into an almost required stance of regret and nostalgia for the past.
"The Foresters Arms," especially, is a conventional
elegy on progress as represented by acres of concrete suburbs, focusing on the new chrome pub of
the title that pays lip service to an older England but
is "Deaf to the echo of a horn's long call/And

Saint Augustine or an anonymous humble pest such
as the Pine Processionary.

In terms of tone and atmosphere, however,
the volume explores the same kinds of aridity as its
predecessor: both the physical aridity of the Libyan
desert and the corresponding spiritual aridity of the
Saint Augustine poems, "Augustine at Carthage"
and "Retractions: Hippo," poems of resignation
and disillusion. In "Sidi Abeid" the reader encounters the same dispiriting accoutrements as before—
weeds, adders, sand, "splinters, fragments, the
wreck/Salvaged from strewn lives," while "At the
Italian Cemetery, Benghazi" the familiar picture of
defeat and neglect is ironically heightened by contrast with Mussolini's empty rhetoric of 1935.

Even without the North African connection
the tone tends to be dispirited. Thus "Circus" exposes the disparity between the poet's daughter's

sounds of men with axes felling trees." "Reformation," in its final stanza, seems to lament the destruction of a pre-Reformation unity and its division into "small meeting houses,/Reformed parishes and tabernacles,/Bethesdas and the whole wide countryside,/All split seven ways in sect and congregation." "At Dunkeswell Abbey" on the other hand ultimately seems more concerned with energy than unity, the same anarchic power that he enthusiastically invokes in "Sea":

> It's coming back, it's gathering its windy breath
> To stride back up its beaches, to knock again
> Heavily hammering at its lost sea-bed
> Now calling itself America or Europe,
> Names to be carried awhile, till they tumble back
> Into the boiling mess that started it all.

What is new or restored in *Inscriptions* is a facet that for want of a better term may be called confessional in that the poems refer to some intensely personal experience: several poems, notably "Elsewhere," "Dead Metaphors," and even perhaps "The Bonfire," establish a setting, a symbol, and then leave it, without comment. All that is clear in "Elsewhere," for instance, is that happiness, pain, and other intense emotions are from an interior world for the unidentified "you" whom the poet addresses, while "Dead Metaphors" seems to refer to a nonrelationship, something that might have been. Very different kinds of confessions, then, from those in *The Owl in the Tree*, and somehow much more personal: Thwaite's command of tactile detail is now at times subordinated to a dreamlike quality, perhaps at its most explicit in "At the Window," which seems to end with a vision of his own death.

Two of the book's most striking poems hinge on art's relationship to life. "Ode" ends with the poet's finding Pindar's ode more real than the physical remnants of the heroic life it celebrates, while "Soldiers Plundering a Village" effectively suspends until the last two lines the fact that this scene of supposedly modern warfare comes from a Flemish painting from 1632. In a kind of writing Thwaite used before to good effect in "Lesson," and was to employ again, he is content to present a situation economically and then, instead of commenting upon it, to juxtapose another situation or fact that makes its own, often sardonic or ironic, comment. Also interesting is that both poems use lines that are, or sound, shorter and certainly allow less of the polysyllabic adjectives and adverbs that sometimes impede the flow of Thwaite's more obviously ambitious writings.

New Confessions, which followed *Inscriptions* in 1974 and included two poems from the previous volume, is not in any sense a comfortable book. Thwaite's prefatory note says that this group of poems employing the persona of Saint Augustine "would also be a personal book of meditation and transmutation," and certainly the book's human interest derives from carefully brought-out parallels: "I sit here, in the garden, at his recorded and recording age." Nevertheless, because Thwaite has an experience of North Africa in common with Augustine, it is not always clear where the early Christian persona ends and the contemporary poet begins. Then too, the form of the book is unusual for Thwaite, comprising fifty passages written in a mixture of prose and poetry. While he admitted to Orr that he was shy of any "extended schematic writing," he had, as early as 1962, in a *London Magazine* interview, expressed a wish to "write long meditative poems, using immensely elaborate stanzas, and . . . even longer narrative poems using a relaxed and fluent verse. . . ." *New Confessions* certainly qualifies, although for readers who have otherwise encountered only Thwaite's discursive prose, some of the prose passages, used mostly for the more directly tactile autobiography, may surprise by their somewhat mannered virtuosity:

> Night of commemoration and celebration, a triumph, a carnival. Heaped fires smoulder and explode on the swart horizons of a winter night, and the sparks are lobbed upwards above shadowy and flaring trees. Dazzling, consumed in brilliance, fitful among the stars, driven to the perimeter of their own light, extinct.

What strikes one most, however, is the neat cadencing, more so, in fact, than in the verse sections. The book does include some technical innovations—for Thwaite at least—in the mildly alliterative four-beat line, of which Auden had popularized more emphatic versions in the 1930s, but it is not an experiment that seems to lead anywhere.

One senses that, as the *Times Literary Supplement* reviewer observed, "the first person poems in which Mr. Thwaite and Augustine appear to be seen as identical are more important than the objective portraits of Augustine alone," and that the aspects of the saint's life to which Thwaite feels most drawn are those connected with his preconversion youth. Thus the stress on dreams, the night, chastity, and lewdness produces at times lines of such striking directness as "I am stunned like an eel in a skillet with pure desire." Intermittently, too, one comes across a muscularity of language that may owe something to the recent example of Geoffrey Hill's 1968 volume, *King Log*, but *New Confessions* remains a strange amalgam, and when one encounters Eliotesque quasi pomposity in such lines as—

> That would be a mistake: to suppose
> Liberty exacts only gifts of selfishness
> Or secrecy always shrouds something disreputable
> Is to miss the will's strange armoury of chances

—it is as if Thwaite could not really decide on his true voice in this book.

The issue of voice seems to be sidestepped temporarily in the next volume, *A Portion for Foxes* (1977), a collection of mainly lyric pieces, although the book does introduce or bring into sharper focus some aspects of Thwaite's poetic character. If such straightforward humor as appears in "Essays in

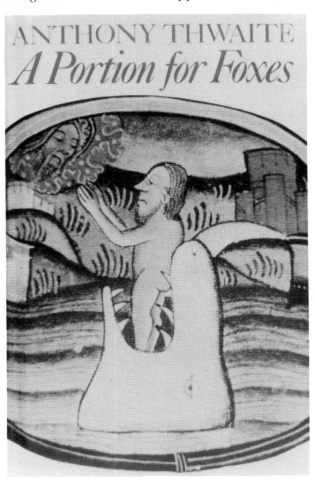

Front cover for Thwaite's 1977 collection of poems that Roy Fuller praised for their "verbal power, to which is allied a technique always sound, never merely showy"

Criticism" and "On consulting 'Contemporary Poets of the English Language' " is mild and unmemorable, and if the howlers and misquotations that enliven "A Girdle round the Earth," a poem on teaching Shakespeare to nonnative speakers in Libya and Japan, are predictably but pleasantly amusing, the irony in "Remembering a Poet" is far sharper than before in its portrayal of the artificiality of fame, of hangers-on, and of the media's interest in biographical tidbits: "She has no father, he no fame except/That once he knew her father. . . ." Throughout the book the poet seems ready to come forward more directly in his own person, not just in recognized roles, such as parent (as in *The Owl in the Tree*), but also taking stands of praise, disapproval, and confession. Thus sharply in "Heptonstall: New Cemetery" he comments on the Sylvia Plath cult:

> No, I was not a man who "knew her well,"
> As many did who kiss and mostly tell.
> . . . .
> You sent me small and formal notes which give
> A brisk air of the bright competitive.

As one of those "who stayed alive through habit and through grace," he is frankly contemptuous of "the acolytes and their lies."

The positive values that Thwaite sets against such cult adulation emerge in his poem "For Louis MacNeice," one of the poet's mentors in his early days as a BBC producer from 1957 to 1962. Although the poet now despises his earlier Boswell self "with deferential eyes/Who saw you as a lion on display," he dedicates his belated tribute (for a memorial volume to MacNeice) "To a Muse who watches, listens, is aware/Of every sell-out, every careless word,/Each compromise, each syllable that's blurred/With vanity or sloth. . . ."

A similar sharpness carries over to wider social themes, most notably in "Marriages," which remains one of Thwaite's best, most passionately felt poems. Even the last two tercets, which at first sight seem over-dramatized, are made to fit by an effective use of verses movement into an atmosphere already uncompromisingly established:

> Let no man put asunder . . . Hanging there
> On glistening hooks, husbands and wives are trussed,
> Silent, and broken, and made separate
>
> By hungers never known or understood,
> By agencies beyond the powers they had,
> By actions pumping fear into my blood.

The personal application of the last line is close to

the confessional mode, while "Spool"—which again uses the tercet, now rhymed—comes fully within that mode and repeats the first stanza as the last:

> Envy and sloth, envy and sloth:
> The two-pronged pincer and the shortened breath,
> The sour mouthful, the finished youth.

To dwell on these poems, however striking, would be to distort the shape of the book as a whole. For, although Thwaite himself, in conversation with the present writer, admits to this confessional element, he denies that it is a conscious direction in his later poetry, and because the book in general is far calmer, more relaxed, providing in fact a good cross section of Thwaite's mature styles and interests. These include exercises in the historical manner, such as "At the Indus," about history coming to a stop, or "Stereoscope: 1870." Some poems, such as "Witch Bottles" or "Digging a Saxon Cemetery," basically repeat the themes of many of the Libyan archaeological pieces. (Yet "Rescue Dig," about an ultimately unsuccessful eleventh-hour search for buried artifacts before they are to be bulldozed for some modern redevelopment, is one of the few poems that actually conveys the excitement of the dig.) Several poems, such as "Boundaries," make the inevitable contrast between past and present. Apart from these poems there are a few that revert to the first part of *The Stones of Emptiness* in their clotted tactility. "By the Sluice" shows how water "pulses like a skin, at dusk / Is shaken like dusty silk," but here as elsewhere ("Hearing Japanese Again" and the title poem) the point is the poet's awareness of the cruelty and ferocity hidden beneath apparently tranquil surfaces. Thus, when, in poems such as "The Simple Life," the poet praises a countryside where "All things are reconciled, the past is calm" and "hours and days like this, / Steady and still," the reader does well to reserve judgment. Thwaite has given a broad hint in "Simple Poem," presumably written for one of his daughters: "Don't ask me in return if I have said / All that I meant, or whether it is true."

Another new direction, much noticed by reviewers, is represented by the first two poems in the book, "The Unnameable," an exploration of the uncanny, and "The Procession," where the basic metaphor is left for the reader to decipher. A third poem, "On the Mountain," recreates an epiphany, something unusual in Thwaite's work: its image is the sudden eruption from a mountainside of a hundred swallows, that then flew off. But most interesting in some ways, for it is a poem that one could imagine several other contemporary British poets writing, but not Thwaite, is "Jack," which originally appeared by itself in pamphlet form. Spoken by someone of Thwaite's mother's generation, his mother herself or perhaps an aunt, it tells matter-of-factly of the hospitalization and subsequent death of her brother Jack. What Thwaite does here, and in doing so perhaps builds upon the albeit unconscious movement toward confessional material, is to delineate a personal past, something that eludes scholarly interest and goes directly to family feeling, as

> Round the shadowy room
> Children and grandchildren are silent too,
> Life standing like a weight we cannot move.

Victorian Voices (1980) in a way picks up where "Jack" left off, by choosing several personas with varied voices to represent facets of a period only just beyond the reach of Thwaite's family's oral history. Thwaite has stated that the only personae in which he is interested are those with whom he can identify himself. Since as a person and as a poet he strikes people as being "highly organized," because he relies on received aesthetic, domestic, and to a certain extent religious props, even though he constantly questions them, he can feel more spiritually at home in the Victorian period, can understand and identify with the spiritual troubles of writers such as George Eliot, Matthew Arnold, and Arthur Clough. *Victorian Voices* is a tour de force, a collection of fourteen monologues by Victorian figures who were prominent but mostly not in the very front rank. Some, such as Philip Henry Gosse (Edmund's father), will be familiar to devotees of Victorian literature; others will be known only to the readers of memoirs and footnotes; but together they manage to encompass several branches of literature, social reform, colonial administration, the clergy, the plastic arts, and antiquarianism, and to involve not just Great Britain herself but also Libya, Italy, and Japan over a period of some sixty years. Some of the major issues of the time emerge quite naturally from these monologues—fundamentalist adherence to biblical literalism despite Lyall and Darwin, the emancipation of women, the morality of imperialism—and yet for whatever reason the section that comes across most sharply is "Seventy Years a Beggar," adapted from Henry Mayhew's *London Labour and the London Poor* (1861-1862).

In rejecting the neo-Browning label, claiming that he has "no gift for the dramatic, for dramatizing," Thwaite has described *Victorian Voices* as "inward poems": "they are all poems about *me*." At the same time the personae certainly allow him to escape what, quoting Roy Fuller, he calls the "tyranny of the I-lyric" for which he feels revulsion. Like many of Browning's dramatic monologues, Thwaite's are written in iambic pentameter. Although at times he has made a conscious effort not to use this meter, he feels nonetheless that perhaps he "ought to stick with what comes naturally." All three aspects, the confessional, the persona, and the iambic pentameter, make *Victorian Voices* his most sustained and his most immediately accessible longer work to date.

Yet the method of these self-portraits-at-one-remove raises a crucial issue, focused perhaps by the following lines from section five, "Parables from Nature," supposedly spoken by Margaret Gatty, a prolific writer for children:

> O Observation—though restricted now
> To Ecclesfield, this room, these walls, this bed—
> How I have used you, for diviner use!
>
> In parables and emblems all things spell
> Lessons for all of us—my humble gift.
> Every true story of humanity
> Contains a moral, wrapped and neatly tied
> Like an unopened parcel for a child.
> We are all children in the eyes of God.

Is this impersonation, or pastiche? Can one practice such skillful ventriloquism without either genuine sympathy (which, on the basis of the rest of his work one must doubt) or a quite savage contempt?

Other sections do not raise this issue quite so pointedly. His Marquess of Dalhousie, Governor-General of India, successfully exposes himself and government policy in passages such as the following:

> Opium stands high—
> On each *per mensem* sale the Government
> Gains well. The punishment we meted out
> To Rani and to Bunnoo is rewarded—
> The Rani people whom Sir Colin thrashed
> Last May, destroying valley, stoup and roup,
> Have just come in with turbans in their hands
> Begging forgiveness, offering allegiance,
> Submitting to our fortress. Our success
> In sowing dissension between tribe and tribe,
> Twixt Mussulman and Sikh, Hindoo and all,
> Is clear: suspicion reigns, and union
> Is hopeless between any. Peace and plenty!

Perhaps it may be carping to say that these lines are

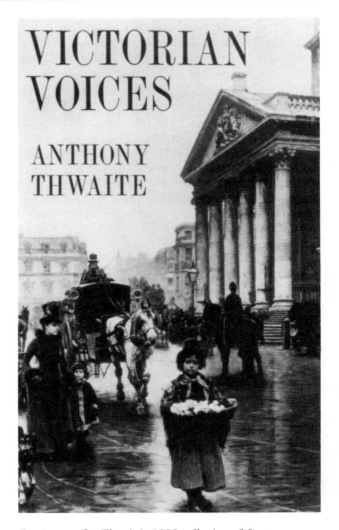

Front cover for Thwaite's 1980 collection of fourteen monologues. Despite their various historical speakers, Thwaite calls them "all poems about me."

almost too good an example, but it seems that such an administrator might have been more circumspect even in letters home. On the whole, the effort of sympathy in the end of the eighth section, "A Message from Her," spoken to George Meredith by his estranged wife, Mary Ellen (about whom Meredith's sequence *Modern Love* was written), is more impressive:

> This is how
> Art will remember us, not in the ways
> That stretched and broke us through those racking days
> But in the mode that's apt and modish now:
> Art for Art's sake . . . Forsaken, you set down
> A set of tablets permanent as stone.

(4 — cont.)

Fine feathering, ~~jaspings~~ rib-work, the antique ornate
Crossed with the sturdy native English style,
Slumped to mere jobbery, plain coarse flower-pots,
Nothings by anyone for anyone,
No individual pride, no sense of ~~the~~ the
Grandeur ~~that~~ I ~~my~~ gave a title to — "Unique
Art Pottery Works of Castle Hedingham"
("The Royal Art"; after Queen Anne's visit).
Zion bewails her pitiful estate —
"Esteemed as earthen pitchers", meaning held
As low as dirt. And yet our dirt is clay,

Grog, slurry to be fashioned into lives
As ~~variable~~ vivid as the ~~shapes~~ mind overlaid ~~shaped~~
~~out of the~~ shapes ~~that are~~
into forms for the
sunny-side.

I was a wisp, a nothing, on my own,
Commemorated with an iron crown.

Reading *Victorian Voices* one cannot deny the dexterity with which the poet moves from one personality to another, nor the sense of relative ease and familiarity that he brings to the task.

Yet certain problems remain for Thwaite, not just in this book but throughout his oeuvre. Of these the foremost concerns verse movement: if the iambic pentameter line, the staple meter of blank verse, is an obvious choice for his increasingly frequent excursions into autobiographical monologue, it is nonetheless, as anyone who has attempted it will testify, difficult to write well precisely because it is so close to ordinary spoken speech that it comes too easily. Four hundred years after Shakespeare British poets need to be more consciously concerned than Thwaite appears to be, to vary line length, tempi, and stress, and to build as much variety of verse movement into his verse

paragraphs as possible. His work has always displayed virtuosity in terms of the stanza forms and rhyme schemes that he has taken over or invented, and increasingly in later volumes he has written powerfully in shorter, not necessarily lyric lines. If, as Peter Porter finds, the continuing thread in Anthony Thwaite's poetry is "his concern for technical accuracy," perhaps what is needed now, despite his professed dislike of "minimalist" poetry, is a stripped-down, more dramatic basic medium, involving possibly a shorter line, certainly new ways of breaking up the very seductive mellifluousness, the adagio plangencies, of traditional English blank verse, so that his longer, more ambitious pieces can match the energy of such poems as "Lesson," "Marriages," or "Jack." But, if his poems are only occasionally taut enough to be truly memorable, he can never write below a certain level of competence. His interests are wide, his comments nearly always graceful, insightful, intelligent, and witty.

Charles Tomlinson
(8 January 1927-　)

Hugh Kenner
Johns Hopkins University

BOOKS: *Relations and Contraries* (Aldington, Kent: Hand & Flower Press, 1951);

The Necklace (Oxford: Fantasy Press, 1955; revised edition, London & New York: Oxford University Press, 1966);

Solo for a Glass Harmonica (San Francisco: Westerham Press, 1957);

Seeing is Believing (New York: McDowell, Obolensky, 1958; London: Oxford University Press, 1960);

Versions from Fyodor Tyutchev, 1803-1873, with an introduction by Henry Gifford (London: Oxford University Press, 1960);

A Peopled Landscape (London & New York: Oxford University Press, 1963);

Castilian Ilexes: Versions from Machado, by Tomlinson and Gifford (London & New York: Oxford University Press, 1963);

Poems: A Selection, by Tomlinson, Tony Connor, and Austin Clarke (London & New York: Oxford University Press, 1964);

American Scenes and Other Poems (London & New York: Oxford University Press, 1966);

The Poems as Initiation (Hamilton N.Y.: Colgate University Press, 1968);

The Matachines: New Mexico (Cerillos, N.M.: San Marcos Press, 1968);

To Be Engraved on the Skull of a Cormorant (London: The Unaccompanied Serpent, 1968);

Penguin Modern Poets 14, by Tomlinson, Alan Brownjohn, and Michael Hamburger (Harmondsworth: Penguin, 1969);

The Way of a World (London & New York: Oxford University Press, 1969);

American West Southwest (Cerillos, N.M.: San Marcos Press, 1969);

Words and Images (London: Covent Garden Press, 1972);

Written on Water (London: Oxford University Press, 1972);

Renga: a Chain of Poems, by Octavio Paz, Jacques Roubaud, Edoardo Sanguineti, and Tomlinson, English translations by Tomlinson (New York: Braziller, 1972; Harmondsworth: Penguin, 1979);

Ten Versions from Trilce, by Tomlinson and Gifford (Cerillos, N.M.: San Marcos Press, 1974);

The Way In and Other Poems (London, New York &

Judith Aronson

Toronto: Oxford University Press, 1974);

In Black and White (Cheadle: Carcanet, 1976);

Selected Poems 1951-74 (Oxford & New York: Oxford University Press, 1978);

The Shaft (Oxford & New York: Oxford University Press, 1978);

Airborn/Hijos del Aire, by Tomlinson and Paz (London: Anvil, 1981);

The Flood (Oxford & New York: Oxford University Press, 1981);

Some Americans: a Personal Record (Berkeley, Los Angeles & London: University of California Press, 1981);

Isaac Rosenberg of Bristol (Bristol: Historical Association, 1982);

Poetry and Metamorphosis (Cambridge: Cambridge University Press, 1983);

Sense of the Past: Three Twentieth Century British Poets (Liverpool: Liverpool University Press, 1983);

Translations (Oxford: Oxford University Press, 1983);

Notes from New York and Other Poems (Oxford: Oxford University Press, 1984).

Charles Tomlinson is the first poet to have learned a way of being distinctively English by mastering an idiom markedly international. Consequently he can write English, in England, as though it were a foreign tongue of amazing resources, at his thorough if somewhat wary command. (Flaubert had learned to write French in a similar spirit.) Stone and water are two of his archetypal images, and language, which can be like water (seductive, compenetrant, omniform), can also be like stone (obdurate, carvable, laudably *other*).

He connects "Little-Englandism" with "that suffocation which has affected so much English art ever since the death of Byron." One way to suffocate is to seal the doors and windows. For a long time, American literature was thought of, in both countries but especially in England, as English literature that by accident had been written somewhere else. Then if (like *Leaves of Grass*) it was not acceptably English, it was barbarous. But in the twentieth century international modernism, of which the language was English (*Ulysses, The Cantos*), sheltered and helped individuate three distinct national literatures, American, Irish, English, with a common dictionary but demonstrably separate traditions. England became a province, one of three. The reality of this event was longest resisted in London, being tantamount to the loss of a literary empire.

In the opening pages of *Some Americans* (1981) Tomlinson charmingly details his own liberation from a falsely defined Englishness. A boy out of the provinces (Staffordshire), he learned from accidental encounters with pages of Ezra Pound, Marianne Moore, Wallace Stevens: also Hart Crane, Janusfaced. Details that stuck in his head bespoke unfamiliar qualities: "Dividing off of parts of language"; "perceptual accuracy." And he relates such discoveries to "looking at Cezanne." In his 1951 *Relations and Contraries*—a book, chiefly of unadventurous quatrains—just one poem (he says) points to "the path into which American writing was leading me":

> Wakening with the window over fields,
> To the coin-clear harness-jingle as a float
> Clips by, and each succeeding hoof-fall, now remote,
> Breaks clean and frost-sharp on the unstopped
>   ear. . . .

(A *float* is a wagon laden with, for instance, milk cans.) Not only is "the unstopped ear" an homage to Pound's *Hugh Selwyn Mauberley*, the meter is un-Englishly syncopated. Then: "The hooves describe an arabesque in space,/A dotted line in sound that falls and rises." Sound (in the head) is intimate; sight (out beyond) detaches; to turn this acoustic perception into a visible "dotted line" is to cut it off from a whole poetic of acoustic intimacy, the likes of Keats's lines "Forlorn! The very word is like a bell/To toll me back from thee to my sole self." No, "my sole self" is not the domain of Tomlinson's poem, which ends,

> And space vibrates, enlarges with the sound;
> Though space is soundless, yet creates
> From very soundlessness a ground
> To counterstress the lilting hoof fall as it breaks.

In positing something to see but nothing the camera could see—rather, something a postcubist painter might show us—that early poem adumbrates Tomlinson's mature effects. Other poems in *Relations and Contraries* try for the "metaphysical" decor that seemed in those Eliotic times the acceptable (Donne-sanctioned) way to be "modern." That intention, though dated now, was not wasted. A "metaphysical" poem is formally detached from the continuum of just looking or just ruminating, and though Tomlinson soon lost interest in cat's-cradle wit he did not cease to prize the formal detachment. Always, a Tomlinson poem, in what he would later discover was the way of the American Objectivists, is an occasion, an undertaking: a something as much itself as a clock or a painting, even when it wears the look of responding or reporting.

In the early work, such portents of individuation are subdued by formalisms of midcentury British practice. All these Tomlinson, aided by examples from Wallace Stevens, seems to have discarded as it were overnight. One would hardly guess that *Relations and Contraries* (1951) and *The Necklace*

Dust jacket for Tomlinson's 1963 collection, which led Cyril Connolly to call him "a poet with an acute intelligence" and a "most exciting talent"

(1955) are by the same author. Such abruptness can be hard on people who expect poetry to muddle along by judicious gradualism. The publishers of *The Necklace*, judging correctly that existing taste would be baffled, commissioned a foreword from Donald Davie. Having begun, "These poems require no introduction," Davie filled a need for more introductory words than are to be found in the book he was introducing. The incident is worth recalling as a measure of the book's originality; for in *The Necklace* (from Wallace Stevens's line, "The necklace is a carving not a kiss"), we encounter a sudden utter liberation from insular taste. (Recall that in 1955 Stevens had not so much as been published in England.)

> Warm flute on the cold snow
> Lays amber in sound
> . . . .
> The sage beneath the waterfall
> Numbers the blessings of a flute;
> Water lets down
> exploding silk.
> . . . .
> Pine-scent
> In snow-clearness
> Is not more exactly counterpoised
> Than the creak of trodden snow
> Against a flute.

Yes, it is easy now to say how that remembers "Thirteen Ways of Looking at a Blackbird" (it is even called "Nine Variations on a Chinese Winter Setting"). But one significant detail owes nothing to Stevens. The lines "Pine scent/In snow-clearness" exactly quote the title of a Chinese picture Tomlinson saw at eighteen. "If I had possessed Miss Moore's scrupulousness it would have been printed in quotation marks." To treat the phrase as found object was an American maneuver. Browning's English conscience had not been satisfied till The Old Yellow Book was processed into words of his own. But Pound lifted Sigismundo Malatesta's post bag bodily. Once a poet has admitted verbatim quotation, with or without quotation marks, he has relinquished the obligation to coerce each word as though they all had to be *his* words. (Even Eliot when he quoted ironically was once thought to be plagiarizing.) And so alien is this method to the practice of Wallace Stevens that its presence in the *Necklace* poems diminishes any claim that these poems are but Stevens in pastiche. Tomlinson was learning from writers who did not necessarily learn from one another.

A lesser poet would have lingered indefinitely

with the methods of *The Necklace*. Once achieved, they afford an easy access to copiousness. But by the time *The Necklace* was in print Tomlinson was well launched into something once again new, his first major collection, *Seeing is Believing*. This was published only in 1958, moreover in America. English publishers had declined it reflexively, quite as they would have declined an electric eel.

> *The Atlantic*
> Launched into an opposing wind, hangs
>   Grappled beneath the onrush,
> And there, lifts, curling in spume,
>   Unlocks, drops from that hold
> Over and shoreward. The beach receives it,
>   A whitening line, collapsing
> Powdering-off down its broken length. . . .

Continuing the first line from the title is a device traceable to Marianne Moore's "The Fish" (another water poem); but the powerful metrical mimesis is not derived from her nor from Stevens but from—from what? At a guess, from potentialities sensed in *Beowulf*. That is one way to use academic learning.

Tomlinson read English literature at Cambridge, 1945-1948 (and French, and German; and of course he had Latin). American poets had begun to show the classroom's stamp in Pound and Eliot's generation, and the tradition persists (Charles Olson, Louis Zukofsky, Guy Davenport). It was not till postwar that a like phenomenon began to be discernible in England (Tomlinson, Donald Davie). True, Tennyson was at Cambridge, but we do not take account of what he learned there, save that Arthur Hallam was prizeworthy, and what Sam Johnson learned at Oxford was to get out of it. Davie and Tomlinson by contrast have not only learned what they do not mind us discerning but have even spent their lives teaching: Davie now at Vanderbilt, Tomlinson at Bristol.

Seeing is Believing is an amazing book. Near its center is "Farewell to Van Gogh":

> The quiet deepens. You will not persuade
>   One leaf of the accomplished, steady, darkening
> Chestnut-tower to displace itself
>   With more of violence than the air supplies
> When, gathering dusk, the pond brims evenly
>   And we must be content with stillness.
>
> Unhastening, daylight withdraws from us its shapes
>   Into their central calm. Stone by stone
> Your rhetoric is dispersed until the earth
>   Becomes once more the earth, the leaves
> A sharp partition against cooling blue.

Front cover for Tomlinson's 1969 collection, which Robert Creeley called "A highly intelligent book by a highly intelligent man"

Farewell, and for your instructive frenzy
    Gratitude. The world does not end tonight
And the fruit that we shall pick tomorrow
    Await us, weighing the unstripped bough.

Six lines, five lines, four lines, the stanzas diminish with the day. Evening shadows will lengthen at their own pace, and no urgency of Van Gogh's will hasten them. "The world does not end tonight": a valuable lesson, in the heyday of Dylan Thomas. And "Stone by stone/Your rhetoric is dispersed" is an early appearance of a central Tomlinson image, the obduracy of stone. It is an image with affinities in Pound's Canto IV:

And she went toward the window,
        the slim white stone bar
Making a double arch;
Firm even fingers held to the firm pale stone;

or, in his Canto LXXIV:

stone knowing the form that the carver imparts it
the stone knows the form
sia Cythera, sia Ixotta, sia in Santa Maria dei
   Miracoli
     where Pietro Romano has fashioned the bases.

Stone is itself: resistant: the other: that which whim cannot subdue, appropriate, transmute. A poem collected in 1963, "The Picture of J. T. in a Prospect of Stone," wishes a child "the constancy of stone" and continues,

—But stone
    is hard.
       —Say, rather
it resists
    the slow corrosives
      and the flight

Front cover for Tomlinson's 1972 collection of poems that suggest the difficulty, and challenge, of capturing visual appearances

of time
    and yet it takes
        the play, the fluency
from light.

Here "takes" means partly "subtracts" but mostly "receives," and the poem, remembering in its title Marvell's "Picture of Little T. C. in a Prospect of Flowers," remembers too how it has been three centuries since a poet could write "See with what simplicity/This nymph begins her golden days!" and not sentimentalize some Alice. Marvell ends with an oblique hint at infant mortality— "Lest Flora . . . /Nip in the blossom all our hopes and thee." Tomlinson, in a time less easily floral, has the child emerge

    from between
        the stone lips
of a sheep-stile
    that divides

    village graves
and village green

and reverts to this moment as his poem ends:

    but let her play
her innocence away
    emerging
        as she does
between
    her doom (unknown)
        her unmown green.

There "unmown" too is a word with Marvell's stamp. In this 1963 collection, *A Peopled Landscape,* Tomlinson, his apprenticeship behind him, is resuming the British side of his heritage. He commences to draw on resources unavailable to American poets, for whom single words cannot have such power to evoke exact areas of reference. Though Pound has potent single words, the occasions they remember exist not so much in an available tradi-

THE TREE
This child, shovelling away
what remains of snow—
a batter of ash and crystals—
knows nothing of the pattern
his bent back lifts
above his own reflection:
it climbs the street-lamp's stem
and cross-bar, branching
to take in all the lines
from gutter, gable, slates
and chimney-crowns to the high
pillar of a mill chimney
on a colourless damp sky:
there in its topmost air
and eyrie rears that tree
his bending sends up
from a treeless street, its roots
in the eye and in the net the shining
flagstones spread at his feet.

The violence that we do to the world about us has always been one of the themes of Charles Tomlinson's poetry. Thus, the way in now lies through a typically ruined post-war townscape. The places of this new volume – places where men have taken purchase on, humanized, or wrecked their surroundings – range from the south-west, where the poet now lives, to the industrial midlands where he was born, southwards to Provence and north to the Hebrides. Tomlinson has often been described as a philosophic poet and as a poet of perception. He is also a witness to our history, and if many of these poems are tragic in mood, several provide a humorous commentary on the passing scene.

Photograph: Ken Lambert, Camera Press London

Oxford University Press   ISBN 0 19 211842 0   £1.25 net in UK

Covers for Tomlinson's 1974 collection, a Poetry Book Society Choice

tion as in the parts of it his own fifty year's poem has already appropriated. *The Cantos* had to create a tradition for themselves. An English poet has not that responsibility.

Still, Tomlinson's tradition does not all come ready-made. In Pound's way, he lets us see him extend it. If the title and some of the diction of "The Picture of J. T." remember post-Civil-War England, the poem's lineation derives from the three-ply stanza William Carlos Williams, then still living, had invented in "The Descent":

> For what we cannot accomplish, what
> is denied to love,
>   what we have lost in the anticipation—
>   a descent follows
> endless and indestructible.

"J. T."—his own child, the poet specifies; scholars

Front cover for Tomlinson's 1978 collection of poems that demonstrate the poet's new willingness to open his writing to linguistic chance

Front cover for Tomlinson's 1981 book, in which the title poem evokes the place where much of the book was written, the poet's home beside a tributary of the Severn

must guess who the Marvell child may have been— lives in an Anglo-American century, and though her "village green" ("unmown") cannot but be English, idioms have altered. So also, since 1945, have dooms. "Her doom (unknown)" is a phrase with special torque amid our various and specific knowledges of death.

Much of *A Peopled Landscape* was written after a first visit to the United States. It sees its English matter with new eyes, for reconstituting with new techniques. One thing the title says is that much American landscape, notably in the Southwest, that draws Tomlinson, is distinctively unpeopled. So what does it mean, where there are abundant people, to locate them in their landscape? It means, for instance, the strange harmonious assault of "Walking to Bells," where immemorial English churchyard sounds (Tennyson's "mellow lin-lan-lone") are distanced by the subtle conceit of a breaking wave:

> The spray of sound
> (Its echo rides
> As bodied as metal
> Whose echoes'
> Echo it is)
> Stunned, released
> Where the house-walls
> Stand or cease
> Blows, or does not
> Into the unfilled space
> Accordingly; which
> Space whose Adam wits
> Slept on till now,
> Kindles from cold
> To hold the entire
> Undoubling wave
> Distinct in its jewelled collapse,
> And the undertone
> Sterner and broader than such facile beads
> Gainsays
> Not one from the toppling hoard its tensed back
> heaves.

Here people are walking, here are house walls, and here at no great distance is always the sea. (No place in England is far from salt water.) Poe's "Tintinnabulation of the bells bells bells" was placeless, contextless: an early American showing-off. In Tomlinson's poem a single long sentence with enjambed interruptions remembers Milton; "accordingly" remembers the chord in its own etymology; since sound does come in "waves," "undertone" can decorously recall "undertow"; and the short ("American") lines attain rest in a crowded iambic pentameter that resolves all the sound in remembering four centuries of British mastery.

That is a minor poem and a concentrative triumph. Its sonorities and internal rhymes and off-rhymes rethink the meaning of "sonority."

Tomlinson spent 1962-1963 as visiting professor at the University of New Mexico in Albuquerque, where the harsh light and the desert spaces offered his language new challenges. *American Scenes and Other Poems* (1966) is a book of places, people, reticences, encountered presences. It ranges south into Mexico, west to San Francisco, northeast to Connecticut, even to Philadelphia, setting for the consummate "Garland for Thomas Eakins," a catena of nine epigrammatic parts:

> . . . What does the man
> who sees
> trust to

> if not the eye? He trusts
> to knowledge
> to right appearances.

In none of his collections is the poet's reliance on visual material more evident: to perceive, even through language, is to *see* accurately. In its successor, *The Way of a World* (1969), along with such a tour de force of his visual method as the title poem, we find poems that depend on accurate hearing, notably of American voices; moreover, prose poems that exploit textures of diction. In a coda, "The Chances of Rhyme," he draws our attention to the mixture of fortuity and necessity that characterizes language.

> Yes. We are led, though we seem to lead
> Through a fair forest, an Arden (a rhyme
> For Eden). . . .

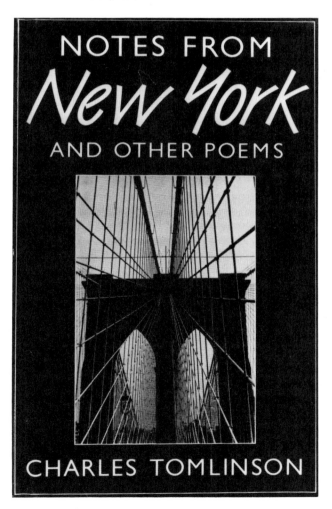

Front cover for Tomlinson's 1984 collection of poems set in New York, the West of England, Europe, and Mexico

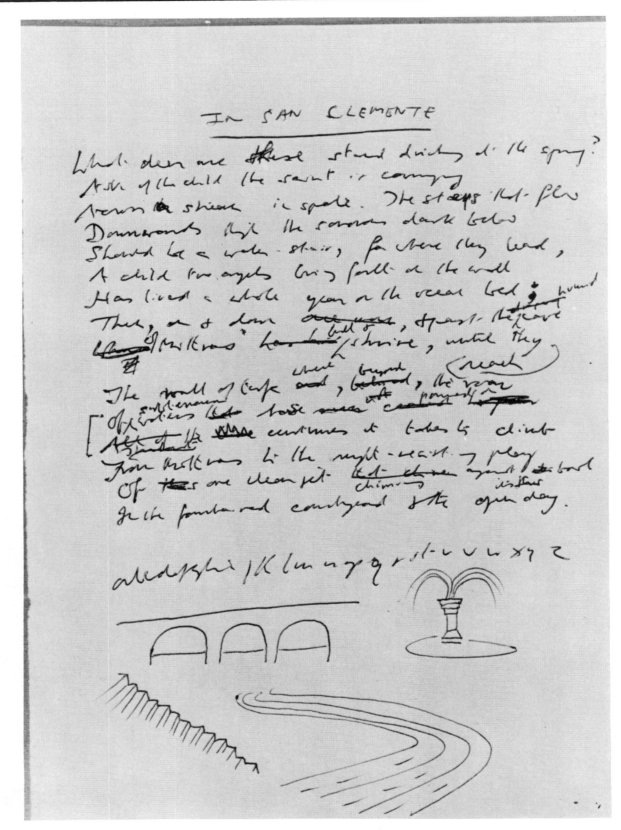

Draft for a recent poem (the author)

"We are led, though we seem to lead": in its acoustic concurrences, we can discern *our language* speaking *us*, as when, in English, "must"—necessity—rhymes with "dust"—mortality.

To appraise such phenomena is to estrange oneself from the language somewhat, in the way of international modernism. Not long after leaving Cambridge, Tomlinson rooted himself in Gloucestershire, and his American and other travels have always been conducted with the security of a man who knows where his home is. One could easily gather from his volumes enough poems of his home region to lend him a spurious but convincing identity as the poet of an adopted region, like Wordsworth in the Lake Country. But that has been only one phase of his poetic identity. In April 1969 he was exercising quite a different one; he, Octavio Paz, Jacques Roubaud, and Edoardo Sanguineti worked for five intense days in a Paris hotel on a long collective four-language poem derived from Japanese rules. It was published in 1972 as *Renga*, along with Tomlinson's English version of the whole.

Four poets, four languages, four cultures, four lives, were submerged in the formalisms of a language game somewhat related to the sonnet sequence. (The scheme called for twenty-eight poems, but the twenty-eighth is blank; Sanguineti's "silence was his sonnet.") Of his own credentials for participating, Tomlinson remarks that when he was in school British children were taught not to use "I"

in their compositions. In one sense a parable of Europe's poetic unity, *Renga* is unique and fascinating, still not assimilated by readers or (presumably) altogether by the participants. Though Tomlinson's post-*Renga* work is as carefully controlled as ever, the control opens itself in a new way to chances, accidents, gratuitous givens.

Thus in "Near York" (*The Shaft*, 1978) a fault in a windowpane "keeps rippling and releasing tense horizons" in ways a shift of the eye will rectify—"As if this place could be pried out of now,/As if we could fly in the face of all we know." And the idiom, "fly in the face," takes substance from a glimpse of wind-borne lapwings. Also the rhyme of Eden and Arden, noted in "The Chances of Rhyme" a decade previously, can now generate an idyllic poem, "In Arden," where, we are told, "No acreage of green-belt complacencies/Can keep Macadam out."

A new willingness to open the poem to linguistic chance comports with delight in the origins of the chances. Thus sidereal things are at the root of "consider"—

Consider! and you con the stars for meaning
Sublime comes climbing from beneath the threshold
Experience? you win it out of peril,
The pirate's cognate. . . .

No living English poet in the mid-1980s has such a repertoire at his command.

John Tripp

(22 July 1927-   )

Michael J. Collins
Georgetown University

SELECTED BOOKS: *Diesel to Yesterday* (Cardiff: Triskel Press, 1966);

The Loss of Ancestry (Llandybie: Christopher Davies, 1969);

The Province of Belief: Selected Poems 1965-1970 (Llandybie: Christopher Davies, 1971);

Bute Park and Other Poems (Cardiff: Second Aeon Publications, 1971);

The Inheritance File (Cardiff: Second Aeon Publications, 1973);

Collected Poems 1958-78 (Swansea: Christopher Davies, 1978);

Penguin Modern Poets 27, by Tripp, John Ormond, and Emyr Humphreys (Harmondsworth: Penguin Books, 1979);

For King and Country (Swansea: Swansea Poetry Workshop, 1980);

Passing Through (Bridgend: Poetry Wales Press, 1984).

OTHER: Letter to J. P. Ward, 9 January 1980, *Poetry Wales,* 15 (Spring 1980): 49-51.

John Tripp was born in Bargoed, a town some fifteen miles north of Cardiff in Glamorgan, Wales, to Henry Paul and Muriel Williams Tripp. His family moved to Whitchurch, in Cardiff, when he was still a boy, and he completed his schooling at the Whitchurch Senior School, Cardiff. From 1945 to 1948 he served as a sergeant in the Royal Army Pay Corps. He later attended Morley College in London, where he received a diploma in moral philosophy in 1963.

His early life in Wales has had a lasting influence on his poetry. "The major themes in my work," he once wrote, "have to do with Wales, its history and people, from the viewpoint of one who is extremely conscious of his roots. I have tried to create a small document about my country, its harsh past, its difficult present, and its chances for the future— including the preservation of the Welsh language."

When he was released from the army he settled in London and began a career as a journalist, working as a news researcher and subeditor for the BBC from 1951 to 1958, as a press officer for the Indonesian Embassy from 1958 to 1967, and as an information officer for the Central Officer of Information from 1967 to 1969. At the same time, while living in London, he was writing poetry deeply rooted in Wales, and he became a member of the London branch of a newly formed Guild of Welsh Writers. In 1966 The Triskel Press brought out his first collection of poems, *Diesel to Yesterday,* the second in its continuing series of volumes by Anglo-Welsh poets. As Roland Mathias has pointed out, the late 1960s gave evidence of a "new spirit abroad amongst Anglo-Welsh writers" for they had come to feel a new sense of poetic and political possibility for Wales. In 1969 Tripp resigned his position in London and, like a number of other Anglo-Welsh writers at the time, went home to live permanently in Wales. He settled in Whitchurch as a free-lance writer and became literary editor of the magazine *Planet* at its founding in 1970. He was awarded Welsh Arts Council Bursaries in 1969 and 1972 to support his writing.

Diesel to Yesterday is in many ways a remarkable collection. Containing only sixteen poems, it reflects, in the words of the introduction by John Stuart Williams, "an exile's keen feeling for his own land. His themes are the old ones of Wales invaded by foreign soldiers in the past and 'the English pound' today." The title poem, the best in the collection, makes clear the qualities and concerns of the volume as a whole. The rain at the border is, as Richard Poole puts it, "omnipresent in John Tripp's Wales." The speaker, arriving in rain at Newport on the southeastern edge of the country, witnesses the decay of an urban, industrial landscape. Plump English tourists passing through the unguarded border on a visit to Wales are seen as "bacilli." Knowing nothing of the history and ancient culture of the nation, unaware they have even crossed a border, they recall the crude accoutrements of the modern vacation: cheap cameras, fast food, the stinking diesel. But the place they visit is equally corrupt: as Tripp puts it in "Anglo-Welsh Testimony," "we have heard the English pound/whistling to us, and have answered."

In the last stanza of "Diesel to Yesterday," the speaker recognizes that his "disdain" grows out of his own sense of exile, of being "caught," as he once wrote, "between two cultures, and well aware of a vacuum of disinheritance." The speaker is forever outside: he cannot be a part of the world he witnesses on the road into Newport nor can he recover the old Welsh world he longs for, "the lost day before dignity went,/when all our borders were sealed."

The Wales of *Diesel to Yesterday* offers few reasons to rejoice. In a poem called "The Vale of Glamorgan," the area in which John Tripp was born, the speaker finds little consolation in the industrial prosperity that has been artificially implanted upon the ruins of the past:

In this dominion of wind and sea, once turbulent,
slowly tamed by alien steel and limp from inbreeding;
among those dunes where a Tudor king
(he who began with everything
                    and frittered it all away)
gutted the abbeys and scattered the heretics;
. . . .
there a land would seem to have quietly died,
its contours blurred on the maps, unvisited
                    in or out of season,
the pits to the north belatedly thriving,
the steel as priceless as ingots,
its wind-socked Norman keeps and crumbled ruins
sole testimony to a harrowed past.

Again, the poem offers an exile's vision: alienated from the industrial present that brings another kind of destruction and from the culture and traditions of the past that should rightfully be his, the speaker has no world of his own, no community in which to rest and draw strength. The village "on the rim of the world," which he describes in "A Parish," though "bleak, dull and deserted," seems, with its historic and traditional links to the past, preferable to the belated prosperity of Glamorgan.

> Those broken farms, the church brambled-over
> and the parson wheezing his days out
> before a decimated flock of the old
> put this place on the rim of the world.
> Another century creeps in the streets.
> . . . .
> It is all very bleak, dull and deserted.
> I hope they keep it this way.

Progress in Wales has traditionally meant industrialization and the alien commercialism that accompanies it: "I have never recovered," Tripp wrote in 1980, "from the sight, many years ago, of a rusty Coca-Cola sign creaking outside an abandoned chapel in the Rhondda."

As the poems in *Diesel to Yesterday* make clear, John Tripp's poetry is formally plain and spare, approaching the restrained, unadorned language of ordinary speech. Unlike Dylan Thomas, whose work, for good or ill, has influenced many Anglo-Welsh poets, John Tripp is suspicious of the ornate use of language in poetry. "One has tried," he once wrote, "to keep a cold eye and a warm heart on the raw material—which is often recalcitrant—to find a union of reason and emotion in pulling away from the sentimental nostalgia and discursive rhetoric of much of the poetry common to the overstating Celt. Our problem has always been one of economy."

The language of the poems is appropriate for one who speaks more immediately and directly about Wales than most of his Anglo-Welsh contemporaries and whose vision of the world is finally bleak and ironic. Looking back in 1980 to the years during which he wrote the poems in *Diesel to Yesterday,* John Tripp recalled that "some of us were so full of burning anger 15 years ago that we filled whole books with it. . . . I felt we had to warn that something terrible was going to happen, without being conscious of making literary emeralds for tomorrow. . . . In my own case it was written very fast in fulminating heat, disgust, outrage and despair, and any other foul mood you care to mention, which probably flawed the early work, but this didn't seem to matter against the larger issue of a nation going down the drain. There was only the urgency of finding a solution to our desperate predicament (which we are still in) as a forgotten, second-rate province." The poems in *Diesel to Yesterday* are the poet's attempts to warn the nation, as he does in "Soliloquy for Compatriots," that its distinct culture and heritage are being annihilated:

> We even have our own word for God
> in a language nourished on hymn and psalm
> as we clinched to our customs and habitats.
> All those decades ago
> in the chapels of the scarred zones,
> lean clergymen made it quite clear
> He had singled us out as his chosen.
> He would care for the beaten Welsh people.
> But now the strangers come to bang more nails
> in the battered coffin of Wales.
> Their sleek cars
> slam up the passes and through the green vales,
> the bramble shudders from the screaming exhausts.

As its title suggests, John Tripp's next volume, *The Loss of Ancestry* (1969), continues the themes of *Diesel to Yesterday*. The title poem, which stands at the beginning of the collection, again opens at the border, now blurred, "where once a straight line/ cut clean as a knife," and it warns that Wales may be destroyed from within as well as without:

> Cold the wind, and cold
> the looming prospect
>   as a nation cuts its roots.
>   History
> that puts a great statesman in the same
>   plane crash with a defecting bankrupt,
> that brought the Welsh an English bible
>   and forgets the names of its failures,
> has no time for whimpered excuse.
>   It neither cares nor feels
> as we let what need not happen
>   come to pass.

The poem laments the loss of the distinct culture and the defining heritage of Wales. As the border becomes blurred, a leveling materialism merges the two nations: the Welsh strive for money and status as an English world defines it. The games on the "sacred turf" at the Arms Park National Rugby Stadium are the only events through which the Welsh express a sense of national identity. Wales is becoming, by its own choices, indistinguishable from the bland, suburban world that is England.

"Family Supper" puts the speaker in touch with his personal heritage and celebrates the mundane realities that fill the lives of ordinary men and women. As the line about "the timelessness of custom" suggests, his people draw their strength from an unconscious but profound connection with their heritage and traditions:

> Grouped over ham and pickles,
> none here has heard of Pound

or Wittgenstein. With philosophy I fought
for years, but now the cutting edge
of argument is suet against their truth.
I believe in their quick kindness,
the timelessness of custom,
the simple plod of this remnant
that sees them through twenty weddings and griefs.

Tripp's third collection, *The Province of Belief: Selected Poems 1965-1970* (1971), includes fourteen of the sixteen poems in *Diesel to Yesterday* and thirty-six previously uncollected. While the familiar themes continue in the new poems, some of them, such as "Snap at Barry 1934," "On My Fortieth Birthday," and "My Courtship of Miss Roberts," bring a new, lighter, and more playful tone to Tripp's work. In the last, the speaker describes courting Miss Roberts as a "dance/the ritual steps of courtship/as it used to be done—/cock and hen in gentility's trance," and describes afternoon tea in the garden:

Miss Roberts wore pastel shifts
    and a medallion for the Barry swim.
She liked to quote Rupert Brooke
    and like Ava Gardner
had a cleft in her chin.
    We would sit very quiet until the orange sun sank
and mother brought out the tea.
    Cucumber triangles and peace
and responsibility smiling at me.

One of the most moving and effective poems in *The Province of Belief*, "End of a Farrier," like some of Tripp's other poems, describes loss and destruction justified by money and putative "progress," but it seems a deeply personal poem as well. The speaker describes the destruction of his father's forge to make way for a new highway, and remembers,

Here once the children stood for hours
wide-eyed at the hunter's kick, shod pony, Shire
and the stunning Palomino. Deep-voiced men slid
from their expensive saddles, and men in pink
share a flask before the blood hunt.

Then, seeing his father being paid for the property by "the man in the bowler and grey suit," he realizes that, like those horses, his father,

is now out to grass himself,
silently plotting to pack his gaping calendar.
We walk home together in the rain
away from forty years of his life.

The last two lines particularly make clear the terrible impact of industrialization on a single individual.

Bute Park and Other Poems (1971), a small collection of poems about Cardiff by John Tripp and photographs of the poet by Barrie Rendell, was followed in 1973 by *The Inheritance File*, a collection of portrait poems with illustrations by Martin Dutton. "These poems and prose-poems," Tripp wrote in an introductory note, "for the most part, are short elegies to several poets and novelists, written over a period and assembled as a collection at the friendly persuasion of the publisher." The book includes poems on A. E. Housman, Dylan Thomas, and F. Scott Fitzgerald to name just three, and while similar poems had appeared in his two previous volumes, their collection here reflects Tripp's increasing interest in two of the traditional forms of Welsh poetry—the elegy and the portrait poem.

Most of the poems in *Collected Poems 1958-78*, published by Christopher Davies in 1978, were written over the previous ten years and had not been collected before. Although much of his early anger has subsided, Tripp's tone and manner in the new poems remain essentially the same. The range of subject and focus, however, is wider, and while Wales is still very much at its heart, the collection seems on the whole rather less immediately political or nationalistic. "Thin Red Line," for example, recalls some of Tripp's earliest poems, but it seems finally quieter and more personal, as the poet describes a visit to a "little school on the moor," where "the teacher is making a last/stand" in the battle for the preservation of the Welsh culture:

Introductions are made: the stale visitor
chugging up the coast to analyse a page
of Auden, or to read my own guilt.
They whisper and giggle, only stay quiet
when I shout lines like a barker
at a fair . . . Then it is over, we take
weak tea and say nothing. We both know
we are outnumbered, keeping a flag flying.

While it might have been written almost anywhere in the modern, industrialized, English-speaking world, the poem unmistakably reflects the contemporary situation in Wales. Teacher, poet, and pupil have been cut off from the language and traditions that fostered in Wales a public, communal poetry. While both teacher and poet believe in its value, neither the Anglo-American Auden nor the Anglo-Welsh speaker, both of whom are themselves displaced persons, can provide the poetry

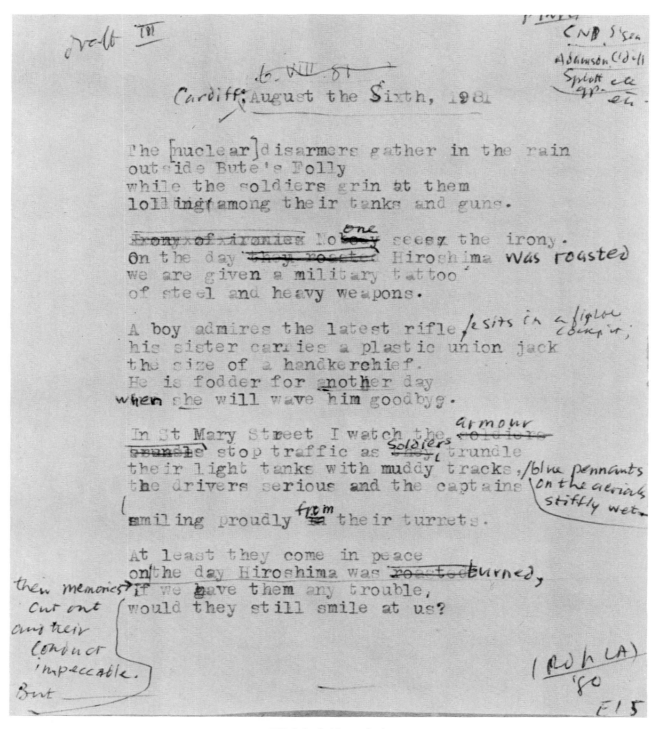

Third draft (the author)

that might play, as Welsh poetry once did, an integral role in the ordinary life of the community. The language and traditions of the past have been gradually eroded by the leveling hegemony of English money and language. Wales is now simply another bland, undistinguished corner of the Anglo-American world.

Among the best poems in the collection are

"Airfield," in which the speaker pays tribute to airmen of World War II for what Jeremy Hooker calls "their fealty to a national cause," and three remarkably unsentimental elegies for animals—"Tomcat," "Welsh Terrier," and "Badger." In the first, the speaker celebrates the tough, alien independence of a tomcat, who, surviving on the outskirts of the settled world, resisting the placid comforts of docile obedience, suggests the stance the Welsh might adopt in an effort to withstand the leveling force of Anglicization and keep their nation alive.

Collected Poems 1958-78 was well received in Wales. Richard Poole wrote a long review for the Spring 1979 issue of *Poetry Wales* in which he analyzed Tripp's achievement over twenty years. Writing in the *Anglo-Welsh Review* of the same year, Jeremy Hooker reversed his earlier judgment of Tripp and called him "one of the most arresting and moving of contemporary Anglo-Welsh poets."

Since the publication of *Collected Poems 1958-78,* Tripp has continued to write and publish his poetry in and out of Wales. In 1979 a selection of his poems (most of which had been included the year before in *Collected Poems*) appeared in *Penguin Modern Poets 27,* and in 1980 the Swansea Poetry Workshop published a short sequence called *For King and Country.* New poems have appeared consistently in, among other places, *Poetry Wales* and the *Anglo-Welsh Review,* and a new collection, *Passing Through,* was published in 1984 by Poetry Wales Press.

John Tripp has been a major figure in Anglo-Welsh poetry since the publication of *Diesel to Yesterday* in 1966. His work is highly regarded in Wales, in part for its sharp, telling particulars in a language appropriate to its subject, and in part for its passionate commitment to the nation and its people. If, as David Annwn suggested in his review of *For King and Country,* John Tripp has neither the range nor the sophisticated grasp of language to be called a major poet, he nonetheless has produced over the last twenty years a distinguished body of work that deserves to be read not only in Wales, but throughout the English-speaking world.

Reference:
Richard Poole, "The Poetry of John Tripp," *Poetry Wales,* 14 (Spring 1979): 72-82.

Gael Turnbull
(7 April 1928-)

George Johnston

SELECTED BOOKS: *Trio,* by Turnbull, Eli Mandel, and Phyllis Webb (Toronto: Contact Press, 1954);

The Knot in the Wood and Fifteen Other Poems (London: Revision Press, 1955);

Bjarni, Spike-Helgi's Son and Other Poems (Ashland, Mass.: Origin Press, 1956);

A Libation (Glasgow: The Poet, 1957);

With Hey, Ho. . . . (Ventura, Cal.: Migrant Press, 1961);

To You, I Write (Worcester, U.K.: Migrant Press, 1963);

A Very Particular Hill (Edinburgh: Wild Hawthorn Press, 1963);

Twenty Words: Twenty Days: A Sketchbook and a Morula (Birmingham: Migrant Press, 1966);

A Trampoline: Poems 1952-1964 (London: Cape Goliard, 1968; New York: Grossman, 1968);

I, Maksoud (Exeter: University of Exeter, 1969);

Scantlings: Poems 1964-69 (London: Cape Goliard, 1970; New York: Grossman, 1970);

Finger Cymbals (Edinburgh: Satis, 1971);

A Random Sapling (Newcastle upon Tyne: Pig Press, 1974);

Wulstan (Bradford: Blue Tunnel, 1975);

Witley Court Revisited (Malvern: Migrant Press, 1975);

Residues (Pennsett: Grosseteste, 1976);

Thronging the Heart (N.p.: Aggie Weston, 1976);

If a Glance Could Be Enough (Edinburgh: Satis, 1978);

Rain in Wales (Edinburgh: Satis, 1981);

A Gathering of Poems, 1950-1980 (London: Anvil, 1983);

From the Language of the Heart (Glasgow: Mariscat Press, 1983).

OTHER: Hector de Saint Denys Garneau, *Nine Poems,* includes translations by Turnbull and Jean Beaupré (Iroquois Falls, Ontario, 1955);

Gilles Hénault, *Seven Poems,* includes translations by Turnbull and Beaupré (Iroquois Falls, Ontario, 1955);

Roland Giguère, *Eight Poems,* includes translations by Turnbull and Beaupré (Toronto: Contact Press, 1955);

Paul Marie Lapointe, *Six Poems,* includes translations by Turnbull and Beaupré (Toronto: Contact Press, 1955);

"Charlotte Chapel, the Pittsburgh Draft Board and Some Americans," *Poetry Nation Review,* no. 28 (1982): 9-11.

Jonathan Williams

Gael Turnbull is a British poet of considerable and various achievement, a friend of poets and a small publisher. His poetry is experimental and adventurous in style, yet it speaks with a clear, consistently recognizable, and always poetic voice. His transatlantic connections and affinities have been important to him, both personally and in his writing, and he has had a steadily widening group of devoted readers on both sides of the Atlantic, many of them poets, who have admired the assurance and vivacity of his style, the variety of his rhythms—always kept in hand by a sensitive and decorous ear—and the compassion and seriousness that underly the normal geniality of his tone. His writing has been almost entirely poetry, except for some short theatrical pieces.

Gael Lundin Turnbull's background is Scottish. He was born in Edinburgh in 1928. His father, Ralph Gale Turnbull, is a Scot, born in Berwick-upon-Tweed, and through him Gael Turnbull is a hereditary freeman of Berwick. His mother, Anne Lundin Turnbull, was born in Minnesota of Swedish immigrant parents. From 1940 to 1944, the family lived in Winnipeg, Canada, where his father, a Presbyterian minister, had charge of a church during World War II. Gael Turnbull's upbringing may be detected in unobtrusive biblical allusions and evidences of the Shorter Catechism in his poetry.

After leaving Winnipeg, he studied natural science at Cambridge University, where he received a B.A. in 1948, and then returned to America to take a degree in medicine at the University of Pennsylvania (1951). While he was in medical school, he had three poems published in the *Pennsylvania Literary Review,* a student publication. He married an American, Jonnie Draper, on 7 June 1952, and they have three daughters and one granddaughter. They have recently separated amicably.

After completing his medical studies, Turnbull practiced medicine in Iroquois Falls, Ontario, Canada, from 1952-1955, and his first postgraduate poems were published in the Canadian magazine *Northern Review* in 1952. In 1954 a group of his poems was published in *Trio,* with the work of Canadian poets Phyllis Webb and Eli Mandel. Turnbull's style is already evident in these poems; many of them are rhymed and all show a respect for form which has stayed with him, though his metrics have generally become freer, and he has developed some fine open rhythms, of short lines and also of long cadences. He has expressed his satisfaction with many of these *Trio* poems, particularly the defter, more epigrammatic ones, though he included only one, and that greatly modified, in his first large collection, *A Trampoline* (1968).

While still in Canada, he also published translations from four French-Canadian poets, Hector de Saint Denys Garneau, Gilles Hénault, Roland Giguère, and Paul Marie Lapointe, in pamphlets in 1955. These, and later readings of French poetry of Apollinaire, René Char, and Jean Follain especially, and informal, unpublished translations, had an early and lasting influence on his style and choice of subject.

Through a Canadian poet-friend, Raymond Souster, he came in touch with Cid Corman, who was then publishing the first series of his magazine *Origin* (1951-1957). Corman has been a continuing friend, though mostly by correspondence. Having his poems published in *Origin* and *Black Mountain Review,* Turnbull came to know the work of many Black Mountain poets and many of the poets themselves, exchanged views with them, and shared their general attitude to poetry. In an article in *Poetry Nation Review* he writes of his friendship and correspondence with Robert Creeley. He was at first not attracted to Creeley's work, which he saw in *Origin,* but on Corman's advice he went back to the poem again and came to admire it: "I gradually came to 'hear' the poem in a way that I had never 'heard' before. It fascinated me even as I could not logically understand how it worked. There was also a music which I could not scan but which radiated delight. I continued to have reservations (as I still do) that, in Swift's words, 'It shall pass for wondrous deep, for no better reason than 'tis wondrous dark.' At the same time, there was a 'light' in it which cast an essential illumination beyond any grammatical logic." In the same article he gives an entry from his journal ("dated about 1953 or 1954"): "Creeley comes very close to having done what I would like to do—one is always conscious of the living man, in activity, in common-place situations—yet the result is never common-place. . . ."

William Carlos Williams was another poet whose work he valued after having at first been put off by it. International in spirit, Turnbull did not readily sympathize with Williams's intense Americanism. Having made the effort to read him again, he went further and persuaded the English poet Charles Tomlinson to have a second look at Williams's poetry (Tomlinson is another English poet, like Turnbull, to have important American friendships and affinities).

In 1956, when he had just returned to England, Origin Press published his *Bjarni, Spike-Helgi's Son and Other Poems,* a pamphlet of poems on subjects taken from the sagas. Dramatic mono-

Front wrapper for the 1963 collection of ten poems by Turnbull, illustrated by Alexander McNeish

logues in cadenced rhythms, they include one of his strongest poems, "An Irish Monk on Lindisfarne." Sympathy, a willingness to project himself imaginatively into the feelings and sufferings of others, has characterized much of Turnbull's poetry. He shares this gift with Raymond Souster. The forms of these monologues and their rhythms are Turnbull's own, but he has been aware of predecessors in Robert Browning and Ezra Pound.

In England Turnbull felt alone, for some while, with his American sympathies, but he discovered fellows in Roy Fisher, Basil Bunting, Charles Tomlinson, and others. He made some effort to circulate books by American and Canadian poets that he was enthusiastic about, and to bring this particular transatlantic world to the attention of English poets, who, in general, seemed hardly aware of its existence. The circulation of the books was carried on in a more-or-less organized way, and the venture was given a name, Migrant Books. A circular, advertising titles that Turnbull had bought from Divers Press, Origin Press, and Jargon Books, was sent to people on a small mailing list supplied by W. Price Turner, editor of the *Poet*, in Glasgow. Poets whose books were distributed by Migrant Books in England and Canada and the United States included Cid Corman, Charles Olson, Irving Layton, Robert Creeley, and William Bronk.

In 1958 the Turnbulls moved to Ventura, California, mainly because there were few jobs for doctors of his generation in England at the time. They lived there from 1958 to 1964, and acquired a new friend in Hugh Kenner, who was a neighbor. Migrant Books suspended operations, but in Ventura Turnbull began publishing the little magazine *Migrant,* the first issue of which appeared in 1959. There were eight issues in all, which appeared at two-month intervals. The magazine was distributed free, though contributions were received from readers to help pay production and mailing costs. While the magazine was international, with readers and contributors on both sides of the Atlantic, Turnbull's chief interest was now in the British end of the venture. Because he felt somewhat exiled in California, he used *Migrant* as a way of keeping in touch with poets in England and Scotland particularly. Michael Shayer in Worcester served as a contributing editor.

Turnbull and Michael Shayer also began publishing pamphlet collections, some by writers who had been attracted to the magazine. One of the better-known of these pamphlets was Ian Hamilton Finlay's *The Dancers Inherit the Party* (1960), of which a second edition had to be printed. The publication

of these pamphlets was continued after Turnbull returned to England in 1964, when Roy Fisher joined him and Michael Shayer in the venture. The value of their efforts to many American and British poets is hard to estimate. Roy Fisher has expressed his gratitude for Turnbull's stimulating and enlightening presence.

Turnbull's long poem *Twenty Words: Twenty Days: A Sketchbook and a Morula,* first published in the April-May 1965 issue of *Poetry* (Chicago), is his most ambitious poem of the 1960s. Migrant Press reprinted it as a pamphlet in 1966, and it was later included in *A Trampoline.* Though he has written poems or poem sequences employing comparable technical conditions, he has not repeated its form; yet it is characteristically his poem. Each of the poem's twenty, thirty-to-thirty-five-line stanzas is composed around twenty words, chosen at random and representing in an unspecified way twenty days. Each stanza is made up of meditations on a particular word, given in clauses or participial phrases or prepositional phrases, between which the connecting tissue is a syntax of association, sometimes merely through the key word. The meditations are personal, often autobiographical; there are brief narratives describing or merely alluding to friends' doings or the poet's problems quoted from letters and responses to them, and interjected observations on things in general. The poem seems a medley at first, but it turns out to be a labyrinth—as it is called in the fifteenth poem—through which the poet's voice, with its rhythms and seductive tones, beckons the reader, as he proceeds among its divergent ways, following the poet's clue. The comparison is approximate, for the poem does not take the reader from an entrance to an exit, nor does it bring us to a Minotaur. Here is the whole of number fifteen:

> "I'm sure I can find
> a thing of some kind,
> a good kind of thing
> to do with my string"

the forward path of the poet into the labyrinth—
                                                                                        not
a poet, be it noted, but *the* poet, that flourish—
                                                                                        but
Theseus used his to find his way back—
                                an INTELLECTUALISM—

as a prism to spread the light for its parts (but looked
through one sees only a jumble)—
                                a great fankle, sometimes,
to be unravelled—

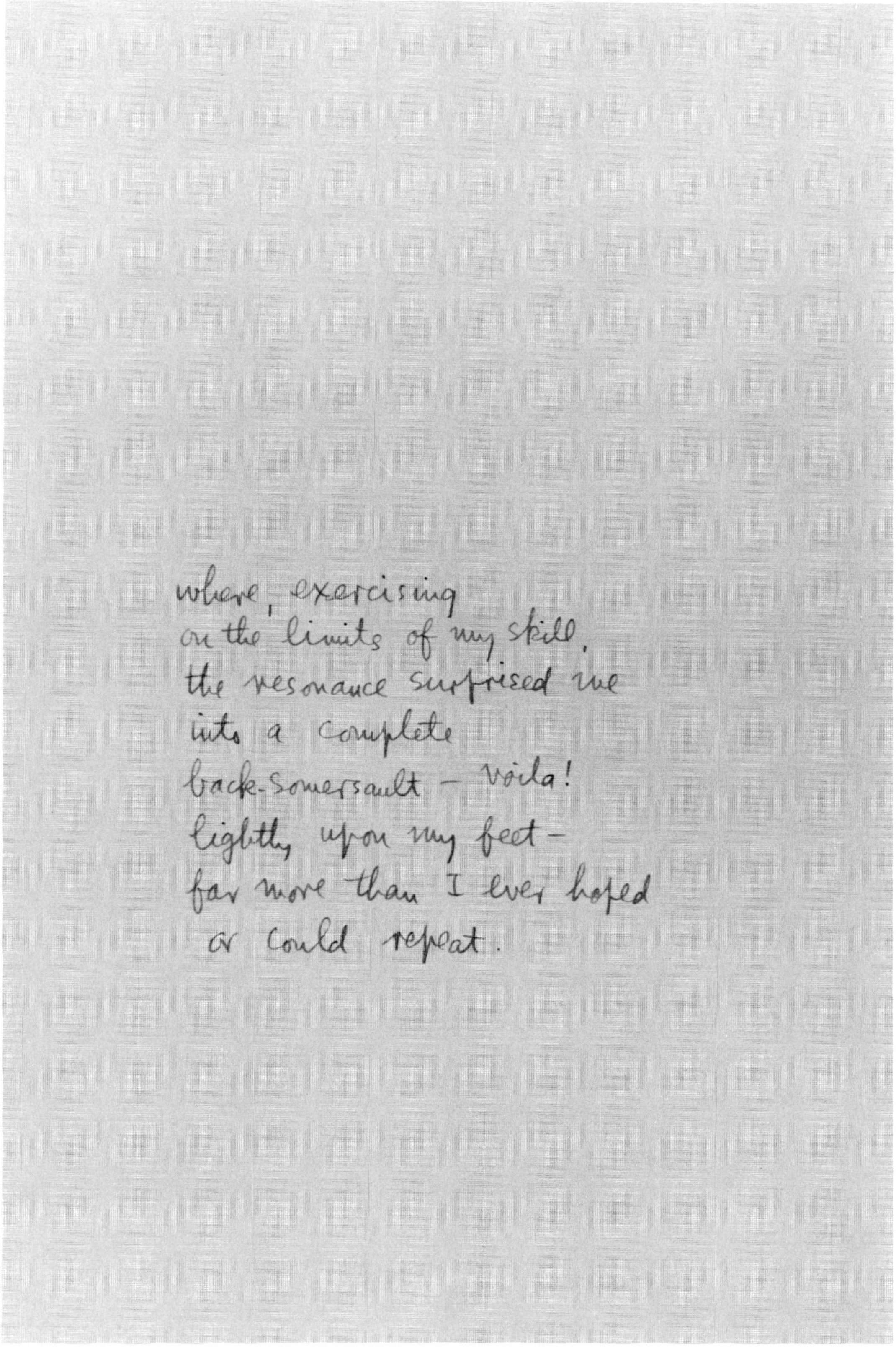

where, exercising
on the limits of my skill,
the resonance surprised me
into a complete
back-somersault — voila!
lightly upon my feet —
far more than I ever hoped
or could repeat.

Holograph poem inscribed by the author in twenty-six special copies, lettered A-Z, of A Trampoline

or a spider, hanging its web for what
might be snared, arrogant in patience, and sticky—
                                                              or a
child, collecting bits of twine, knotting them end to
end—

       (how big will it get)?

       "with a big ball of string
       I could do anything!"

This section is open-ended. The connectives that would join each succinct element into a statement are missing, and the turns of thought from one element to another are frequently abrupt. It is one of twenty questions in a poem whose continuing note is questioning, but there is nothing puzzling or obscure about the poems, though they do call for thinking out; the allusions and associations are fresh, the separate phrases and clauses are presented with clarity and seriousness; and the steady rhythms, Turnbull's own, but having the Authorized Version of the Bible in their background, are urbane and persuasive.

In Turnbull's first full-length collection, *A Trampoline: Poems 1952-1964* (1968), awarded the Alice Hunt Bartlett prize by the Poetry Society in London in 1969, conciseness is given equal prominence with open-endedness. The book includes, among other poems, "An Irish Monk on Lindisfarne," some of the poems from *Bjarni*, and *Twenty Words: Twenty Days*. Of the eight brief poems at the beginning of the book, six are taken virtually unaltered from a 1955 pamphlet, *The Knot in the Wood*. A seventh, "One Word," is a reduced version of "To the Point, for Once," which was published in *Trio*. The six lines of "One Word"—

One word and clearly
and from the heart

when I had swum my utmost
and felt my breath give out

was enough
as the water lapped my mouth.

—represent ten lines of "To the Point, for Once." The reduction is for the sake of brevity, but also for allusiveness, leaving the point of the poem to be inferred. The epigrammatic allusiveness of all eight of these poems is not as common in Turnbull's poetry as narration or drama. Even in these poems the tone is likely to be query, curiosity, caprice, or,

not infrequently, celebration. Form seems to be self-effacing in Turnbull's poetry, played down by the candor and urbanity of his tone of voice, yet the serious attention he gives it is apparent in the variety of his work, and the firmness and consistency that carries through it all and supports its ease of manner.

Caprice is represented in two sections in the book, "Diversions" and "Six Fancies." These show most clearly the influence of the French poets he had been reading. The lightheartedness and occasional whimsicality of their tone are deceptive. There is a pervasive melancholy in all the poetry, along with a cheerfully fatalistic acceptance of the puzzling vagaries of life. There is no bitterness and scarcely a hint of existential anxious brooding. An occasional touch of harsh realism, usually drawn from his experience as a doctor, is startling in its contrast with the level tone of voice in which it is told.

There are as many verse forms and rhythms as there are poems in the "Diversions" section, all but one poem of which is written in free verse. The rhythms of some are prose rhythms, but in a strung-out uncomplicated syntax that invites the reader to chant the lines. The deliberately prosaic tone of the poems in "Six Fancies" contrasts with the absurdity of their themes. The laconically simple sentences and clauses, through their brevity and repetitions, set up a rhythm that is sustained gracefully through the section.

The prose poem "A Case" is written with economy and its tone of voice is poetic, though with a mixture of concern and clinical detachment. It was distantly inspired by René Char's "Madeleine à la veilleuse"; the experience and the idiom of "A Case" are Turnbull's own, however, and the connection between the two poems is not readily apparent. "At Mareta" is also a fine poem. Its social conscience is far from typical; Turnbull is not a political poet.

Many of the poems in *Scantlings: Poems 1964-69* (1970), Turnbull's second full-length collection, are personal, in the sense that they refer to the poet's private emotions or are addressed to his friends. Composed with restraint and delicacy of feeling, the poems are masterly in form. Their language is clear and pure, and the handling of the brief lines and of the spaces between the words is skillful. There are also formally ingenious and witty poems in this collection, and some of the more personal poems are scattered among them.

Turnbull is fond of setting up a technical condition to be fulfilled, as in *Twenty Words: Twenty*

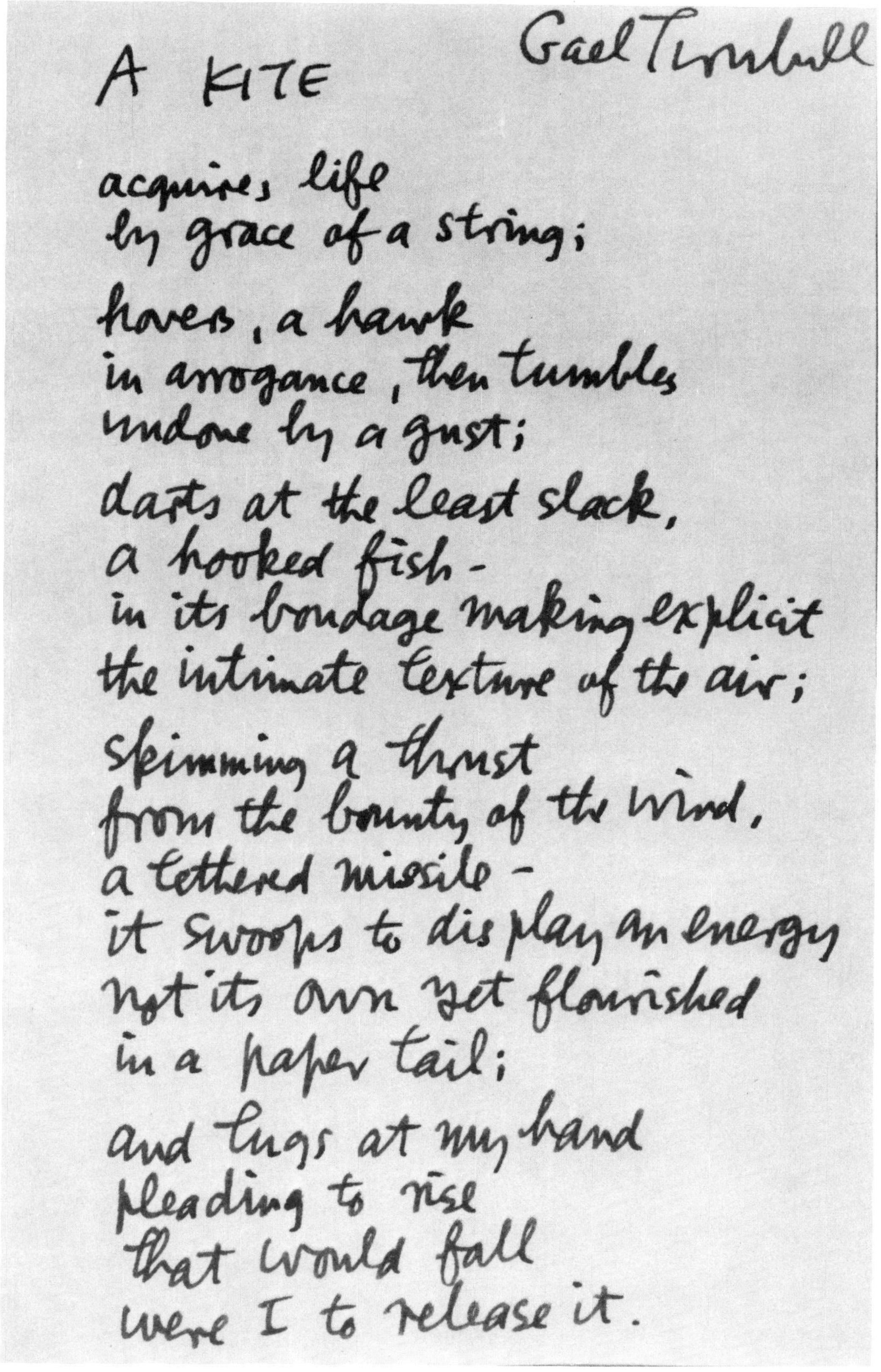

A KITE

Gael Turnbull

acquires life
by grace of a string;

hovers, a hawk
in arrogance, then tumbles
undone by a gust;

darts at the least slack,
a hooked fish -
in its bondage making explicit
the intimate texture of the air;

skimming a thrust
from the bounty of the wind,
a tethered missile -
it swoops to display an energy
not its own yet flourished
in a paper tail;

and tugs at my hand
pleading to rise
that would fall
were I to release it.

Fair copy (the author)

Days, in which the subject of each section was chosen at random. The poems addressed to his poet friends in *Scantlings* all contain, as a condition, references to a wall or walls. The final poem in the book is a long one, made up of a number of brief lines paired in many different combinations. The first line of each pair is a noun with an indefinite article; the second line is a phrase, or perhaps two phrases. The nouns and phrases are so chosen that all their different combinations are poetic, and the poem as a whole is a formal achievement.

The volume is arranged with thoughtful artistry. The first seven poems are various in form and subject and include a finely touched personal poem, "It's Dark," written in his most economical style; a meditation on John Bunyan's *Grace Abounding to the Chief of Sinners* (1666); a poem on Louis Riel; recollections of his term as a doctor in the Ontario Northland; and a vivid dramatic presentation of conflicting passions, "After Catullus."

Between *Scantlings* and the publication of *A Gathering of Poems, 1950-1980* in 1983 Turnbull published many poems in magazines and pamphlets. The variety of form and subject represented in these poems is as great as ever and their artistry is at his highest level. A long poem, *Residues* (1976), published by Grosseteste Press, with a second part, called *Thronging the Heart,* also published as a pamphlet in 1976, is probably his most important poem. A successor to "Twenty Words: Twenty Days," it is more intricate and, in form and content, both deeper and more comprehensive.

Turnbull has also written some sketches for theatrical presentation and otherwise indulged his bent for theater in Morris dancing, acting, and organizing some local community festivities. In the spring of 1979 he was commissioned to do three school broadcasts for the BBC on his old and continuing love, the literature of the Norsemen. Out of these broadcasts came another fine longer piece, a translation of Egil Skallagrimsson's *Sonatorrek*—his lament for his son—which he has written in an alliterative verse that approximates the original meters.

A comprehensive selection from all his poetry, *A Gathering of Poems* gives the most satisfactory and enduring impression of his work to date. In his article in *Poetry Nation Review,* Turnbull expresses a feeling of detachment now from his early American and Canadian enthusiasms, and it is true that there is more of the British in his poetry since *A Trampoline,* more of Bunting and Hugh MacDiarmid than of Williams. Yet it would be hard to locate a dividing line and harder to establish an influence. He has always been a careful and delighted poet, he has always respected and loved words, and the same voice is always audible in all his writing, generous in its affections and enthusiasm, unjaded, candid, but with a decent and also professional reticence, somewhat melancholy, honest and poetic.

Reference:

Review of *Residues, Poetry Information* (London), no. 16 (Winter 1976-1977).

Frederick Turner
(19 November 1943-   )

Frederick Feirstein

BOOKS: *Deep Sea Fish* (Santa Barbara: Unicorn Press, 1968);

Birth of a First Son (Goleta, Cal.: Christopher's Books, 1969);

The Water World (Santa Barbara: Christopher's Books, 1970);

Shakespeare and the Nature of Time (Oxford: Oxford University Press, 1971);

Between Two Lives (Middletown, Conn.: Wesleyan University Press, 1972);

Counter-Terra (Santa Barbara: Christopher's Books, 1978);

A Double Shadow (New York: Berkley, 1978);

The Return (Woodstock, Vt.: Countryman Press, 1981);

The Garden (Washington, D.C.: Ptyx Press, forthcoming 1985);

The New World (Princeton: Princeton University Press, forthcoming 1985);

Natural Classicism (New York: Paragon House, forthcoming 1985).

OTHER: William Shakespeare, *Romeo and Juliet*, edited by Turner (London: London University Press, 1972).

PERIODICAL PUBLICATIONS: "A Structuralist Analysis of *The Knight's Tale*," *Chaucer Review*, 8 (Spring 1974): 279-296;

" 'Mighty Poets in their Misery Dead': a Polemic on the Contemporary Poetic Scene," *Missouri Review*, 4 (Fall 1980): 77-96;

"Replies to criticisms of 'Mighty Poets,' " *Missouri Review*, 5 (Winter 1981-1982): 191-197;

"Kit Marlowe's Testament," *Bennington Review*, no. 12 (1982): 14-22;

"The Carnival Revolution," *Ontario Review*, 16 (Spring-Summer 1982): 93-97;

"The Neutral Lyre: Poetic Meter, the Brain, and Time," by Turner and Ernst Poppel, *Poetry*, 142 (August 1983): 277-307;

"Escape from Modernism," *Harper's*, 269 (November 1984): 47-55.

Frederick Turner is a poet, science-fiction novelist, literary critic, and philosopher of science. He was also coeditor and then editor of the *Kenyon Review* from 1978 to 1983 and an associate professor of English at Kenyon College from 1972; in 1985 he was appointed Founders Professor of Art and Humanities at the University of Texas at Dallas. His poetry integrates his vision as a student of the sciences with his narrative and poetic skills. His book-length poem *The Return* (1981) has helped to bring both fiction and extended narrative back into poetry, and his latest book, *The New World* (forthcoming in 1985), has gone a long way toward reviving the epic form in American and British poetry.

Turner has had poems, stories, and articles published in periodicals such as *Poetry*, the *Yale Review*, *Shenandoah*, *Kenyon Review*, *Ontario Review*, *Cumberland Poetry Review*, *Missouri Review*, *Corona*, and *Poetry Nation Review*.

Turner was born in Northamptonshire, England, to Edith L. B. Turner and Victor Witter Turner, a renowned anthropologist. During World War II, Victor Turner became a conscientious objector and was assigned to the extremely dangerous noncombatant job of digging up unexploded Nazi bombs. The family was impoverished and lived in a gypsy caravan. Frederick Turner's poetry is full of exotica and descriptions of vast spaces and light— all of which might have been influenced by the family's moving to Africa when Turner was seven. At that time, his father was doing fieldwork for his Ph.D., and the family spent three years living in a Zambian village. There Turner developed a lifelong appreciation of the beautifully civilized qualities of tribal life, and many of his poems satirize the sentimental notions modernist and postmodernist artists have about "innocent primitives."

The Turners returned to England when Turner was eleven. The return was an unhappy one for him, and his work often hints at a longing for an old world in the guise of a new one, one with highly developed tribal values—of family, loyalty, honor, and spirituality.

Victor Turner tried to find these values for himself and his family in Catholicism, which he had come to see as a parallel to the Ndembu religion he loved. Turner converted along with the rest of his family, and perhaps in an attempt to recapture the lost African world he missed, began writing poetry. His juvenile poetry was both mystical and full of imaginary worlds. He read science fiction omnivorously at this time, along with English religious poetry, particularly the poems of Gerard Manley Hopkins. He studied Hopkins' and Robert Bridges' metrics as well and, at sixteen, began to experiment with the sprung rhythm that he was later to employ in *The Return* and *The New World*.

The independence of mind that his father exhibited in his work and life Frederick Turner began to manifest in his own way as he grew to manhood. He found himself attracted to renaissance literature for its breadth of vision, its adventurousness, and its profound humanity, and he matriculated at Christ Church, Oxford, to study the renaissance, particularly Shakespeare's work, intending to teach and practice the craft of poetry. But the England he found himself to be living in was not the one of his imagination. It seemed not at all like the one of his sixteenth-century poet-heroes, not at all the place for a poet wanting to declare himself in the vital tradition of Christopher Marlowe.

Turner found on a trip to America in 1961 the energy, the commercial bustle, and the scientific explosiveness that had made Elizabethan England an exhilarating environment for an ambitious poet. At first he tried to reproduce the American experience in England, as many young people of his generation did (for instance the Beatles pounding out American rhythm and blues to Liverpool listeners). Some of the poems in Turner's *Between Two Lives* (1972), including "The Ajax Power-man" and "The Old Black Convertible," try to translate the American spirit into Oxfordshire. But he knew he could not go on living between two lives, and in 1967, after receiving a B.A. (1965), a B. Litt. (1967), and an M.A. (1967) from Oxford, he moved to America. Married since 25 June 1966 to Mei Lin Chang, a student of modern languages at Oxford, Turner joined the English department at the University of California in Santa Barbara. At twenty-three he became one of the youngest assistant professors in the University of California system.

Characteristically, he began to look for a *via nuova* for himself in creating fiction. In poetry he moved away from the confessional mode and began to create characters and dramatic situations. In religion he began to create his own theology, one that would later become the inspiration for his book *The Garden* (forthcoming in 1985).

Correspondingly, his aesthetic was developing. The later poems in *Between Two Lives* are fictional, as is almost all of *Counter-Terra* (1978). The clearest indication of what Turner's aesthetic was to become is what he selected to quote on the back of *Counter-Terra*: "*Fiction,* or *invention,* is the core of poetry, without which poetic 'truth' of any kind is impossible. The mathematician, the philosopher, the linguist, said Philip Sidney, . . . all merely imitate nature; 'Only the poet, disdaining to be tied to any such subjection, lifted up with the vigor of his own invention, does grow in effect into another Nature, in making things either better than Nature bringeth forth, or, quite anew, forms such as never were. . . .' "

The Return (written in 1976; published in

1981) is set in 1976, and its hero-narrator is an American journalist who is about to expose the Drug Lords plundering Indochina. He and a Chinese photographer he has fallen in love with pose as archaeologists exploring a dig on the Plain of Jars, but their deception is discovered by their host, the General, one of the powerful heroin dealers, and they are imprisoned. Continually injected with drugs, they are on the way to becoming slaves of their captor, when Laos falls and the General is murdered. Released by their guard, who wants them to help him make his way to America, they begin a wild flight across Southeast Asia in search of freedom.

As George Steiner says in the introduction to the book, "*The Return* is a gripping tale of adventure, of broken pontoons, and ice-fields, of hunters and fatigue. With the authority of obviousness, Fred Turner reclaims for poetry its antique privilege of heroic action, its right and, perhaps, primal compulsion to tell a story more sharply, with more economy than can that later idiom which is prose."

Turner's metric, developed from his adolescent experiments with Hopkins's sprung rhythm, helped to manage these effects. In *The Return* he juxtaposes two meters, creating a continuous anapestic or dactylic flow through verse paragraphs, usually in twelve syllable lines. This form allows for variety and change of pace as well as narrative speed, which is augmented by his use of idiom; it is also as dramatic as the Homeric rhythm.

But *The Return* is much more than an adventure story. It becomes, by its lyrical end, "a prothalamion," as Steiner says, "a song sung before and in honour of a nuptial (its points of contact with Spenser are real). It is an account of an education to love." But not to love merely a woman—as the hero does—and to marry her, but to love the way of life postwar America was tentatively trying to create. That love Turner renders both somberly and comically, his flexible meter allowing him to shift tone and mood with great ease.

In an outrageously joyous list the hero declares that "What we miss are the bourgeois trivia of Capitalism;/the smell of a new house, fresh drywall, resin/adhesive, vinyl, new hammered studs; ground coffee/in a friend's apartment in San Francisco . . . ," and Turner has the audacity to include the values and affectations of the underground Left: "the romance/of revolutionary groceries bought at the A & P,/delicious living underground like Superman,/nobody knowing our real identity, doomed/and shaded by the deadly influence of kryptonite/wielded by J. Edgar Hoover and the

CIA/. . . even the Movement was full of the American Romance."

The romance of *The Return* ends on a fictional note that was to become actual. Perhaps inspired by the action of his hero who founds a literary magazine in an attempt to help revivify America culturally, Turner with Ronald Sharp began to lay plans for the resurrection of the *Kenyon Review*. The review, he hoped, would embody the values of his hero—and become the basis of an American renaissance after the "dark ages" of the 1960s and Vietnam. As an editor Turner discovered writers much like himself who had by necessity worked in isolation for fifteen to twenty years writing dramatic and narrative poems, often in strict metrical form, marrying science to art in their visions, and countering in their essays as well as in their poems the nihilism of their contemporaries. Perhaps the clearest statement of his principles as editor was the Spring 1983 issue which was to be his last.

While he was engaged in reviving the *Kenyon Review*, Turner was also writing the poems of his next book, *The Garden*—an integrated collection of lyrical poems and philosophical aphorisms that rises to a religious-scientific vision. The book is divided into three sections, each of which is devoted to a different god in Turner's theology. Pan, the god of Pantheism, the world as god, embodies the physical world and its past. It is in Pan's world that Turner lays out the aesthetic boundaries of his garden, which becomes a metaphor for the writing of poetry: "To weed a garden is to become one of the forces of natural selection. . . . Poetry is a gardening or cultivation of the language. . . . All the great cultural florescences began when the purpose of gardening changed from food for the body to food for the spirit. Poetry begins with 'anthologies'—flower collections. . . . American culture will begin when the first American garden for the spirit is planted. Gardens remind us that the purpose of art is joy." The aphorisms expand and vary this simple metaphor and outline Turner's larger religious, and scientific view of the universe: "Our language is not a single code, but a concentrically nested series of codes, including the codes of animal behavior, the DNA molecule, the periodic table of elements, the 'periodic table' of elementary particles, and the necessary axioms of mathematics. . . . The history of the universe is the history of language. . . . The universe is a single cumulative act of self-utterance. . . . Flowers are the tongues of the world, that we teach to speak. . . . Flowers are the sexual organs of plants. . . . Sexuality is utterance. . . . Nature invented death at the same moment as it in-

Hic opus, hic labor est.

Those so many ways I have tried to come ~~upon you~~
to you, Vic, through dream, ~~through~~ through discipline, ~~of~~ thought,
words, art, yet always you remain as dumb
as if your mouth were choked with bread, your throat
a ~~broke~~ box; through the heart's portals of kin,
through ~~those~~ groves or hilltops where we would walk
when you were alive, and ~~talk~~ ~~sanely~~ out and in
of ~~the~~ ~~every~~ world's labyrinths we'd ~~spin the~~ spin the talk:
those ways have all come up dead ends, my Vic,
and though in the dreams you turn your brown eyes
and smile, and something seems to ~~try~~ work your cheek,
and your nice small ~~little~~ hands bend back in such wise
as ~~they~~ ~~would~~ when you set ~~you got~~ in earnest out to speak:
yet ~~always~~ you're as ~~still~~ as myths, as mute ~~as~~ as sighs.
                                         Stilled

Working draft (the author)

vented sex. Sex was a way of internalizing mutation into the organism; death was therefore necessary, to internalize selection. . . . The spade with which we divide a clump of irises is an organ of reproduction. . . . We are living in Paradise."

The second section of *The Garden* is the domain of the god Yahman who represents everything outside the garden's boundaries. He is zero, absolute negation, the future, Death. In Turner's next book-length poem, *The New World*, Yahman is the god of the religious fundamentalists, in love with death and denial. The protagonists of *The New World* follow Turner's third god Sperimenh, who represents the evanescent process of growth, the growing moment of the present. It is Sperimenh who is given the last word, the final section of "The Garden."

The New World is a long science-fiction epic, set in America four hundred years in the future. As Turner says in a screenplay treatment of the poem: "The world's fossil and nuclear fuels have been spent, its metallic ores exhausted, and much of its population either departed for the stars or slaughtered in the great twentieth and twenty-first century pogroms against the middle class. But high civilizations, based on a technology of solar and wind power, glass and resin chemistry, microprocessors and bioengineering, still flower on the earth. War is waged by mounted knights in resinite armor, with lasers and swords. The ancient institution of the nation-state, obeying the same historical laws that brought it into existence, has collapsed, and the human race has discovered new forms of political organization: the Riots—violent matriarchies based in the ancient cities, whose members have no incest-prohibitions and no money, are addicted to the ultimate psychedelic joyjuice, and have almost lost the power of human language. . . . the Burbs—populations descended from the old middle class, whom the Riots hold hostage and use as slaves to produce their food, luxuries, and joyjuice . . . the Mad Counties—religious theocracies, dominated, in North America, by fanatical fundamentalists . . . and the Free Counties—independent Jeffersonian aristocratic democracies, where art, science, and the graces of human life are cultivated to their highest, as in classical Athens, Renaissance Florence, and Heian Japan."

The plot of the poem is as exciting as the exposition. It is full of extraordinarily beautiful passages that lyrically or philosophically transcend the action. The metric is a 5-stress line with a varying amount of unstressed syllables. Its effect, like the metric of *The Return*, allows Turner to shift mood easily—from brutal battle to delicate love to hymns in praise of natural beauty.

Turner resigned from the editorship of the *Kenyon Review* in late 1982. He continues to work in other ways as an editor and poet.

Reference:

Aaron Kramer, Donald Hall, Louis Simpson, Diane Wakoski, Theodore Weiss, David Perkins, and Robert Bly, "Responses to Frederick Turner," *Missouri Review,* 5 (Winter 1981-1982): 171-190.

Jeffrey Wainwright

(19 February 1944-   )

Jon Glover

BOOKS: *The Important Man* (Newcastle upon Tyne: Northern House, 1970);
Heart's Desire (Manchester: Carcanet Press, 1978);
Selected Poems (Manchester: Carcanet Press, 1985).

OTHER: Jon Silkin, ed., *Poetry of the Committed Individual,* includes poems by Wainwright (Harmondsworth: Penguin, 1972);

Poetry Introduction 3, includes poems by Wainwright (London: Faber & Faber, 1975);
Michael Schmidt and Peter Jones, eds., *British Poetry Since 1970,* includes poems by Wainwright (Manchester: Carcanet Press, 1980), pp. 208-212;
Blake Morrison and Andrew Motion, eds., *The Penguin Book of Contemporary British Poetry,* in-

cludes poems by Wainwright (Harmonds-worth: Penguin, 1982);

Schmidt, ed., *Some Contemporary Poets of Britain and Ireland,* includes poems by Wainwright (Manchester: Carcanet Press, 1983), pp. 29-31;

Peter Robinson, ed., *Geoffrey Hill: Essays on His Work,* includes an essay by Wainwright (Milton-Keynes: Open University Press, 1985), pp. 100-111.

PERIODICAL PUBLICATIONS: "Geoffrey Hill's *King Log,*" *Stand,* 10, no. 1 (1968): 44-49;

"Ezra Pound's Prose," *Stand,* 15, no. 3 (1974): 46-48;

"Poetry and Revolution," *Agenda,* 13 (Winter-Spring 1975): 53-64;

"Editorial," *Stand,* 17, no. 1 (1975): 4-6;

"Geoffrey Hill's 'Lachrimae,'" *Agenda,* 13 (Autumn 1975): 31-38;

Contribution to a symposium, *Agenda,* 14, no. 3 (1977): 32-35;

"The Poetry of Peter Levi," *Agenda,* 14, no. 4 (1977): 82-93;

"The Politics of Literature," *PN Review,* no. 5 (1977): 52-54;

"William Wordsworth at Briggflatts," *Agenda,* 16 (Spring 1978): 37-45;

"Geoffrey Hill's *Tenebrae,*" *Agenda,* 17 (Spring 1979): 4-11;

"'The Silence Round All Poetry,'" *Poetry Review,* 69, no. 1 (1979): 57-59;

"Naiveté over Realism—Jon Silkin's *The Peaceable Kingdom,*" *Poetry Review,* 69, no. 4 (1980): 3-7;

"Shelley's Political Poetry," *PN Review,* no. 20 (1981): 35-38;

"Reading the Americans: Apart and Together," *PN Review,* no. 21 (1981): 22-25;

"The Poetry of W. S. Graham," *Parnassus,* 9 (Fall-Winter 1982): 242-252;

"William Carlos Williams' Lyric Poetry," *Akros,* 17, no. 49 (1982): 28-41;

"Linkwords," review of Tony Harrison's *Selected Poems, Poetry Review,* 74, no. 3 (1984): 73-75.

Jeffrey Wainwright has become widely respected as a poet and critic since his work first appeared in periodicals during the 1960s. His poetry has developed with an unswerving self-conscious discipline that has gone hand in hand with the critical integrity shown in articles in *Agenda, Stand,* and *PN Review.* His critical consciousness and his feelings for the morally precarious nature of poetry have led him to publish relatively few poems, but those collected in *Heart's Desire* (1978) have enor-

Jeffrey Wainwright

mous internal energy as well as making a range of demands on the reader which belies their scale.

Wainwright was born in Stoke-on-Trent, in the English Industrial Midlands, to Sidney and Nellie Wainwright. Attending the grammar school where Charles Tomlinson had been a pupil, he had developed an interest in writing as well as in reading widely in modern poetry before he went to study English at the University of Leeds in 1962. The mid-1960s was a period of exceptional poetic opportunity in Leeds. Geoffrey Hill was lecturing at the university and Peter Redgrove, as Gregory Fellow in Poetry, ran creative writing seminars which Wainwright attended. Jon Silkin, former Gregory Fellow, was editing the international literary quarterly *Stand* in Leeds with the poet Ken Smith. Poets came to read from all over Britain and from further afield, for example Robert Creeley and Andrei Voznesensky.

After graduating in 1965 and obtaining his M.A., with a thesis on William Carlos Williams, in 1967 he went to teach at the University of Wales in Aberystwyth, where, apart from a year at Long

Island University (1970 to 1971), he remained until 1972. Since then he has been a senior lecturer in English at Manchester Polytechnic. He is married with two children.

Wainwright's earliest published poems, which remain uncollected and which he considers mere juvenilia, appeared in the Leeds weekly poetry magazine *Poetry and Audience* while he was a student there. "Poem" (concerning a rural survivor figure Like R. S. Thomas's "A Peasant"), "Harlech Castle," "The Fruit and the Flowers," and "The End of Lord Franklin's Expedition" show both independence from the many possible powerful influences at Leeds and from conventional student subjects. The presence of so many influential figures confirmed Wainwright's own belief that poetry ought to be relevant to the larger, political world rather than a means of private self-expression. However, such a theory of impersonality or "commitment" is not without its paradoxes; and it is perhaps significant that the "outer world" that he evokes in these early poems is harsh, lonely, and only explored tentatively. It is by no means a world of simple political programs; and it is interesting that his later poems develop the early themes of isolation, failure, and delusion within the context of ideals—often those of social egalitarianism or socialism ("Thomas Muntzer"), or as a critique of "patriotic" history ("Three Poems on the Battle of Jutland").

"The Fruit and the Flowers" (*Poetry and Audience*, 1964) is one of the best of his early poems. The poem evokes the sense of perturbed wonder felt by a farm boy, accustomed to the mere "circle of work," when he visits a lady and her daughters to take

grain

For the house, and the weight of the sack,
Still in his arms, he looked at the flowers,
Risked dark feeling fingers over the petals.

For the majority of the poem the poet dwells sympathetically on the limitations of traditional working life, which is nevertheless dignified and complete. Yet, he feels for the boy's awe at the notion of luxury, a culture above, yet dependent on, the world of labor. It is significant that, whether the vision here is formed by the opening pages of D. H. Lawrence's *The Rainbow* (1915) or by a reading of Marx, the poem is successful as a dramatic entity, and it gains by leaving much unsaid in its characteristic focus on isolation. Interestingly, the gardener figure, who seems to represent the exploited work-

er but also someone more knowing and more vital than the employer, reappears later in the "Death of the Mill-Owner," the fourth section of the sequence "1815"; in "The Garden Master"; and "The Forest of Fontainebleau," the third section of the sequence "Sentimental Education." Wainwright ironically identifies his own art as part of the luxurious, unnecessary superstructure supported by the gardener. He is, in this sense, an "owner." Yet, however guilty he may feel at this position ("Aware as I am of my own / Glibnesses, repetitions, minor faults . . .") he would like the poems themselves to shock, to intrude obstinately like the gardeners' or the woodsmen's adders into the complacent middle-class world.

Wainwright's mature poems began to appear in *Stand* in 1966 and were first collected in *The Important Man* in 1970. This pamphlet consists of four sequences, "Three Poems on the Battle of Jutland 1916," "1815," "Sentimental Education," and "The Garden Master." The sequence form seems to fulfill the requirements of maintaining each poem as a short, finely drawn picture while permitting an imaginative spaciousness and an interdependence which gradually adds pressure to each component.

What strikes the reader immediately about "H.M.S. Invincible," in "Three Poems on the Battle of Jutland 1916," is its extraordinary rationing of charged imaginative pictures, which enforce a sense of emotional commitment, set against a restraint in language, which allows one to "see through" to the original event:

Shoals of North Sea cod
Are interrupted by an Admiral
Swallowing their live water.
He dies screaming
In broad fathoms among
Coal shovels and scalded stokers
Suddenly washed of their dust.

Within only seven lines are twists of vision in which each potential for reaction is marked out, by an appropriate tone that is then denied in the next line. The cod "interrupted" by a drowning admiral might seem grotesquely funny, and yet one is immediately brought up short by the next line, "He dies screaming." Again, the pace changes, and the slow-motion descent of coal shovels and stokers through the "broad fathoms" makes the picture distanced and almost surreal. Involving and distancing elements are thus intermingled and deliberately confused by the short lines, the line breaks, and by the refusal to assent to the luxury of language that might merely lament:

> The facade
> *Invincible,* bow and stern,
> Subsides: two hulks.

Such finality seems both banal and tragic. Sentimental eloquence is not all that is fended off by deft counterpointing. The sarcasm and absurdity of political cartoon is both invoked and then stripped of its containing ease by its immediate surroundings, as in "Summary," in the same sequence:

> A padre rescues a parrot
> From plucked extinction.
>
> Fisher shifts for his grave
> But his dream just holds.

Though "1815" is a poem of only sixty lines, it is divided into four sections, each telling a separate, complementary story. It is in a sense a study of socially required sacrifice, if suicide can be called sacrifice. Set in the year of the English victory over Napoleon at Waterloo it rewrites history so as to interleave the deaths of a mill girl, of soldiers in battle, and of a mill owner. The conventional accounts of the period in which England asserts military and industrial might are characterized— or caricatured—in the background of "The Mill-Girl":

> Waterloo is all the rage;
> Coal and iron and wool
> Have supplied the English miracle.

But that "miracle" indulges itself in the conspicuous consumption of people; they become, for official purposes, "the fallen." The social and political energy that organizes the mass sacrifice keeps it in its place as much by the deflection of language as by physical oppression, and, when death appears unnatural or intrusive, as in the case of the mill-girl's body floating in the canal, one feels that Wainwright sees this event too as containable: tragic, individual and uncommunicating, the body becomes the "property" of the lock keeper who finds her as part of his routine occupation: "He is an important man now."

The lock keeper, the "Important Man" of the pamphlet's title, is perhaps an image of the poet. Disturbed and inflated by his discovery of the uncomfortable realities of history the poet's imagination is as close to vanity as is the lock keeper's. Secure in their social functions, helping to keep

Front cover for Wainwright's first collection, four sequences later included in Heart's Desire

things flowing, they both watch the results of others' agonies. Too late to help, they nevertheless acquire a momentary importance as discoverers and celebrators, giving meaning, for what it is worth.

The messages of history may not be worth much, of course, compared with present pleasures. The lock keeper is "Bothered by his wife/From a good dinner," to pull in the girl's body. And, in "Sentimental Education," the next sequence, the poet compares "eel stew,/Chicken, hard bread, and wine sharp on the tongue" with news of "revolution" read about in the newspapers. Material security is compared with the dubious self-confidence of long-distance political concern and the comfortable *frisson* at the thought of losing a loved one in some social upheaval. This poem and the other two in the "Sentimental Education" sequence openly acknowledge, for perhaps the first time, that even sincerely felt guilt at one's role in history is dependent on a privileged narrative position. The poem's very manipulative impersonality is permitted only by their author's middle-class life. Guilt, irony, and political anger will not suffice alone for a moral atonement without an admission that turning the events of history into aesthetic objects is likely to result in duplicity or even treachery. Will the active commitment be forthcoming? Will the real as opposed to the imagined intrusive demand be handled with such care and insight? Wainwright admits a mocking doubt:

> God knows it I am with you! all your trials
> And your vexations and how you weigh them
>   here
> Bear upon me. But these your lithe spokesmen—
> Too salutory, too quick. Show them to
> Students, the educated poor, and tourists
> Looking for something to amuse their friends.

The poems in *The Important Man* were collected with newer poems in *Heart's Desire* in 1978. The principle additions were three more long poems or poem sequences, "Thomas Muntzer," "Five Winter Songs," and "Heart's Desire." "Thomas Muntzer" concerns a sixteenth-century German radical and visionary who was captured and executed in the Peasant War. Wainwright's treatment of this historical theme is more expansive than is permitted in his earlier poems. It also fixes firmly on the vision and voice of the eponymous hero. Had the pared-down, continually deflecting style of "Three Poems on the Battle of Jutland 1916" and "1815" been less confidently handled one might have said that this new expansiveness marked a greater confidence. Yet Wainwright is not rejecting his old methods as technically inadequate nor have his concerns changed. In fact, in "Thomas Muntzer," there is a concentration on the themes of illusion, political power, and imaginative treachery that were important components of the earlier poems:

> Sometimes on clear nights I spread my arms wide
> And can fly, stiff but perfect, down
> Over this pond just an inch above the surface.

Muntzer acts as his own deflector; the moment he says, "This is not/A vision," the reader feels a desperate tension in his voice. There is need for the narrator to undermine each picture since the mind of Muntzer and the world about him crackle with uncertainty. The concluding stages, a chaste but majestic invocation of Muntzer's torture and death, again unite the poet's sense of his own place in history, both living it and making it, with the central historical figure, as he does in his earlier poems. This time, however, the result is neither wry nor distrustful; the powerful temptation to "justified" illusion is no longer just the subject's but clearly, and with a firm bitterness, that of both poet and subject:

> History, which is Eternal Life, is what
> We need to celebrate. Stately tearful
> Progress. . . . you've seen how I have wept for it.

"Heart's Desire" perhaps represents a change in emphasis so great that it is really a change of substance. While many of the elements of earlier poems are still there, their very persistence seems to have posed new problems and new challenges. A critical unveiling of the poet's personal integrity now no longer follows ironically in the train of an outgoing, political thrust toward the re-interpretation of history but as an internalized, ritual drama. While the world of actual battle formed the foreground of many of the earlier poems, now the fight has been placed in a formal and tautly balanced mode in which the poet's internal struggles find a bleak peace through identifying with the tentative, brave, and painful desires of previous writers. Federico García Lorca, Lope de Vega, William Wordsworth, and others appear not merely as historical figures but to help to crystallize the dialogue of dream and disillusion, love, and pain. There is no longer a contrast between the forces of history which destroy and the innocence of the victim. Having assumed guilt the mind recognizes its own contrary forces of energy, desire, and destruction, as in "The Fierce Dream":

> The mind swoons to see again
> How it contrives
> Its own dismay.

In "Despair (Desesparada)" "We fight—to want our own desires—/Our dealing hearts and flying brain." The formal perfection of these poems requires the same slow reading and hard-won familiarity that is needed to piece together the incongruous tableaux of "1815." But the forms, employing for the first time rhyme, represent a new relationship with the burden of history: they appear sometimes simple, even simplistic, but paradoxically they invoke a highly wrought contact with the tight drumskin of form stretched and tuned under sufferings of other ages. After the foregrounding of this drum in the battle of Frankenhausen in "Thomas Muntzer": "*dran dran dran* we have the sword—the purity/Of metal—the beauty of blood falling," it is reshaped in "Illumination" into the rhythmic pulse of poignant love poems:

> That is her lover lying there,
> And she beside him lying close.
> They do not speak, or move, or touch.
> The lucid grass between them flows.

"Some Propositions and Part of a Narrative" begins to explain Wainwright's new view of the rôle of love in his consciousness of history and death, but, ironically, another part of the fiction (in truth, a world of experience that supplants explanation) intrudes. Oddly, then, although these poems have become more formal, they also represent not an escape from the world of fact but a recognition of it, a recognition which of course does not make living any easier.

Although *The Important Man* received little critical attention, *Heart's Desire* was widely reviewed. Some found it humorless and obscure, others, too political. Martin Dodsworth in the *Guardian*, however, called it "the best first collection to have been published in the last ten years," and went on: "Wainwright's irony is neither evasive nor callous, and permits the splendour and the pathos of Muntzer's discovery to ring out in the line 'I find I am a god, like all men.' The poem is a masterpiece, and the book is indispensable." There were also sensitive reviews by John Cassidy in the *Poetry Review*, by Anne Stevenson in the *Times Literary Supplement* and Julian Symons in the *Sunday Times*. "Thomas Muntzer" was the subject of a lengthy discussion by Rodney Pybus in *Stand*. In a broad attack on what she sees as the conservatism of recent English poetry Marjorie Perloff attacks Wainwright, and "Thomas Muntzer," in particular, maintaining that it is technically inept, lacking in historical sense, and a thinly disguised mask for the author. It has also been suggested, however, that the poem fits integrally into Wainwright's clear patterns of technique and theme, and it would therefore seem that Perloff is coming to "Thomas Muntzer" with as much ignorance of the required approaches as she accuses the British of in their supposed distaste for the modernist masters. Students of the impact of Ezra Pound's "A Few Don'ts by an Imagiste," may like to note, however, that while Perloff claims that "it isn't even good prose . . . neither graphic nor suggestive," Martin Dodsworth talks of Wainwright's using "The restraint and accuracy of the best imagist poetry."

Since the appearance of *Heart's Desire*, the long, historical poem "George III Speaking in his Madness" has been broadcast by the BBC and published in *PN Review* in 1982. All the poems he has written since 1978 are collected in *Selected Poems* (1985). The inclusion of his work in *British Poetry Since 1970* (1980) and *The Penguin Book of Contemporary British Poetry* (1982) confirms Jeffrey Wainwright's position as one of the important poets of his generation.

In November 1984 and March 1985 his English version of Charles Péguy's *Le Mystère de la Charité de Jeanne d'Arc*, adapted by Jean-Paul Lucet, was performed at the Other Place in Stratford-upon-Avon and in Newcastle upon Tyne by members of the Royal Shakespeare Company. He has also done an English stage version of Denis Diderot's *Les Amours de Jacques le Fataliste*, adapted from the novel by Francis Huster, and he was recently appointed Judith E. Wilson Fellow at the University of Cambridge for the autumn term of 1985.

Ted Walker
(28 November 1934-   )

Julian Gitzen
Victoria College

BOOKS: *Those Other Growths* (Leeds: Northern House, 1964);

Fox on a Barn Door (London: Cape, 1965; New York: Braziller, 1966);

The Solitaries (London: Cape, 1967; New York: Braziller, 1967);

The Night Bathers: Poems 1966-8 (London: Cape, 1970);

Gloves to the Hangman: Poems 1969-72 (London: Cape, 1973);

Burning the Ivy: Poems 1973-77 (London: Cape, 1978);

The Lion's Cavalcade, by Walker and Alan Aldridge (London: Cape, 1980);

The High Path (London: Routledge & Kegan Paul, 1982).

TELEVISION: *Big Jim & The Figaro Club,* BBC, 1981;

Getting On, BBC, 1982.

PERIODICAL PUBLICATIONS: "Estrangement," *New Yorker,* 46 (13 June 1970): 30-35;

"As May Be," *New Yorker,* 48 (29 April 1972): 40-44;

"Cosher and the Sea," *New Yorker,* 51 (30 June 1975): 28-29;

"The Last of October," *New Yorker,* 55 (22 October 1979): 36-39.

©*Edward Lucie-Smith;*
courtesy of Bernard Stone,
The Turret Book Shop

Along with poets such as Ted Hughes, Jon Silkin, Peter Redgrove, R. S. Thomas, and Seamus Heaney, Ted Walker has contributed much to the revitalizing of British nature poetry. Ranging over the Sussex seacoast of his birth and drawing his subjects almost exclusively from the out-of-doors, he combines verisimilitude of observation with evocativeness and double entendre in lyrics shaped in traditional metric and stanzaic forms.

Walker's early years were to prove immensely important to his poetic development. His continuing deep attachment to his family and to scenes of his childhood colors both his poems and fiction. Walker was born in 1934, in Lancing, Sussex, the first child of Edward Joseph and Winifred Edith Walker. Although the beaches were mined and closed to civilians during World War II, Walker and his friends were able to return to them at the war's end. The poet reports that he enjoyed "all kinds of sea fishing—trotlining and beach-casting, even shrimping and beachcombing for crabs after gales." He adds: "Between our house and the beach was the Widewater, a brackish lagoon . . . [which] contained eels, sticklebacks, and was the haunt of many different varieties of waterfowl. My 'territory' was really the foreshore, between high- and low-water marks. But also I roamed the immediate hinterland—rather unkempt arable and grazing pastures. . . . When I was a little older, I began to explore further afield into the chalk hills of the South Downs."

From his father, a carpenter by trade, the boy "learned to prize that which is well made." His father also encouraged young Walker's interest in reading, supplying money for books from his modest earnings: "Even when he was out of work in the thirties, he always found a couple of shillings a week for books." Walker's autobiography, *The High Path* (1982), also mentions the father's own small library, which included a series of books entitled *The Natural History of the World in Pictures*. There Walker "discovered that I shared this earth also with such as tree-climbing crabs and devil-fish, zebra and warthog. . . . Most of my first published poems were to be about animals. The excited curiosity which was to engender them had been sparked." The boy's education also continued more formally in primary school in Shoreham-by-Sea. Somewhat to his own disappointment, he won admission to Steyning Grammar School, thereby ending, it seemed, his chances of becoming a tradesman like his father. He went on to study French and Spanish at St. John's College, Cambridge, from which he graduated with an honors B.A. in 1956.

Although he had written both poetry and prose from early childhood, Walker reports that he "kept nothing and published nothing until (I think) 1963." While still a schoolboy he discovered the work of T. S. Eliot, the first, and for a time the only, modern poet with whom he was to be acquainted. Eliot "was important to me in the sense that I realised, through him, poetry was not a dead or even a moribund art . . . but was flourishing; and that what I was trying to do was not an anachronism in the 20th century." While having "admired and found helpful" a list of poets various enough to include Samuel Taylor Coleridge, Alfred Tennyson, Robert Frost, Thomas Hardy, W. H. Auden, Pierre de Ronsard, Paul Verlaine, Arthur Rimbaud, and García Lorca, the poet feels most deeply indebted to F. L. Lucas's *The Decline and Fall of the Romantic Ideal* (1936), from which he learned "the principles I have tried to follow ever since: to blend elements of the *classical* (as far as disciplined form is concerned) with my incurable *romanticism* of outlook, with the *realism* which springs from close observation of the world."

Walker's emergence as a published poet occurred when, in his late twenties, he returned to live on the Sussex coast. He recalls, "It was the rediscovery of the coast . . . which prompted the release of poems which had been a long while forming. Having found my true voice, almost by accident—experimenting with new metres and stanza forms—and then finding my subjects as though mint-new, I was able to begin." His first collection, a pamphlet entitled *Those Other Growths* (1964), offers impressive evidence of a mature and accomplished talent. It opens with "By the Saltings," a portrait of a low-tide beach at dawn which remains one of his finest works and closes with "Porpoises," perhaps the single most widely known of Walker's poems. His first full-length collection, *Fox on a Barn Door* (1965), includes all seven of the pieces contained in *Those Other Growths* and derives its title from the unfortunate fox described in one of them, "Easter Poem."

At first glance Walker might be mistaken for a follower of Ted Hughes, a celebrant of instinctive and ruthless energy exemplified by the porpoises, "frenzied, intent as athletes," which "never stop, never sleep," or by the enormous skate "pulsing with irritation" as it snaps a fisherman's line. Closer inspection reveals that Walker has marked out two related subjects which are to characterize his future work: first, a nameless apprehension, evidently compounded of a fear of death and a dread of loneliness; second, the pains and pleasures of solitude. Walker himself identifies his early thematic concerns as "fear and loss which looks for the beauty that remains among the ruins of lost faith, lost innocence, and lost animal strength." Like the persona of "By the Saltings," he stands "alone/ . . . and as fearful/as some crab beneath some stone." "Song for my Children" portrays him as fated "to meet my fear by/the dark water." His fear is heightened by a spiritual desolation, the conviction that religious faith amounts to "superstition" combined with a residual yearning for "some comet fall of insight/in the chasm of this night/to light me my loneliness" ("On the Sea Wall"). Those poems which concern his own experiences frequently portray him as a lonely figure silhouetted in dim light. Sharing to an unusual degree the universal feeling that night is lonelier than day, Walker chooses dusk, darkness, or first light as backdrops for numerous poems, while the vastness of the ocean frequently intrudes to heighten the sense of loneliness. Not only human beings but animals also are featured in solitude, like the powerful carp which hurls himself across "a pond too small for him" or the ferocious conger eel which has "lived alone, eating all spies and intruders" until he is hauled into a fishing boat.

Front cover for Walker's first collection, seven poems later
included in Fox on a Barn Door

If solitude is a necessary condition, it is not without its potential rewards. Though it fosters loneliness, solitude also offers the freedom to exercise fancy or imagination. *The High Path* recalls the early development of Walker's own penchant for solitude. While in primary school he "became more and more of a solitary . . . independent, aloof, reflective, an observer." He enjoyed getting away alone in a flat-bottomed boat on the "Widewater" fronting his family home: "The moment I cast off, I was beyond anybody's reach. I could row myself to solitude in the evening, anchoring near the swans' island." This same romantic hunger for undisturbed reverie animates the man in "Skimmers," who stops on a beach to reminisce with a shell-throwing boy, then continues "alone,/shuffling up the pea-beach track/on shores of his mind's making." In "Estuary" the speaker remembers how in boyhood he came upon "a bark broken/in three

across the open/mudflat" and imaginatively pictured the "terror" which had prevailed on board as the ship broke apart in a storm. So, in adulthood, he "would wish to be alone/with the loneliness of then," free both to recreate the shipwreck in his imagination, and to "efface" that frightening vision.

Walker's interest in mental and emotional states combined with his preference for sensuous imagery leads him to embody abstractions in tangible form. "Terrains Vagues," for instance, draws a geographical parallel: "At the edge of any town/ and the edge of any life/are tracts we never build on." Beginning, "Our fears, like starlings, gather/ with the dusk," "Starlings" draws an extended analogy between our secret fears and those "sacristan black" birds which roost "untouchable by night" and at sunrise leave behind them an "uneasy calm."

"Starlings" is characteristic also in using one of Walker's favorite forms, the tetrameter line arranged in six-line stanzas. The author's commitment to traditional forms has never been more evident than in *Fox on a Barn Door,* which, in addition to experiment with terza rima and the sonnet, deliberately rings the changes on the rhyming variations offered by the six-line stanza, "Skimmers" alone supplying five distinct rhyme patterns for its total of seven stanzas.

The popularity of Walker's work probably owes less to such formal dexterity than to its descriptive power. An old-fashioned realist, he excels at the sharply observed and metaphorically colored detail, such as the "sores/of orange rust" formed by bolts driven through wooden breakwaters, the timbers of which are speckled at low tide with "an eczema/of pink and white barnacles/and mussels of midnight blue" ("Breakwaters"). Walker examines his subjects intently enough to notice that the ears of a dead fox are "snagged with burdock" and "his dry nose/plugged with black blood" ("Easter Poem"). He is capable, too, of intense verbal energy, as in this portrait of a female porpoise feeding on mackerel:

When she dives her flukes lie poised
on the surface an instant
as she breaks another back
among the perfervid shoal
with an automatic snap

of appalling, fluted jaws.

Fox on a Barn Door remains perhaps Walker's best-known volume. It established him as one of England's finest young nature poets. Most of its

There were seaweeds that popped and greasily oozed; seaweeds that looked dead until you suspended them in a pool and saw their filigrees open and dance; and best of all was the eel-grass, like a drenched and matted fur hiding the nakedness of the breakwaters. I would stand among the spars, my cheek pressed to the eel-grass, listening to the hiss of the barnacles draining, my legs feeling the sharp edges of mussels that grew like bunches of indigo fruit low down. At such moments, I must suppose, the images of my first poems were formed: then, and when I would lie tiredly where the pebbles wet the sand, my eyes closed, my fingers round a brittling oyster shell, hearing the gulls and sand-martins and the skirr of something dry and weightless as it skittered along over the stones. I was to remember all that during the years while I grew into a boy, while the beach was sown with mines — a forbidden place for Germans to swarm over. Above all I should remember the smell, the conflicting freshness and sourness of it all; the blood of broken lugworms on my palms, and then my running through the foam at the water's fringes for the huge rinse and cleansing of the sea.

Fair copy of a passage from The High Path *(the author)*

Dust jacket for Walker's 1970 collection, which includes translations from Spanish, French, Italian, and German as well as his own poems

reviewers pointed to resemblances between Walker and Hughes. Predictably, not all critics were pleased by the effects. While considering the volume "worth paying attention to," Francis Hope of the *New Statesman* objected that "the striking of violent poses is [not] a substitute for emotional force." M. L. Rosenthal, in contrast, sounded a far more encouraging note: "Though gentler than Hughes, and closer sometimes to sentimentality, Walker has a similar muscular precision of phrasing and movement. . . . Seldom has a young poet's first volume crackled with such acute perceptions."

The Solitaries (1967), which followed, maintains the concerns of *Fox on a Barn Door*. The volume's title expresses its dominant theme, which is supported by numerous portraits of single, isolated animals and humans. When confronting death, which often enforces a mournful solitude upon survivors, Walker adopts the wistful elegiac tone which will characterize much of his subsequent writing. While "Crocuses" may bravely celebrate a spring flower's "vital gift of waste," the poet con-

tinues to regret his losses, and "Clay" leaves no doubt about the omnipresence of death and oblivion:

> Earth, consuming our
> small imprints on her,
> heals every lesion;
>
> soon our intrusion
> will be sucked under.

"Elegy for a Trotliner" honors a figure who remained something of a loner, but whose passing leaves the poet even more lonely and haunted by "the barren whistle" of the seashore wind.

In *The Night Bathers* (1970) Walker includes translations among his own poems, and the range of languages offered testifies to his long experience as a student and teacher of languages. There are translations from Spanish (Lope de Vega, García Lorca, Pablo Neruda), from French (Paul Verlaine, Charles Leconte de Lisle), from Italian (Eugenio

Montale), and from German (Friedrich Hölderlin and Rainer Maria Rilke). His own topics, essentially occasional in character, resemble those of the first two volumes, but the poems adopt a slightly altered autobiographical stance, as the author increasingly portrays himself as husband and father. When *The Night Bathers* appeared, Walker had already been married fourteen years. He fell in love with and proposed to Lorna Ruth Benfell when he was only fifteen years old. The couple were married on 11 August 1956, the year of his graduation from Cambridge. They have four children. Both emotional and physical separations from family members the poet accepts as regretfully necessary. In "The Night Bathers" he walks as "a stranger" along the coast of "alien, emptying Wales," while his son "worries at sleep" after an irritating afternoon's rivalry with his father. His son's gesture of independence is perhaps a necessary rite of manhood, resembling Walker's own boyish defiance when he ignored his father's command to come out of the water, swimming instead "deep into banks of sea-fret/too far to have to answer him." Reviewers recognized *The Night Bathers* as a modest departure from the first two volumes. While he saluted the poet's effort "to extend that fairly narrow range of observation which had previously kept him on the seashore or just inland," and paid tribute to "a group of good family poems," Alan Brownjohn was disturbed by what seemed to him the author's excessive neatness and control. Ronald Hayman was less reserved, congratulating Walker for "refusing to go on doing what he has already done well" and for "experimenting with different voices."

A reader encountering the increased autobiographical material in *The Night Bathers* can better appreciate Walker's claim that his fiction "complements" his poems, for his short stories, approximately thirty of which have appeared in the *New Yorker*, are strongly autobiographical and richly flavored with details of the landscape and people of the Sussex coast. When collected, these scattered pieces acquire something of the appearance of a journal. Uniformly Chekhovian in structure, they concern commonplace events and experiences of daily life and are devoted largely to revelation of character. Most of the stories employ a first-person narrator. In combination they offer helpful insights into the poet's personal interests and testify forcefully to the depth of his ties both to his family and to the region of his birth.

Gloves to the Hangman (1973) marks a change in its author's viewpoint. His gaze has turned away from the sea, and he has assumed the perspective of

a countryman keeping a watchful eye upon weather and the seasons. Several titles, such as "After drought," "August," "Snow in southern England," and "A celebration for autumn," are indicative. While weather and seasonal imagery have featured in previous poems, here the seasons have emerged as a dominant subject in their own right. In "Letter to Barbados," reminiscent of Horace, the poet writes contentedly to his brother of seasonal activities:

> This morning I made
> A first cut of the grass since autumn.
> It smelt sweet in the sun, in the swathe
> Where I left it to dry.

A favorite setting of the poems in *Gloves to the Hangman* is the poet's traditional Sussex house and garden, which serves as the central locale for the next book, *Burning the Ivy* (1978). The gardener-poet has discovered an appropriate Frostian image to complement his increasing attraction to the subject of his own craft. Gardening and poetry writing certainly have much in common. Walker's large garden is attractively landscaped, lovingly tended, and highly colored with blossoms. Questioned about his gardening, he modestly replied, "I can't claim to be an expert gardener. . . . I do like growing flowers, vegetables and fruit, and I do know a fair bit about gardening, but I am lazy and forgetful and untidy and therefore can never be very successful. The *point* of my garden is that I foster my sanity there. . . . What attracted me to this house when we moved here fifteen years ago was the garden and its high encircling wall of warm brick. . . . In a sense, the walled garden became a kind of extended metaphor of life itself, of temporary endeavour and small achievement. Unhappinesses crept over my wall from the outside, however I tried to hack them back; within the boundaries, small joys would briefly flourish. The garden is where I can be private, sealed off. It is what I most prize—the juxtaposition of Nature and Man; like the foreshore, a meeting-place between the wild and the tamed. . . . It is where I keep in touch with the elemental forces, see the seasons pass, get my hands dirty. I fight God there. Some hope I've got." Surveying his "emptied apple-trees" on New Year's Eve, the speaker of "Gardener" promises himself that "One more fortnight of surfeit/surely will come." That he is thinking not only of fruit and vegetables but of new poems is underlined by the presence of a companion piece, "Perfidious Euterpe," addressed to the muse of lyric poetry. "Logs" portrays Walker at one of his favorite activities—starting a fire. Here is a further parallel to his art, for only suitable fuel arranged with skill can produce a good fire. Similarly, the lyric poet pays dearly for the brief blaze and pleasant afterglow enjoyed by his readers:

> I dread my craft, crabbed
> words obdurate as sodden
> bark: yet love the morning
>
> scent of pear, the smoulder.

As confirmed by the three elegies in this volume, Walker never forgets that the elemental forces with which he keeps in touch bring loss as well as gain. Whether as friend, poet, or gardener he is haunted by the persistence of "feeble, savage-rooted growths" which "pick at the fabric of happiness" ("Elegy for an old acquaintance"). Though he cuts back the ivy which swarms up his garden wall, it "will grip again, cannot be kept out" ("Ivy"). Still,

for so long as he lives and is able, the task is his, and he is grateful to perform it, resigning it at last to others, just as he too has taken over from preceding generations. It is, as he says, a classical perspective.

Formally, *Burning the Ivy* differs noticeably from *Fox on a Barn Door*. While not abandoning tetrameter, Walker has lengthened his meters, working often in a loose pentameter and even in hexameter. To further increase rhythmic variety, he moves from the extremes of free verse to the rigid syllabic regularity of the sequence "Creatures of a zodiac," which consists of twelve perfectly equal sections of fifteen lines each with seven-syllable lines throughout (complete with a seven-syllable title). In brief, Walker remains receptive to both new subjects and different forms. Considering the extent of its new departures, it is fitting that *Burning the Ivy* should center upon the subject of the poet's craft. No doubt as professor of English literature and creative writing at New England College in Arundel, Sussex, a post he has held since 1971,

Covers for Walker's 1978 collection, poems that, for the most part, are set in the poet's Sussex house and garden

Walker has had abundant opportunities to consider the details of his craft.

Despite formal variations, however, Walker's posture remains meditative and elegiac. His normal tone is that of an enlightened Horatian conversationalist. On the rare occasions, such as "Pig pig" and "Letter to Marcel Proust," when he ventures into a callously brutal or hearty vernacular voice, the effect is likely to prove less bracing than embarrassing, perhaps because the strident tone seems so entirely out of character. His wide powers of observation and metaphorical inventiveness do not conceal that his subjects are limited in range and that, as indicated, he is either unable or unwilling to attempt great tonal versatility. While formalism has served him well, he has justifiably reproached himself for excessive "gentility" and zeal for tidiness. Indeed, for a self-confessed romantic, he maintains relentless emotional control. The very candor of such self-criticism, however, lends integrity and strength to poems which have reached an appreciative audience, and have earned him numerous awards, including the Eric Gregory and the Cholmondeley awards, the Campion Prize, and election as Fellow of the Royal Society of Literature. While *Fox on a Barn Door* still marks perhaps the zenith of his critical acclaim, the succeeding volumes have much to offer, and Walker's undiminished creative powers virtually assure that further awards are in store.

References:

Marius Bewley, "Poetry Chronicle," *Hudson Review*, 19 (Autumn 1966): 479-489;

Philip Legler, "Three Poets," *Poetry*, 109 (March 1967): 411-415;

Laurence Lieberman, "The Expansional Poet: A Return to Personality," *Yale Review*, 57 (Winter 1968): 258-271.

Andrew Waterman

(28 May 1940-   )

Neil Powell

BOOKS: *Living Room: Poems* (London: Marvell Press, 1974);

Last Fruit (Hitchin: Mandeville Press, 1974);

From the Other Country (Manchester: Carcanet Press, 1977);

Over the Wall (Manchester: Carcanet Press, 1980);

Out for the Elements (Manchester: Carcanet Press, 1981; Atlantic Highlands, N.J.: Humanities Press, 1981).

OTHER: "The poetry of Geoffrey Hill," in *British Poetry Since 1970*, edited by Peter Jones and Michael Schmidt (Manchester: Carcanet Press, 1980), pp. 85-102;

The Poetry of Chess, edited by Waterman (London: Anvil Press, 1981).

PERIODICAL PUBLICATIONS: "Ulsterectomy," *PN Review*, 3 (1977): 21-23;

"Notes on the Blue Guitar," *PN Review*, 8 (1978): 32-38.

Although Andrew Waterman's first collection of poems did not appear until he had reached the far from precocious age of thirty-four, his subsequent output has been astonishing in quantity and, recently, impressive in quality. It is unusual enough for a poet to produce collections in successive years, as Waterman did in 1980 and 1981; it is the more extraordinary when the title poem of *Out for the Elements* (1981) consists of 178 rhymed stanzas occupying ninety pages of a very substantial book. "Out for the Elements," the sequence, is a major achievement in other more important ways too, in technique and intention a cumulative piece of writing toward which Waterman's earlier poems can clearly be seen to lead.

Born in 1940, Andrew John Waterman grew up in South London suburbia so frequently and tellingly evoked in his poems. When he was nine, his adoptive father, Leonard Waterman, left the household; he himself left the home, maintained by Olive Smith Waterman, at seventeen. For seven years he did an assortment of clerical and manual jobs before going to Leicester University as a mature student in 1963. He graduated in 1966 with a first-class degree in English, and since 1968 he has taught in Coleraine, County Londonderry, at the New University of Ulster—the "other country" of his second book—where he is now a senior lecturer in English. He has one son, Rory, by his former wife Angela Eagle.

Much romantic and postromantic English poetry consists of fragmented autobiography, but this is especially true of Waterman's work. His recurrent theme is the landscape, or rather townscape, of late-twentieth-century suburban life— "These rained-on corners, pubs, or dusty streets"—and his subject matter tends to be, in a not necessarily pejorative sense, circular and repetitive. The stance, established at the very start of *Living Room* (1974), is one of wary observation: much of his poetry's distinctive flavor comes from the nervous juxtaposition of observed present and remembered past, evidence and autobiography. Where recollection fails, documentation takes over: "I cannot even remember/that other girl's face (I could check, I have photographs)." Waterman is constantly checking perception against evidence, suspicious that either might fail him or reveal only a partial truth.

Living Room, which was favorably received on its appearance in 1974 (it had the unusual distinction for a first collection of being selected as a Choice of the Poetry Book Society), maps out a territory which is explored rather than enlarged in the subsequent books: autobiographical poems from Waterman's London childhood (for instance, "Mother") to his present-day life in Ulster ("Derry Images 1968-1971"); poems which rely heavily on the demotic and conversational (such as "Two Railway Portraits"); poems whose subjects ("The New Young") or titles ("Waterman & Co") suggest the influence of Philip Larkin. In fact, Waterman's earlier work lacks Larkin's formal crispness and adopts a quite different kind of abrasive stance:

> Sweep us away who were young, it is time for the
>   young.
> Across the park a haze
> of dust. They are demolishing buildings.
> Like a frayed leaf blown to settle out of the heat,
> one old woman. She is an orphan,
> her whole world passed away.

Despite the vitality and the acute details (the wick-

edly ambiguous "They" in the third line, for instance), there is an impatience about this writing which suggests irritation rather than anger or concern. Anything approaching lyricism is stifled by both style and subject: thus, "Dingle" begins with a celebration of "great mountains weltering into the sea, surgings of rock and cloud," of "clochans, ring-forts, earthworks, burial grounds," but before the end of the poem we have descended to the village shop, where

> ancient gutturals are drowned
> by the television dumped
> among stacked Kelloggs, Surf, Flash, Alka-Seltzer.

The piling-up of rather tawdry details—in this case, brand names—to evoke the ephemeral quality of contemporary life is typical; even in the finely judged poem "Gardens," which concludes *Living Room,* the author's earliest horticultural memory turns out to be of the child who "bought seeds/at Woolworth's in vividly illustrated packets," and the reflections on different kinds of gardens are made from a precarious and ironic vantage point, "looking out of whatever rooms I've got/at some rubbly yard with bins."

Waterman's third book, *From the Other Country* (1977), is a disappointing one: partly because the range is predictably similar to his first, despite some forays into academic satire; partly because what previously appeared to be demotic freshness in Waterman's style now reveals itself as prosodic slackness. The author is evidently aware of this: among the seriously flawed poems in *From the Other Country* are "The Old, Cast Up on Lawns" and "Suburban Eden," both of which appear in much tighter, recast forms in *Out for the Elements.* The main focus has shifted somewhat from Waterman's London past to his Derry present. "Summer Truce" recalls W. H. Auden's "The summer holds . . ." and seems perfunctory by comparison, but the tighter anecdotal forms of "North Derry Nocturne" are more successful:

> I load the Bendix—round
> and round all goes in the wash—
> and walk down Prospect Road
> to raise my glass in the Anchor:
>
> the old familiar faces,
> the University matters.
> These horses of instruction!
> Where are the wiser tigers

of wrath? Outside and headed
this way last evening, a car
blew up: they found an arm
tattooed "for God and Ulster."

Elsewhere, "A New Babel" scores some effective if hardly momentous points against university English departments, but here (as in "The Tasserty File" from *Over the Wall*) the satirical mode which depends upon names such as Hack, Popgun, Glib, Potsmoke, and Drosse seems strained; Waterman's narrative skills are more usefully applied—as "North Derry Nocturne" at once compactly and eloquently suggests—to the contradictions of real life.

    The best poems in *Over the Wall* (1980) find Waterman at once exploring those contradictions and making increasingly supple use of traditional

Front cover for Waterman's 1980 collection, poems that display the poet's ability to forge satisfying wholes from disparate, apparently random bits of experience

meters, settling into the relaxed iambic of "Harmonies of Islington":

> "Look at that plane!"—a dark shell tipped with lights
> aimed slant above the flats' brute lines.
> And you, just five, "It's going to crash the moon."
>
> We watch. It hits. It is of course the moon
> endures (the plane sunk back beneath the horizon),
> frailly to intimate through pearls and blues
>
> of evening its conceivable angle on
> what's spoilt, waste, broken, moved among down here;
> collecting my past hour's wanderings.

There is an echo, not for the first time in Waterman's work, of Robert Frost's "Acquainted with the Night" here (and perhaps of Sidney's famous sonnet on the moon); and there seem to be traces of Frost's manner—isolation mellowing into the elegiac—in other poems too, such as "In Highgate Wood":

> A flicker of sun through leaves in Highgate Wood,
> this moment of recognition: I who know
> no kin find myself open intently
> in a willed, almost religious relinquishing.

But the most striking achievement in *Over the Wall* is the growth of that inclusiveness already implied: the ability to forge satisfying wholes from disparate, apparently random bits and pieces of experience. In the splendid (though enravelled and hence unquotable) "Playing through Old Games of Chess," Waterman's characteristic method of chronological association is extended to become historical rather than autobiographical in scope, while the vulnerably truthful "On the Mend" looks forward to the method of "Out for the Elements."

    Out for the Elements (1981) consists of four sections: the second is a somewhat miscellaneous collection of short poems and the third an attractive if garrulous piece called "Anglo-Irish," but the first and last are Waterman's most impressive achievements so far. "Given Worlds," which opens the book, displays both formal skill and a certain nerve, for several of the twenty short pieces are earlier poems recycled. The result is successful and a little discomfiting: a distillation of much in the earlier books, which, the reader now realizes needed just this kind of compact rewriting. The nature of the process is clearly exemplified by comparing these lines from the earlier version of "Suburban Eden"—

And one can never go back.
Only to look: it is still going on,
on a frail rectangle of grass shaken out
where cloud-shadows pass boys are chasing a ball
    about,

girls call from the benches, the ball hangs
in the same arc over the same bough,
the foot aches to kick, held by fear
as of breaking glass.

with their counterparts in "Given Worlds":

And one cannot return, except
to look: shrunk, all's still going on;
girls call, the ball rolls loose; my foot
holds back. One kick might shatter glass.

Though less detailed, the second version is more exact, more evocative and technically far more sharply defined and self-disciplined than the first; it also, quite simply, makes more sense.

However, it is the long title sequence which concludes Waterman's most recent book, which is his finest work yet: "Out for the Elements" is his *Prelude* and might well have been subtitled "The Growth of a Poet's Mind"—a connection which may serve to remind us that, above and beyond the echoes of Frost or Larkin, the figure which stands most majestically behind Waterman's poetry is Wordsworth's. "Out for the Elements" borrows its stanzaic form from Pushkin, but its autobiographical method and its fidelity to ordinary speech are true to the principles of the preface to the *Lyrical Ballads*. The writing is both relaxed and assured within the tight stanzaic form, and the poem's ambitious range is announced in its opening stanza:

Starry tonight, and repetitious
sea harrassing the empty strand,
as when it first cast adventitious
staggering life upon the land;
through sleights of wondrous generation
since to attain a consummation
in filaments of light I see
stacked on the Prom: humanity
with all its complex apparatus,
deep-freezers, televisions, cars,
banks, supermarkets, churches, bars,
shows what once kindled to create us
subtilised now to a weird grace-
note shimmering on time and space.

Waterman handles the form with equal confidence when incorporating conversation (sometimes running through several stanzas) and, in this case, a

Front cover for Waterman's 1981 book. The long title sequence has been praised as his finest work yet and a major poetic achievement.

direct acknowledgement of his Wordsworthian allegiance:

"We're five, my kids and me. There's Maire
who I was talking of, she's great.
Sean died at three months, he'll be four, a
beautiful son. Martine and Kate
I lost at fifteen days. September
they're two, the twins. Oh, I remember
all their birthdays, to me they stay
alive and growing every day."
Cellophane in the ashtray crackles
as she stubs her cigarette, flares
brilliant as magnesium. There's
life answering academic jackals
who, reading Wordsworth, have demurred
at "We are Seven" as absurd.

As with "Given Worlds," there is a degree of recy-

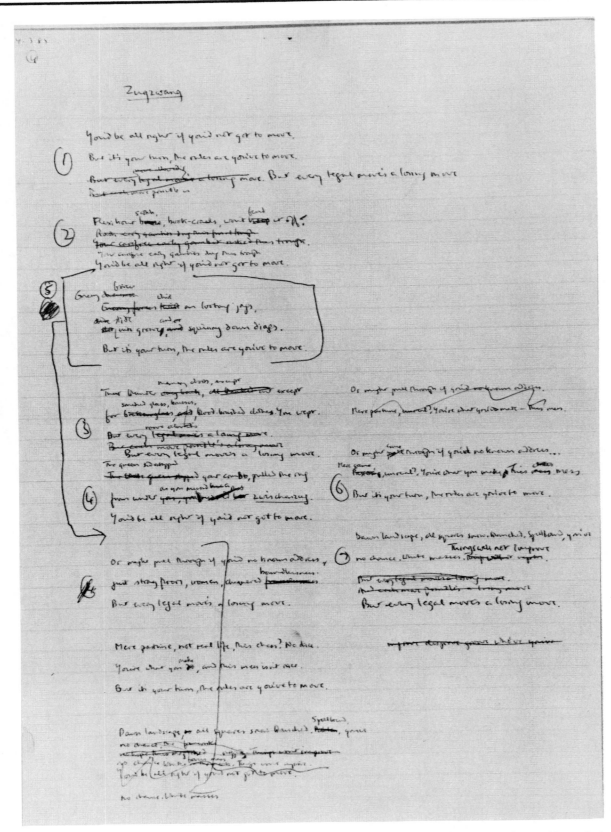

Draft and final typescript for a recently completed poem (the author)

Zugzwang.

You'd be all right if you'd not got to move.
But it's your turn, the rules are you've to move.
But every legal move's a losing move.

Enemy forces whirl on looting jags,
slide into groove, and squinny down diags.
You'd be all right if you'd not got to move.

That blunder memory aborts — except
for smashed glass, bruises, blood-brushed clothes. You wept.
But it's your turn, the rules are you've to move.

The queen sidestepped your combo, pulled the rug
from under as you missed her zwischenzug.
But every legal move's a losing move.

Flexihour scotch, book-crawls, won't fend it off.
Your carefree early gambit dug this trough.
You'd be all right if you'd not got to move.

Or might pull through if you'd no known address,
just stray floors, lovers, chequered boundlessness.
But it's your turn, the rules are you've to move.

Mere pastime, not real life, this chess? No dice.
You're what you make, this mess no paradise.
But every legal move's a losing move.

Dawn's landscape, all squares snow-blanched. Spellbound, you've
no chance. White masses. Things will not improve.
You'd be all right if you'd not got to move.

Andrew Waterman
March 1985

cling from earlier poems in "Out for the Elements," which is unsurprising in view of the sequence's autobiographical reach. But there *are* surprises, of the most overwhelmingly ironic kind, for author and reader alike: for at stanza 77, almost halfway through the sequence, Waterman abruptly discovers that "life has ways of interrupting/poetry." Until this day in March 1980, he had been unable to discover the identity of his actual parents:

> Once, chancing past the building where
> all births are registered, I wandered
> inside, but my enquiries there
> drew a blank. My adoptive father,
> not seen since I was nine for rather
> intricately sad reasons, died
> late last year. I was notified.
> "From his papers" proof of my actual
> parentage comes, astounds my day:
> Nolan, Dermot and Moyra (nee
> Enright). Both Irish. A strange factual
> fluke for me to assimilate.
> I sit, and let it resonate.

Not only does this have obvious implications for Waterman's recurrent theme of Anglo-Irishness: it is also satisfyingly apt, given his poetic stance, for "art" to be so magnificently upstaged by "life."

Of course, there are flaws in "Out for the Elements": the verse form, over this length, naturally imposes strains, and there are some lapses of tone ("But I wouldn't scoff," says Waterman inadequately, having just scoffed at the aspirations of his former South London friends). Nevertheless, it remains an unusually ambitious enterprise, carried out more successfully than one would have thought at all probable: a skillful and accessible long poem, conventionally autobiographical yet wholly contemporary in tone and range, it is among the most impressive achievements in recent English poetry. As Grevel Lindop noted in the *Times Literary Supplement*, "If someone in a century or so would like to know what it was like to live in Britain in the 1980s, he could do worse than turn to *Out for the Elements*." It will be a hard act for Waterman to follow.

Robert Wells

(17 August 1947-   )

Kathleen Henderson Staudt
Drexel University

BOOK: *The Winter's Task* (Manchester: Carcanet Press, 1977).

OTHER: Jim Hunter, ed., *Modern Poets Five: C. H. Sisson, Andrew Waterman, Craig Raine, Robert Wells, Tom Paulin, Andrew Motion*, includes notes by Hunter and Wells (London: Faber & Faber, 1981);
Vergil: The Georgics, translated by Wells (Manchester: Carcanet Press, 1982).

PERIODICAL PUBLICATIONS: "Nine Poems," *PN Review*, 5, no. 2 (1977): 54;
"For Pasolini," *PN Review*, 5, no. 4 (1978): 26;
"Leaving" and "Nothing But the Flicker of Leaf Shadow," *PN Review*, 6, no. 4 (1979): 46;
"Virgil's Fourth Georgic," *PN Review*, 8 (Winter 1981): 22-26.

Robert Wells, one of a number of young poets currently published by the *PN Review* and Carcanet Press, has been praised most often for the classical purity of form and subject in his poetry. Deeply influenced by long study of Greek and Latin poetry, his style is lucid and carefully wrought. His orientation to the world is at once objective and also morally engaged.

For his commitment to formal clarity, Wells is frequently associated with his friends and contemporaries Clive Wilmer and Dick Davis. Thom Gunn and Yvor Winters have also been cited as modern poets whose ideas harmonize with Wells's own practice, and one can detect echoes of the British preromantics—especially William Collins, Thomas Gray, William Cowper, and James Thomson—in the landscape poems of *The Winter's Task* (1977). Nonetheless, Wells's style is finally a particular and original one, developing in calm, stable, and transparent forms a modern pastoral vision deeply rooted in the landscapes of Exmoor, on the Devon-Somerset border, and of the Licenza Valley in the Sabine Hills outside Rome.

Wells was born in Oxford, the son of a classical don and teacher at the university. From about his tenth year, his education consisted largely of translating between English and Greek or Latin, and his poetic style testifies to this long devotion to the classics. Wells read classics and English at King's College, Cambridge, from 1965 to 1968. During this period, he became close friends with fellow poets Clive Wilmer, Dick Davis, and Michael Vince. Between 1968 and 1979, after completing his studies at Cambridge, Wells worked as a forester on the coast of Exmoor, North Devon, and later as a teacher of English in southern Italy and in Iran. The landscapes of Exmoor and southern Italy are brought to life vividly in *The Winter's Task.*

The title poem of this collection, which focuses on the figure of a woodcutter working alone in Exmoor, offers an extended meditation on the virtues of solitary labor in nature. As in many poems in this volume, the protagonist is described in the third person, so that despite the details of his consciousness, the poetic self is objectified. The poem emphasizes the changelessness of the natural landscape despite the passage of time and the efforts of human energy. Ultimately, it celebrates the laborer's pursuit of work for its own sake, as he moves out of himself and lays hold of a fundamental and objective reality:

> For hand in hand with hope, life in his hands,
> And clothed in powerful youth, he turns aside
> From local ambition, even from the abyss
> Of human feeling, though to stand at loss,
> Frustrate or joyous amid the idle paths
> Where nature cancels history, where strength
> Of body is the means toward its own end;
> And is the strongest he will ever be.

The laborer achieves fulfillment, not in self-absorption and introspection, like so many romantic solitaries, but in completing one task and moving on to the next, engaging the world actively through hard work. Hence the protagonist struggles "to break/the tryst of self-possession," to shake off both childhood memories and existential doubts about the final value of the products of his labor. The poem concludes by discovering in the task a deeper

way of apprehending and embracing a reality and purpose beyond the self.

"The Winter's Task," with its twelve stanzas, is the longest and most ambitious poem in the volume. The other poems, however, demonstrate a remarkable mastery of the brief (4-6 line) lyric. Such poems as "His Thirst," "The Bathing Place," "Off the Path," "Waterfall," "At the Well," and "After Haymaking" rely on vivid and concisely expressed images to convey the simple sensuous pleasures of the worker's life. Others develop more specifically the effort to find within work a core of reality which would lift the individual worker out of the self-absorbed "abyss of human feeling" into the stately peace of the landscape. As the poem "The Knot" suggests, discovering this core of being in nature is analogous to achieving "self-possession,"

Front cover for the 1979 edition of Wells's first book. Robert Nye, reviewing the 1977 edition, hailed Wells, as "one of the best young poets now writing."

but it involves moving beyond the subjective world:

> The knot cuts across however far
> You cut back the wood,
> A deep engraining. The figure moving there
> Is not where your passion centres
> But is a likeness of the shape
> That itself moves inside you.

The second stanza of the poem, however, acknowledges that apprehension of this core of being will upset the inward-turning impulses of the ego. This theme is also developed in the next poem in the volume, "The Changeling," a sensitive account of childhood betrayal, nightmarish history and insomnia. These two poems immediately precede the title poem, which seems to offer a corrective to the introspective urges they express.

The tension between the conflicting demands of inner self and outer world is summarized well in "Not Like the Fields," which also exemplifies the spare, meditative style of some of Wells's shorter poems:

> His nature was mild like the fields.
> It was the soft turf under his tread,
> The alteration of weather.
>
> But desire was in his nature too
> And that was not like the fields.

This desire which hinders harmony with the landscape takes two different forms in Wells. In poems such as "The Changeling" and "The Knot," one senses an inner turmoil, rooted in childhood dreams and disappointments, which the maturing protagonist struggles to master. Elsewhere, in "Angel," "Virginity," and the quartet of brief lyrics consisting of "Bonfire," "His Thirst," "Love's Default," and "The Stream," the poet describes a desire for human love which is limited by the laborer's sparse and solitary life. A few of these poems invoke an absent loved one, as in, for example, "Morning." Two poems in the collection, "The Trance" and "Deus Loci," record with almost mystic intensity the intuition of a hidden but compelling divine presence in the landscape. Thus "Deus Loci" invokes a deity who "is on the edge of appearing, and is withheld / only by so slight a thing as his absence." But if human and divine absence can evoke a sense of presence and love in the empty landscape, Wells also records the laborer's frequent sense of solitude in the company of his fellow workers. "Lost Company," "Cattlemen," "On the Hillside," and "The

First Thing," for example, reflect in various ways on the pleasures of solitude which one finds both in company and in unexpected separations from one's fellows.

The contemporary pastoral vision comes into sharper focus in a group of poems toward the end of the volume—"Disco," "While Dancing," "Expectations," and "At the Back of His Mind," which look longingly at rural life from the perspective of the modern urban world. "Outside," "Vendemmia," and "Gran Sasso" recall in loving and literal detail the sounds and shapes of rural southern Italy. *The Winter's Task* ends with a few experiments in less typical themes and forms, notably in the final two poems. "The Last Caliph" is based on an incident from Persian history and traceable, perhaps, to Wells's time in Iran. The final poem, "Chinese Dish," demonstrates Wells's attraction to the clarity and fluidity of Chinese poetry, which he has read in translation by A. C. Graham, Arthur Waley, and Ezra Pound.

Given the classical lucidity evident in *The Winter's Task,* it is not surprising to find that Wells's most recent work has been a translation of Vergil's *Georgics* completed while he was teaching English at Leicester University, from 1979 to 1982. His introduction to this volume provides useful insights into the things he most appreciates in classical poetry and the qualities he strives to achieve in his own work. He expresses admiration, for example, for Vergil's valuation of hard work as a means to discover "the mind that is present in matter and the sympathies that bind things together" and for the Vergilian analogy between the labor of the farmer and that of the poet. His account of Vergil's style suggests a source of his own commitment to clarity, accuracy, and objectivity in poetry: "Vergil's clarity is not a clarity of surface—it has not that sharpness of edge and line that Ezra Pound has taught us to look for. To read Vergil is like looking down through very clear water; one is barely conscious of the surface, but the objects on the riverbed are made to shine. Bathed in his sensibility the world has a subdued brightness, like pebbles underwater, all their colours enlivened."

The initial response to Wells's translation of the *Georgics* has been positive, and as poems in their own right, Wells's versions effectively transmit to the English speaking reader the pleasure that he has found in the Latin poet's style and rural themes. Among the many examples one might cite is the beginning of the fourth Georgic, where the poet tells the beekeeper what animals to keep away from the hive:

Keep away the lizards with bright green scaly backs
And harmful birds like the bee-eater and swallow,
Its breast-feathers stained by Procne's hands for a sign.
These do great damage, snatching the bees from
    flight—
Sweet morsels to stop their nestlings' gaping throats.
There should be water close by, pools green with moss,
And a small stream running shallowly through the
    grass.

This passage demonstrates well the economy and smoothness of the translator's verse as well as his skill in capturing the life, variety, and color of the Latin poet's rural world.

In addition to the translations from Vergil, Wells has published a number of other poems in *PN Review* since the appearance of *The Winter's Task*. Notable among these is "For Pasolini," a poem in memory of the Italian poet, which vividly describes a decaying and disorderly landscape, reflecting elegiacally on the loss of the antique virtues celebrated both in Pasolini's early work and in *The Winter's Task*. The elegiac tone of this poem, critical of life in the modern world, indicates one of the more recent directions of Wells's poetry. He also hopes to do further work on classical translation, perhaps of the work of Theocritus.

Although Robert Wells is still young and his work quite recent, a number of readers have hailed him as one of the most important and promising talents of his generation. Perhaps because of his long devotion to the classics and to the landscapes he loves, he brings to poetry a sincerity, discipline, freshness, and depth of moral vision that many of his contemporaries welcome.

References:

David Middleton, " 'Men in Dark Times': Three New British Poets," *Southern Review*, 15 (Summer 1979): 585-604;

Michael Schmidt, "The Time and the Place," *Kenyon Review*, new series 3 (Summer 1981): 9-31.

Hugo Williams

(20 February 1942-   )

Michael Hulse

BOOKS: *Symptoms of Loss: Poems* (Oxford & New York: Oxford University Press, 1965);
All the Time in the World (London: Alan Ross, 1966; Philadelphia: Chilton, 1968);
Poems (London: The Review, 1969);
Sugar Daddy (Oxford & New York: Oxford University Press, 1970);
Some Sweet Day (Oxford & New York: Oxford University Press, 1975);
Love-Life (London: Deutsch/Whizzard Press, 1979);
No Particular Place to Go (London: Cape, 1981);
Writing Home (Oxford & New York: Oxford University Press, forthcoming 1985).

OTHER: *London Magazine Poems 1961-1966*, edited, with contributions, by Williams (London: Alan Ross, 1966);
Hermine Demoriane, *Life Star*, translated by Williams (London: London Magazine Editions, 1968; New York: Coward-McCann, 1968);
Blake Morrison and Andrew Motion, eds., *The Penguin Book of Contemporary British Poetry*, includes poems by Williams (Harmondsworth: Penguin, 1982).

Hugo Williams's biggest popular success came with *No Particular Place to Go* (1981), a travel book relating the poet's journey from East to West in the United States and back again. An engaging, funny, and frank book, it has also been published in paperback by Picador. His major effort, however, has been in poetry, and his first three full-length collections in particular—*Symptoms of Loss* (1965), *Sugar Daddy* (1970), and *Some Sweet Day* (1975)—represent what may be the finest work produced in one of the two main schools associated with the *Review* (later the *New Review*). One of these schools can be seen as including the somewhat baroque wit of John Fuller, James Fenton, and Clive James, writing in a tradition with clear links to W. H. Auden; the other

Hugo Williams

imagery of some of Williams's poems (including "The Actor," "The Stage is Unlit," "Revolving Stage," and "First-Night"), and the poet's present work in progress promises to deal at greater length with this material; it is intended as a semi-autobiographical sequence, dealing also with his father and the acting life. Hugo Williams's brother has in fact also gone on the stage, but the young Hugo was actively discouraged by his father, though he admits to a lingering desire.

Hugo Williams was educated at Eton College (1955-1960) and, during this time, he wrote his first poems, some of which were accepted for publication by the *London Magazine;* and in 1960 he joined this magazine as an editorial assistant. Two years later he left again, to spend some twenty months traveling around the world. These travels are recorded in *All the Time in the World* (1966), a mild-mannered and perceptive travel book written later in London from notes. Often it reads as if a street-wise urchin had been given an education in poetic journalism. New Year 1963 found Williams on shipboard from Venice to Greece; from there he traveled across the Middle East, driving down through the desert to Kuwait. This experience, only slightly transfigured, appears in "Crossing a Desert":

> This truck puts an end to dreams,
> How we arrive in great cities,
> Simply by wishing on their names:

and, in the closing lines,

> And after all, it is fear. A scampering
> For the burrow. I can only cross
> This wilderness because I know
> That it is part of a return, that long ago
> I made the outward journey in a dream.

If the quasi-mythic undertones of this poem suggest deeper veins of meaning, the understated uncertainty nonetheless must hold interpretation in check. This mild sense of mystery is a characteristic Williams note.

Williams traveled on through India and South East Asia (see the poem "Beginning to Go," which appears to record an affair with a woman named Lily in Thailand) to Japan and Australia, and then sailed home (see the two short "Tahitian Poems"). If the section on Australia was the weakest part of this first travel volume, the country's effect settled more noticeably into Williams's poetic imagination. "The Hitch Hiker" recollects roadside boredom:

discernible school, of which Williams has been an accomplished member, placed an emphasis on seeing the everyday and ordinary in bare, minimalist rhetoric, giving an impression of 1950s restraint slightly stripped. This group of writers included the *Review*'s editor, Ian Hamilton, and David Harsent and Colin Falck as well as Williams. It would perhaps do insufficient justice to Williams to see his poetry only in these terms, since indeed his earliest and most recent work show other pressures and directions, but it is useful to remember that this poet's claim on attention comes not only from his poetry itself but also from a position in the influential literary establishment, at least in the late 1960s and early 1970s.

Hugo Williams was born in 1942 at Windsor in Berkshire, the son of Hugh Williams, an actor-playwright, and Margaret Vyner Williams. Hugo Williams has testified to the fascination the acting life held for him, with its backstage excitement, makeup, costumes, and girls, and still, with that antiacademicism often seen in writers, he says: "This is nearer poetry than universities for me." A theater background is present in the settings and

Roadsides are desert islands. There
You are cast up like driftwood,
Dependent on the tides and moods
Of motorists, and there you stay,

Flotsam and jetsam of the highway.

"Aborigine," examining a man who is "Beautiful in the manner of his country," appeared first in *Symptoms of Loss* and then, with minor amendations, reappeared in *Sugar Daddy*, under the title "The Dreamtime," as the last of a six-part sequence headed "Aborigine Sketches." Of these six poems, "Mission" presents a total—if one-sided—image of a continent and typifies Williams's clipped, emblematic style. Now "embalmed in charity," the mission was founded by "Misguided German Christians," who now are buried "an inch/under the dusty sand," barren soil that will never be tilled "or broken with laughter." The living exist in a similar milieu:

All day the families of matchstick children
Shift like hour hands round eucalypts.
Hazed in flies, a bleary wolfhound
Shambles across the courtyard—ratbag
Mascot of some disgraced regiment in exile.

Having returned to London, Williams spent some months of 1965 as a staff writer for the *Telegraph Magazine* (March to July), and on 9 October 1965 he married a Frenchwoman, Hermine Demoriane. Their one daughter, Murphy, to whom *Some Sweet Day* is dedicated, was born the following year, and husband and wife collaborated on an account of the pregnancy, which Williams translated into English. Also in 1966 he went back to the *London Magazine*, where he worked as assistant editor until 1970. These years, which followed the publication of his first collection of poems and travel volume, also marked the beginnings of his association with the *Review*, and brought the poet the first of his several prizes: an Eric Gregory Award in 1966 and an Arts Council Bursary in the same year. Of his early poetry, probably the best-known is "The Butcher," in which the sensitive "rosy young" butcher, "with white eyelashes/Like a bullock," appears "hurt by the parting sinews" when he carves veal for the poet and his wife. "I think he knows about my life," the poet writes. "How someone/With a foreign accent can only cook veal." The butcher's smile, as he hands the poet his package, "Is the official seal on my marriage." The power of this brief observation comes from its unsettling sense of menace below the surface of everyday domestic events, as if happiness were in the keeping of other people. The latent question of the negative dimensions present in human relationships is sometimes more openly explored in Williams's work, though rarely to such evocative effect.

In 1969 Williams's father died, leaving his poet son a legacy of fondness for the theater as well as an inscription on the flyleaf of a travel book, *Eye of Day*, by Sir Lawrence Olivier's son: "His father may be a better actor than I am. May you be a better writer than he is." The following year saw the publication of Hugo Williams's next major collection, *Sugar Daddy*, which earned him a Cholmondeley Award in 1971. In *Sugar Daddy* the cult of brevity becomes excessive, with many poems no more than four lines, but the more successful poems, often anecdotal yet laden with insight, create the reverberations we associate with the poet's finest work. "The Couple Upstairs," for example, develops the random observation of the wife leaving the house rapidly, into a perception of the mysterious connections that link lives to those of others:

they seemed inviolate, like us,
Our loves in sympathy. Her going

Thrills and frightens us. We come awake
And talk excitedly about ourselves, like guests.

Here and elsewhere, Williams has a talent for touching nerves, for seeing in two words ("like us") the essential instability of worlds, for finding the right, questioning image ("like guests").

The 1970s were less favorable to Williams than his period of increasing ascendancy in the 1960s. He has read from his work, taught casually, and for the first six months of 1972 worked as a staff writer for *Realités* in Paris. In 1973 he joined in an Arts Council reading tour of Israel (Tel Aviv, Jerusalem, and Haifa) of which he recalls: "It was two days after the Lod Airport massacre and we shuddered at the bullet holes in the departure lounge." In 1975 he was for a time an editorial assistant with the *New Review*, and throughout the 1970s he was variously involved in writers-in-schools tours of England and residencies at the Arvon Foundation, a British creative writing organization. Otherwise, as Williams puts it, "The real background story of the last ten years is a record-breaking dole-run which I am now cold-turkeying."

The middle of the decade was marked by the publication of *Some Sweet Day*, a less convincing collection than *Symptoms of Loss* and *Sugar Daddy* and one in which the *Review* cult of brief minimalism for the first time seems to be coming into conflict with the writer's expressive wishes. The most interesting note in this book is a movement toward a vaguely oriental angle to the word, so that the charge of mystery that is always in Williams's work takes on an almost Japanese rhetoric, as in the opening lines of "Cherry Blossom":

> Delicate red flames
> Are finding their way
>
> Out of the dark cherry branches.
> They have discovered the sky!
>
> Already they expect the clouds
> To reward their fidelity.
>
> O cherry tree, guest of the sunset,
> Is this your or my day?

If this oriental manner was a workable compromise with his own talent, Hugo Williams seems nonetheless to have recognized that a different approach might be more rewarding; and the final demise of the *New Review* in 1979, marking the end of an era that had already been superseded, coincided with the publication of his next volume of poetry, *Love-Life* (1979). Here the oriental strain is still present, but the poet has added to it an imagination charged with the street-life sense and perceptive power that can also be seen in his 1981 travel book, *No Particular Place to Go.* Accepting the contexts and cultural predilections to which his own preferences incline him, Williams writes poems whose obvious contemporary relevance in no way offends against the more fragile frames he uses. This tendency can be seen, for example, in "Confessions of a Drifter," which is subtitled "(after Tu Mu 803-852 A.D.)":

> I used to sell perfume in the New Towns.
> I was popular in the saloons.
> Professional women slept in my trailer.
> Young salesgirls broke my heart. For ten years
> I never went near our Main Office.

If poems such as "Stagefright" remember his father and look forward to the sequence at present in progress, most of the pieces in *Love-Life* are what the title promises: explorations of love and sex. These areas of experience, always important to Williams, seem at the end of the 1970s to have grown in significance in both his personal life and his poetry, so that *No Particular Place to Go,* which recounts near-penniless Greyhound travel in the United

Front cover for Williams's 1979 collection, winner of a Geoffrey Faber Memorial Prize

States, with a handful of poetry readings jostled off the page by accounts of women and brief affairs, appears to be the most necessary reading to accompany recent poems such as "The Best in the World" or "The Spring of Sheep." The first of these speaks of Young America and its happiness—

> You girls whose talk is all of Pop,
> You're showing off to us
> In your halter-tops and slacks.

The second is a mock-modest account of his visit, packed with "Pro-Plus Rapid Energy Tablets," to a girl friend:

> I practised laughing in the window of the bus,
> but I laughed on the other side of my face
> when I saw her riding her pony
> in her beatnik pullover.

If these poems are anecdotal and finally not of the greatest significance, it is important to realize that in them Williams is developing in a direction new to him, toward a lengthier, more leisurely examination of personal experience. Without being confessional or embarrassing, his recent poems are among the finest he has written, the best of them no doubt being "Tangerines," which took second prize in the 1980 National Poetry Competition. In this poem he evocatively recreates his postwar childhood, the mysteriousness of his parents' night life, and the irresistible call of another place or another time:

> They sent me sword-shaped eucalyptus leaves
> And purple, pre-war flowers, pressed

Between the pages of my first letters. One year
A box of tangerines arrived for me from France.
I hid behind the sofa in my parents' bedroom,
Eating my way south to join them.

In 1979 *Love-Life* won its author the Geoffrey Faber Memorial Prize, and in 1981 the University of East Anglia appointed him its writer in residence for the session. If these good omens are accompanied by a resurgence in his poetic imagination, we can expect a good deal of rewarding poetry from Williams in the future.

Clive Wilmer
(10 February 1945-   )

David E. Middleton
Nicholls State University

BOOKS: *Shade Mariners: Dick Davis, Clive Wilmer, Robert Wells* (Cambridge: Gregory Spiro, 1970);

The Dwelling-Place (Manchester: Carcanet Press, 1977);

Devotions (Manchester: Carcanet Press, 1982).

OTHER: *Poetry Introduction 2*, includes poems by Wilmer (London: Faber & Faber, 1972);

Michael Schmidt, ed., *Ten English Poets: An Anthology*, includes poems by Wilmer (Manchester: Carcanet Press, 1976), pp. 67-75;

Miklós Radnóti, *Forced March: Selected Poems*, translated, with an introduction and notes, by Wilmer and George Gömöri (Manchester: Carcanet Press, 1979);

Thom Gunn, *The Occasions of Poetry*, edited, with an introduction, by Wilmer (London: Faber & Faber, 1982);

John Ruskin, *Unto This Last, and Other Writings*, edited, with an introduction, by Wilmer (London: Penguin/Manchester: Carcanet Press, forthcoming 1985).

PERIODICAL PUBLICATIONS: "Clive Wilmer on New Poetry," review of Thom Gunn's *Moly* and other books, *Spectator*, 29 May 1971, pp. 742-744;

"Exorcising the Ghost," review of *Tennyson*, by

Christopher Ricks, *Spectator*, 2 September 1972, pp. 364-365;

"Rooted in the Past," review of *Selected Poems: 1923-67*, by Jorge Luis Borges, *Spectator*, 19 May 1973, pp. 622-623;

"In the Distance," review of *In the Distance*, by Dick Davis, *PN Review*, 4, no. 1 (1976): 41-42;

"A Net of Stars," review of *Selected Poems*, by Janos Pilinsky, *PN Review*, 4, no. 3 (1977): 34-36;

"Preaching to the Converted," letter to the editor in response to Donald Davie, *PN Review*, 4, no. 4 (1977): 54-55;

"Definition and Flow: A Personal Reading of Thom Gunn," review-essay on *Jack Straw's Castle*, by Thom Gunn, *PN Review*, 5, no. 3 (1978): 51-57;

"Daedalus and Icarus: A Note on the Poetry of John Heath-Stubbs," *Aquarius*, 10 (1978): 98-100;

"Exile and Ambassador," review of *The Watchman's Flute*, by John Heath-Stubbs, *PN Review*, 6, no. 3 (1979): 26-28;

"Note," on John Taverner and "Antiphonal Sonnets," *PN Review*, 6, no. 4 (1979): 46;

"Leaving the Burning City: on the work of Czeslaw Milosz," *New Statesman*, 24 October 1980, pp. 25-26;

"White Spaces," review of *Modern Hungarian Poetry*, edited by Miklós Vajda, *London Magazine*, 20 (February-March 1981): 134-139;

Clive Wilmer

"The Rational Mystic," review of *An Introduction to the Poetry of Yvor Winters,* by Elizabeth Isaacs, *Times Literary Supplement,* 14 August 1981, p. 930;

"Adventurer in Living Fact: The Wilderness in Winters' Poetry," *Southern Review,* new series 17·(Autumn 1981): 964-971;

"An Art of Recovery: Some Literary Sources for Geoffrey Hill's *Tenebrae,*" *Southern Review,* new series 17 (Winter 1981): 121-141;

"Between Silences," review of *Poems,* by Paul Celan, translated by Michael Hamburger, *PN Review,* 8, no. 3 (1981): 26-29;

"John Ruskin: Life or Works?," review of *John Ruskin: The Passionate Moralist,* by Joan Abse, *PN Review,* 8, no. 4 (1981): 24-25;

"Masters in Modernism," review of *Some Americans: A Personal Record,* by Charles Tomlinson, *Times Literary Supplement,* 5 February 1982, p. 141.

Clive Wilmer, poet, translator, editor, and regular contributor of book reviews and essays to British periodicals, is most closely associated with *Poetry Nation Review* whose editor, Michael Schmidt, also publishes Wilmer's poetry through his Carcanet Press. Wilmer's first full-length book of poetry, *The Dwelling-Place* (1977), has been praised for its thematic unity and for its technical mastery of traditional forms. Tennyson, the mature Yvor Winters, Allen Tate, and the earlier formalism of Thom Gunn are the governing spirits of the volume's antithetical strains of stoic rationalism and the longing for a lost heroic past. In *Devotions* (1982), Wilmer displays a wider, more affirmative range of sensibility. John Ruskin, David Jones, Geoffrey Hill, the later Gunn, and the Winters with a keen eye for natural detail inform the poet's new concern with the relation between sensation and intellect, between the natural world and human language, as these antiphonal pairs mutually define and nourish one another. *Devotions* continues Wilmer's elegiac lamentation for lost traditions, but a clear-eyed celebration of the otherness of natural beauty, of the sacramental character of language, art, and human labor, and of a naturalist's concern for the rightful interplay of man and the world widens the poet's thematic range even as the use of free verse extends his technical mastery without prejudice to those traditional forms which still dominate the second volume. Both *The Dwelling-Place* and *Devotions* contain poems whose sensuous intensity is matched and controlled by an intellectual content whose lucid complexity is rare in contemporary verse.

Clive Wilmer was born on 10 February 1945 in Harrogate, Yorkshire. His family, however, is from South London, North Surrey, and the poet spent his childhood in a London still gutted by the German air raids of World War II. Wilmer feels deeply moved by his childhood experience of modern war's destruction of public edifices celebratory of other times and larger values. Born in 1882, Wilmer's father, a civil servant, was in his sixties when the poet was born, and he died in 1948 before Wilmer's fourth birthday. Thereafter, his mother raised the poet and his sister in modest circumstances. Judging from certain poems, one sees Wilmer as an intelligent, imaginative child, somewhat given to a Victorian dream of the chivalric Arthurian past.

Wilmer attended Emmanuel Grammar School in South London (1956-1963) and then King's College, Cambridge (1964-1967), on an open scholarship. He was graduated with first-class honors in English and won an Honourary Senior Scholarship. After spending 1968 learning Italian while teaching at the British Institute in Florence, Wilmer returned to Cambridge (1968-1971) to do research on a still unfinished thesis entitled "Symbolic Landscape in Tennyson's Poetry." Since leaving Florence, Wilmer has served for a time as poetry critic for the *Spectator* and has supervised for the English faculty at Cambridge, specializing in classes in practical criticism, and, after spending 1971-1972 at the Oxford School of English in Padua and then at the University of Padua at Verona, has taught English to foreigners at the Cambridgeshire College of Arts and Technology and at the Bell School of Languages. From 1973 until the present, Wilmer has been on the full-time staff at the Bell School but has done some teaching elsewhere and has taken leave without pay to do writing. He is married and has two children.

In *The Dwelling-Place* (which contains eight of the thirteen poems that Wilmer contributed to *Shade Mariners*, 1970) Wilmer shares with other British poets active in the 1960s and 1970s (Hill, Seamus Heaney, David Jones) a desire to rediscover history in the aftermath of empire, two world wars, and the establishment of the welfare state. In his introductions to *British Poetry Since 1960* (1972) and *British Poetry Since 1970* (1980), Michael Schmidt notes that the best contemporary British poets are "historical in imagination" and ready to use the "old and serviceable prosodic skills" of traditional forms that animated past poetry. Concern with the past, Schmidt says, enables poets "to see places and events in their full human complexity, to re-imbue with human warmth facts which have turned cold, to make earlier lives and earlier struggles part of a present which they illluminate." And, in response to twentieth-century barbarism, as Alan Brownjohn notes in "English Poetry in the Early Seventies," the poet must cultivate "a rational, sceptical temperament" to oppose "the machinery of horror" with "the commonwealth of decency."

This antithesis of present skepticism and a loving search through history for clues to personal, national, and human identity appears in *The Dwelling-Place* as well as in a number of Wilmer's occasional prose pieces. In the introduction to his translation of the poems of Miklós Radnóti, Wilmer sees the Hungarian poet, who was executed by firing squad during World War II, as "an individual talent . . . moulded by historical events" which at the same time may be seen "discerning meaning in the events, even as it is transformed by them." Using the Hungarian equivalent of classical meters and the classical form of the eclogue, Radnóti affirmed civilized order in the midst of barbarism: "the expression of thought and feeling within the clear but flexible order of the classical hexameter came to seem a moral act" while his use of the eclogue showed "his commitment . . . to the humane order of the Classical tradition." Wilmer also found this combination of history and rationality in Thom Gunn's *Moly* (1971). Praising Gunn's "highly classical limpidity" as a way of controlling poems that were "obsessive, introspective, ruled by the past," Wilmer defined Gunn as "a poet of the intellect" whose poems are "forms of the conscious intelligence." One can see the influence of Yvor Winters, in varying degrees, on the work of both Gunn and Wilmer. Wilmer has called the American critic "the apostle of classical form and lucidity." Winters's antipantheistic poem "The Slow Pacific Swell" Wilmer has recommended for its "neoclassicism," as "an antidote to the oceanic vision." In Winters's poetry of an American wilderness devoid of history, Wilmer sees the type of the rational humanist whom he praises in *The Dwelling-Place:* "the poet as frontiersman who carries the heritage of civilization, rational intelligence, into the primeval wilderness, the unknown."

For Wilmer, then, the poet is a man of conscious intelligence and moral courage. Although he explicitly rejects the romantic idea of the poet as unacknowledged legislator of the world, Wilmer sees the poet, especially the modern poet, as a martyr of conscience and sensibility. He praises Czeslaw Milosz as an instance of the poet as "solitary witness" to human values in a totalitarian age. Radnóti, too, is "an example of the poet as witness" whose "encounter with history [is] an accomplishment of the modern poet's destiny." Of all who use language now, the poet is the purest truth teller, a fact which accounts for "the ethical power of poetry." This Wintersian emphasis on reason, moral choice, and the efficacy of traditional forms disciplines Wilmer's nostalgia for lost traditions, a nostalgia which explains Wilmer's love of Tennyson, especially the *Idylls of the King* (1859-1885).

In a review of Christopher Ricks's *Tennyson,* Wilmer highlights Tennyson's paradoxical nature, the disguising of personal views behind impersonal subjects from history and myth, and, quoting Ricks, Tennyson's "deep need to express a counterview" against the official, surface theme. Such a "counterview" or development by antithesis—or what Wilmer later calls "antiphony" or "polyphony" after the sixteenth-century English composers of church music he admires—explains Wilmer's own development from the Wintersian stoic of *The Dwelling-Place* to the naturalist-sacramentalist and Adamic namer-and-evoker of being in *Devotions.* Indeed, Wilmer's comments on the *Idylls of the King* illuminate his own heroic poems: "*Idylls of the King* will appear as the *Paradise Lost* of the 19th century. . . . It is a very elaborate, artificial structure, full of archaic language and mannered syntax; but these effects are part of a great poet's endeavour to draw into a centre an order that he feels to be breaking-up and starting to drift beyond the reach of his understanding. The battle in which the Arthurian order collapses is surely one of the greatest passages in English poetry."

Wilmer's defense of archaism as a valid rhetorical device calls to mind his very occasional employment of archaisms in his own poetry. After Donald Davie attacked him for this use, Wilmer replied in a 1977 letter to *PN Review* that just as "we

are glad of the holiness that archaism confers" on the King James Bible's somewhat deliberately dated language, so poetic archaisms may affect us. In his use of archaic forms, Wilmer says that he is trying "to re-awaken in the reader some sense of the human loyalties latent in words that, thankfully, he is still able to understand."

Despite Davie's reservations, critical commentary on the poems in *The Dwelling-Place* was mainly affirmative. In his introduction to *Shade Mariners,* Tony Tanner saw in Wilmer's earlier poems "the human need to achieve and maintain some enduring outline" informed by "the ambiguity of what we inherit from our warlike ancestors." He found in Wilmer's poems "a dream of heroism" and "fictions of valour" whose remoteness from us instigates a "melancholy stoicism." In the *Times Literary Supplement,* John Mole praised *The Dwelling-Place* for its

Clive Wilmer
The Dwelling-Place

Dust jacket for Wilmer's first full-length collection, which Blake Morrison praised for its dramatization of the "struggle between the forces of light (past civilization) and darkness (impending anarchy)"

"antique gravity" and its awareness of "the precarious balance between order and chaos." Neil Powell in his *Carpenters of Light* (1979) cited the book for "virtues of clarity and control allied to a confidence in language and a welcome degree of seriousness about the business of making poems." In "Young Poets in the 1970s," Blake Morrison noted that the book "dramatizes in poem after poem a struggle between the forces of light (past civilization) and darkness (impending anarchy). Bright fragments of order, reason, and art are shored up against the 'encroaching forest' of ruin and despair." Mole and Morrison did have some criticisms: Mole objected to an "oppressively sententious" tone in some poems while Morrison regretted that Wilmer seemed to feel, almost unhealthily, that our "sole source of comfort is the past."

The book's epigraph, from John Ruskin, is extremely appropriate: "A man's religion is the form of mental rest, or dwelling-place, which, partly, his fathers have gained or built for him, and partly, by due reverence to former custom, he has built for himself; consisting of whatever imperfect knowledge, may have been granted, up to that time, in the land of his birth, of the Divine character, presence, and dealings; modified by the circumstances of surrounding life." From this seminal remark grow the themes of Wilmer's first book: the importance of tradition and inheritance, stoic rationalism before the chaos of nature and the barbarism both within and without the mind, the need for heroic action in the public sphere of life, the search for religious experience, the importance of art as a preserver of civilized codes of behavior and modes of thought, and a tentative movement toward one of the central concerns of *Devotions*, the right relation of nature to the human mind that celebrates nature's otherness by knowing and defining that otherness by which the mind is simultaneously linked to and separated from that world it looks upon.

"The Dedication" to *The Dwelling-Place* muses on the poet's early loss of his father. Symbol of inherited tradition and an ultimate divine authority, the absent father teaches the poet "what a child could never see:/That I must never hope to be/The master of my dwelling-place." "Prologue (1965-70)," the first of the volume's two sections, contains poems set either in ancient history, including Roman Britain and Saxon England during the Viking invasions, or in the poet's childhood during which time he knew older people—a storyteller, a grandfather, his elderly Victorian father—who linked him to the nineteenth century. "The Exile" is a parable of a leader who erected a citadel against political chaos, barbarians, and nature, only to be betrayed by his own people. Returning from exile years later, he finds the citadel (civilization) in ruins: "Poppies revive,/In the wall they spatter, spectres of old blood." "Chiaroscuro" is an abstract study in the light and dark imagery that dominates the volume. Though aware of the dark, the poet affirms the light which is "opening outward, opening more and more." "The Invalid Storyteller" recounts the poet's childhood visits to an old man who imbued him with stories of heroic action, the stories becoming more tragic as the sick man weakened. A more vigorous form of inheritance comes from the blacksmith grandfather in "The Sparking of the Forge." Imitating his predecessor's honorable craft, the poet in the practice of his art is a blacksmith of words.

"Genealogy" is a sequence of five poems on inheritance, examining how one's nature is a mixture of the good and evil received from those who went before. "Ghost King" sees the poet's dead father as the Genius of the land he lies beneath. "East Anglican Churchyard" meditates on the confluence of sea and land, Viking and Christian worlds, in this graveyard on the fens. "The Sons of the Invaders" praises the poet's Norse forebears for the heroism of their southward voyage and for their draining of the marshes. Yet their Viking brutality was passed on as well, so that the poet wonders what the land now "yields us/Their richness, and their ghosts, malignant blooms:/Ghosts of our fathers, or our fathers' crimes?" "The Portrait" is a meditation on a picture of a father born in Victoria's India, an emblem of the stern willfulness that created the empire yet lived on into the uncertainties of the depression and two world wars. "Victorian Gothic" closes the sequence by musing on the immoral divergence between the Gothic style's spiritual aspiration and the industrial slums of rampant laissez-faire capitalism wherein the nineteenth-century workers usually lived. Ruskin's belief that an age's morality is visible in its architecture informs this poem.

The "Prologue" section closes with three poems on the stoical endurance of the civilized man. "Northward" tells of a hunter's fishing skills that enable him to survive the winter as he "breaks a hole in the ice,/Fishes in darkness," while "The North Legion" investigates the mind of a Roman legionnaire stationed in England. Fighting both winter ice and the wild, he carries the burden of civil order into the woodlands, where the Britons "come with silence/And with icy pain./They come to smash the barriers between / The dark repelled by armour and the dark entrenched within." In "The Ruined Abbey," one of Wilmer's finest poems, the monks of the early Middle Ages embody human values in the very stone that naturally resists a human imprint. They wrested meaning from the moors: "And so from the stone of landscaped minds, they fashioned / A form for those meanings, a form / That arched over meaningful air. / According to their time they shaped it / With massive grace. / And in the face of evil, weathers and decay / Its essence constant in the shiftings of ages." Fallen in ruin, the abbey divides into dust and silence, pure matter and pure divinity, void of human mediation, "lapped by the speechless howl of winds." Exemplifying again Ruskin's belief that architecture reveals an age's moral temper, this poem establishes the monks' heroic act of mind and will as an analogue for what man still might do today.

The second section of *The Dwelling-Place*, "The Clearing (1969-75)," contains a number of poems in praise of historic or mythic figures who bravely chose to uphold civilized values. "The Rector" commends a naturalist-priest whose poetry and sermons sought to link the Book of the Word with "the other book, creation" and who kindly ministered to his flock as well. In "Chivalric Monument" Wilmer recalls his childhood yearning to imitate knightly heroes, something that seems impossible to the adult. "The Wedding of St. George and Princess Sabra" and "Andromache" examine the hero in victory, over the slain dragon, and in defeat, after Troy's fall. In the moving shorter poem "Arthur Dead," Wilmer argues for the survival of the ideal of Camelot. Though Arthur is dead, his knights remain Good Samaritans: "Yet those few, who halting at the wayside / Kneel to victims of the terror, / Salvage thus, from desolation which they ride in, / Love and honour." The double poem "In Malignant Times" praises a seventeenth-century English doctor who refused to participate in the English civil war and a Lutheran minister in Germany who preached in defiance of Hitler. The first spoke with "chaste formality" and the second found that "speech was action" and that a "calm voice" would overcome Nazi "hysteria and pride": in both cases, language rightly used sets apart the civil man from the brute and the fanatic. "Of Epitaphs" ends with a series of poems on heroic will as the poet meditates on the tombs of the dead who, because they believed in absolutes, could be the kind of valiant men of action that our own divided minds make it hard for us to be: "We, sceptics in our wisdom, miss their

vice / Whose virtue, being substantial, could suffice."

Other poems in section two address the problem of the relation of human consciousness to nature. A girl's suicidal union with nature in "The Lake" is firmly rejected as romantic excess, while the boy in "The Riches," who surfaces from the ocean with treasure to display in sunlight seems the type of the mind inquiring into nature, or into itself. In "The Well" the poet sees his face mirrored in the water, but he does not jump into the well: man's place is in the world, but human boundaries must be maintained. Should mankind die out of nature, "there is only the old perspective into endless dark / with silence at the source." In "Bird-Watcher," a lovely poem that foreshadows a central idea of *Devotions*, the naturalist marvels at the bird's instinctive return with the new season. Yet he knows that the bird's "instinct to his knowledge corresponds," that he remains "the landscape's eyes," and the bird departs into a world where the naturalist is alien: it "veers off to vanish where the human ends." Wilmer rejects both romantic pantheism and modern scientific rationalism in regard to nature. Man is the Adamic custodian of a world which reveals some but not all of the beauty and spiritual essence of its creator. Man's duty is not to lose his human identity by totally merging with nature; rather, nature and language interact in the creation of poetic metaphor in such a way that both man and nature become more vitally themselves by means of the interchange. Man should be the shepherd of the world.

"To the Undeceived" is a vigorous attack on those who ridicule the poet for seeking "the dim / Outline of order" in "the crumbling palaces / And shady temples" of the past. These decadents who cultivate a fascination with barbarism would, the poet suggests, commit suicide like Romans if the barbarians actually arrived. "Sanctuary" is a stirring account of the building of Torcello Cathedral in Venice, a stronghold against eastern hordes and lashing sea waves: "immemorial, grey ghost-marauders / That broke on the shore, grey spume of the ancient sea." In "The Clearing," Wilmer wonders how long human reason can endure as guard at the forest's edge and whether reason's succumbing to exhaustion and despair might give back the "clearing" of civilization to "the anarchic wood." Reason, of course, is ultimately not enough, as in "The Grail Knight," where, the knight tells his lady he must leave her to find the Grail, the "light's source" that informs their love. Later, after seeing the Grail, the knight finds in a pool in the woods his own illumined face matched with his lady's "redeeming underwater eyes" and finds divinity in her love for him.

The Dwelling-Place closes with "Saxon Buckle," a poem whose subject is a warrior who fashioned out of gold the gleaming heads of the very forest beasts he fears. The buckle's light keeps back "the encroaching forest night/Where monsters and his fear dwell." By making images of the beasts, he deprives them of power: his primitive fear transformed by the creating mind into "an object for his contemplation." Thus, art and the mind raise humanity up from the beast, and then keep the beast at bay.

Clive Wilmer's second book of poems, *Devotions,* which appeared in 1982, expands upon his first volume both in theme and style. Sections one and three contain poems in traditional forms, but section two is made up of poems in free verse. (Section three also contains the prose meditation "A Woodland Scene"). This stylistic shift reflects Wilmer's new emphasis on the need to supplement the derived propositions of ratiocination with the intense immediacy of experienced sensation. Also present is widening concern for the relation between language and the world; for the Wordsworthian concept of "natural piety"; for a Ruskinian devotion to naturalism, moral architecture, beauty in the craftsmanship of all man-made things; and a sacramental attitude toward the created world reminiscent of David Jones's; and, incorporating all of these concerns, a desire to write poems that, in a Heideggerian sense, evoke being from the world by the antiphonal method of composition, a musical analogy that finds necessary the use of paradox, ambiguity, irony, and pun to contain within the poem the manifold diversities of human experience.

Wilmer's book reviews and essays, as is so often the case with poets, are in part hidden arguments for his own practice. In his more recent prose, one can detect evidences of the expansions in technique and idea that make *Devotions* a worthy successor to Wilmer's astonishingly mature first volume. Wilmer has observed Thom Gunn's movement from strict to open forms as well as Yvor Winters's earlier, opposite movement from open to strict forms to be attempts by both poets to broaden the content and range of feeling of their poems. In a 1971 review of Gunn's *Moly,* Wilmer notices in Gunn a new desire to "derive meaning from sensation" by seeing "intelligence and the senses as

allies." In an important review-essay on Gunn's *Jack Straw's Castle,* Wilmer reaffirms his original faith that traditional forms "will continue to be called upon to embody the products of concentrated thought, to give the semblance of immutable form to immutable verities"; but he appears more receptive to free verse which "seems to discover its meanings as it proceeds, as if the poem is a sequence of thought enacted before us, affected by the moment: a sense of thought (and poem) as *process.*" Gunn's more recent preference for Ezra Pound's forma over Winters's propositions Wilmer sees as a need to balance "rational intelligence" with "our more elementary, animal consciousness."

In a 1981 essay on wilderness and the frontiersman in Winters's poetry, Wilmer traces a reverse movement in Winters. To the extent that the American wilderness is more threatening than the English "pastoral landscape, friendly to man," Wilmer understands Winters's frontiersman's "intense wonder in the face of nature's otherness and the fear of it," yet he praises Winters as an early conservationist ("The California Oaks"), as a poet whose sensuous response to nature was intense though fearful, and, in a 1981 review of a critical study of Winters's poetry, Wilmer reminds us that Winters's early poems in free verse are "mystical: ecstatic immersions of the self in the detail of sensory experience" and that in his later, antipantheistic poems "the mystery of being itself remained his central concern."

The poet's knowledge of the mystery of being is entangled with his sense of the necessity yet inadequacy of language as an instrument of perception. In a review of a translation into English of the poetry of Paul Celan, Wilmer describes Celan's view of the poet as a Heideggerian Orpheus who evokes being from the world by way of language, his words dependent on a creator's Word as his own being depends on being itself. Thus, for Celan, the "central riddle" is "the relation of language to the world" and the need for "bridging the gap" between the two. That Celan's desire may be excessively hopeful, however, is made clear in Wilmer's comments, in a 1982 *Times Literary Supplement* review of Charles Tomlinson, that although language and the world are deeply and necessarily interdependent, their mutual healths depend on our not insisting that they try to merge into one. Wilmer thus redefines Wordsworth's "natural piety" to serve a modern poet such as himself: "the piety is no longer felt to have transcendental implications but expresses itself as a respect for particulars, for the otherness of

SAXON BUCKLE
        in the Sutton Hoo treasure

His inlaid gold hoards light :
A gleaming thicket to expel,
With intricacy worked by skill,
the encroaching forest might
Where monster and his fear dwell.

Gold forest tangles twined by will
Become a knot that closes in
The wild beasts that begin
Beyond his habitation.
An object for his contemplation.

— From which three rivets gaze :
A beast's head forested within,
That clasps his swordbelt to his breast
By daylight, and before his eyes,
By hearthlight, stills unrest.

Manuscript for the last poem in The Dwelling-Place *(the author)* things. It involves a recognition that the world is simply not available to language . . . [and that] though the world would exist if language never had been, nevertheless, the world would have no existence for the speaking animal if it were not for the assaults his language makes upon it."

This new stress on the relationship between intellect and sensation, language and world, shows that Wilmer is striving for a widely inclusive vision of the role of the intelligent poet in the modern age. Wilmer wants to be what he once called his profoundest influence, Ruskin: "He was, in the broadest sense, an 'ecological' thinker . . . incapable of regarding any particular as independent of its context." Like the postsymbolist Winters and the older Thom Gunn, Ruskin, too, sought to understand the objects of sense and the processes of mind as parts of a larger, whole event—"vividly particularized detail [seen] within a larger conceptual framework." This desire for inclusive vision marks the development within Wilmer of a religious sensibility, which had earlier been held in check by stoic rationalism or troublingly displaced from an Anglicanism the poet seems unwilling either to reject or accept totally. In a 1979 review of new poetry by John Heath-Stubbs, Wilmer approves of the poet's use of musical analogies as metaphors of cosmic order. In Heath-Stubbs's Artorius (Arthur), Wilmer sees "the poet as king, the dreamer and creator of civic order," a veritable "generator of culture" (flower, fauna, art, religion). Ideally, the poet would be able to adopt a "sacramental" view of creation, as did David Jones, so that his poems would heighten the metaphysical reality of the creatures of the world in the very "act of naming" them. The religious dimension of such naming is clear in Wilmer's comment, in an important review-essay on Geoffrey Hill's Tenebrae, concerning Rilke: "when Rilke in the ninth Duino Elegy meditated on the relation between familiar objects in their mystery and the names we address them with, he was attempting through poetry to reclaim the material world for the spiritual nature of man." Hill's similar concern, says Wilmer, leads him to desire "a wider form of antiphony" in which the paradoxical opposites of experience—Catholic/pagan, spirit/flesh, action/vision, history/epiphany—can be contained within the poet's "possibility of certain utterance." The search for such resolving utterance is the task of Wilmer's Devotions.

A passage from its single prose meditation, "A Woodland Scene," holds the key to the title of Devotions. Thinking of a mid-Victorian landscape painting, the poet finds it "Ruskinian, too, in the implied continuity of the given world with whatever a mesh of boughs and branches, contained within an arbitrary rectangle, can itself contain. Speaking, then, of the world at large, the picture expounds no painter, is devotional." Earlier, in reviews of the poetry of Pilinsky and Borges, Wilmer had employed the term "devotional" to describe a poet's celebratory preservation of some portion of tradition or natural beauty that, having sustained mankind in the past, is currently threatened with annihilation.

One object of Wilmer's devotion is lost tradition. "On the Demolition of the 'Kite' District" attacks modern Conservatives who conserve nothing in their sponsorship of the needless destruction of "Good rooms, good walls of weathered brick." "After A Cremation" deplores the absence of the beautiful cadences and phrasings of the Anglican burial service: in its place the inarticulate whir of the efficient crematorium furnace. The powerful poem "For the Fly-Leaf of a King James Bible" celebrates the civilizing beauties of a central text, now greatly displaced, that links humanity to the whole Western past by its consummate language: "A rhythm draws the mind/ . . . to older scores:/Lollard and Saxon drafts; Latin behind,/A plainchant barely heard." "The Retreat" sympathizes with a friend who, as an adult, cannot inherit his own childhood innocence, while "Beyond Recall" describes a poet (Gunn) who cannot seem to recapture in language the ideal beauties lost in the past. The lost tradition of chivalric heroism that dominated The Dwelling-Place reappears here in only two poems, "Among Bric-A-Brac" and "An Autumn Vision": the first, a rumination on a toy knight (The Disinherited Knight from Walter Scott's Ivanhoe) repurchased in adulthood; the second, a dream amid bombed-out London of a grave of a dead knight whose wrongs live unavenged in the inaccessible past. Also, in "Il Palazzo Della Ragione" the poet sees in a carved figurine on Padua's Palace of Reason an emblem of rational enlightenment which remains "beyond our time to emulate,/Though one may celebrate." Reason, however, is not "a final wisdom/As of Christ or the Buddha." Other poems deal with Wilmer's need for religious experience versus a rational skepticism that he is understandably reluctant to evade.

In "The Advent Carols" Wilmer with sadness declines to believe that the Word became incarnate at Bethlehem: all his hope is in the poet's language as it encounters the world it came from: "For the one sanctuary, now, is the word not/Made flesh— though it is big with child, invaded/By the dumb world that was before it was." In "Near Walsingham" the poet dismisses the miracles of saints for the beauty of creation as the central miracle: "Where water had already blessed the land / Saints chose to pray." "To a Modern Mystic" admonishes one who believes that the divine is remote from the world simply because the world's many-sided diversity seems at odds with the pure self-unity of the disincarnate Word. "The Fall" is an epigrammatic parable which says that man exiled God from Eden when man adopted a basely materialistic view of nature.

"Mosque" rejects a purely abstract religious art that omits the necessarily human perspective on the world. Illumination comes to man as much from a sacramental kneeling under the sky as from arabesques, minarets, and domes. Wilmer's insistence that we accept our human positioning in creation continues in "Narcissus, Echo," where Narcissus's excessive love for the absolute merges with self-love, while Echo pines away for him in the natural world where such love as hers should be rightly consummated: "He knelt to the one pure idea, / Self-love; the perfect sacrifice. / / She calls and calls to him, till all / The vacant world resounds with love." In contrast, "My Great-Aunt, Nearing Death" lovingly portrays the embodiment of charity in a particular human being, while "Pony and Boy" is an imagistic sketch of the distinction between being in nature (the pony) and consciously observing nature (the boy).

"Bindweed Song" and "Wild Flowers" near the end of section one and "The Natural History of the Rook" at the beginning of section three are poems in traditional forms that enclose section two, a series of poems on birds written in free verse. Wilmer finds in flowers and birds latent significances which it is the responsibility of the poet, through language, to release. In "Bindweed Song" and "Wild Flowers" the spontaneous adornment of wasteground by brilliant flowers seems both a criticism of human mismanagement and a compensatory gift. In section two, poems such as "Migrant" and "Wasteground" praise the splendid brilliance and sudden appearance of redwing and goldfinch—alluring specimens of nature's alien beauty. "Predator" celebrates the hawk's brutal skill as it readies itself to kill a rodent: "master of earth and blood—/ poised / in the blue, the master of the air." Though talking civilly with a friend on Keats's Hampstead Heath as this violence occurs, the poet can admire what he would not be, for, as he says elsewhere, "what is feared with reason, love / Need not renounce." Similarly, "Beside the Autobahn" wonders at the owl's primeval ability to pick out the

Front cover for Wilmer's 1982 book. The title refers to the poet's task of celebrating and preserving some portion of the traditional and natural beauty that is threatened with annihilation in the modern world.

rodent's scurrying feet amid the traffic's roar.

The two "Aerial Songs" muse on a thrush's morning song and a blackbird's evening song: the first has adapted itself to the unnatural forest of television aerials, while the second reminds us of the "greenwood/ . . . / . . . dark and other" out of which we have partially emerged. "Natural Selection" is an ecological condemnation of human waste that may cause humankind to select itself out of existence, along with the birds who, like the house martins, depend on us, leaving only derelict buildings for the hardy sparrows to inhabit. "A Victorian Cemetery" finds in the rooks circling over the buried dead a natural analogue to the peacefulness and rest the energetic Victorians so longed for at the end. The most substantial of these free-verse bird poems is "On the Devil's Dyke," which closes section two. Walking along the dyke that imposes human boundaries and thus human meanings on a land and on creatures oblivious to such orderings, the poet imagines the larks singing of this overlap of worlds: "*you, / a man, live in a place. More, / in a palimpsest of places: / landscape history creed the word. / Through us you may infer those / other worlds your map / and composite of places must at best / imply. / Worlds often glimpsed / beyond your earthworks, ramparts, palisades.*" The first poem in section three concludes these naturalist poems with a powerful blank-verse commendation of Charles Waterton (1782-1865) who established the world's first wildlife refuge. Both nature and mind benefited from the act: "He made himself / a sanctuary / the mind / Questing could enter into, haunt in freedom, / And dwell in, freed of its own hauntings." Echoing, while exultantly reversing, the last stanzas of Keats's "To Autumn" and Wallace Stevens's "Sunday Morning," Wilmer ends the poem with deep affirmation: "Blithe you were / From your high perch to watch the darting turquoise / Spear the still pool, to hear the barn-owl screech / No special doom to man, and see the rooks / Fly overhead in the dawn light to pass / Into the still-remote, unmediated / Variety of inhuman atmosphere."

Two outstanding poems on art and life in section three of *Devotions* are "The Parable of the Sower" and "Chinoiserie: The Porcelain Garden." The first is a meditation on a figure in a Victorian stained-glass window. The beautiful colors are those which the artist used to add human meaning and a sacramental aura to a task objectively arduous and to which the land remains oblivious. Human presence, perception, and value are melded with the land through the artist's vision: "The vision is of a vision that transfigured / Perspectives on the bare field; but with skill / The craftsman has contained, / Edged, the unearthly glow." The craftsman colors the scene "with his need / For things to mean—the word / Secreted in the seed." "Chinoiserie" addresses figures on a bowl that represent the permanence of natural beauty when abstracted into art. Like Keats and the Grecian urn, Wilmer slyly reproves the figures for the aesthetically inhuman existence they represent: "There you look on, and we glimpse paradise: / A dream of beauty and a form of dearth. / One touch of pain, unmimed, might turn to vice / Your virtues. Beauty is gloss. Like constant ice, / Polar, yet of the earth." Art is of the earth, as the bowl is made of earthen clay: though art strives toward permanence, its true focus is creation— God's art—the world of time and change.

Possibly the best poems in *Devotions* are the two "Antiphonal Sonnets." Their subject is John Taverner, sixteenth-century English composer of religious music who later renounced Catholicism to become an iconoclastic Protestant. The first sonnet is a reaction to Taverner's Respond "Dum transisset sabbatum," a musical setting of Mark 16:1-2, sounds whose spiritual beauty might transfigure our perception of the world: "it would be like . . . / . . . setting eyes for the first time / On the world, ours, yet other." Based on a passage in a letter from Taverner to Cromwell ("according to your lordship's commandment the Rood was burned on the seventh day"), the second sonnet recounts the Protestant Taverner's entry on horseback into his former church to destroy the Catholic images in defense of "a simple disembodied word, the truth." Now beauty is found not in the transcendental harmonies of a mass but in "hoofbeats in the nave, / The radiant shower of glass, a mace that knocked / Devotion from her pedestal, the flames / That burnt the rood in the broad light of day." Like the polyphonic strains of renaissance church music, the truth, and beauty of life, for Wilmer, can be most wholly known through an art that unites these and all the other opposites of experience. Just as Taverner the Catholic and Taverner the Protestant each fastened on a portion of the truth, or the whole truth under varying semblances, so Wilmer, in *Devotions*, seeks to develop antithetically from the stoicism and Tennysonian nostalgia of *The Dwelling-Place* to a naturalist's affirmation of the sacramental nature of creation. There, the poet's central role is to foster through his words the true relation between man and the world fathered forth by the primal unitary Word. In the divine Logos all "counterviews" and "antiphonies" polyphonically collapse at last, into their silent origin, the divine.

References:

Dick Davis, "Islands and Caves," review of *Forced March: Selected Poems*, by Miklós Radnóti, translated by Clive Wilmer and George Gömöri, *London Magazine*, 20 (April-May 1980): 126-128;

David Middleton, "Beyond the Merely Modern: New Poetry from Britain," review of *Forced March: Selected Poems*, by Miklós Radnóti, translated by Wilmer and George Gömöri, and other volumes, *Southern Review*, new series 17 (Winter 1981): 214-224;

Middleton, "Men in Dark Times," review-essay on *The Dwelling-Place*, by Clive Wilmer, and other volumes, *Southern Review*, new series 15 (Summer 1979): 585-604;

Middleton, "The Poetry of Clive Wilmer," *Sequoia* (Spring 1985);

John Mole, "Dim Outlines of Order," review of *The Dwelling-Place*, by Clive Wilmer, and other volumes, *Times Literary Supplement*, 13 January 1978, p. 38;

Blake Morrison, "Young Poets in the 1970s," in *British Poetry Since 1970*, edited by Michael Schmidt and Peter Jones (Manchester: Carcanet Press, 1980), pp. 147-150;

Neil Powell, *Carpenters of Light: Some Contemporary English Poets* (Manchester: Carcanet Press, 1979), pp. 138-140;

Tony Tanner, Introduction to *Shade Mariners* (Cambridge: Gregory Spiro, 1970).

Appendix

Small Presses in Great Britain and Ireland, 1960-1985

The years since 1960 have witnessed a steady growth in the number of small presses specializing in the publication of poetry. The emergence of a mass audience for poetry in the 1960s also helped to popularize the writing of verse, and the small-press movement developed, at least in part, because the increasing number of poets had sharpened the competition for publication by larger commercial houses. Small presses have helped to launch a number of important poets by providing an opportunity for first publication in book form. The production quality of small-press books has been consistently high; the sense of the book as artifact is often shown in the use of high-quality paper and graphics. Also, the close relationship possible between writers and publishers has provided for greater artistic cooperation and control.

Each of the following entries describes the history and aims of a small press. Addresses are included for the presses that are still in operation. Other presses, which did not provide information, are listed at the end of this appendix.

—Vincent B. Sherry, Jr.

H
I
P
P
O
P
O
T
A
M
U
S

P
R
E
S
S

Check List of Books and Pamphlets in Print

1984/5

HIPPOPOTAMUS PRESS

BLOODAXE BOOKS

New Books & Complete List
SPRING 1983 - SPRING 1984

ANGELA CARTER HART CRANE EVA FIGES B.S. JOHNSON SHENA MACKAY

FICTION POETRY DRAMA LITERATURE

FLEUR ADCOCK DAVID CONSTANTINE JENI COUZYN TOM PAULIN

PIG PRESS

pig. n. A sixpence; a policeman; a journalist; a piece of an orange; soiled goods returned to manufacturer.

(from a dictionary of slang)

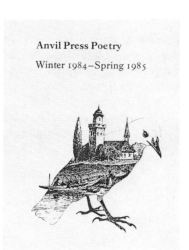

Anvil Press Poetry

Winter 1984–Spring 1985

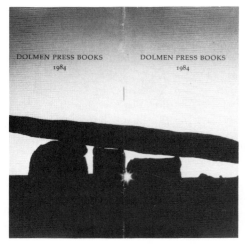

DOLMEN PRESS BOOKS
1984

DOLMEN PRESS BOOKS
1984

PETERLOO POETS

1984/85
STOCKLIST
BOOKS IN PRINT & FORTHCOMING
PETERLOO POETRY CASSETTES
ASSOCIATE MEMBERSHIP SCHEME

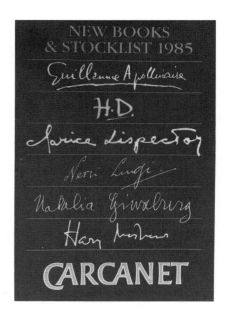

NEW BOOKS
& STOCKLIST 1985

Guillaume Apollinaire

H·D·

Clarice Lispector

Nervi Lingi

Natalia Ginzburg

Hary Mathews

CARCANET

The Mandeville Press
2 Taylor's Hill, Hitchin, Herts, SG4 9AD

A group of short poems is often at its best in a pamphlet....
The Mandeville Press adds to these virtues some of its own;
flawless printing and tactful, scrupulous attention to design.

Times Literary Supplement

Agenda Editions (1971-)
Editors: William Cookson and Peter Dale
5 Cranbourne Court
Albert Bridge Road
London SW11 4PE

Agenda Editions was founded in 1971. Our first book was Peter Dale's translation of François Villon, *The Legacy and other poems*. The aim was to publish the kind of poetry which the magazine *Agenda* believes in.

The most significant books we have published are *The Roman Quarry*, David Jones's posthumous writings; *The Kensington Mass*, David Jones's last, unfinished poem, which was also included in *The Roman Quarry;* Peter Dale's *Mortal Fire*, published in association with Ohio University Press; also his sonnet sequence, *One Another;* Anne Beresford's *Footsteps on Snow* and *The Curving Shore*. I should also like to draw your attention to Geoffrey Hill's *The Mystery of the Charity of Charles Peguy*. It is certainly one of the most important poems we have published.
                                        —*William Cookson*

Akros Publications (1965-)
Duncan Glen
25 Johns Road
Radcliffe-on-Trent
Nottingham NG12 2GN

Akros Publications was founded by Duncan Glen in 1965 to publish new Scottish poetry. To date (May 1985) the imprint has published 118 titles, and although most of them are poetry there are also pamphlets of literary criticism, two novels, and one collection of short stories in Scots. Akros Publications is perhaps first thought of as a publisher of poetry in Scots, but in fact a bibliography of the imprint reveals at least an equal number of collections of poetry in English.

In addition to publishing books and pamphlets Akros Publications published fifty-two numbers of the internationally recognized poetry magazine *Akros* (August 1965 and October 1983). A free magazine entitled *Aynd* is now being published, edited by Duncan Glen (who also edited *Akros*).

Among the imprint's more famous collections of poetry are *Cantrips* (1968), and *Selected Poems 1943-1974* (1975), by Alexander Scott; *Clytach* (1972, by Alastair Mackie); and a whole range of books by Duncan Glen including *In Appearances* (1971), *Realities Poems* (1980), and *On Midsummer*

Evenin Merriest of Nichts? (1981). John Herdman's two novels, *A Truth Lover* (1973) and *Pagan's Pilgrimage* (1978), have received high critical acclaim. The anthology *Modern Scots Verse 1922-1977* (1978), edited by Alexander Scott, performed a unique service by bringing together the best of poetry in Scots of the "MacDiarmid" years of Scottish poetry.
                                        —*Duncan Glen*

Reference:
Duncan Glen, *Forward from Hugh MacDiarmid: or, mostly out of Scotland, being fifteen years of Duncan Glen/Akros Publications* (Preston: Akros Publications, 1977).

Anvil Press Poetry Ltd
Peter Jay
69 King George Street
London SE10 8PX

Anvil Press Poetry was founded in 1968 by Peter Jay. It developed from a poetry magazine *New Measure* (1965-1969), which he edited as a student at Oxford University. Initially the object was to publish these new poets who were being overlooked by commercial houses; gradually the scope of the press has broadened, and it is now an eclectic specialized publisher of new poetry and poetry in translation with a list of about 150 titles. The press became a limited company in 1980 with Peter Jay as managing director.

The more important British poets published by Anvil include Gavin Bantock, Tony Connor, Dick Davis, Harry Guest, Anthony Howell, Peter Levi, E. A. Markham, Matthew Mead, F. T. Prince, Peter Russell, Michael Schmidt, Gael Turnbull, and Peter Whigham. Anvil has published such American poets as Jane Cooper, Louise Glück, Donald Justice, John Matthias, and Stanley Moss. Among Anvil's European poets are Johannes Bobrowski, Odysseus Elytis, Ivan V. Lalić, János Pilinszky, Salvatore Quasimodo, Tadeusz Różewicz, George Seferis, and Nichita Stănescu.
                                        —*Peter Jay*

Canongate Publishing Ltd (1973-)
Managing Director: Stephanie Wolfe Murray
17 Jeffrey Street
Edinburgh, EH1 1DR

Canongate Publishing Ltd. was founded in 1973, its remit being to publish good literature (fiction and poetry) in Scotland.

While not publishing Scottish authors and poets exclusively, Canongate's most successful titles to date have originated in Scotland. Although their publishing scope has widened for commercial reasons, their reputation both at home and abroad has been based to a considerable extent on its distinguished poetry list by poets both young and old.

The older Scottish poets on their list include that greatest of Gaelic poets, Sorley Maclean, and Naomi Mitchison. Alastair Reid (of *New Yorker* fame) follows, whilst the younger award-winning poets include Valerie Gillies, Walter Perrie, and Andrew Greig.

Canongate has also published two important poetry anthologies: *Scottish Love Poems*, edited by Antonia Fraser, and *Modern Scottish Gaelic Poems*, edited by Donald MacAulay, both of which have been published in the United Kingdom and North America.   —*Stephanie Wolfe Murray*

Carcanet Press Ltd (1969-   )
Michael Schmidt
208-212 Corn Exchange Buildings
Manchester M4 3BQ

Carcanet was founded in 1969, grew out of a university magazine and developed into a coordinated list which includes new poetry, translations, "re-discoveries," "lives and letters," and fiction. Our aim was to publish "the exceptions," those excellent writers who had escaped from or had been excluded by the "mainstream" and whom we considered to be central despite their marginal treatment. We were also keen to introduce a new generation of younger poets which we did successfully and, I trust, continue to do.   —*Michael Schmidt*

Poets whose work has been published by Carcanet include John Ash, Edmund Blunden, Alison Brackenbury, Gillian Clarke, Elizabeth Daryush, Donald Davie, Keith Douglas, G. S. Fraser, Michael Hamburger, John Heath-Stubbs, Elizabeth Jennings, Christopher Middleton, Edwin Morgan, Andrew Motion, I. A. Richards, Edgell Rickword, C. H. Sisson, Iain Crichton Smith, Jeffrey Wainwright, Andrew Waterman, Robert Wells, and Clive Wilmer.   —*Editor*

Dedalus Press (1985-   )
46 Seabury
Sydney Parade Avenue
Sandymount
Dublin 4

The Dedalus Press was established in April 1985 to publish collections of poetry in finely designed and carefully printed editions. Collections of poetry by new and established writers will be published, and a special feature of The Dedalus Press will be the publication of internationally known poets in English translation by Irish writers.
                                          —*Dedalus Press*

The Dedalus Press's first three publications were *Age of Exploration* by Conleth Ellis, *A Bright Mask: New & Selected Poems* by Robert Greacen, and Tomas Tranströmer's *The Wild Market Place*, translated by John F. Deane. *Winter in Meath* by Deane and *The Walking Wounded* by Rory Brennan will be published in autumn 1985.   —*Editor.*

Dolmen Press Ltd (1951-   )
Director: Liam Miller
The Lodge
Mountrath
Portlaoise

The Dolmen Press was founded in Dublin in 1951 as a small hand press to publish the works of Irish writers in Ireland as well as works of Irish interest by writers from other countries. Since then over three hundred titles have appeared with the Dolmen imprint and the list, which has a strong emphasis on poetry, includes many of the foremost Irish writers of today. The scope of the list has broadened over the years and now includes books on art and crafts, bibliography, history, literary criticism, and drama as well as original writing in prose and verse.

Several Dolmen books have been choices and recommendations of the Poetry Book Society in London; Thomas Kinsella's *Another September* (1958) being the first to be so honoured. Other awards to books and authors have included the AE memorial award, the Kavanagh award, and the W. H. Smith award, given to Kathleen Raine's book of poems, *The Lost Country* in 1972, the first occasion on which a book of poems received that distinguished prize.

The best known book from the Dolmen Press is probably Thomas Kinsella's translation of the old Irish epic *The Tain*, first issued in a limited edition in 1969 and in paperback in 1971; since then the book has never been out of print and is now going into its ninth printing. It has also appeared in German translation in both East and West Germany. A notable feature of *The Tain* is the accompanying brush drawings by the distinguished Irish painter Louis le Brocquy, of which there are one hundred and thirty in the limited edition, and thirty, selected from these, in the paperback. A new library edition with all the original drawings appears in a full cloth binding this year.

For its first thirty years the press printed almost all its own books and achieved a reputation for design and printing which was marked by several design awards in Ireland, and a bronze medal at the Leipzig book fair in 1979. Since 1980 Dolmen books have been printed at various presses.

As to significant poetry, I feel the works of Thomas Kinsella and John Montague, the Collected Austin Clarke (now out of print, but represented by a selection made by Thomas Kinsella), Padraic Colum's *The Poet's Circuits*, the collected poems of Denis Devlin, the *Poems* of Padraic Fallon, and our large anthology translated from the Irish: *An Duanaire, Poems of the Dispossessed 1600-1900*, being a hundred poems selected and arranged by Sean O'Tuama, with verse translations by Thomas Kinsella, are perhaps the most important.

—*Liam Miller*

Enitharmon Press (1968-   )

Alan Clodd
22 Huntingdon Road
East Finchley
London N2 9DU

Enitharmon Press's first title was published in 1968 and since that time about one hundred books have been issued; more than two thirds of these have been poetry, but a series of monographs on George Gissing and three titles on the Powys brothers have also been published as well as a few books of letters, reminiscences, literary criticism, bibliography and related subjects, and one novel.

In my poetry publishing one of my aims was to publish the work of women poets and to attempt to draw attention to the work of some poets I considered to have been undeservedly forgotten, or underestimated.

I consider that the most significant poetry titles I have published are *Artorius* by John Heath-Stubbs, *The Ballad of the Outer Dark* by Vernon Watkins, *The First-Known & Other Poems* by Frances Bellerby, *The Oval Portrait* by Kathleen Raine, and *A Man Afraid* by Jeremy Reed. I would also like to mention David Gascoyne's two remarkable books *Journals 1936/7* and *Paris Journal 1937/9*.

—*Alan Clodd*

Fantasy Press (1952-1963)

Oscar Mellor

Fantasy Press was founded by Oscar Mellor in 1952 at his home in Swinford, Eynsham, Oxford. Its most significant publications were the thirty-five untitled pamphlets in the Fantasy Poets series (1952-1957), many of which were the first books of now-important poets. The first eight were designed and printed by Mellor and Roger Smith. After number eight all the Fantasy Press publications were printed by Mellor alone. Assistant editors for the series were Michael Shanks (numbers 1-8), Donald Hall (numbers 9-18), George MacBeth (numbers 19-24), Anthony Thwaite (numbers 25-29), and Bernard Bergonzi (numbers 30-35).

In addition to the Fantasy Poets series the press published the little magazine *New Poems*. The first four issues (Autumn 1952-Summer 1953), edited by Donald Hall, were followed by two undated issues, the first edited by Jonathan Price and Geoffrey Hill and the second edited by Price alone. It also published the *Oxford Poetry* anthologies (1953-1960), whose editors included Anthony Thwaite, Adrian Mitchell, John Fuller, Donald Hall, and Geoffrey Hill. Other Fantasy Press books and pamphlets include: Donald Hall, *Exile* (1952); Elizabeth Jennings, *Poems* (1953); Thom Gunn, *Fighting Terms* (1954); George MacBeth, *A Form of Words* (1954), Donald Davie, *The Bride of Reason* (1955); Kingsley Amis, *The Evans Country* (1962); George MacBeth, *Lectures to the Trainees* (1962), and Peter Dale, *Walk from the House* (1962). In 1962 Mellor moved the press to his new home in Oxford, but the following year, when he went to live in Exeter he retired from publishing.

The Fantasy Poets Series:
1. Elizabeth Jennings (1952)
2. Pearce Young (1952)
3. James Price (1952)
4. Donald Hall (1952)
5. Simon Broadbent (1952)
6. Peter Dale Scott (1952)
7. Paul West (1952)
8. F. George Steiner (1952)
9. Lotte Zurdorfer (1952)
10. Martin Seymour-Smith (1952)
11. Geoffrey Hill (1952)
12. Adrienne Cecile Rich (1952)
13. Michael Shanks (1952)
14. Michell Raper (1952)
15. A. Alvarez (1952)
16. Thom Gunn (1953)
17. Anthony Thwaite (1953)
18. Arthur Boyars (1953)
19. Donald Davie (1954)
20. Jonathan Price (1954)
21. Philip Larkin (1954)
22. Kingsley Amis (1954)
23. Richard Selig (1954)
24. Adrian Mitchell (1954)
25. J. E. M. Lucie-Smith (1954)
26. John Holloway (1954)
27. Richard Drain (1955)
28. Laurence D. Lerner (1955)
29. Daibhidh Mitchell (1955)
30. H. S. Eveling (1956)
31. Mark Holloway (1956)
32. Richard Aldridge (1956)
33. Kenneth Wood (1956)
34. Dennis Keene (1957)
35. Richard Kell (1957)

Reference:

John Cotton, *Oscar Mellor: The Fantasy Press* (Hitchin: Dodman, 1977).

—*Editor*

Ferry Press (1964-   )
Andrew Crozier
177 Green Lane
London SE9

The Ferry Press has published books of a high standard with rare consistency. Libraries which take an interest in contemporary English poetry should buy everything it prints. . . .   —David Trotter,
The Making of the Reader (Macmillan, 1984)

The Ferry Press was established in 1964 by Andrew Crozier. Throughout its existence one purpose of the press has been to publish work the editor himself wished to read in book form, and in its early years the press published the work of several American writers, including Robin Blaser, Fielding Dawson, and Peter Schjeldahl. The first publication of an English poet was *Mmm . . . Ah Yes* (1967) by John James, and from this time the press began to publish the work of several other English poets, including J. H. Prynne, Douglas Oliver, John Temple, Peter Riley, David Chaloner, and Chris Torrance. By the early 1970s it was evident that the editorial policy of the press had an established direction, and that it should concentrate its efforts towards the publication of writing by these and other English poets of related interest. This writing does not represent any closely defined theoretical position, although the writers in question are in general sympathetic to one another's work by virtue of similarities in their preoccupations and goals, nor is it exclusively associated with the Ferry Press, which has cooperated editorially and practically with other publishers operating broadly similar policies, including Grosseteste, Great Works, Street Editions, Délires, and Allardyce, Barnett.

Reference to "this writing" might seem to imply a polemical stance. This is not primarily intended, but it may perhaps help to say that this writing is in important respects unlike (and often implicitly critical of) that sponsored by the poetry lists of the large commercial houses, though its differences may not readily be perceived as considerable and viable in their formal and rhetorical procedures by readers who cannot recognize, in the poetry to which their attention is directed by the major systems of information and validation, certain deeply marked homogeneities of style and sensibility. It is only from a position out with current received opinion that the discursive enclosure of English poetry over the last three decades is apparent. This is not a theme for choice to dwell on: it is often however necessary to draw attention to such differences when introducing this writing to new readers in order to establish that what appears (as it still often does) problematic by virtue of being unheard of is not therefore without validity and unworthy of attention. Matters of more substantial import—the writing's intelligence, its variety, range of feeling, and breadth of reference, above all the meanings produced by the modes of writing themselves—are then best left to be discovered by the reader. A few significant titles still in print:

Peter Ackroyd, *London Lickpenny; Country Life*
Anthony Barnett, *Fear and Misadventure & Mud Settles*
John James, *Berlin Return*
Douglas Oliver, *The Diagram Poems*
J. H. Prynne, *Down where changed*
Peter Riley, *Lines on the Liver*
John Temple, *The Ridge*.

—*Andrew Crozier*

Goliard Press (1965-1967)
Barry Hall and Tom Raworth

The Goliard Press was started in London in 1965 by Barry Hall, a painter and engraver, and Tom Raworth, a poet whose Matrix Press had, between 1959 and 1964, printed and published the magazine *Outburst* and small books by Edward Dorn, Anselm Hollo, David Ball, and Piero Heliczer. The aim of both presses was to introduce new and interesting work, mainly poetry but not neglecting prose and graphics, to Britain.

Between 1965 and 1967 Goliard Press produced books by Elaine Feinstein, Aram Saroyan, Tom Clark, Ron Padgett, Charles Olson (his first book published in the United Kingdom), and Tom Raworth; as well as printing books for other small publishers (Basil Bunting's *Briggflatts* for Fulcrum Press as one example). In 1967 the press was taken over by Jonathan Cape Ltd., becoming Cape-Goliard. Not wishing to work for a large publisher, Raworth then left; but Barry Hall continued to produce a remarkable series of poetry books, including several already accepted by himself and Raworth (Jeremy Prynne's *Kitchen Poems*, Paul Blackburn's *In, On, or About the Premises*, Charles Olson's *Maximus* poems, Neruda's *We are Many*). The press ceased production in the early 1970s.

—*Tom Raworth*

Grosseteste Press (1966-   )
Tim Longville
Robertswood
Farley Hill
Matlock
Derbyshire

Grosseteste Press was founded in 1966 and has since published around seventy titles as well as, since 1968, fifteen volumes (about 3,000 pages) of the literary magazine *Grosseteste Review*.

Like most small presses, it was founded by a group of friends (John Riley, Gordon Jackson, Tim Longville) to publish, initially, their own work and the work of other friends and acquaintances which they admired.

The *Descriptive Catalogue* issued on the press's tenth anniversary in 1975 deliberately describes its later operations in terms derived from that opening intimacy:

> A little press is little. *Some* apples. No, but seriously: I mean, it's me and him; or you.
> Little in numbers. In the numbers of those who run it or of those who buy, beg or borrow its productions. Little and close. Little and close out of interest. Particular-ness. No fuss (about "principles": you know, salvation's something else) but no fluff (about what to do or why), either. That is, Mr. Armstrong to the woman asking about rhythm, *Lady, if you gotta ask, you ain't never gonna know.* I'll tell you, though, what you do know (don't you?): we publish what we love, want readers who will, also. Seriously. Some apples, you agree?
> . . . This sounds personal and is meant to but isn't trivial. The person with the personal interest is the person we operate for and in terms of. At either end.

Time and mortality have reduced the founding group to one (Tim Longville), but the intentions, then as now, remain as (deliberately) vague and as (deliberately) precise.

Volumes of poetry the press has published by poets from the United Kingdom include:

Almost all of the individual volumes by John Riley as well as the 520-page volume of his *Collected Works*, edited after his death by Tim Longville.
J. H. Prynne: *The White Stones.*
John James: *The Welsh Poems; Berlin Return.*
Roy Fisher: *Nineteen Poems And An Interview.*
Gael Turnbull: *Residues.*
Peter Riley: *Linear Journal; Tracks And Mineshafts; Two Essays.*
David Chaloner: *Hotel Zingo.*
John Hall: *Between The Cities; Days; Meaning Insomnia.*
Thomas A. Clark: *Twenty Poems.*
Ralph Hawkins: *Tell Me No More And Tell Me.*

Peter Philpott: *Some Action Upon The World.*
Anthony Barnett: *Titular.*
Nick Totton: *Radio Times.*
Tim Longville: *Pigs With Wings; Spectacles, Testicles, Wallet And Watch; Between The River And The Sea; To Intimate Distance; Seven Elephants And One Eye.*

—*Tim Longville*

Hippopotamus Press (1975-   )
Editor: Roland John
26 Cedar Road
Sutton, Surrey

The Hippopotamus Press was founded in 1975 as a pamphlet press specializing in the work of the unknown and neglected. Now we publish full collections in paperback and cloth editions. Although we have published established poets like Peter Dale, and will continue to do so, our main aim is to find new work.

The Hippopotamus Press is not tied to any group, nor coterie, nor are we followers of a particular poetic dogma. We try to publish the best manuscripts that we receive. We are interested in modern poetry by those who have learned from the Modernist tradition of Pound-Eliot and who have found their own path forward. We have published work in formal metric as well as much looser forms. The Hippopotamus Press offers a wide variety of books and pamphlets by poets working in different styles. We have published poetry by William Cookson, G. S. Sharat Chandra, Peter Dent, Peter Dale, Lotte Kramer, Shaun McCarthy, and many others.

—*Roland John*

Keepsake Press (1958-   )
Roy Lewis
26 Sydney Road
Richmond
Surrey TW9 1UB

Originally, The Keepsake Press, was founded by myself and my teenage daughters to learn printing and design, using the poetry of friends as suitable texts, a classic starting point for a private press.

However, the friends introduced *their* friends who were poets, and so the venture developed of its own momentum. The only aims I have had (my daughters are now elsewhere and married) is to bring out first editions of authors, both established

and unestablished, whose work interests me, and which fitted into a format of a small edition. Everything being done on hand or treadle press, mostly by hand, everything had to be small scale—and this suited poetry because it is very difficult to sell more than 200-400 copies of a booklet of lyric poems.

I have consciously sought to make my books very much private press books in style, especially by getting artists to provide decoration or visual counterpoint. (They include John Piper, for example, and the late Duncan Grant.) Besides booklets of poetry and verse, the press brought out between 1972 and 1979 thirty-nine issues of *Keepsake Poems,* a single poem and an illustration on a single folded sheet with an appropriate cover and envelope. Among the poets represented in this collection are Vernon Scannell, Anne Tibble, M. Crossley-Holland, G. Wightman, Peter Porter, Charles Causley, Anne Stevenson, D. M. Thomas, Roy Fuller, Gavin Ewart, George MacBeth, Alan Bold, Gordon Symes, and Thomas Blackburn.

Among the poets whom I have published in about forty books and booklets are: John Heath-Stubbs, Edward Lowbury, James Simmons, Gavin Ewart, John Press, Stanley Cook, Ahmed Ali, David Holbrook, and Martin Booth.

I have not confined myself to modern poetry, however, and, for example for the U.S. Bicentennial published a long hitherto unknown and unpublished poem about the American Revolutionary War written by Charles Wesley in 1782. I have also published the remarkable poem translations of Horace's *Epodes* by John Penman. —*Roy Lewis*

Mandeville Press (1974-   )
Peter Scupham and John Mole
2 Taylor's Hill
Hitchin
Hertfordshire SG4 9AD

The Mandeville Press is a private press, founded in 1974 by Peter Scupham and John Mole with the aim of publishing new poetry from both established and little-known authors. The editors have looked for poets working in modes which demonstrate formal qualities and a sense of literary continuity; the editors are their own letterpress printers, and over the last decade have produced four or five items a year, including pamphlet collections, small anthologies, and collections of poems on cards. They see the function of the press as providing a bridge between magazine publication and the full-length collection provided by a major publishing house. They aim to produce crisply and attractively printed pamphlets, enlivened with accompanying graphics where appropriate. The collections are modestly priced, and the print runs are usually between 200 and 400 copies. The editors have taken particular pleasure in producing the work of poets whose output is small, but in their opinion, distinguished: poets neither young nor fashionable enough to attract media attention, but whose qualities deserve recognition. Recent publications have included:

Twists of the Way, Geoffrey Grigson.
To Go Hidden, Patric Dickinson.
Mandeville's Travellers, an Anthology.
Selected Poems, Michael Riviere.
A Love for Four Voices, Anthony Hecht.
The January Divan, John Fuller, with accompanying graphics by George Szirtes.
The Last Picnic, K. W. Gransden.
Years, Bernard Bergonzi.
The Corridor, C. H. Sisson.
Man Dancing with the Moon, Freda Downie.

—*Peter Scupham*

Menard Press (1971-)
Anthony Rudolf
8 The Oaks
Woodside Avenue
London N12 8AR

The Menard Press started life as a magazine, *The Journals of Pierre Menard*, with its accompanying *Notebooks of Pierre Menard*. Numbers one, three and four of the *Journals* and numbers one and eight of the *Notebooks* plus a special *June Diary of Pierre Menard* (The Curse of Babel) came out irregularly in 1969 and 1970 on dates which did not coincide with the dates on the preprinted covers. The magazine's name was derived from a marvellous short story by Borges, *Pierre Menard, Author of Don Quixote*.

The Menard Press itself was born in 1971. The primary concern remained that of the magazine: poetry in translation. Over the years about half of our literary titles came into this category, but quite a lot of original poetry was published. We also published some fiction and literary criticism and three sets of postcards. Including the *Journals*, ninety-six titles have been published.

In 1980 Menard began publishing anti-nuclear pamphlets and in 1983 ceased publishing poetry.

—*Anthony Rudolf*

Reference:
Anthony Rudolf, *From Poetry to Politics: The Menard Press 1969-1984* (London: Menard Press, 1984).

Migrant Press (1957-)
Gael Turnbull
25 Church Walk
Ulverston
Cumbria LA12 7EN

Migrant Press began with Gael Turnbull as Migrant Books in 1957 in Worcester, England, trying to distribute some books from Divers Press, Jargon, and Origin Press, and publishing a small selection of poems by Robert Creeley, *The Whip*. It continued as the magazine *Migrant* (eight issues 1959-1960), jointly edited and published by Michael Shayer in Worcester and Gael Turnbull in Ventura, California. Then, as Migrant Press, from Worcester and later with Roy Fisher from Birmingham, it published a series of pamphlets and books, including first collections by Pete Brown, Edward Dorn, Ian Hamilton Finlay, Roy Fisher, Anselm Hollo, Matthew Mead, and Michael Shayer, as well as items by Basil Bunting, Hugh Creighton Hill, Edwin Morgan, and Gael Turnbull.

By 1966 there were a number of other small presses publishing similar poetry in Britain, and although Migrant Press has continued to publish occasional items, the need that had brought it into existence was being met elsewhere. Its most recent publication is a long poem by John Adlard, *Sobieski in Autumn* (1985).

—*Gael Turnbull*

Northern House (1964-)
Jon Silkin
19 Haldane Terrace
Newcastle upon Tyne NE2 3AN

Northern House publishes mostly small collections of poetry by new or established poets. Each of the pamphlets contains ten to sixteen poems, often a group written to one theme. Occasionally larger volumes are published and their number will be increasing in the future. Each work is in an attractive format and low-priced. Northern House is associated with *Stand*, the literary quarterly based in Newcastle upon Tyne. It was started by Dr. Andrew Gurr and Ken Smith with Jon Silkin at the small hand press, English department, University of Leeds.   —*Jon Silkin*

Books published by Northern House include Geoffrey Hill, *Preghiere;* Ken Smith, *Eleven Poems;* Ted Walker, *Those Other Growths;* Tony Harrison, *Earthworks* and *Newcastle is Peru;* Michael Hamburger, *In Flashlight* and Hamburger's translation of *Poems* by Hans Magnus Enzensberger; Roy Fisher, *The Memorial Fountain;* Jon Silkin's translation of *Against Parting* by Natan Zach and the second edition of Silkin's *Flower Poems;* Sorley Maclean, *Dain Do Eimhir/Poems to Eimhir*, translated by Iain Crichton Smith; Tony Connor, *Seven Last Poems from the Memoirs of Uncle Harry;* and Roger Garfitt, *The Broken Road.*   —*Editor*

Phoenix Pamphlet Poets (1968-1972)
Peterloo Poets (1976-)
Harry and Lynn Chambers
Treovis Farm Cottage
Upton Cross
Liskeard
Cornwall PL14 5BQ

Harry Chambers' launching of Peterloo Poets as a major independent press in 1976 came as a natural development from his apprentice years of editing two series of the little magazine *Phoenix* (1959-1975) and as a logical expansion from the production of nineteen substantial pamphlets in the Phoenix Pamphlet Poets series (1968-1972). Peterloo Poets was first launched in 1972 as a hardback series, edited by Harry Chambers but published by E. J. Morten, a South Manchester bookseller who withdrew from the enterprise after the production of only four volumes. The relaunching of Peterloo Poets in 1976 as Harry Chambers' own imprint was made possible by his being awarded a small grant from the Arts Council of Great Britain, which has maintained an increased level of support into the mid-1980s. In the years 1976-1985 over sixty volumes have been produced, mainly in laminated paperback with Baskerville typeface.

From its inception Peterloo Poets aimed at publishing "poetry of quality by new or neglected poets" and carried as house colophon an engraving—taken from a "Bibliophily in Caricature" supplement to the *American Book Collector*—of a balding man, waist-deep in water but also immersed in a book, and protected by what is now recognized as the Peterloo umbrella. Several new poets discovered and given first volumes by Peterloo turned out to be writers aged about fifty or so.

Peterloo has also been anxious to discover and publish good young poets and is proud to have on its lists first volumes by Peter Bennet, Humphrey Clucas, Peter Forbes, John Gohorry, Philip Gross, Stuart Henson, David Jacobs, John Levett, William Scammell, I. P. Taylor, and Landeg White.

In 1979 Peterloo made a significant shift in publication policy. Previously it had existed to give an author an opportunity for a first volume only, while poets who had made their mark through publication by Peterloo then passed on, if they were lucky, to one of the larger publishing houses.

In 1983 Harry Chambers produced the first of what is hoped to be a continuing series of Peterloo Poetry Cassettes. No. 1 features U. A. Fanthorpe and Elma Mitchell each introducing and reading a forty-five-minute selection of poems. No. 2 (1984) features William Scammell and Elizabeth Bartlett each introducing and reading a thirty-five-minute selection of poems. Each cassette is accompanied by a text booklet of all the poems read.

Peterloo Poets is a two-person press. All the creative work—choice of poets, appearance, typeface, house-style, cover illustration/design etc.—is done by Harry Chambers, whilst his wife, Lynn, deals with mail orders, computerized records, contracts, etc.

Most Significant Titles

I. Peterloo Poets:
Peter Scupham/*The Snowing Globe* (1972)
John Mole/*The Love Horse* (1973)
Elma Mitchell/*The Poor Man In The Flesh* (1976)
Edmond Leo Wright/*The Horwich Hennets* (1976)
F. Pratt Green/*The Old Couple: Poems New & Selected* (1976)
U. A. Fanthorpe/*Side Effects* (1978, 1979, 1982, 1984) over 2,000 copies sold
U. A. Fanthorpe/*Standing To* (1982)
U. A. Fanthorpe/*Voices Off* (1984)
John Latham/*Unpacking Mr Jones* (1982, 1985)
Elizabeth Bartlett/*A Lifetime of Dying* (1979)
William Scammell/*Jouissance* (1985)
John Latham/*From The Other Side Of The Street* (1985)
David Jacobs/*Terminus* (1984)
I. P. Taylor/*The Hollow Places* (1980)

Landeg White/*For Captain Stedman* (1983)
John Gohorry/*A Voyage Round The Moon* (1985)

II. Phoenix Pamphlet Poets:
Glyn Hughes/*Love On The Moor* (1968)
Seamus Heaney/*A Lough Neagh Sequence* (1969)
Michael Longley/*Secret Marriages* (1968)
Derek Mahon/*Ecclesiastes* (1970)
Stanley Cook/*Form Photograph* (1971)
Peter Scupham/*The Small Containers* (1972)

III. *Phoenix:*
No. 11/12 Philip Larkin double issue (Autumn & Winter 1973/74)

—*Harry Chambers*

Pig Press
Editors: Richard and Ann Caddel
7, Cross View Terrace
Neville's Cross
Durham DH1 4JY

Pig Press is "an enterprising northern press [publishing] some of the most important modern and modernist poets" *(Time Out,* January 1981). Amongst the list are writers such as Asa Benveniste, Robert Creeley, Paul Evans, Roy Fisher, Harry Guest, Lee Harwood, Barry MacSweeney, Tom Pickard, Carl Rakosi, and Gael Turnbull. However, Richard and Ann Caddel (the editors and organizers of Pig Press since its birth in 1972) would suggest that the success of the press lies not in its famous or established poets, but in its publishing of new or little-published writers, both British and American—it is this which caused one reviewer (Jeff Nuttall, *Guardian,* 21 March 1981) to note that "Pig produces so much material that can't be ignored."

Amongst the not-so-well known writers in the current list, the editors would wish to draw attention to the work of Tony Baker, John Seed, and George Evans—not for their similarities, but for their contrasts and differences. In as much as we have any policy at all, it is to publish the widest range of exciting writing available to us. Although we are a small press, with small circulation, our hope is to break down barriers between the "specialist" and the "general reader"—the common denominator of Pig Press books is, hopefully, their readability.
—*Richard Caddel*

References:
Richard Caddel, "Pig Press—A Beginner's Guide," *Association of Little Presses Newsletter* (August 1979);
Paul Green, "Pig Press," *Small Press Review* (forthcoming);
Jeff Nuttall, "In Praise of Northern Pigs," *Guardian* (London), 21 March 1981;
Aidan Semmens, "Pigs is Equal," *Sunderland Echo,* 5 May 1983;
Anne Stevenson, "But Pigs is Equal . . . ," *Arts North* (February 1984).

Poet & Printer
Alan Tarling
30 Grimsdyke Road
Hatch End
Middlesex HA5 4PW

Poet & Printer from 1965 has been a one-man operation collaborating with whichever English-speaking poet seemed the best at the time. Although some thirty pamphlets, paperbacks, and hardbacks have been made at the press, always inexpensive and rather utilitarian, I claim no literary originality in my selection and would prefer to be thought of as one who attempted to popularize pamphleteered poetry as superior to the relatively ponderous hardbacks squeezed out of their authors by bigger publishers.

As with most small presses (I suspect) there has been an element of exploitation of poetry for my own crafty ends (in short, I like making books by letter-press and traditional ways of sewing and binding), but I nevertheless feel greatly honoured by many poets who have allowed me to present their work, from Ted Hughes and Peter Redgrove to Robert Shaw and Alan Dixon.

My next full-scale book, "Twenty Years at a Poetry Press," is a chronology of the press's activities, and I start setting it in 1986. —*Alan Tarling*

Rivelin Press (1974-1984)
Rivelin Grapheme Press (1984-   )
Directors: Snowdon Barnett, David Tipton, and
   Winston Barnett
199 Greyhound Road
London W14 9SD

Rivelin Grapheme Press was formed in March 1984 in London. It is the successor of Rivelin

Press, which was formed in Bradford in 1974.

Rivelin Press, when it started published pamphlets, and over the years as the press became more established the quality of the standard of publication improved. When Rivelin Grapheme Press was started, its intention was and remains to publish only books of poetry, rather than pamphlets, and so far we have published twelve titles. The range of poetry covered is extremely wide. For example we have published a first volume of poetry by a woman writer, Anna Taylor, called *Fausta*, which is a long continuous poem, being a feminist interpretation of the Faust legend. On the other hand, more recently, we have published a first collection by another woman writer, Isobel Thrilling, called *The Ultrasonics of Snow*, which is a collection of many years of her writing. She has won a number of poetry competitions and prizes.

One of the other aims of the press is to bring to the attention of English readers the work of distinguished South American poets, and in October 1984 we published *Recife,* which was a translation by Eddie Flintoff of the poems of Manuel Bandeira.

One of the Rivelin titles was called *Looking at the Mona Lisa,* which is a collection of poems by Rosario Castellanos translated by Maureen Ahern. I am pleased to say that that sold out quickly, and in April 1986 we hope to bring out a much fuller volume of her works which (for the purpose of continuation and tradition) we are calling *Looking at the Mona Lisa and other poems.*

We have published since 1974 almost sixty titles and they are extremely varied and cover all types of poetry. In October 1985 we are publishing an anthology called *Purple & Green,* a collection of thirty-three women poets, as well as another anthology by some young English poets called *SIX—the Versewagon Poetry Manual.*

The aim of Rivelin Grapheme Press is to publish eight poetry titles a year, and one of our specialties is to encourage the first publication in book form of new writers.

In addition we are also interested very much in bringing to the attention of the English reader the extremely important work which has been done in South America over the last twenty to thirty years.
—*Snowdon Barnett*

Salamander Press Edinburgh Ltd. (1981-)
Managing Director: Tom Fenton
Directors: Mary Fenton, James Fenton,
  John Fuller
113 Westbourne Grove
London W2 4UP

The Salamander Press was founded in 1981 as a private press, printing and publishing poetry. Our aim at first was to produce well designed and printed books but at accessible prices, the sort of thing poets could sell at their readings, that students could afford and would want to collect.

The first three poetry titles were *A German Requiem* by James Fenton (pamphlet), *A Free Translation* by Craig Raine, and *Independence* by Andrew Motion (all 1981 and all printed letterpress by myself). In 1982 I added John Fuller to the list with his collection *Waiting for the Music* and two young Scottish poets, Kathleen Jamie and Ron Butlin. Since then we have followed the pattern of publishing work by established and important poets and introducing new poets, though the press has also started to publish drama, fiction, and nonfiction.

Our most important publications are probably: *The Memory of War* (1982) and *Children in Exile* (1983) by James Fenton (both now available as one volume from Penguin in the United Kingdom and from Random House in the United States and Canada); *Dangerous Play: poems 1974-1984* (1984) by Andrew Motion; *Poems 1963-1983* by Michael Longley (1985). I am also very proud of our first publication of an American poet, *Difficulty* by William Logan (1984), which I understand will be published in the United States this year by David Godine.

In 1983 the Salamander Press was incorporated as the Salamander Press Edinburgh Ltd, and in 1984 we moved our offices to London.
—*Tom Fenton*

Second Aeon Press (1966-1974)
Peter Finch

Second Aeon magazine and its attendant publications ran from 1966 to 1974 and published over one hundred items. These ranged from twenty-one issues of the periodical through an array of books and booklets to the *No Walls* broadsheets, a kind of poetry wallposter. The magazine was the head in this operation and the press the tail. Between them they became one of the most significant small presses in Britain during the period. Dedicated to publishing a true reflection of literary, mainly poetic, activity they included all the important British writers, a vast array of American ones, introduced a good range of European and other work in English translation, and had a strong bias towards the experimental. The magazine was also important for its survey activities, listing other small press products and magazines worldwide in its "small press scene."

Some of the writers published included Charles Bukowski, Peter Redgrove, Allen Ginsberg, Dannie Abse, Bob Cobbing, William Wantling, Tom Phillips, Octavio Paz, García Lorca, Dick Higgins, D. M. Thomas, Robert Bly, Cid Corman, John Digby, Pavese, Meredith Monk, Charles Plymell, John Wain, Paul Celan, William Burroughs, Theodore Enslin, Tom Pickard, Peter Porter, Edwin Morgan, Christopher Middleton, R. S. Thomas, Barry Macsweeney, and Douglas Blazek. Significant individual publications include *Typewriter Poems*, edited by Peter Finch and published in conjunction with Something Else Press Inc.; *For Jack Kerouac*, edited by Peter Finch; *Songsignals*, a folder of visual poetry by Bob Cobbing; *Greek Images*, by Alexis Lykiard; *Love's Journeys*, by Peter Redgrove; *10,000 rpm and diggin it*, *Sick Fly*, and *San Quentin's Stranger*—the first significant publications of the late William Wantling; *Lilith Prints*, by D. M. Thomas, and *Bute Park* and *The Inheritance File*, by John Tripp.   —*Peter Finch*

Turret Books (1965-　)
Bernard Stone
The Turret Book Shop
42 Lamb's Conduit Street
London WC1N 3LJ

Since he founded Turret Books in 1965, Bernard Stone, with the help of editor Edward Lucie-Smith during the first ten years of the press's existence, has published about one hundred limited editions of poetry by both new and well-known writers. Among the poets whose work he has published are Ted Hughes, Sylvia Plath, Louis Zukofsky, John Hollander, Lawrence Durrell, Charles Causley, George MacBeth, Barry Cole, and Peter Straub. The most recent Turret Book is a limited edition of *Fluff* by Christopher Logue.
          —*Editor*

Writers Forum (1963-　)
Bob Cobbing
89A Petherton Road
London N5 2QT

Writers Forum began in November 1952 and has met regularly ever since. From the first it has endeavoured to be experimental and professional. It has concerned itself with "the limits of poetry" including "graphic displays, notations for sound and performance, as well as semantic and syntactic developments, not to mention fun."

The group began publishing *AND* magazine in 1954; and regular publishing of booklets by members and others in 1963. To date, 351 items have been published, including one record and four cassettes. Members who have been published include: Jeff Nuttall, Lee Harwood, Bob Cobbing, Bill Griffiths, Paula Claire, Clive Fencott, Maggie O'Sullivan, Herbert Burke, Jeremy Adler, and Bill Butler.

Nonmembers whose work has been published include: Eric Mottram, Peter Finch, Allen Fisher, Ken Edwards, Geraldine Monk; Ruth Rehfeldt (East Germany), Ernst Jandl (Austria), B. P. Nichol (Canada), Jiří Valoch (Czechoslovakia); John Cage, Allen Ginsberg, Anselm Hollo, Dom Silvester Houédard, Stefan Themerson, and Claude Pelieu. A significant publication was *Concerning Concrete Poetry* by Bob Cobbing and Peter Mayer.

The press has also published four issues of *Kroklok*—a magazine/anthology of sound poetry.

Publications are now distributed by *New River Project*, which also stages monthly jamborees of mixed media events in which Writers Forum members play a prominent part.   —*Bob Cobbing*

Other Small Presses

Black Staff Press Ltd
3 Galway Park
Dundonald
Belfast BT16 0AN

Bloodaxe Books Ltd
Directors: Neil Astley, Simon Thirsk
P.O. Box 1SN
Newcastle upon Tyne NE99 1SN

Gomer Press
Directors: J. Huw Lewis, John H. Lewis
Llandysul, Dyfed SA44 4 BQ

Sycamore Press
John Fuller
4 Benson Place
Oxford OX2 60H

Ulsterman Publications
James Simmons
15 Kerr Street
Portrush
County Antrim

Wild Hawthorn Press
Ian Hamilton Finlay
Stonypath
Dunsyre
Carnwath
Larnarkshire

Books for Further Reading

Adams, Sam, ed. *Ten Anglo-Welsh Poets*. Cheadle: Carcanet Press, 1974.

Allott, Kenneth, ed. *The Penguin Book of Contemporary Verse. 1918-60*, revised edition. Harmondsworth: Penguin, 1962.

Alvarez, A., ed. *The New Poetry*. Harmondsworth: Penguin, 1962; revised and enlarged, 1966.

Astley, Neil, ed. *Ten North-East Poets*. Newcastle: Bloodaxe Books, 1980.

Bedient, Calvin. *Eight Contemporary Poets*. London, New York & Toronto: Oxford University Press, 1974.

Berke, Roberta. *Bounds Out of Bounds: A Compass for Recent American and British Poetry*. New York: Oxford University Press, 1981.

Bold, Alan, ed. *Cambridge Book of English Verse 1939-1975*. Cambridge: Cambridge University Press, 1976.

Bradbury, Malcolm. *The Social Context of Modern English Literature*. Oxford: Blackwell, 1971; New York: Schocken, 1971.

Brown, Merle. *The Double Lyric: Divisiveness and Communal Creativity in Recent English Poetry*. New York: Columbia University Press, 1980.

Conquest, Robert, ed. *New Lines*. London: Macmillan/New York: St. Martin's, 1956.

Conquest, ed. *New Lines 2*. London: Macmillan, 1963; New York: Macmillan, 1963.

Dale-Jones, Don, and Randal Jenkins, eds. *Twelve Modern Anglo-Welsh Poets*. London: University of London Press, 1975.

Davie, Donald. *Articulate Energy: An Inquiry into the Syntax of English Poetry*. London: Routledge & Kegan Paul, 1955.

Davie. *Purity of Diction in English Verse*. London: Chatto & Windus, 1952.

Davie. *These The Companions: Recollections*. Cambridge: Cambridge University Press, 1982.

Deutsch, Babette. *Poetry in Our Time*, revised and enlarged edition. Garden City: Doubleday, 1963.

Dodsworth, Martin, ed. *The Survival of Poetry*. London: Faber & Faber, 1970.

Ellmann, Richard, and Robert O'Clair, eds. *The Norton Anthology of Modern Poetry*. New York: Norton, 1973.

Enright, D. J., ed. *The Oxford Book of Contemporary Verse, 1945-1980*. Oxford & Melbourne: Oxford University Press, 1980; New York: Oxford University Press, 1980.

Finn, F. E. S. *Poems of the Sixties,* introduction by Norman Nicholson. London: Murray, 1970.

Finn. *Poets of Our Time*. London: Murray, 1965.

Finn, ed. *Here and Human: An Anthology of Contemporary Verse.* London: Murray, 1976.

Fraser, G. S. *Essays on Twentieth Century Poets.* Leicester: Leicester University Press, 1977.

Fraser. *The Modern Writer and His World,* second revised edition. London: Deutsch, 1964.

Grubb, Frederick. *A Vision of Reality: A Study of Liberalism in Twentieth Century Verse.* London: Chatto & Windus, 1965.

Haffenden, John. *Viewpoints: Poets in Conversation with John Haffenden.* London: Faber & Faber, 1981.

Hall, Donald, Robert Pack, and Louis Simpson, eds. *New Poets of England and America.* Cleveland & New York: Meridian, 1957.

Hall and Pack, eds. *New Poets of England and America, Second Selection.* Cleveland: Meridian, 1962.

Hamilton, Ian. *The Modern Poet: Essays from "The Review."* London: Macdonald, 1968.

Hamilton, ed. *A Poetry Chronicle: Essays and Reviews.* London: Faber & Faber, 1973.

Heath-Stubbs, John, and David Wright, eds. *The Faber Book of Twentieth-Century Verse,* second revised edition. London: Faber & Faber, 1975.

Hollander, John, ed. *Poems of Our Moment.* New York: Pegasus, 1968.

Holloway, John. *The Charted Mirror: Literary and Critical Essays.* London: Routledge & Kegan Paul, 1960; New York: Horizon Press, 1962.

Homberger, Eric. *The Art of the Real: Poetry in England and America Since 1939.* London: Dent, 1977; Totowa, N.J.: Rowman & Littlefield, 1977.

Horovitz, Michael, ed. *Children of Albion: Poetry of the Underground in Britain.* Harmondsworth: Penguin, 1969.

Jones, Peter, and Michael Schmidt, eds. *British Poetry Since 1970: A Critical Survey.* Manchester: Carcanet Press, 1980; New York: Persea, 1980.

King, P. R. *Nine Contemporary Poets: A Critical Introduction.* London: Methuen, 1979.

Larkin, Philip, ed. *The Oxford Book of Twentieth Century English Verse.* Oxford: Clarendon Press, 1973.

Lindsay, Maurice, ed. *Modern Scottish Poetry: An Anthology of the Scottish Renaissance.* Manchester: Carcanet Press, 1976.

Lucie-Smith, Edward, ed. *British Poetry Since 1945.* Harmondsworth: Penguin, 1970; revised and enlarged, 1985.

Lucie-Smith, ed. *Holding Your Eight Hands: An Anthology of Science Fiction Verse.* Garden City: Doubleday, 1969; London: Rapp & Carroll, 1970.

Lucie-Smith, ed. *The Liverpool Scene.* London: Rapp & Carroll, 1967; New York: Doubleday, 1968.

Lucie-Smith, and Philip Hobsbaum, eds. *A Group Anthology.* Oxford: Oxford University Press, 1963.

Matthias, John, ed. *23 Modern British Poets.* Chicago: Swallow, 1971.

Moore, G. H. *Poetry To-Day*. London: Longmans, Green, 1958.

Moorish, Hilary, Peter Orr, John Press, and Jan Scott-Kilvert. *The Poet Speaks: Interviews with Contemporary Poets*. Edited by Orr. New York: Barnes & Noble, 1966.

Morrison, Blake. *The Movement: English Poetry and Fiction of the 1950's*. Oxford: Oxford University Press, 1980.

Morrison, and Andrew Motion, eds., *The Penguin Book of Contemporary British Poetry*. Harmondsworth: Penguin, 1982.

O'Connor, William Van. *The New University Wits and The End of Modernism*. Carbondale: Southern Illinois University Press, 1963.

Ormsby, Frank, ed. *Poets From The North of Ireland*. Belfast: Blackstaff Press, 1979.

Powell, Neil. *Carpenters of Light: Some Contemporary English Poets*. New York: Barnes & Noble, 1980.

Press, John. *A Map of Modern English Verse*. London: Oxford University Press, 1969.

Press. *Rule and Energy: Trends in British Poetry Since the Second World War*. London & New York: Oxford University Press, 1963.

Ries, Lawrence. *Wolf Masks: Violence in Contemporary Poetry*. Port Washington, N.Y.: Kennikat Press, 1977.

Robson, Jeremy, ed. *The Young British Poets*. London: Chatto & Windus, 1971.

Rosenthal, M. L. *The New Poets: American and British Poetry Since World War II*. New York: Oxford University Press, 1967.

Rosenthal, ed. *The New Modern Poetry: An Anthology of American and British Poetry Since World War II*, revised edition. New York: Oxford University Press, 1969.

Rosenthal, ed. *100 Postwar Poems: British and American*. New York: Macmillan, 1968.

Schmidt, Michael. *A Reader's Guide to Fifty Modern British Poets*. London: Heinemann/New York: Barnes & Noble, 1979.

Schmidt, ed. *Eleven British Poets*. London: Methuen, 1980.

Schmidt, ed. *Some Contemporary Poets of Britain and Ireland*. Manchester: Carcanet Press, 1983.

Schmidt, ed. *Ten English Poets: An Anthology*. Manchester: Carcanet Press, 1976.

Schmidt, and Grevel Lindop, eds. *British Poetry Since 1960: A Critical Survey*. Oxford: Carcanet Press, 1972.

Sharkey, John J., ed. *Mindplay: An Anthology of British Concrete Poetry*. London: Lorimer, 1971.

Silkin, Jon, ed. *Poetry of the Committed Individual: A Stand Anthology*. London: Gollancz, 1973.

Simmons, James, ed. *Ten Irish Poets*. Cheadle: Carcanet Press, 1974.

Spender, Stephen. *The Thirties and After: Poetry, Politics, People (1933-1970)*. New York: Random House, 1978.

Summerfield, Geoffrey, ed. *Worlds: Seven Modern Poets*. Harmondsworth: Penguin, 1974.

Thurley, Geoffrey. *The Ironic Harvest: English Poetry in the Twentieth Century.* London: Arnold, 1974.

Thwaite, Anthony. *Essays on Contemporary English Poetry: Hopkins to the Present Day.* Tokyo: Kenkyusha, 1957. Revised as *Contemporary English Poetry: An Introduction.* London: Heinemann, 1959.

Thwaite. *Poetry Today: 1960-1973.* Harlow: Longman, 1973.

Thwaite. *Twentieth Century English Poetry.* London: Heinemann, 1978; New York: Barnes & Noble, 1978.

Wain, John, ed. *Anthology of Contemporary Poetry: Post-War to the Present.* London: Hutchinson, 1979.

Walsh, Chad, ed. *Today's Poets: American and British Poetry Since the 1930's,* revised and enlarged edition. New York: Scribners, 1972.

Weatherhead, A. Kingsley. *The British Dissonance: Essays on Ten Contemporary Poets.* Columbia & London: University of Missouri Press, 1983.

Williams, Hugo, ed. *London Magazine Poems 1961-1966,* introduction by Alan Ross. London: Alan Ross, 1966.

Contributors

Edward Broadbridge.. *Paderup College*
Joseph Browne .... *West Chester University*
J. E. Chamberlin.. *University of Toronto*
Caroline L. Cherry ....*Eastern College*
Michael J. Collins ....*Georgetown University*
Lester I. Conner.. *Chestnut Hill College*
Neil Corcoran... *University of Sheffield*
Thomas Dilworth ....*University of Windsor*
Brian Donnelly ....*Carysfort College*
Karen Dorn ....*London, England*
Frederick Feirstein ....*New York City, New York*
Roger Garfitt .... *Ross-on-Wye, England*
Julian Gitzen.. *Victoria College*
Jon Glover ....*Bolton, England*
Michael Grant.. *University of Kent at Canterbury*
John Haffenden ....*Sheffield University*
Wayne E. Hall .... *University of Cincinnati*
Maurice Harmon...*University College, Dublin*
Michael Hulse..*Oxford, England*
Alan Jenkins ....*London, England*
George Johnston .... *Chateaugay, New York*
Hugh Kenner ....*Johns Hopkins University*
Christopher Levenson .... *Carleton University*
Tim Longville..*Farley Hill, England*
Paul Mariani .... *University of Massachusetts / Amherst*
Robyn L. Marsack ....*London, England*
Margaret B. McDowell .... *University of Iowa*
David E. Middleton ....*Nicholls State University*
James J. Murphy .... *Villanova University*
Neil Powell.. *Baldock, England*
John Press..*Frome, England*
Lawrence R. Ries..*Skidmore College*
Kit Robinson...*Berkeley, California*
Robert B. Shaw .... *Mount Holyoke College*
Ken Smith..*London, England*
Stan Smith .... *Dundee University*
Kathleen Henderson Staudt .... *Drexel University*
William S. Waddell, Jr. ....*St. John Fisher College*
Alan Young ....*Timperley, England*
Toby Silverman Zinman ....*Philadelphia College of Art*

Cumulative Index

Dictionary of Literary Biography, Volumes 1-40
Dictionary of Literary Biography Yearbook, 1980-1984
Dictionary of Literary Biography Documentary Series, Volumes 1-4

Cumulative Index

DLB before number: *Dictionary of Literary Biography*, Volumes 1-40
Y before number: *Dictionary of Literary Biography Yearbook*, 1980-1984
DS before number: *Dictionary of Literary Biography Documentary Series*, Volumes 1-4

C

D

E

F

G

K

L

O

S

T

W

Y

Z